seen any
good films
lately?

if you have

and would like to know more about them and the cinema generally, then the British Film Institute can help

● The **Information and Documentation Department** offers research facilities with an index of 160,000 films and a collection of 20,000 books and pamphlets.

● The **National Film Archive** contains over 20,000 films of historic, artistic and scientific interest and a stills collection of over 700,000 photographs.

● The Institute publishes **Sight and Sound**, the international film quarterly and the **Monthly Film Bulletin** and **British National Film Catalogue**, both invaluable reference works.

● The **Distribution Library** has over 2,000 titles about the history and art of film and television available for hire.

● The **Educational Advisory Service** offers assistance to teachers of film courses at all educational levels.

if you haven't

but would like to, the BFI can help there too

• The **National Film Theatre** shows 1,000 films a year – the best of world cinema – and has a members' riverside restaurant and bar.

• The **Regional Department** is involved in over forty Regional Film Theatres and the work of the Regional Arts Associations.

• The **Central Booking Agency** offers a comprehensive service for film societies and educational bodies.

• If you want to make a film, and have a script and some experience, why not contact the BFI **Production Board**, 42/3 Lower Marsh, London S.E.1.?

and, of course, there's the LONDON FILM FESTIVAL held every November with over 40 new features – the pick of the year's other film festivals and many films by new directors.

Further details on these and all BFI activities from:
Membership Department (1FG2)
British Film Institute
81 Dean Street London W1V 6AA
Telephone: 01-437 4355 ext. 42

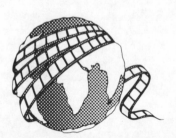
4

5

"THE LOOK OF THINGS TO COME"

THE FABLE OF HE AND SHE

I HEARD THE OWL CALL MY NAME

TWO CITIES: LONDON AND NEW YORK

A contemporary portrait of urban living in two international capitals offers a thought-provoking study in contrasts. New production in the "Comparative Cultures" series. Color—23 min.

THE HANDY DANDY DO-IT-YOUR-SELF ANIMATION FILM

Award Winner: American Film Festival

Three young students show the simple basics of making Super 8 animated movies. From a new series "The Young Filmmakers." Color —11 min.

WRITE FOR COMPLETE CATALOG

LEARNING CORPORATION OF AMERICA

1350 AVENUE OF THE AMERICAS NEW YORK, NY 10019

CANADA: Marlin Motion Pictures, Ont. GREAT BRITAIN: Rank Film Library, Middlesex

Sales
Exhibition
Distribution
Television

CONTEMPORARY FILMS

Britain's leading
Film Specialists
for World·wide
distribution

CONTEMPORARY FILMS LTD
55 GREEK STREET
LONDON W1V 6DB

INTERNATIONAL
FILM GUIDE
1976

Edited by Peter Cowie

Associate Editor: Derek Elley
Television Editor: David Wilson

The Tantivy Press,
108 New Bond Street, London W1Y 0QX.
A. S. Barnes & Co.,
South Brunswick & New York.

leaders in the field of
SWEDISH CINEMA

currently available

HUGS AND KISSES · DUET FOR CANNIBALS · TO LOVE

SAWDUST AND TINSEL · JOURNEY INTO AUTUMN

THE BOOKSELLER WHO GAVE UP BATHING · I AM CURIOUS—YELLOW

I AM CURIOUS—BLUE · YOU'RE LYING · MISS JULIE · THE RITE

MY SISTER, MY LOVE · BLUSHING CHARLIE · CLOSE TO THE WIND

DEAR JOHN · DOG DAYS · LE VIOL

shorts

LOVE & TV · PARKING AUTOMATION · THE KARLSSON BROTHERS

JOHAN EKBERG · SWEDISH CINEMA CLASSICS · NEW

SWEDISH CINEMA · MODERN SWEDISH CINEMA

also five films by Ralph Lundsten

ALIEN WORLD · EMS No I · NATURE AHOY

THE HEART IS BURNING · THE TRAVELLER RECALLS

for future release

THE PISTOL (Jiri Tirl) · FOREIGNERS (Johan Bergenstrahle)

THE TEMPTATION (Ivo Dvorak) · ONE ARMED BANDIT (Peter Kruse)

PURGATORY (Michael Meschke) · TROLL (Vilgot Sjoman)

Free catalogue on request - 20p. p & p would be appreciated

280 Chartridge Lane, Chesham, Bucks. HP5 2SG

Tel. Chesham (STD 02405) 3643

Choice of Films 1974/75

1. *The Passenger/Professione: Reporter* (Antonioni—Italy/France/Spain).
2. *Scenes from a Marriage/Scener ur ett äktenskap* (Bergman—Sweden).
3. *The Conversation* (Coppola—U.S.A.).
4. *Survival of the Fittest/Faustrecht der Freiheit* (Fassbinder—West Germany).
5. *The Magic Flute/Trollflöjten* (Bergman—Sweden).
6. *The Godfather Part II* (Coppola—U.S.A.).
7. *Lancelot du Lac* (Bresson—France).
8. *A Woman under the Influence* (Cassavetes—U.S.A.).
9. *Akenfield* (Hall—Britain).
10. *Shazdeh Ehtejab* (Farmanara—Iran).
    Sunday Too Far Away (Hannam—Australia).

Film Guide Liaison

Africa and Third World: Viggo Holm Jensen
Argentina: Alberto Tabbia
Australia: David J. Stratton
Austria: Goswin Dörfler
Belgium: Paul Davay, Francis Bolen
Brazil: Jaime Rodrigues
Canada: Gerald Pratley
China: Peter Davey
Egypt: Abdel Moneim Saad
Eire: Pat Billings
England: David McGillivray
Finland: Kari Uusitalo
France: Michel Ciment
Germany (BRD): Edmund Luft

Greece: Mirella Georgiadou
Hongkong: Verina Glaessner
Hungary: Robert Bán
India: Chidananda Das Gupta, Uma da Cunha
Indonesia: Baharudin A. Latiff
Iran: Hagir Daryoush
Israel: Ze'ev Ravnof
Italy: Lino Miccichè
Japan: Naoki Togawa
Lebanon: Leon Torossian
Malaysia: Baharudin A. Latiff
Mexico: Tomás Pérez-Turrent
New Zealand: Lindsay Shelton

Norway: Jan E. Holst
Peru: John Beauclerk
Poland: Bolesław Lutosławski
Romania: Manuela Gheorghiu
South Africa: Lionel Friedberg
Sri Lanka (Ceylon): Philip Coorey, Amarnath Jayatilaka, D. B. Warnasiri
Spain: Roger Mortimore
Switzerland: Felix Bucher
Syria: Mohamed Rida
Turkey: Giovanni Scognamillo
U.S.A.: Stuart Rosenthal
Venezuela: Jacobo Brender
Yugoslavia: Ronald Holloway

EDITOR:
Peter Cowie

ASSOCIATE EDITOR:
Derek Elley

ADVERTISING MANAGER:
Susan Andrews

EDITORIAL ASSISTANCE:
Miles Smith-Morris

Editorial and business offices: The Tantivy Press, 108 New Bond Street, London W1Y 0QX, England. Telephone: 01-499 4733.

Directors of the Year

1964	1965	1966	1967
Visconti	Fellini	Kurosawa	Franju
Welles	Ray (S)	Rosi	Losey
Truffaut	Buñuel	Demy	Polanski
Wajda	Malle	Brooks	Frankenheimer
Hitchcock	Kubrick	Haanstra	Torre Nilsson

1968	1969	1970	1971
Widerberg	Bondarchuk	Anderson	Donskoi
Ivens	Forman	Chabrol	Kazan
Lumet	Jancsó	Ichikawa	Melville
Němec	Penn	Pasolini	Oshima
Antonioni	Tati	Skolimowski	Schorm

1972	1973	1974	1975
Bertolucci	Bergman	Boorman	Altman
Donner	Bresson	Gaál	Ferreri
Kozintsev	Makavejev	Godard	Has
Rohmer	Resnais	Huston	Lester
Troell	Schlesinger	Ivory	Sjöman

Copyright © 1975 by The Tantivy Press

U.S. Library of Congress Catalogue Card No. 64-1076

SBN 0-904208-01-X (U.K.)
SBN 0-498-01718-4 (U.S.A.)

Text set in 10/10 pt. Photon Times, printed by photolithography, and bound in Great Britain at The Pitman Press, Bath

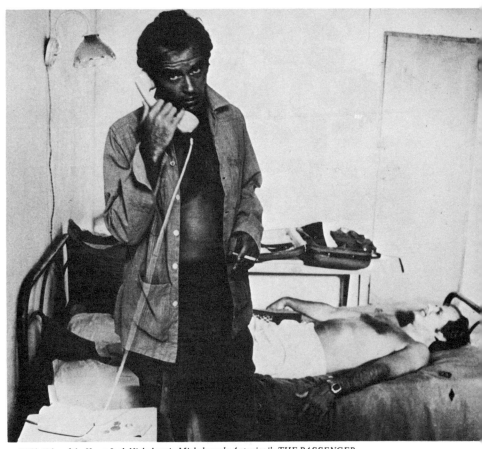

IFG's Film of the Year: Jack Nicholson in Michelangelo Antonioni's THE PASSENGER

IVAN VASILYEVICH

SEMURG

FRONT WITHOUT FLANKS

SOVEXPORTFILM

HEAD OFFICE: **14, KALASHNY PEREULOK,
MOSCOW,
U.S.S.R.**

LONDON OFFICE: **10 KENSINGTON PALACE GARDENS,
LONDON W.8.
ENGLAND.**

18

Guide to Contents

THE BOAT starring Chic Murray, a 35mm E/col production for theatrical release in 1975. This 30 minute comedy is written and directed by Laurence Henson and photographed by Eddie McConnell.

International Film Associates (Scotland) Ltd.
19 North Claremont Street Glasgow G3 7NR

World Survey

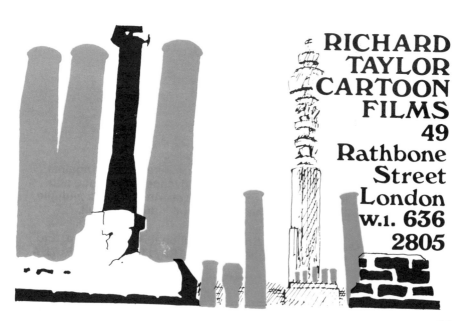

List of Films Reviewed

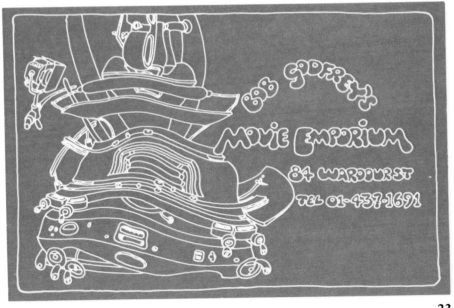

Lasst uns machen

Leave us alone

Foutez-nous la paix

*Why does the young public in Denmark crowd to see LEAVE US ALONE — not only once, but several times? Because more than anything it is **their** film - a film about their love and their violence - in a language which they know and understand. This may be one of the secrets behind the tremendous success of LEAVE US ALONE.*

Leave us alone

a box office success for sale

35mm Eastmancolor 90 mins

please contact:
STEEN HERDEL, FILM & TV PRODUCTION, NYGARD TERRASSERNE 242D
3520 FARUM
TLF. (01) 95 49 19

WYATTANEO

Wyatt Cattaneo Productions Limited 22 Charing Cross Road London WC2
836 5104/5 Cutting room 836 6800   *Directors* Ron Wyatt, Tony Cattaneo

THE LONDON INTERNATIONAL FILM SCHOOL is

the international centre for education and training in film and television production; situated in London's Covent Garden it welcomes students from all countries. The long established, intensive, two year Diploma Course in film continues and the School will also provide a full time Diploma Course in Television to the same high standard. Tuition, Production and Aesthetic Studies are designed to make graduates fully professional in their creative work. All members of the faculty are professional workers in film or T.V. See details under "Film Schools". The School is a company limited by guarantee, managed by the Board of Governors elected by the members, among whom are students and staff.

1976 courses commence:

January 12th   ●   April 26th   ●   September 27th

Terms are twelve weeks.

Write to Student Counsellor, F.I.
THE LONDON INTERNATIONAL FILM SCHOOL LTD
24-26, Shelton Street, London, WC2H 9HP. England.
Telephone 01 240 0168. Cables ARTACTION Ldn WC2

THE CINEMA OF FRANK CAPRA
An Approach to Film Comedy
by Leland A. Poague

Frank Capra is analyzed and lauded for his outstanding achievement as a comic artist. His directorial genius is evidenced throughout each one of his classic movies. The quality control of performances, scenes, sets, music, shots — everything has that unmistakable Capra touch; and now it can be seen that the Capra genius can be evaluated in the literary sense. There are 185 stills of memorable scenes and famous actors, and a complete Capra filmography. $19.95 £8.50

HOLLYWOOD PROFESSIONALS
Volume 4: Tod Browning and Don Siegel
by Stuart Rosenthal and Judith M. Kass

Volume 5: King Vidor, John Cromwell, and Mervyn LeRoy
by Clive Denton and Kingsley Canham

This popular series continues with studies of major figures in the history of Hollywood. Their films are evoked in text and pictures with careful analyses of their most important films. Movie fans and students of the cinema alike will learn from and enjoy these well-researched volumes which contain detailed filmographies and a wide range of rare illustrations. $2.95   £1.25   each volume

THE VAMPIRE FILM
by Alain Silver and James Ursini

The Vampire Film is a detailed study of the vampire myth. Concentrating on the various manifestations of the vampire in films from all parts of the world, the book also discusses earlier appearances in folklore and literature. An extensive filmography and more than 100 illustrations help to make this a most attractive and valuable contribution to film literature. $10.00 £4.25

5 DIRECTORS OF THE YEAR

Michael Cacoyannis

Who would have ever predicted a decade ago that Michael Cacoyannis, the most "international" of Greek directors, would find himself at the centre of Greece's patriotic and political campaign for the Cyprus cause, with the label of the *engagé* film-maker on his sleeve? Yet a quick survey of Cacoyannis's career prior to *Attila 74* reveals that underneath the stylistic perfection of, say, *Electra* and *The Trojan Women*, the folklorish characteristics of *Zorba the Greek* and *Stella*, and the Kubrickian allegory of *The Day the Fish Came Out*, there is strong evidence of his involvement in the social and political reality of his native land and an ever-present desire to shock and attack to put the Greek people on guard against its own weaknesses and complexes.

MICHAEL CACOYANNIS was born on June 11, 1922, in Limassol, Cyprus. After his secondary education at a Greek Gymnasium, his father Sir Panayotis Loizou Cacoyannis, who achieved distinction as an attorney and a public servant, enrolled him at

Gray's Inn in London to study Law. The young Michael, who, by the time he was thirteen, had staged his first productions using his brother and two sisters as cast and family friends as his audience, did not dare to tell his father that he wanted to enter the theatre instead. His dream was fulfilled, however, when he passed the Bar: the Second World War broke out and he remained in England to produce Greek programmes for the BBC, while studying drama at the Central School of Dramatic Arts. In 1949 he joined the Old Vic, making his acting *début* as Herod in Oscar Wilde's "Salome." Although rather successful, he suddenly gave up his acting career in 1951 to become a writer and director.

Unable to raise production money to film his first screenplay ("Our Last Spring," based on "Eroica," a novel by Greek writer Kosmas Politis), Cacoyannis returned to Greece in 1953. He made friends with Dimitris Horn, Elli Lambetti and George Papas, three very popular stage actors who

Faster Visual Presentation

Speed is decisive. For example in television. News items and world-wide communications are effective only if the current is truly presented. And yet, satellites and giant trans-mitters are not enough. The film material for illustrations and copies must be processed equally quickly to be newsworthy.

Agfa-Gevaert, the European organisation in film manufacture, has such films.

The Olympic Games in Munich are proof. Most of the filmed events which were seen throughout the world, day and night, on the Tele-vision screens were covered on Agfa-Gevaert material.

Agfa-Gevaert offers the professional film makers what they need. Not just individual products, but a fully developed, progressive, easy to use film system. Negative and reversal films, optical and magnetic sound films, films for theatre and TV prints, filters and chemicals. And a service which such a programme requires. A service famous for its quality. Agfa-Gevaert – the professionals' partner.

Agfa-Gevaert N.V.
B-2510 Mortsel (Belgium)

introduced him to a producer and assumed the leading parts in his first film, *Windfall in Athens*.

Conceived as a vehicle for the actors, the film (a lottery comedy about a girl, a boy and an older man) recalled in atmosphere French works of the period. Somehow it was something more than just another light-hearted romantic story, as it managed to combine fairy-tale charm and freshness with a subjective realism (the best scenes were shot on location in the streets of Athens) that cast a smiling eye on a society recovering from the wounds of the German Occupation and the Civil War, tasting again the sweet fruits of pleasure and success. The film was remarkably well received both in Greece and at the Edinburgh Film Festival, where Cacoyannis was welcomed as a prodigiously talented newcomer.

To an American reviewer, Cacoyannis described *Stella*, his second and altogether more ambitious feature, as "a very primitive film, purely Athenian." The definition is accurate as regards the environment and minor parts but certainly cannot be extended to the central character. Stella, a *bouzouki* singer and dancer who abhors marriage, defies the

Melina Mercouri in Cacoyannis's STELLA

Elli Lambetti and George Foundas in THE GIRL IN BLACK

rules of conventional morality, and pays for a
freedom denied by the men who love her, is
far apart from the "ordinary" contemporary
Athens woman, a splendid reflection of the
temperament of the protagonist, Melina Mercouri, beautifully controlled in this her first
film role. *Stella* shows Cacoyannis finding his
way in matters both of subject and technique.
There is a pervasive sense of atmosphere that
allows the characters to become an organic
part of the streets and houses used for location (the scene with Stella triumphantly riding

an open truck to show the neighbours her
lover's gift, a piano, is among the funniest and
best observed), and the folklore material
(chiefly *bouzouki* dances and music by
Manos Hatzidakis) is dexterously used to
enliven the melodramatic plot. The "pure"
tragic element takes over in the finale, with the
chorus of neighbours gathering round the
couple as Stella dies in the arms of her lover.

The Girl in Black, a simple story of
frustrated love between a boy from Athens
and a girl on an island, uses the conventions of

a typical romance only to undermine them. The film is built as a tragedy from start to finish, and the moving portrait of the proud, disillusioned heroine, victimised by her hostile surroundings, is for Cacoyannis a pretext to unearth the myths and taboos, traditions and rituals, the social and individualistic tendencies, the prejudices, obsessions and underdevelopment, all present in Greek provincial life. Elli Lambetti's performance has a mysterious, fascinating quality, and the sad autumnal tones of the island of Hydra, captured by the camera of Walter Lassally (who was to collaborate with Cacoyannis on all his major works), build a climate of emotional misery and underlying despair that breaks out in sudden bursts of uncontrolled violence. To quote Cacoyannis: "I have been accused of showing violence to the hilt. But violence is the logical outcome of the repressive relationships which exist within the society and the family." The film closes with a tragic episode (several children are drowned in a boat-ride and the visitor from Athens is held responsible) in which non-professionals play an active part. "The scene was achieved by working up the local women to a frenzy of despair and then hurling the camera among them, shouting instructions and re-arranging patterns with feverish urgency, while everyone responded with that extraordinary alertness which is only possible in moments of tremendous general tension."

A Matter of Dignity (1957), acclaimed by the London critics as the best film of that year, again featured Elli Lambetti in the role of a girl sacrificing her personal life to social hypocrisy. The Greek quality of the film and its importance lies, however, in the character of the maid—an excellent performance by Helen Zafiriou, the mother in *The Girl in Black*—and the semi-documentary scenes shot on Tinos, where a religious ceremony,

Elli Lambetti and Helen Zafiriou in A MATTER OF DIGNITY

similar to that of Lourdes, takes place every year. With a handful of international prizes to his credit it was easy for Cacoyannis to find foreign backing for *Our Last Spring*, his very first script, based on the novel by Kosmas Politis, about adolescents challenging the hostile adult world. The film was not a success, but the final scene of the funeral games organised by the hero during the passing of his dead friend's *cortège* is worthy of the best of Cacoyannis.

Involved for the second time in the big commercial world and the multi-lingual productions he so dreaded, Cacoyannis had another bitter experience with *The Wastrel (Il relitto)*, a melodrama filmed in Italy and presented at the Cannes Festival under the colours of Cyprus. Van Heflin (as the jealous husband) and Franco Fabrizi were the partners of Elli Lambetti, rigid and cold and very unlike her real self.

Back in Greece, Cacoyannis embarked on a long-cherished project: a new approach to ancient drama "in order to explore the tragic element that has been evident in my work and which is partly content and partly form." Cacoyannis turned to Euripides, and for his adaptation of *Electra* set out to translate visually his favourite author's "extraordinary technique of opening up the action to establish a dramatic situation and then focusing in on his characters at such close range that you feel you are looking straight into their souls." Few words are spoken during the opening scenes of Agamemnon's arrival in Argos and his assassination; moments of absolute stillness are followed by passages of frenetic violence.

Sound, mixed with the musical score of Mikis Theodorakis, plays a predominant part in the establishment of the frozen atmosphere of grief and desolation when Electra is expelled from the palace and is seen leading the humble life of a peasant wife in a small rocky village. Cacoyannis uses the desolate landscape as a stage against which the incidents of the drama unfold, but there is never any false sense of distance between the film and the spectator. As Walter Lassally's camera relentlessly explores Irene Papas's hermetically-sealed face for signs of unrelieved suffering, the audience is urged to adopt the reactions of the chorus of black-

Alan Bates and Anthony Quinn in ZORBA THE GREEK

Irene Papas and Aleka Katseli in ELECTRA

dressed village women who follow Electra's journey. Rich in virtuoso passages and dazzling stylistic effects, *Electra* marks the peak of Cacoyannis's career. The film won a special prize at Cannes, some twenty additional international awards, and an Oscar nomination, and its American release in 1963 coincided with Cacoyannis's first triumphal stage production in New York: "The Trojan Women" by Euripides, which he had staged the preceding summer at the Festival of the Two Worlds in Spoleto, was presented at the off-Broadway Circle-in-the-Square Theatre.

In 1964 Cacoyannis broke his three-year absence from the cameras with *Zorba the Greek*, shot on location in Crete with an international cast. For his adaptation of Kazantzakis's novel (about an intellectual and a strange vagabond who helps him rediscover the primitive world of the island of Crete and his real self), Cacoyannis played three winning cards: leaving behind Kazantzakis's exploration of the Greek soul, he concentrated on the picturesque and folklorish elements of the plot, the devilish vitality of the larger-than-life Zorba figure, and the violence of the dramatic climaxes. The film was an immediate commercial success, won three

Katharine Hepburn and Geneviève Bujold in THE TROJAN WOMEN

never made a real super-production, a very expensive film. I work usually with a small unit of technicians, mostly Greeks. Most of the big stars that have appeared in my films, e.g. Katharine Hepburn or Vanessa Redgrave in *The Trojan Women*, chose to work with me not for money but because they really wanted to play the roles. In 1967 I made *The Day the Fish Came Out*, a black comedy about nuclear weapons, because I thought I had something to say on the role the Great Powers play in the fate of small countries. The film was shot in Greece and banned by the *régime* that took over some months later. It was a commercial failure, probably because at the time nobody had the courage to joke with such subjects. Cancer and the atomic threat were taboo. Now *The Day the Fish Came Out* is having a new lease of life in France. They show it at the Cinémathèque and the Cinémas d'Art et d'Essai and the young love it. Four years later I made *The Trojan Women* in Spain, as a kind of tribute to those who were fighting the Fourth Reich of Greece. The *cinéma-vérité* technique I used in *Attila 74* [a compassionate full-length colour documentary made in Cyprus to mobilise domestic and foreign opinion against the crimes committed on his home island] is not so far from the improvisation process I have used for certain scenes in all my major films. If I have been at all successful in my attempt to understand and make other people understand what *was* going on and what *is* going on in Cyprus, this I no doubt owe to being able in the interviews with the protagonists and victims of the Cyprus tragedy to come very near the people I had to film, make them feel comfortable, make them forget I am someone else besides a shocked witness. At the same time I had to control my own emotions and be on the look-out to catch the unexpected reaction, the moment of naked truth."

Oscars, and obtained enthusiastic reviews by such critics as Bosley Crowther, who wrote about the episodes of the young widow's slaughter in the middle of the village square and the looting of the dying courtesan's hotel by the local women: "These are incidents that Cacoyannis has staged with such intense reality that they fairly paralyze the senses for brief spells ... Quinn is Adam in the Garden of Eden, Odysseus in the windy plains of Troy. He is a little bit of a Nijinsky and a good bit of Tom Jones ..." There was also the other side of the coin, though: Cacoyannis was accused of having betrayed the spirit of the original, the Greeks (depicted as barbarians) and his artistic integrity; all for the sake of big co-production interests.

In a personal interview, Cacoyannis told me about this second period of his career. "I have always acted as producer, director, writer and editor of my films. Nobody ever interfered in the picture I wanted to make. I usually have no difficulty in finding foreign backing, but this is only because my films never run beyond schedule. In fact I have

A striking shot from Cacoyannis's ATTILA 74

Cacoyannis had embarked on the preparation of *The Third Marriage*, a biting and occasionally savage critique of lower-middle-class society based on a novel by Kostas Tahtisis, when the Cyprus tragedy broke out. Now, after *Attila 74*, priority will be given perhaps to *Iphigenia in Aulis*, from the tragedy by Euripides, a project that dates back to 1961, before the filming of *Electra*. With his mastery of form and wealth of psychological insight, Cacoyannis has made a fair claim to be ranked with such internationally renowned directors as Fellini and Bergman. In a longer perspective, it is very likely that his distinctive awareness of Greece and the Greek situation, and his capacity to rise above it and bring into the open the anguish of a dying, disappearing world of settled ethical and social traditions, will ensure him his continuing place in the cinema.

MIRELLA GEORGIADOU

CACOYANNIS FILMOGRAPHY

Cacoyannis is uncredited editor on all his films. In 1974 he directed a two-hour teleplay, *The Story of Jacob and Joseph*, for American TV, filmed in Israel, with Keith Michell, Tony Lo Bianco, Julian Glover, Harry Andrews and Alan Bates.

1953

KYRIAKATIKO XYPNIMA/SUNDAY AWAKENING/WINDFALL IN ATHENS. Script and direction: MC. Photography: Alvise Orfanelli. Art Direction: Yannis Tsarouhis. Asst. Dir: Anis Nohra. Players: Elli Lambetti (*Mina*), George Papas, Dimitris Horn, Margarita Papageorgiou, Tasso Kavadia, Sapfo Notara, Haris Pateraki. For Milas Films. 95 mins. On 16mm: Contemporary (G.B.), Audio Brandon (U.S.).

1955

STELLA. Script and direction: MC, from the play "Stella with the Red Gloves" by Iakovos Kambanellis. Photography: Kostas Theodoridis. Asst. Ed: George Tsaoulis. Music: Manos Hatzidakis (played by a folk orchestra conducted by Vasilis Tsitsanis). Art Direction: Yannis Tsarouhis, Vlasis Kaniaris. Asst. Dir: Anis Nohra. Players: Melina Mercouri (*Stella*), George Foundas (*Miltos*), Alekos Alexandrakis (*Alekos*), Voula Zoumboulaki (*Anneta*), Sofia Vembo (*Maria*), Dionisis Papayannopoulos (*Mitsos*), Hristina Kalogerikou (*Miltos's Mother*), Tasso Kavadia (*Alekos's Sister*), Kostas Karalis-Kakavas (*Antonis*). Produced by Vasilis Lambiris and Sotiris Milas for Milas Films. 95 mins.

1956

TO KORITSI ME TA MAVRA/THE GIRL IN BLACK. Script and direction: MC. Photography: Walter Lassally. Music: Argyris Kounadis (guitar: Gerasimos Miliaresis). Prod. Sup. and asst. dir: Anis Nohra. Players: Elli Lambetti (*Marina*), Dimitris Horn (*Pavlos*), Helen Zafiriou (*Froso, her Mother*), Anestis Vlahos (*Brother*), Notis Peryalis (*Antonis*), George Foundas (*Hristos*), Stefanos Stratigos (*Panagos*), Nikos Fermas, Thanasis Vengos. Produced by Vasilis Lambiris for Hermes Films. 120 mins. On 16mm: Audio Brandon (U.S.).

1958

TO TELEFTEO PSEMA/THE FINAL LIE/A MATTER OF DIGNITY. Script and direction: MC. Photography: Walter Lassally. Music: Manos Hatzidakis. Art Direction: Yannis Tsarouhis. Players: Elli Lambetti (*Hloi*), George Papas (*Father*), Helen Zafiriou (*Maid*), Michael Nikolinakos (*Mr. Galanos*), Athina Milhailidou (*Mother*), George Sarri (*Aunt*), Dimitris Papamihail (*Markos*), Minas Hristidis (*Shipowner*). For Finos Films. 95 mins.

1959

OUR LAST SPRING/EROICA. Script and direction: MC, from the novel "Eroica" by Kosmas Politis.

Photography: Walter Lassally. Editing: Fred Burnley, MC. Music: Argyris Kounadis. Art Direction: Yannis Tsarouhis. Players: Alekos Mamatis (*Alekos*), Jennie Russell (*Monica*), Panos Goumas (*Loizo*), Patrick O'Brian (*Stefanos*), Marie Ney (*Governess*), Nikiforos Naneris (*Dimitri*), Stathis Giallelis, Jane Cobb. Produced by MC. 121 mins.

1960

THE WASTREL/IL RELITTO/HAMENO KORMI/ETSI ESVISE I AGAPI MAS. Script: Fred Wakeman, Suso Cecchi D'Amico, MC, from a novel by Wakeman. Direction: MC. Photography: Piero Portalupi. Music: Angelo Francesco Lavagnino. Art Direction: Enrico Equini. Players: Elli Lambetti (*Liana*), Van Heflin (*Duncan Bell*), Franco Fabrizi (*Rudi Veronese*), Michael Stellman (*Cam*), Fosco Giachetti (*Jug Hardy*), Tiberio Mitri (*Macniff*), Paul Muller (*Fatso*), Clelia Matania (*Betsy*), Aldo Pini (*Doc*), Annie Gorassini (*Monique*). Produced by Angelo Ferrara for Lux/Tiberia. 115 mins.

1961

ELEKTRA/ELECTRA. Script and direction: MC, from the tragedy by Euripides. Photography: Walter Lassally. Asst. Ed: Leonidas Antonakis. Art Direction: Spiros Vasiliou. Asst. Dir: Vasilis Mariolis, H. Hristidis. Players: Irene Papas (*Elektra*), Yannis Fertis (*Orestes*), Aleka Katseli (*Klytemnestra*), Fivos Razis (*Egisthos*), Manos Katrakis (*Tutor*), Notis Peryalis (*Elektra's Husband*), Takis Emmanouil (*Pylades*), Theano Ioannidou, Helen Karpeta. Produced by MC in collaboration with Finos Films for United Artists. 120 mins. On 16mm: FDA (G.B.), UA: 16 (U.S.).

1964

ZORBA THE GREEK/ALEXIS ZORBAS. Script and direction: MC, from the novel by Nikos Kazantzakis. Photography: Walter Lassally. Music: Mikis Theodorakis. Art Direction: Vasilis Fotopoulos. Players: Antony Quinn (*Zorbas*), Alan Bates (*Writer*), Lila Kedrova (*Madame Ortense*), Irene Papas (*Widow*), George Foundas (*Mavrantonis*), Takis Emmanouil (*Manolakas*), Sotiris Moustakas (*Mimithos*), George Voyatzis (*Pavlis*), Helen Anousaki (*Lola*). Produced by MC for 20th Century-Fox. 141 mins. On 16mm: FDA (G.B.), Films Inc. (U.S.).

1967

THE DAY THE FISH CAME OUT. Script and direction: MC. Photography (DeLuxe Color): Walter Lassally. Music: Mikis Theodorakis. Art Direction: Spiros

Vasiliou. Dances: Arthur Mitchell. Costumes: MC. Asst. Dir: Tom Pevsner. Main title: Maurice Binder. Players: Tom Courtenay (*Navigator*), Sam Wanamaker (*Elias*), Colin Blakely (*Pilot*), Candice Bergen (*Electra*), Ian Ogilvy (*Peter*), Dimitris Nikolaidis (*Dentist*), Nikos Alexiou (*Goatherd*), Patricia Burke (*Mrs. Mavroyannis*), Paris Alexander (*Fred*), Arthur Mitchell (*Frank*), Marlena Carrere (*Goatherd's Wife*), Tom Klunis (*Mr. French*), William Berger (*Man in Bed*), Kostas Papakonstantinou (*Manolios*), Dora Stratou (*Travel Agent*), Alexander Lykourezos (*Director of Tourism*), Tom Whitehead (*Mike*), Walter Granecki (*Base Commander*), Demetris Ioakimides (*Policeman*), Lynn Bryant, James Connolly, Assaf Dayan, Robert Killian, Derek Kulai, Alexis Mantheakis, Raymond McWilliams, Michael Radford, Peter Robinson, James Smith, Grigoris Stefanides, Peter Stratful, Kostas Timvios, Herbert Zeichner (*Tourists*). Presented by International Classics. 109 mins. On 16mm: Films Inc. (U.S.).

1971

THE TROJAN WOMEN. Script and direction: MC, from the tragedy by Euripides. Photography (Eastmancolor): Alfio Contini. Music: Mikis Theodorakis. Art Direction: Nicholas Georgiadis. Special Effects: Basilio Cortijo. Asst. Dir: Stavros Konstantarakos, José María Ochoa, Roberto Cirla. Players: Katharine Hepburn (*Hekuba*), Geneviève Bujold (*Kassandra*), Vanessa Redgrave (*Andromache*), Irene Papas (*Helen*), Brian Blessed (*Talthybios*), Patrick Magee (*Menelaos*), Alberto Sanz (*Astyanax*), Pauline Letts, Rosalind Shanks, Pat Becket, Anna Bentick, Esmeralda Adam, Maria Garcia Alonso, Nilda Alvarez, Victoria Ayllon, Elizabeth Billencourt, Margarita Calahora, Elena Castillo, Anna María Espejo, Maria Jesús Hoyos, Conchita Leza, Margarita Matta, Mirta Miller, Conchita Morales, Virginia Quintana, Yvette Rees, Carmen Segarra, Esperanza Alonso, Consolation Alvarez, Adela Armengol, Gloria Berrogal, Maria Borge, Carmen Cano, Renée Eber, Katie Ellyson Gwendoline Kocsis, Maureen Mallall, Ivi Mavridi, Livia Mitchell, Ersie Pittas, Catherine Rabone, Clara Sanchiz, Laura Zarrabeitia (*Chorus*), Maria Farantouri (*Singer*). Produced by MC and Anis Nohra for Josef Shaftel Productions. 111 mins. On 16mm: Ron Harris (G.B.), Swank (U.S.).

1975

ATTILA 1974. Script and direction: MC Photography (colour): Sakis Maniatis. 2nd Unit Phot: Nikos Kavoukidis, Katharine Leroy. Music: Mihalis Hristodoulides. Produced by MC. 98 mins.

The death scene from STELLA

Cover portrait of Michael Cacoyannis by Stathis Y.

John Cassavetes directing A WOMAN UNDER THE INFLUENCE

42 5 DIRECTORS: CASSAVETES

John Cassavetes

While John Cassavetes has been the subject of much critical debate over the years, neither admirer nor disparager has ever accused him of predictability. When his dark horse *Shadows* won the Critics Award at the 1960 Venice Film Festival, Cassavetes was hailed as the harbinger of an American New Wave. Sixteen years and six films later actor-writer-director Cassavetes has evolved a distinctly personal style, but one which refuses to conform to any tide (a fact which has never endeared him to American distributors). In the years of *Easy Rider* and *Zabriskie Point* he was dissecting bourgeois marriage and the ageing suburbanite; and he flagrantly glorified the actor as *auteur* at a time when Hitchcock's "cattle" theory was in vogue. Despite a neo-experimental liking for the hand-held camera and grainy texture, Cassavetes has evinced a singular disinterest in both composition and *genre*—subjects which are preoccupying his peers. He stands virtually alone among the "new" Hollywood directors in his searing, compassionate evocation of that most neglected of species: the middle-aged, middle-class, middle-brow American.

JOHN CASSAVETES was born on December 9, 1929, in New York, the son of Greek immigrants. His father a Harvard-educated businessman with a knack for making and losing millions, Cassavetes was raised in *Husbands* territory, the Long Island towns of Sands Point and Port Washington. One of his most vivid recollections from childhood is of how he chipped his teeth in a fight and, unable to afford caps, refused to smile for years—an anecdote which makes one speculate on the strained smiles and laughter in his films. At Colgate University the plays of Robert E. Sherwood spurred Cassavetes to enroll at the New York Academy of Dramatic Arts, from which he graduated in 1953. Unable to find work on Broadway, Cassavetes drifted into James Dean-type roles on television and slowly made his way into such films as *The Night Holds Terror* and *Edge of the City*. Cassavetes still considers himself a "professional" actor and an "amateur" director, as most of his films have been financed by his acting career. In 1956 he began conducting a "method" workshop for unemployed actors, and in an interview on *Night People*—a late-night music and talk show—he mentioned the possibility of turning an especially successful improvisation into a film. Small contributions began pouring in from listeners, and thus began *Shadows*.

Shadows is still the film Cassavetes is most fond of (though he judges *Woman under the Influence* his best), and it is certainly his most fragile, endearing work. Starring unknowns Lelia Goldoni, Hugh Hurd, and Ben Carruthers, it is Cassavetes's only fully-improvised script and his solitary investigation of youth to date. Set in the Broadway area of Manhattan, *Shadows* contains most of the elements that turn up in the later works: the Pirandellian framework (all the actors and actresses play themselves); the shakey, hand-held camera; the myopic lens; the pre-eminence of character over structure and actor over audience. Centring around a parentless black family in which the sister and younger brother pass as whites, *Shadows* is also Cassavetes's most *nouvelle vague*-ish film, highly reminiscent of Chabrol's *Les cousins* in its juxtaposition of the callow and the vulnerable nature of youth. A rites of passage film, *Shadows* takes all its characters to the brink of understanding and leaves them at a moment of revision.

Despite the rough texture of the cinematography, the camera is more docile in *Shadows* than in the later works. There is a swift but elegiac sequence in Central Park and a lengthy stroll through the Sculpture Garden at the Museum of Modern Art: two of the very few outdoor sequences in Cassavetes's *oeuvre*. The jazz background music of Charles Mingus and Shafi Hadi complements the syncopated rhythm of the improvisation itself, and the hysteria implicit in Lelia's laughter and the fear and violence thinly sheathed by Benny's apparent passivity are *motifs* that will recur again and again, particularly in *Faces* and *Husbands*.

Following the success of *Shadows*, Paramount contracted Cassavetes to make a series of artistic, low-budget films, a partnership which came swiftly to a halt with the failure of *Too Late Blues*—a commercial version of the first film, which pleased neither critics nor the public. Stanley Kramer produced Cassavetes's third film, an underestimated picture (Cassavetes himself finds it sentimental—a result of the producer's cutting) starring Judy Garland and Burt Lancaster in a semi-documentary on afflicted children, told with classical Hollywood pans and zooms and a steadied camera. Despite its overt didacticism, *A Child Is Waiting* is a surprisingly moving and provocative statement, suggesting much more than the traumas of the retarded child. In one rather understated sequence a father deplores the fact that the most his son can aspire to is a life as a dish-washer or basket-weaver. The response—" I often wonder how far the rest of us get"—echoes throughout all of the more sophisticated, more idiosyncratic works.

A Child Is Waiting marked the end of Cassavetes's pandering to distributors, and, with the exception of *Minnie and Moskowitz*, all his other films have been independent projects—the finances accrued from friends, unsalaried actors, and predominantly his own resources. (In the case of *Woman under the Influence* Cassavetes had to mortgage his house, and the venture is only now beginning to pay off.) Even with *Minnie and Moskowitz* Cassavetes gave Universal a run for their money: when he disapproved of their publicity campaign, he began holding his own press screenings.

Faces was shot in eight months and released four years later. Featuring John Marley (winner of Best Actor in Venice), Lynn Carlin, Seymour Cassel, and Gena Rowlands (Cassavetes's off-screen wife), it was greeted with raves and verbal tomato throwing, but little in between. It is his most comprehensive, least elastic film—an uncompromising dissection of a fourteen-year-old middle-class marriage in the grainy, *cinéma-vérité* style of *Shadows*.

The "morning after" scene in *Faces* has been likened to Lelia Goldoni's similar sequence in the earlier film. The comparison could not be more unjust. Lelia, in what is probably Cassavetes's most poignant vignette, is experiencing the first tremors of life—an intimation of potential ecstasy and commensurate despair, while the Lynn Carlin character is affirming her own mortality. Her vomiting is really much closer to that of the men in *Husbands*: an impotent recoiling from the limitations dictated both by her society and by her own emotional framework.

Despite its bourgeois setting, *Faces* is no more social commentary than *Husbands*, a

Gena Rowlands and John Marley in FACES

film in which Cassavetes joins Ben Gazzara and Peter Falk in a tale of three suburbanites who take off on a four-day binge after the funeral of their fourth buddy. Like *Faces*, *Husbands* is both fully scripted and highly improvisational, with the emphasis on actors and undermining of technique. Though it focuses on the narcissism of three men-children in search of an inaccessible freedom, it contains such a wealth of feeling on so many levels that it has been hailed by no less a feminist than Betty Friedan as a Women's Lib film! *Husbands* reinvestigates the validity of the nuclear family: although only one wife is portrayed (and she in an unfavourable light),

the presence of all three is keenly sensed. Cassavetes's ribald humour strains to over-indulgence at times, but his characters are never cruel merely for the sake of crudity. (Peter Falk's salacious mockery of the old lady gambler is thus just as revealing as Cassavetes's calculated indifference to the vulnerability of his "one-night-stand.") The pseudo-intimate laughter between the sexes rings as strident as the shared jokes of the husband and wife in *Faces*, and the inconclusive ending once again underscores the director's aversion to polemics.

Minnie and Moskowitz, Cassavetes's "entertainment" film, is an *hommage* to the sentiment of old Hollywood, updated and surprisingly upbeat. The chronicle of a mismatched romance, *Minnie and Moskowitz* comes complete with Humphrey Bogart clips, nostalgic tunes ("I Love You Truly"—a nice tribute to Capra's *It's a Wonderful Life*), and happy ending. Starring Gena Rowlands and Seymour Cassel (not to mention half the Rowlands–Cassavetes brood and the two grandmothers as well), it is the improbable saga of the WASP and the car parker, told in Technicolor with a fidgity camera and refreshing bravado. Like Martin Scorsese's *Alice Doesn't Live Here Anymore*, *Minnie*

and Moskowitz is replete with darker undertones (the eccentric blind date, the withering bridesmaid, the suicidal wife); but it marks a momentary relenting of the intransigence of Cassavetes's universe, and the result is a picaresque comedy, rooted in anything but realism.

A Woman under the Influence, which opened at the 1974 New York Film Festival, represents the director's latest and finest work thus far. Once again an exploration of middle-class (this time lower middle-class) marriage at metaphysical crossroads, *Woman under the Influence* is Cassavetes's first confronta-

Peter Falk, Ben Gazzara, and John Cassavetes enjoy their drinks in HUSBANDS

Peter Falk and Gena Rowlands on the set of A WOMAN UNDER THE INFLUENCE

tion with the awesome nature of connubial love. While the final image of *Faces* is of husband and wife enunciating their raw mutual distaste on a cramped, dank, staircase, *Woman under the Influence* leaves Gena Rowlands and Peter Falk undressing for bed—imperfectly wed, but committed. Here Cassavetes's always superior acting is elevated to the sublime with Gena Rowlands's flailing, inarticulate Mabel masterfully encapsulating the ambivalence and the depth of the ailing female—liberated or not—and Peter Falk brilliantly interpreting the flawed, loving nature of the man who almost unwittingly betrays her.

Here more than ever Cassavetes's denigration of style is a style in itself: his indifference to landscapes and long shots serving to underscore the *huis clos* of his universe. With *Woman under the Influence* John Cassavetes reasserts himself as one of the most important film-makers working in America today. Eschewing intellectual, social and cosmic correlatives, he has created a cinema of intuition, a world devoted to the mysteries of idiosyncrasy. It is the wisdom of his feelings rather than the selective realism of his camera that has made metaphor of retarded child, ageing jazz musician, and atrophied mother alike; and it is his perverse integrity that denies his audience answers—easy or complex.

DIANE JACOBS

(The author would like to thank Swank Motion Pictures, Audio Brandon Films, and the Museum of Modern Art, for screening certain Cassavetes pictures in preparation for the above article.)

CASSAVETES FILMOGRAPHY

Cassavetes's acting appearances in films other than his own are as follows: *Taxi* (1953), *The Night Holds Terror* (1955), *Crime in the Streets* (1956), *Edge of the City/A Man Is Ten Feet Tall* (1957), *Affair in Havana* (1957), *Saddle the Wind* (1958), *Virgin Island* (1958), *The Webster Boy* (1962), *The Killers* (1964; made for TV), *The Devil's Angels* (1967), *The Dirty Dozen* (1967), *Rosemary's Baby* (1968), *Gli intoccabili/Machine Gun McCain* (1968), *Roma come Chicago/Bandits in Rome* (1968), *If It's Tuesday, This Must Be Belgium* (1969), *Capone* (1975).

1960

SHADOWS. Script and direction: JC. Photography (16mm): Erich Kollmar. Editing: Len Appelson, Maurice McEndree. Music: Charles Mingus (saxophone: Shafi Hadi). Players: Lelia Goldoni (*Lelia*), Ben Carruthers (*Ben*), Hugh Hurd (*Hugh*), Anthony Ray (*Tony*), Rupert Crosse (*Rupe*), Tom Allen (*Tom*), Dennis Sallas (*Dennis*), David Pokitellow (*David*). Produced by Maurice McEndree for Cassavetes–McEndree–Cassel. 81 mins. On 16mm: Audio Brandon (U.S.).

1961

TOO LATE BLUES. Script: JC, Richard Carr. Direction: JC. Photography: Lionel Lindon. Editing: Frank Bracht. Music: David Raksin. Art Direction: Tambi Larsen. Players: Bobby Darin (*John "Ghost" Wakefield*), Stella Stevens (*Jess Polanski*), Everett Chambers (*Benny Flowers*), Nick Dennis (*Nick*), Rupert Crosse (*Baby Jackson*), Vince Edwards (*Tommy*), Val Avery (*Frielobe*), J. Allen Hopkins (*Skipper*), James Joyce (*Reno, the Barman*), Marilyn Clark (*Countess*), Allyson Ames (*Billie Gray*), June Wilkinson (*Girl at Bar*), Cliff Carnell (*Charlie, the Saxophonist*), Seymour Cassel (*Red, the Bassist*), Dan Stafford (*Shelley, the Drummer*), Richard Chambers (*Pete, the Trumpet-Player*). Produced by JC for Paramount. 103 mins.

1962

A CHILD IS WAITING. Script: Abby Mann, from his own story. Direction: JC. Photography: Joseph LaShelle. Editing: Gene Fowler Jr. Music: Ernest Gold. Production Design: Rudolph Sternad. Players: Burt Lancaster (*Dr. Matthew Clark*), Judy Garland (*Jean Hansen*), Gena Rowlands (*Sophie Widdicombe*), Steven Hill (*Ted Widdicombe*), Bruce Ritchey (*Reuben Widdicombe*), Gloria McGehee (*Mattie*), Paul Stewart (*Goodman*), Lawrence Tierney (*Douglas Benham*), Elizabeth Wilson (*Miss Fogarty*), Barbara Pepper (*Miss Brown*), John Marley (*Holland*), June Walker (*Mrs. McDonald*), Mario Gallo (*Dr. Lombardi*), Frederick Draper (*Dr. Sack*). Produced by Stanley Kramer (Larcas Productions) for United Artists. 104 mins. On 16mm: FDA (G.B.).

1968

FACES. Script and direction: JC. Photography: Al Ruban. Editing: Al Ruban, Maurice McEndree. Music: Jack Ackerman. Song: Charles Smalls ("Never Felt Like This Before"). Art Direction: Phedon Papamichael. Players: John Marley (*Richard Forst*), Gena Rowlands (*Jeannie Rapp*), Lynn Carlin (*Maria Forst*), Fred Draper (*Freddie*), Seymour Cassel (*Chet*), Val Avery (*McCarthy*), Dorothy Gulliver (*Florence*), Joanne Moore Jordan (*Louise*), Darlene Conley (*Billy Mae*), Gene Darfler (*Jackson*), Elizabeth Deering (*Stella*), Dave Mazzie, Julie Gambol. Produced by Maurice McEndree. 130 mins. On 16mm: Walter Reade (U.S.).

1970

HUSBANDS. Script and direction: JC. Photography (DeLuxe Color): Victor Kemper. Sup. Editing: Peter Tanner. Art Direction: René D'Auriac. Players: Ben Gazzara (*Harry*), Peter Falk (*Archie*), JC (*Gus*), Jenny Runacre (*Mary Tynan*), Jenny Lee Wright (*Pearl Billingham*), Noelle Kao (*Julie*), Leola Harlow (*Leola*), Meta Shaw (*Annie*), John Kullers (*Red*), Delores Delmar (*Countess*), Peggy Lashbrook (*Diana Mallabee*), Eleanor Zee (*Mrs. Hines*), Claire Malis (*Stuart's Wife*), Lorraine McMartin (*Annie's Mother*), Edgar Franken (*Ed Weintraub*), Sarah Felcher (*Sarah*), Antoinette Kray ("*Jesus Loves Me*"), Gwen Van Dam ("*Jeannie*"), John Armstrong ("*Happy Birthday*"), Eleanor Gould ("*Normandy*"), Carinthia West (*Susanna*), Rhonda Parker (*Margaret*), Joseph Boley (*Minister*), Judith Lowrey (*Stuart's Grandmother*), Joseph Hardy ("*Shanghai Lil*"), K. C. Townsend (*Barmaid*), Anne O'Donnell (*Nurse*), Gena Wheeler (*Nurse*). David Rowlands (*Stuart Jackson*). Produced by Al Ruban for Columbia. 154 mins. (G.B.: 142 mins). On 16 mm: Swank (U.S.).

Peter Falk in A WOMAN UNDER THE INFLUENCE

1971

MINNIE AND MOSKOWITZ. Script and direction: JC. Photography (Technicolor): Arthur J. Ornitz, Alric Edens, Michael Margulies. Editing: Fred Knudtson. Music: Bob Harwood. Players: Gena Rowlands (*Minnie Moore*), Seymour Cassel (*Seymour Moskowitz*), Val Avery (*Zelmo Swift*), Tim Carey (*Morgan Morgan*), Katherine Cassavetes (*Sheba Moskowitz*), Elizabeth Deering (*Girl*), Elsie Ames (*Florence*), Lady Rowlands (*Georgia Moore*), Holly Near (*Irish*), Judith Roberts (*Wife*), JC (*Husband*), Jack Danskin (*Dick Henderson*), Eleanor Zee (*Mrs. Grass*), Sean Joyce (*Ned*), David Rowlands (*Minister*). Produced by Al Ruban for Universal. 115 mins. On 16mm: Universal 16 (U.S.).

1974

A WOMAN UNDER THE INFLUENCE. Script and direction: JC. Photography (M-G-M Color): Mitch Breit, Chris Taylor, Bo Taylor, Merv Dayan, Caleb Deschanel. Editing: Tom Cornwell, Elizabeth Bergeron, David Armstrong, Sheila Viseltear. Music: Bo Harwood. Art Direction: Phedon Papamichael. Players: Peter Falk (*Nick Longhetti*), Gena Rowlands (*Mabel Longhetti*), Matthew Cassel (*Tony Longhetti*), Matthew Laborteaux (*Angelo Longhetti*), Christina Grisanti (*Maria Longhetti*), Katherine Cassavetes (*Mama Longhetti*), Lady Rowlands (*Martha Mortensen*), Fred Draper (*George Mortensen*), O. G. Dunn (*Garson Cross*), Mario Gallo (*Harold Jensen*), Eddie Shaw (*Doctor Zepp*), Angelo Grisanti (*Vito Grimaldi*), James Joyce (*Bowman*), John Finnegan (*Clancy*), Hugh Hurd (*Willie Johnson*), Leon Wagner (*Billy Tidrow*), John Hawker (*Joseph Morton*), Sil Words (*James Turner*), Elizabeth Deering (*Angela*), Jacki Peters (*Tina*), Elsie Ames (*Principle*). Produced by Faces International Films (Sam Shaw). 155 mins.

Francis Ford Coppola with Gene Hackman between takes on THE CONVERSATION

Francis Ford Coppola

None of the directors at work in the American "new wave" can match the Protean talent of Francis Ford Coppola. In terms of financial achievement, he has outstripped with *The Godfather* even such giants as *Gone with the Wind*. In April 1975 *two* of his films, *The Godfather Part II* and *The Conversation*, were nominated for Best Picture in the Academy Awards, with Coppola winning a personal Oscar as Best Director. And few of those who hailed Coppola as an *auteur* following the release of *The Godfather* were aware that this gifted director was also a screenwriter (*This Property Is Condemned, Patton*, etc.) and production mentor for a still younger generation of movie-makers like George Lucas and John Milius.

FRANCIS FORD COPPOLA (pronounced "cope-ella") was born on April 7, 1939, in Detroit, Michigan. His father, Carmine Coppola, was first flute under Toscanini in the NBC Symphony Orchestra, and conducted the music with various shows on tour throughout the country. From an early age, Coppola expressed an interest in plays and musicals, and at ten he was already experimenting with sound in his home movies. While still in college, he wrote the book and lyrics for "The Delicate Touch". But it was at the University of California, Los Angeles, where he studied film, that Coppola began to shape his future career. He wrote a screenplay, *Pilma, Pilma,* which won a Samuel Goldwyn Award in 1962 but was never produced, and he wrote and directed a stage production of "Aymonn the Terrible." Then, thanks to his "doing the dub" for Roger Corman on a Soviet science fiction movie, he began a vital collaboration with the young prince of Z-films. Coppola was a kind of Man Friday to him. He supervised the sound on *The Young Racers*; he polished the dialogue on *The Tower of London*. Corman's cynical batch of horror movies has always masked a keen and intuitive appreciation of good cinema. His encouragement of Coppola is one indication of this; so is his purchase of *Cries and Whispers* for release in the United States. In 1962, Corman gave the twenty-two-year-old Coppola the chance to direct *Dementia 13*. This horror movie, entitled *The Haunted and the Hunted* in Britain, startlingly prefigures *The Godfather*. The Halloran family, reunited in an ancestral Irish castle, shares with the Corleones an unmitigated desire for power and a taste for violent solutions, "Despite a limited budget and conventional approach," wrote an anonymous critic in "Monthly Film Bulletin," "the atmosphere of mystery and midnight wanderings is well-sustained, and the settings ... are imaginatively handled."

There ensued a period of cinematic chores for Coppola—scripting, re-writing, production work—and it was not until 1966 that he contrived to make another film, *You're a Big Boy Now*. It was a gamble, and Coppola earned a mere $8,000 for writing and directing the picture, but when it was screened at Cannes in 1967, it undoubtedly caused a stir among international critics. Agreeably stamped with the influence of Dick Lester, John Cassavetes, and the French New Wave, the movie tells the story of a pint-sized Portnoy who comes to New York and takes a job in the Public Library. His attempts to master

Above: DEMENTIA 13
Below: Peter Kastner skating through the book stacks in YOU'RE A BIG BOY NOW

an innate shyness and adolescent fear of girls lead to one farcical situation after another, and witty observations coruscate throughout the film. The dialogue has a strange, delightful wackiness, and the spectacle of Bernard's chasing a kite in Central Park, or roller-skating his way through the hushed echelons of the Library, is riotously amusing. There are songs by John Sebastian that slide deftly into the plot, and the actors, from Peter Kastner to Rip Torn, from Julie Harris to Elizabeth Hartman, perform with effervescent zeal. One's impression of Coppola that May in Cannes was of an alert, ebullient director, ready to take risks to achieve an unpretentious laugh.

The film raised Coppola's prestige at Warner-Seven Arts, and he was offered *Finian's Rainbow*, a musical that had first appeared on Broadway in the Forties and had evinced a winsome charm with its leprechauns and its crock of gold. At first Coppola thought that he could shoot the production in Kentucky, using genuine backgrounds. He was soon told by the studio, however, that his cameras would be restricted to the backlot. He was disillusioned, but still managed to stage the songs with aplomb and edit them with a precision that makes his early fondness for Eisenstein readily understandable. The film flopped, and Coppola was lucky enough to have his next production already financed and under way.

He would probably agree that *The Rain People* was his first self-determined movie, and the poor release pattern accorded the film by Warners still irks him. The budget ran to $750,000, and shooting was accomplished entirely on location in eighteen states. James Caan, whom Coppola knew from Hofstra College days, plays the mentally injured pro footballer who encounters Shirley Knight's pregnant housewife. Both have fled their anchorage in life; each responds to the other in a remarkably sincere, unaffected way, and Coppola's sympathetic direction eschews forthright sexual language. Yet it remains a *film maudit*, abandoned by the studio in the wake of *Finian's Rainbow*, and its failure marks the nadir of Coppola's fortunes. His American Zoetrope studio in San Francisco was brought to the brink of extinction when Warners withdrew their financial support, and Coppola, by his own admission, was "penniless" when Paramount offered him *The Godfather*. Zoetrope as a name, however, has endured, with George Lucas as its favourite son. Coppola was the guiding force behind *THX 1138* and *American Graffiti*, two pictures that established Lucas as an exciting off-Hollywood talent.

One of the major reasons for the success of *The Godfather* in the States was undoubtedly its appeal to the ethnic consciousness of so many Americans. For all its modern violence and sophistication, the film is really a paean, not so much to the Mafia as to the pioneer spirit that enabled generations of Italians to sail to the U.S.A., settle, and establish a new caste of iron-clad proportions. While never glorifying the exploits of "the Black Hand," *The Godfather* does probe thoughtfully into the grand tradition of the Italian families, and in early set-pieces like Sandra's *alfresco* wedding at Long Beach, the film captures the dizzy romance of the family celebrations. Cinematographer Gordon Willis imbues the images with a crisp, sunburned glow (dismissed by many naive critics as bad lab work), so that even when the action switches to Sicily (in an oddly moving dissolve from the Don's regretful face on his sickbed), there is little change in tone. It is as though the Corleones had shifted not only their family but also the very texture of their age-old environment to the United States.

Fred Astaire with Petula Clark in FINIAN'S RAINBOW

Although off-screen for much of *The Godfather's* three hours, Marlon Brando looms over the film. His performance as Don Vito gives off a fading grandeur, casual gestures invoking instant obedience, the voice hoarse and weary. It is Brando's Don who embodies the saving grace of the Corleones, the honour among thieves and the inviolability of the family.

There are small flaws stemming from the inevitable compression of the novel. Richard Conte's Barzini is a tailor's dummy with hardly a line of dialogue to his credit, and one never grasps in the film that Michael is secretly jealous of Tom Hagen's closeness to Sonny, with the result that the expulsion of Tom as *consigliore* is puzzling to anyone unfamiliar with the book. Even in *Part II*, the love-hate attitude extended towards Hagen by Michael is weakly articulated.

Against this one can set the uncanny

Marlon Brando and Al Pacino in THE GODFATHER

John Marley awakes to find the horse's head in his bedclothes

prescience of the production, with the Gallo-Columbo gang war erupting in the Mulberry Street murder a few days after the film opened in New York in 1972.

The Godfather was conceived, directed, and edited with an altogether more assured flair than any of Coppola's previous films. Inevitably, there remained the suspicion that this was a "fluke," a stroke of luck rather than a work of genius. Coppola's answer was to withdraw to San Francisco and quietly shoot the film that may well be the masterpiece of the American Seventies: *The Conversation.* From the first, protracted zoom shot, peering down into San Francisco's crowded Union Square, Coppola stimulates the susceptibilities of his audience.

Known in the surveillance trade as "the best bugger on the West Coast," Harry Caul is fiercely independent, his workshop in a disused warehouse a miracle of home engineering, a litter of elaborate devices that can penetrate the thickest curtain of crowd noise and street music to eavesdrop on a couple's conversation. Like the photographer in *Blow-Up,* however, Harry finds that his technical prowess can detect, but cannot comprehend, the message . . . . Warned by the Kafka-esque "Director's Office" to hand over the tapes in return for cash without further questions, he reacts by going to Confession for the first time in months and by launching his own private investigation into the crime he is certain will be committed. His job afflicts him like an ulcer; during the party in his workshop after a Convention-floor meeting with his arch-rival, Moran, he experiences revulsion against the whole, furtive, dis-

Allen Garfield, Elizabeth MacRae, and Gene Hackman in THE CONVERSATION

tasteful business. Triumphs, like the taping of a Presidential scandal in 1968 recalled with admiration by Moran, suddenly appear like sins to Harry's Catholic nature. His self-confidence, hitherto impregnable, is shattered when Moran manages to plant a microphone on him with insolent ease. And the ironic climax of *The Conversation* shows how Harry, the solitary individual whose professional life is devoted to the invasion of other people's privacy, is himself violated in the selfsame fashion. He dismembers his apartment in a frantic effort to locate the "organisation's" bugging device, and then retreats into a paranoid limbo, playing his beloved saxophone and dwindling into futility and insignificance, like Andreas Winkelmann at the end of *The Passion of Anna*. It is a ritual dismantlement, the final demonstration of Harry's quest for his own origins and the source of his guilt.

According to Coppola, the twin in-fluences on his first treatment were Herman Hesse (Harry Haller/Harry Caul) and *Blow-*

Up, but the film reeks of the Watergate era. Not just in the specific notion of bugging, but in the wider sense of lives being manipulated from within what Coppola has termed the "citadel of power."

The most remarkable feature of the film is its deployment of *in*human devices and technology to investigate a *human* predicament. Harry is, ultimately, more mysterious and intriguing than the tape he dissects. He has the same awareness of inner shame as a Graham Greene victim; each of his most treasured possessions—the plastic mac, the saxophone, the statuette of the Virgin Mary—strikes a response in the spectator, symbolises a life-style, dovetails the personal and the impersonal ... In spite of these vibrations, however, Harry remains a tantalising figure. His girlfriend fails to fathom his obsessions. He remains immune to Moran's persistent provocation in the workshop sequence. And finally, aided and abetted by Coppola, he obscures the truth from the audience in an indeterminate welter of reportage, dream, and hallucination. Someone is killed. That is indubitable. But the various versions of the murder in Room 773 are convulsive efforts on the part of Harry's subconscious to find a visual metaphor for his own deep-down disquiet.

The Godfather Part II, like *The Conversation*, is set in a visual equivalent of G minor: intense, searching, mature. It begins with Michael Corleone in close-up, accepting the silent oath of fealty from a member of the family. Clearly, Michael is to hold the centre of the stage. Like Brando in the first part, however, Al Pacino has comparatively few scenes in which to make his impact, for the narrative flutters about like a caged bird. One moment we are in Sicily at the turn of the century, witnessing the murder of Don Vito's mother in bright sunlight; the next we are at Lake Tahoe, Nevada, celebrating the first communion of Michael's son. There are long sections describing the early years of the Don in New York, and there is even a kind of flashback to the first film, showing the Corleone family round the Sunday dinner table, berating Michael for joining the Marines.

Coppola rightly rejects the suggestion that *The Godfather* and its sequel set out to exalt and exonerate the Mafia. "For me," he says, "the Mafia is just a metaphor for America. It is transplanted from Europe; it is a capitalistic, profit-seeking body; it believes that anything it does to protect and sustain itself and its family is morally good." Kay, ironically the weakest character in both films, becomes the vicarious spectator who is confronted with the most monstrous and calculating aspects of the Corleone family. In *The Godfather* she is transfixed by Michael's hypnotic personality, and is eventually willing to accept a lie so shattering, and so shameless, that its utterance comes as the perfect closure to the film. In *Part II*, she threatens to leave Michael and they have bloodcurdling quarrel that ends with the new Don's revelation that he would rather kill her than her escape with his children. It is in moments like these that the Mafia's code of violence defeats itself, like incest, and as Coppola observes Michael's brooding face in close-up in the final shot of *Part II*, there is no sense of cheap cathartic release. This heinous individual has coldly eliminated all his enemies, including his own brother. Beyond his profile, there extends only a dark wood, like the sombre background to a Caspar David Friedrich painting.

If there is a hero in *The Godfather Part II*, it is the young Don Vito, establishing his power in the teeming streets of Little Italy with a discreet, strategic patience. Appropriately, the cinematography in these scenes bears a golden sheen; the interiors are refulgent with ochreish light, and the music of Nino Rota heightens the mood of lost romance. The film may lack the homogeneity and cohesion of its predecessor, but the explosions of sex and violence that light up *The Godfather* give way here to a pervasive sense of dread and anguish. Like Harry Caul, Michael has stripped away everything and everyone that appears hostile to him, and he is left a solitary, reflecting on a hectic past and a sunless future. Even *Consigliore* Tom Hagen is estranged. Kay has been banished. Fredo, Frankie, and Hyman Roth have been eliminated. Just as Harry fails to realise that the bugging device may be lodged in his saxophone, so Michael cannot perceive the seeds of nemesis within his own character. This, in the final analysis, is what fascinates Coppola in all his pictures—the motivation that urges someone to become a mobster, an eavesdropper, or merely a stack boy in the New York Public Library. Other American directors have had similar preoccupations.

Coppola supervises the Cuban Street sequence in THE GODFATHER PART II

But Coppola's recent films manifest a quite extraordinary sophistication. He has acquired, like the most personal of the European *auteurs*, an Olympian tolerance of human foibles, and a cinematic style that is increasingly distinguished by its poetic gravity and restraint.

PETER COWIE

(Portions of this article have appeared in the form of reviews in "Focus on Film." The author gratefully acknowledges the permission of that magazine to reprint the material.)

COPPOLA FILMOGRAPHY

Coppola's screenplay work is as follows: *This Property Is Condemned* (1966), *Paris brûle-t-il?* (1966), *Reflections in a Golden Eye* (1967, uncredited early work), *Patton* (1970), *The Great Gatsby* (1974). He also wrote the following unfilmed scripts while at Seven Arts: *The Disenchanted, The Fifth Coin, My Last Duchess*. Coppola is also credited as Associate Producer on Roger Corman's *The Terror* (1963),

1963

DEMENTIA 13/THE HAUNTED AND THE HUNTED. Script and direction: FFC. Photography: Charles Hannawalt. Editing: Stewart O'Brien. Music: Ronald Stein. Art Direction: Albert Locatelli. Players: William Campbell (*Richard Haloran*), Luana Anders (*Louise Haloran*), Bart Patton (*Billy Haloran*), Mary Mitchell (*Kane*), Patrick Magee (*Justin Caleb*), Eithne Dunn (*Lady Haloran*), Peter Read (*John Haloran*), Karl Schanzer (*Simon*), Ron Perry (*Arthur*), Derry O'Donovan (*Lillian*), Barbara Dowling (*Kathleen*). Produced by Roger Corman for Filmgroup/AIP. 81 mins. (G.B.: 73 mins.). On 16mm: Audio Brandon (U.S.).

1967

YOU'RE A BIG BOY NOW. Script: FFC, from the novel by David Benedictus. Direction: FFC. Photography (Eastmancolor): Andy Laszlo. Editing: Aram Avakian. Music: Bob Prince. Songs: John Sebastian (sung by The Lovin' Spoonful). Art Direction: Vassele Fotopoulos. Choreography: Robert Tucker. Players: Peter Kastner (*Bernard Chanticleer*), Elizabeth Hartman (*Barbara Darling*), Geraldine Page (*Margery Chanticleer*), Julie Harris (*Miss Thing*), Rip Torn (*I.H. Chanticleer*), Tony Bill (*Raef*), Karen Black (*Amy*), Michael Dunn (*Richard Mudd*), Dolph Sweet (*Policeman Francis Graf*), Michael O'Sullivan (*Kurt Doughty*).

Produced by Phil Feldman (Seven Arts) for Warner-Pathé. 97 mins. On 16mm: Columbia-Warner (G.B.), United Films (U.S.).

1968

FINIAN'S RAINBOW. Script: E. Y. Harburg, Fred Saidy, based on their musical play (music: Burton Lane; lyrics: E. Y. Harburg). Direction: FFC. Photography (Technicolor, Panavision, presented in 70 mm): Philip Lathrop. Editing: Melvin Shapiro. Music Direction: Ray Heindorf. Production Design: Hilyard M. Brown. Choreography: Hermes Pan. Players: Fred Astaire (*Finian McLonergan*), Petula Clark (*Sharon McLonergan*), Tommy Steele (*Og*), Don Francks (*Woody*), Barbara Hancock (*Susan the Silent*), Keenan Wynn (*Judge Billboard Rawkins*), Al Freeman Jr. (*Howard*), Brenda Arnau (*Sharecropper*), Avon Long, Roy Glenn, Jerster Hairston (*Passion Pilgrim Gospellers*), Louis Silas (*Henry*), Dolph Sweet (*Sheriff*), Wright King (*District Attorney*). Produced by Joseph Landon (Warner Bros./Seven Arts) for Warner-Pathé. 144 mins. On 16mm: Columbia-Warner (G.B.), United Films (U.S.).

1969

THE RAIN PEOPLE. Script and direction: FFC. Photography (Technicolor): Wilmer Butler. Editing: Blackie Malkin. Music: Ronald Stein. Art Direction: Leon Ericksen. Players: James Caan (*Kilgannon*), Shirley Knight (*Natalie*), Robert Duvall (*Gordon*), Marya Zimmet (*Rosalie*), Tom Aldredge (*Mr. Alfred*), Laurie Crews (*Ellen*), Andrew Duncan (*Artie*), Margaret Fairchild (*Marion*), Sally Gracie (*Beth*), Alan Manson (*Lou*), Robert Modica (*Vinny*), Produced by Bart Patton and Ronald Colby (Coppola Company Presentation) for Warner Bros./Seven Arts. 101 mins. On 16mm: Warner Gallery (U.S.).

1972

THE GODFATHER. Script: Mario Puzo, FFC, based on the novel by Puzo. Direction: FFC. Photography (Technicolor): Gordon Willis. Editing: William Reynolds, Peter Zinner, Marc Laub, Murray Solomon. Music: Nino Rota (conducted by Carlo Savina). Production Design: Dean Tavoularis. Art Direction: Warren Clymer. Players: Marlon Brando (*Don Vito Corleone*), Al Pacino (*Michael Corleone*), James Caan (*Sonny Corleone*), Richard Castellano (*Clemenza*), Robert Duvall (*Tom Hagan*), Sterling Hayden (*McClusky*), John Marley (*Jack Woltz*), Richard Conte (*Barzini*), Diane Keaton (*Kay Adams*), Al Lettieri (*Sollozzo*), Abe Vigoda (*Tessio*), Talia Shire (*Connie Rizzi*), Gianni Russo (*Carlo Rizzi*), John Cazale (*Fredo Corleone*), Rudy Bond (*Cuneo*), Al Martino (*Johnny Fontane*), Morgana King

(*Mama Corleone*), Lenny Montana (*Luca Brasi*), John Martino (*Paulie Gatto*), Salvatore Corsitto (*Bonasera*), Richard Bright (*Nerì*), Alex Rocco (*Moe Greene*), Tony Giorgio (*Bruno Tattaglia*), Vito Scotti (*Nazorine*), Tere Livrano (*Theresa Hagen*), Victor Rendina (*Philip Tattaglia*), Jeannie Linero (*Lucy Mancini*), Julie Gregg (*Sandra Corleone*), Ardell Sheridan (*Mrs. Clemenza*), Simonetta Stefanelli (*Apollonia*), Angelo Infanti (*Fabrizio*), Corrado Gaipa (*Don Tommasino*), Franco Citti (*Calo*), Saro Urzi (*Vitelli*). Produced by Albert S. Ruddy (Alfran Productions) for Paramount. 175 mins. On 16mm: Columbia-Warner (G.B.), Films Inc. (U.S.).

1974

THE CONVERSATION. Script and direction: FFC. Photography (Technicolor): Bill Butler. Editing: Walter Murch, Richard Chew. Music: David Shire. Production Design: Dean Tavoularis. Technical Advisors: Hal Lipset, Leo Jones. Players: Gene Hackman (*Harry Caul*), John Cazale (*Stan*), Allen Garfield (*Bernie Moran*), Frederic Forrest (*Mark*), Cindy Williams (*Ann*), Michael Higgins (*Paul*), Elizabeth MacRae (*Meredith*), Harrison Ford (*Martin Stett*), Mark Wheeler (*Receptionist*), Teri Garr (*Amy*), Robert Shields (*Mime*), Phoebe Alexander (*Lurleen*), Robert Duvall (*The Director*). Produced by FFC and Fred Roos (Coppola Company/Paramount) for CIC. 113 mins. On 16mm: Columbia-Warner (G.B.), Films Inc. (U.S.).

1974

THE GODFATHER Part II. Script: FFC, Mario Puzo, from the novel by Puzo. Direction: FFC. Photography (Technicolor): Gordon Willis. Editing: Peter Zinner, Barry Malkin, Richard Marks. Music: Nino Rota (conducted by Carmine Coppola). Production Design: Dean Tavoularis. Art Direction: Angelo Graham. Players: Al Pacino (*Michael Corleone*), Robert Duvall (*Tom Hagen*), Diane Keaton (*Kay Adams*), Robert De Niro (*Vito Corleone*), John Cazale (*Fredo Corleone*), Talia Shire (*Connie Corleone*), Lee Strasberg (*Hyman Roth*), Michael V. Gazzo (*Frankie Pentangeli*), G. D. Spradlin (*Seantor Pat Geary*), Richard Bright (*Al Nerì*), Gaston Moschin (*Fanucci*), Tom Rosqui (*Rocco Lampone*), B. Kirby Jr. (*Young Clemenza*), Frank Sivero (*Genco*), Francesca De Sapio (*Young Mama Corleone*), Morgana King (*Mama Corleone*), Mariana Hill (*Deanna Corleone*), Leopoldo Trieste (*Signor Roberto*), Dominic Chianese (*Johnny Ola*), Amerigo Tot (*Michael's Bodyguard*), Troy Donahue (*Merle Johnson*), John Aprea (*Young Tessio*), Joe Spinell (*Willi Cicci*), Abe

Vigoda (*Tessio*), Tere Livrano (*Theresa Hagen*), Gianni Russo (*Carlo Rizzi*), Maria Carta (*Vito's Mother*), Oreste Baldini (*Vito Andolini, as a Boy*), Giuseppe Sillato (*Don Francesco*), Mario Cotone (*Don Tommasino*), James Gounaris (*Anthony Corleone*), Fay Spain (*Mrs. Marcia Roth*), Harry Dean Stanton (*First FBI Man*), David Baker (*Second FBI Man*), Carmine Caridi (*Carmine Rosato*), Danny Aiello (*Tony Rosato*), Carmine Foresta (*Policeman*), Nick Discenza (*Barman*), Father Joseph Medeglia (*Father Carmelo*), William Bowers (*Senate Committee Chairman*), Joe Della Sorte, Carmen Argenziano, Joe Lo Grippo (*Michael's Buttonmen*), Ezio Flagello (*Impresario*), Livio Giorgi (*Tenor in "Senza Mamma"*), Kathy Beller (*Girl in "Senza Mamma"*), Saveria Mazzola (*Signora Colombo*), Tito Alba (*Cuban President*), Johnny Naranjo (*Cuban Translator*), Elda Maida (*Pentangeli's Wife*), Salvatore Po (*Pentangeli's Brother*), Ignazio Pappalardo (*Mosca*), Andrea Maugeri (*Strollo*), Peter La Corte (*Signor Abbandando*), Vincent Coppola (*Street Salesman*), Peter Donat (*Questadt*), Tom Dahlgren (*Fred Corngold*), Paul B. Brown (*Senator Ream*), Phil Feldman (*First Senator*), Roger Corman (*Second Senator*), Yvonne Coll (*Yolanda*), J. D. Nichols (*Attendant at Brothel*), Edward Van Sickle (*Ellis Island Doctor*), Gabria Belloni (*Ellis Island Nurse*), Richard Watson (*Custom Official*), Venancia Grangerard (*Cuban Nurse*), Erica Yohn (*Governess*), Theresa Tirelli (*Midwife*), and James Caan (*Sonny Corleone*). Produced by FFC (A Coppola Company Production) for Paramount. 200 mins. On 16mm: Columbia-Warner (G.B.), Films Inc. (U.S.).

Hackman at work in THE CONVERSATION

Rainer Werner Fassbinder

Godard apart, no other European director of the last ten years or so has made such an explosive impact as Rainer Werner Fassbinder. The fuse, though, was slow-burning, the explosion itself a delayed action. Although Fassbinder's cinema has had a few consistent champions since his first feature in 1969 (particularly in his native Germany, but also in Britain), it was not until *Fear Eats the Soul*—his thirteenth feature—shared the Critics' Prize at Cannes in 1974 that Fassbinder became a name to be reckoned with on the international critical circuit. Fassbinder himself would appreciate the irony. When his first film, *Love Is Colder than Death*, was virtually booed off the screen by the audience at the 1969 Berlin festival, he coolly predicted that it was only a matter of time before that audience would change its mind. And so it has been. Astonishingly prolific (he has made more films in six years than many directors have made in a lifetime), supremely indifferent to critical fashion, Fassbinder is a genuine subversive.

RAINER WERNER FASSBINDER was born on May 31, 1946, in Bad Wörishofen, Bavaria. After leaving school he was variously employed, and eventually found his way to the Munich "Action Theatre," a fringe theatre group with a developing reputation for iconoclastic productions. A year later, in 1968, he founded his own unit, characteristically christened "Anti-Theatre" and including several members (Hanna Schygulla, Kurt Raab, Peer Raben) of the group which was later to become his film-making ensemble. The "Anti-Theatre" style was a slap in the face to a West German theatre sleep-walking through the cosy complacencies of the postwar economic miracle: sparse *décor*, uninflected performance, an idiosyncratic and irreverent approach to the classics. The style is recorded on film, in Jean-Marie Straub's *The Bridegroom, the Comedienne and the Pimp*, which includes a condensed version of the Anti-Theatre's production of Ferdinand Bruckner's "Krankheit der Jugend."

The influence of Straub can be detected in Fassbinder's first feature, *Love Is Colder than Death* (he had previously made two short films): a mostly static camera, grey, grainy images, an implied though distanced critique of the "capitalist" ethics of a gangster syndicate. The film also reveals, in embryonic form, two further preoccupations which were later to become key elements in Fassbinder's style. First, there is an affinity with Godard in the use of theatrical mannerisms to challenge and subvert the conventions of cinematic language (the film often looks like *Bande à part*, but its syntax is closer to the later, more experimental Godard). And secondly there is a fascination—shared of course by Godard—with the idiom of the Hollywood "*genre*" film, and particularly those films made in the decade after the Second World War.

Certain of the themes of this first feature—the effect of an outsider on the complacency of a group, the internecine tensions which both sustain and undermine group identity, the sudden eruption of casual violence—were more confidently realised in Fassbinder's next film, *Katzelmacher*. Superficially dealing with the effect on the oc-

Doris Mattes, Lilith Ungerer, Hanna Schygulla, and Fassbinder in KATZELMACHER

cupants of a Munich apartment block of a Greek immigrant worker who rents one of the apartments, the film can also be seen as a critical commentary on the moral and political state of a postwar Germany basking in the sun of the economic miracle. Fassbinder himself plays the immigrant worker (he frequently appears in his own films), who like many of the protagonists of his later films first intrigues and finally falls victim to the group whose latent frustrations ("ordinary Fascism") he unwittingly lays bare.

Formally, *Katzelmacher* exemplifies a recurring feature of Fassbinder's cinema: a

balance, often precarious and usually discomforting, between the highly stylised and the almost naturalistic. It is present in two further films which both parody and subvert the conventions of the Hollywood gangster movie. *Gods of Plague*, about a gangster just out of jail (characteristically, the gangster is black in a Munich underworld iconographically denoted by white trenchcoats), includes several archetypal gangster film sequences, all chairoscuro lighting and choreographed action. But the dialogue is offbeat, even atonal; and in a typical Fassbinder conjunction of banality and violence, the final shoot-out is staged not in the mean streets of the city but among the shelves of a supermarket loaded with the artefacts of a consumer society. In *The American Soldier* the gangster figure is a German-American veteran of Vietnam, returning to Munich as a hired killer; and again the conventional gangster film *motifs* are inverted, as the killer mechanically despatches his victims in a setting characterised by the moral and physical limbo of hotel rooms, bars and station left luggage lockers.

Violence, emotional as well as physical, frequently occurs as a catalyst in Fassbinder's films. It is often used as both a formal and a thematic pivot: a sudden and unexpectedly elegant camera movement in the middle of a mostly static film, or an eruption of emotion in an atmosphere devoid of it. In *Why Does Herr R. Run Amok?*, for instance, Fassbinder describes a circle round the rigid patterns of social convention which is Herr R.'s version of lower middle-class existence: a steady job, family and friends, the trite, enervating minutiae of a superficially comfortable life. The pace is unpunctuated, the style uninflected, which both emphasises the tension concealed just beneath the surface and makes both unexpected and inevitable the moment when that tension snaps, as Herr R. impulsively murders his wife and child and hangs himself.

Fassbinder's eye for faces: WARUM LÄUFT HERR R. AMOK?

Pent-up aggression does not always find this terminal release. In *Rio das Mortes* (one of the several films Fassbinder has made for television) it is thwarted, as a girl pulls a gun from her handbag but decides not to use it. In *Whity* an all-purpose mulatto servant is shown the light by a prostitute and murders his masters, but the road to freedom ends as a dance of death in the desert. Both these films reveal an articulation of the various stylistic devices which Fassbinder had been developing in his earlier work. Apparently casual, unnuanced passages alternate with striking artifice; dialogue is mannered, and delivered in a slow, monotonous diction which, like other Fassbinder trademarks, has

the effect of both distancing and engaging the audience. Like the melodramas of Douglas Sirk (an unmistakable and much quoted point of reference), Fassbinder's films play on—and frequently confound—their audience's expectations and susceptibilities. Fassbinder repeatedly focuses attention by distracting the viewer from a scene's natural focal centre—a device used with studied application in two further films for television, *Die Niklashauser Fahrt* and *Pioniere in Ingolstadt*, where anachronistic costumes and emblems announce both the artificiality and the timelessness of the films' only superficially particular themes (respectively, revolution through the ages, and the essential

Crise de coeur: THE MERCHANT OF FOUR SEASONS

Margit Carstensen in THE BITTER TEARS OF PETRA VON KANT

despotism of men in uniform).

The "distanciation" achieved by this very conscious use of artifice finds its most complete expression in *Beware of a Holy Whore*, a bitterly self-critical film about the making of a film (it was made immediately after *Whity*, and reflects a time of crisis in Fassbinder's film-making ensemble). Set in a Spanish hotel, the film draws an endless, enclosing arc round the emotional cannibalism of puppet-like actors and technicians waiting for a temperamental director to give them life. This incestuous, hermetically sealed world, emphasised by the tangible claustrophobia of the hotel setting, represents Fassbinder's comment on his films up to this point: it is a world of artifice and artificial emotion, a world which inevitably excludes—the film implies—the political and social realities of the world outside this hive of narcissism. It was as though, like Godard, Fassbinder was announcing that he had been seduced by form and that in his subsequent films he intended to refine his style and address himself to a larger public on subjects which would be more directly relevant to their everyday lives. Characteristically, Fassbinder made this announcement by making a film.

The larger public certainly came, though perhaps not for the reasons that Fassbinder

El Hedi Ben Salem in FEAR EATS THE SOUL

conflict and the development of a political awareness (factory workers, a sit-in at a public library). These TV films are considerably more optimistic in mood than any of Fassbinder's previous work. Which can hardly be said of his next feature film, *The Bitter Tears of Petra von Kant*. Originally written for the theatre, this film has a single setting, the baroque artifice of a fashion designer's apartment, and in style is at once ornamental and refined. Like much of his work, the film centres on the differences between ambition and achievement, the professed ideal (the fashion designer's doomed attempt to construct a perfect relationship with another woman) and the reality of behaviour. And here more than ever *décor* is both formally and thematically central—most evidently in the enormous mural of baccanalian love which mockingly looks down on the games people play in the name of love.

Fassbinder's next three films all focus in their different ways on the notion of love thwarted by what people think it should and should not be. In *Fear Eats the Soul* it is the love of an odd couple—a Moroccan immigrant worker and an ageing charwoman—circumscribed and finally destroyed by social convention and the expectations of innate prejudice. In *Effi Briest*, adapted from the minor classic by Theodor Fontane and magisterially filmed in black-and-white, it is again the frustrations engendered by society's norms which destroy even the chance of love. And in *Martha*, a brooding melodrama of possessiveness and Fassbinder's most direct bow to Sirk, it is the traps sprung by auto-suggestion which suffocate even the chance of love.

Any interim report on Fassbinder is in danger of being overtaken by several new films (see review below of his latest film at the time of writing), such is the extraordinarily

might have wished. It was with his next films that Fassbinder at last achieved widespread critical recognition—and he would be the first to be wary of that. All the same, his next film is noticeably simpler in style. *The Merchant of Four Seasons* is a return to the territory of *Why Does Herr R. Run Amok?*, the thwarted ambitions of family life. Again the dialogue is unshaded, the settings contracted into vicious circles of conflict. But in this story of an unassuming little fruit-seller, oppressed by the women in his life and finally drinking his way to oblivion while his family babbles unconcernedly around him, Fassbinder gets closer to a direct involvement with his characters than in any of his previous films.

There is a similar formal directness in the series of five television films (known collectively as *Eight Hours Don't Make a Day*) which Fassbinder was making at this time. Here again the subjects are internecine family

Margit Carstensen in MARTHA

prolific rate at which he works. He continues to work in television and the theatre while making three or four films a year. It would be unsafe at this stage to predict any future direction for his films. But one thing is certain: at twenty-nine Fassbinder has established himself as one of the most original and consistent of his generation of film-makers. His films, immersed in the language of an older cinema, have given it a wholly new inflection.

DAVID WILSON

At right: Hanna Schygulla in Fassbinder's screen version of EFFI BRIEST

FAUSTRECHT DER FREIHEIT
(Survival of the Fittest)

Script: Rainer Werner Fassbinder, Christian Hohoff. Direction: Fassbinder. Photography (colour): Michael Ballhaus. Editing: Thea Eymèsz. Music: Peer Raben. Players: Rainer Werner Fassbinder, Peter Chatel, Karlheinz Böhm, Harry Baer, Ulla Jacobsson, Barbara Valentin. For Tango Film/Filmverlag der Autoren. 123 mins.

Where *The Bitter Tears of Petra von Kant* unfolds in a world governed by Lesbian responses, Fassbinder's *Survival of the Fittest* is set in a homosexual milieu. The primary element in the film, however, is the struggle between the classes, a contest which, maintains Fassbinder, is much more vividly reflected in homosexual relationships than it would be in a "normal" environment. The rise and fall of the unfortunate Fox is plotted in bold, gaudy strokes. Dismissed from an ailing circus, he stakes his last scrap of money on a lottery ticket—and wins half a million marks. He quickly rises in homosexual circles, his new-found wealth a lodestone for lovers. Inevitably, when the money is exhausted, Fox is cast aside with merciless ease. Fassbinder's camera leaves Fassbinder's Fox moribund on the cold floor of a Munich subway station, his pockets picked by two predatory urchins. Society has masticated and then expectorated the misfit.

The story is, like most of Fassbinder's subjects, melodramatic and banal. Yet such is his mastery of performance, tone, colour, music, and rhetoric that the film is intensely gripping. He has absorbed the influence of Hollywood with aplomb. When, for instance, Fox returns contritely to his lover's apartment, and bends over the baroque bed to declare his devotion, one recalls the fervour of Lana Turner in Sirk's *Imitation of Life* or Michael Gordon's *Portrait in Black*.

Fassbinder with Barbara Valentin in SURVIVAL OF THE FITTEST

Fassbinder's originality lies in his ability to boil down the artifice of most conversations, so that even the shortest sequences (in the mud-baths, or in the bazaar at Marrakesh) reverberate with cogent meaning.

PETER COWIE

FASSBINDER FILMOGRAPHY

This filimography does not list Fassbinder's work either on radio (since 1970) or in the theatre (since 1967) or on video for TV (since 1970). His appearances as an actor in films other than his own are as follows: as Mallard in Paul Vasil's *Tonys Freunde* (*Tony's Friends*, 1967), Freder the Pimp in Jean-Marie Straub's *Der Bräutigam, die Komödiantin und der Zuhälter* (*The Bridgegroom, the Comedienne and the Pimp*, 1968), Man in Uniform in Dieter Lemmel's *Alarm* (1969), Heini in Franz Peter Wirth's *Al Capone im deutschen Wald* (*Al Capone in the German Forest*, 1969), Baal in Volker Schlöndorff's *Baal* (1969), a Mechanic in Korbinian Köberle's *Frei bis zum nächsten Mal* (*Free Until the Next Time*, 1969), Flecklbauer in Reinhard Hauff's *Matthias Kneissel*, a Peasant in Volker Schlöndorff's *Der plötzliche Reichtum der armen Leute von Kombach* (*The Sudden Fortune of the Poor People of Kombach*, 1970), Man at Shop Window in Rudolf Thome's *Supergirl* (1970), Wittkowski in Ulli Lommel's *Zärtlichkeit der Wölfe* (*Tenderness of Wolves*, 1973).

1965

DER STADTSTREICHER/THE CITY BUMS. Script and direction: RWF. Photography (16mm): Josef Jung. Players: Christoph Roser, Susanne Schimkus, Michael Fengler, Thomas Fengler, Irm Hermann, RWF (*Man in Urinal*). Produced by Roser-Film. 10 mins.

1966

DAS KLEINE CHAOS/THE SMALL CHAOS. Script and direction: RWF. Photography: Michael Fengler. Players: Marite Greiselis, Christoph Roser, Lilo Pempeit, Greta Rehfeld, RWF (*Gangster*). Produced by Roser-Film for Filmverlag der Autoren. 9 mins. (originally 12 mins.).

1969

LIEBE IST KÄLTER ALS DER TOD/LOVE IS COLDER THAN DEATH. Script and direction: RWF. Photography: Dietrich Lohmann. Editing: Franz Walsch. Music: Peer Raben, Holger Munzer. Art direction: Ulli Lommel, RWF. Players: Ulli Lomell (*Bruno*), Hanna Schygulla (*Joanna*), RWF (*Franz*), Hans Hirschmüller (*Peter*). Katrin Schaake (*Woman in Procession*), Peter Berling (*Illegal Arms Dealer*), Hannes Gromball (*Customer with Joanna*), Gisela Otto (*First Prostitute*), Ingrid Caven (*Second Prostitute*), Ursula Strätz (*Fat Prostitute*), Irm Hermann (*Sunglasses Saleswoman*), Les Olvides (*Georges*), Wil Rabenbauer (*Jürgen*), Peter Moland (*Leader of Syndicate*), Anastassios Karalas (*Turk*), Rudolf Waldemar Brem (*Policeman on Motorcycle*), Yaak Karsunke (*Commissioner*), Monika Stadler (*Girl*), Kurt Raab (*Shop Supervisor*). Produced by Antiteater-X-Film for Filmverlag der Autoren. 88 mins. On 16mm: New Yorker Films (U.S.).

KATZELMACHER. Script and direction: RWF. Photography: Dietrich Lohmann. Editing: Franz Walsch. Music: Peer Raben (from Schubert). Art direction: RWF. Players: Hanna Schygulla (*Marie*), Lilith Ungerer (*Helga*), Elga Sorbas (*Rosy*), Doris Mattes (*Gunda*), RWF (*Jorges*), Rudolf Waldemar Brem (*Paul*), Hans Hirschmüller (*Erich*), Harry Baer (*Franz*), Peter Moland (*Peter*), Hannes Gromball (*Klaus*), Irm Hermann (*Elisabeth*), Katrin Schaake (*Woman on Highway*). Produced by Antiteater-X-Film for Filmverlag der Autoren. 88 mins.

1970

GÖTTER DER PEST/GODS OF PLAGUE. Script and direction: RWF. Photography: Dietrich Lohmann. Editing: Franz Walsch. Music: Peer Raben. Art direction: Kurt Raab. Players: Harry Baer (*Franz*), Hanna Schygulla (*Joanna*), Margarethe von Trotta (*Margarethe*), Günther Kaufmann (*Günther*), Carla Aulaulu (*Carla*), Ingrid Caven (*Magdalena Fuller*), Jan George (*Policeman*), Marian Seidowski (*Marian*), Yaak Karsunke (*Commissioner*), Micha Cochina (*Joe*), Hannes Gromball (*Supermarket Head*), Lilith Ungerer (*Girl in First Cafe*), Katrin Schaake (*Occupier of Second Cafe*), Lilo Pempeit (*Mother*). RWF (*Porn-Buyer*), Irm Hermann, Peter Moland, Doris Mattes. Produced by Antiteater for Filmverlag der Autoren. 91 mins.

WARUM LÄUFT HERR R. AMOK?/WHY DOES HERR R. RUN AMOK? Script: improvised by Michael Fengler, RWF. Direction: Michael Fengler, RWF. Photography (colour, 16mm): Dietrich Lohmann. Editing: Franz Walsch, Michael Fengler. Music: Christian Anders ("Geh' nicht vorbei"). Art direction: Kurt Raab. Players: Kurt Raab (*Herr R.*), Lilith Ungerer (*His Wife*), Amadeus Fengler (*Their Son*), Franz Maron (*Chief*), Harry Baer, Peter Moland, Lilo Pempeit (*Colleagues in Office*), Hanna Schygulla (*School Friend*), Herr and Frau Sterr (*Father and Mother*), Peer Raben (*School Friend*), Carla Aulaulu, Eva Pampuch (*Record Salesgirls*), Ingrid Caven, Doris Mattes, Irm Hermann, Hannes Gromball (*Neighbours of the R. Family*), Peter Hamm, Jochen Pinkert (*Commissioner*), Eva Madelung (*Chief's Sister*). Produced by Antiteater and Maran-Film for Filmverlag der Autoren. 88 mins.

DER AMERIKANISCHE SOLDAT/THE AMERICAN SOLDIER. Script and direction: RWF. Photography: Dieter Lohmann. Editing: Thea Eymèsz. Music: Peer Raben. Song: RWF, Peer Raben ("So Much Tenderness"). Sung by: Günther Kaufmann. Art direction: Kurt Raab, RWF. Players: Karl Scheydt (*Ricky*),

Kurt Raab in TENDERNESS OF WOLVES

Elga Sorbas (*Rosa*), Jan George (*Jan*), Margarethe von Trotta (*Chambermaid*), Hark Bohm (*Doc*), Ingrid Caven (*Singer*), Eva Ingeborg Scholz (*Ricky's Mother*), Kurt Raab (*Ricky's Brother*), Marius Aicher (*Policeman*), Gustl Datz (*Police Chief*), Marquard Bohm (*Private Detective*), RWF (*Franz*), Katrin Schaake (*Magdalena Fuller*), Ulli Lommel (*Gypsy*), Irm Hermann (*Whore*). Produced by Antiteater for Filmverlag der Autoren. 80 mins.

DIE NIKLASHAUSER FAHRT/THE NIKLASHAUSER DRIVE. Script and direction: RWF, Michael Fengler. Photography (colour, 16mm): Dietrich Lohmann. Editing: Thea Eymèsz, Franz Walsch. Music: Peer Raben, Amon Düül II. Art direction: Kurt Raab. Players: Michael König (*Hans Böhm*), Michael Gordon (*Antonio*), RWF (*Black Monk*), Hanna Schygulla (*Johanna*), Walter Sedlmayr (*Parson*), Margit Carstensen (*Margarethe*), Franz Maron (*Her Husband*), Kurt Raab (*Bishop*), Günther Kaufmann (*Peasant Leader*), Siggi Graue (*First Peasant*), Michael Fengler (*Second Peasant*), Ingrid Caven (*Girl Crying*), Elga Sorbas (*Weak Girl*), Carla Aulaulu (*Epileptic Girl*), Peer Raben (*Monsignore*), Peter Berling (*Executioner*), Magdalena Montezuma (*Penthesilea*). Produced by Janus Film und Fernsehen for WDR TV. 86 mins. First shown on WDR TV.

1971

RIO DAS MORTES. Script: RWF, from an idea by Volker Schlöndorff. Direction: RWF. Photography (colour, 16mm): Dietrich Lohmann. Editing: Thea Eymèsz. Music: Peer Raben. Art direction: Kurt Raab. Players: Hanna Schygulla (*Hanna*), Michael König (*Michel*), Günther Kaufmann (*Günther*), Katrin Schaake (*Katrin, Hanna's Friend*), Joachim von Mengershausen (*Joachim, Katrin's Friend*), Lilo Pempeit (*Günther's Mother*), Franz Maron (*Hanna's Uncle*), Harry Baer (*Michel's Colleague*), Marius Aicher (*Master*), Carla Aulaulu (*Customer*), Walter Sedlmayr (*Secretary*), Ulli Lommel (*Car Dealer*), Monika Stadler (*Tourist Office Employee*), Hanna Axmann-Rezzori (*Patroness*), Ingrid Caven, Kerstin Dobbertin, Magdalena Montezuma, Elga Sorbas (*Hanna's Colleagues*), Kurt Raab (*Petrol Pump Attendant*), Rudolf Waldemar Brem (*Customer in Bar*), Carl Amery (*Librarian*), RWF (*Man Dancing with Hanna in Discotheque*), Eva Pampuch (*Friend*). Produced by Janus Film und Fernsehen/Antiteater-X-Film. 84 mins. First shown on ARD TV.

PIONIERE IN INGOLSTADT/PIONEERS IN INGOLSTADT. Script: RWF, from the work by Marieluise Fleisser. Direction: RWF. Photography (colour): Dietrich Lohmann. Editing: Thea Eymèsz.

Music: Peer Raben. Art direction: Kurt Raab. Players: Hanna Schygulla (*Berta*), Harry Baer (*Karl*), Irm Hermann (*Alma*), Rudolf Waldemar Brem (*Fabian*), Walter Sedlmayr (*Fritz*), Klaus Löwitsch (*Sergeant*), Günther Kaufmann (*Max*), Carla Aulaulu (*Frieda*), Elga Sorbas (*Mariel*), Burghard Schlicht (*Klaus*), Gunther Krää (*Gottfried*). Produced by Janus Film und Fernsehen/Antiteater for ZDF TV. 87 mins. First shown on ZDF TV.

WHITY. Script and direction: RWF. Photography (colour, CinemaScope): Michael Ballhaus. Editing: Franz Walsch, Thea Eymèsz. Music: Peer Raben. Art direction: Kurt Raab. Players: Günther Kaufmann (*Whity*), Hanna Schygulla (*Hanna*), Ulli Lommel (*Frank*), Harry Baer (*Davy*), Katrin Schaake (*Katherine*), Ron Randell (*Mr. Nicolson*), Thomas Blanco (*Fake Mexican Doctor*), Stefano Capriati (*Judge*), Elaine Baker (*Whity's Mother*), Mark Salvage (*Sheriff*), Helga Ballhaus (*Judge's Wife*), Kurt Raab (*Pianist*), RWF (*Guest in Saloon*). Produced by Atlantis Film/Antiteater-X-Film for Berliner Synchron. 95 mins.

WARNUNG VOR EINER HEILIGEN NUTTE/BEWARE OF A HOLY WHORE. Script and direction: RWF. Photography (colour): Michael Ballhaus. Editing: Franz Walsch, Thea Eymèsz. Music: Peer Raben, Gaetano Donizetti, Elvis Presley, Ray Charles, Leonard Cohen, Spooky Tooth. Art direction: Kurt Raab. Players: Lou Castel (*Jeff, the Director*), Eddie Constantine (*Himself*), Hanna Schygulla (*Hanna, the Actress*), Marquard Bohm (*Ricky, the Actor*), RWF (*Sascha, the Producer*), Ulli Lommel (*Korbinian, the Production Manager*), Katrin Schaake (*Scriptgirl*), Benjamin Lev (*Candy, the Spanish Production Manager*), Monika Teuber (*Billie, the Make-Up Girl*), Margarethe von Trotta (*Production Secretary*), Gianni Di Luigi (*Camera Operator*), Rudolf Waldemar Brem (*Chief Electrician*), Herb Andress (*Coach*), Thomas Schieder (*Jesus, the Electrician*), Kurt Raab (*Fred*), Hannes Fuchs (*David*), Marcella Michelangeli (*Margaret*), Ingrid Caven (*Extra*), Harry Baer (*Her Husband*), Magdalena Montezuma (*Irm*), Werner Schroeter (*Dieters, the Photographer*), Karl Scheydt, Tanja Constantine, Maria Novelli, Enzo Monteduro, Achmed Em Bark, Michael Fengler, Burghard Schlicht, Dick Randall, Peter Berling, Tony Bianchi, Renato dei Laudadio, Gianni Javarone, Peter Gauhe, Marcello Zucche. Produced by Antiteater-X-Film (W. Germany)/Nova International (Rome) for Filmverlag der Autoren. 103 mins. On 16mm: New Yorker Films (U.S.).

1972

HÄNDLER DER VIER JAHRESZEITEN/THE MERCHANT OF FOUR SEASONS. Script and direction: RWF. Photography (colour): Dietrich Lohmann.

Irm Hermann in THE BITTER TEARS OF PETRA VON KANT

Editing: Thea Eymèsz. Music: Rocco Granata ("Buona notte"), archive material. Art direction: Kurt Raab. Players: Hans Hirschmüller (*Hans the Fruiterer*), Irm Hermann (*Irmgard, his Wife*), Hanna Schygulla (*Erna, the First Sister*), Andrea Schober (*Child*), Gusti Kreissl (*Mother*), Kurt Raab (*Brother-in-Law*), Heide Simon (*Second Sister*), Klaus Löwitsch (*Harry*), Karl Scheydt (*Anzell*), Ingrid Caven (*Big Love*), Peter Chatel (*Doctor*), Lilo Pempeit (*Customer*), Walter Sedlmayr (*Fruit-Cart Seller*), Salem El Hedi (*Arab*), Hark Bohm (*Policeman*), Daniel Schmid, Harry Baer, Marian Seidowski (*Three Competitors*), Michael Fengler (*Playboy*), RWF (*Zucker*), Elga Sorbas (*Marile Kosemund*). Produced by Tango Film for Filmverlag der Autoren. 89 mins. First shown on ZDF TV. On 16mm: Cinegate (G.B.); New Yorker Films (U.S.).

DIE BITTEREN TRÄNEN DER PETRA VON KANT/THE BITTER TEARS OF PETRA VON KANT. Script and direction: RWF. Photography (colour): Michael Ballhaus. Editing: Thea Eymèsz. Music: The Platters, The Walker Brothers, Verdi. Art direction: Kurt Raab. Players: Margit Carstensen (*Petra von Kant*), Hanna Schygulla (*Karin Thimm*), Irm Hermann (*Marlene*), Eva Mattes (*Gabriele von Kant*), Katrin Schaake (*Sidonie von Grasenabb*), Gisela Fackeldey (*Valerie von Kant*). Produced by Filmverlag der Autoren. 124 mins. On 16mm: Cinegate (G.B.); New Yorker Films (U.S.).

ACHT STUNDEN SIND KEIN TAG/EIGHT HOURS DON'T MAKE A DAY (episodes: **JOCHEN UND MARION, OMA UND GREGOR, FRANZ UND ERNST, HARALD UND MONIKA, IRMGARD UND ROLF**). Script and direction: RWF. Photography (colour, 16mm): Dietrich Lohmann.

Editing: Marie Anne Gerhardt. Music: Jean Gepoint (=Jens Wilhelm Petersen). Art direction: Kurt Raab. Players: Gottfried John (*Jochen*), Hanna Schygulla (*Marion*), Luise Ullrich (*Oma*), Werner Finck (*Gregor*), Anita Bucher (*Käthe*), Wolfried Lier (*Wolf*), Christine Oesterlein (*Klara*), Renate Roland (*Monika*), Kurt Raab (*Harald*), Andrea Schober (*Sylvia*), Thorsten Massinger (*Manni*), Irm Hermann (*Irmgard Erlkönig*), Wolfgang Zerlett (*Manfred*), Wolfgang Schenck (*Franz*), Herb Andress (*Rüdiger*), Rudolf Waldemar Brem (*Rolf*), Hans Hirschmüller (*Jürgen*), Peter Gauhe (*Ernst*), Grigorios Karipidis (*Giuseppe*), Karl Scheydt (*Peter*), Victor Curland (*Master Kretzschmer*), Rainer Hauer (*Superintendant Gross*), Margit Carstensen, Christiane Jannessen, Doris Mattes, Gusti Kreissl, Lilo Pempeit (*Wives in Episode Two*), Katrin Schaake, Rudolf Lenz, Jörg von Liebenfels (*Lessors in Episode Two*), Ulli Lommel, Ruth Drexel, Walter Sedlmayr, Helga Feddersen, Heinz Meier, Karl-Heinz Vosgerau, Peter Chatel, Valeska Gert, Eva Mattes, Marquard Bohm, Klaus Löwitsch, Hannes Gromball, Peter Märthesheimer. Produced by WDR TV. 101 mins./100 mins./92 mins./88 mins./89 mins. First shown on WDR TV over the period October 1972—March 1973.

1973

WILDWECHSEL/GAME PASS. Script: RWF, from the play by Franz Xaver Kroetz. Direction: RWF. Photography (colour): Dietrich Lohmann. Editing: Thea Eymèsz. Music: Beethoven. Art direction: Kurt Raab. Players: Jörg von Liebenfels (*Erwin*), Ruth Drexel (*Hilda, his Wife*), Eva Mattes (*Hanni, their Daughter*), Harry Baer (*Franz*), Rudolf Waldemar Brem (*Dieter*), Hanna Schygulla (*Doctor*), Kurt Raab (*Chief*), Karl Scheydt, Klaus Löwitsch (*Policemen*), Hedi Ben Salem (*Friend*), Irm Hermann, Marquard Bohm (*Police Officers*). Produced by Intertel for SFB TV. 102 mins. First shown on SFB TV.

WELT AM DRAHT/WORLD ON A WIRE (in two episodes). Script: Fritz Müller-Scherz, RWF, from the novel by Daniel F. Galouye. Direction: RWF. Photography (colour, 16mm): Michael Ballhaus. Editing: Marie Anne Gerhardt. Music: Gottfried Hüngsberg, and archive material. Art direction: Kurt Raab. Players: Klaus Löwitsch (*Fred Stiller*), Mascha Rabben (*Eva*), Adrian Hoven (*Vollmer*), Ivan Desny (*Lause*), Barbara Valentin (*Gloria*), Karl-Heinz Vosgerau (*Siskins*), Günter Lamprecht (*Wolfgang*), Margit Carstensen (*Schmidt-Gentner*), Wolfgang Schenck (*Hahn*), Joachim Hansen (*Edelkern*), Rudolf Lenz (*Hartmann*), Kurt Raab (*Holm*), Karl Scheydt (*Lehner*), Rainer Hauer (*Stuhlfaut*), Ulli Lommel (*Rupp*), Heinz Meier (*Weinlaub*), Peter Chatel (*Hirse*), Ingrid Caven, Eddie Constantine, Gottfried John, Elma Karlow, Christine Kaufmann,

SURVIVAL OF THE FITTEST: Peter Chatel (right) chooses clothes in a boutique, with Fassbinder's use of the mirror suggesting the narcissism of the moment

Rainer Langhans, Bruce Low, Karsten Peters, Katrin Schaake, Walter Sedlmayr, El Hedi Ben Salem, Christiane Maybach, Rudolf Waldemar Brem, Peter Kern, Ernst Küsters, Peter Moland, Doris Mattes, Liselotte Eder, Solange Pradel, Maryse Dellannoy, Werner Schroeter, Magdalena Montezuma, Corinna Brocher, Peter Gauhe, Dora Karras-Frank. Produced by WDR TV. 99 mins./101 mins. First shown on WDR TV.

1974

ANGST ESSEN SEELE AUF/FEAR EAT OUT SOUL/FEAR EATS THE SOUL/ALI. Script and direction: RWF. Photography (colour): Jürgen Jürges. Editing: Thea Eymèsz. Music: archive material. Art direction: RWF. Players: Brigitte Mira (*Emmi*), El Hedi Ben Salem (*Ali*), Barbara Valentin (*Barbara, the Barmaid*), Irm Hermann (*Krista*), RWF (*Eugen, her Husband*), Karl Scheydt (Albert), Elma Karlowa (*Frau Kargus*), Anita Bucher (*Frau Ellis*),

Gusti Kreissl (*Paula*), Walter Sedlmayr (*Herr Angermeyer the Grocer*), Doris Mattes (*His Wife*), Liselotte Eder (*Frau Münchmeyer*), Marquard Bohm (*Herr Gruber*), Katharina Herberg (*Girl in Bar*), Rudolf Waldemar Brem (*Customer in Bar*), Peter Moland (*Chief in Car Workshop*), Margit Symo (*Hedwig*), Peter Gauhe (*Bruno*), Helga Ballhaus (*Yolanda*), Elisabeth Bertram (*Frieda*), Hannes Gromball. Produced by Tango Film for Filmverlag der Autoren. 93 mins. On 16mm: Cinegate (G.B.), New Yorker Films (U.S.).

MARTHA. Script and direction: RWF. Photography (colour, 16mm): Michael Ballhaus. Editing: Liesgret Schmitt-Klink. Music: archive material. Art direction: Kurt Raab. Players: Margit Carstensen (*Martha Salomon*, née *Hyer*), Karlheinz Böhm (*Helmut Salomon*), Gisela Fackeldey (*Mother*), Adrian Hoven (*Father*), Barbara Valentin (*Marianne*), Ingrid Caven (*Ilse*), Ortrud Beginnen (*Erna*), Wolfgang Schenck (*Chief*), Günter Lamprecht (*Dr. Salomon*), Peter Chatel (*Kaiser*), Salem El Hedi (*Hotel Guest*), Kurt Raab (*Em-*

Above: a boudoir scene, redolent of Hollywood, from EFFI BRIEST

bassy Secretary), Rudolf Lenz (*Porter*). Produced by WDR TV. 112 mins. First shown on WDR TV.

EFFI BRIEST. Script: RWF, from the novel by Theodor Fontane. Direction: RWF. Photography: Dietrich Lohmann, Jürgen Jürges. Editing: Thea Eymèsz. Music: from Saint-Saëns and others. Art direction: Kurt Raab. Players: Hanna Schygulla (*Effi*), Wolfgang Schenck (*Baron Geert von Instetten*), Karlheinz Böhm (*Privy Councillor Wüllersdorf*), Ulli Lommel (*Major Crampas*), Ursula Strätz (*Roswitha*), Irm Hermann (*Johanna*), Lilo Pempeit (*Luise von Briest, Effi's Mother*), Herbert Steinmetz (*Herr von Briest, Effi's Father*), Hark Bohm (*Gieshübler, the Chemist*), Rudolf Lenz (*Privy Councillor Rummschüttel*), Barbara Valentin (*Marietta Tripelli, the Singer*), Karl Scheydt (*Kruse*), Theo Tecklenburg (*Pastor Niemeyer*), Barbara Lass (*Polish Cook*), Eva Mattes (*Hulda*), Andrea Schober (*Annie*), Anndorthe Braker (*Frau Pasche*), Peter Gauhe (*Cousin Dagobert*), RWF (*Narrator*). Produced by Tango Film for Filmverlag der Autoren. 141 mins. Only Hanna Schygulla, Wolfgang Schenck and Karlheinz Böhm speak their own lines.

1975

FAUSTRECHT DER FREIHEIT/SURVIVAL OF THE FITTEST. Script: RWF, Christian Hohoff. Direction: RWF. Photography (colour): Michael Ballhaus. Editing: Thea Eymèsz. Music: Peer Raben. Players: RWF (*Fox*), Peter Chatel (*Eugen*), Karlheinz Böhm (*Max*), Harry Baer (*Philip*), Adrian Hoven (*Father*), Ulla Jacobsen (*Mother*), Christiane Maybach (*Hedwig*), Peter Kern, Hans Zander, Kurt Raab, Irm Hermann, Ursula Strätz, Elma Karlowa, Barbara Valentin, Bruce Low, Walter Sedlmayr, Evelyn Künneke, Ingrid Caven, Marquard Bohm, Liselotte Eder. Produced by Tango Film for Filmverlag der Autoren. 123 mins.

MUTTER KÜSTERS FAHRT ZUM HIMMEL/ MOTHER KÜSTER'S TRIP TO HEAVEN. Script and direction: RWF. Players: Brigitte Mira, Ingrid Caven, Gottfried John, Karlheinz Böhm, Margit Carstensen, Irm Hermann, Armin Meyer. Produced by Tango Film/Filmverlag der Autoren.

Krzysztof Zanussi

The concerns of most film-makers emerge from a cultural background. The landscape of Krzysztof Zanussi, however, is mapped out in scientific terms; himself a lapsed physicist, Zanussi brings to the cinema a rare grasp of the problems faced by scientists in the post-war world. Where other directors concentrate on characters, Zanussi dwells on ideas. Where others, like Wajda or Fellini, are creatures of passion, Zanussi is nothing if not a moralist. In this respect, his only peer is Eric Rohmer, whose area of reference is literary while Zanussi's is geometric.

KRZYSZTOF ZANUSSI was born on July 17, 1939, in Warsaw. From 1955 to 1959 he took physics at the University of Warsaw, and in 1956/57 he completed a film study course there under Aleksander Jackiewicz. Soon he was directing amateur films in the student society, AKF. Zanussi also read philosophy at Kraków during this period, and dabbled in the theatre. The success of Ingmar Bergman left a deep and stimulating impression on him. Here was a man who had proved that film-making could be a way of life, a means of fulfilling one's vision. So in 1960 Zanussi joined the directing department of PWSTiF at Łódź, and six years later he earned his diploma with *Death of a Provincial*, which won awards at Venice, Mannheim, Vallodolid, and Moscow.

Unlike most prentice works, *Death of a Provincial* offers a template for Zanussi's future films. He is habitually concerned with the meeting of two people, two attitudes, two ages. Climatic conditions also intrigue him—this film, like *Structure of Crystals* and much of *Illumination*—being marked by an almost palpable coldness and the enveloping silence of snow. A young man arrives at a monastery to study, and observes the ritualistic routine around him with detachment and, at first, nonchalance. But gradually he becomes fascinated by an elderly monk, whose infirmity and refusal to admit defeat touch the younger man. A soul seems to have been isolated, laid out for analysis prior to transmigration, and Zanussi suggests the psychic bond between the two men with a bold device: a box of matches on the youth's cell table flares up abruptly of its own accord as if to signal the moment of the old monk's death. The boy wanders disconsolately into the chapel, and crashes his arm down on the organ keys, the peal embracing all his sense of loss and exasperation. The film's lingering impression is not, however, a depressing one. "I believe," says Zanussi, "that one cannot appreciate life without appreciating death."

The psychological impact of one human being on another is again to the forefront in *Face to Face*, a short made for TV by Zanussi in 1967. The sour, taciturn individual who is awakened by his morning call at 6.45 A.M. and moves lethargically through the business of dressing, washing, and making breakfast with his wife, finds himself distracted (and finally shaken) by a stranger who by sheer chance impinges on his life.

Glancing out of his apartment window, he catches sight of a struggle between two men on a nearby rooftop. A few minutes later, he sees one of the strangers climbing perilously down the "well" in the centre of the block; even then, his curiosity is only mildly aroused. But as he watches the fugitive crawl

The plea at the window, in FACE TO FACE

The aged monk in DEATH OF A PROVINCIAL

desperately, inexorably, towards his bathroom window, he finally recognises the threat to his complacency—and shuts the window in the face of the unwelcome visitor as firmly as a hangman pulls his lever. There is a long scream, a thud, the pigeons wheel and scatter, and neighbours emerge to inspect the tragedy. Our morose anti-hero survives another bout of nagging from his wife and leaves for work . . .

Zanussi has demonstrated, this time in a highly subjective manner, how each man is indeed an island, hostile to invaders from without. In *Face to Face*, the camera accompanies the action like an invisible warden, prowling through the apartment, spurting forward over the window-sill in anticipation of the fugitive's fall, and then creeping back into the room with embarrassment. The film is only twenty-five minutes in length, but it is a searching study of moral cowardice.

The Structure of Crystals was Zanussi's first feature movie, and established him as a new force in Polish cinema. The tension in the film stems from the clash between two fundamentally dissonant approaches to life. Jan and Marek are old college friends. Jan has married, and works as a meteorological observer in a remote country area. The meeting of these two contemporaries—Marek with his ambition and urban sophistication, Jan the calm, contented provincial— is counterpointed with scientific references. "Nature has been outdistanced by man," claims Marek confidently in a lecture at the local institute, but as he drives away through the snow-covered fields, he must shield his eyes against the glare of the morning sun, as if unable to cope with its intensity. The contrast between artificial and genuine crystals that Marek discusses during the same lecture parallels the situation and outlook of the two friends: it is in fact Marek whose life is founded on a false notion of liberty; he is too obsessed with the struggle for recognition in life to be able to contemplate his crystal-like soul. Jan, on the other hand, has arrived at a certain degree of fulfilment.

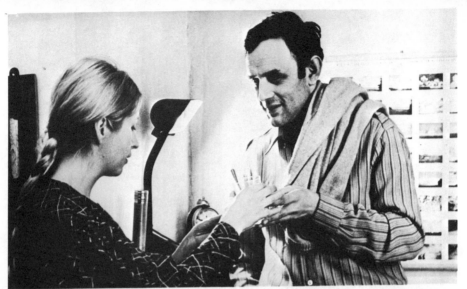

Zanussi's characters usually belong to the same generation as himself. Jan and Marek are both in their thirties, both conscious that this is a vital watershed in their existence. Anna, the wife, hovers between the two men, like a particle drawn to two magnetic fields. For her, Marek represents the dynamism and excitement of the outside world; but her rhythm ultimately matches Jan's the better.

The Structure of Crystals is a film built on conversation, and on the spaces betwen the sentences. Like the Yugoslavian *Rondo*, with which it has many affinities, it is Chekhovian in its reticence. There is a feeling of emotions coursing beneath the bland surface of the friends' reunion. If for Astruc the camera is merely a pen, for Zanussi it is a microscope, in the lens of which are reflected the curious forces that shape our lives.

As a reaction against the asceticism of *Structure of Crystals*, Zanussi wrote the screenplay of *Family Life* in a theatrical idiom. "I wanted it to be more traditionally constructed, more academic in form," he says. Yet the director's preoccupations remain essentially the same as before. Wit, the young industrial designer summoned home, like Bobby Dupea in *Five Easy Pieces*, by a crisis in his father's health, is stamped by much the same egotism as Marek is in Zanussi's earlier film. His city routine has robbed him of the luxury of self-analysis, and as he succumbs by the hour to the pressures and complexes that surround his relatives, so he becomes more and more frustrated by his failure to escape his heritage. This young hero of scientific Socialism despises his bibulous father, patronises his aunt and his wayward

Opposite: Barbara Wrzesińska and Andrzej Żarnecki in STRUCTURE OF CRYSTALS (above); Daniel Olbrychski in FAMILY LIFE (below)

sister, and dismisses the notion of rejoining the small family business (private enterprise, though still permitted in Poland, is regarded with scorn by most people there). The atmosphere of the decrepit house, however, with its weird memories, slowly takes him in its grip. As he departs from Chorzów, Wit is seen in close-up through the train window; suddenly he is aware of a twitch in his left eye and, like us, he knows that it is a mark of Cain, identical to his father's affliction. At first he scowls in fear and anger, then finally he laughs and turns away, at peace with himself and his lot for the first time in the film. Perhaps he recalls his father's words, "Everyone's got his measure. You can't surpass yourself."

Family Life reveals a distinct development in Zanussi's technical imagination. He changes focal lengths with economy and intelligence, and his careful control of lighting captures the oppressive languor of the old house. An autumnal sun laps in through the windows, cobwebs and ancient family photographs are picked out discreetly, clocks resound in every room, and the father makes a terrifying entrance, shuffling forward through a doorway, his bulky figure etched in menacing silhouette by a hidden rear light.

Behind the Wall, made for Polish TV, is typical of Zanussi in its contact between two very different personalities and the moral challenge that they represent to each other. A research scientist is persuaded by his superior to interview a neurotic young woman applying for a post at the biochemistry institute where he works. They both happen to live in the same apartment block, and by degrees—truculently on his part, eagerly on hers—the slow fire of a relationship is kindled. Over tea and brandy they converse in awkward spasms. They discover a common interest in classical music; yet they part on a

Maja Komorowska in BEHIND THE WALL

note of mutual misgiving. The next morning, as the man shaves lazily and drinks his coffee, he learns that the woman has attempted to commit suicide. He hurries to her apartment and, in a bedside sequence directed and acted with consummate delicacy, a transference of roles seems to occur: now it is the man who is anxious for companionship, and the woman who radiates a placid and altogether unexpected aura of security.

For Zanussi, then, life consists primarily of the search for companionship, and even in such a mundane B-thriller as *The Catamount Killing* (based on a novel by James Hadley Chase and shot in Vermont over a six-week period in 1973), this theme is dominant. The young bank manager (Horst Buchholz) is more interested in achieving control over his accomplice (Ann Wedgeworth) than in escaping with the $250,000 payroll. The film has not been edited to Zanussi's satisfaction, and suffers from banalities and poor dialogue, but there are moments that betray a talent at work. For instance, when Buchholz shares a picnic with his mistress and tells her in obviously hackneyed phrases of the happiness she so richly deserves, Zanussi moves the camera downwards to show the woman's hands in confusion, crumbling together lumps of dark earth.

Illumination begins, as *Family Life* concludes, with a young man's awareness of his physical envelope. Franciszek is undergoing his medical prior to entering the University of Warsaw. "We attain wisdom through enlightenment of the mind," says his professor, defining the Augustinian concept of illumination. The next ten years or so of Franciszek's life are recounted by Zanussi with a density and a concision that speak not only of personal involvement but also of artistic maturity on the director's part. Like a physician inspecting a cardiograph, Zanussi concentrates on the peaks and troughs in the Faustian experience of his young hero. There is the excitement of university education and the encounter with a mature mistress; a climbing expedition in the mountains when a close friend is killed; his army training; a shotgun wedding and then the awesome fascination of

A moment of happiness for Franciszek and his wife in ILLUMINATION

awaiting his first child; a traumatic spell as a hospital orderly in which he realises how the human brain and body are violated with casual ease; a rupture, soon healed, with his wife; and finally the piercing pain in his chest that heralds the onset of heart disease. Zanussi leaves him relaxing happily with his family beside a lake, just another man in swim-trunks with the seeds of death growing inevitably within him. One thinks of the words of Franciszek's mistress: "We are not so important as we seem to be." Zanussi's men are not given to self-pity, but they do yearn for an interlude in which to assess their progress, to question the values by which they live, and to find a moral justification for their behaviour. [With savage irony, the non-professional actor chosen by Zanussi to play Franciszek was himself killed in a climbing accident in the Himalayas at the end of 1974.]

Zanussi's most recent work, *Quarterly Balance*, insists on this *motif*, this striving after absolute truth, and stars one of the director's favourite actresses, Maja Komorowska. The film relies, however, on a familiar theme—the wife who toys briefly and painfully with the idea of self-liberation and a love affair outside her modest domestic and office world. It has moments of exquisite emotional feeling, but its characters are conventional and somewhat literary in conception.

Zanussi is not typical either of show business or of his generation. He is a restrained, abstinent, neatly-dressed individual who is extremely articulate about his own films. But his work could never be called abstract or insensitive. Each of his major characters is much more than the sum of his organs, limbs, and myriad cells; each evinces a soul that, like the enfeebled monk's in *Death of a Provincial*, flies mysteriously towards us for friendship and protection.

PETER COWIE

ZANUSSI FILMOGRAPHY

Besides several student works at university during the Fifties, Zanussi has also directed the following shorts since graduating from PWSTiF (Łódź) in 1966: the documentaries *Przemyśl* (1966) and *Maria Dąbrowska* (1966), the education film *Komputery (Computers,* 1967), and the documentary *Krzysztof Penderecki* (1968; for TV). His early fictional film *Tramwaj do nieba (Tram to the Sky,* 1958), co-directed with Wincent Ronisz, won the main prize at that year's Amateur Film Festival. His other fictional works are as follows:

1966

ŚMIERĆ PROWINCJAŁA/DEATH OF A PROVINCIAL. Script and direction: KZ. Photography: Jan Hesse. Music: Adam Walaciński. Players: Władysław Jarema (*Provincial*), Jerzy Jogałła (*Curator*). Produced for PWSTiF. 28 mins. Diploma work.

1967

TWARZĄ W TWARZ/FACE TO FACE. Script: KZ, Edward Żebrowski. Direction: KZ. Photography: Jerzy Wójcik, Franciszek Kądziolka. Music: Adam Walaczyński. Players: Piotr Pawlowski (*Man*), Justyna Kreczmar (*Woman*), Maria Andrzej Zawada (*Fugitive*). Produced by "Tor" Film Unit. 25 mins. For TV.

1968

ZALICZENIE/ATTESTATION. Script: KZ, Edward Żebrowski. Direction: KZ. Photography: Tadeusz Wieżan. Music: Jerzy Maksymiuk. Players: Aleksander Bardini (*Professor*), Daniel Olbrychski (*Student*), Jadwiga Colonna-Walewska (*Professor's Wife*). Produced by "Tor" Film Unit. 28 mins. For TV.

1969

STRUKTURA KRYSZTAŁU/THE STRUCTURE OF CRYSTALS. Script: KZ (literary collab.: Edward Żebrowski). Direction: KZ. Photography: Stefan Matyjaszkiewicz. Music: Wojciech Kilar. Players: Barbara Wrzesińska (*Anna*), Andrzej Żarnecki (*Marek*), Jan Mysłowicz (*Jan*), Władysław Jarema (*Grandfather*). Produced by "Tor" Film Unit (Jerzy Owoc). 77 mins.

1970

GÓRY O ZMIERZCHU/MOUNTAINS AT DUSK. Script: KZ, Edward Żebrowski. Direction: KZ. Photography: Sławomir Idziak. Mountain climbing photography: Andrzej Galiński, Jerzy Surdel. Music: Wojciech Kilar. Players: Jerzy Kreczmar (*Professor*), Marek Perepeczko (*Jan*), Maja Komorowska (*Jan's Wife*), Andrzej Zawada (*Andrzej*). Produced by "Tor" Film Unit. 27 mins. For TV.

1971

ŻYCIE RODZINNE/FAMILY LIFE. Script and direction: KZ. Photography (Eastmancolor): Witold Sobociński. Music: Wojciech Kilar. Art Direction: Tadeusz Wybult. Players: Daniel Olbrychski (*Wit*), Jan Kreczmar (*Father*), Halina Mikołajska (*Aunt*), Maja Komorowska (*Bella*), Jan Nowicki (*Marek*). Produced by "Tor" Film Unit (Jerzy Buchwald). 92 mins.

ROLA/ROLE. Script: KZ, inspired by the story by Magda Szabó. Direction: KZ. Photography (Eastmancolor): Jan Hesse. Music: Wojciech Kilar. Players: Jan Kreczmar (*Father*), Daniel Olbrychski (*Son*), Jan Ciecierski (*Neighbour*), Anna Milewska (*Sister*). Produced by "Tor" Film Unit (Jerzy Buchwald) for ZDF (W. Germany). 28 mins. For TV.

ZA ŚCIANĄ/BEHIND THE WALL. Script: KZ, Edward Żebrowski. Direction: KZ. Photography: Jan Hesse. Editing: Urszula Śliwińska. Music: Beethoven (Piano Concerto No. 5). Art Direction: Tadeusz Wybult. Players: Maja Komorowska (*Anna*), Zbigniew Zapasiewicz (*Doctor*), Eugenia Herman (*Secretary*), K. Machowski (*Assistant*), Jan Kreczmar (*Professor*). Produced by "Tor" Film Unit (Jerzy Buchwald). 58 mins. For TV. On 16mm: Film Images (U.S.).

1972

HIPOTEZA/DIE HYPOTHESE/ HYPOTHESIS. Script and direction: KZ. Photography (Eastmancolor): Edward Kłosiński. Editing: Urszula Śliwińska. Music: Wojciech Kilar. Art Direction: Teresa Barska. Players: Jerzy Zelnik (*Professor*), Danuta Rinn (*His Wife*), Stanisława Celińska (*Victim*). Produced by "Tor" Film Unit (Jerzy Buchwald, Janina Krassowska) for ZDF (W. Germany) and Polish TV. 28 mins. For TV.

1973

ILUMINACJA/ILLUMINATION. Script and direction: KZ. Photography (Eastmancolor): Edward Kłosiński. Editing: Urszula Śliwińska. Music: Wojciech Kilar. Art Direction: Stefan Maciąg. Scientific Advisors: Prof. Władysław Tartarkiewicz, Prof. Iwo Birula-Białynicki, Dr. Jerzy Mycielski, Dr. Sylwester Porowski, Dr. Bogdan Mielnik, Dr. Władysław Turski, and Dr. Łukasz Turski. Players: Stanisław Latałło (*Franciszek Retman*), Małgorzata Pritulak (*Małgosia*), Monika Dzienisiewicz-Olbrychska (*Agnieszka*), Edward Żebrowski (*Doctor*), Jan Skotnicki (*Patient*), Jadwiga Colonna-Walewska (*Franciszek's Mother*), Professor Włodzimierz Zonn (*Zonn*), Dr. Włodzimierz Zawadzki (*Assistant*), Kryzysztof Ernst (*Assistant*), Irena Horecka (*Patient's Mother*), Jerzy Illasiewicz (*Physicist*), Julian Klemerus (*Climber from Mountains*), Alina Korniejowska (*Woman*), Marcin Latałło (*Son*), Andrzej

Mikulski (*Physician*), Andrzej Mellin, Tomasz Misztela (*Workers*), Włodzimierz Okrasa (*Acquaintance*), Jacek Petrycki, Włodzimierz Włodarski (*Witnesses*), Michał Tarkowski (*Driver of Hospital Car*), Ryszard Wachowski (*Man from the Dream*), Krystyna Wojciechowska (*Girl*), Jerzy Vaulin (*Boss*), Joanna Żółkowska (*Girl at Window*). Produced by "Tor" Film Unit (Jerzy Buchwald). 91 mins. On 16mm: Contemporary Films (U.K.).

1974

THE CATAMOUNT KILLING. Script: Julian and Sheila More, from the novel "I'd Rather Stay Poor" by James Hadley Chase. Adaptation: Krzysztof Zanussi. Additional dialogue: Samuel Reifler. Photography (Movielab Color): Witold Sobociński. Editing: Ilona Wasgint. Music: Wojciech Kilar. Production Design: Ruffin Barron Bennett. Players: Horst Buchholz (*Mark Kalvin*), Ann Wedgeworth (*Kit Loring*), Chip Taylor (*Ken Travers*), Louise Clark (*Iris Loring*), Patricia Joyce (*Alice Craig*), Polly Holliday (*Miss Pearson*), Stuart Germain (*Mr. Hardy*), Rod Browning (*Easton*), Peter Brandon (*Marthy*), Lotti Krekel (*Helga*), Alexander Bardini (*Petrol Pump Attendant*), Ernest Martin (*Rudy*), Leon Carter (*State Trooper*). Produced by Manfred Durniok Produktion for Film und Fernsehen (W. Germany) and Nat Rudick (U.S.A.). 102 mins. Shot in English in the U.S.A.

1975

BILANS KWARTALNY/QUARTERLY BALANCE. Script and direction: KZ. Photography (Eastmancolor): Sławomir Idziak. Editing: Urszula Śliwińska. Music: Wojciech Kilar. Art Direction: Tadeusz Wybult. Players: Maja Komorowska (*Marta*), Piotr Fronczewski (*Jan*), Marek Piwowski (*Jacek*), Halina Milołajska (*Róża*), Zofia Mrozowska (*Jan's Mother*), Barbara Wrzesińska (*Ewa*), Mariusz Dmochowski (*Director*), Chip Taylor (*Ewa's Husband*), Eugenia Herman (*Zofia*), Elżbieta Karkoszka (*Maria*), Celina Mencner (*Halina*), Krzysztof Machowski (*Rowing Instructor*), Małgorzata Pritulak (*Ania*), Danuta Rinn (*Irena*), Kazimiera Utrata-Lusztig (*Jadzia*), Stefan Szmidt (*Holidaymaker*), Jerzy Fryżlewicz (*Vice-Director*), Antonina Girycz (*Basia*), Zbigniew Jankowski (*Helmsman*), Mieczysław Kołodziejczyk (*Skiing Instructor*), Marcin Mroszczak (*Ania's Boy*), Leszek Mystkowski (*Cleaner*), Joanna Poraska (*Old Neighbour*), Jan Sieradziński (*Bosun*), Józef Wieczorek (*Taxi-Driver*). Produced by "Tor" Film Unit (Jerzy Buchwald). 98 mins.

(*We gratefully acknowledge the help of Mr. Zanussi in personally checking and authenticating this filmography*).

Above: ILLUMINATION, Franciszek visits the monastery in his search for peace
Below: Maja Komorowska in QUARTERLY BALANCE

WORLD SURVEY

Algeria

by Viggo Holm Jensen

In 1974/75 ten feature length films were produced in Algeria. *Patrouille à l'est* by Amar Laskri, *Sueurs noires* by Sid Ali Mazif, *Libération* by Mourad Bouchouchi and Farouk Beloufa, *Zone interdite* by Ahmed Lallem, *Les médailles* by Lamine Merbah, *L'héritage* by Mohamed Bouamari, and *Chronique des années de braise* by Mohamed Lakhdar-Hamina are all concerned with problems related to the War of Liberation.

Leila Shenna and Yorgo Voyagis in CHRONIQUE DES ANNEES DE BRAISE, which won Algeria the Palme d'Or at Cannes in 1975

Les vacances de l'inspecteur Tahar and *Hassan Terre s'évade*, by Moussa Haddad and Mustapha Badie, are comedies. Ali Ghalem, who previously dealt with the problems of foreign workers in France, has made a new film on the same subject called *L'autre France*. In the many films concerned with the War of Liberation there are two themes: an official celebration of the twentieth anniversary of the November Revolution in Algeria, and an opportunity to view the war as a part of the people's culture, with implications for the future.

The winning of the Grand Prix at Cannes in 1975 with *Chronique des années de braise* should help Algerian films on the world market.

Argentina

by Alberto Tabbia

Officials and superficial observers stress the fact that in the 1974/75 season Argentinian films earned several international prizes—a Berlin Silver Bear for *La Patagonia rebelde*, three San Sebastian prizes for *Boquitas pintadas*, something in Karlovy Vary for *Quebracho* and something in San Remo for *Gente en Buenos Aires*, as well as the first Oscar nomination ever for an Argentine film, *La tregua*. (All of these titles were covered in IFG 1975.) Most reflect, though, an attitude to subject-matter and film production that had it roots in the climate of 1973, one that seems each time more difficult to sustain in the present.

Before and immediately after the 1973 elections a new film law was prepared, by all the professional associations concerned, that would have assured more rational aid as well as a credit policy, with special consideration for beginners and projects of artistic intent. During that short spell of optimism the draft was studied in Congress but not passed, perhaps on account of the import-limiting measures it included and its anti-censorship stance: something that did not seem unrealistic during the time when *Last Tango in Paris* and *State of Siege* opened. (The first was later seized, the second had its certificate cancelled by the new censorship board.) As things stand in the first half of 1975, projects under way are either those that would have been produced before 1973, i.e. films with strong names (whether stars, best-selling novels or a major subject), and an occasional prestige venture or cheap quickie that is pre-sold to an intended market.

Unrelenting inflation and currency devaluations have made production costs soar while admission prizes have been kept frozen or allowed only slight increases. Now, more than ever, an Argentine film, in order to make a profit, has to be seen by a substantial part of the country's population. At the same time, the film-workers' union has enforced new rules for minimum crews and wages that should guarantee full employment but make it impossible to envisage small ventures outside the established industry. The only allowances made are for 16mm, insofar as such works do not aspire to any kind of commercial release.

Censorship, always a household word, has resulted in several projects being abandoned, while others undergo drastic changes.

Luisina Brando in LOS GAUCHOS JUDÍOS, directed by Juan José Jusid

The interrelation of all stages in film-making, from pre-production to release, leads easily enough to the most effective kind of self-censorship: though the law does not entertain any special credit policy, and only guarantees obligatory showing of a quota of Argentine films and an aid proportional to the number of tickets sold, it is customary to have new projects submitted to the censors to prevent an unwelcome last-minute red light or to know where the eventual objections to a film will lie. The original scenario for Torre Nilsson's *El pibe Cabeza* (*Big-Head Kid*), albeit a minor effort, was thought to "glorify crime"; this study of a Thirties small-time crook had to be softened in such a way that the already shaky script left the director visibly disinterested.

Something like "nostalgia" has been forced on Argentine films by the impossibility of discussing present-day behaviour and situations with a degree of dramatic interest while still eluding the censor. But not only subject-matter has been coming back. People too, and some of interest. Hugo Fregonese, who made some promising, above-average Argentine films in the Forties, then left for Hollywood and later pursued an unstable career in Europe. *Más allá del sol* (*Beyond the Sun*) is his second film since he returned to Argentina; the first one, two years ago, was *La mala vida* (*The Wrong Side of the Tracks*). From a more recent past there is José Martínez Suárez, who in the early Sixties made two isolated attempts at social criticism, the second a very ambitious and biting film: *Dar la cara* (*Stand for Something*). Away from the industry since 1963, he has come back, with two comedies that at least have a refreshing approach to *genre* conventions.

The only newcomer whose *début* is awaited with interest is Ricardo Luna, scriptwriter and personal assistant to Torre Nilsson in the late Fifties and early Sixties, who makes a belated but very ambitious first feature with *Los orilleros* (*Riverside Men*), one of two unfilmed though published scenarios by Borges and Bioy Casares. Borges, who thirty years ago complained that nobody cared about his original scripts, has seen in recent years a wave of adaptations, both here and in Europe, where already a host of quotations (by Godard, Resnais, Nicolas Roeg and others) has assured him cult status among cinephiles. His name also works as a prestige guarantee. As such it has been widely

Alfredo Alcón in EL PIBE CABEZA, directed by Leopoldo Torre Nilsson

publicised at home by the producers of *El muerto* (*The Dead One*), an adaptation of his short story of the same name. Bioy Casares, who had also haunted European films since French critics discovered his shadow lurking behind *L'année dernière à Marienbad*, and whose *Morel's Invention* surfaced during the 1974 Directors' Fortnight at Cannes, is having his *Diario de la guerra del cerdo* (*Diary of the Pig War*), a very difficult novel, directed by Torre Nilsson. But not only internationally known writers have been carried along by this trend. The box-office success of *La tregua* (*The Truce*), already a best-seller as a novel by the Uruguayan writer Mario Benedetti, has had its producers trying to revive the portmanteau film format in order to accommodate three of his short stories.

Such a rigid industrial frame supposes less a particular subject-matter than a certain approach to all subject-matter. Outside its safety devices there is little to be found—for instance Leonardo Favio's *Nazareno Cruz y el lobo* (*Nazareno Cruz and the Wolf*), an extravaganza that carries one step further the director's inclination for outdoor full-blown lyricism, already noticeable in his previous half-historical half-mythical *Juan Moreira*. His new film is an intriguing white elephant—nearly one year in production, colossally expensive, and still without a release-date. At the other end, there is nothing like the lively parallel cinema that a few years ago still made its dissident voice intermittently heard, though a project that might be classified as such is *Alicia en el país de las maravillas* (*Alice in Wonderland*), previously called, more eloquently, *Alice in the Country of Underdevelopment*. It is shot in 16mm and its director is Eduardo Pla.

LOS GAUCHOS JUDÍOS
(The Jewish Gauchos)

Script: Oscar Viale, based on the book by Alberto Gerehunoff. Direction: Juan José Jusid. Photography (Eastmancolor): Juan Carlos Desanzo. Music: Gustavo Beytelman. Players: Dora Baret, Pepe Soriano, Luisina Brando, Víctor Laplace. María Rosa Gallo, Adrián Ghio, Luis Politti, Osvaldo Terranova, Golde Flami, China Zorrilla, Gustavo Luppi, Gina María Hidlago, Raúl Lavié, Jorge Barreiro, Oscar Viale, María José Demare, Arturo Maly. A Film Cuatro Production. 120 mins.

A colourful, unique phenomenon in Argentinian social history was the immigration, between the 1880s and 1900, of Russian and Eastern-European Jews, who arrived as settlers to work the land given to them by the government: a stark contrast to the accepted image of Jewish immigrants as business-oriented city dwellers, to which they conformed both in the United States and in Argentina during the present century. Alberto Gerchunoff (1883–1950) arrived as a child from Russia, and years later was to become a well-known writer and journalist. His book of recollections and vignettes "Los gauchos judíos" (1910) coined a name for that fairly large stream of turn-of-the-century immigration. The screenplay had to incorporate the poetic observations of Gerchunoff's prose into a collective narrative, without losing its wealth of episodic detail. From the appearance of a samovar in an incongruous countryside setting, to the circumcision ritual, a country wedding where the bride is abducted by a gaucho, and a striking scene where the settlers move as if about to dance among their freshly disembarked belongings, there is a rich visual, emotional and dramatic content to the film. The focus is provided by a teenager who, like the author, made his own the new entourage his elders had to adapt to. Though not a musical, the film includes several song-and-dance scenes that also illustrate the process of assimilation. A most unusual film in its Argentinian context, *Los gauchos judíos* has great dignity in its treatment of subject-matter that could easily lend itself to coyness or demagogy, as well as being solid professional entertainment. This is Juan José Jusid's third feature as a director, and a brilliant departure from the small-scale chamber drama of his previous *Tute cabrero* (1968) and *La fidelidad* (1970). He has had, on this occasion, the outstanding contribution of cinematographer Juan Carlos Desanzo and one of the film's co-producers is Leopoldo Torre Nilsson.

ALBERTO TABBIA

Facts and Figures

The big money-makers of the year 1974, and their attendance figures on first run, were: *The Sting* (George Roy Hill)—1,021,672 spectators; *The Exorcist* (William Friedkin)—583,376; *A Touch of Class* (Melvin Frank)—563,454; *La tregua* (Sergio Renán)—414,636; *La Patagonia rebelde* (Héctor Olivera)—379,453.

recent and forthcoming films

(Ail films are in colour)

LA GUERRA DEL CERDO (The Pig War). Script: L. Pico Estrada, B. Guido, L. Torre Nilsson. Dir: Torre Nilsson. Based on the novel by Adolfo Bioy Casares. A Capricornio production. A big city is shaken by urban guerrillas as the Young People set out to exterminate the Old Ones.

NAZARENO CRUZ Y EL LOBO (Nazareno Cruz and the Wolf). Script: L. Favio, Zuhair Juri. Dir: Leonardo Favio. A Choila production. Between folklore and myth a pampas werewolf plays hide-and-seek with the Devil.

One of the most expensive, as well as less predictable, ventures in recent Argentinian cinema.

LOS ORILLEROS (Riverside Men). Script: Jorge Luis Borges, Adolfo Bioy Casares, R. Luna. Dir: Ricardo Luna. An Alamo Film production. Love, death and the cult of courage and chance among turn-of-the-century Buenos Aires tough guys. First feature by the director.

MÁS ALLÁ DEL SOL (Beyond the Sun). Script: H. Fregonese, V. Proncet, P. Palant based on original of A. Pérez Pardella. Dir: Hugo Fregonese. A Telecine SA production. A biopic of Jorge Newbery, pioneer Argentinian flyer, and by local standards a blockbuster—period planes rebuilt, and careful technical research.

LA RAULITO. Script: J. C. Gené, J. M. Paolantonio. Dir: Lautaro Murúa. A Helicón production. Case history of a girl who, though not homosexual, choses to dress and live as a man until the law finally has her committed.

EL PIBE CABEZA (Big-Head Kid). Script: L. Pico Estrada, B. Guido, L. Torre Nilsson. Dir: Torre Nilsson. A Lumiere production. The tragi-comic exploits of a popular Argentinian criminal of the Thirties, with large doses of period colour and local humour.

LOS MUCHACHOS DE ANTES NO USABAN ARSÉNICO (Yesterday's Guys Used No Arsenic). Script: J. Martínez Suárez, Augusto Giustozzi. Dir: Martínez Suárez. A Victoria production. Faded film star and companions see their suburban villa invaded by an enterprising girl who is a real-estate agent. A would-be comic *Sunset Boulevard*.

YO MATÉ A FACUNDO (I Killed Facundo). Script: Isaac Aizenberg. Dir: Hugo del Carril. A Bejolu production. A new attempt to revise accepted values in Nineteenth-century Argentinian history. This version stands for provincial *caudillos* and against the liberal federal government.

LOS ANOS INFAMES (The Infamous Years). Script: César Tiempo, U. P. de Murat, based on original by José Dominiani. Dir: Alejandro Doria. A Glori-Art production. Corruption in politics and journalism, as well as period *dolce vita* in Buenos Aires between 1938 and 1942.

LOS CHANTAS (The Phonies). Script: Norberto Aroldi. Dir: José Martínez Suárez. A Victoria production. Picaresque adventures of urban con-men, with snatches of social criticism.

LAS SORPRESAS (Surprises). Script: based on three short stories by Mario Benedetti. Dir: Luis Puenzo, Alberto Fischermann. D. C. Galettini. A Tamames-Zemborain production. Three episodes of everyday drama and comedy.

ACABEMOS DE UNA VEZ (At Long Last Come). Script: Ricardo Talesnik. Dir: Rafael Cohen. A Rafael Cohen production. A series of comedy episodes centred on the strategies to overcome feminine frigidity.

EL GRITO DE CELINA (Celina's Cry). Script: Mario David, based on short story by Bernardo Kordon. Dir: David. A Cono Sur production. Rural drama involving a possessive mother-in-law, her two weak sons and the murder of her daughter-in-law.

TRIÁNGULO DE CUATRO (Four-Sided Triangle). Script: María Luisa Bemberg. Dir: Fernando Ayala. An Aries production. Adultery among the smart set.

LOS DÍAS QUE ME DISTE (The Days You Gave Me). Script: Julio Mauricio. Dir: Fernando Siro. A Mural production. Middle-aged, middle-class housewife falls for a younger man, the neighbourhood butcher: a straight-faced attempt at soap-opera.

ADONDE MUERE EL VIENTO (Where the Wind Dies) and **SEIS PASAJES AL INFIERNO (Six Tickets to Hell).** Dir: Fernando Siro. Both with John Russell, the first with Tippi Hedren and the second with Mala Powers. Two English-speaking quickies for the horror market. Produced by Mural SCA.

LA HORA DEL SOL (Hour of the Sun). Script: R. Kuhn, Eduardo Gudiño Kieffer. Dir: Rodolfo Kuhn. A Neci production. A tale of fantasy and superstition shot on location in the province of Corrientes.

EL MUERTO (The Dead One). Script: F. Ayala, H. Olivera, Juan Carlos Onetti. Dir: Héctor Olivera. Based on a short story by Jorge Luis Borges. An Aries production. Turn-of-the-century struggle for power inside a smugglers ring on the Brazilian border. Co-produced with Spain.

Australia

by David J. Stratton

Feature film production is certainly on the increase in Australia (as the following list of recent and forthcoming films will amply indicate) but whether or not there really is a boom, is right now really hard to decide.

Films are certainly being made, but they are not finding the audiences that were expected for them. Apart from the first *Alvin Purple* film (whose astonishing success was noted last year) and *The Adventures of Barry Mackenzie*, Australian films are almost certainly not going to recover their costs without generating considerable overseas sales. With this in mind, the Department of the Media organised an expensive, Canadian-style junket to the 1975 Cannes Film Festival which certainly made some impact though the full results are not available as yet.

What *is* disturbing is that the best film of last year, Peter Weir's *The Cars That Ate Paris*, was so atrociously handled by its (American) distributor on its first release in Melbourne that it still hasn't surfaced in Sydney more than a year after its triumphant screening at the 1974 Sydney Film Festival. Weir has been able to make another film, *Picnic at Hanging Rock*, which promises to be even better than *Cars*, and since a distributor participated in production this time, the same fiasco is not expected to be repeated. Another talented film-maker, Michael Thornhill, four-walled his controversial look at Australian prejudices between the two world wars—*Between Wars*—and did much better than anybody expected; but still nowhere near enough to cover production costs. The new films of the active Hexagon company (*Petersen, Alvin Rides Again*) have done quite well, but not as well as had been hoped: the latest Hexagon film, a thriller called *End Play*, is now awaiting release. Terry Bourke's horror film with Judith Anderson, *Inn of the Damned*, has been awaiting release for over a year now; Ken Hannam's *Sunday Too Far Away*, David Baker's *The Great McCarthy* and Tom Jeffrey's *The Removalists* will be out just after this copy flies off to London; while Richard Franklin's rather stylish *The True Story of Eskimo Nell* has just opened to very unfavourable reviews in Sydney—its fate is uncertain.

Certainly many (not all) Australian film critics seem to delight in attacking locally made films (*The Cars That Ate Paris* was particularly shamefully treated) and this strange attitude certainly doesn't help to attract audiences.

A comprehensive retrospective of Australian film production which formed a part of this year's Sydney Film Festival has helped to create a new awareness of our cinema history and to discover that several of the films of the Twenties, Thirties and even Forties and Fifties weren't as bad as we'd been led to believe—in fact some were astonishingly good. So there *is* a tradition to be lived up to.

It has been a year of political in-fighting and dramas of all kinds, with the ineffectual Minister for the Media finally shifted to another portfolio. As I write, it has just been announced (amid the expected flak) that the Prime Minister's Private Secretary has been appointed Head of the Media Department. The formation of an Australian Film Commission, with powers to handle distribution as

well as to take over the activities of the Film Development Corporation, is also seen as a positive sign for the future. But whatever happens eventually, these are certainly exciting times; though the pessimists note that if the Labour Government loses at the next election the boom might well become a bust overnight—comments from the shadow spokesman for media and cultural matters have been hardly inspiring.

Censorship, once a major bugbear of Australian filmgoers, has eased until all but *Deep Throat* is freely available: indeed, the present Australian censorship system is far freer and more sensible than that currently practised in Britain.

This continues to be a major market for American films (running almost neck and neck with the British market with its far larger population): the popular American features (*Chinatown, The Godfather Part II*, etc.) enjoy spectacularly long runs. The market is less open for foreign language films, though there is always a reasonable variety available. Over the last year an attempt has been made—with Federal Government support—to take a selection of films from the Sydney and Melbourne Film Festivals to a series of small country towns. Though not financially successful, the scheme will be repeated and enlarged in 1975.

In this period of uncertainty, when literally anything can happen to the Australian film industry, it will indeed be interesting to see what will be reported in this section in a year's time. It's anybody's guess.

PICNIC AT HANGING ROCK

Script: Cliff Green. Direction: Peter Weir. Photography (colour): Russell Boyd. Editing: Max Lemon. Players: Rachel Roberts, Dominic Guard, Helen Morse, Jacki Weaver, Win Roberts, John Jarratt, Jack Fegan, Vivian Gray, Kirsty Child, Anne Lambert, Karen Robson, Jane Vallis. Executive Producer: Pat Lovell. Produced by Hal & Jim McElroy for BEF/South Australian Film Coporation.

Uncompleted at the time of going to press, *Picnic at Hanging Rock* is confidently expected to be the big feature film breakthrough we've all been waiting for, a film that is both intelligent and stylish and also commercial both in Australia and overseas. The story, based on a novel by Joan Lindsay, takes place on St. Valentine's Day, 1900, when a party of girls from an exclusive boarding school in Victoria went for a picnic at Hanging Rock, a famous local landmark, and some of them never returned. The interesting casting includes Rachel Roberts as the school's English headmistress and Dominic Guard (the boy in Losey's *The Go-Between*) as an English youth whose life is crucially affected by the mysterious disappearances.

THE GREAT McCARTHY

Script: John Romeril, David Baker. Direction: David Baker. Photography: Bruce McNaughton. Editing: John Scott. Players: John Jarratt, Judy Morris, Kate Fitzpatrick, Barry Humphries, Peter Cummins, Bruce Spence, Max Gillies, Chris Heywood, Sandra McGregor, Denis Miller. Executive Producer: Richard Brennan. Produced by David Baker for Stoney Creek Films.

Adaptation of Barry Oakley's popular novel about the misadventures of an Australian rules football player. Very funny in spots, and with some splendid performances.

THE TRUE STORY OF ESKIMO NELL

Script: Alan Hopgood, Richard Franklin. Direction: Richard Franklin. Photography: Vincent Monton. Music: Brian May. Editing: Andrew London. Players: Serge Lazareff, Max Gillies, Grahame Bond, Ellie McLure, Elke Neidhart, Abigail, Victoria Anoux, Bob Horsfall. Produced by Richard Franklin, Ronald Baneth for Filmways.

A modest, but within its own limits very successful, sex comedy with gutsy performances and plenty of bawdy humour. Vincent Monton's photography, recapturing Australia's goldrush era, is extremely handsome.

YAKKITY YAK

Script and direction: Dave Jones. Photography: Gordon Glenn. Players: Dave Jones, Peggy Cole, John Flaus, Peter Carmody. Produced by Dave Jones.

Rich, complex, funny look at the problems of an egotistical film-maker and his reluctant actors and crew.

THE LOVE EPIDEMIC

Script and direction: Brian Trenchard-Smith. Players: John Ewart, Ros Spiers, Michael Laurence, Barry Lovatt. Produced by Alan Finney, for Hexagon.

A semi-dramatised documentary on venereal disease.

SUNDAY TOO FAR AWAY

Script: John Dingwall. Direction: Ken Hannam. Photography (colour): Geoff Burton. Editing: Rod Adamson. Music: Patrick Flynn. Players: Jack Thompson, Reg Lye, Max Cullen, Peter Cummins, John Ewart, Robert Bruning, Sean Scully, Jerry Thomas, Ken Shorter, Lisa Peers, Gregory Apse. Produced by Gil Brealey, Matt Carroll for South Australian Film Corporation.

Unquestionably *the* Australian feature film of the year, *Sunday Too Far Away* not only

scooped the pool at the Australian Film Awards but also participated in the Directors' Fortnight at Cannes. An honest, splendidly acted and perceptively written piece of Australiana, it deals with the relationships between a group of shearers working on an isolated sheep station in the mid-Fifties. The film blends semi-documentary material of the shearers at work with rich comedy and, with the death of an old shearer (memorably played by veteran Reg Lye), also reaches a high level of drama. In spite of some rather jagged editing, *Sunday Too Far Away* is an auspicious entry into feature production on the part of the South Australian Film Corporation.

THE REMOVALISTS

Script: David Williamson, from his play. Direction: Tom Jeffrey. Photography: Graham Lind. Editing: Anthony Buckley. Players: Peter Cummins, Kate Fitzpatrick, Jacki Weaver, John Hargreaves, Chris Heywood, Martin Harris. For Margaret Fink.

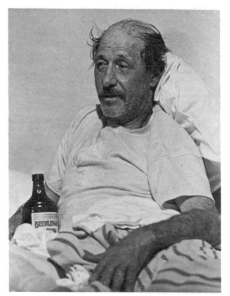

Reg Lye in SUNDAY TOO FAR AWAY

Like *Sunday Too Far Away*, production of *The Removalists* was marred by disputes between producer and director. Yet both films have triumphed over these problems, and this excellent version of David Williamson's play is a highly successful blend of theatre and cinema. The plot, involving a couple of paranoid policemen trying to help a pair of ladies apparently in distress, bristles with superb dialogue and a sextet of fine actors give marvellous performances.

PLUGG

Script and direction: Terry Bourke. Photography: Brian Probyn. Music: Bob Young. Editing: Rod Hay. Players: Peter Thompson, Cheryl Rixon, Norman Yemm, Reg Gorman. Produced by Ninki Maslansky, for Romac Films.

A comedy, set in the Western Australian capital Perth, involving a bumbling private eye's efforts to close down the Pussycat Escort Agency.

SCOBIE MALONE

Script: Casey Robinson. Direction: Terry Ohlsson. Photography: Keith Lambert. Editing: Bill Stacey. Players: Jack Thompson, Judy Morris, Noel Ferrier, Victoria Anoux. Produced by Casey Robinson, for Kingcroft Productions.

Jack Thompson plays the title character, a Sydney policeman, in this adaptation of Jon Cleary's book "Helga's Web."

END PLAY

Script and direction: Tim Burstall. Photography: Robin Copping. Editing: David Bilcock. Players: George Mallaby, John Waters, Ken Goodlet, Robert Hewett,

Kevin Miles, Charles Tingwell, Belinda Giblin, Reg Gorman. Produced by Tim Burstall, for Hexagon.

A thriller, adapted from a story by Russell Braddon, about two brothers, one a paraplegic, suspected of murdering a hitch-hiker.

THE BOX

Script: Tom Heggardy. Direction: Paul Eddy. Photography: Wayne Williams. Editing: Phil Reid. Players: George Mallaby, Fred Betts, Belinda Giblin, Ken James, Judy Nunn, Ken Snodgrass, Geraldine Turner, Cornelia Francis, Robin Ramsay. Produced by Ian Jones for Crawford Productions.

A feature film adapted from a popular, long-running TV series about the private lives of people who work for a big Melbourne television station.

THE GOLDEN CAGE

Script and direction: Ayten Kuyululu. Photography: Russell Boyd. Editing: David Huggett. Players: Sait Memisoglu, Kate Sheil, Ilhan Kuyululu, Ron Haddrick, Kerry Anne Scott. Produced by Ilhan Kuyululu, for Independent Artists.

A drama about two Turkish migrants to Australia and the fateful love affair one of them has with a Sydney girl.

CADDIE

Script: Joan Long. Direction: Donald Crombie. Photography: Peter James. Players: Helen Morse, Takis Emmanuel. Produced by Anthony Buckley.

A drama, set in the Twenties, about the struggles of a young woman and her two children.

ANGEL GEAR

Script: Lewis Baypnas. Direction: Esben Storm. Photography: Mike Edols. Players: John Ewart, John Waters, Justine Saunders. Produced by Lyn Bayonas, for Quinkan Films.

Story of a truck-driver and a hitch-hiker on a long cross-country haul.

THE FIRM MAN

Script and direction: John Duigan. Photography: Sasha Trikojus. Editing: Tony Patterson. Players: Peter Cummins, Eileen Chapman, Peter Carmody, Chris McQuade, Max Gillies, Bruce Spence. Produced by John Duigan.

Story of a middle-aged businessman who joins a mysterious political organisation known as "The Firm."

Film Australia News

The most important film made by Film Australia over the past year has been a co-production with the National Film Board of Canada—*Mr. Symbol Man*, directed by

Australian Film Institute

EXHIBITION: the AFI operates an alternative film circuit. FESTIVALS: the AFI provides Australian films for international festivals and organizes the annual Australian Film Awards competition. DISTRIBUTION: the AFI distributes quality films and exchanges films with other sources.

79 - 81 Cardigan Street, Carlton South, Victoria, Australia, 3053. Telephone: (03) 3476888. Cables: 'FILMINSTITUTE MELBOURNE'.

Bruce Moir and Bob Kingsbury. Their subject is Charles Bliss, a remarkable man who devised a new international language based solely on basic symbols and, after a lifetime of battling for recognition, finally found his ideas being accepted in Canada. Bliss, who lives with his brother in a Sydney suburb, comes across as a tenacious fighter, yet a thoroughly warm, funny and delightful personality. It is criminal that, at the time of writing, this superb film has been rejected by all the local television networks. Jane Oehr ran into Department of Education trouble with her film *Stirring*, a study of an experimental teaching class which is discussing the issue of corporal punishment. Also interesting is *One-weft Double-cloth*, directed by James Coffey, which explores through a progression of woven images, the work of a weaver, a potter and a blacksmith. Finally, a handsome production by David Haythornthwaite which won the St. Finbarr Prize for the Best Short Fiction Film at the 1975 Cork Film Festival, *A Steam Train Passes*, a romantic reminiscence of a steam train that leaves Sydney for Western N.S.W. from the present time to times long past.

South Australian Film Corporation

Gil Brealey and his colleagues in Adelaide are undoubtedly euphoric over the highly successful screenings so far of their first feature film *Sunday Too Far Away*, both in the Directors' Fortnight in Cannes and also as the opening night film at the Sydney Film Festival. Their second feature, *Picnic at Hanging Rock*, should be at least equally successful.

The standard of films coming from the Corporation is very high, with the outstanding non-feature of the year being *Who Killed Jenny Langby?*, directed by Donald Crombie, an analysis of the reasons for the suicide of a working-class housewife, with a memorable performance from Julie Dawson as the housewife (she won the 1974/75 Australian Film Award for Best Actress) and an equally effective contribution from Peter Cummins—who has emerged as probably the best Australian character actor around—as her husband. On a lighter level, the Corporation co-produced (with the National Film Board of Canada) *The Players*, an often hilarious look at the experiences of the Stratford Theatre Players on tour in Australia.

Focus on Shorts

The Rouben Mamoulian Award for the Best Australian Short Film was presented (by Philippe Mora, director of *Brother Can You Spare a Dime?*) to Jane Oehr for her remarkable documentary *Niugini—Culture Shock*, which deals with the massive impact of Western culture on the people of Papua, New Guinea. Winners of the year's Greater Union Awards for Australian Short Films were Frank Shields's *The Breaker* (Documentary), about an Australian adventurer who died during the Boer War; Russell Mulcahy's *Contrived Mind Flashes* (General), an overlong but often spectacular experimental film which attempts to get into the minds of its characters; and Ken Cameron's *Sailing to Brooklyn* (Fiction), a highly accomplished (and rather erotic) short story about a young schoolteacher's affair with one of his pupils.

Other interesting short films, in a rather good year, include Chris Noonan's *Bulls*, an

Charles Bliss in MR. SYMBOL MAN, a co-production between Film Australia and the National Film Board of Canada

excellent adaptation of an Alan Marshall short story about a little girl's irrational fear of the bull on her father's property; Graham Shirley's *Lanshan*, which re-creates a somewhat bizarre period of Australian history when escaping convicts believed China was attached to the Australian mainland and set out to find safety there; James Ricketson's *It Wasn't Going to Happen to Me*, a remarkable documentary about the last months of a wealthy businessman who has discovered he is dying

of cancer; and *Circuit* by Gillian Burnett, a highly personal but rather uneven film about the breakup of a relationship and its intense emotional effect on the woman involved, with beautiful performances from Robyn Nevin and Arthur Dignam. Three experimental films should also be included here; Paul Winkler, with *Chants* and *Brick Wall*, proves again that he is the most original short film-maker working in Australia today, if only he could exert a little more discipline and tighten his films; and *We Should Call It a Living Room* ... by Aleksander Danke, Joan Grounds, David Lourie and David Stewart, is a dazzling and perfectly executed little exercise in which an empty room literally comes to life before our eyes with lush shrubbery emerging from the walls, floor, ceiling and furniture.

Australian Film Institute

The Australian Film Institute was established in 1958, and its principle aims are to encourage the art of film, to encourage a wider distribution of different types and styles of film or video within the community, and to conduct or participate in film festivals, exhibitions and similar activities and to assist in the procurement and exchange of films between Australia and overseas countries.

To this end, the Institute operates a distribution service (the Vincent Library) which distributes Australian and foreign films both locally and overseas; organises the Australian Film Awards competition, an annual event attracting considerable attention; administers the Experimental Film and Television Fund in collaboration with the Australia Council (providing almost $325,000 annually for independent and *avant-garde* film production). Again with funds provided by the Australia Council, the Institute established in mid-1974 ten Community Access Video Centres across Australia as well as two sophisticated Video Resource Centres in Sydney and Melbourne. The video scheme is loosely based on the Canadian "Challenge for Change" programme, and is intended to provide for people within individual communities at grass roots level, the facilities to use portable video equipment in order to produce tapes depicting problems within their own areas, and thereby bring these problems to the attention of community and government leaders.

With the number of quality films finding distribution in Australia declining each year, the Institute moved to rectify the situation by opening the first of a nation-wide chain of "art houses" in Melbourne which, coincidently have also made a point of exhibiting certain Australian films of artistic merit. The Institute has, as a result, begun to rapidly expand its collection of foreign films for programming in its cinemas. Within twelve months from now, the Institute will have opened another three of these cinemas.

Over the past twelve months the Institute has provided numerous Australian entries in international festivals, as well as an Australian Film Week.

The Australian Film Institute is philosophically investigating its role and function in relationship to both the general public and the film and video community. Towards this end a new constitution, which will ensure that the Australian Film Institute is responsive to a wide number of interests, is currently being instituted.

Austria

by Goswin Dörfler

Nothing has changed on the Austrian film scene during the past five years. The long-promised parliamentary act (aimed at encouraging Austrian films) which was put forward five years ago, has still not been placed before the house. Not even a definite draft has appeared. New elections are due in the autumn of 1975, thus shelving for years any hope for an improvement in the situation.

This is why there really is *no* Austrian film production and will be none in the near future. The few movies that are made each year are of neither commercial nor artistic importance internationally speaking. They are trivial experiments by ambitious amateurs and film students, or films in part or wholly financed by TV as cheap programme fillers, as shabby sex films, or as German or Italian co-productions (only one director really figures here—Franz Antel/François Legrand). It is encouraging, however, that occasionally among the amateur-experimental

films something interesting emerges, worthy of screening at a festival. But these efforts cannot really change the pattern of Austrian cinema.

The eight films listed below represent the entire Austrian output in 1974. Internationally it may seem a gloomy picture, but it reflects the cinema-going habits of the Austrians themselves. In 1973 there were 23,886,386 spectators (including 7,966,827 in Vienna), and in 1974 these figures again dropped slightly. The number of cinemas has declined too, from 228 in Vienna in 1953 to a mere 97 now. The number of TV licences is on the increase, with 1,848,950 in circulation at the end of 1974—5% more than in 1973. This is hardly surprising, as Austrian Television (ORF) offers strong competition to the cinema after the so-called "Radio Reform" (synonymous with politically controlled TV and radio). Due to a lack of original programmes, talent, and initiative (not to

Walter Bannert in DIE GLÜCKLICHEN MINUTEN DES GEORG HAUSER

A scene from UNDINE 74, with Werner Pochath

mention a sense of responsibility), the TV has to be content with an increasing number of movie screenings—ten per week on average, some of them quite recent releases.

Even the number of films released in Austria is declining. Against 357 new openings in Vienna in 1973 (1959: 520!), only 341 made their way to the cinemas in 1974. Of these, 98 were American, 64 West German, 53 Italian, 36 French, 28 Hongkong(!), 27 English, 7 Spanish, 6 Soviet, and the remainder from smaller countries. These films were on offer from 26 distributors.

Even the activities of a few, more or less non-commercial organisations with cultural ideals cannot flourish properly in Austria. There is little domestic interest. And the annual "Viennale," a festival for the Viennese (inquiries to: Kulturamt der Stadt Wien, A 1080 Vienna, Friedrich Schmidt-Platz 5), does not improve matters much—although several interesting films have been screened—*Still Life* (Iran), *Lancelot du Lac* (France), *Illumination* (Poland), *The Cars That Ate Paris* (Australia). The Film Weeks organised by foreign embassies (such as the excellent Soviet Week in April, or the retrospective of Pierre Etaix at the Institut Français, at which the director himself was present) are unfortunately also of little help. The efforts of "Aktion Der gute Film," a non-profit organisation helping to show films that might otherwise be ignored (e.g. Zeman's *Invention for Destruction* or Tanner's *Retour d'Afrique*), do not achieve the success they deserve (inquiries to: Neubaugasse 25, A1070 Vienna).

The most successful work in this field is still performed by the Austrian Film Archive, with their annual summer retrospectives in Laxenburg Castle near Vienna. A complete tribute to Fred Astaire was very popular here in 1973, and this summer a retrospective of 26 Austrian directors was combined with an exhibition from May to September. (Inquiries to: Rauhensteingasse 5, A 1010 Vienna.) Yet the irony is that it is not so much the films that attract visitors as the castle and its grounds—an excursion into bygone times of which Austrians still dream. The cinema, alas, is not accepted by the court . . .

recent films

DAS MANIFEST (The Manifest). Experimental film. Script: Gotthard Boehm. Antonis Lepeniotis, Wilhelm Diem. Dir: Lepeniotis. Players: Gerald Florian, Günther Hauser, Peter Garell, Dieter Schrage. Prod: Cinecoop-Filmproduktion, Vienna. Released February 22, 1974.

PROTOKOLL EINER MONTAGE (Protocol for a Montage). Experimental film. Script and dir: Sepp Jahn, Edith Hirsch. Players: Dieter Haspel, Helene Hebda, Silvia Huerlimann. Firtz Silberbauer. Prod: Jahnfilm-Produktion, Vienna. Released March 14, 1974.

UNDINE 74. Romantic drama. Script: Ted Rose, Josef Czech, from the short story by De la Motte-Fouqué. Dir: Rolf Thiele. Players: Werner Pochath, Elisabeth Flickenschildt, Ingo Thouret, Angela von Radloff. Prod: MINA-Film, Vienna/CARO, Munich/TIT, Berlin. Released April 19, 1974.

ABENTEUER EINES SOMMERS (Summer Adventure). Family film. Script: Veit Heiduschka, Kurt Nachmann, from the novel by Alexander Sacher-Masoch. Dir: Helmut Pfandler. Players: Matthias Habich, Marte Harell, Fred Liewehr, Fritz Muliar. Prod: Star-Film. WDS-Film, Vienna/ORF. Released April 25, 1974.

DIE GLÜCKLICHEN MINUTEN DES GEORG HAUSER (The Happy Minutes of Georg Hauser). Experimental film. Script: Dieter Schrage, Wilhelm Diem, Mansur Madavi. Dir: Madavi. Players: Walter Bannert, Ernst Epller, Lore Heuermann, Christine Heuer. Prod: Cinecoop-Filmproduktion, Vienna. Released July 14, 1974 (at Karlovy Vary Festival).

WENN MÄDCHEN ZUM MANÖVER BLASEN (When Girls Trumpet for Manoeuvres). Military sex farce. Script: Florian Burg. Dir: Franz Antel. Players: Rinaldo Talamonti, Alena Penz, Alexander Grill, Nina Frederik. Prod: Neue Delta-Filmproduktion, Vienna/Lisa-Film, Munich. Released August 23, 1974.

DAS LEBEN ANTON BRUCKNERS (The Life of Anton Bruckner). Documentary. Script and dir: Hans Conrad Fischer. Prod: FFF-Produktion Salzburg/Berchtesgaden. Released September 1, 1974.

STOSSTRUPP VENUS—5 MÄDCHEN BLASEN ZUM ANGRIFF (Venus Raiders—5 Girls Trumpet the Attack). Sex farce. Script: Willy Pribil. Dir: Georg Keil. Players: Michael Maien, Nina Frederik, Alena Penz, Franz Muxeneder. Prod: Günter Köpf Filmproduktion, Vienna/TIT Filmproduktion, Munich. Released September 13, 1974.

Austrian Distributors

Atlantic Film
Neubaugasse 25
1070 Vienna.
Austria Film
Neubaugasse 25
1070 Vienna.
Commerz Film
Neubaugasse 25
1070 Vienna.
Constantin Film
Siebensterngasse 37
1070 Vienna.
Czerny Film
Neubaugasse 1
1070 Vienna.

DAFA Film
Lindengasse 43
1070 Vienna.
Favorit Film
Neubaugasse 38
1070 Vienna.
FZ Stadthalle Wien
Neubaugasse 35
1070 Vienna.
Germania Filmverleih
Neubaugasse 4
1070 Vienna.
Gloria Filmverleih
Neubaugasse 25
1070 Vienna.

Jupiter Film
Neubaugasse 25
1070 Vienna.
Oefram Film
Neubaugasse 36
1070 Vienna.
Roxy Filmverleih
Neubaugasse 25
1070 Vienna.
Universal Film
Neubaugasse 38
1070 Vienna.

Belgium

by Paul Davay

Over the past year cinema attendance figures have shown a slight rise, due in no small measure to the impact of the Brussels International Festival held for the second time in January 1975 to great public acclaim. A non-competitive event, its sole objective is to showcase certain films which have already been bought by distributors—a good idea, judging by the festival's success. Other reasons for the rise in attendances have been the development of smaller, more luxurious cinemas, and the increase in the number of films of a sensationalist nature—"disaster" pictures and sex-films. All this, however, has not helped the distribution of Belgian films within the country. On the one hand,

exhibitors refuse to programme works on which they are not assured of a good return, and on the other, only dare to show films like Robbe De Hert's *Camera Sutra* on bad box-office occasions. Finally, although there is no censorship in Belgium, the Ministry of Economic Affairs do not give tax rebates on works which they classify as "immoral" or too controversial. Thierry Zeno's *Vase de noces* recently fell a victim to this ruling. In fact, the last Belgian film to make any impression at the box-office was Roland Verhavert's *Le conscrit* (particularly in Flanders).

If there were more *cinémas d'art-et-essai*, Belgian films would be able to find more outlets; as it is, there is only one (in

Still from SOUVENIR OF GIBRALTAR, produced by Y.C. Aligator Film, Brussels

Brussels)—and that with a mere fifty seats . . . Its director hopes to open two others soon, and there is also talk of setting up a Maison du Cinéma, showing films for "connoisseurs." There is, then, some room for hope. The only other outlets open to Belgian film-makers lie in the "ghetto" of the Musée du Cinema, the Maisons de la Culture, and the Days, Weeks and Rencontres du Jeune Cinema organised by Right and Left in the capital and provinces. The situation is all the more regrettable in the light of the financial aid granted by the two Ministries of Culture (see separate article), which has resulted in fifteen films being currently in various stages of production. Despite enjoying such official aid, however,

certain directors have met great obstacles created by bureaucratic tardiness: Jean-Jacques Andrien, for example, has only recently managed to complete *Le mensonge* (working title: *Le fils d'Amr est mort*).

One consolation is that Belgian films are beginning to be sold abroad more, mostly thanks to the initiative of organising a Film Market at the Tenth Belgian Film Festival. Almost twenty foreign film critics, from a dozen countries, attended the festival, which showcased two years' production (30 features, 180 shorts) and showed the world that our film-makers are capable of as many conventional and stereotyped films as the rest—well-made, also, but for the most part sticking to a facile romanticism which, when it does abandon its nostalgic or passive stance, perverts the subject-matter by skirting the issues or lacking real development. To all appearances, no Belgian has any problems, only leaving the conformist mainstream to indulge in the fantastic or "audacious." One of the merits of Benoît Lamy's *Home, Sweet Home* was that it did *not* set its sights so low, did not lose its way in a facile sense of style, but still managed to relate everyday details in an interesting way.

Henri Xhonneux's *Souvenir of Gibraltar* (the script of which won a prize) was similarly successful. The story of a young film-maker who decides to direct a picture in which the leading characters are his brother (a boxer) and his parents (butchers in a small provincial town), the film has a delicate humour full of small allusions to everyday life, drawn in rapid brush-strokes and touched by an authentic feel which comes from filming in real locations in Brussels and (his family) in Welkenraedt. The picture is fictionalised autobiography: Xhonneux's own brother plays the boxer, and his wife, the comedienne Margrit, plays the film-maker's wife; as the parents, Annie Cordy and Eddie Constantine are models of simplicity and observation.

That apart, there is not much else worth remembering from recent productions from within the System, apart from Frans Buyens's *Wondershop*, a fairy-tale of uneven quality but full of clever ideas and with a pretty score by Arsène Souffriau. Very popular with child audiences, it has the great merit of making them think while entertaining at the same time and does not preach any moral lessons.

Two fine works have been produced by the French-language RTB TV, the products of two men who worked together for a long time but have now gone their own ways. *Histoire d'un oiseau qui n'était pas pour le chat*, by Jean-Jacques Péché, tells of the crises of conscience in two women, one a Belgian worker who enters a beauty contest, the other a Palestinian teacher who takes part in a hijacking. Pierre Manuel's *Les belles manières* describes the change of a young idealist into a conformist. Each director, working with non-professionals, attempts to reconcile *cinéma direct* with the fictional film based on real events. Both pictures survive projection on cinema screens.

As for independent productions, there have been two very personal works on 16mm. Chantal Akerman, in *Je, tu, il, elles,* lucidly scrutinises herself, some men, and a girl-friend from whom she seeks affection, in the form of a three-part meditation—austere, dense, and showing original talent. In *Le saigneur est avec nous* Roland Lethem abandons the provocative stance of his previous works for a violent condemnation of the fascism inherent in every domain of social life. It is a splendid mixture of disparate elements, seasoned by a feel for both satire and dialectics.

Willeke van Ammelrooy in LA DONNEUSE

recent films

LES BELLES MANIERES. Script and dir: Pierre Manuel. Phot (16mm, Gevacolor): Manu Bonmariage. Music: Etienne Gilbert, Marc Deneyer (guitar). Players: Yves Vasseur, Jacqueline Hamers, Christiane Renard, Léon Rucuoy, Léon Hecq, René Francis, Raymond Coumans. 90 mins. French language. For RTB (Brussels).

LA DONNEUSE. Script and dir: Jean-Marie Pallardy. Phot (colour): Jacques Ledoux, Maurice Kaminsky, Christian Depovere. Players: Willeke van Ammelrooy, Jean-Marie Pallardy, Beba Lončar, Louise Allard, Pierre Valery, André Koob, Bernard Musson, Georges Dobagne, Jean Gillard, Guy D. Len. 90 mins. French language. For Eurafi (Brussels) Films JMP (Paris).

LES FILLES DU GOLDEN SALOON. Script: H. L. Rostaine, H. B. de Boitselier, W. Russel. Dir: Pierre Taylou. Phot (Eastmancolor): Raymond Heil. Music: Daniel White. Players: Sandra Julien, Alan Spencer, Claude Bregeon, Evelyne Scott, Alice Arno, Gilda York, France Nicolas, Gilliane Pascal, Roger Darton. 90 mins. French language. For Brux International Pictures (Brussels)/Eurociné (Paris).

LA FLUTE A SIX SCHTROUMPFS. Script: Peyo and Yvan Delporte. Dir: Eddy Ryssack. Music: Michel

Legrand. Animated film. 90 mins. French language. For J. Dupuis and Belvision (Brussels).

LES GASPARDS. Script and dir: Pierre Tchernia. Phot (Eastmancolor): Jean Tournier. Music: Gérard Calvi. Players: Michel Serrault, Philippe Noiret, Charles Denner, Michel Galabru, Annie Cordy, Chantal Goya, Prudence Harrington, Gérard Depardieu, Daniel Ivernel, Jean Carmet, Roger Carel. 90 mins. French language. For Les Films de la Seine (Paris)/Albina Productions (Paris)/ORTF (Paris)/Belvision (Brussels).

GOLDEN OPHELIA. Script and dir: Marcel Martin, from a novel by Ward Ruyslinch. Phot (Eastmancolor): Ralf Boumans. Music: Charles Aznavour, Etienne Verschueren. Set dec: Antoine Geyskens. Players: Henk van Ulsen, Ward De Rawet, Bettina Dubbeld, Bob van der Veken, Joanna Geldof, Léo Dewals, Ann Petersen. 80 mins. Dutch language. For Promofilm (Brussels).

HISTOIRE D'UN OISEAU QUI N'ETAIT PAS POUR LE CHAT. Script and dir: Jean-Jacques Péché, Pierre Mertens. Phot (Eastmancolor, 16mm): Manu Bonmariage, Gérard Collet. Music: Fairuz and Al-Safi. Players: Jannik Urbain, Mireille Vicat, Khiti Benhachem, Gisèle Bruart, Constantin Constantinidis, Salim Tamer. 80 mins. French language. For RTB (Brussels).

ISABELLE DEVANT LE DESIR. Script: J. P. Berckmans, Jacques De Decker, from a novel by Maud Frère. Dir: Jean-Pierre Berckmans. Phot (Eastmancolor): Henri Decae. Music: Claude Luter, Yannick Singery. Set dec: Philippe Graff. Players: Anicée Alvina, Jean Rochefort, Mathieu Carrière, Annie Cordy, Francine Blistin, Etienne Samson, Sophie Barjac, Anne-Marie Ferrières. 90 mins. French language. For Art et Cinéma (Brussels)/Elan Films (Brussels)/Lira Films (Paris).

JE, TU, IL, ELLES. Script and dir: Chantal Akerman. Phot (16mm): René Fruchter. Players: Chantal Akerman, Niels Arestrup, Claire Wauthion. 80 mins. French language. For Chantal Akerman (Brussels).

KIM OI! Script and dir: Pham-Lai. Phot (Eastmancolor): Lucien Suscky. Music: from Thailand. Players: Ngoc Suong, Quoc Tuan, Nguyen Thi Luu, Pham-Lai, Brigitte Dessars, Claudia Sylva, Fernandin, Christian Rouckhout. 75 mins. French language. For Dainam International Films (Mons).

LE NOSFERAT. Script: M. Rabinowicz, Yvette Michelems. Dir: Maurice Rabinowicz. Phot (Gevacolor): Jean-Jacques Mathy. Music: Marc Héroeut, René César. Set dec: Raymond Renard. Players: Véronique Peynet, Maïté Nahyr, Martine Bertrand, Guy Pion, Quentin Milo. 90 mins. French language. For Les Films du Groupe de Chambre (Brussels).

PONT BRULE. Script: G. Henderickx, Marcel van Maele. Dir: Guido Henderickx. Phot (Eastmancolor): Walther van den Ende. Music: Alain Pierre. Set dec: Philippe Graff. Players: Malka Ribovska, Jan Decleir,

Yves Beneyton, Doris Arden, Charles Jansses, Paul Meyer. 90 mins. Dutch and French languages. For Pierre Films (Brussels)/Visie (Meise).

LE PREMIER ETE. Script: J. Correa, Charles-Laurent Gondanoff. Dir: João Correa. Phot (Eastmancolor): Jean Rosenbaum. Music: Henri Seroka. Players: Trille Jorgensen, Claude Huart, André Daufel, Nadia Vasil, Olivier Mathot, Marcel Portier, Marc Sand. 100 mins. French language. For Cocibel (Brussels)/Orpham (Paris).

SOUVENIR OF GIBRALTAR. Script: H. Xhonneux, François-Xavier Morel. Dir: Henri Xhonneux. Phot (Eastmancolor): Michel Houssiaux. Music: Tucker Zimmerman. Players: Annie Cordy, Eddie Constantine, Armand Xhonneux, François-Xavier Morel, Eric Muller, Margrit, Manda Hartmann. Set dec: Oscar Morle, Philippe Graff. 90 mins. French language. For Aligator Films (Brussels)/Tanagra Productions (Paris).

APRES LE VENT DES SABLES. Script and dir: Claude Zaccai. Phot (Eastmancolor): Walter Lassally. Set dec: Michael Bastow. Players: Ronald Guttman. Pierre Laroche, Alexandre von Sivers, Roland Mahauden, Assaf Dayan. 90 mins. French language. From Timber Films (Brussels)/Cyadmarc (London).

WONDERSHOP. Script: F. Buyens, Guido Staes. Dir: Frans Buyens, Guido Staes, Dirk van den Eynden. Phot (Gevacolor): Fernand Tack, Walter Smets. Music: Arsène Souffriau. Set dec: Luc Monheim. Players: Romain Deconinck, Yvonne Delcour, Eva Kant, Brick Andersen, Peter Duvour, Aagje Dolhain, Julien Schoenaerts, Wannes van de Velde, Wies Andersen. 65 mins. Dutch language. For Crea (Antwerp).

JEANNE DIELMAN, 23 QUAI DU COMMERCE, 1080 BRUXELLES. Script: Chantal Akerman. Phot (color): Babette Mangolte. Players: Delphine Seyrig, Jan De Corte. 210 mins. French language. For Paradise Film (Brussels).

LA FLEUR ET LE FUSIL. Prod and dir: Gérard Valet. Phot (colour, 16mm): André Goeffers. French language. Feature-length documentary on North Vietnam.

Belgian Distributors

Art et Essai:

Cinevog Films
10 rue des Palais
1030 Brussels
Progrès Films
286 rue Royale
1030 Brussels.

L'Action Cinématographique
30 rue de l'Etuve
1000 Brussels.
Groupe Nouveau Cinema
68 rue du Prince Royal
1050 Brussels.

Underground:

Unité de Distribution
19 rue Murillo
1040 Brussels.
Bevrijdingsfilms
4 Quentin Metsysplein
3000 Leuven.

Official Bodies

Ministère de la Culture Française
Emile Cantillon, chef du Service Cinéma
138 avenue de Cortenberg
1040 Brussels
(Tel: (02) 735.60.40).

Ministerie voor Nederlandse Cultuur
Juul Anthonissen, hoofd van de Filmdienst
158 Kortenberglaan
1040 Brussels
(Tel: (02) 735.60.40).

Ministère des Affaires Etrangères
Gérard Legros, chef du Service Cinéma
2 rue des Quatre-Bras
1000 Brussels.

Film Festivals

Festival National du Film Belge
32 avenue de l'Astronomie
1030 Brussels.

Film International Antwerp
437 Bisschoppenhoflaan
2100 Deurne.

Prix L'Age d'Or
Cinémathèque Royale de Belgique
23 Ravenstein
1000 Brussels.

Pierre Clémenti in LE MENSONGE, directed by Jean-Jacques Andrien

LE MENSONGE

Script and direction: Jean-Jacques Andrien. Photography (Eastmancolor): Giorgos Arvanitis, Georges Barsky. Music: Monteverdi, and Tunisian music. Art Direction: Philippe Graff. Players: Pierre Clémenti, Claire Wauthion, Malcolm Djuric. For Les Films de la Drève (Brussels)/Unité 3 (Paris). 90 mins. French and Arab dialogue.

Since 1966, the year of the "discovery" of André Delvaux, the Belgian cinema has waited a long time for another name on which to build its international reputation. It now has one, however, in Jean-Jacques Andrien (born 1944), one of the most brilliant pupils of INSAS, where he studied under Delvaux, Ghislain Cloquet, Michel Fano and Antoni Bohdiewicz. *Le mensonge* tells the simple story of a man (Pierre Clémenti) who realises that his life to this point has been a lie: the mysterious death of a fellow pickpocket from Maghreb, a death for which he feels he may be responsible, makes him leave his wife (Claire

Wauthion) and son in Brussels to go on a voyage of self-discovery in a South Tunisian village. The film is constructed as a succession of long, beautifully photographed takes which, while eschewing pictorialism, have a remarkable density and air of mystery. Andrien orchestrates his resources with musical skill, combining an elaborate soundtrack with dialogue and camera movement. *Le mensonge* is a refreshing work which owes nothing to contemporary styles, and while taking the form of a spare, austere meditation upon its subject, is free of intellectualism for its own sake. With this his first feature, art house audiences will discover in Andrien a director of great quality.

PAUL DAVAY

FRANS BUYENS (born 1924, at Temse) is a multilingual Flemish film-maker whose mind never ceases to swarm with original ideas. Of working-class origins, completely self-taught, he acquired an enviable cultural education thanks to his intellectual curiosity and innate gifts. His interests remain wide-ranging: numerous essays on Belgian and foreign artists, plays for the theatre, several novels, short stories, children's books, science fiction works, as well as founding and running a *théâtre satirique* in Anvers and working as a scriptwriter, director and reporter on TV. Buyens has made many shorts on socially important personalities—Jean Jaurès (1959), the engraver-painter Frans Masereel (1959 and 1969), the writer Vercors (1967), the tapestry-maker Gaspard De Wit (1968) and the economist Ernest Mandel (1972). In the feature field he was the first Belgian director to attempt an "engaged" work—*Combattre pour nos droits* (1961), about striking workers, shown at Poretta Terme, Leipzig, Florence, Venice and Tel-Aviv. Other works have mirrored his concern with the problems of the real world. In *Allemagne, terminus Est* (1964) he looked at the GDR through Western eyes, while in *Dialogue ouvert* (1971) a visit to the Breendonck concentration camp gave him the opportunity to bring together the reactions of the younger generation and of those Belgians who had experienced the Nazi occupation. Buyens does not neglect the medium of fiction, however: *Chacun de nous* (1971) employed a free format which allowed its comedians to improvise on the theme of integration and submission by the individual to the social structure. More recent works, on the other hand, have used rigorously detailed scripts: *Zigzag* (1973), *Où toussent les petits oiseaux* (1974) and the children's film *Wondershop*. These films are dream-like in structure, with music and dance intervening more than once. It could be that Buyens is our sole *fabuliste*, despite the fact that he uses little in the way of money to transform his ideas into gold.

PAUL DAVAY

Frans Buyens

ROLAND VERHAVERT (born May 1, 1927, in Melsele) spent his early years in Anvers, where he studied commercial science. His first job was as an accountant, but he soon became enamoured of the cinema, writing in magazines and founding with Karel Simons in 1947 "Het Linnen Venster," a film society in Anvers which had a brief but brilliant life. In Brussels, at the Cinémathèque de Belgique, he gained experience in compiling anthologies of classic films, and on Flemish TV he was responsible for *Première*, a programme reviewing new releases. Verhavert began his film-making career through the usual channels of commissioned documentaries and fictional shorts, finally making his first feature-length work, *Meeuwen sterven in de haven (Seagulls Die in the Harbour)*, in 1955. The film was a genuine collective effort, signed jointly by Rik Kuypers, Ivo Michiels and Roland Verhavert: a man-on-the-run thriller set in Anvers, the shortcomings of the story were compensated for by a fine sense of atmosphere. Since then Verhavert has made great strides: he is a professor of the RITCS film school and president of the Belgian Association of Film and TV Artists; and as well as having his own production company (Visie) with which he encourages younger talent, he also finds time to work for other concerns.

Roland Verhavert

Verhavert's films include *Schwarz weiss blues*, *Allemande in Herbst*, and *Das specifische Gewicht* (1962), documentaries on Ruppelmonde, Brussels and Gand, and fictional shorts like *Albisola mare savona* (1963), *Wat nu, oude man?* (1964), *De luitenant*, *Kerkhofblommen* (1964), and *De geboorte* (1968). Since *Meeuwen sterven in de haven* he has made three more feature-length films: *Het afschied (Farewell*, 1966) from a fine novel by his friend Ivo Michiels, *Rolande* from Herman Tierlinck's melodramatic and sarcastic novel, and *De loteling* from a work by Henri Conscience, a popular novelist of the last century.

Verhavert has shown a consistent interest in filming Flemish literature, and is currently working on a screen version of Félix Timmermans's "Pallieter." His interest is, however, far from regional, his universal outlook underlined by his use of multilingual dialogue and introduction of foreign actors. His interest in the past prefigured by many years the current nostalgia vogue, and, most importantly, Verhavert works within the Belgian tradition, with image and sound combining in true harmony.

FRANCIS BOLEN

Films Aided by the Ministry of French Culture

In IFG 1975 we dealt briefly with the system of "Aid" given by the (Belgian) Ministry of French Culture. It remains to be noted that this Aid can be granted also to films co-produced between a Belgian company and one or more foreign companies, and not only to wholly indigenous productions. During the financial year 1974/75 the Ministry financially assisted the following films:

Feature Films: *La trame* (Claude Zaccai—Timber Films), *Il vogue vers l'Amérique* (Chantal Akerman—Showking Films), *Moi, Tintin* (Henri Roanne and Gérard Valet—Pierre Films), *Souvenir of Gibraltar* (Henri Xhonneux—Y.C. Aligator Film), *Les frontières du rêve ou Jean-Pierre, Anne et Juliette* (Jacques Faber—Films du Bélier).

Shorts: *L'arbre à cames a perdu ses feuilles* (Jean Agulhon—Flashbird), *La Pub* (Michel Clarence—Flashbird), *Le quatrième homme* (J. van Koekenbeek—Alpha 67 Films), *Savez-vous que vous feriez une merveilleuse ingénue?* (Pierre Dupont—Showking Films), *Les marcheurs d'Entre Sambre et Meuse* (Henri Storck), *Juste* (J. P. Ferbus), *Luxembourg* (J. P. Grombeer), *Retro* (Richard Olivier), *Les marionnettes à sang chaud,* (Yvan Lemaire), *Troubles* (Hugo Ké), *Quand le loup n'y est pas* (Carlo Binstock).

First works*: *Luc Bunni a disparu* (Gilles Moniquet), *Le mariage de Jean* (R. De Longueville), *L'innocente victime* (J. L. Lamy), *Le petit train* (Henri Slepon), *La musique au fil du temps* (A. Rarrbo), *Da Capo* (Christian Fontaine), *Projet d'un court métrage* (J. M. Houdemond), *Visite* (S. Szlingerbaum), *La Marge* (Ivan Segard), *Jeanne* (Dominique Miauton), *La disparition* (Francis de Laveleye), *La fleur de papier* (Ph. Defalle), *Un aller sans retour* (C. Garreau), *NBC* (Annick Leroy), *Rochassiers* (J. M. Cresse), *Valentine et le parti* (Georges Lebouc), *Un cadre pour photo* (Rafael Serenellini), *La visite* (M. Meerbergen).

At the beginning of 1975 the minister, Henri-François van Aal, apportioned 38,000,000 Belgian francs to the Aid scheme, enough for participation in five or six features and a certain number of 16mm shorts. Encouragement will also be given to works on Super-8, without forgetting the annual prize for Best Screenplay and organisation of Belgian film weeks abroad in co-operation with the Flemish minister and Minister for Foreign Affairs.

At the end of April 1975 the minister announced his intention of creating within the department a special team responsible, on the one hand, for publicising the financial scheme to producers and, on the other, for helping them gain distribution abroad.

Eddie Constantine (left) in SOUVENIR OF GIBRALTAR

* "Pre-aid" (L'aide avant) for a first work usually allows the film-maker to make a short on 16mm which will serve as a modest visiting-card to a potential producer for a more ambitious project.

Films Aided by the Ministry of Dutch Culture

In principle the Aid offered by the (Belgian) Ministry of Dutch Culture does not differ from that on the French side—in a country in which two linguistically-different communities live side by side (three, if one includes the district bordering on Germany, where German is the majority tongue and is officially recognised as such). In fact, Flemish Aid was introduced several months before French; in IFG 1974 a list was published of Flemish films which had received assistance up to the end of 1973.

For the financial year 1974/75 the distribution of monies was as follows: *Pallieter* (R. Verhavert, 7,000,000 francs), *Het lege huis/The Empty House* (N. van der Heyde, 5,143,131), *Musica* (N. van der Horst, 5,314,407), *Verbrande brug/Burnt Bridge* (G. Henderickx, 6,482,619), *De riolentocht Journey into Sewers* (D. van den Eynden, 809,685), *Science Fiction* (G. Henderickx, 1,090,000), *Salt Canyon Massacre* (J. De Hert, 1,169,835), *Avonturen van alledaagse held/Adventures of an Everyday Hero* (L. van de Velde, 1,500,000), *Marnix Gijsen achterna/Looking at Marnix Gijsen* (J. Claes, 290,000).

From her budget for the coming year, Mme. Rika De Backer, Minister for Dutch Culture, has apportioned 37,100,000 Belgian

Malka Ribovska in VERBRANDE BRUG, directed by Guido Henderickx

francs in Aid for Flemish films (eventually to be co-produced with foreign companies) and 3,400,000 francs for their promotion abroad.

FRANCIS BOLEN

Bulgaria

by Ivan Stoyanovich

The past year has been one of stabilisation in Bulgarian cinema: 300,000 people a day went to see the 160-170 feature films and several hundred shorts shown in cinemas. In a country of only 8,500,000, admissions totalled 110–112,000,000 or an average figure of 13 visits per head of population. The number of cinemas has already topped 3,600 and it is a significant fact that interest in Bulgarian films has particularly increased. Six years ago they were seen by only 6–7,000,000 people, whereas today the figure is nearing the 20,000,000 mark.

Up to the end of 1975 Bulgarian filmgoers were able to see about 170 new films, of which 19 were Bulgarian, 50 Soviet, 65 from the remaining Eastern European countries and 40 from the West. Films like *The Highway* (dir: St. Dimitrov), *Eternal Times* (Assen Shopov), *With Nobody* (Ivanka Grubcheva), and *That Real Man* (A. Obreshkov) showed the efforts made by the state to develop the country and the working man in new society. *Doomed Souls*, by Vulo Radev from the novel by Dimiter Dimov, reflected social problems and personal con-

Still from VILLA ZONE

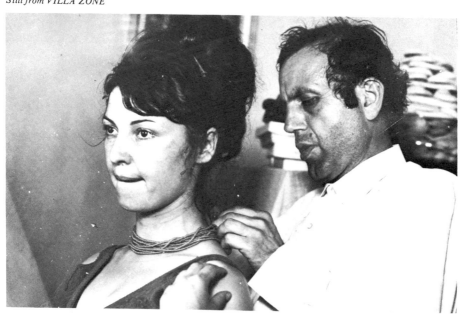

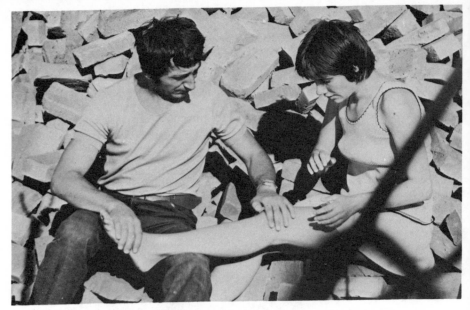

Still from STRONG WATER

flicts during the period of the Spanish Civil War—valid even today, was one which stood out with its contemporary ring and artistic power. Present-day problems were well handled in the films *Villa Zone* (Eduard Zahariev), *Strong Water* (Ivan Terziev), *A Man Like Us* (Lyudmil Kirkov), *Sweet and Bitter* (Ilya Velchev) and *The Investigating Magistrate and the Wood* (Ranghel Vulchanov).

Two films about the anti-fascist resistance and revolutionary struggles of the recent past have entered production: *The Last Battle*, an epic tale of partisan life from the "Memoirs" of Vesselin Andreyev, directed by Zacco Heskia, and *Amendment to the Defence of the Realm Act* (dir: Lyudmil Staikov), a keen study of social problems

linked with the political events of 1923/25.

Bulgaro—Soviet co-productions play an important role in Bulgarian output. *Communists*, directed by Yuri Ozerov (known for the *Liberation* series), is an epic story of international activity and aid by revolutionary forces during the years of Fascism; *The Soldier of the Transport Unit*, directed by Igor Dobrolyubov, concerns the roots of Bulgaro—Soviet friendship. Both are now finished. *Loyalty for Loyalty*, directed by Nikola Korabov and devoted to the centenary of the Russo—Turkish War of Liberation, and *Men of the Blue Flame*, which tells of the building of the U.S.S.R.—Bulgarian gas pipeline, are now being shot.

For the future director Hristo Hristov is preparing *The Cyclops*, which deals with the psychological problems of a man who holds in his hands the power of arms and is at the same time full of humanism and a love of peace. Hristov is well-known for his films *A Tree without Roots*, *The Last Summer* and *Iconostasis* (together with Todor Dinov), all well received both at home and abroad. Binka Zhelyazkova, known for *We Were Young* and *The Last Word*, has turned to contemporary matters for the first time, seeking a link between the generations of today and yesteryear (*The Swimming Pool*). The Marmorev Brothers (*Exams at Any Old Time*, *With Children at the Seaside* and *Hedgehogs Are Born without Bristles*) are turning to comedy this year: their script, *Two Dioptres of Far-Sightedness*, is being directed by Peter Vassilev. Contemporary themes are also the concern of directors Dimiter Petrov (*The Day's Beginning*), Peter Donev (*The Memorable Day*) and Georgi Roudarov (*To Eat the Apple*). The film *Bouna* (*The Riot*), deals with a village riot which took place at the beginning of the century (dir: Willy Tsankov).

Bulgarian films have been particularly successful with prizes abroad. The works of Hristo Hristov, *The Last Summer*, *A Tree without Roots* and *Anvil or Hammer*, were recently awarded prizes at Atlanta (U.S.A.), San Remo and Avelino (Italy) and Karlovy Vary (Czechoslovakia). Nikola Korabov's *Ivan Kondarev* won a prize in San Remo; Ivanka Grubcheva's *Exams at Any Old Time* brought four prizes back from Gijon (Spain); and Binka Zhelyazkova's film *The Last Word* enjoyed great success in Cannes. In addition, the cartoons *De Facto* (Donyo Donev) and *The Carbon Paper Pirate* (Radka Buchvarova), and Hristo Kovachev's documentary *Builders* won major prizes in Oberhausen, Leipzig and Gijon.

During the year Bulgarian films were shown abroad in all the East European countries, as well as in West Germany, Peru, Syria, Greece, Algeria, Tunis, London, San Francisco, Mexico, Spain, Portugal and Scandinavia. The largest sales to the West were made to the U.S.A., France, Ireland, Canada, Spain, Portugal, West Germany, Britain, Switzerland and Belgium.

VULO RADEV graduated from the Department of Cameramen at VGIK in Moscow, later revealing his talents in that direction best in *Tobacco*, directed by Nikola Korabov. In 1964 Radev transferred to direction, *The Peach Thief* (from Emilian Stanev's novella) marking his *début*. A poetic and tragic work directed against the horrors of war, *The Peach Thief* was chosen for the 1965 Venice Film Festival, and has since been highly acclaimed both at home and abroad. In 1966 Radev shot *The Tsar and the General*, from a screenplay by Lyuben Stanev, the following

Vulo Radev

year turning his attention fo the theme of anti-Fascist resistance with *The Longest Night* (screenplay by Vesselin Branev). In 1970 he shot *Black Angels* (from Mitka Grubcheva's book "On behalf of the People," awarded First Prize at the 1970 Karlovy Vary Festival. Making use of the World Exposition in Osaka in 1971, Radev made an interesting feature about the way of life, customs and ethics of the Japanese people (*The Roots of the Rising Sun*). *Doomed Souls*, after the novel of the same name by Dimiter Dimov, is Vulo Radev's most recent work. Set during the Spanish Civil War, it concerns the tragic love of an Englishwoman, Fanny Horn, and a priest, Father Luis Eredia.

LYUDMIL STAIKOV graduated from the Dramatic Institute in Sofia, having trained as an actor, and later finished at the Institute's Production and Direction Department. From 1960 to 1965 he worked as an actor and producer at the National Theatre of Bourgas, his first job being a dramatisation of "The Adventures of Huckleberry Finn," in which he played the part of Tom Sawyer. In 1964 he was awarded the prize for production at the Review of National Theatres in Sofia, and his last work for the theatre was a production of Salinger's "Catcher in the Rye" at the Theatre for Youth in Sofia, a most successful venture which stayed in the Theatre's repertory for four seasons. Since 1965 he has been working as a director at Bulgarian Television, directing many documentaries, musical films, short features, etc. He is at present artistic director

Still from Radev's latest film, DOOMED SOULS

of the "Mladost" (Youth) Group, one of three at the Feature Film Studio. *Affection* (1973) was his first feature film, concerning the problems of present-day youth and the hard road travelled to form a mature personality. At the Moscow Eighth Film Festival the film won a gold medal. Together with scenarist Anghel Vagenshtine, Lyudmil Staikov is now engaged on his second feature, *1925*, which takes its subject from Bulgaria's most recent revolutionary past.

Useful Address

Inquiries regarding the distribution of Bulgarian films in the U.S.A. may be directed to International Film Exchange Ltd., 159 West 53rd Street, New York, N.Y. 10019.

Lyudmil Staikov

Still from EXAMS AT ANY OLD TIME

Canada

by Gerald Pratley

In Toronto, Montreal, Winnipeg, and to a lesser degree, Vancouver, the year has been marked by great conferences and confrontations between trade and professional organisations, unions, guilds and societies, and any number of government officials, both major and minor, during which the participants put forward their views on what should be done to save "the industry." The Secretary of State's Film Department appears to have remained quite unmoved by the storm, but the provincial governments of Ontario and Quebec have responded, although not quite in the manner anticipated. Ontario, which has formed a Ministry of Culture, has promised legislation to bring about quotas and levies by mid-summer. When the Ministry was asked how the box-office levy would be administered, an official thought it would be "a good idea" to let the Americans have it to make films in Ontario! The Government of Quebec, pressed for years by the trade to bring in a Film Act to protect Canadian (Quebec?) films, has done just that, but with such stringent government control that it amounts, according to the organisations which asked for it, to legislation akin to totalitarian rule! For the moment, this continuing serial adventure ends here. The trade, both English-speaking and French-speaking, has achieved one impressive result, and that is unanimity. Governments have defended their lack of action on the grounds that the many organisations representing the various parts of production didn't know what they wanted, and all spoke with different voices contradicting each other. They have changed this by presenting a united front, and by the time next year comes around, the battle may have been won (a) to improve methods of finance, (b) to make access to cinemas less difficult than it is now. The Federal Government did heed the call to restore previously disallowed tax concessions, but on a more sensible basis. Producers can now write off 100% of capital costs providing the motion picture represents "significant Canadian participation." This is to prevent promoters "writing off" films with American stars, directors, writers.

There are many film-makers, members of the public, and officials connected with the trade, however, who feel that quotas, levies and other schemes have come too late. With theatres now charging $3.50 admission prices, only "big" pictures which promise audiences some immediate satisfaction are drawing good attendances. The smaller film, no matter how excellent, about which audiences are not sure of "their money's worth," is ignored, because the public knows that within a very short space of time it will be showing on television. Discussions are taking place which deal with the possibilites of Canadian features being made primarily for CBC TV, without commerical interruptions, financed jointly by the CBC and the CFDC. This has been the pattern in Germany for the past few years. There appears to be no reason why it could not work in Canada, and provide our film-makers with regular employment. Talented directors such as Jutra and Shebib could have matched Fassbinder's output by now!

During the past seven years of its existence the CFDC has invested $17.2 million in production, representing 160 mo-

ONTARIO FILM INSTITUTE

CINEMATHEQUE DE L'ONTARIO
at the Ontario Science Centre

770 Don Mills Road, Toronto, Canada.

Ministry of Culture, Government of Ontario.

From LES ORDRES, which shared in the directing prize at Cannes in 1975

tion pictures. It has prompted private investors and producers to make available another $52 million. Of its $17 million odd, the CFDC has earned back $2.7 million on its investments, a 15% return. The fact that so little has been recovered is not really important when considering the work and experience which the money provided, and that it made possible a Canadian presence on the world's screens and in a home market traditionally swamped with American movies. The CFDC completed its 1974/75 fiscal year by investing $3.5 million in 24 movies. Of these, 11 were low-budget productions, not necessarily for showing in cinemas, but more suited for television and, in effect, providing opportunities to first film-makers (the first of these

projects to be successful was Brian Dalmude's remarkable *Sudden Fury*); four were major English-track films from Toronto and nine were major French-track films from Montreal. During this period the CFDC earned back a record $830,000, a $50,000 increase over the previous year. Of the total, between $100,000 and $200,000 came from sales to TV networks and a large part of the remainder came from the success of *Duddy Kravitz* (see IFG 1975) and two commercial U.S.-Canadian pot-boilers, *Black Christmas* and *Sunday in the Country*. The CFDC's executive secretary, Michael Spencer, who has long advocated a quota system, has also declared that a 5% levy against box-office grosses would make all the difference to the

amount of money available for production. The huge sum of $180 million was taken in at cinema box offices last year, most of which left the country. "Five per cent of that is $9 million and this sum, with the FDC's money, would help to make 25 features per year, or one per million of our population. It works this way in other countries, why not here?"

Cinema Canada

The Secretary of State's Department may get low marks when it comes to helping film-makers in Canada, but few would deny that at festivals, the Festivals Office, under Jean Lefebvre, has achieved remarkable results in making Canadian films known to audiences abroad. Last year, the Bureau co-ordinated approximately 800 entries in 100 festivals. Undoubtedly, its greatest success is at Cannes, where its organisation of trade shows, press participation (under David Novek), receptions, and producer-distributor relations, is reliable, efficient, impressive and a model other countries have followed.

notable new films

ACTION: THE OCTOBER CRISIS. Dir: Robin Spry. Documentary. 90 mins. NFB. A reconstruction using actual material filmed at the time of the kidnapping of James Cross and the murder of Pierre Laporte, in 1970, together with a history of the separatist movement in Quebec. A forceful, sympathetic and honest account.
BLACK CHRISTMAS. Dir: Robert Clark. Players: Keir Dullea, Olivia Hussey, Margot Kidder. 93 mins. Horror film in which an "unspeakable something" terrorises girls in a university residence (U.S. title: Silent Night, Evil Night).
DREAMLAND. Dir: Donald Brittain. NFB. Documentary. 90 mins. A well-made and well-researched history of motion picture production in Canada from 1895–1939.

Lightly told, it contains much rare and valuable footage from films long since gone and forgotten.
GINA. Dir: Denys Arcand. Players: Gabriel Arcand, Céline Lomez, Frédérique Collin. 100 mins. Based partly on his own experiences as a documentary film-maker, Denys Arcand has made an ironic study of a unit shooting a film on conditions in a textile factory, and of their involvement with a striptease girl.
IT SEEMED LIKE A GOOD IDEA AT THE TIME. Dir: John Trent. Players: Anthony Newley, Stephanie Powers, Isaac Hayes. Broadly-played and farcical comedy relating to local politics, tangled marital affairs, and anything else which just seems to come along.
LES ORDRES. Dir: Michel Brault. Players: Hélène Loiselle, Jean Lapointe, Guy Provost. 107 mins. An affecting, dramatised account of the experiences of people taken to prison under the War Measures Act during the October crisis of 1970 in Montreal. In its accumulation of significant and human details is conveyed honestly and fairly the humiliation of innocent people, caught up in the backlash of a violent period. (Michel Brault shared the Director's Prize at Cannes, 1975.)
POUR LE MEILLEUR ET POUR LE PIRE. Dir: Claude Jutra. Players: Jutra, Monique Miller, Monique Mercure, Pierre Dufresne. 93 mins. A minor work from this important film-maker, this is nevertheless a deft, light, whimsical comedy about love and marriage, romance and reality, filmed with insight and imagination.
SUDDEN FURY. Dir: Brian Damude. Players: Dominic Hogan, Gay Rowan, Dan Hennessy. 95 mins. A vivid, tense and ingenious "first feature" in which an innocent man is turned into a murderer through his involvement with a married couple.
LES VAUTOURS. Dir: Jean-Claude Labrecque. Players: Gilbert Sicotte, Monique Mercure, Carmen Tremblay. 98 mins. A young man becomes an unwitting pawn in an artful political game played out during the corrupt régime of Premier Maurice Duplessis of Quebec.
WHY ROCK THE BOAT. Dir: John Howe. Players: Stuart Gillard, Ken James, Tilu Leek, Henry Beckman, Budd Knapp. Sean Sullivan, Patricia Gage. 111 mins. NFB. A splendid comedy about a young reporter working on a Montreal paper in the Forties, based on the actual experiences of the writer, William Weintraub.
Others: four Québecois comedies: Les aventures d'une jeune veuve (Roger Fournier), La pomme, la queue et les pépins (Claude Fournier), Tout feu tout femme (Gilles Richer), Les beaux dimanches (Richard Martin); a minor horror, The Parasite Murders (David Cronenberg), two children's films, Lions for Breakfast (William Davidson), Wings in the Wilderness (Dan Gibson), and two interesting social dramas in a minor key, Montreal Main (Frank Vitale) and The Hard Part Begins (Paul Lynch).

Ontario Film Theatre

Monthly programme booklets attest to the continued excellence and intelligence of the programmes at this leading Canadian film theatre, which was established and developed thanks to Gerald Pratley (author of this section). There are now branches of the OFT in Brockville, Dryden, Hamilton, and Windsor. International screenings have covered France, Czechoslovakia, Switzerland, Spain, and Finland among other countries, and guest speakers add to the importance of the occasion several times each season. There are shows for Senior Citizens, and during opening hours at the Science Centre the auditorium offers children's film and animation and short subjects. Admission is extraordinarily cheap by current standards, and a trip to the Ontario Science Centre must be obligatory for all visitors to Toronto.

PETER COWIE

A still from GUITARE, a new Canadian film for children released by Faroun Films of Montreal. In addition to a range of fine entertainment pictures for children, Faroun also distributes around 100 adult features, including nine by Fassbinder

Leading Independent Distribution Companies

Alliance Film Distribution Ltd.
651 Yonge Street
Toronto, Ontario M4Y 1Z9
Ambassador Film Distributors Ltd.
Suite 400
88 Eglinton Avenue East
Toronto, Ontario
**Association coopérative
de productions audio-visuelles**
96 ouest, rue Sherbrooke
Montréal, Québec H2X 1X3
Astral Films Ltd.
Room 3, 5800 Monkland Street
Montréal, Québec H4A 1G1
Bellevue Film Distributors Ltd.
277 Victoria Street
Toronto, Ontario M5B 1W6

Canadian Filmmakers Distribution Centre
406 Jarvis Street
Toronto, Ontario M4Y 2G6
Ciné-Art Distributing Co. Ltd.
Suite 600
800 de Maisonneuve Blvd. East
Montréal, Québec H2L 1Y6
Cinepix Inc.
8275, rue Mayrand
Montréal, Québec H4P 2C8
Citel Inc.
321, avenue Querbes
Montréal, Québec H2V 3W1
Compagnie France Film
1405, rue Alexandre de Sève
Montreal, Québec H2K 1V3
Coopérative des cinéastes indépendants

CAN WE HELP ?

The Canadian Film Institute was founded in 1935 to encourage and promote the study, appreciation and use of motion pictures and television in Canada. The CFI operates the National Film Theatre which screens, throughout Canada, cultural film programmes, retrospectives and the best Canadian and foreign films. Our publications division produces FILM CANADIANA which annually provides complete documentation on all films made in Canada. We also publish monographs on Canadian and International films and filmmakers. Our distribution library is Canada's largest, with over seven thousand titles listed in some forty catalogues. Whatever your requirements are concerning film in Canada, we can help. For further information please write to: Frederik Manter, Executive Director.

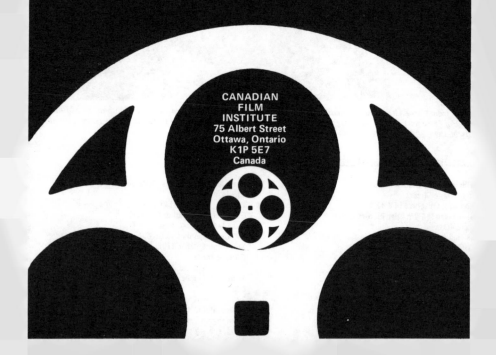

CANADIAN
FILM
INSTITUTE
75 Albert Street
Ottawa, Ontario
K1P 5E7
Canada

Still from Denys Arcand's GINA

2026 est, rue Ontario
Montréal, Québec H2K 1V3
Crawley Films Ltd.
409 King Street West
Toronto, Ontario M5V 1K1
Elliott Distribution
1227 Richards Street
Vancouver, British Columbia V6B 3J3
Eurofilm Ltée/Ciné-France distribution Ltée
690 ouest, rue Lagauchetière
Montréal 101, Québec
Faroun Films (Canada) Ltée
136A est, rue Saint-Paul
Montréal, Québec H2Y 1G6
Les Films Mutuels
225 est, rue Roy
Montréal, Québec H2W 1M5
Glen-Warren Productions Ltd.
9 Channel Nine Court
Agincourt, Ontario

International Film Distributors Ltd
5801 avenue Monkland
Montréal, Québec H4A 1G4
International Tele-Film Enterprises
47 Densley Avenue
Toronto, Ontario M6M 2P5
J.A. Lapointe Films Inc.
4651, rue Saint-Denis
Montréal, Québec H2J 2L5
New Cinema Enterprises Corp. Ltd.
35 Britain Street
Toronto, Ontario M5A 1R7
Phoenix Film Inc.
651 Yonge Street
Toronto, Ontario M4Y 1Z9
Premier Operating Corp.
215 Victoria Street
Toronto, Ontario
Prima Film Inc.
Bureau 205

135 est, rue Sherbrooke
Montréal, Québec H2X 1C5
George Ritter Films Ltd.
2264 Lakeshore Blvd. West
Toronto, Ontario M8V 1A9
Saguenay Film
Suite 570
102 Bloor Street West
Toronto, Ontario M5S 1M8
Société Micro-Cinéma Ltée
4651, rue Saint-Denis
Montréal, Québec H2J 2L5
La Société nouvelle de cinématographie
Suite 600
800 est, boul. de Maisonneuve
Montréal, Québec H2L 1Y6
Wildlife Film Distributors Ltd.
Suite 402
66 Wellesley Street East
Toronto, Ontario M4Y 2E3
Zodiak Film Co. Ltée
Suite 115
5165 ouest, rue Sherbrooke
Montréal, Québec H4A 1T6

*Above: from the Canadian production, SUDDEN FURY,
a first feature directed by Brian Damude
Below: Pan Tung-tzu and his mother welcome the Red
Army to their village in BRIGHT RED STAR*

China

by Peter Davey

This year's report is confined to a factual listing for two reasons: nothing particularly new seems to have emerged at this juncture in Chinese cinema, and extra comment on the notes below is unnecessary since they speak for themselves.

recent films

At the Festival of Documentary Film on July 1, 1974—the aim of which was a mass campaign to learn from the examples of Taching and Tachai—the following films were shown:

TACHING—RED BANNER ON THE INDUSTRIAL FRONT.
TACHAI—RED BANNER ON THE AGRICULTURAL FRONT.
TACHAI FIELDS. A two-part scientific/educational film.
TACHAI FLOWERS IN FULL BLOSSOM IN HSUYANG COUNTY. Scientific/educational.
SPECIAL SERIES ON THE CRITICISM OF LIN PIAO AND CONFUCIUS—NO. 8. A short documentary in the series in which Taching workers criticise the fallacy that the high-born are wise and the low-born fools.

At the Peking Festival (and in other parts of China) on October 1, 1974, the following features were released:

BRIGHT RED STAR. See synopsis below.
FROM VICTORY TO VICTORY. See synopsis below.
A STEEL GIANT. No information available.
SILVER NEEDLES UNDER THE OPERATING LAMP. No information.
LEATHER SAFETY BELT. No information.
STORY ABOUT A COMPOUND. No information.

Of the five new documentaries shown only two titles are available:

THE PEOPLE OF HUIHSIEN COUNTY ARE DOING FINE.
THE CHENGTU-KUOMING RAILWAY.

Of the thirteen new scientific and Educational films shown only the following titles are known:

PETROLEUM.
HIGH YIELDING FIELDS IN TIBET.

During 1974 new colour films of the operas *Fighting on the Plain* and *Azalia Mountain* were shown throughout China. The former depicts the struggle against Japan during the War of Resistance on the plains of Northern China. In the latter Ko Hsiang, a woman Party member, is sent to Azalea Mountain in the the spring of 1928 to reorganise a force of peasants and incorporate it into the Revolutionary Army. The heroine has to struggle against reactionary landlord forces, saboteurs and wrong-headed revolutionaries. Both operas include sung and spoken passages as well as difficult acrobatic and dance movements, so characteristic of the revolutionary opera in the new China.

Synopses of Recent Feature Films

RECONNAISSANCE ACROSS THE YANGTZE. This and the following film, *From Victory to Victory*, are both colour revisions of films with the same titles made twenty years earlier. The original themes and story-lines remain more or less intact, but aim at a clearer exposition of Mao's military strategy and tactics. *Reconnaissance across the Yangtze* describes events in the spring of 1949, on the eve of the final defeat of Chiang Kai Shek's army. A scouting detachment crosses the Yangtze to gather intelligence in preparation for a forced crossing of the river. With the active support of guerrillas and the local people it achieves its objective. Many vivid scenes eulogise the revolutionary heroism of the People's Liberation Army in action. (This film was not apparently shown at the 1974

October Festival, but was widely distributed during 1975).

FROM VICTORY TO VICTORY. Produced by the Peking Film Studio. Main characters: The Division Commander; Chao Yu-min, female head of Tao Chun village; Kao, Commander of the First Battalion; Grandma Chao; the Divisional Political Commissar. The film takes its inspiration from historical events in early 1947 when the Kuomintang Army of Chiang Kai Shek changed its tactics from an all-out offensive to attacks against key sectors, in this case two liberated areas in East and North-West China. The PLA on the East China front abandons northern Kiangsu, retreats to Shantung Province and waits its chance to defeat the enemy in mobile operations. A small unit disguised as the PLA's main force is sent out to stop the enemy on the southern front at the Tasha river, later preventing them at Mount Motien from reinforcing their northern contingent. The main force of the PLA wipes out isolated enemy forces in the Fenghuang Mountains on the northern front. The enemy forces in the south retreat; the PLA moves forward swiftly, takes the Chiangchunmiao Railway Station and cuts off their retreat. The PLA encircles the main enemy force and destroys it, sector by sector. The film illustrates the strategy of "concentrating a superior force to destroy the enemy forces one by one" and at the same time is intended as a criticism of Lin Piao's six tactical principles during the War of Liberation.

BRIGHT RED STAR. Produced by the August First Film Studio. Main characters: Pan Tung-tzu, the eleven-year-old son of a poor peasant and the film's hero; Pan Hsing-yi, the hero's father; the hero's mother; Hu Han-san, tyrannical village landlord; Wung Ming, a Left opportunist; Wu Hsiu-chu, a Red Army soldier; Grandpa Sung; Chun Ya-tzu, a friend of the hero and of about the same age. This adaptation of a novel of the same name is set during the period of the Second Revolutionary Civil War. In 1931 the Red Army comes to Pan Tung-tzu's home village. There the villagers celebrate their liberation and the founding of a democratic government of workers and peasants. Tung-tzu is active in expropriating the landlord's land and dividing it among the poor. He joins the Children's Corps. Owing to the erroneous leadership of Wung Ming, the Red Army is unable to break the Kuomintang encirclement and is forced to leave the Central Revolutionary Base and begin the Long March. The hero's father gives the boy a red star before leaving with the army. Soon after, news comes that Mao's line has won out over Wang Ming's opportunist tactics. Wu Hsiu-chu, a red army fighter who has stayed behind to lead the guerrilla force, tells the boy's mother about decisions made by Mao and the Party Central Committee at the Tsunyi Conference. One night the landlord and his gang suddenly appear when the boy's mother is telling the news

to the villagers. She dies a heroine's death in covering the retreat of the others, and Wu Hsiu-chu now takes on the job of looking after the young Tung-tzu. One day the guerrillas attack the village. Aided by Grandpa Sung, the boy tears some planks from a wooden bridge and cuts off the enemy, who then surrender. The landlord replies by imposing a blockade preventing the guerrillas from getting their essential supply of salt. The boy hero tricks the guard, passes through the blockade, and brings the salt up the mountain to the revolutionary fighters. The Party sends Tung-tzu to a rice store in Yaowan as an apprentice, where he sends out information, sinks the rice-boats of the enemy, and in co-ordination with the guerrilla attack on Yaowan kills the landlord Hu Han-san. The film ends with the resounding victory of Mao's policies on the anti-Japanese national united front. The Red Army units south of the Yangtze are ready to march to the front to resist the Japanese invasion. Tung-tzu's father comes to escort Wu Hsiu-chu and his unit. Father and son meet again and the boy joins the Red Army.

Pan Tung-tzu, young hero of BRIGHT RED STAR

Colombia

by Jacobo Brender

Film activity started in Colombia as early as 1912. Two years later the first silent feature, the very primitive *The Triumph of Faith* directed by Italian cameraman Floro Maco, appeared, showing the progress of the town of Baranquilla. During the Twenties fictional topics were handled by the Spaniards Moreno Garzón, Mejía Robledo, Acevedo and others. A novel of frustrated love, *Aura/The Violets* by Vargas Vila, was successfully brought to the screen by Vicente Di Doménico in 1923. Closely following it came the same director's *Like Dead People*, a melodrama that impressed audiences less. *La Maria*, an earlier tear-jerker based on a novel by Jorge Silva and directed by Alberto de Diestro and Maximo Calvo, was the decade's biggest hit, and *Love, Duty and Crime* (1924), by Pedro Moreno Garzón, tried in vain to repeat its success. In all, no more than fifteen features were made during the silent era, and at the end of the Twenties production came to a halt due to the total lack of technical equipment.

As late as 1939 the first locally-filmed sound feature, *Flowers of the Valley* directed by Maximo Calvo, stimulated the production of about three dozen works up to 1971. Most notable were two films directed by Gabriel Martínez (*The Nightwatchman* and *There in the Sugarmill*), *Lovely Colombia* by Camilo Correa, *Roots of Stone* by José M. Arzuaga, *Pan-American Games* by Diego Leon Giraldo, *Three Colombian Stories* by Luzardo and Mejía, *Harder Boys!* by Zingarelli, *Street Angel* by Diaz Urquiza, *The Taciturn* by Jorge Gaitan, *Passing the Meridian* and *The Crossing* by Arzuaga, *Aquileos Vengeance* by Ciro Durán, and *The River of*

Tombs by Luzardo. Co-productions with Mexico, Spain or Venezuela feature strongly in Colombian cinema, and in spite of the fact that cinema legislation has now been passed only three to four features are being made in the country. Short documentaries, however, are being made in abundance.

new and forthcoming films

UNA TARDE ... UN LUNES (On a Monday Afternoon). First episode: *Al dia siguente (The Next Day)*. Script, dir, prod: Alberto Giraldo Castro. Phot: Julio Luzardo. Players: Dora Franco, Miguel Torres, Ananias Cruz, Carmen Chaux. Second Episode: *Una tarde... un lunes*. Script, dir, prod: A. Giraldo Castro. Phot: Fernando Laverde. Players: Karina, Gabriel Londoño, Danilo Abadia. Third episode: *Fin de semana (Week-End)*. Script, dir, prod and phot: Julio Luzardo. Players: Franky Linero, Beatriz Mejia, Eduardo Osorio. For Cineproducciones 70. An erotic feature about seduction: a young man who matures through a love affair with a woman; the woman who returns to reality through a new experience; an old man who lives in the past; a man who pretends to be a Don Juan but is really a frustrated lover ...

Still from Luis Alfredo Sanchez's EL ORO ES TRISTE

AURA o LAS VIOLETAS (Aura or The Violets). Script, dir, phot: Gustavo Nieto Roa, from the novel by María Vargas Vila. Music: Blas Emilio Atehortúa. Art dir: Gonzalo Mahecha. Prod: Nieto Roa, Max Castillo, Gladys Estrella Riaña. Costumes: Maria Luisa Lignarolo. Players: Cesar Bernal, Martha Stella Calle, Ugo Armando, Ana Mojica, Marina Veslin, Omar Sanchez. For Producciones Mundo Moderno. A romantic love story, already filmed in 1923.

PRESTAME TU MARIDO (Lend Me Your Husband). Script and dir: Julio Luzardo, based on a book by Luis Enrique Osorio. Players: Julio Cesar Luna, Lyda Zamora, Consuelo Luzardo, Franky Linero, Luis Fernando Orozco, Jaime Santos, Fernando Corredor, Roberto Reyes. A comedy.

CAMILO EL CURA GUERILLERO (Camilo the Guerilla Priest). Dir, prod, edit: Francisco Norden. Phot (colour): Gustavo Nieto Roa. Music: Jacqueline Nora. Players: the priest Camilo Torres himself, and his political contemporaries. For Norden. Feature documentary about a real-life popular communist priest who renounced his priesthood, and fought and died as a guerilla in vain.

DIOS Y YO (God and I). Script: Gabriel García Márquez. Dir: Ramiro Meléndez. Important project written by the well-known writer.

important shorts

EL ORO ES TRISTE (Gold Is Sad). Script and dir: Luis Alfredo Sanchez. Phot (colour): Hernando González. Edit: Natalia Jartovskaia de Sánchez. Assist: Alfonso Lara. Music: Esteban Cabezas, Alejandro Gómez. Sung by: Leonor González, Mina and Piero. For Boliveriana Films. Musical documentary.

LA PATRIA BOBA (Stupid Fatherland). Script, dir, prod: L. A. Sanchez. Phot (colour): Hernando González. Text: Daniel Samper. Player: Silvia Gómez. For Boliveriana Films. Documentary.

EL CASO TAYRONA (The Tayrona Case). Dir: Diego León Giraldo. Text and edit: Antonio Montaña. Sound: Elmer Carrera. Documentary.

CUANDO LA SAL PIERDE SU SABOR (When Salt Loses Its Taste). Script and dir: Manuel Franco. Phot (Eastmancolor): Gustavo Barrera. Music: Gustav Mahler (Fifth Symphony), Lara. Players: non-professional actors. For AV Asociasos. Scientific documentary about venereal disease, its dangers, the social problem it presents, how to avoid it, etc.

CORRALEJAS DE SINCELEJO (Feasts of Sincelejo). Dir: Ciro Durán, Mario Mitrotti. Phot: Luis Eduardo Cuesta. Edit: Mitrotti, Durán. For Uno. Description of the ignorant and frustrated inhabitants of a small backward village who take part in a "feast" in which bulls are let loose on illiterates.

CARTA AJENA (Another's Letter). Script: Silvia Patiño. Dir and phot (colour): Diego Leon Giraldo. For Bolivariana Films.

EL PAÍS DE BELLA FLOR (The Land of Beautiful Flowers). Dir: Fernando Laverde. Music: songs by Picofino. Animated short with puppets, showing the confrontation of man against machine, individuals against the heartless mechanisation of labour.

LOS ENCOSTALADOS. Dir: Gabriela Samper. Assist: Hernando Sabogal, René Capucha. Phot: Jorge Silva. Documentary.

Y SE LLAMARÍA COLOMBIA (It Will Be Called Colombia). Colour, 35mm. Dir: Francisco Norden. Narrator: Carlos Muñoz.

ENTREVISTA SOBRE PLANAS (Interviews on Planas). Script and dir: Martha Rodriguez, Jorge Silva. Phot: Jorge Silva. Assist: Gustavo Perez. Revealing interviews with Indians of the Plana region.

CHIRCALES. Script: Martha Rodriguez. Dir and prod: Martha Rodriguez and Jorge Silva. Phot and edit: Jorge Silva. 42 mins. For Rodriguez-Silva. Ethnographic investigation of working conditions and methods of the Chircales region.

RHAPSODY IN BOGOTÁ. Dir: José Maria Arzuaga. Colour. Documentary. Winner of the award "La Perla de Cantábrico" at San Sebastian Film Festival.

MADE IN COLOMBIA. Dir and prod: Manuel Bousquets Emiliani. Phot: Enrique Forero. Edit: Manuel José Alvarez. Documentary.

CALI: TOWN OF AMERICA. Dir: Diego León Giraldo. For Boliveriana. Documentary.

LA CASA DE BOLIVAR (Bolivar's House). Dir: John Dennis. For Boliveriana. Documentary.

Denmark

by Martin Drouzy

With the exception of two works which will be discussed separately, all twenty films released in Denmark within the last year have been made either by old, established directors or else by completely new and untried people. In the latter category, is *La' os være*, by Lasse Nielsen and Ernst Johansen, about a group of children on a desert island and their cruelities when left to themselves. The film is grim entertainment, and unfortunately reveals no clear intentions on the part of the directors; it has justifiably been classified as "X." *Tag det som en mand, frue* (*Take It Like a Man, Ma'am*) differs from the remainder of the year's films in having been made by a women's collective called "The Red Sisters"; this comprises Mette Knudsen, Li Vistrup and Elisabeth Rygård, who are jointly responsible for both screenplay and direction. The three "sisters" have succeeded in making a popular and entertaining film about women and sex roles in society: perhaps they try to say too much at once, but their infectious humour and lack of aesthetic pretentiousness make it a particularly effective work; it is both engaged and engaging without being solemn or presumptuous.

Peter Refn and Esben Høilund Carlsen both belong to the same category of untried film-makers. Refn's first feature film, *Violer er blå (Violets Are Blue)* was premiered at the Cannes Festival (see separate biography). Esben Høilund Carlsen's thriller *19 røde roser (19 Red Roses)* is a competent first work in a *genre* in which Danish film directors have hitherto shown very little competence. A few critics raised their eyebrows at the film's queer mixture of cynicism and sentimentality, but at all events it is an example of solid, respectable craftsmanship that bears witness to the director's professionalism. Carlsen, who studied at the Danish Film School, provides striking proof of the fact that in recent years prospects for new Danish film-makers have become considerably brighter.

At the other end of the spectrum are several well-known veterans. Erik Balling has finished the sixth in his popular Olsen Gang series, this time entitled *Olsen-bandens sidste bedrifter (The Olsen Gang's Last Escapade)*. In light comedy style, it is as vivacious and quality-conscious as its forerunners, and even though the title—and the film's ending—would indicate that the series has now

finished, Balling has found it hard to abandon
his trio of small-time crooks and is already at
work on the next in the series.

Hagen Hasselbalch is also not exactly
unknown in Denmark. He has been making
documentary films for over thirty years and
has a great many valuable short films of informative or educational character to his credit.
Yoga—a Road to Happiness (partly self-
financed) is his longest film to date, a feature-
length documentary about an Indian guru,
Swamiji Narajanananda, who recently settled
in Denmark, gathered a flock of obedient disciples around him and founded an Indian
monastery in Jutland. Through interviews
and idyllic visuals Hasselbalch illustrates the
various yoga methods; however, the material
and controversial person of the guru himself
ensure that the didactic tone of the film gains
the upper hand, and though the aim of the
work is to present yoga as concerned with the
expansion of consciousness, the means
employed betray this aim and border on in-
doctrination. It is a case of the documentary
transformed into a commercial.

Henning Carlsen, after his
characteristically Danish *Man sku' være
noget ved musikken* (*Oh, to be on the
bandwagon*), has become the country's first
director to join the Common Market with *En
lykkelig skilsmisse* (*A Happy Divorce*). This
film is the result of a Danish-French co-
production agreement, with the technical
crew from Denmark and almost the entire
cast from France. Like the majority of
Carlsen's films, *A Happy Divorce* is
professionally made and extremely well acted.
But has the director, in describing the cynical
self-satisfaction of the *bourgeoisie*, been
hampered by his new environment and the
previous work of French colleagues, particularly Chabrol? In any event, the film lacks
what was formerly Henning Carlsen's

From Hagen Hasselbalch's YOGA—A ROAD TO HAPPINESS

The funeral scene from LEAVE US ALONE

From the outrageously funny Danish satire, TAKE IT LIKE A MAN, MA'AM!

strength—familiarity with the people and *milieu* he is representing, and an intensity of personal observation. This respectable but cool work is hardly likely to convince the opponents of the EEC as to the blessings of the Common Market in the sphere of filmmaking. *A Happy Divorce* is merely the result of a bad marriage.

The expectations which Carlsen's film aroused have been fulfilled, however, by *Per*, one of the two most sympathetic and sensational Danish films of 1975. The other is *Det gode og det onde* (*Good and Evil*) by Jørgen Leth (see profile). *Per* was directed by Hans Kristensen, who like Leth is neither well-established nor entirely new to film work.

Kristensen wrote his own screenplay and retained the same leading character from his first film, *Flugten* (*The Escape*): a young swindler from a semi-slum district of Copenhagen who cons his way through life by turning on his own personal charm. This time he falls in love with a married woman who moves in upper-class circles, but when relations with this rich, corrupt *milieu* break down, Per finds himself more isolated than ever. Once again Kristensen shows his rare knack for combining an action-packed story with an ability for drawing human portraits. With this film he confirms his position as the most gifted natural talent in Danish cinema today.

Ole Ernst and Agneta Ekmanner in PER

PER

Script and direction: Hans Kristensen. Dialogue: Hans Hansen. Photography (Eastmancolor): Dirk Brüel. Editing: Christian Hartkopp. Music: Gunnar Møller Pedersen. Players: Ole Ernst, Agneta Ekmanner, Frits Helmuth. For Asa–Panorama/Erik Crone–Hans Kristensen. 104 mins.

The problem facing small national film industries today is that they must somehow match the slickness and technical sophistication of Hollywood pacesetters like *The Godfather*, *The French Connection*, and *Chinatown*. Hans Kristensen's *Per* has achieved the rare distinction of attracting a large and discriminating audience in its own country. It is a polished thriller, sustained more by its players than by its plot—which creaks badly and melodramatically. Per is pinched for money, and ingenuous to a fault. He gladly accepts a bribe to set fire to a businessman's premises, and when the venture goes awry he finds himself out of his social depth and temptingly shacked up with the businessman's wife in a hideaway across the water, in Skåne. Both Ole Ernst, as the coarse, clumsy, but lovable Per, and Agneta Ekmanner, as the elegant *bourgeoise* who responds to his charm, act intelligently and amusingly. During their long scenes together in the cottage, the air of social hostility gradually gives way to a mutual understanding. But the realities of the class war reassert themselves in the aftermath, and Per is left to tramp away disgruntled in the dawn light, as cold and as impoverished as he was at the start of the film. Dirk Brüel's photography is outstanding by Danish standards, and it's a pity that Kristensen perpetuates the conventional image of corruption and wild parties, a picture taken to grotesque extremes in the performance of Frits Helmuth as the scheming capitalist.

PETER COWIE

Diana Benneweiss in Jørgen Leth's GOOD AND EVIL

DET GODE OG DET ONDE (Good and Evil)

Script and direction: Jørgen Leth. Photography: Henning Camre. Editing: Franz Ernst. Music: Gunnar Møller Pedersen. Players: non-professionals. For Jørgen Leth/Nina Crone. 83 mins.

Leth's films are almost without parallel in modern movie-making. In one sense they are pure experiments, both in form and thought. In another way, they are conservative and ascetic. One tableau follows another, each expressing a thought or a concept: Good Thoughts, Bad Thoughts, Feelings, Words, Necessary Actions, Unnecessary Actions. Leth has a gift for isolating the genuine properties of certain objects—a washing machine in some bushes, for instance—and one can readily appreciate that his favourite art is poetry. *Good and Evil* is, in spite of its calm surface, a *searching* film, a meditation on the apparent contradictions of life. It fragments one's daily actions into a series of logical steps; Leth is a cinematic scientist, analysing the system that governs all our responses.

PETER COWIE

LA' OS VAERE
(Leave Us Alone)

Script: Lasse and Carsten Nielsen. Direction: Lasse Nielsen and Ernst Johansen. Photography (colour): Andreas Fischer-Hansen. Editing: Lars Brydesen. Music and songs: Lars Ørsted and Lasse Lunderskov "Kino Filmmusic." Players: non-professionals. For Steen Herdel Film & TV Production.

The two directors of *Leave Us Alone* knew a great deal about children's behaviour and not so much about film-making when they embarked on this project. And there are moments of theatrical clumsiness that mar the verisimilitude of the setting (an island off Denmark where a group of schoolchildren deliberately hide from the authorities). Some of the dialogue (discussions of the soul's fate after death, etc.) is fatuous, too. But the best thing about the film is the spontaneity of ths children's acting, which compares favourably with the performances in Peter Brook's *Lord of the Flies.* They improvised most of their dialogue, and this may explain why the film has had such a tremendous success among a teenage audience in Denmark. The message of *Leave Us Alone* is in the title. If the children are given a chance, they will reveal their true character. "Let them learn for themselves, let them love, leave them alone." For Steen Herdel's independent production unit, this movie is a small but significant triumph.

PETER COWIE

Jørgen Leth

JØRGEN LETH (born 1937) differs from the majority of other film-makers in Denmark by virtue of his versatility. He formerly worked as a journalist, with jazz, sport, the cinema and theatre as his special areas of interest. He has published several volumes of poetry, directed plays, written radio plays and made films. Artistically, he is something of a one-man band. In the spring of 1968 he founded, together with a number of friends who wished to experiment outside traditional film production, a group whose aim was to make films collectively. In 1971/72 he was appointed to the post of producer to the then Short Film Council, and was twice given a grant of 500,000 kroner with which to produce films. He was also given sole responsibility for selecting those projects he wished to see put into motion. During those two years he supported (and discovered) a number of talented new film-makers, and something like a dozen interesting experimental films were made. Since 1963 he himself has made an impressive series of shorts which should have won him wider public recognition long ago. It is only during the past few years, however, that his name has come to the forefront, largely on account of *Stjernerne og vandbærerne* (*Stars and Water Carriers*, 1974), a ninety-minute film about the cyclist Ole Ritter and his performance in the Giro d'Italia in 1972. Jørgen Leth's latest work, *Det gode og det onde* (*Good and Evil*, 1975) serves to confirm his position as a filmic experimenter who has gradually come to master his own very personal form of expression. This could be described as a "dehumanised shooting technique and composition," since one of its most marked traits (particularly in his most recent film) is that the visuals are strikingly one-dimensional in style, lacking perspective and clinically cleansed of unnecessary detail. Leth seems to be fascinated by the surface values of things and people, divorced from their material surroundings.

Peter Refn

PETER REFN (born 1940) started as an assistant director and since 1965 has drawn attention to himself by importing and show ing in his own cinema a number of films which in one way or another are "different". His first work, *Eftermiddagsgæsten* (*The Stolen Feast,* 1963), a thirty-minute short, was also different: it tried to describe a gay party for young people in Denmark in an un-Danish fashion, namely as "a baroque tale." His next film, *Kort fra Danmark* (*Denmark between Danes*, 1972) was in an equally untraditional style, the revelation of life in Denmark and the way it is sold to tourists at once ironical and disrespectful. It caused a storm of indignation amongst its sponsors and was rejected—at all events as an advertising film. Since then it has been translated into a great many languages and shown on French, British and German

TV—to the delight of the managing director of the Danish Tourist Association!

Violer er blå (Violets Are Blue), Peter Refn's first feature-length film (1975), is marked by the same approach: a combination of warm interest and endistancing of sympathy and irony. The film, which could also be called *Love's Not a Thing to Be Trifled With*, bearing as it does quite a strong resemblance to Eric Rohmer's *contes moraux*, describes the conflict between a romantic view of love and a cruder, sexual conception. A girl (Lisbeth Lundquist) cannot be bothered to go to bed with her "co-habitor" (they have been living together, unmarried, for five years) but happily does so with other men and other girls, even cultivating an elderly homosexual antique dealer. The film mingles the frivolous and the dramatic quite deliberately and alternates between long, contrived, almost literary conversations and entirely relaxed and apparently improvised scenes. It contains self-irony and is yet engaged, and in its criticism of ingrained prejudices manages to be both semi-pornographic and semi-"socialistic."

Art House Focus

The **Danish Film Museum** (Store Søndervoldstræde) is a haven for film enthusiasts in Copenhagen. Quarterly brochures, attractively printed and illustrated, set out the various seasons. Spring 1975 saw tributes to D. W. Griffith, the western, silent films in Denmark, and socially committed films of the Thirties. Being one of the world's foremost archives, the Danish Film Museum can enliven its programmes with rare items that would never reach a commercial art house.

Peter Refn, who built up the Camera cinema into one of the best art houses in Scandinavia, has now developed the **Grand** (in Mikkel Bryggersgade) as a first-run theatre for pictures like Fassbinder's *Angst essen Seele auf*, *Zandy's Bride*, *Flesh for Frankenstein*, and Steen Herdel's production of *Leave Us Alone*. The Grand was originally a theatre

Still from Peter Refn's VIOLETS ARE BLUE

for the Royal Danish Court, and was founded by Urban Gad. He and his wife ran the cinema for fifty years. Now there are 340 seats in the auditorium, and seven performances daily.

Other Danish cinemas worth noting are Ulrik Uhrskov's **Repriseteatret** (in Holte), Henning Carlsen's complex of quality theatres at **Dagmar** (Jernbanegade 2), and the **Alexandra** (Gammel Torv).

Film Clubs in Denmark

The film clubs form a genuine alternative to the commercial cinemas in Denmark. There are some sixty, spread throughout the country, with a combined membership not far short of 15,000. The parent organisation is the SDF (Sammenslutningen af Danske Filmklubber). Apart from the actual film booking, the SDF imports good films that for some reason or another have been overlooked by commercial distributors. The SDF arranges contacts between Danish and other Scandinavian film clubs in order to exchange important titles—on a loan basis—the language differences in the subtitles not being of vital importance. For further information, contact Jørgen Westergård, the Secretary, Sammenslutningen af Danske Filmklubber, Vester Alle 15, 8000 Århus C, DK Denmark.

Egypt

by Abdul Moneim Saad

Egyptian cinema during 1974 showed several healthy signs: long runs for individual films and record box-office takings. Previously, producers had tried to extend a film's run from a fear that its reputation abroad might suffer; in 1974 this was not necessary—works like *Bamba Kasher, Brothers . . . but Enemies* and *Bedour* were carried over because they took more than the minimum receipt of £1,800 a week. In response to this heartening situation (which, however, has led to a pile-up of films awaiting release), the Cinema Organisation is now up-rating some second-class cinemas like "Pigale" and "Capitol" to first-class status. In the regions smaller centres continue to be built (600-800 seats) so as to ease the pressure on first-class cinemas and put an end to overcrowding.

A total of forty-two films were released during the 1974 season, the same number as last year. Most notably, works by younger directors (Nader Galal, Ashraf Fahmy) were as popular as those by more established figures (Hassan El Imam, Hussam Eldine Mostafa, Atef Salem, Barakat and Hassan El Seifi).

The October War figured in many productions (*The Great Devotion, The Bullet Is Still in My Pocket, Bedour*), while others dealt with social or political themes: *The Bird,* with political life in Egypt just before the June 5 defeat; *The Back Stairs*, with the nationalist movement during the Thirties. Pure melodrama was not to be found; generally it was amalgamated with song-and-dance, as in Hassan El Imam's *My Story with Times* and *Bamba Kasher*. Comedy and farce were well

Faten Hammama, Egypt's leading female star

represented by *In Summer We Must Love, The Happy Marriage* and *The Most Beautiful Days in My Life,* while the problems of the individual unable to adapt himself to the community found comic expression in films like *The Pleasant Bridgegroom, 24 Hours' Love* and *A Widow on Her Wedding Night.* Traditional action films were few and far between; martial arts films like *The Heroes and the Giants,* imitative of Japanese and Hongkong productions, took their place.

The Year's Top Ten

MY STORY WITH TIMES. Dir: Hassan El Imam. Prod: Saut El Fan. Players: Warda, Rushdi Abaza.

TORTURE ON SMILING LIPS. Dir: Hassan El Imam. Prod: Ramses Naguib. Players: Nagwa Ibrahim, Mahmoud Yassin.

BAMBER KASHER. Dir: Hassan El Imam. Prod: Emad Hamdi. Players: Nadia El Guindi, Samir Sabry. Featuring the songs of Sayed Darwish (sung by Soad Mohamed).

BROTHERS ... BUT ENEMIES. Dir and prod: Hussam Eldin Mostafa. Players: Nadia Lotfi, Nour El Sherif.

THE BULLET IS STILL IN MY POCKET. Dir: Hussam Eldine Mostafa. Prod: Mourad Ramses Naguib. Players: Nagwa Ibrahim, Mahmoud Yassin. Authentic film about the October War, showing the withdrawal, the crossing and break-through of the Barlev Line.

BEDOUR. Dir: Nader Galal. Prod: Mary Queenie. Players: Naglaa Fathi, Mahmoud Yassin. Feature attempting to mix narrative with the October War; includes footage from the documentary *Resistance,* showing the crossing.

WHERE'S MY MIND? Dir: Atef Salem. Prod: Abbas Helmi. Players: Soad Hosni, Mahmoud Yassin.

THE HOUR STRIKES TEN. Dir: Barakat. Prod: Abbas Helmi. Players: Nahed Sherif, Mahmoud Yassin.

A WOMAN IN LOVE. Dir: Ashraf Fahmy. Prod: Mohamed Ragaii. Players: Shadia, Hussein Fahmy.

A TRIP IN WONDERLAND. Dir and prod: Hassan El Seifi. Players: Nabila Ebied, Mohamed Awad.

Stars and Capital

The Egyptian star system is reminiscent of old Hollywood, with an established *cadre* of top stars (rather than directors) guaranteed to attract audiences. This front-line group may last some four or five years. The country's leading actress, Faten Hammama, enjoys a privileged position in this star system. She stands apart from the rest of the group and has learned to choose her roles carefully and selectively, thus remaining consistently popular through the years. Others will work on as many as four or five films at the same time, encouraged by producers who wish to take advantage of their crowd-pulling success. Male stars such as Mahmoud Yassin, Hussein Fahmy or Nour El Sherif, tend to exhaust the market at a more rapid rate than actresses and fall from favour quicker. After Faten Hammama the most popular actress at the moment is Soad Hosnei, who has recently shot to success from small roles.

American and European films are rarely released in Egypt now that domestic films are grossing such high profits. Lebanese capital still plays a strong role in the Egyptian film industry since starting to encourage Egyptian producers about two years ago (Itani Films, one of the biggest distributors in Lebanon, has backed some fifty Egyptian films in the last two years). Often a loan is in exchange for distribution rights throughout the Arab world. Whether the industry would slump as a result of any withdrawal of this capital is open to conjecture. If the current boom continues as it is, it could be that Egyptian cinema will soon become self-sufficient again.

MOHAMMED RIDA

Madiha Kamel (right) in the Egyptian production, IN SUMMER WE MUST LOVE

Eire

by Pat Billings

During a year in which film activity in Ireland was virtually at a standstill, the one bright ray of hope came with the announcement that the government had decided to set up a state-sponsored company to run Ardmore Studios. As reported in the previous edition of IFG, the government had stepped in to save the Ardmore complex from the land speculators and the move, while welcomed, was greeted with some misgivings by those technicians and film-makers who had been earning a somewhat precarious living from the Irish motion picture industry. Many of their doubts have since been dispelled, however, by the government's subsequent moves. Appointed as managing director of the new company was Sheamus Smith, a man of many years experience in various facets of the Irish television service, RTE. Chairman of the company is John Boorman who, on the basis of *Deliverance* alone, must be regarded as one of the most creative forces in present-day cinema. His subsequent production, *Zardoz*, was made entirely in and around Ardmore Studios whose facilities he has also used for post-production work. Boorman has also lived in Ireland, within a few miles of the studios, for several years and therefore has valuable practical experience of the pros and cons of making films in this country. Ardmore's prospects as a viable centre for the production and servicing of Irish-based films now seem better than they have done for many years, and future development there is awaited with considerable eagerness.

In recent years, Dublin has seen a growing tendency towards the closure of its suburban cinemas in favour of the opening of newer, considerably smaller houses within a half-mile radius of the city's main thoroughfare. Several of the larger city-centre theatres have also been altered to embrace two, three and, in one case, four smaller cinemas. The Odeon (Ireland) group, which controlled several first-run houses and even more second-run houses in Dublin itself and in provincial cities, gave news of further developments with its cinema chain. Having closed six of its oldest and most-popular cinemas in suburban Dublin, Odeon (Ireland) announced that a third cinema would be incorporated in its city-centre twin-houses, The Savoy, and that the smaller Corinthian cinema, also in the city centre, would be twinned. The Corinthian, a favourite film spot for many years, had become affectionately known to Dublin's more-enthusiastic filmgoers as "The Ranch" because of its almost unbroken addiction to the humble "cowboy picture" or western. The closure by Odeon of its principal cinema in Cork City, which also went under the name of the Savoy, cast a shadow of doubt over the 1975 Cork Film International. The film festival had had a close association with the Savoy since its inception and the luxuriously-appointed theatre had played host to the festival's various activities and visiting celebrities for many years. The Savoy always put on its finest garb at festival time and its magnificent foyer and impressive staircases gave celebrities—and young people in particular—a reminder of what the traditional "cinema palace" was really like. The Savoy in Cork closed its doors at the end of January 1975 and its 2,000 seats remained in their quiescent, upright position until the festival director successfully negotiated for the temporary re-opening of the theatre to accommodate the 1975 festival during eight days in June. A new home will have to be found for the Twenty-First Cork Film International in 1976.

Perhaps the most welcome aspect of filmgoing in Ireland during 1975 was the unmistakable upswing in admissions to the country's many cinemas. The filmgoing habit—once Ireland's *second* most popular pastime—seems to be returning to its former vigour after a somewhat alarming period of relative inertia over the past ten years. Those who have made a study of the situation agree that it is the quality of the fare on offer that is drawing the public back. Throughout the period under review *The Sting* proved to be the most successful attraction with Irish audiences.

England

by David McGillivray

The true state of the British film industry is currently anybody's guess. To judge from the widely conflicting reports circulating in 1974/75 it might almost have seemed that a plot had been devised to confuse some foreign enemy, while the truth lay buried under lock and key in a Whitehall vault.

First the bad news. Particularly sad for those who remember palmier days was the almost complete collapse of the studio system. During the period under review Shepperton auctioned off most of its stock, Elstree closed six of its nine stages, Bray teetered on the verge of bankruptcy, and Pinewood (last of the big studios to remain fully operational) was threatened by the construction of a motorway. It is generally accepted that this situation has arisen out of a growing international preference for location work. But in Britain there has been a marked decrease in film production on *and* off location and, in January 1975, this reached an all-time low when only three major films were shooting in this country. The economic crisis was partly to blame, but partly is the operative word. The larger companies also seemed drastically out of touch wth popular taste and accordingly the cream of Britain's directorial talent (with the exception of Ken Russell) continued to work abroad, while overseas earnings for British films hit rock bottom. In an effort to halt the decline Films Minister Eric Deakins began a campaign to encourage more British participation in foreign productions. There is now every indication that British co-productions with France, Italy and West Germany will eventually become the rule rather than the exception.

Despite many indisputably disturbing facts, however, the prevailing mood was far from one of gloom and despair. By many standards the Big Film of 1974 was the thoroughly British *Murder on the Orient Express*, which was made in a British studio with a largely British cast and a considerable amount of British money. By all accounts it continues to make enormous profits and will almost certainly encourage similar big budget experiments.

THE RANK ORGANISATION

PRODUCTION
PROCESSING
DISTRIBUTION
EXHIBITION

THE RANK ORGANISATION
38 South Street, London W1A 4QU

Telephone: 01-629 7454   Telex: 263549

Against all the apparent odds, in fact, finance for *certain* productions appeared to be readily available. In December 1974 Sir Lew Grade declared that in 1975/76 he intended to spend £20,000,000 on a programme of film and television projects. In March 1975 both 20th Century-Fox and the BBC publicised plans to back British films. And the appearance of *A Bigger Splash* and *A Private Enterprise* (both of which restored faith in creative British cinema) seemed to prove that it was possible to launch even "uncommercial" ventures. But perhaps the most positive sign that all was not lost was the announcement that, in 1974, the number of admissions to British cinemas had risen for the first time in twenty years (to approximately 143,270,000). It seems that British cinema is destined to challenge British theatre for the title of The Thing That Wouldn't Die.

TOMMY

Script and direction: Ken Russell, from the opera by Pete Townshend, with additional material by John Entwistle and Keith Moon. Photography (colour): Dick Bush. Editing: Stuart Baird. Art direction: John Clark. Players: Ann-Margret, Oliver Reed, Roger Daltrey, Elton John, Eric Clapton, Keith Moon, Jack Nicholson, Robert Powell, Paul Nicholas, Tina Turner. For the Robert Stigwood Organisation, distributed by Hemdale. 108 mins.

It would be pointless to try and commend *Tommy* to anyone with a built-in aversion to Russell, ear-shattering pop music, or both. But for the rest, here is an imaginative rock opera brought to near perfection by a visual director of the highest order. *Tommy* features a theme (deaf, dub and blind boy is cured by accident and hailed as a messiah) tailor-made for Russell improvisations. The surprise lies in his comparative restraint. A new prologue showing Tommy's mother and father snatching precious moments together during

Richard Roundtree and Peter O'Toole in MAN FRIDAY, a Keep Films production in association with ABC Entertainment and ITC

the Second World War is treated with just the right amount of *Brief Encounter*-style romanticism. The relatively few ultra-flamboyant sequences (including one in which a television set explodes baked beans over an ecstatic Ann-Margret) seem perfectly in keeping with the emotive spirit of the original. Although the quality of Russell's inventiveness has never been higher, it is his discipline that makes *Tommy* his most satisfying film to date. Credit must also be given, however, to the familiar brilliance of Russell's associates. Dick Bush's

FILMLINKS LTD

FOR EXCLUSIVE REPRESENTATION OF
HIGHEST QUALITY
INTERNATIONAL FILMS

representatives:

ROME ⎫
PARIS ⎭   **Harry Baird**

MUNICH   **Janusz von Pilecki**

LONDON ⎫   **Frankie Dymon Jnr**
NEW YORK ⎭   **Charles Bartholomew**

HEAD OFFICE
5/7/9 Beadon Rd., Hammersmith Broadway, London W6 0EA
Telephone 01-741/0011/1004   Telex 934386

ravishing colour photography has been unsurpassed by anything else on British screens this year, and costumier Shirley Russell must surely be the only serious contender for the mantle of Margaret Furse. Of the performers, Ann-Margret reveals a musical and dramatic range hitherto untapped. And among a considerable number of personalities co-opted from the current pop scene, Elton John and the electrifying Tina Turner both give performances that suggest they will be reappearing shortly in solo vehicles.

DAVID McGILLIVRAY

BROTHER, CAN YOU SPARE A DIME?

Script and direction: Philippe Mora. In colour and black-and-white. Editing: Jeremy Thomas. For VPS/Goodtimes, distributed by VPS. 109 mins.

During the past year the first British "TV films" began to appear. They were largely undistinguished, but *Brother, Can You Spare a Dime?* (backed by the BBC, who screened it just prior to its West End opening) was a typically thorough, rewarding piece of film archaeology by Philippe Mora. In the style of his earlier work (*The Double-Headed Eagle* and *Swastika*), Mora has pieced together, entirely without editorial comment, footage from newsreels and feature films in order to give an overall impression of a period of recent history (in this case the years of the American depression). Chronologically arranged, the material speaks for itself. The rarer snippets (Orson Welles, for instance, making an unsuccessful attempt to appear repentant as he apologised for throwing the country into turmoil with his "Martian" broadcast) are worth their weight in gold, while the quite valid contrasts drawn between the destitution of the workers and the in-

Triangle Film Productions Ltd

Associated with **L'EDITION FRANCAISE CINEMATOGRAPHIQUE** Paris

Specialise in Anglo-French and Anglo-Italian
co-production of short and feature films

"MIDNIGHT EPISODE"
"LEONARDO DA VINCI"
"VAN GOGH"
"MOLIERE"
"BERNARD SHAW"
"CHOPIN"

"CHINESE THEATRE" (Eastmancolor)
"TEIVA" (Eastmancolor)
"THE SIXTH DAY OF CREATION" (Eastmancolor)
"FINALE"
"PARADE"
"CORSICA" (Eastmancolor)
"SEEDS IN THE WIND"
"SALVADOR DALI" (Eastmancolor)
"EDITH PIAF"
"VENICE—ETERNAL CITY?"

In Preparation:

"SHELLEY—THE REBEL"
"L'AME EN PEINE"

Directors Théodora Olembert   Jan Read   Rodney Phillips

15 Oslo Court, Prince Albert Rd. London N.W.8. 01-722 5656

domitable optimism of Hollywood are often intensely moving. It is extraordinary that some critics should have taken Mora to task for his lack of "objectivity," for he has a unique talent for clarifying history and making it utterly fascinating.

DAVID McGILLIVRAY

LITTLE MALCOLM AND HIS STRUGGLE AGAINST THE EUNUCHS

Script: Derek Woodward, from the play by David Halliwell. Direction: Stuart Cooper. Photography (Kodakcolor): John Alcott. Editing: Ray Lovejoy. Art direction: Edward Marshall. Players: John Hurt, John McEnery, Raymond Platt, David Warner, Rosalind Ayres. For Subafilms/Apple Films, distributed by Multicetera Investments. 110 mins.

David Halliwell's play, about the sexual and artistic frustration often to be found lurking behind the bombast of the student revolutionary, has no greater admirer than former Beatle George Harrison, who entirely financed this film version. Highly thought of on the Continent, it was belatedly and timidly released in this country at the beginning of 1975, and proved to be an excellent stage-to-screen adaptation. Gone is the important claustrophobic atmosphere of the original play, but in its stead is a meticulous attention to detail that succeeds almost as well in evoking the chilly squalor suffered by the grantless art student. The new settings for Malcolm's pathetic plot to avenge his expulsion from art school consist of a strikingly bleak collection of Victorian ruins in the Huddersfield area, lovingly photographed by John (*Clockwork Orange*) Alcott, who seems especially taken by the visual splendour of breath vapour. American director Stuart Cooper (a young actor previously seen as one of *The Dirty Dozen*), appears totally *au fait*

The Akashic Record

A COSMOLOGICAL THRILLER BY JANE ARDEN AND JACK BOND IN PRODUCTION LONDON

An Indigo Production
6 — Chemin Louis Pictet
Vernier — Geneva. Switzerland

with his surroundings and, on one occasion, is resourceful enough to play a complete scene—Malcolm's oration to his fellow students—on a hilltop in order to take advantage of a genuine blizzard. The players, all looking appropriately white and sickly, are superb throughout.

DAVID McGILLIVRAY

OVERLORD

Script: Christopher Hudson and Stuart Cooper. Direction: Stuart Cooper. Photography: John Alcott. Editing: Jonathan Gili. Music: Paul Glass. Players: Brian Stirner, Davyd Harries, Nicholas Ball, Julie Neesam. For the Imperial War Museum/James Quinn. 85 mins.

This is one of the most original and affecting British films since *It Happened Here*.

Although the title suggests a picture of epic proportions, there is a very subdued quality to *Overlord*. The apprenticeship of young Tom in the British army just before D-Day is described with the poignance and the lyricism of a poem by Sassoon or Owen. Some startling footage from the Imperial War Museum is dovetailed into the film with consummate skill by Jonathan Gili, but there is no attempt to dwell on the brutality of war. Instead, Cooper and his co-screenwriter Chris Hudson show how a young man's sensibilities react to the discipline and isolation of

OVERLORD, with Brian Stirner (right), the British film that won a Silver Bear at Berlin 1975

FIFTY YEARS OF FILM SOCIETIES

FILM   SOCIETIES
SHOW   THE   FILMS
YOU   WANT   TO   SEE

why not join one?
                    or even start one?

It is easier than you think!

For details, see the "special section" in this

guide, or get in touch with:

The British Federation of Film Societies
81 Dean Street   London W1V 6AA   437 4355

army training. "It's like being part of a machine that gets bigger and bigger while we get smaller and smaller, until there's nothing left of us," writes Tom to his parents in a farewell letter that, ironically, must be burnt for security reasons on the eve of the "the Longest Day." *Overlord* is couched in a tranquil, melancholy tone that recalls Wordsworth's "Intimations of Immortality," and the perfectly judged score by Paul Glass carries the stamp of Elgar or Vaughan Williams. The film strives too hard for the lyrical and the symbolical touch, and Tom's encounter with a girl at a dance hall introduces a sentimental twinge at odds with the cool, dispassionate observation of the rest. *Overlord*, nonetheless, takes Stuart Cooper's career a step further forward, and it will be interesting to see what *genre* he essays next.

PETER COWIE

The love scene from OVERLORD

A PRIVATE ENTERPRISE

Script: Peter K. Smith and Dilip Hiro. Direction: Peter K. Smith. Photography (colour): Ray Orton. Editing: Peter K. Smith and Charles Rees. Art direction: Matthew Knox and Peter Harvey. Players: Salmaan Peer, Marc Zuber. For BFI Production Board, distributed by Cinegate. 78 mins.

Over the years the BFI Production Board has received more brickbats than bouquets for the types of films (indulgent/worthless/unfinished) it has chosen to finance. Its caprices were partially vindicated by the appearance in 1974 of *A Private Enterprise*, a splendid film by any standards, which secured showings at the London Film Festival and, later, at London's new art house, the Gate. The film, possibly the first to take as its subject Britain's Indian community, is a brave and worthwhile effort, produced on a budget which, although lower than those of most sex films, never undermines the material. For this, all credit to director Peter K. Smith who, with his co-writer Dilip Hiro, conveys perfectly every dramatic, humorous and tragic facet of integration. The story revolves around a representative young Indian immigrant (the excellent Salmaan Peer), unable to relate to the cultural and social traditions of his own society, yet equally unable to adapt to the English way of life. Such is the delicacy of the treatment that the final shot—of an English woman distastefully shifting her baby out of reach as the Indian tries to caress it—does not seem overstated.

DAVID McGILLIVRAY

recent and forthcoming films

THE MAN WHO FELL TO EARTH. Dir: Nicolas Roeg. Players: David Bowie, Rip Torn, Buck Henry. For Lion International.

CONDUCT UNBECOMING. Script: Robert Enders, from the play by Barry England. Dir: Michael Anderson. Players: Trevor Howard, Susannah York, Christopher Plummer, Richard Attenborough, Michael York, Stacy Keach. For British Lion.

MAN FRIDAY. Script: Adrian Mitchell. Dir: Jack Gold. Players: Peter O'Toole, Richard Roundtree. For ITC/Keep Films/American Broadcasting Entertainment.

SEVEN MEN AT DAYBREAK. Script: Ronald Harwood. Dir: Lewis Gilbert. Phot: Henri Decae. Players: Timothy Bottoms. Martin Shaw, Nicola Pagett. For Warner Brothers.

THE MAN WHO WOULD BE KING. Script: John Huston and Gladys Hill, from the story "The Man Who Would Be King" by Rudyard Kipling. Dir: John Huston. Phot: Oswald Morris. Players: Michael Caine, Sean Connery, Christopher Plummer. For Columbia/Allied Artists.

LISZTOMANIA. Script and dir: Ken Russell. Phot: Peter Suschitzky. Players: Roger Daltrey, Sara Kestelman. Ringo Starr, Paul Nicholas, Fiona Lewis, Veronica Quilligan, Rick Wakeman. For VPS.

SHOUT AT THE DEVIL. Script: Wilbur Smith, Stanley Price, Alistair Reid, from the novel by Wilbur Smith. Players: Roger Moore, Lee Marvin, Barbara Parkins, Ian Holm. For Michael Klinger.

INSIDE OUT. Script: Judd Bernard and Stephen Schneck. Dir: Peter Duffell. Phot: Johnnie Coquillon. Players: Telly Savalas, Robert Culp, James Mason. For Judd Bernard.

AN ACE UP MY SLEEVE. Script: Jesse Lasky Jr. and Pat Silver, from the novel by James Hadley Chase. Dir: Ivan Passer. Players: Omar Sharif, Karen Black, Joseph Bottoms. For Gloria.

THE ADVENTURES OF TOM JONES. Script: Jeremy Lloyd. Dir: Cliff Owen. Players: Nicky Henson, Trevor Howard, Terry-Thomas, Arthur Lowe, Joan Collins. For Chromebridge.

THE SELLOUT. Script: Murray Smith and Jud Kinberg. Dir: Peter Collinson. Players: Oliver Reed, Richard Widmark, Sam Wanamaker, Gayle Hunnicutt. For Joseph Shaftel/Grandgrange.

THE HUMAN FACTOR. Script: Peter Powell and Tom Hunter. Dir: Edward Dmytryk. Phot: Ousama Rawi. Players: John Mills, George Kennedy, Rita Tushingham, Barry Sullivan. For Bryanstone/Eton.

THE ADVENTURES OF SHERLOCK HOLMES' SMARTER BROTHER. Script and dir: Gene Wilder. Players: Gene Wilder, Dom De Luise, Leo McKern, Madeline Kahn, Marty Feldman. For 20th Century-Fox.

Art House Focus

Outside London, apart from the admirable network of **Regional Film Theatres** (write to the BFI, 81 Dean Street, London W1V 6AA for a complete up-to-date list), there are not many genuine art houses. The Arts Cinema in Cambridge is still worth visiting during the university terms, but it is London that offers the widest selection of new and old films to the movie buff. Visitors should consult "What's On in London," which has a complete guide to all films being screened as well as ample coverage of entertainments, restaurants, and night-clubs, or "Time Out," which is strong in its film coverage and aims at the younger radical reader.

The **Academy Cinemas** (167 Oxford Street) have long been renowned for the distinction of their programmes, chosen by George Hoellering and Ivo Jarosy. There are new foreign and English-language films of the highest calibre in Academy One and Academy Two (*Distant Thunder, Black Holiday, Medea,* and *The Spirit of the*

Beehive since our last edition, for example),
and revivals in Academy Three. There is a
restaurant attached to the Academy, two
bars, and a film bookstore in the foyer.

In Mayfair, **The Curzon** reigns supreme,
both in terms of programmes and comfort.
Air-conditioned throughout, and with
luxurious armchairs, the Curzon is one of
those few establishments that can rival a
theatre for atmosphere and flair in presentation (the large screen and excellent sightlines
are characteristic of the thought that has gone
into the planning of the Curzon). *Alice
Doesn't Live Here Anymore, California Split,
Le fantôme de la liberté, What?,* and *Scenes
from a Marriage* have all been shown here
recently.

The leafy Drayton Gardens, in South
Kensington, is the site of the **Paris Pullman,**
an intimate home for such recent films as
Illumination, Pirosmani, A Bigger Splash,
and *Akenfield.* Shorts are particularly well-
chosen here, and there are late night shows in
addition to the regular daily programmes. The
Paris Pullman is the only London cinema that
reminds one of the best French art houses.

The **National Film Theatre** is really the
hub of film activity in London, almost in spite
of its awkward location beneath Waterloo
Bridge on the South Bank. It is the home of
the annual London Film Festival, and
throughout the year shows over one thousand
different features from around the world.
There are long seasons as well as short
tributes, and programmes are intelligently
divided between the large NFT One and the
smaller, more intimate NFT Two. An innovation since 1974 has been the "Junior NFT,"

which presents a matinee every Saturday for young people.

In Knightsbridge, **The Minema** (next to the Berkeley Hotel) is a sumptuous repertory house that is not only the home of some first-class films but also ideal for private film seminars, company meetings, and executive conferences.

The legendary **Everyman Cinema** in Hollybush Vale, Hampstead, is by far the oldest art house in London, and continues a serene repertory of the classics, both vintage and modern, from Clair to Bergman, and from Eisenstein to Satyajit Ray. No visit to London is complete without a pilgrimage to the Everyman.

The Gate Cinema, in Notting Hill Gate, has established a *niche* for itself in barely a year. Not only has it courageously screened the works of Rainer Werner Fassbinder (*Fear Eats the Soul* and *The Bitter Tears of Petra von Kant*); it has proved that this young German director could become as popular as Bergman with London audiences. Another fine Gate presentation was the double bill of *The Mattei Affair* and *Knots*.

The **ICA,** in The Mall, maintains its policy of booking quality films thanks to the international knowledge and discriminating taste of Derek Hill. And **The Electric Cinema** in Portobello Road is still in action with all manner of seasons and repertory offerings, enabling the student to catch up with an old movie he might have missed.

British Specialised Distributors

Anthony Morris (London) Ltd.
142 Piccadilly
London W1V 0HJ.

British Film Institute
42–43 Lower Marsh
London S.E.1.

Cinegate Ltd.
70 Portobello Road
London W11.

Concord Films
Nacton
Ipswich, Suffolk.

Connoisseur Films Ltd.
167 Oxford Street
London W1R 2DX.

Contemporary Films Ltd.
55 Greek Street
London W1V 6DB.

Curzon Film Distributors
38 Curzon Street
London W1.

Darvill Associates Ltd.
280 Chartridge Lane
Chesham, Bucks.

Eagle Films Ltd.
35 Soho Square
London W1V 5DG.

ETV Films Ltd.
247 Upper Street
London N1 1QR.

Gala Film Distributors Ltd.
15–17 Old Compton Street
London W.1.

The Other Cinema Ltd.
12–13 Little Newport Street
London WC2H 7JJ.

Pleasant Pastures
57 Greek Street
London W1

VPS (Visual Programme Systems)
21 Great Titchfield Street
London W1P 7AD.

Finland

by Kari Uusitalo

Unfortunately, there is not much to report about production in the 1974/75 season—only three feature-length films were released, less than at any other time since the 1932/33 season. There are signs, however, that this poor result reflects a temporary rather than a permanent condition. At the time of writing, available information leads one to expect once more over half-a-dozen Finnish films during the 1975/76 season. The roster of directors will probably again include both Jarva and Mollberg, who did not surface during the past year.

Of the three Finnish films released during the year, the one deserving prime mention is *Jouluksi kotiin* (*Home for Christmas*), directed by Jaakko Pakkasvirta. Now forty, Pakkasvirta had directed three feature-length works previously, but this fourth effort undoubtedly crowns his career to date. *Home for Christmas* deals with the life of workman Urho Suomalainen and his family during one crucial year. Suomalainen has been building houses all his life, but he has never been able to afford a decent place of his own to live. In desperation, he decides to build his own house, his timetable calling for occupancy by Christmas. His dream comes true, but only in

part—Urho Suomalainen himself does not live to see the day of completion . . . Although Pakkasvirta's outlook on life still seems to consist only of contrasting blacks and whites, his characterisation is now much richer and warmer.

The biggest popular success of the season was scored by Spede Pasanen's farce *Viu-hah hah-taja* (*The Whizzer*), about a couple of characters who land in Finland in a flying saucer, take on human shape and have a number of whacky adventures. As is customary in Spede Pasanen's films, the humour is largely verbal. Direction was entrusted to Ere Kokkonen, whose name is familiar from many previous Spede comedies.

The third new Finnish work of the season was Seppo Huunonen's tragic-comic thriller *Karvat* (literally, *The Hairs*), a free adaptation of Lionel White's novel "Obsession." The director-producer of the big hit a couple of seasons ago, *Lampaansyöjät* (*The Sheep Eaters*), seems to have struck the wrong chord this time—*Karvat* attracted only small audiences and the critics also have serious reservations about the picture's merits.

Total box-office admissions in 1974 fell

Jörn Donner returns to filmmaking with

THREE SCENES WITH INGMAR BERGMAN
90 minutes, 16 mm/color

THE WORLD OF INGMAR BERGMAN
50 minutes, 16 mm/color

SWEDEN. A LOVELETTER
Ready in 1976

Jörn Donner Productions. Ten years of creative production.
Pohjoisranta 12, SF-00170 Helsinki 17, Finland.
Phone 661212. Cables DONNPROD/Helsinki.

below ten million for the first time since talkies were introduced—the national total amounted to 9,630,000, an alarmingly low figure. One reason was probably that domestic production fell so sharply: one hopes that next year we can send in a brighter report again.

recent and forthcoming films

RAKASTUNUT RAMPA (Cripple in Love). Dir: Esko Favén, Tarja Laine. Players: Vesa-Matti Loiri, Riitta Räty. Prod: Ilkka Lehtonen for Filmisyndikaatti.
KESÄN MAKU (A Taste of Summer). Dir: Asko Tolonen. Players: Virpi Uimonen, Juha Hyppönen. Prod: Pentti Helanne for Filmi-Jatta.
MIES JOKA EI OSANNUT SANOA EI (A Man Who Couldn't Say No). Dir: Risto Jarva. Players: Antti Litja, Kirsti Wallasvaara, Matti Ruohola. Prod: Kullervo Kukkasjärvi for Filminor.
UUNO TURHAPURO II (Dopey Numbskull Useless-Brook II). Dir: Ere Kokkonen. Players: Vesa-Matti Loiri, Marjatta Raita. Prod: Spede Pasanen.
PERHE (The Family). Dir: Anssi Mänttäri. Players: Lasse Pöysti, Birgitta Ulfsson. Prod: Jörn Donner Productions.
ANTTI PUUHAARA. Dir: Heikki Partanen. Prod: Partanen and Rautoma.
THE FUSE. Dir: Clive Donner. Players: Raquel Welch, Elke Sommer, Robert Wagner. Prod: Michelangelo Productions, Roxy Film, Filmi-Jatta.
LUOTTAMUS, eli Lenin ja Suomi (Confidence, or Lenin and Finland). Dir: Viktor Tregubovich, Edvin Laine. Players: Kirill Lavrov, Vilho Siivola, Innokenti Smoktunovski, Evgenian Pleshkite, Yrjö Tähtelä, Yrjö Paulo, Matti Ranin, Jussi Jurkka, Jarno Hiilloskorpi. Prod: Nikolay Eliseev for Lenfilm and Mauno Mäkelä for Fennada-Filmi.

Art House Focus

In Helsinki, the **Uusi Orion**, in the Eerinkatu, specialises in first-class French films, while **La Scala,** in the North Esplanade, owned by Suomi Filmi, also has a distinctive policy, with good first-runs pre-eminent. The new **Maxim,** with two cinemas under one roof, has offered Helsinki moviegoers such master-

Seppo Huunonen (background), director of OBSESSION, with Mikku Majanlahti, the leading actor

pieces as *Cries and Whispers* and *The Conversation*, as well as unusual features like *The Paper Chase* and *Stubby*. There is completely automatic projection equipment, and the seats are exceptionally comfortable.

In Turku, the country's former capital, there is the **Astor,** with 100 seats and a repertory programme, and the **Boston,** with 320 seats. Both these Turku houses are programmed by Aito Mäkinen, himself a prominent Finnish director.

Focus on Shorts

Aito Mäkinen's *The Bridge*, which won the Grand Prix at the Fifteenth International Industrial Film Festival in 1974, is a cogent,

The Maxim Two, the newly opened art cinema in Helsinki, part of the Kinosto Oy circuit and based faithfully on the original 1909 theatre design

beautifully edited history of a northern suburb of Helsinki during the first phase of industrialisation in Finland. It sounds dry as dust, but in fact there is a human fascination about the subject, and about the way in which Mäkinen brings the historical aspects to life, through still photographs and an intelligent soundtrack. As an educational film, it is exemplary, and is based on Heikki Waris's doctoral thesis on economic and social history in Finland.

ORGANISATIONS

Elokuva- ja televisiokasvatuksen keskus—Centre of Film and TV Education in Finland. Founded 1958. Address: Vyökata 10, SF–00160 Helsinki 16.
Elokuva- ja tv-opiskelijat—Film and TV Students. Founded 1972. Address: Kamerataiteen laitos, Vesitorni 1 D, SF-00240 Helsinki 24.
Elokuvakontakti—Film Contact. Founded 1970. Purpose: to promote the production and distribution of noncommercial films. Address: Vyökatu 10, SF-00160 Helsinki 16.
Mainoselokuvatuottajain liitto—Advertising Film Producers' Association of Finland. Founded 1966. Address: Mariankatu 26 C 28, SF-00170 Helsinki 17.
Suomen elokuva-arkisto—The Finnish Film Archive. Founded 1957. Address: Eteläranta 4 B, SF-00130 Helsinki 13.

SUOMI - FILMI OY

(est'd 1918)
Finland-Helsinki 12, Bulevardi 12

DISTRIBUTORS of domestic and foreign films
—35 & 16mm & 8mm
—commercials as well

LABORATORIES, color and black/white
—35 & 16mm & 8mm
—domestic and foreign

CINEMA CIRCUIT
all over the country

PRODUCTION DIVISIONS
—domestic and foreign
—35 & 16mm & 8mm
—feature films (over 150 made)
—sponsored films (over 2300 made)
—documentaries
—commercials

Recording and dubbing services, magnetic and optical

Special sound effects

Rental equipment services

Preview theatres

Video services

OVER 50 YEARS LEAD IN CREATIVE FILMSERVICE

Suomen elokuvakerhojen liitto—The Federation of Finnish Film Societies. Founded 1956. Address: Eteläranta 4 B, SF-00130 Helsinki 13.
Suomen elokuvasäätiö—The Finnish Film Foundation. Founded 1969. Address: Kaisaniemenkatu 3 B 25, SF-00100 Helsinki 10.
Suomen elokuvatuottajat—The Finnish Film Producers. Founded 1973. Address: c/o Mia Seiro, Iso-Roobertinkatu 3–5 A 25, SF-00120 Helsinki 12.
Suomen elokuvatyöntekijät—The Association of Finnish Film Workers. Founded 1972. Address: Kaskenkaatajantie 16 B 21. SF-02100 Espoo 10.
Suomen elokuvateatterinomistajain liitto—Finnish Cinema Owners' Association. Founded 1938. Address: Kaisaniemenkatu 3 B 29, SF-00100 Helsinki 10.
Suomen elokuvatoimistojen liitto—The Finnish Film Distributors' Association. Founded 1937. Address: Kaisaniemenkatu 3 B 24, SF-00100 Helsinki 10.
Suomen filmikamari—Finnish Film Chamber. Founded 1923. Central business organisation of the Finnish film industry. Address: Kaisaniemenkatu 3 B 29, SF-00100 Helsinki 10.
Suomen filmivalmistajien liitto—Finnish Film Producers' Association. Founded 1945. Address: Kaisaniemenkatu 3 B 29, SF-00100 Helsinki 10.
Suomen kaitaelokuvaajain liitto—Finnish Society of Amateur Film Makers. Founded 1955. Address: Kauppiannkatu 2 B 16, SF-00160 Helsinki 16.
Tampereen elokuvataide—Society for Film Art in Tampere. Founded 1969. Organises, among others, the Tampere International Short Film Festival. Address: PO Box 305, SF-33101 Tampere 10.

STATE INSTITUTIONS

Taideteollinen korkeakoulu, Kuvallisen viestinnän laitos, Elokuva- ja tv-linja—Institute of Industrial Arts, Faculty of Visual Communication, Film and TV Studies. Founded 1959. Aesthetically-based educational institution giving courses in the fields of film and television. Address: Vesitorni 1 D, SF-00240 Helsinki 24.
Valtion elokuvatarkastamo—State Board of Film Censorship, and **Valtion elokuvalautakunta**—State Film Board. Founded originally in 1919. Entrusted with the task of censoring films in advance. Address: Jaakonkatu 5 B, SF-00100 Helsinki 10.
Valtion kamerataidetoimikunta—State Camera-Art Commission. Founded 1964. Duties include promoting creative and performing arts connected with films, knowledge of and interest in such arts, and timely research of significance from the standpoint of the arts. Address: c/o Ministry of Education, Rauhankatu 4, SF-00170 Helsinki 17.

Rauni Mollberg

RAUNI MOLLBERG (born 1929) is known to the Finnish public for both his work in the theatre and his achievements as a TV and film director. Mollberg attended the Finnish Theatre School from 1948 to 1950, and afterwards worked as an actor and director for thirteen years in the municipal theatres of Joensuu and Kuopio. In 1963 he entered television in the capacity of director. His best-known TV films are *Lapsuuteni* (*My Childhood*), dating back to 1967, and *Tehtaan varjossa* (*In the Shadow of the Factory*, 1969), both of which, in four parts, are based on novels by Toivo Pekkanen. Mollberg's latest TV productions include the eight-part serial *Pääluottamusmies* (*The Shop Steward*, 1970/71), *Sotaerakko* (*The War Recluse*, 1972), which has a Second World War setting, and the comedy *Siunattu hulluus* (*Blessed Madness*, 1975), which is his most recent work. Mollberg's film career has been short but brilliant. In 1963 he was commissioned to direct a short documentary film

Filminor Film Company: eleven features in thirteen years. From l. to r: Risto Jarva, Juha-Veli Äkräs, Timo Linnasalo, Erkki Peltomaa, Orvokki Taivalsaari (seated), Matti Kuortti, Antti Peippo and Kullervo Kukkasjärvi

entitled *Kuopio* (the name of an old town in the Finnish lake district). Ten years later, as an independent producer, he made the feature film *Maa on syntinen laulu* (*The Earth Is a Sinful Song*), which, based on the controversial youthful novel by the late Timo K. Mukka, he also directed himself. This picture was unanimously admired by the critics, and on the home circuit in Finland alone it has gained over 700,000 admissions (or about 15% of the total population of the country). Mollberg's plans call for starting a new film in the latter half of 1975.

Jaakko Pakkasvirta

JAAKKO PAKKASVIRTA (born 1934) worked his way through college by, among other things, appearing as an extra in Finnish films of the Fifties; at the same time, he was head of the Student Theatre in Helsinki. In 1958 he won his first major role—in Jack

Witikka's *Mies tältä tähdeltä* (*The Man from This Planet*). He next took the male leads in Maunu Kurkvaara's *Rakas* (*Beloved*, 1961), and *Meren juhlat* (*The Feast out at Sea*, 1963). The following year, Pakkasvirta collaborated with Risto Jarva in directing the feature *Yö vai päivä* (*Night or Day*) and in 1964 with Jarva and Spede Pasanen in directing the farce *X-Paroni* (*Baron X*), in which he played one of the two leading roles. In 1965 Pakkasvirta starred in Jarva's feature-length *Onnenpeli* (*Game of Chance*).

His *début* as a fully-fledged director was in 1968 with *Vihreä leski* (*Green Widow*), a film that cast a sharp eye on the social problems of Finnish suburbia. His *Kesäkapina* (*Summer Rebellion*), released in 1970, attacked the "consumer fascism" prevalent in Finnish society, and the 16mm feature *Niilon oppivuodet* (*Niilo's Apprenticeship*, 1971) took a critical look at the country's educational system. Since 1971 Pakkasvirta has been running his own production company (Filmityö Oy) and has directed several shorts for it. His finest directorial achievement so far is *Jouluksi kotiin* (*Home for Christmas*), released early this year (1975).

PRODUCTION COMPANIES

Elokuva Oy Filminor
Luotsikatu 3 C 17
SF-00160 Helsinki 16.
Fennada-Filmi Oy
Kaisaniemenkatu 2 B
SF-00100 Helsinki 10.
Filmi-Jatta Oy
Aleksanterinkatu 21 A
SF-00100 Helsinki 10.
Filmiryhmä Oy
Kruunuvuorenkatu 5 F
SF-00160 Helsinki 16.
Filmisyndikaatti Ilkka Lehtonen Oy
Mikonkatu 13, piha
SF-00100 Helsinki 10.

Filmituotanto Spede Pasanen Oy
Fredrikinkatu 61
SF-00100 Helsinki 10.
Eloseppo Oy
Korkeavuorenkatu 2 B
SF-00140 Helsinki 14.
Jörn Donner Productions Oy
Pohjoisranta 12
SF-00170 Helsinki 17.
Käpyfilmi Oy
c/o Mikko Niskanen
Iso-Roobertinkatu 35–37 G 88
SF-00120 Helsinki 12.
Power Pictures Partanen & Rautoma
SF-02550 Evitskog.
Rauni Mollberg
Siltakatu 2 A
SF-33100 Tampere 10.
Suomi-Filmi Oy
Bulevardi 12
SF-00120 Helsinki 12.

FILM DISTRIBUTORS

Oy Warner Columbia Films Ab
Pohjois-Esplanadi 33
SF-00100 Helsinki 10.
OY MGM-Fox Ab
Hallituskatu 17 B
SF-00100 Helsinki 10.
Suomi-Filmi Oy
Bulevardi 12
SF-00120 Helsinki 12.
Oy Cinema International Corporation Ab
Korkeavuorenkatu 47
SF-00130 Helsinki 13.
Adams-Filmi Oy
Mikonkatu 13 A
SF-00100 Helsinki 10.
Kosmos-Filmi Oy
Mannerheimintie 16
SF-00100 Helsinki 10.
Oy Valio-Filmi Ab
Kasarminkatu 48 B
SF-00130 Helsinki 13.

Oy United Artists Films Ab
Mikonkatu 13 A
SF-00100 Helsinki 10.
Lii-Filmi Oy
Kaisaniemenkatu 1 C
SF-00100 Helsinki 10.
Kamras Film Agency
Korkeavuorenkatu 45 A
SF-00130 Helsinki 13.
Republic-Filmi Oy
Kaisaniemenkatu 1 C
SF-00100 Helsinki 10.
ABC- Kinot Mäkinen & Nurmi
Box 31
SF-20101 Truku 10.
Filmipaja Oy
Kaisaniemenkatu 2 B
SF-00100 Helsinki 10.
Finnkino Oy
Pohjoisranta 12
SF-00170 Helsinki 17.
Oy Magna-Filmi Oy
Temppelikatu 6 B
SF-00100 Helsinki 10.
Väinän Filmi Oy
Kaisaniemenkatu 2 B
SF-00100 Helsinki 10.
Helsinki-Filmi Oy
Etelä-Esplanadi 22 A
SF-00130 Helsinki 13.
Kino-Filmi Oy
Mikonkatu 9
SF-00100 Helsinki 10.
Ky Mårten Kihlman
Laivurinkatu 33 C 69
SF-00150 Helsinki 15.
Fenno-Filmi Oy
Kaisaniemenkatu 2 B
SF-00100 Helsinki 10.
Filmimies Oy
Kaisaniemenkatu 1 C
SF-00100 Helsinki 10.
Meridian Films
Telakkakatu 1 C
SF-00150 Helsinki 15.

France

by Michel Ciment

Paradoxically, the Cannes Film Festival, by far the most important event of its kind, is unable each year to give a fair account of the French cinema which is, arguably, after the American and the Italian cinemas, one of the most interesting in the world. In 1975 the selection was not as scandalous as it was the previous year (when Bresson, Pialat, Rivette, Franju, Corneau, Girod, Makavejev *et al.* were excluded!), but failed to satisfy. If it

aroused less ire, it is simply because the annual crop was not of a particularly high quality, though the production has never been so abundant. 234 films were made in 1974 (against 200 in 1973) and among them 137 (against 97 last year) with French money exclusively. But in spite of the increase in production costs the average movie budget went down (1.50 million francs against 1.56) and 73 films (as against 43 last year) were

Still from Marguerite Duras's INDIA SONG, with Delphine Seyrig (left)

made on a budget of less than a million francs.

This is due, of course, to the boom in cheaply-made porno films. The incredible inflation in this relatively new market raises serious problems to the extent that in many provincial towns half (or more) of the films being programmed belong to this category. The government which, in spite of ambiguous statements, has never completely abandoned the censorship regulations but has loosened them considerably, has decided to practice an economic censorship in refusing to sex films the automatic financial help given to the producers of every film made in France. This decision is inadequate, for who will set the standards of what is or is not pornographic? Once more some judges will decide what is to be seen by the adult audience. The only sound regulation would be to oblige the producers of porno films to pay their crew according to the Unions' standards which would increase their production costs and slacken their outputs. Most nudies gain money because they are so cheaply made. The evidence of this new trend has been spectacularly demonstrated by *Emmanuelle* which has been the most successful film released in Paris in 1974: 1,342,921 tickets, followed by: *The Sting* 1,154,952, *Les valseuses* (*Going Places*) 950,209, *La moutarde me monte au nez* 844,363, *Robin Hood* (Walt Disney) 802,513, *Vincent, François, Paul . . . et les autres* 791,776, *La gifle* 655,092, *The Exorcist* 655,092, *Papillon* 536,787, *Lacombe Lucien* 528,373. One should add, for the first months of 1975: *The Towering Inferno*, *The Man with the Golden Gun*, *Earthquake* and Henri Verneuil's *Peur sur la ville*.

This list shows no marked difference (except *Emmanuelle*) to the one published in recent editions of IFG. French comedies are still very popular together with American "action" films, the latter allowing the U.S. film in-

LES PETITES AMOUREUSES, directed by Jean Eustache

dustry to regain some of the ground lost in the last years. Paris is still a unique town for the film buff, who was offered 607 new films in 1974 (against 557 in 1973). But among them only 92 had an attendance of more than a hundred thousand and 200 films (one third) had an audience of less than 10,000! The production and distribution inflation is not finding an outlet at the exhibition level. Potential spectators just don't follow up and the provinces tends to confirm in a much more drastic way the Paris results. Most arthouse films or simply foreign products (apart from *kung-fu*, spaghetti westerns and nudies) are never shown outside Paris.

For the professional observer, though, the landscape has been extremely varied and offers food for thought. The interest in politics among younger people has led to many films dealing with controversial problems. The growing role of women and their stand against the current state of society have been witnessed in their collaboration on several of these particular films: *La folle de Toujane* by René Vauthier and Nicole Le Garrec, on the fight of Bretons for their cultural identity, *Histoires d'A* by Charles Belmont and Marcelle Issartel, on abortion; *Mai 68*, by

Gudie Lawaets; *La fête aujourd'hui, la fête demain* by Maria Koleva, on the annual celebrations of the Communist paper "L'Humanité"; *Au nom de la race*, by Marc Hillel and Clarissa Henry, on the Nazis' breeding of a "pure" race; *Kashima Paradise*, by Yann Le Masson and Benie Deswartz, on the Japanese peasants' fight against the building of an airport; *Le ghetto expérimental*, by Jean-Michel Carré and Adam Schneider, on the University of Vincennes; and Jérôme Kanapa's *La république est morte à Dien-Bien-Phu*, on the Indochina War.

These documentaries or montage films reveal an increasing awareness of political and social problems which is confirmed by a series of fiction films often labelled under the tag of "nouveau naturel," a new "spontaneity" in shooting the film and directing actors, background and people looking more "natural" than in the more "classical" productions. This concept of "spontaneity" is a very fragile and artificial one. It is often due to the small production budget. Aesthetically it usually represents a new type of naturalism. It is true that these films have been paying attention to people rarely seen on the screen: villagers as in Pascal Thomas's *Le chaud lapin*; a factory worker who burns himself to death because his boss wants him to have his long hair cut (Philippe Condroyer's *La coupe à dix francs*, from a real event); the plight of a young widow and her child (Pierre Jallaud's *La chaise vide*); a peasant becoming politically conscious (Jean-Daniel Simon's *Il pleut toujours où c'est mouillé*); a worker's sentimental life (Dugowson's *Lily aime-moi*). These films do not always avoid offering new stereotypes, such as Boisset's *Dupont-Lajoie* on the racism of the average Frenchman. Their approach is often sensitive but limited. Their scope is

narrow and for all the critical comments about their novelty they represent an old French tradition that goes back to Clair and Pagnol. In the best of cases we have *Les doigts dans la tête* by Jacques Doillon, a *Design for Living* among young workers, a *ménage à trois* without the Lubitsch touch but with a rare humour and a sense of the difficulties of modern life and the birth of new morals and manners.

There is a new conformism in "political" subjects and, ironically, the only victim of a short critical backlash was the much overrated Costa-Gavras who started the trend. His *Section spéciale* about the exceptional jurisdictions created by the Vichy *régime* to comply with the German occupation is a heavy-handed movie but neither better nor worse than his other films and did not deserve the abuse that it received after the applause of the past.

Some directors have tried to go into less frequented territory: Robert Benayoun's *Sérieux comme le plaisir* leads his three characters, a girl (Jane Birkin) and two boys through the paths of a fantasy world full of incongruous gags, and Claude D'Anna's *Trompe l'œil* is an exercise in the interplay of reality and illusion influenced by Hitchcock and surrealism.

As usual, visitors from abroad have brought their audacity to the very safe French scene. Buñuel's *Le fantôme de la liberté* is a companion piece to his *Charme discret de la bourgeoisie*, an "open" film, amusing but also deeply disturbing, a synthetic view of society by a sceptical, materialistic old master. Andrzej Żuławski, a pupil of Wajda, has instilled his Polish romanticism into his adaptation of a French novel. His *L'important c'est d'aimer* aroused much controversy. Its lyrical excesses, its morbid sense of life made it an extremely exciting film to watch, and had the

Bruno Cremer and Charlotte Rampling in LE CHAIR DE L'ORCHIDEE

very qualities lacking in Patrice Chéreau's *La chair de l'orchidée* adapted from James Hadley Chase. The wonder boy of the French stage failed to create on screen the decadent atmosphere *à la* Visconti that was supposed to surround his *film noir* plot. Among the newcomers, Chéreau created the greatest disappointment but none of the 29 first films really revealed a major talent.

There were some confirmations, however, particularly Bertrand Tavernier who, after the success of his first feature *L'horloger de Saint-Paul*, embarked on a very bold enterprise, a historical movie about the Régence, that period of French history between the death of Louis XIV and the advent of Louis XV. *Que la fête commence* shows a dazzling display of talents in its portrayal of politics, economics, sexuality and human relationships at the beginning of the Eighteenth Century. Tavernier's scope has broadened and makes us even more confident of his future. Eustache's *Mes petites amoureuses*, though not as striking as *The Mother and the Whore*, confirms his talent and is a return to his first films about the French provinces. Almost Bressonian in its restraint and the neutral tone of its per-

Philippe Noiret and Jean Rochefort in Bertrand Tavernier's QUE LA FETE COMMENCE

formers, it has some remarkable sequences (the seduction of a young girl on a country road for instance) but fails to achieve a real style of its own.

If I was rather severe with Chabrol recently, I must admit to having been impressed by his latest opus, *Les innocents aux mains sales* (which has been incredibly slighted by the press), a thriller so abstract in its development that it reminds us of Fritz Lang. Previously, Chabrol had made a very "personal" film, *Une partie de plaisir*, written by Paul Gégauff who also played in it (together with his ex-wife), the portrait of a monstrous he-man which was ambivalent, half-admiring, half-critical, but was marred by the interpretation of Gégauff, the simple-mindedness of the script and a confusion of attitude.

Another "classical" director, Claude Sautet, produced with *Vincent, François, Paul . . . et les autres* what is probably his best film. Through four main characters and without the help of a linear story, he extends on the screen his usual world of the outskirts of Paris. The passage of time, the crisis of the individual, the pressures of social life, the oppositions of generations, are given a physical presence by a director whose mastery of the

Still from LILY AIME MOI

Romy Schneider and Fabio Testi in Andrzej Żulawski's L'IMPORTANT C'EST D'AIMER

medium from scriptwriting to direction of actors and sense of rhythm is, within his limits, almost perfect. At the other extreme of the aesthetic spectrum Marguerite Duras has finally given a satisfying form to an artistic enterprise (which has already yielded five films). *India Song* is Marienbad revisited, a ballet of shadows, life seen in a mirror, the triumph of incantation and stylised cinema. It is liable to annoy many with its literary viewpoint, its contrapuntal use of sound and image, but no one can deny its accomplishment.

Many famous French directors did not offer any new film to the public. Some were busy writing. Truffaut gathered a sample of his critical writings in "Les films de ma vie"; Bresson distilled his aphorisms in "Notes sur le cinématographe"; Astruc recalls his career in "La tête la première" and Rohmer published the "literary" text of his *Six Contes Moraux*. To make us forget their latest cinematographic ventures, Marcel Carné (*La vie à belles dents*) and Roger Vadim (*Les mémoires du diable*) also turned autobiographers. This outpouring of books testifies to the vitality of the French cinema book market (though not on a par with the Anglo-Saxon one). No doubt that the bumper issue of "Communications" on psychoanalysis and cinema (a very interesting collection of texts by Barthes, Bellour, Kuntzel, etc.) will nourish academic film writing all over the world for years to come. Christian Metz has turned for a time from linguistics to the study of Freud.

The French cinema magazines, always fighting among themselves, have, for once, come to an agreement and signed a text in common ("Cahiers du Cinéma," "Positif," "Ecran 75," "Cinéma 75," "Image et Son," "Téléciné"), asking for the foundation of a National French Film Institute, an organisation severely lacking at present which would offer a library, an accessible archive, with the possibility for students of films to analyse them and the arrangement of extensive retrospectives.

recent and forthcoming films

SOUVENIRS D'EN FRANCE. Script: André Techiné, Marilyn Goldin. Dir: André Techiné. Phot: Bruno Nuytten. Players: Michel Auclair, Jeanne Moreau, Marie-France Pisier. Prod: Stéphan Film.

CE CHER VICTOR. Script: Robin Davis, Patrick Laurent. Dir: Robin Davis. Phot: Yves Lafaye. Players: Bernard Blier, Jacques Dufilho, Alida Valli. Prod: Les Productions de Daunou.

SECTION SPECIALE. Script: Jorge Semprun. Costa-Gavras, from the writings of Hervé Villeré. Dir: Costa-Gavras. Phot: Andréas Winding. Players: Louis Seigner, Michel Lonsdale, Pierre Dux, Claude Pieplu, Jean Champion. Prod: Reggane Films/Artistes Associés (Paris)/Goriz Films (Rome)/Janus Films, (Frankfurt).

ALOISE. Script: Liliane De Kermadec, André Techiné. Dir: Liliane De Kermadec. Phot: Jean Penzer. Players: Delphine Seyrig, Isabelle Huppert, Roger Blin. Prod: Unité Trois.

LA BRIGADE. Dir: René Gilson. Players: Brigitte Fossey, Edward Wojtaszek, Jean Bouise. Prod: Sofracima.

INDIA SONG. Script and dir: Marguerite Duras. Phot: Bruno Nuytten. Players: Delphine Seyrig, Michel Lonsdale, Mathieu Carrière, Claude Mann. Prod: Sunchild Productions/Les Films Armorial.

LE SAUVAGE. Dir: Jean-Paul Rappeneau. Players: Yves Montand, Catherine Deneuve. Prod: Lira Film, Paris/Nassau Film Studios.

L'ARGENT DE POCHE. Dir: François Truffaut. Prod: Les Films du Carrosse/Les Productions Artistes Associés.

L'ARBE DE GUERNICA. Dir: Arrabal. Players: Maria-Angela Melato, Rob Faber, Jean-François Delacour.

L'INCORRIGIBLE. Script: Michel Audiard. Dir: Philippe De Broca. Players: Jean-Paul Belmondo. Prod: Les Films Ariane/Mondex Films/Cerito-Films.

LE VIEUX FUSIL Script: Pascal Jardin, Robert Enrico. Dir: Robert Enrico. Players: Romy Schneider, Philippe Noiret. Prod: Mercure Productions.

LE GRAND DELIRE. Script and dir: Dennis Berry. Players: Jean Seberg, Yves Beneyton, Wolfgang Preiss, Pierre Blaise. Prod: Paris Cannes Production.

LE JUGE ET L'ASSASSIN. Dir: Bertrand Tavernier. Players: Philippe Noiret, Michel Galabru. Prod: Lira Films.

VOYAGES DE NOCES. Dir: Nadine Trintignant. Players: Jean-Louis Trintignant, Stefania Sandrelli. Prod: Lira Films.

PROVIDENCE. Script: David Mercer. Dir: Alain Resnais. Players: Dirk Bogarde. Prod: Action Films–Citel Films.

DR. FRANCOISE G. Script: André Brunelin, from the novel by Noelle Loriot. Dir: Jean-Louis Bertucelli. Players: Annie Girardot. Prod: Action Films–Citel Films.

LE TESTAMENT. Dir: André Cayatte, from the novel by Francis Ryck. Prod: Paris Cannes Production.

IL FAUT VIVRE DANGEREUSEMENT. Dir: Claude Makovski. Players: Annie Girardot, Claude Brasseur, Sydne Rome. Prod: Les Films de la Chouette/Nelly Kaplan/Claude Makovski.

UN DIVORCE HEUREUX. Script: Benny Andersen. Henning Carlsen. Dir: Henning Carlsen. Players: Jean Rochefort, André Dussollier, Daniel Ceccaldi, Bulle Ogier. Prod: Dagmar Distribution (Copenhagen)/ UGC–ORTF–Mag Bodard (Paris).

DUNE. Dir: Alejandro Jodorowsky, from the novel by Frank Herbert. Prod: Michel Seydoux/Camera One.

LE CHAT ET LA SOURIS. Script and dir: Claude Lelouch. Players: Michèle Morgan, Serge Reggiani, Philippe Léotard. Prod: Les Films 13.

L'HISTOIRE D'ADELE. Script: François Truffaut, Jean Gruault, S. Schiffman. Dir: François Truffaut. Players: Isabelle Adjani, Sylvia Marriot, Bruce Robinson. Prod: Les Films du Carrosse/Les Artistes Associés.

MIRAGES. Script: Pascal Aubier, C. Gion. Dir: Pascal Aubier. Players: Brigitte Fossey, Paulette Frantz, Germaine Montéro. Prod: Films de la Commune (Pascal Aubier).

L'IBIS ROUGE. Script and dir: Jean-Pierre Mocky, based on a novel by Frédéric Brown and André Ruellan. Players: Michel Simon, Michel Serrault, Michel Galabru. Prod: M Films/Les Films de l'Epée.

LE MALE DU SIECLE. Script: Claude Berri, Jean-Louis Richard based on an idea by Miloš Forman. Dir: Claude Berri. Players: Juliet Berto, Claude Berri, Hubert Deschamps, André Rouyer. Prod: Reen Productions/Christian Fechner Films.

F FOR FAKE

Script: Orson Welles, Oja Palinkas. Direction: Welles (additional footage by François Reichenbach). Photography (Eastmancolor): Christian Odasso, Gary Graver. Editing: Marie-Sophie Dubus, Dominique Engerer. Players: Welles, Oja Kadar, Elmyr de Hory, Clifford Irving, François Reichenbach, Joseph Cotten. For Planfilm. 90 mins.

In a celebrated "New Yorker" article, Pauline Kael explained that *Citizen Kane* was really by Herman Mankiewicz, not by Orson Welles; her questionable argument was that Mankiewicz had written so many poor scripts before coming up with a masterpiece. She also traced the relationship between *Kane* and German expressionism via Gregg Toland, who had photographed Peter Lorre in *Mad Love*. One shudders to think what authorship she should assign for *F for Fake*, a pseudo-documentary, *montage* film which incorporates material shot by François Reichenbach in Ibiza about artist-forger Elmyr de Hory being interviewed by forger-to-be Clifford Irving (of Howard Hughes fame). Welles encases the Reichenbach material in his own, makes it his own, seemingly implying both that forgers are artists in their own right and that "genuine" artists have something of the forger in them. The trouble is that Welles's genius is largely spent on one sequence of the film, in which he appears dressed in a black cloak and a black hat as a conjurer performing tricks to an audience of children on a station platform. After that he seems to take a holiday: the final twenty minutes, with the obviously fake reconstitution of an obviously fake love affair between Picasso and beautiful Oja Kadar, are ponderous padding, masochistic self-derision. Genius may well be manipulative; not all manipulation is a work of genius.

JACQUES SEGOND

LE FANTOME DE LA LIBERTE
(The Phantom of Liberté)

Script: Luis Buñuel, Jean-Claude Carrière. Direction: Buñuel. Photography (Eastmancolor): Edmond Richard. Editing: Hélène Plemiannikov. Players: Adriana Asti, Julian Bertheau, Jean-Claude Brialy, Adolfo Celi, Paul Frankeur, Michel Lonsdale, Pierre Maguelon, François Maistre, Hélène Perdrière, Michel Piccoli, Claude Piéplu, Jean Rochefort, Bernard Verley, Monica Vitti, Milena Vukotic. For Greenwich Films. 104 mins.

In the opening sequence of *The Phantom of Liberté*, the Spanish patriots about to be shot by Napoléon's soldiers shout "Vivan las

LE FANTOME DE LA LIBERTE

cadenas!" ("Long live chains!"), which Buñuel himself translates as "Down with liberty!" The scene brings to mind Goya's "Tres de Mayo," both because of the similar subject matter and of the ambiguous relationship between Reason and Liberty. In Goya's painting the firing squad, representing geometrical reason, is surrounded by darkness; patriotic passion is suffused with light. Buñuel also must be torn between the anti-clerical, progressive but oppressive French, and his obscurantist, "tyranny-loving" fellow-countrymen. The rational and the irrational, the repressive and the revolutionary, certainly have the knack of exchanging places. Picture postcards of tourist spots are seen as obscene; defecation is standard social practice but one asks for the way to the dining-room in hushed tones. The loose narrative structure of *Phantom* closely resembles that of *Discreet Charm of the Bourgeoisie*: it is a picaresque structure without a *picaro*, a narrative equivalent of the free association of ideas. The butts are also similar to those of *Discreet Charm*: mostly people wearing uniforms or religious costumes (emblems of Reason) but bent on proving that there is nothing quite as irrational as Reason. Hence, a final reversal of accepted values: in its very unexpectedness, oppressive Reason does stand for Liberty after all, and the satire is often gentle rather than biting. The opening sequence has a power which is not really sustained by the rest of the film.

JACQUES SEGOND

LA GUEULE OUVERTE
(The Mouth Agape)

Script: Maurice Pialat. Direction: Pialat. Photography (Eastmancolor): Nestor Almendros. Editing: Arlette Langmann, Bernard Dubois. Players: Nathalie Baye, Hubert Deschamps, Philippe Léotard, Monique Mélinand. For Lido Films-Films La Boétie. 80 mins.

In IFG 1975 Michel Ciment mentioned *La gueule ouverte* and called it "outstanding"; since the film is still in need of a British distributor even after its London Festival presentation, I should like to return to it briefly. Maurice Pialat is fifty and did not direct his first feature (*L'enfance nue*, seen here only on television) until 1968. He was a painter for some years and this training is apparent in both *L'enfance nue* and *La gueule ouverte*—a "painter of reality" in the tradition of Vermeer and Chardin. His sets and films generally are not picturesque, but tend toward the still-life study which endows things with spiritual meaning; at the same time, their vivid colour and earthy richness set them poles apart from Bresson's more intellectualised *oeuvre*, which they superficially resemble. *La gueule ouverte* is rooted in the tradition of Auvergne, the volcanic core of the French province where Pialat was born and where the film was shot. The Romanesque churches of Auvergne (such as the one where the funeral takes place) have a dark, ageless quality. The catholicism of Auvergne has a strong regional, almost

pagan, flavour, together with a sense of fate. *La gueule ouverte* is a pagan film in its suggestion that death and the rather disgusting process of physical decay call for (sometimes equally disgusting) outbursts of life and sex to redress the balance. The implied outlook is profoundly conservative; brooding pessimism made flesh, colour and Mozart.

JACQUES SEGOND

VINCENT, FRANÇOIS, PAUL . . . ET LES AUTRES

Script: Jean-Loup Dabadie, Claude Néron, Claude Sautet, from a novel by Claude Néron. Direction: Sautet. Photography (Eastmancolor): Jean Boffety. Editing: Jacqueline Thiédot. Players: Yves Montand, Michel Piccoli, Serge Reggiani, Gérard Depardieu, Stéphane Audran, Ludmilla Mikael, Marie Dubois, Antonella Lualdi, Catherine Allégret. For Lira Films-President. 118 mins.

As the title makes clear, Sautet's latest film follows in the *unanimiste* tradition of its predecessors. Though there is, undoubtedly, a main character (Montand as Vincent), whose multifold crises (material: bankruptcy; sentimental: estrangement from wife and then from girl-friend; medical: heart attack) we follow through the film, the focus could just as easily be provided by Paul (Reggiani) or Jean (Depardieu), most important among the unmentioned "others." Least likely would be François (Piccoli), because the material he would provide would certainly be less congenial, out of tune with Sautet's and the other characters' generosity. *Vincent* is about comradeship, collective friendship, though it also examines a number of marital relationships (notably the admirable one between Reggiani and Antonella Lualdi) and aims at social description; like Sautet himself, the film is rooted in the twilight zone of *la banlieue*, the suburbs, and draws on the rich terrain of second-generation Italian immigrants, an element made believable and moving by the main actors. Beautifully acted and photographed, adequately accompanied by Philippe Sarde's score, it has the sweep but not the insight of a social fresco. We cannot believe that François, an over-ambitious and over-successful physician, would be free to spend week-end after week-end with his friends. Typically, Sautet started by mitigating the pessimism of Claude Néron's novel; he is a romantic artist posing as a realist.

JACQUES SEGOND

French Specialised Distributors

Plan Film
30 avenue de Messine
75008 Paris.

Cinéma Service
2 Cité Trévise
Paris 9.

Ursulines Distribution
6 rue de Monceau
Paris 8.

Grands Films Classiques
16 rue de Boulainvilliers
Paris 16.

Capital Films
57 bis rue de Babylone
Paris 7.

Etoile Distribution
99 avenue Mozart
Paris 16.

N.E.F. (Claude Nedjar)
92 Champs-Elysées
Paris 8.

MacMahon Distribution
5 avenue MacMahon
Paris 17.

Medicis Distribution
6 rue de Monceau
Paris 8.

Art du Siècle
24 rue Godot de Mauroy
75009 Paris.

German Democratic Republic

In May 1975, the GDR participated for the first time in the official competition at Cannes, with Egon Günter's version of *Lotte in Weimar*. Lilli Palmer played Lotte with an unaffected grace that must have put her in line for the Best Actress award, and there were some visual felicities in the production too—the costumes, for instance, and Jutta Hoffmann's sad glissade on the ice rink when she hears of her beloved's engagement to another girl. Certainly *Lotte in Weimar* demonstrated that the GDR can now offer films with production values the equal of any country's.

The film also emphasised that in the GDR the adaptation of works from literature is vital. The possibilities for film production are largely dependent—as far as quality and quantity are concerned—on the availability of writers. Several authors, such as Günther Rücker, Wolfgang Kohlhaase, Helmut Baierl, Jochen Nestler and Manfred Freitag, work permanently at the DEFA studios. Others make just one or two films each. Since 1960

Export and import of feature films, documentary films, children's films, popular science films and animated films · Besides we execute your orders for negative development and printing in black/white and colour for 8 mm, 16 mm, 35 mm and 70 mm, as well as all production works and synchronizations for 70 mm films · In addition we export scientific films for general education, for professional schools, high schools and universities, and 8 mm and 16 mm films for home projectors. · On your request we may execute your orders for publicity films and German synchronizations

DEFA-AUSSENHANDEL
1058 BERLIN, MILASTRASSE 2
German Democratic Republic

Lilli Palmer in LOTTE IN WEIMAR

there have been a number of artistic teams at DEFA, headed by a central management board. These teams achieve with comparatively large degree of independence the artistic development of a literary subject and its adaptation to the screen. The role of the dramaturgs is crucial, and their responsibilities are divided into areas of cultural policy and aesthetics as well as production economy and organisation.

In the late Fifties DEFA began to co-operate with GDR Television so that both branches could work to full capacity. Today, more than 80% of staff at the DEFA Studio for Feature Films have passed an examination as skilled workers, or are graduates from either technical schools or colleges. The Studio is headed by a Director General, who has at his disposal an Art Director, a director responsible for production, a director in charge of technology, and a director for economical matters. The staff amounts to some 2,400 people. The Studio has all the necessary production facilities, including a lab for the development of samples in black-and-white, lighting, image and sound techniques, workshops for set preparation and construction, a costume department, and a research department. At present there are thirty directors and eighteen scriptwriters at work permanently in the Studio. The aim is that at least 30% to 50% of all films produced should deal with the contemporary problems of the GDR. The country's workers, who participate in the management and development of factories and plants, can find their dilemmas mirrored in such recent films as *Too Skinny for Love*, *Josef, for Example*, *Looping*, and *Suse Dear Suse*.

Apart from *Lotte in Weimar*, literary adaptations of the past year or two include *Die Wahlverwandtschaften* (*Elective Affinities*) and *Goya* (based on the novel by Leon Feuchtwanger).

To date, DEFA has produced around 600 feature films, several of which have been released abroad. The Studio intends to increase its work in the co-production field, and a series of films has recently been made about the Red Indian struggle for independence, in collaboration with the U.S.S.R., Romania, and Czechoslovakia.

recent and forthcoming films

JOHANNES KEPLER. Dir: Frank Vogel, from a book by Freitag and Nestler. Players: Raimar Johannes Baur, Kurt Böwe, Dieter Franke, Karin Gregorek.

JAKOB THE LIAR. Dir: Frank Beyer. Players: Vlastimil Brodsky, Erwin Geschonneck.

TILL EULENSPIEGEL. Dir: Rainer Simon. Script: Christa and Gerhard Wolf. Players: Winfried Glatzeder, Cox Habbema, Eberhard Esche.

WOLZ. Script: Günther Rücker. Dir: Günter Reisch. Players: Regimantas Adomaitis, Heidemarie Wenzel, Stanislav Lyubshin.

"... VERDAMMT, ICH BIN ERWACHSEN ..." Script: Günter Mehnert. Dir: Rolf Losansky. Players: Ralf Schlösser, Angelika Herrmann, Frank Wuttig.

APACHEN. Script: Gojko Mitic, Dr. G. Kolditz. Dir: Dr. G. Kolditz. Players: Gojko Mitic, Milan Beli, Leon Niemczyk, Colea Rautu, Else Grube-Deister.

HANS RÖCKLE UND DER TEUFEL. Script: Gudrun Deubner. Dir: Hans Kratzert. Players: Rolf Hoppe, Peter Aust, Simone von Zglinicki.

FÜR DIE LIEBE NOCH ZU MAGER? Script: Jochen Nestler, Manfred Freitag. Dir: Bernhard Stephan. Players: Simone von Zglinicki, Ursula Staak, Christian Steyer.

ORPHEUS IN DER UNTERWELT. Script and dir: Horst Bonnet. Players: Gerry Wolff, Dorit Gäbler, Rolf Hoppe, Achim Wichert.

WIE FÜTTERT MAN EINEN ESEL? Script: Maurycy Janowski, Roland Oehme, Dieter Scharfenberg. Dir: Roland Oehme. Players: Manfred Krug, Karla Chadimova, Fred Delmare, Rolf Hoppe.

LIEBE MIT 16. Script: Gisela Steineckert, Rainer Simon. Dir: Herrmann Zschoche. Players: Simon von Zglinicki, Heinz-Peter Linse, Martin Trettau.

Useful Address

Inquiries regarding the distribution of films from the German Democratic Republic, in the U.S.A., may be directed to International Film Exchange Ltd., 159 West 53rd Street, New York, N.Y. 10019.

Egon Günter, director of LOTTE IN WEIMAR

Germany (BRD)

by Edmund Luft

Cinema in the Federal Republic during recent year has shown two main tendencies. On the one hand, the film industry is inclined to bypass the home market by aiming at too low a cultural level. On the other, representatives of progressive cinema and the *film d'auteur* are all too often marooned in esoteric areas. Their work rarely comes up to audiences' expectations and is duly buried in late night TV programmes.

Even the newly introduced law for the advancement of good films, which since early 1974 has been aimed at giving generous aid to projects, partly in connection with TV, has not so far induced any artistic achievement. After one year's activity by the FFA (Filmförderungsanstalt), the trade magazine "Filmecho/Filmwoche" reports, in April 1975, that nothing of importance has occurred. At no other time during recent years were there fewer worthwhile films being made or seen in the West German film market.

This harsh judgement needs some modification. Now, as always, the German film scene does have some artistic forces with international potential. Hans-Jürgen Syberberg created a three-hour, superbly-produced feature, *Karl May*, about the fate of the German author whose adventure novels have been best-sellers for decades, and whose life was overshadowed by violence and intrigue. The leading part in this colourful epic is played by none other than the director Helmut Käutner. He now excels, as he did in his youth, in ironic character roles. The film, produced by TMS, Munich, ran for several months in Paris.

Alexander Kluge and Edgar Reitz, too, have offered a new form of contemporary satire: *In Gefahr und höchster Not bringt der Mittelweg den Tod* (*In Danger and Greatest Distress, the Middle Course Brings Death*). They describe the life of a young person in the midst of violent sociological conflict. This often amusing, often bitter documentary kaleidoscope, is set in the concrete metropolis of Frankfurt am Main. (Produced by Reitz-Kluge Filmproduktion, Munich.) The talented young directors Bernard Sinkel and Alf Brustellin achieved an impressive popular hit with their comedy *Die Interessen der Bank können nicht die Interessen sein, die Lina Braake hat* (*The Bank's Interests Cannot Be Those of Lina Braake*). The film deals with the fate of an old woman who is forced out of her flat by the ruthless action of a credit bank, and is sent to an unpleasant old people's home. With the help of an elderly, incapacitated finance manipulator, she manages to outwit the bank and win a new home. There is wit and charm in this movie; in parts it recalls René Allio's *La vieille dame indigne*. It also contains cameo appearances from two of the country's most distinguished veteran players: Lina Carstens, who was in the film version of Kleist's *Zerbrochenem Krug* in 1937, plays the determined old lady, and Fritz Rasp, a screen heavy since the days of Fritz Lang, excels as the sneering financial expert. (Produced by U.L.M. Bernhard Sinkel Filmproduktion, Munich.)

Then Werner Herzog, whose *Aguirre, Wrath of God* attracted international attention, won the Special Jury Prize in Cannes for

Bruno S. in *JEDER FÜR SICH UND GOTT GEGEN ALLE*, Werner Herzog's prize-winning film, released throughout the world by Cine-International, Munich

The Enigma of Kaspar Hauser, a film concerned with the clash between the individual and a conservative society. Kaspar Hauser was "a wild child," found at the beginning of the Nineteenth century in southern Germany. Through a strange blend of cinematic visions and demonstrative, often symbolic re-enactments, Herzog attempts to portray the tragedy of animal innocence in a *bourgeois* society. His interesting film adds richness to the various literary and cinematic variations on the theme of *l'enfant sauvage*. (Produced by Werner Herzog, Munich.)

Like Herzog, newcomer Ulf Miehe completed his *John Glückstadt* (based on a novel) with the aid of a quality award from

A characteristic still from Jan Němec's much underrated satire, THE LOWCUT BACK, released through Cine-International, Munich

the Ministry of the Interior (DM 200,000–300,000). Munich producer Heinz Angermeyer, particularly interested in the successful arthouse film, gave him the chance to direct a social drama from a book by the North German poet Theodor Storm (1817–1888). It has Zolaesque overtones, and describes the fate of a small town worker in the stiff society of the previous century. His fight, his very existence as an outsider, exposes cracks in a narrow-minded community. (Produced by Independent Film, Heinz Angermeyer and Marran Film.)

Probably the finest artistic achievement of the German cinema in 1975 occurred through a collaboration between literature, film, and TV. Wim Wenders (*The Goalkeeper's Fear of the Penalty*) took a script by the prominent author Peter Handke and made *Falsche Bewegung* (*Wrong Move*), a modern version of Goethe's "Wilhelm Meister" theme. Wenders shows a melancholy journey through Germany by his young would-be author. The film is a fable, full of poetic elements; it is an odyssey of grief and helplessness. Quite apart from the symbolic film language, the performances are captivating. The jury for the annual Bundesfilm prize honoured the entire ensemble, Rüdiger Vogeler, Hans Christian Blech and Ivan Desny, with a "Golden Film Strip." (Produced by Solaris Film- und Fernsehproduktion, Munich, with Peter Genée.)

In the semi-documentary area, the Berlin producer and director Ottokar Runze was outstanding. He shot *Im Namen des Volkes* on location with the inmates of a penal institution. This fascinating film seeks to shed light

on the problems of court procedure and the execution of sentences, and makes use of the self-critical group work of the prisoners themselves. Runze's socio-political role switching, and his demonstration of an "argument free of domination," were among the most startling aspects of the 1974/75 season. (Produced by Ottokar Runze Filmproduktion, Berlin.)

In any survey of the film scene in the Federal Republic in 1975 there are a few promising signs for the future of cinema. Although the inclination towards investment in the production sector has fallen back, there are still about eighty features being produced each year. Attendances are stabilising, however. There are some 3,000 cinemas at-

tracting about 144 million spectators annually. In certain big cities there has been a noticeable increase in the number of spectators, mostly in the under-25 age group, and especially from the intelligentsia. At the same time TV is losing its appeal. There is a noticeable stalemate between the two media, which had long believed themselves to be locked in competition. Efforts to find a formula for constructive collaboration within the framework of the FFA have led to the above-mentioned agreement between the two TV bodies, ARD and ZDF, and the film industry. Television is investing some 34 million marks in projects of economic and artistic quality during the next few years. The results are anxiously awaited.

some recent films

UNORDNUNG UND FRÜHES LEID (Disorder and Early Sorrow). Script and dir: Franz Seitz, from the novel by Thomas Mann.

EISZEIT (Ice Age). Dir: Peter Zadek. Players: O. E. Hasse, Helmut Qualtinger, Heinz Bennent.

TAL DER WITWEN (Valley of the Widows). Script: Volker Vogeler, Thomas Schamoni. Dir: Vogeler. Players: Hugo Blanco, Tilo Brückner, Judy Stephen, Harry Baer. Prod: Michael Fengler/Volker Vogeler in Filmverlag der Autoren/Luis Megino P.C.

KARL MAY. Script and dir: Hans-Jürgen Syberberg. Players: Helmut Käutner, Kristina Söderbaum, Käthe Gold, Attila Hörbiger. Prod: TMS-Film, Munich.

DER MÄRTYRER—DR. KORCZAK UND SEINE KINDER (The Martyrs—Dr. Korczak and His Children). Script: Joseph Gross, from the novel by Alexander Ramati. Dir: Aleksander Ford. Phot: Jerzy Lipman. Players: Leo Genn, Orma Porat, Ohad Kaplan, Benjamin Völz. Prod: Artur Brauner, Berlin/Jacob Alkob, Tel Aviv.

DIE ANTWORT KENNT NUR DER WIND (The Answer's in the Wind). Script: Manfred Purzer. Dir: Alfred Vohrer. Phot: Petrus Schloemp. Players: Marthe Keller, Maurice Ronet, Karin Dor, Walter Kohut. Prod: Roxy-Film, Munich/Paris-Cannes-Film, Paris.

IN GEFAHR UND GRÖSSTER NOT BRINGT DER MITTELWEG DEN TOD (In Danger and Greatest Distress, the Middle Course Brings Death). Script and dir: Alexander Kluge and Edgar Reitz. Phot: Edgar Reitz and Alfred Hürmer. Players: Dagmar Böddrich, Jutta Winkelmann, Norbert Kentrup. Prod: RK-Film, Munich.

FALSCHE BEWEGUNG (Wrong Move). Script: Peter Handtke, based on "Wilhelm Meisters Lehrjahre," by Goethe. Dir: Wim Wenders. Phot: Robby Müller. Players: Rüdiger Vogler, Hanna Schygulla, Hans-Christian Blech, Ivan Desny. Prod: Solaris-Film/Peter Genée.

HAUPTLEHRER HOFER. Script and dir: Peter Lilienthal, from a story by Günther Herburger. Phot: Kurt Weber. Players: André Watt, Sebastian Bleisch, Kim Parnass, Gerhard Sprunkel. Prod: FFAT im Auftrag des WDR.

DAS NETZ. Dir: Manfred Purzer, from the novel by Hans Habe. Players: Mel Ferrer, Klaus Kinski, Andrea Rau. Prod: Roxy for Constantin Film.

DER STERNSTEINHOF. Prod: Roxy for Constantin Film.

POTATO FRITZ. Dir: Peter Schamoni.

ANSICHTEN EINES CLOWNS (The Clown). Dir: Vojtěch Jasný, from the novel by Heinrich Böll. Phot: Walter Lassally. Prod: Independent/MFG/WDR.

LINA BRAAKE UND DIE INTERESSEN DER BANK . . .

DIE VERLORENE EHRE DER KATHARINA BLUM. Dir: Volker Schlöndorff and Margarethe von Trotta. Players: Angela Winkler, Mario Adorf, Dieter Laser. Prod: Bioscop/Orion/WDR for CIC.

MITGIFT. Dir: Michael Verhoeven. Prod: Sentana/WDR.

DAS RUCKENDEKOLLETE. Dir: Jan Němec. Players: Kai Fischer, Barbara Neilsen, Hans von Borsody. Prod: FILIAG/FIP Munich.

DIE VERROHUNG DES FRANZ BLUM (The Brutalisation of Frank Bloom). Script: Burkhard Driest from his own novel. Dir: Reinhard Hauff. Players: Jürgen Prochnow, Eik Gallwitz, Burkhard Driest, Tilo Brückner. Prod: Bioscop-Filmproduktion, Munich.

INKI. Dir: George Moorse. Phot: Gerard Vandenberg. Players: Angelika Bender, Louis Waldon, Alexander McDonald. Prod: Barbara Moorse Workshop/Bayerischer Rundfunk.

DER LETZTE SCHREI. Dir: Robert van Ackeren. Phot: Dietrich Lohmann. Players: Barry Foster, Delphine Seyrig, Kirstie Pooley, Peter Hall, Udo Keir. Prod: Inter-West-Film, Berlin.

Art House Focus

The **Arsenal** (Welserstrasse 25, 1 Berlin 30) is one of Europe's most adventurous film theates, on a par with the NFT in London and the AFT in Washington. Each month the programmes are mouth-watering—not only films from all over the world, but also

seminars and retrospectives, and during the Berlin Festival the Freunde der deutschen Kinemathek is the guiding force behind the "Forum" of Young Cinema. Occasional booklets, researched with meticulous care, are issued to coincide with certain seasons at the Arsenal.

Members of the Arbeitsgemeinschaft Neue Deutscher Spielfilm-produzenten e.V.

Robert van Ackeren Filmproduktion
Kurfürstendamm 132A
1 Berlin 31.
action 1 GmbH, Gustav Ehmck
Bahnhofstrasse 100A
8032 Gräfelring.
Basis Film GmbH
Adolf-Martens-Str. 2A
1 Berlin 45.
Bioskop Film GmbH
Türkenstr. 95
8 Munich 40.
BMC-Film
Michael and Christian Blackwood
Schraudolphstr. 9
8 Munich 40.
Uwe Brandner Filmproduktion
Friedrich-Herschel-Str. 17
8 Munich 80.
Delta Circus 1
Ulf von Mechow
Hohenzollernstr. 3
1 Berlin 39.
DKS-Film
Kauzner & Selle oHG
Schellingstr. 33
8 Munich 40.
FFAT GmbH
Dr. Norbert Kückelmann—Peter Lilienthal
Franz-Joseph-Str. 9
8 Munich 40.
Filmverlag der Autoren
Tengstr. 37
8 Munich 40.
Film 16, Helmut Rings Filmproduktion
Pittingerstr. 23
8025 Unterhaching.
Roger Fritz Filmproduktion
Ohmstr. 8
8 Munich 40.

Gall Filmproduktion GmbH
Am Herrensee 10
8911 Pürgen.
GKS-Film- und Fernseh-Produktion
Karl Schedereit
Ohmstr. 16
8 Mucich 40.
Hallelujah Film GmbH
Türkenstr. 95
8 Munich 40.
Rob Houwer Film
Viktoriastr. 34
8 Munich 40.
Inter West Film GmbH
Wenzel Lüdecke
Mühlenstr. 52
1 Berlin 46.
Werner Herzog Filmproduktion
Lichtengerstr. 9
8 Munich 60.
Iduna-Film Produktionsgesellschaft & Co.
Amiraplatz 1
8 Munich 2.
Institut für Filmgestaltung Ulm e.V.
Am Hochstr. 8
79 Ulm.
Janus Film
Film- und Fernsehvertriebs GmbH
Paul-Ehrlich-Str. 24
6 Frankfurt am Main.
Kairos-Film
Dr. Alexander Kluge
Schumannstr. 64
6 Frankfurt am Main.
Roland Klick Filmproduktion
Isabellastr. 35
8 Munich 40.
Klaus Lemke Filmproduktion
Elisabethstr. 38
8 Munich 40.

Lux-Film
Boris von Borresholm
Mauerkircherstr. 18
8 Munich 27.
Vlada Majić KG Filmproduktion
Beethovenstr. 3
43 Essen.
Margo-Film
Marangosoff
Georgenstr. 53
8 Munich 40.
Barbara Moorse Workshop
Römerstr. 14
8 Munich 40.
Hansjürgen Pohland Filmproduktion
Forststr. 16
1 Berlin 37.
Edgar Reitz Filmproduktion
Agnesstr. 14
8 Munich 40.
Pik-7-Film
Karlsgarten 20
1 Berlin 44.
Christian Rischert Filmproduktion
Giselastr. 13
1 Munich 40.
Peter Schamoni Filmproduktion
Mauerkircherstr. 184
8 Munich 81.
Volker Schlöndorff Filmproduktion
Obermaierstr. 1
8 Munich 22.
Werner Schröter Filmproduktion
Krepelinstr. 63
8 Munich 40.
Haro Senft Filmproduktion
Siegesstr. 1
8 Munich 40.

Sentana Film GmbH
Herzog-Christoph-Str. 10
8022 Grünwald.
Isolde Stapenhorst Filmproduktion
8021 Icking.
Ula Stöckl Filmproduktion
Agnesstr. 14
8 Munich 40.
Hans-Rolf Strobel Filmproduktion
Viktor-Scheffel-Str. 19
8 Munich 40.
Studio 1 Werner Grassmann KG Filmproduktion
Heinrich-Barth-Str. 4
2 Hamburg 13.
Syrinx-Film
Horst Bienek
Isarweg 2
8012 Ottobrunn.
tango-film
Rainer Werner Fassbinder
Elisabethstr. 38
8 Munich 40.
Karin and Rolf Thome Filmproduktion
Uhlandstr. 46
1 Berlin 31.
tms-film
Dr. Hans-Jürgen Syberberg
Genter Str. 15A
8 Munich 40.
U.L.M. Filmproduktion III
Agnesstr. 14
8 Munich 40.
Visual-Film
Elke Haltaufderheide
Widenmayerstr. 1
8 Munich 22.
Bernhard Wicki Filmproduktion
Weisgerberstr. 2
8 Munich 40.

Members of the Verbandes Deutscher Spielfilmproduzenten e.V.

CCC-Filmkunst GmbH & Co., KG
Verl. Daumstr. 16
1 Berlin 20.
Corona-Filmproduktion GmbH
Freystr. 4
8 Munich 40.
KG Divina-Film GmbH & Co.
Karlsplatz 5
8 Munich 2.

Eichberg-Film GmbH
Herzog-Rudolf-Str. 1
8 Munich 22.
Ilse Kubaschewski Filmproduktion und Vertrieb
Karlsplatz 5
8 Munich 2.
International Film GmbH
Schützenstr. 1
8 Munich 2.

Lisa-Film GmbH
Widemayerstr. 48
8 Munich 22.
Neue Münchener Lichtspielkunst GmbH
Pienzenauer Str. 17
8 Munich 81.
Paramount-Orion-Filmproduktion GmbH
Herzogspitalstr. 13
8 Munich 2.
Rapid-Film GmbH
Schützenstr. 1
8 Munich 2.
Rex-Film Bloemer & Co.
Sachsendamm 65
1 Berlin 62.
Rialto-Film Preben Philipsen GmbH & Co. KG
Bismarckstr. 108
1 Berlin 12.
Roxy-Film GmbH & Co. KG
Schützenstr. 1
8 Munich 2.
Franz Seitz Filmproduktion
Beichstr. 8–9
8 Munich 40.
Studio-Film GmbH
Postfach 11 20
2106 Bendestorf Kr. Harburg.
Terra Filmkunst GmbH
Albert-Rosshauptr.-Str. 73
8 Munich 70.
Thalia-Film GmbH
Beichstr. 8–9
8 Munich 40.
Transcontinent-Filmproduktion GmbH
Marschallstr. 1
8 Munich 40.

Film Export Companies

Atlas International Film GmbH & Co.
Burgstr. 7
8 Munich 2.
Hans-Joachim Boldt,
Export-Import-Coproduktionen
Löwengrube 10
8 Munich 2.
Dr. Roland Cämmerer Filmvertrieb
Leopoldstr. 18
8 Munich 40.
Cine-International Filmvertrieb GmbH & Co.
Leopoldstr. 18
8 Munich 40.

Exportfilm Bischoff & Co. GmbH
Albert-Rosshaupter-Str. 73
8 Munich 70.
Gloria-Film Produktions- und Vertriebs GmbH & Co.
Karlsplatz 5
8 Munich 2.
Eginhart Hillenbrand
Pacellistr. 7
8 Munich 2.
Klann-Film GmbH & Co. Filmvertriebs KG
Bundesallee 35
1 Berlin 31.
Omnia Deutsche Film Export GmbH
Herzog-Rudolf-Str. 1
8 Munich 22.
Pegasus Film GmbH
Kurfürstendamm 229
1 Berlin 15.
Produktion 1 im Filmverlag der Autoren (PIFDA)
GmbH & Co.
Tengstr. 37
8 Munich 40.
Roxy-Film GmbH & Co. KG Export
Brienner Str. 1
8 Munich 2.
Hans Schubert Weltvertrieb
Pacellistr. 7
8 Munich 2.
Transocean International Film-und Fernseh GmbH
Brienner Str. 1
8 Munich 2.
Dieter-Wahl-Film
Poccistr. 3
8 Munich 2.

Other Useful Addresses

Export-Union der deutschen Filmindustrie e.V.
Langenbeckstr. 9
62 Wiesbaden.
Gilde Deutscher Filmkunst-Theater e.V.
Neureutherstr 29
8 Munich 40.
Freunde der deutschen Kinemathek e.V.
Welserstr. 25
1 Berlin 30.
(*Distribution, and Arsenal film theatre*)
Arbeitsgemeinschaft der Filmjournalisten e.V.
(*West German section of FIPRESCI*)
St. Martin-Str. 44
8 Munich 90.

GREEK FILM CENTRE

GREEK FILM CENTRE S.A.
- A Hellenic Industrial Development Bank Subsidiary Company.
- Production of movie and TV films, facilities to foreign producers.
- Complete technical and financial network and participation in foreign co-productions.

Greece

by Mirella Georgiadou

If the purpose of a domestic festival is to mirror all that is happening or going to happen in a country's cinema, then the Fifteenth Thessaloniki Festival, held exactly two months after the collapse of the junta regime, was a big success indeed. The atmosphere was similar to that of Cannes in 1968: discussions, heated contestations, new young film-makers with their enthusiastic and hyper-critical followers. The main targets were naturally censorship, authoritarian rules, police presence at the festival, the prize system, and preferential treatment to the "establishment" in seating allocation. There was, however, only one basic complaint: that they ceased to be regarded as "intruders" to the official events (as in junta times) and be given the right to participate in a democratic selection of the programme.

The selection itself (apart from the shorts, which were less interesting than last year) was very satisfactory, proving that Greek cinema is not lacking in either vitality, courage or variety. All except one of the ten features were by young newcomers and, despite being shot during the last and darkest months of the junta's rule, mostly dealt with politically taboo subjects (*Kierion, Megara, The Reason Why, Gazoros*). The two most exciting revelations, however, were *The Colours of the Rainbow* and *Model* (see reviews), both "non-engaged" works which carefully concealed their various messages. Finos Films' *The Trial of the Judges* represented the world of the commercial companies; an historical picture with political overtones (see IFG 75), it did not lack courage in either script or treatment, but was badly received due to its production by the older establishment. Unless the suggestion that Thessaloniki has two separate competitions (one for the new generation, the other for traditional cinema) is accepted, it is doubtful whether "commercial" producers and directors will risk presenting their works there in the future.

All parties are agreed, however, on two points. Firstly, the time is now ripe for a total reappraisal of the rigid censorship system which strangled the industry and press during the junta years (even IFG fell a victim of this policy: my report last year had several cuts and "optimistic ameliorations" imposed at the last minute). A new draft for the constitution is now being discussed in parliament; everyone in the industry will need to fight very hard to safeguard their rights and exclude restrictive measures such as script censorship, export bans, and censorship for adults Secondly, there is also a need for a general reform of the tax system. Since attendance has been sinking, it is clear that the economy is no longer influenced by the cinema's financial contribution, and it would thus be no great sacrifice for the state to reduce drastically the Entertainment Tax (an extraordinary 40% on admission tickets) and abolish all extra or special taxes.

The taxation of domestic films is another matter. Commercial film-makers claim that *all* Greek films should be exempt from charges if the state is really willing to revitalise the industry back to the golden days of the Sixties. Younger film-makers, however, are of the opinion that *only* quality or experimental films deserve aid and exemption, arguing that

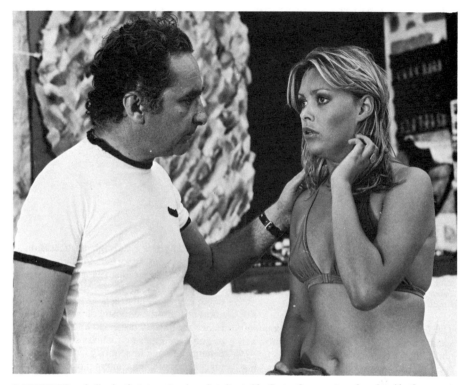

GANGSTERS, a thriller for the international market, directed by Costas Carayannis and produced by Carayannis-Caratzopoulos Co.

the state protection granted to the big companies during the junta era led to a monstrous situation: while it is clear that quality and art films will play a bigger role in the future in Greek cinema, the money-prizes and subsidies they receive at the moment are of no value, particularly when combined with the problems of financing, distribution and lack of control on imports. Statistics speak eloquently here: about a dozen new foreign productions are premiered each week in the Athens-Piraeus area, against one or two domestic films (many sex thrillers, the last refuge of the local industry).

During the first four months of the 1974/75 season the three biggest foreign box-office hits—*Z, State of Siege, La grande bouffe*—achieved a total of 774,880 admissions, while the top three commercial Greek pictures (out of twenty-nine released)—*The Trial of the Judges, A Law-Abiding Citizen, Dream-Lovers* (all by Finos

Films)—scored 210,245 entries. Four independently produced quality films—*Megara, Kierion, The Reason Why, Gazoros*—scraped together 29,276.

In a first effort to overcome the present crisis the Ministry of Industry appointed the right man at the right place: the Greek Film Centre (the old General Film Enterprises rebaptised to stress its break with the junta past) is now run by George Tzavellas, the eminent director of *Antigone* and *The False Pound Sterling*. A man of rare talent, intelligence and energy, much admired by both young and old, Tzavellas is expected to perform wonders of organisation. The Greek Film Centre's role will largely consist of granting low-interest loans and offering co-production opportunities and technical facilities to both Greek and foreign, commercial and independent film-makers.

O THIASOS
(The Troupe)

Script and direction: Thodoros Angelopoulos. Photography (colour): Giorgos Arvanitis. Music: Loukianos Kilaidonis. Players: Eva Kotamanidou, Vangelis Kazan, Stratos Pahis, Aliki Georgouli, Petros Zarkadis, Kiriakos Katrivanos, Grigoris Evangelatos, Kostas Stiliaris, Maria Vasiliou. 230 mins.

The Greek director Thodoros Angelopoulos seems to be increasing his range with each film. After *Reconstruction* and *Days of '36* comes *The Troupe*, nearly four hours long, which attempts nothing less than an impressionistic political history of Greece from 1939 to 1951—but not necessarily in that order. Angelopoulos's protagonists are a rather tatty little theatrical company who take their play "Golfo the Shepherdess" around the villages and are constantly interrupted by the disruptive intrusion of outside events. As a symbolic device, it works well, and the director adds an extra dimension by giving the company's leading actress some of the characteristics (and family problems) of Elektra.

The film's main achievement is to translate the essential edginess of a society which has passed through a succession of *régimes*, veering from Left to Right, into images which are as disturbing as the events themselves. One group of insurgents sweep down empty night streets to be answered by another from the opposite direction; political rallies are quickly dispersed by a distant rally of gun-fire; opposing factions shout out their defiance in song in a smoky café. Using long takes and sweeping camera movements in the Jancsó manner, Angelopoulos builds up some impressive visual *coups*, holding great crowds of people in long shot and then isolating his troupe as they gamely chant their way down a snowy hillside. Occasionally, near the beginning, the stylisation and extremely slow tempo verge on the pretentious but, as the film moves into its final stages, one complex piece of stage management follows another and the saga of betrayal and revenge takes on the aspect of a bitter, modern Odyssey. Superb colour photography, plus three direct-to-camera monologues which are both daringly placed and movingly performed.

JOHN GILLETT

From the widely-acclaimed, four-hour film by Angelopoulos, THE TROUPE

MODEL

Script and direction: Kostas Sfikas. Photography (colour): George Kavayas. Set: Sfikas, Kavayas. Factory-yard and figure construction: Nikos Papadakis, Yannis Papadakis, Vasilis Spahos. Designers: Zoi Keramea, Vanghelis Hrysovitsiotis, Hristos Santamouris. Screenwriter: Thanos Grammenos. Rhythm: Leni Keramea. Produced by George Papalios, Anna Sfika and the Contemporary Cinema Co. 105 mins.

This was the revelation of the 1974 Thessaloniki Festival, an experimental work revolutionary in style and concept, received by the majority of the local audience as an indecipherable enigma. The film has no sound or actors, and only a single set representing a factory yard: robot-like faceless human figures walk slowly by a long corridor, plastic household items forming the production chain. Kostas Sfikas, who made a great impression some years back with his shorts *Thira* and *Dawn over Thira*, has attempted to X-ray our civilisation on film, analysing the implacable process that transforms mankind into negotiable goods and mere accessories of an industrial machine.

MIRELLA GEORGIADOU

TA HROMATA TIS IRIDOS
(The Colours of the Rainbow)

Script and direction:Nikos Panayatopoulos.
Photography (colour): Nikos Kavoukidis. Editing: Takis
Davlopoulos. Music: Stamatis Spanoudakis. Set dec:
Dionisis Fotopoulos. Players: Nikitas Tsakiroglou,
Vanghelis Kazan, George Dialegmenos, Helena Kirana,
Takis Voulalas, Christina, Anghelos Theodoropoulos,
Flore Derain, George Moschidis, Alekos Deliyannis.
Produced by George Papalios. 100 mins.

By far the most "finished" work, artistically
and thematically, in current Greek cinema,
The Colours of the Rainbow deserves special

*THE COLOURS OF THE RAINBOW, directed by
Nikos Panayotopoulos*

attention both for its confirmation of
Panayatopoulos's mastery of the medium and
for its demonstration that it is possible to
make films which fill the gap between art and
entertainment. The story concerns the sudden
appearance one day of a mysterious stranger
who interrupts filming of a commercial: the
man disappears into the sea and while
everybody is encouraged by the authorities to
try and put the disturbing incident out of their
minds, a member of the crew, a musician,
carries out a lone investigation which leads
him in search of his true self. The film ends
with the musician disappearing into the sea,
like the ghost he was seeking.

To quote the director himself, the film is
an operetta, with a libretto and a mocking
hommage to the American gangster film and
western. In approaching his material from
this angle, however, Panaytopoulos takes the
route followed nowadays by French directors
prominent during the Sixties: there is a distinctly Truffautesque flavour about the highly
flexible scenario—its light-heartedness,
refined sensuality, piquant humour, relaxed
manner and dexterity in changing moods.
Nikos Kavoukidis's photography is first-rate,
and praise is due to the stage actor Nikitas
Tsakiroglou for interpreting a character
straight from the comic-book strips.
MIRELLA GEORGIADOU

recent and forthcoming films

ANATOMIA MIAS LISTIAS (The Gangsters). Script: Thanassis Livaditis. Dir: Kostas Karayannis. Mus: Yannis Spanos. Players: Sereta Wilson, Gareth Forwood, Kostas Karageorgis, Alekos Tzanetakos, Minas Hristidis. For Carayannis-Caratzopoulos. A thriller for the international market, shot in Greek and English.

HRONIKO TIS KIRIAKIS (A Sunday Chronicle). Dir: Takis Kanellopoulos. The eighth picture by the acclaimed romantic poet of Sixties Greek cinema (*The Sky, The Excursion*). A nostalgic throw-back to the world of childhood, in six episodes.

DI'ASIMANDON AFORMIN (The Reason Why). Script and dir: Tasos Psarras. Phot: Stavros Hasapis. Edit: Takis Davlopoulos. Mus: folksongs (arr. by Domna Samiou). Set dec. and cost: Julia Stavridou. Players: Mihalis Boyaridis, Stelios Kapatos, Byron Tsaboulas, Vana Fitsori, George Fourniadis, Lazaros Aslanidis, Hristos Fitsoris. For George Papalios. 120 mins. An honourable *début*, and at times very convincing piece of engaged cinema, by a young director from Thessaloniki with three outstanding shorts to his credit. With stage actors mingling with native residents, the films tells in a realistic manner of a true event in Northern Greece back in 1953, when a tobacco-planter was murdered for betraying a community's pact of solidarity not to sell their product to buyers offering low prices.

THE NOAH. Script, dir and prod: Daniel Bourlas. Phot: Jerry Kalogeratos. Players: Robert Strauss, Geoffrey Holder, Sally Kirkland, David Bourlas. For The Noah Films. 107 mins. An ambitious project by Greek-American Bourlas, a political parable dealing with the atomic threat. Noah, a corporal in the American Army and the last man alive on earth, assumes a God-like role and recreates a new civilisation. As history repeats itself, however, he destroys his creation.

MEGARA. Script and dir: Sakis Maniatis, George Tseberopoulos. Phot (part colour) and edit: Sakis Maniatis. 75 mins. For George Tseberopoulos. Reportage about the last days of a rich rural village near Athens, evacuated to make way for an oil refinery.

GAZOROS SERRON. Script and dir: Dimitris Hatzopoulos. Phot: Vanghelis Iliopoulos. Mus: George Papadakis. For "Cinetic" Ap. Papaefstathiou & Co. 77 mins. Documentary about a village in Northern Greece, made on a budget of about 100,000 drachmas.

KIERION. Script: Kostas Sfikas, Dimosthenis Theos. Dir and prod: Theos. Phot: George Panousopoulos. Edit: Vanghelis Serdaris. Players: Anestis Vlahos, Dimos Starenios, Stavros Tornes, Helen Theofilou, Elli Xanthaki, Kiriakos Katsourakis, Titika Vlahopoulou, Kostas Sfikas, Grigoris Masallas. For George Papalios.

SONGS OF FIRE, in liberated Athens. Melina Mercouri is in the group

86 mins. This prize-winner at Thessaloniki was started in 1966, but after filming was interrupted by the coming of the colonels, the first version was completed outside Greece and shown at Venice in 1968. The technical defects in this second "re-arranged" version give the film an "unfinished" quality which curiously reinforces its strength. Many questions are left open about the political motives behind the mysterious death of an American journalist. The film stands between the political thrillers of Costa-Gavras and the polemical pictures of Rosi and Petri.

I FONISSA (The Murderess). Script: Dimos Theos, Kostas Ferris, from the novel by Alexandros Papadiamantis. Dir: Ferris. Phot (colour): Stavros Hasapis. Edit: Yanna Spiropoulou. Mus: Stavros Logaridis. Art dir: Tasos Zografos. Players: Maria Alkeou, Dimitra Zeza, Fivos Taxiarhis, Natalia Alkeou, Elpidoforos Gotsis, Kostas Darlasis, Helen Ioannou, Anthi Kariofilli. For Semeli Films. Adaptation of Papadiamantis's modern masterpiece by a young director who worked for seven years with French film-makers like Jean-Daniel Pollet and Philippe Garrel. About an old peasant women on Skiathos who murders young women. Exotic, overpowering visuals.

TRAGOUDIA TIS FOTIAS (Songs of Fire). Dir: Nikos Koundouros. Phot (colour): Nikos Kavoukidis, Nikos Adamopoulos, Paflos Filippou, Sirrakos Danalis, Nikos Gardelis, Sakis Maniatis, Aristidis Karydis Fuchs. Edit: Fuchs, Koundouros. For Finos Films. After seven years of self-exile Koundouros (*Young Aphrodites, The Face of Medusa*) returned last summer to make this feature documentary about the first days of liberation from the junta. Film opens with two concerts by Theodorakis,

Yannis Markopoulos, Stavros Xarhakos and other popular composers at the Panathinaikon and Karaiskaki sports grounds. Koundouros covers the entire emotional spectrum in his portrayal of a nation suddenly released from fear and restraint.

Greek Producers and Distributors

C. Carayannis-A. Caratzopoulos
42 Themistokleous St.
Athens.
A notable director and producer, Carayannis and his associate have in preparation several films for the international (mainly British and American) market. In the distribution field the firm has scored many successes, such as with Pontecorvo's *Battle of Algiers* and Costa-Gavras's *Z*, the top money-maker of the season.

Th. Damaskinos-V. Mihailides Co.
96 Akadimias St.
Athens.
Distributors.

Finos Films
53 Chiou St.
Athens.
The oldest production company in Greece, owning two stages and up-to-date laboratories and equipment. There are many Finos productions dubbed into English and French available for the international market.

George Papalios
167 Alkiviadou St.
Piraeus.
A shipowner, Papalios entered the production market with several shorts and features directed by the Seventies' "new wave".

United Artists of Greece and Cinema International (Universal and Paramount) representatives
4 Gambetta St.
Athens.

Art House Focus

There are three good art cinemas in Athens: Alkyonis, Alex and Studio. **Alkyonis** and **Alex**, which operate under the same direction, presented several Russian classics in their 1974/75 season (among others Eistenstein's *October*, *Battleship Potemkin*, *Ivan the Terrible* and *Bezhin Meadow*, and Dovzhenko's *Earth*), the Russian *Hamlet* and *Othello*, a

week dedicated to the recent production of six Soviet republics, Munk's *Man on the Track*, Pasolini's *Teorema*, Buñuel's *La fièvre monte à El Pao*, Oshima's *The Ceremony*, and several Greek features like *Songs of Fire* by Nikos Koundouros, *Face to Face* by Roviros Manthoulis and *Bloko* by Ado Kyrou. After the relaxation of censorship, **Studio** specialised in first-run showings of political pictures from Brazil, Chile (the University of Santiago's documentary *When the People Awake* and Patricia Guzman's *La repuesta de Octubre*), the U.S.A. (among others, Emile de Antonio's *In the Year of the Pig*, *Millhouse: A White Comedy*, Linda Firestone's *Attica*, Pintoff's *Dynamite Chicken*), France (Godard's *Les carabiniers*) and Underground classics like Shirley Clarke's *Connection*. A small *salle* upstairs, screening classics from all over the world (Dreyer's *La passion de Jeanne d'Arc*, Christensen's *Witchcraft through the Ages*, Buster Keaton's comedies, etc.), is open free to Studio's audience.

Hongkong and Taiwan

by Verina Glaessner

The flood of martial arts films that made noticeable dents in Western markets in 1972 and reached boom proportions in 1973 brought the Hongkong-based film industry to international notice in a way that previous sporadic screenings at festivals—Chu Shih-ling's *The Secret History of the Ching Court* at Locarno in 1950, the first post-war Hongkong film to be shown in Europe, and Shaw Brothers' *Magnificent Concubine* (by Li Han-hsiang) at Cannes in 1962—could never have hoped to. The films of the charismatic Bruce Lee blazed a trail that both Chinese and Western directors and producers strove to rival and exploit. Inevitably the boom ran itself into the ground—but not before it had revealed a lively popular film industry to rival that of Hollywood in the Thirties and Forties, not only in sheer volume of films produced but in richness, inventiveness and sheer enthusiastic response to the possibilities of the medium.

Historically the Hongkong film industry is a refugee one. The island provided a haven for theatre people fleeing Canton in the Twenties who found themselves drawn to the new art of cinema; for those fleeing Japanese aggression in North China during the Thirties; after the War, for radicals chafing under Kuomintang repression; and finally, after the liberation of Peking, for those film-makers, performers and businessmen unable or unwilling to come to terms with the stringent requirements of the new *régime*. Inevitably it was in Hongkong rather than in the mainland studios that the seeds of Chinese cinema that had burgeoned in Shanghai and other Chinese studios developed, and developed with a notable sense of urgency in the treatment of historical, national and social themes. The pre-occupation with classic literary subjects, myths and folklore can be traced back to Shanghai in the Twenties. The swordplay *genre* that flourished so richly during the mid- and late Sixties can be seen to have derived from the sword-bearing tales of knight errantry mingled with elements of the fantastic and the romantic that were enormously successful during the Thirties. Likewise, the thread of nationalism and anti-Japanese sentiment present in both the martial arts films and historical melodramas finds a parallel in the films made in the face of the Japanese invasion.

The Hongkong industry was the first to recover after the war, and by the late Fifties something like the current film production structure had emerged, with the Shaw Brothers' empire on the one hand, balanced by Motion Picture and General Investments' Cathay Limited (whose studios and position in the league devolved upon Golden Harvest in 1970) on the other; around them, a number of patriotic production companies, most notably The Great Wall Film Company, of varying ambitiousness. For a time The Great Wall led in technical sophistication until, during the early Sixties, Shaw Brothers embarked upon a deliberate policy of technical improvement, lavishing large (by local standards) budgets and much care on remakes of classic Chinese tales. The arrival of sound had led to the development of an exportable Mandarin cinema alongside a popular local Cantonese cinema. In 1962 Hongkong produced some 303 feature films, of which 224 were in

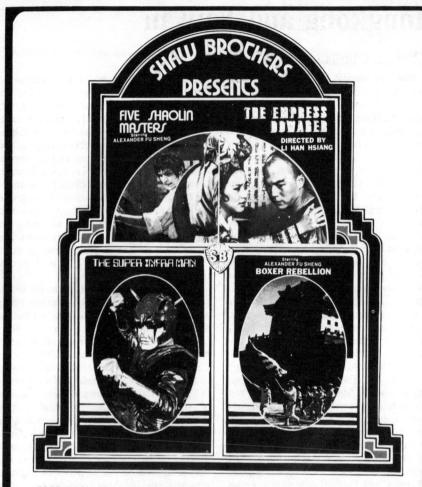

SHAW BROTHERS PRESENTS

FIVE SHAOLIN MASTERS
Starring ALEXANDER FU SHENG

THE EMPRESS DOWAGER
DIRECTED BY LI HAN HSIANG

THE SUPER INFRA MAN

Starring ALEXANDER FU SHENG
BOXER REBELLION

FOREIGN SALES: SHAW BROTHERS (H.K.) LTD.,
                  LOT 220, CLEAR WATER BAY ROAD, KOWLOON, HONG KONG.

FROM SHAWS STUDIO: COMPLETE WITH MODERN FACILITIES — THE LARGEST SELF
                      CONTAINED STUDIO IN THE FAR EAST.

Ti Lung as Tsai Te-chung in Chang Ch'eh's SHAOLIN WU TSU (FIVE SHAOLIN MASTERS)

Cantonese and 42 in Mandarin. Some ten years later the proportion had more than reversed itself. Cantonese films had all-but disappeared from the scene, only to be revived in 1973.

Production, however, remained fairly constant through the early Seventies, if at a numerically lower level than that of the decade earlier (the Cantonese films were often made swiftly on low budgets), apart from a distinct bulge coinciding exactly with the breakthrough of "*kung-fu* movies" into the world market. A total of 137 films were made and released in 1970/71; 126 in 1971/72; 133 in 1972/73; 201 in 1973/74; 148 in 1974/75. (These figures include all films passed by the Hongkong Government Film Censor for distribution both on television and theatrically. They do not include films made in Taiwan, which for the five years stand at 97, 68, 41, 44 and 34 respectively.) In 1966 attendance figures stood at a healthy 98,538,730, a number which declined gradually but unmistakably to 71,279,000 in 1972/73. No figures are available for the next two years as the entertainment tax that provided the source of this information, was abolished. However, it has been estimated that there has been a drop of some 36% in theatre grosses. Likewise the number of cinemas in Hongkong declined from 107 in 1968/70 to 80 in March 1975, with a total of 100,825 seats between

them. The contracting attendance figures and cinema closures were due in large part to rising tickets prices, escalating land values and, most recently, an increasingly desperate and painful unemployment problem. The modestly-budgeted film could still recoup its costs and with luck make a healthy profit on the home market alone. None, however, could still count on the bonanza of international distribution but it was increasingly the more ambitious films that looked to the financial support which, in the current situation, only a wider distribution could guarantee. It remains to be seen whether these films will be able to hold on to the position in the international market established (through brilliance, luck or good management) by the haphazard array of action films which preceded them.

The year 1974/75 found the industry deprived of a sure-fire box office formula. Producers laid off film-workers and expensive

stars and sold films to television. They also began shooting television spin-offs, several of which, as it turned out, proved not at all to be despised. Even the super-light *Gossip Street* (Shaws) carried a degree of charm, while Ch'u Yüan's *House of 72 Tenants* and *Hongkong 73* turned out to be witty social comedies marked by vast galleries of characters and a measure of sly social comment. Another version of the spin-off appeared following the success of the Japanese Toho-style Superman series on television. Shaw Brothers, taking their cue from the Golden Harvest/Concord co-production with Warner Brothers, *Enter the Dragon*, embarked on a series of co-productions with European and American companies, producing films which generally tended to embed martial arts elements in horror, western or comic contexts. If anything, these films simply proved the intractability of martial arts material divested of its very particular moral universe. Lo Wei, director of two of the Bruce Lee films, after having shot a number of winning if slightly erratic comedies for Golden Harvest, left that company to set up Lo Wei's Motion Picture Company with plans to shoot some six to eight films per year for world-wide distribution (three were scheduled for June 1975). Golden Harvest's Raymond Chow meanwhile strengthened the company's role in distribution by taking over Panasia and forging links with Towa, the company which had handled the Lee films in Japan.

Meng Fei, Fu Sheng, Ti Lung, David Chiang and Ch'i Kuan-chün in SHAOLIN WU TSU (FIVE SHAOLIN MASTERS), directed by Chang Ch'eh

Otherwise production runs the gamut from crime thrillers (some based on fact like *The Big Storm*, an examination of recent police corruption scandals, directed by Wu Tze-yuan), to historical and contemporary melodramas, or to love stories—such as the bland Hollywood-style works which stream from the hands of Pai Ching-jui—comedy series such as the "Ah Fook" films, and sex farces of various descriptions. Mainstream Hongkong-Taiwan film-making, in fact, spans the spectrum from the lively to the unambitious, blandly imitative, opportunistic and vacuously formular. More fruitful are the forays into the horror *genre*, social comedy and the historical romance, revived ambitiously in Li Han-hsiang's *The Empress Dowager*. The horror film cannibalises influences as diverse as the Japanese ghost story and Friedkin's *The Exorcist*, blatantly and not unentertainingly remade as *The Devil in Her* by Chang Sen. One of the most characteristic is a frantic compendium of tales called *Blood Reincarnation*, directed by Ting Shan-hsi, which begins on a note of unforgettable hysteria and progresses by degrees to tell a dignified story of the fantastic. Both these films were made by small independent companies and despite the creeping effects of austerity the period has been marked by a continued flowering of independently generated film-making. Michael Hui had an enormous box office success with his *Games Gamblers Play* (the only locally-produced film of 1974 to outgross foreign product), following an earlier appearance in Li Han-hsiang's *The Warlord* and its sequels.

Despite an atmosphere of economic uncertainty the work of directors like King Hu, Li Han-hsiang, Chang Ch'eh and others continue to point quite decisively at the existence of a film culture of undeniable strength and sophistication. King Hu's *The Fate of Lee Khan* proved to be a finely-judged work, a film of wit and perceptiveness in its exploration of the struggles of its primarily female protagonists. This was followed by *The Valiant Ones* and the first public showing of the complete version of *A Touch of Zen* in competition at Cannes in 1975.* Chang

* As of Spring 1975 Hu is embarking on a series of new productions. *I Go, Oh No* is to be about Chinese immigrants employed to work on the railroad in the United States. *Raining in the Mountains* is a philosophic parable in which Buddhism, Confuciansim and Taoism confront each other and are in turn confronted most devastatingly by the incursion of Christianity and Western technology. Two other projects are also in the wind: *The Monkey Goes West* and *The Red Robe General*.

Ch'eh, a Shaw studio director since 1963, set up a Shaw-financed company in 1973 and launched an extraordinary series of productions including *Boxer Rebellion: The Coalition of Eight Foreign Armies against China* which examined a long-neglected subject, and most notably his "Tales of the Shaolin Monastery," a series of films which include *Heroes Two*, the fierce and brilliant *Men from the Monastery*, *Shaolin Martial Arts*, the less successful—artistically not financially—*Five Shaolin Masters* and *Disciples of Shaolin*, films which proved the culmination of the martial arts *genre*. *Men from the Monastery* ranks with the finest work Chang has produced in its examination of the dynamic metamorphosis of history to myth framed in his normal visually and morally satisfying style. Chang is a director preoccupied with the potentials of cinema to explore specifically Chinese subjects. Myth was overtly examined in his *Na Cha the Great* and *The Fantastic Magic Baby*, and as of May 1975 he was engaged in preparing *Hell*, a film merging national drama, action and dance around a mythic plot. Other directors who have been building reputations for themselves include Ch'u Yüan, Li Hsing, Lung Kang and Chang Mei-chün. One can only hope that the growing serious estimation in which the cinema of Hongkong is coming to be held internationally will lead to a great local awareness of the island's film heritage, and that rapid steps will be taken to salvage and preserve films that find themselves in jeopardy once their commercial value has expired.

(Grateful acknowledgements to Mr. T. H. Cheah for help in translating Chinese source material.)

HSIA NÜ
(A Touch of Zen)

Script: King Hu, based on "The Magnanimous Girl" by P'u Sung-ling. Direction: King Hu (=Hu Chin-ch'üan). Photography (colour, scope): Hua Hui-ying. Music: Ng Tai-Kwong. Assistant Director: Miao T'ien. Players: Hsü Feng, Shih Chün, Pai Ying, T'ien P'eng. Hsüeh Han, Ch'iao Hung, Chang Ping-yü, Ts'ao Chien, Wan Chung-shan, Miao T'ien, Chia Lu-shih, Wan Jei, Han Ying-chieh. For Union Film Company. 180 mins.

King Hu's fourth film as a director, *A Touch of Zen*, made in 1968 but only released in its complete form in 1975, is a remarkable and assured reflection on the mesh of historic and philosophic forces that define Chinese culture. Set in the Ming dynasty, a favourite period for Hu and one marked by corruption and the development of a particularly lethal secret police, the film centres on the strange encounter between a local artist and the mysterious woman who takes up residence in a nearby abandoned frontier fortress. The story formed the gist of P'u Sung-ling's cryptic tale in his collection of "Strange Stories from a Chinese Studio," and in filming it Hu has momentously enlarged the scope of the original: *A Touch of Zen* becomes the embodiment of a meditation on philosophy in the form of a ghost story, with full attention paid to the expressive force of the natural landscape through which his protagonists move, and in which Taoism, Confucianism and Buddhism are related to a historical background of political and historical treachery. The central *motif* is the deceptiveness of appearances. Much of the action

A characteristically spectacular and imaginative set-up from King Hu's A TOUCH OF ZEN

takes place in the dark, by torch light, in the confines of the ruined fortress, where visibility is hampered by swirling mists: an environment in which intellectual confidence rings very hollow indeed and in which zen, in the shape of the band of monks whose path crosses and recrosses that of our naive hero, is seen as the portentous disciplining of natural forces. In common with *The Fate of Lee Khan*, *A Touch of Zen* is built around sudden flurries of action that escalate into violence, in which the martial arts are depicted with full regard to their supernatural aspects, and of which the consequences are ever more critical. In its scope, in its technical brilliance and directorial precision and in its evocative performances, especially those of King Hu's regulars Hsü Feng and Pai Ying, *A Touch of Zen* emerges as a major discovery and certainly a landmark in the history of Hongkong cinema.

VERINA GLAESSNER

KUEI MAH SUENG SING (Games Gamblers Play)

Script: Michael Hui, Liu Tien. Direction: Hui. Music: Samuel Hui. Players: Michael Hui, Samuel Hui, Betty Ting P'ei, Lisa Lu (=Lu Yen), James Wong (=Huang Chan), Roy Ch'iao (=Ch'iao Hung), Lu Lan, Li Kun. Produced by Raymond Chow. For Hui's Production Company/Golden Harvest. 100 mins.

Games Gamblers Play is a deceptively broad Cantonese social comedy distinguished not only by its phenomenal box-office success but by the edge and sharpness with which Michael Hui mines and exposes one particularly raw nerve of Hongkong society, illuminating a droll and distinctly quixotic social panorama. His film fastens on gambling as an obsessive fact of life, anchoring its narrative around the wayward progress of the partnership (forged, appropriately, in gaol) between Wen (played by Michael Hui), a confirmed recidivist first glimpsed breaking rocks under the watchful eye of the armed guard, and his ingenuous straightman played by Samuel Hui. Throughout the film the protagonists attempt to relate to various archetypal heroic figures of Chinese lore; the gap provides a source of amusement but desperation is never more than a fraction beneath the surface. The film's scenes of comic fantasy escalate revealingly and naturally from a recognisably grim and realistic environment: jobs are pathetically dead-end or plainly non-existent, the dice is firmly stacked in favour of the other guy. The finale, in which Wen escapes the clutches of the gang by running happily into the waiting arms of the law, suggests that the options open are slim in the extreme. The mirage of a fortune dangles before our fallen heroes as seductive as it is unreachable; the big game, Hui's film suggests, is being played elsewhere. Several sequences are particularly resonant in this way—especially those shot within the casino itself, a suggestively all-embracing and claustrophobic structure, and those within the prison. *Games Gamblers Play*, despite its occasional roughness, is a fair and amusing portrait of the hero in non-heroic guise, working efficiently on both a thematic and a broad slapstick level. It is a film that reveals a fine hand for social satire and bodes extremely well for Michael Hui's future productions.

VERINA GLAESSNER

new and forthcoming films

CHUNG LIEH T'U (The Valiant Ones). Script and dir: King Hu (=Hu Chin-ch'üan). Players: Pai Ying, Hsü Feng, Ch'iao Hung. For King Hu Film Productions.

YING CH'UN KO CHIH FENG-PO (The Fate of Lee Khan). Script and dir: King Hu. Players: Li Li-hua, Hsü Feng, Angela Mao (=Mao Ying), Ch'iao Hung, Pai Ying, Hu Chin, Helen Ma (=Ma Hai-lun), T'ien Feng, Shang-kuan Yen-erh. For King Hu Film Productions.

PA KUO LIEN-CHÜN (Boxer Rebellion). Script: I K'uang. Dir: Chang Ch'eh. Asst. dir: Wu Ma. Players: Fu Sheng, Li Li-hua, Hu Chin, Ch'i Kuan-chün. For Chang's Film Company.

HUNG HAI-ERH (The Fantastic Magic Baby). Dir: Chang Ch'eh. Players: Ting Hua-ch'ung, Hu Chin, Liu Chung-ch'ün. For Chang's Film Company.

HUNG CH'ÜAN HSIAO TZU (Disciples of Shaolin). Script: I K'uang. Dir: Chang Ch'eh. Players: Fu Sheng, Ch'i Kuan-chün. For Chang's Film Company.

MA-K'O P'O-LO (Marco Polo). Script: I K'uang. Dir: Chang Ch'eh. Players: Shih Szu, Ch'i Kuan-chün, Richard Harrison. For Chang's Film Company.

TI-YÜ (Hell). Dir: Chang Ch'eh. Players: David Chiang (=Chiang Ta-wei), Li Lin-lin (in episode *T'ien-shang/Paradise*); Fu Sheng, Chen Ni (in episode *Jen chien/Earth*); Shih Szu, Li Yi-min (in episode *Ti-yü/Hell*). For Chang's Film Company.

PA TAO LOU TZU (The Eight Path Tower—working English translation). Script: I K'uang. Dir: Chang Ch'eh. Players: David Chiang, Ti Lung.

TIEN CHYE EE PIE CHU (The Last Message). Script and dir: Michael Hui (=Hsü Kuan-wen). Players: Michael Hui, Samuel Hui (=Hsü Kuan-chieh), Joseph Ku (=Ku Chia-hui), Eileen Humphreys. For Hui's Film Company.

CH'ING KUO CH'ING CH'ENG (The Empress Dowager). Script and dir: Li Han-hsiang. Players: Lisa Lu (=Lu Yen), Ti Lung, Hsiao Yao, David Chiang, Ivy Ling Po, T'ien Ni. For Shaw Brothers.

HSÜEH TI TZU (The Flying Guillotine). Script: I K'uang. Dir: Ho Meng-hua. Players: Ch'en Kuan-t'ai. For Shaw Brothers.

CH'OU WEN (Scandal). Dir: Li Han-hsiang. Players: Michael Hui, Tanny (=T'ien Ni), Wang Sheng. For Shaw Brothers.

WU T'U WU MIN (Land of the Undaunted). Script: Chang Yung-hsiang. Dir: Li Hsing. Players: Alan Tang (=Teng Kuang-jung), Ch'in Han, Lin Feng-chiao, Wang Yin. For Ma's Film Co.

CHIN FEN SHEN-HSIEN SHOU (The Girl with the Dexterous Touch). Script: I K'uang. Dir: Lo Wei. Players: Chen Chen, Ch'in Hsiang-lin, T'ien Feng, K'o

Chün-hsiung, Lo Wei. For Lo Wei Motion Picture Company.

HSIAO SHANTUNG TAO HSIANGKANG (Shantung Man in Hongkong). Script and dir: Lo Wei. Players: Li K'un, Cheng Shao-ch'iu. For Lo Wei Motion Picture Company.

CHIH TAO HUANG LUNG (The Man from Hongkong). Dir: Wang Yu, Brian Trenchard-Smith. Players: Wang Yu, George Lazenby. For Golden Harvest-BEF.

TA CH'IEN SHIH-CHIEH (My Wacky, Wacky World). Dir: Ting Shan-hsi. Players: Wang Yu, K'o Chün-hsiung, Helen Pan (=P'an Ping-ch'ang). For Golden Harvest.

LIEH SHIH CHI HUA (Operation Regina—working title). Dir: Ting Shan-hsi. Players: Angela Mao, George Lazenby, Wang Yu, T'ien Ni, Helen Pan, K'o Chün-hsiung, Don Berry, Judith Brown. For Golden Harvest.

King Hu

Production and Distribution Companies

Shaw Brothers (HK) Ltd.
Lot 220, Clear Water Bay Road
Kowloon, Hongkong.

Golden Harvest
Room 1412 Tung Ying Building
100 Nathan Road
Kowloon, Hongkong.

Lo Wei Motion Picture Co
Block A, 12F, Milton Mansion
96 Nathan Road
Kowloon, Hongkong.

Ma's Film Company
1 Kwai Chau Street
Kowloon, Hongkong.

Fung Ming Film Co
39 Broadcasting Drive
5th Floor, Block E
Kowloon, Hongkong.

Seasonal Film Corporation
375–381 Nathan Road,
Honour House
15th Floor, Block 5
Kowloon, Hongkong.

Summit Film Productions Ltd
8–10 Granville Road
Prosperity House, Room 802
Tsim Sha Tsui
Kowloon, Hongkong.

Crystalart (HK) Ltd
210 Prince Edward Road
1st Floor
Kowloon, Hongkong.

Park Film (HK) Ltd
Room A, Ho On Mansion,
15th Floor
107 Austin Road
Kowloon, Hongkong.

Chang's Film Co
79 Waterloo Road, 8/F, Room 61
Kowloon, Hongkong.

King Hu Productions
15D Fa Po Street
Yau Yat Chuen, Garden City
Kowloon, Hongkong.

Goldig Films (HK)
Room 2, Block B,
Ho Hung Hing Bldg
12th Floor
Tsim Sha Tsui
Kowloon, Hongkong.

Lo Mar Film Co
141 Prince Edward Road
11th Floor, Block F
Kowloon, Hongkong.

First Film Organisation Ltd
Burlington House, 14th Floor, A–1

Kowloon, Hongkong.

New World Film Productions Co
8 Hammer Hill Road
Kowloon, Hongkong.

Yin's Film Company
146 Prince Edward Road
11th Floor
Kowloon, Hongkong.

Eternal Film Company
1204 Wu Sang House
655 Nathan Road
Kowloon, Hongkong.

Hong Hwa Motion Picture (HK) Co
Flat 7, 8th Floor, Honour House
No. 375–381 Nathan Road
Kowloon, Hongkong.

HK Hsin Wha Motion Picture Co
150 Austin Road, 3rd Floor
Kowloon, Hongkong.

Hsin Hwa Motion Picture Co
Madame Tung Yueh Chuan
3rd Floor, 15 Austin Road
Kowloon, Hongkong.

Fu Kuo Motion Picture Co
Room 403, Seng Shun Mansions
71 Peking Road
Tsim Sha Tsui
Kowloon, Hongkong.

Cathay Organisation
(film distribution only)
PO Box 45
Killney Road
Post Office, Singapore 9.
The Great Wall Film Co
Clear Water Bay
Kowloon, Hongkong.

Publications

Cinemart
36A Cameron Road
4th Floor, Flat C
Kowloon, Hongkong.
The industry's most enterprising magazine, independently run and not affiliated to any production company. Articles are in Chinese, with succinct English translations, on trends in the industry, the work of various directors, interviews with directors and stars as well as the more usual gossipy snippets. Authoritative coverage of independent Hongkong productions.
Golden Movie News
(published by Leung To Kin)
The Four Seas Publication Ltd
122B Argyle Street, 1/Floor

Kowloon, Hongkong.
Essentially the publicity arm of Golden Harvest. Picture coverage of features in production, a comic strip format treatment of one new film per issue, and the usual pin-up pictures, gossip, and news.
Southern Screen
(published by V. C. Shaw)
Hongkong Movie Publications Ltd
Lot 220, Clear Water Bay Road
Kowloon, Hongkong.
The publicity arm of Shaw Brothers, featuring credits and picture spreads of films in production, fan material, etc.
Hongkong Movie News
(published by V. C. Shaw)
(chief editor: Chu Shu Hwa)
Hongkong Movie Publications Ltd
Lot 220, Clear Water Bay Road
Kowloon, Hongkong.
Another Shaws-affiliated magazine.

Information

Television and Films Authority
International Building
24th Floor
Hongkong.

Hungary

by Robert Bán

The reputation of Hungarian cinema has been enhanced during the past year by a number of important international successes. Zoltán Fábri, whose *The Boys of Paul Street* earned him the privilege of being the first Hungarian director to be nominated for an Academy Award, was joined on that list by Károly Makk, with his movie, *Catsplay*. István Szabó's *25 Fireman's Street* was awarded the Grand Prix at the Locarno Festival. In Tehran, Pál Sándor's grotesque comedy, *Football of the Good Old Days*, captured the Special Jury Prize. And the first prize at Mannheim went to *At the End of the Road* by Gyula Maár, who made his *début* with this picture.

As reported in IFG 1975, quite a few top-ranking veteran directors came up with new movies. Fábri's *The Unfinished Sentence*, a supremely successful screen adaptation of Tibor Déry's novel of the same name, was yet one more tribute to the director's exceptionally high craftsmanship and to his sensitive creativity. It proved that, although approaching sixty, he possesses the ability to renew his stock-in-trade, his resources, and medium, and has a capacity for successfully assimilating numerous achievements in modern cinema. András Kovács's *Blindfold* can safely be regarded as a step forward in the director's success-studded career. And Miklós Jancsó, in his latest picture, *Elektreia*—the Hungarian entry at Cannes, 1975—has produced a summing up, a comprehensive synthesis, of the particular *genre* he has created: an extraordinarily suggestive blend of ballet, the musical, and the

"happening," that expresses his attitudes towards socio-philosophical problems.

The name Béla Balázs Studio keeps cropping up in these reports. For about fifteen years now, this special-purpose studio has been playing an important part in the Hungarian film industry, providing an experimental workshop for young, prospective film directors. In the last few years, the budding film-makers who are active in the studio have tended to devote their attention to an attempt to evolve a specifically

Mari Törőcsik in EXPECTANTS

Márta Mészáros's ADOPTION, which won the Golden Bear at Berlin 1975

sociological type of cinema, the observation of reality at close quarters—pinning down, so to speak, all aspects of reality—being their prime interest. *Holiday in Britain*, István Dárday's first feature, was made as the result of such experimenting. The young director won great acclaim in Oberhausen several years ago with a number of shorts that were marked with his unusual signature. His particular style and way of looking at things, which dominated these earlier works, appear to have achieved perfection in *Holiday*, in which Dárday draws forth problems of universal validity from a mundane situation, and his treatment is packed with splendidly observed details and plenty of humour.

In his latest film—*Don't Pull My Beard*—Péter Bacsó continues in the satirical vein of *Bald Head for Bald Head*, the movie that earned him the Grand Prix at Taormina. The two *débutants* of the year are Barna Kabay and Miklós Csányi, both from Hungarian TV. Films in production include Gyula Maár's study of one of the most intriguing personalities of the pioneering era of Hungarian theatre, with Mari Törőcsik (of *Merry-Go-Round* and *Love*) taking the title role; and Tamás Rényi's *When Time Began*, which brings to the screen the bitter political and social struggles of the immediate postwar period; and, above all, István Szabó's *Budapest Tales*, which mirrors the transformation of the social scene in Hungary through the adventures of an odd group of people, thrown together under bizarre circumstances. The film is presented in the form of a poetically, almost surrealistically, conceived play.

Finally, news from another area of filmmaking. Spurred on by the success of *Childe John*, an animated cartoon based on a popular peasant epic written by the Nineteenth-century plebeian, poet-revolutionary Sándor Petőfi, work has begun on a second, full-length animated production, *Mattie the Gooseboy*, another humorous peasant epic.

recent and forthcoming films

JELBESZÉD (Recovery). Script: Judit Máriássy. Dir: Mara Luttor. Phot: János Kende. Players: András Nyiri, Jana Brejchová, Ildikó Jani.
JUTALOMUTAZÁS (Holiday in Britain). Script: Györgyi Szalai, István Dárday. Dir: István Dárday. Phot: Lajos Koltai. Players: Kálmán Tamás, Mme Tamás, József Borsi, Mária Simai.
DUNAI HAJÓS (The Danube Pilot). Script: Miklós Markos, from the novel of Jules Verne. Dir: Miklós Markos. Phot: Iván Lakatos. Players: Gábor Koncz, Gábor Agárdy, István Bujtor, Magda Menszátor.

Still from DON'T PULL MY BEARD

Still from THE DANUBE PILOT

ÖRÖKBEFOGADÁS (ADOPTION). Script: Márta Mészáros, Gyula Hernádi. Dir: Márta Mészáros. Phot: Lajos Koltai. Players: Kati Berek, László Szabó, Gyöngyvér Vigh, Arpád Perlaky.

ERESZD EL A SZAKÁLLAMAT! (Don't Pull My Beard!) Script: Péter Bacsó. Dir: Péter Bacsó. Phot: János Zsombolyai. Players: Tamás Major, Ferenc Kállai, László Helyey, Ildikó Bánsági.

TÜZGÖMBÖK (Start from Zero). Script: Bulcsu Bertha. Dir: Imre Fehér. Phot: György Illés. Players: Gábor Szabó, Nóra Káldi, Bertalan Solti, Ágnes Mészáros, Ferenc Kállai, Hédi Váradi.

VÁRAKOZÓK (Expectants—working title). Script: Imre Gyöngyössy, Barna Kabay. Dir: Imre Gyöngyössy. Phot: János Kende. Players: Mari Törőcsik, Maja Komorowska, Lajos Balázsovits, Erika Bodnár.

DÉRYNÉ, HOL VAN? (Where Are You, Mrs. Déry—working title). Script: Gyula Maár. Dir: Gyula Maár. Phot: Lajos Koltai. Players: Mari Törőcsik, Ferenc Kállai, Mária Sulyok, Lajos Őze, Cecilia Esztergályos, Tamás Major, András Kern, András Kozák.

LEGENDA A NYULPAPRIKÁSRÓL (Legend about the Stewed Hare—working title). Script: Barna Kabay, Imre Gyöngyössy, based on the novel of Józsi Jenő Tersánszky. Dir: Barna Kabay. Phot: György Illés. Players: Siemion Wojciech, Ádám Szirtes, Dezső Garas, Judit Halász, László Helyey, Endre Harkányi, Lili Monori.

VÖRÖS REKVIEM (Red Requiem—working title). Script: Gyula Hernádi. Dir: Ferenc Grunwalsky. Phot: Elemér Ragályi. Players: Miklós Lontai, Attila Kovács, Miklós Dávid, Miklós Dárdányi, György Gonda, András Mészáros, Iván Szendrő.

India

by Chidananda Das Gupta

The censorship gap between India and the rest of the world has widened so much as to isolate us more than ever. Nothing illustrated this more than the Fifth International Film Festival held in New Delhi in January. Although festival films are not checked by the Censorship Board, the authorities marked films with nude scenes "A" (Adult), occasioning a black market spree and near-riot over tickets. It is three years since India cancelled the import licences of American distributors and tried to bring selected foreign films from various countries as a substitute for the Hollywood monopoly. The dismal failure of this policy has now led to a new agreement with the U.S. motion picture exporters, and the monopoly is being fully restored. During the attempt to diversify imports, censorship made it impossible to show films even from Communist countries without extensive cuts. In the meantime, the Indian commercial cinema, although not permitted kissing or nudity, continues to be vulgarly erotic in its own censor-defeating ways.

Probably the most significant development of the year has been the box-office success of Shyam Benegal's *Ankur*, a sensitive film with a strong story-line and the striking new actress Shabana Azmi, and Basu Chatterjee's *Rajanigandha*, whose uncomplicated if unoriginal depiction of real people has taken audiences by storm. These straws in the wind may indicate the future development of good narrative cinema without song-and-dance routines—works not at loggerheads with the box-office like the majority of the products of the Film Finance Corporation. Will "Parallel Cinema," much

debated during the festival, merge into the mainstream and bring about changes from within, instead of striking attitudes borrowed from the minority cinema of the West?

The growth of television, so far confined to large cities and yet to spread to all of them, is now to be extended to rural audiences. By August, 5,000 TV sets placed in villages in twelve selected districts will be receiving programmes bounced off the American Telstar Satellite in a year-long experiment with rural TV. Thereafter India hopes to send up her own satellite in order to expand the service to more and more villages. With the successful production of the first satellite "Aryavata" (named after a Fifth-century mathematician and astronomer) launched by the U.S.S.R., hopes of a wider follow-up to this year's Satellite TV (the SITE programme) experiment have brightened. Ground television is dominated by commercial cinema programmes and affluent set-owners; how far the rural network, when it is fully established, will be able to stay independent of these two factors remains to be seen.

ANKUR (The Seedling)

Script and direction: Shyam Benegal. Dialogue: Pt. Satyadev Dubey. Photography (Eastmancolor): Govind Nihalani, Kamath Ghanekar. Editing: Bhanudas. Music: Vanraj Bhatia. Players: Shabana Azmi, Sadhu Meher, Anant Nag, Priya Tendulkar, Kadar Ali Beg, Agha Mohammed Hussain. Produced by Mohan J. Bijlani and Freni Variava for Blaze Film Enterprises. 120 mins.

Shyam Benegal's first feature bears out his reputation as a documentary film-maker. *Ankur* has a quiet realism in its treatment of

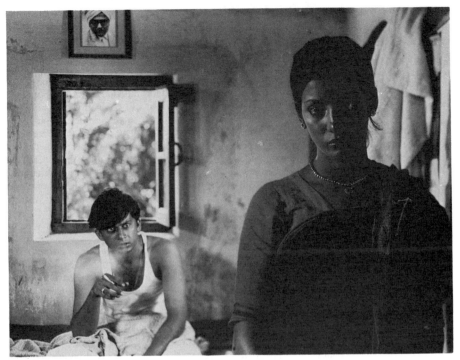
Anant Nag and Shabana Azmi in ANKUR, directed by Shyam Benegal

the age-old exploitation of tenant by landowner which still persists in rural India today. Acting and staging are handled very well: all three of the main characters emerge as rounded personalities, and the slow rhythm of the direction —*à la* Satyajit Ray—holds attention throughout. In this her first film, Shabana Azmi excels as Laxmi, the attractive young wife of the deaf-mute labourer Kishtaya (played equally well by Sadhu Meher); seduced by the landowner's city-bred son, she is hastily dropped when his wife appears on the scene. *Ankur* may be faulted only for its perhaps excessive gentleness; a touch of violence or tension might have given it more power.

CHIDANANDA DAS GUPTA

recent and forthcoming

SONAR KELLA. Satyajit Ray's recent release is a crime story written by himself and filmed in colour, with the accent more on charm than on suspense. Soumitra Chatterjee plays the detective.

JANA ARANYA. Ray is currently filming another story by Shanker (the writer of *Seemabaddha*).

JUKTI TARKA GAPPA. Ritwik Ghatak returns to film-making with an exercise in autobiographical style.

PADATIK. Mrinal Sen's film after *Calcutta 71* deals with the mental state of a revolutionary youth who is hiding in a young woman executive's flat. The revolutionary is played by Dhritiman Chatterjee and the woman executive by Simmi.

CHORUS. Another of Mrinal Sen's political films, episodic in character, with sequences played by noted theatrical actors.

AVISHKAR. Basu Bhattacharya makes another foray into the problems of staying married. This time the husband is played by *matinée* idol Rajesh Khanna and the wife by equally famous Sharmila Tagore.

The Bombay Film Industry

Since the time (just after Griffith) when Dadasaheb Phalke introduced the feature film to India, Bombay has remained the heart of India's film industry. When change hits Bombay, it hits the cinema everywhere in the country—and it has begun to hit Bombay.

Madras is one threat to Bombay's dominance, with 252 productions against Bombay's 141 in 1974. But 125 of Bombay's films were in colour, 50% more than Madras's offerings.

More importantly, Bombay continues to monopolise the country's major film form: the "Hindi feature." During 1974 it produced, on average, one every three days against Madras's total output of only twenty such films. Here is where change has begun to blow.

It is strange that the home of the Hindi film should be Bombay, since the city's state language is Marathi (Maharashtra state has only started encouraging Marathi films this year). Besides a £200,000 Film City project afoot in the suburbs of Bombay, there is also a substantial tax rebate available for Marathi films here where the entertainment tax on the box office runs at 55%. The Hindi film continues to flourish however, nurtured by the Bombay film industry.

The signs of change are becoming clearer, though. While star teams like Dharmendra and Hema Malini reign supreme, new faces and talents like Shabana Azmi and Amitabh Bacchan are stealing the limelight. Two outsiders have proved runaway hits: *Bobby*, featuring unknowns and a lukewarm story, and *Roti, kapada aur makan*, about social inequality. The Hindi film and its followers are slowly drifting away from the old formula of big-name stars, the music of two or three pairs of song writers, and an equal number of playback singers. Song sequences used to be a crucial part of a film's success and budget, with eighty-strong orchestras and exotic locations. In 1974 there was a decline in such sequences, as well as in studio work and big star line-ups. Perhaps the five-month musicians' strike provided an interval for meditation; it certainly halted production and release for quite a while.

The year saw the making of scriptwriters like Gulzar. Subjects improved noticeably with regard to topical matters, social themes, and character analysis. The industry partly ascribes this change to the new liberal policy of the Central Board of Film Censors. Films like *Namak haram* took up the cause of trade unionism, while *Call Girl* and *Prem nagar* were marked by understanding and realistic treatment. The prestigious government National Awards came as a challenge, deliberately by-passing the commercial cinema. Two regional black-and-white, low-budget films won the main awards, their respective leads winning Best Performer. The spokesman for such New Wave films, Mani Kaul, was named Best Director (Kaul also won the coveted Nehru Fellowship, a handsome grant for promoting a specialised area of an art form). A modest Film Finance Corporation work was judged Best Hindi Film.

A ruder blow came with the glittering Bombay Filmfare Awards, based on a public poll conducted amongst readers of the leading film fortnightly, which also gives a Critics'

Award for experimental film. For the first time, *both* awards went to *Rajanigandha*, a deceptively simple film with unknown actors. Jaya Bahaduri, non-glamorous alumna of the State's Film and TV Institute at Poona, won Best Actress and *matinée* idol Rajesh Khanna was named Best Actor, but for a film (*Avishkar*) which did not lay calim to box-office values. Finally, a Bombay documen-tary film-maker, Shyam Benegal, won national acclaim with his first film, *Ankur*. Both *Ankur* and *Rajanigandha* proved the year to be a testing time in another sense: exhibitors and distributors relaxed their stan-dards, opened their doors, and promised more variety for their audiences.

UMA DA CUNHA

Indonesia
by Baharudin A. Latiff

Towards the end of 1974, Indonesian film-makers began to realise that the cinema's pop-ularity was beginning to decline. By early 1975, with the industry practically gasping for breath, its heyday was almost over. The five-year boom had passed like a flash-in-the-pan. The situation was so demoralising that the industry's leading light, Wim Umboh, threatened to go into a temporary self-imposed exile after critics severely attacked his film *Tokoh* (*The Great Lover*). Indonesian film-makers had at last learned the bitter lesson of other prolific industries—quantity habitually kills quality. Producers themselves are to blame for the present crisis. The over-crowding of the profession is made worse by the fact that Indonesians have yet to master the medium; one needs only to sit through the best on offer to draw up a lengthy list of faults.

Foreseeing the inevitable crisis, director Syuman Djaya called on his fellow film-makers to make use of the vast number of literary works which were readily available and would make fine films. Djaya, who had adapted two novels—"Si doel anak betawi" by Abdullah Moeis and "Atheis" by Achdiat Kartamihardja—for the screen, wisely saw

Poster for RAMA SUPERMAN INDONESIA

this as a last resort to save the dying industry. Sadly, his call went unheeded; film-makers still clamoured for original scripts.

There were many reasons for this: first, they cost less; second, adapting from novels would involve the need to compromise with the authors, besides incurring greater financial responsibilities and comparisons by critics between the original and the finished film. Most film-makers only realised the crisis was at their door-step when one particularly good film played for only one night after an eight-month wait for the sixty-plus cinemas in Jakarta. Alarmed, they approached the government for help, conveniently blaming the glut of imported films for their dilemma. Obligingly, as usual, the government reduced the annual import of foreign films from 500 in 1974 to 400 in 1975. Further reduction will continue at the rate of 100 a year henceforth. As a further step, a ruling was imposed requiring all theatres to screen at least two native productions a month.

In 1974, production reached 80 films, an increase of about 30 over the previous year. Producers numbered over 80, 6 of whom were women. It is projected that by the end of the Second Indonesia Plan (1980), domestic production will be running at about 500 films a year. By then imports will be nil. Gaining finance for productions is no problem since the imposition of a government ruling that each imported film has to pay a tax of RP 250,000 (about £250). The money goes to a National Film Production Board from which producers can raise loans of up to RP 7,500,000 (about £950).

At present, tear-jerkers on suffering children are enjoying great popularity. Sandy Suwardi paved the way when he stopped playing villains and turned producer/director with *Ratapan anak tiri* (*Woes of a Step-Daughter*). The film, starring his ten-year-old daughter Faradilla Sandy, broke box-office records everywhere. It also broke the backs of other producers rushing to push imitations on the market while the going was good. Everyone doted on such films showing orphaned, hapless children mistreated by all-and-sundry and facing life loveless and unloved. The future hardly looks promising. Film-makers should take stock of the situation and realise that production of commercial works on a conveyor belt is no sin—as long as they are well done.

recent and forthcoming films

KUNTILANAK (The Vampire). Script and dir: Ratno Timoer. Players: Ratno Timoer, Peggy Monach, W. D. Mochtar, Pancky Suwito, Vanny Pawaka, Harjo Muljo. For P. T. Daya Isteri Film.

RATAPAN RINTIHAN (Cries of Despair). Script and dir: Sandy Suwardi Hassan. Players: Faradilla Sandy, Suzanna, Ratno Timoer, Sofia W. D., Farouk Afero, W. D. Mochtar, Tatiek Tito. For P. T. Serayu Agung Jaya Film.

KEHORMATAN (Honour). Dir: Bobby Sandy. Players: Widyawati, Sophan Sophiaan, Tante Josepha, Dicky Zulkarnaen, Kusno Sudjarwadi, W. D. Mochtar, Kieke Widjaya. For P. T. Surya Indonesia Medan Film.

BOBBY, Script: Arifin C. Noor. Dir: Fritz G. Schadt. Players: Dicky Zulkarnaen, Chitra Dewi, Ratno Timoer, Fifi Young, Agus Erwin, Ismet M. Noor, Yuni Arcan, Roy Marten, H. Mansur Shah. For P. T. Dipa Jaya Film.

TOKOH (The Great Lover). Script and dir: Wim Umboh. Players: Titik Tito, Kusno Sudjarwadi, Emilia Contessa, W. D. Mochtar, Mieke Widjaya, Paula Roemokoy, Ruth Pelupessy. For Aries Film.

SENYUM DIPAGI BULAN SEPTEMBER (Smiles on a September Morning). Script and dir: Wim Umboh. Players: Sukarno M. Noor, Kusno Sudjarwadi, Rachmat Hidayat, Rima Melati, Lenny Marlina, Rano Karno, Dicky Zulkarnaen, Santi Sardi. For Aries Film.

SENYUM DAN TANGIS (Smiles and Tears). Dir: A. Rizal. Players: Lenny Marlina, Kusno Sudjarwadi, Rano Karno, Sofia W. D., Aminah Cendrakasih, Bambang Irawan. For P. T. Surya Indonesia Medan Film.

TIADA WAKTU BICARA (No Time for Talk). Script and dir: Sandy Suwardi Hassan. Players: Sarimah, Idris Sardi, Rachmat Hidayat. For P. T. Serayu Agung Jaya Film.

Iran

by Hagir Daryoush

In spite of an impressive number of awards won within the last year by Iranian feature and short films in major festivals as well as in specialised events, the local film industry is passing through a quiet period.

Production has dropped from an annual 90 features in 1974 to a little more than half that figure. There seems to be two explanations for the decline. First, the freezing of cinema admission prices combined with the rising costs of material, labour and services in a country where films are primarily destined for local consumption, has made film-making a much less profitable enterprise than it was, say, five years ago. Second, many of the producers, directors and writers who have been, and still are, responsible for products pejoratively called "Persian-speaking films," are not prepared or able to cope with the emerging sophistication of the public, which shows positive signs of being fed up with local adaptations of Bombay melodramas or third-rate American thrillers.

Given these prevailing conditions, it seems that an aid law or some other sort of government subvention is now badly needed to prevent a complete standstill. Although no such scheme actually exists in any effective and systematic way, some national organisations have been active in helping the young directors who try to make quality products. One such organisation is the Telfilm Company, wholly owned by the National Radio-Television, which has co-produced, on a 50-50 basis, the majority of films made within the last two years that have been identified as belonging to the "New Iranian Cinema." A recent example of this is the strange and disturbing *Prince Ehtejab* by Bahman Farmanara, which explores life under the Qadjar dynasty, removed from power half a century ago.

Another organisation, a private company with its stock majority held by a national bank, may also prove helpful to the local industry. It is called SACI (for Société Anonyme Cinématographique de l'Iran), and is certainly the most enterprising of the new producers. With enough funds to support its ambitious programme, SACI last year concluded a much-publicised deal with Carlo Ponti to make twelve productions, some of them "super," within three to four years. The company has also been active on the local scene, and the encouraging news that Bahman Farmanara has been appointed its Managing Director may mean that more attention will in future be focused by this company on Iranian talent and on turning out completely Iranian films of quality.

Outside the realm of these two powerful bodies, the New Film Group Co-operative is the only production unit worthy of mention. Working under constant financial pressure and yet with total disregard for commercial considerations, this Co-operative was responsible for Shahid-Saless's *Still Life* and *Far From Home* (the latter co-produced with the Federal Republic of Germany) and will present this year Dariush Mehrjui's *Mina Cycle* and Massoud Kimiai's *Ghazal*, both co-produced with SACI. Although these films have been made with an eye on the foreign market and can hold their own when com-

Societe Anonyme Cinematographique Iran
presents

CO-PRODUCTIONS

"F. FOR FAKE"
Directed by Orson Welles   released

"LA CHAIR DE L'ORCHIDEE"
Directed by Patrice Chereau   released

"THE OTHER SIDE OF THE WIND"
Directed by Orson Welles   in production

"LE DESERT DES TARTARES"
Directed by Valerio Zurlini   in production

"GOLGO 13"
Directed by Junya Sato   released

IRANIAN PRODUCTIONS

"MINA CYCLE"
Directed by Dariush Mehrjui   released

"RUINED"
Directed by Nosrat Karimi   in production

FOR MORE INFORMATION PLEASE CONTACT
SACI, 43 AVENUE DAMGHAN, TEHRAN, IRAN
TELEPHONE: 824979–824985 TELEX: 2325

Jamshid Mashayekhi and Nouri Kassraï in a scene from Farmanara's first film, PRINCE EHTEJAB, which won the Grand Prix at the Tehran International Film Festival 1974

pared with any "artistic" movie from the traditional film-making countries, the *cinéastes* of the Co-op are starting to talk bitterly of "distribution ghettos" and "distribution racism." And indeed, it is a fact that in spite of prizes and critical acclaim won by the New Film Group products, they have not been able to break into even limited "art et essai" circuits, let alone more generalised foreign markets.

recent and forthcoming films

ZIRE POOSTE SHAB (Under Cover of Night). Dir: Fereydoon Goleh. Phot: Barbod Taheri. Players: Morteza Aghili, Suzanne Giller. Prod: Salehi.
MOSSAFER (The Passenger). Dir: Abbas Kiarostami. Phot: Malek-Zadeh. Players: Hassan Darabi, Massoud Zand Beglar. Prod: The Institute for the Intellectual Development of Children and Young Adults.
KHANE-KHARAB (Ruined). Dir: Nosrat Karimi. Phot (colour): Nemat Naghighi. Players: Nosrat Karimi, Zhaleh Sam. Prod: SACI.

SYERA FILMS
Director MEHDI MOSSAYEBI
90 AV. ARBAB DJAMSHID TEHRAN
Tel. 313110–312792

THE PIGEON (TOGHI)
AND BABA SHAMAL (1970)
THE DERVISH (GHALANDAR) (1977)
MAMAL THE AMERICAN
(Box office champion in 1974)

THE VOYAGE COMPANION
(HAMSAFAR) with:
Behrooz Vossoughi (Best Actor Award
in Tehran International Film Festival
1974) also (best actor award in Dehli
International Film Festival 1975) and
Googoosh

And now: BEEHIVE in colour
(Kandoo) by Freydoon Goleh with
Behrooz Vossoughi, Davood Rashidi

ZABIH by Motevasselani with Behrooz
Vossoughi, Djamshid Mashayekhi,
Aram.

IRAN **237**

Parviz Sayyad in FAR FROM HOME, directed by Sohrab Shahid-Saless

GHAZAL. Dir: Massoud Kimiai. Phot (colour): Nemat Haghighi. Players: Fardin, Pouri Banai. Prod: The New Film Group.

TAJROBE (The Experience). Dir: Abbas Kiarostami. Phot: A. Zarrin-dast. Players: Hossein Yarmohammadi, Parviz Naderi. Prod: The Institute for the Intellectual Development of Children and Young Adults.

SHAZDE-EHTEJAB (Prince Ehtejab). Dir: Bahman Farmanara. Phot: Nemat Haghighi. Players: Jamshid Mashayekhi, Nouri Kasraï, Fakhri Khorvash. Prod: Telfilm.

DAR GHORBAT (Far from Home). Dir: Sohrab Shahid-Saless. Phot (colour): Ramin Molai. Players: Parviz Sayyad, Ursula Kessler. Prod: The New Film Group, Tehran/Provobis-Film, Hamburg.

Iranian Film Week in Cannes 1975

Thanks to the energetic efforts of Mr. A. As. N. Ashtiany, the Iranian cinema received international attention and coverage during the Cannes Festival this year. Several shorts were screened, including items from the Institute for the Intellectual Development of Children and Young Adults in Tehran, but interest focused on the features.

The brilliantly-photographed *Tangsir* (*dir*: Amir Naderi) was familiar to those who had attended the New Delhi Festival last year, as was Sohrab Shahid-Saless's *Still Life* to those who had been at Berlin in 1974. But the two films everyone was eager to see were *Prince Ehtejab* and *The Stranger and the Fog*.

Bahman Farmanara's first film, *Prince Ehtejab*, is somewhat reminiscent of Satyajit Ray's *The Music Room* as it observes the declining days of a wealthy man, living in painful solitude in his mansion. Knowing that he must soon die, the Prince recalls the extravagant *régimes* of both his father and grandfather, who were directly related to the Qadjars, the former royal family of Iran. Farmanara shows how each generation has taken cruelty a step forward, from the crude anger of the grandfather to the ruthless psychological torture inflicted on his wife by the Prince himself. The dialogue is full of pretty ironies, the compositions are arresting, and the atmosphere of the old house is perfectly conveyed. Farmanara deservedly won the Grand Prix at the Tehran International Film Festival of 1974 for *Prince Ehtejab* and the film's closing shot, of the doomed man slowly descending a spiral staircase into the dark bowels of his mansion, is hard to forget.

The Stranger and the Fog, which runs for nearly two-and-a-half hours and was some years in preparation, is an epic that owes allegiance to the Japanese cinema of Kurosawa. It is set in some distant historical epoch (unfamiliar even to Iranians), and centres on intolerance in a small seaside village. A stranger arrives in a boat. No one knows why or whence he comes. After an initial period of suspicion, he is accepted by the villagers and marries a young widow. But there is always the feeling that he is being pursued, and the climax of the film describes a running fight between the villagers and five mysterious armed men who come in search of the stranger. The film is shot in colour with an arrogant ease; the camera travels swiftly and fluently alongside running figures, and prowls unerringly through the village huts. This is a grandiose achievement, as successful in its depiction of a primitive life-style as Paradjanov's *Shadows of Our Forgotten Ancestors*. It does not provide a window into contemporary Iranian culture, to be sure, but it does mark Bahram Beiza'i as one of his country's most gifted directors.

PETER COWIE

FILM PRODUCTION AND DISTRIBUTION COOPERATIVE

THE MOST IMPORTANT ORGANISATION FOR MOTION PICTURES IN IRAN

for any further information please contact -

executive director
A.AS.N. Ashtiany
Av. Koushk - Tehran - Iran

Animation in Iran

Although animation has a twenty-year history in Iran, it really only began its active life some four to five years ago. As TV gradually found its way into private homes, and as the Children's Film Festival (from 1966 onwards) grew in stature, so audiences and artists alike became more familiar with animation and its potential. The Institute for the Intellectual Development of Children and Young Adults became a matrix to hold and nurture talents in this field, and even individuals without experience in cartoon work were able to reach a certain international standard. To date 23 animated films, ranging in length from one minute to fifteen minutes, have been completed and have gained prizes abroad.

Moreover, with the expansion of 8mm movie-making, and with an increasing interest in films among young adults, several routine but interesting animated films have emerged from the younger generation in Iran. The Institute, with more than one hundred libraries and cultural centres throughout Iran, has chosen the intellectual development of children and young adults as its major goal. Facilities for making animation films are available, together with specially trained teachers in the *genre*. Out of these circumstances came, in early 1975, the resolve

Massoud Kimiai's THE DEER

to launch an Animation School. Fifteen talented youngsters were selected from five hundred applicants. Subjects taught at the School include: Aesthetics, Photography (Theoretical and Practical), History of Plastic Art, History of Cinema and Animation, Painting, Graphic and Visual Design, Track Film, Camera, Literature, Caricature, Puppet Film, Music, Sound, Film Criticism, Children's Psychology, Animation (Theoretical and Practical).

The course is a two year one. Students for the second year will be selected from among the graduates of the first year, who will be given sufficient training to become professional animators and, eventually, film-makers.

DR. N. ZARRINKELK, Director

THE
ISRAEL FILM CENTRE
invites

film makers to use Israel

filming locations

and

film production services

and to

benefit from the financial

incentives given to film

production in this country

Israel

by Ze'ev Ravnof

Contrary to the usual survey of film production, it seems appropriate to begin this account of the year in Israel by studying the changing trends in audience perception. The 1974/75 period has been significant for the establishment of the *cinémathèque* network in Israel. Though the Israeli Film Archive, founded privately in Haifa by Mrs. Lia Van Leer, has been active for many years, and has undoubtedly contributed to the education of audience response to films, its impact has been marginal, due to circumstances beyond its control. During 1973, new and vital forces appeared on the *cinémathèque* scene—the Israeli Film Institute was established, and the Tel-Aviv municipality created its own *cinémathèque*. The response of the public, mainly among young people, was immediate, enthusiastic, and overwhelming. In fact so outstanding that it created a conflict, both social and legal, between the establishment and the inhabitants of the district near the *cinémathèque*, who claimed that their living conditions were being disrupted. While the Tel-Aviv municipality was lucky enough to be able to move the art house to another location (the City Museum), other councils took action, encouraged by the Tel-Aviv experiment. The Israeli Film Archive in Haifa joined forces, as did the Government, through the Film Centre in the Ministry of Trade and Commerce. As a result, there are now three permanent *cinémathèques* in operation—in Jerusalem, Tel-Aviv, and Haifa. They are based on the stock of films held in Israel, as well as on programmes selected, composed, and brought from abroad. Films are presented with the aid of lecturers, Israelis and others, and a wealth of informational material is printed and circulated. There are weeks devoted to movements in cinema, to directors, to films on a certain subject, as well as to national cinemas. These latter screenings are arranged with the help of the countries themselves; thus, recent weeks have been devoted to Finnish, German, and Dutch movies.

As to film production, the obvious setbacks of the October 1973 war, and the difficult economic situation, acute as they are, have not resulted in collapse. The cameras kept rolling, the foreign cameras as well as the Israeli, without any real interruption. The very fact that the situation did not arouse feelings of hatred and bitterness (which would have doubtless affected the film subjects and styles) is significant and encouraging. The crop for 1974 amounts to ten features—seven Israeli, one co-production, and two foreign productions. As these lines are written, there are three features in production—one Israeli, one co-production, and one foreign production.

Dan Wolman directed his new feature, *My Michael*, based on the book by Amos Oz; the new, immigrant Russian-born director Michael Kalik has made his first Israeli feature, *Three and One*; and Freddy Steinhardt has done a sequel to the adventures of the Greek-born dock worker Salamonico, entitled this time *The Father*. Moshe Mizrachi is finishing his Biblical story, *Rachel's Man*, while Benjamin Hayin is editing his crazy comedy, *The Black Banana*. Otto Preminger's *Rosebud*, made largely in Israel, was released worldwide. Menachem

GOLAN-GLOBUS PRODUCTIONS

NOAH FILMS Ltd.
32 Allenby Road
Tel-Aviv, Israel

AMERIEURO PICTURES
10301 Keswick Avenue
Los Angeles, Calif. 90064, U.S.A.

In release:

'LEPKE' 1974
Tony Curtis
Released worldwide
by Warner Bros.

'FOUR DEUCES' 1974
Jack Palance — Carol Lynley
Release:-
Avco-Embassy and Independent Distributors

'KAZABLAN' 1973
Yehoram Gaon
Released worldwide by M.G.M.

'DAUGHTERS, DAUGHTERS' 1974
Shai K. Ophir
Released by Independent Distributors

1975

Robert Shaw   Richard Roundtree
Barbara Seagull   Shelley Winters

in

'DIAMONDS'
A Menahem Golan Film
Release — Avco-Embassy

In preparation for 1976:

1. MAGICIAN OF LUBLIN
2. THE GOLEM
3. THE JAMES FAMILY
4. HELLO SUCKER!

Golan has completed his international production, *Diamonds*, and George Ovadia quietly put the finishing touches to his two new Mediterranean tearjerkers, *Sarat* and *Day of Judgement*. A special mention should be given to the editorial committee, headed by the writer-poet Haim Guri, who assembled the full-length documentary *The 81st Blow*, which is a compilation of material—as yet unpublished—on Nazis and Jews during the holocaust. The basic idea revolves round the tragic fact that nobody believed the horrors as recounted by the few survivors of the death camps. The facts were simply unacceptable, and this attitude—this 81st blow, as it is called here—resulted in more tragic, passive submissions on the part of the remaining victims. They doubted the truth of the unimaginable horror, branding the stories as hysteria—and went like cattle to the slaughter, with no resistance, exactly according to the Nazi Machiavellian scenario.

While this article is being compiled, two young and dynamic Israeli directors, Yehuda (Judd) Ne'eman and Yitzhak (Zepell) Yeshouroun, are completing their production arrangements for two films, which they are able to make thanks to a government subsidy distributed annually by the Culture and Arts Council for an outstanding script, written by an acknowledged director, either by himself or in collaboration. Both men revealed considerable talent some years ago, Ne'eman in *The Dress* and Yeshouroun in *The Woman in the Next Room*. But the films were box-office flops and they have not received any financial support since then.

Strange as it may sound, looking at the Israeli film scene today, one is tempted to recall the old Hollywood slogan, "Movies are better than ever . . ."

Robert Shaw and Yoseph Shiloah in DIAMONDS, directed by Menahem Golan

Lior Yeini in DANIEL WAX

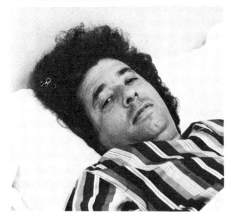

Still from MY MICHAEL

MY MICHAEL

Script: Esther Mor, Dan Wolman, based on the book by Amos Oz. Direction: Wolman. Photography (colour): Adam Greenberg. Editing: Danny Shik. Music: Alex Cagan. Players: Ephrath Lavi, Oded Kotler. For My Michael Film Co. (Alfred Plaine, Shlomi Cohen, David Kipkind). 86 mins.

This is the first Israeli film based on an important contemporary work of literature (translated into twelve languages). The story involves a young couple from intellectual circles in Jerusalem during the Fifties, when the Sinai Campaign was in progress. It is an account of the turbulent personal relationship between two lovers who cannot get along "normally" due to the situation. The woman is a day-dreamer, constantly returning to her childhood and recalling the Arab twins she used to play with. This is the divided Jerusalem, the city prior to 1967, in the words of one character, "A city of enclosed courtyards, its soul sealed up between bleak walls with jagged glass."

ZE'EV RAVNOF

THE FATHER

Script: Eli Tavor, Reuven Bar-Yotam. Direction: Freddy Steinhardt. Photography (colour): David Gurfinkel. Editing: David Troyhartz. Music: Dov Seltzer. Players: Reuven Bar-Yotam, Ze'ev Berlinski, Shai K. Ophir, Yona Eliyan, Meni Pe'er, Koya, Ronith Porath. For Rom El/Shapira Films (Henry Ohana and David Shapira). 100 mins.

The old dock hand, Salamonico, of Greek descent, has retired. He has created a line of successors—two sons and a daughter. All of them are established in a society that is alien and inexplicable to him. He is proud, but remains a kind of outsider. The children are after his old house, an undervalued property, and they try to lure him through kindness to spend his days between them, with them, to provide the means of selling the house and dividing the loot. Old Salamonico is bewildered, sad, and estranged, but he finds an ally in his grandson. It appears that the child is very much like his grandfather. Salamonico has found a link, and so all is not lost. Hope remains.

ZE'EV RAVNOF

Avram Heffner

Profile of a Director

AVRAM HEFFNER was born in Haifa in 1935, studied philosophy and English literature at the Hebrew University in Jerusalem, philosophy and American civilisation at the Sorbonne in Paris, and participated in film workshops at New York City College and NYU. Heffner, who was assistant in Paris to Jacques Becker in *Le trou* and Laszlo Benedek (*Recours en grâce*) began to make shorts in New York, but on his return to Israel in 1963 spent four years writing scripts for other directors and acting on his own account (notably in *Hole in the Moon*, by Uri Zohaz). In 1967 he had his first break—*Slow Down*, a sixteen-minute study of the strange, claustrophobic relationship between two old people, and was awarded a state prize. The film was presented at Venice, Oberhausen, and Melbourne (where it won a prize). Heffner's second short, *Seance* (1970) was a puzzling film that failed to stir real interest. His first feature, *But Where Is Daniel Wax?* (1972), was a revelation, at least as far as film-buffs were concerned, in Israel and elsewhere. Heffner has proved to be a probing director, at once cynical and humane, slightly amused, sometimes vicious, sometimes compassionate, and very individual in his slow-paced way. His style is not yet firmly established, he is remarkably talented. He has a rare and delightful talent for punchlines, reminiscent of artists from Chekhov to Wilder, while his timing is almost impeccable. During his last visit to England (1973/74) he wrote a script entitled *Journey in Europe* which he hopes will be his next film (he is still looking for finance). Meanwhile, he writes books, two of which have been published.

Italy

by Lino Miccichè

At the end of 1974 and beginning of 1975, when the economic crisis, with its repercussions on the mechanisms of financing, had strictly limited credit to the cinema, Italian producers felt they were on the verge of collapse. All the more so, since the Italian people have a strict habit: when the national economy is on the rocks, when petrol is almost as expensive as French perfume, when coffee is sold as if it were filtered gold, people go to the cinema more than ever (perhaps this is the reason why the frailty of the Italian "economic miracle" is coupled by a demand for cinema still running at almost 550,000,000 spectators per year). Providing, that is, the films are available. And producers were biting their nails because the credit squeeze had led to a situation whereby adequate product was not available to meet such a large and ever-rising demand.

Consequently, worthless Italian lire would be converted to Euro-dollars, to the exclusive advantage of the Hollywood majors who normally drew only about 30% of takings on the national market.

Following the bleak prospects of winter, however, the spring breezes brought some improvement to the credit sector, and the number of films going into production gradually increased: 9 in January, 15 in February, 20 in March and almost 60 in the following three months. By the end of June over 100 "national" films had gone into production, while the announcement of the start of shooting on July 14 of Fellini's much-discussed *Casanova* assumed a positive ritual value.

There are also other titles on which to base certain hopes: while Bertolucci is working on the editing of his *Novecento*, Pasolini, continuing his theme (begun outside the cinema) of Fascism and mass psychopathology, is shooting *Salò e le centoventi giornate di Sodoma* which depicts the last days of Fascism under Mussolini (Salò being the capital of the so-called Fascist Republic of 1943–1945) via De Sade; Francesco Rosi, apparently moving away from the journalistic style of cinema adopted in his last two films, is shooting a work based on the polemic novel "Il contesto" by Leonardo Sciascia; Giuseppe Patroni Griffi promises new and luxurious middle-class small-talk in *Divina creatura*; Luigi Zampa is filming another of his "moralistic comedies," *Gente di rispetto*; Tinto Brass emerges from a long period of silence with *Salon Kitty*; Alberto Bevilacqua, who is also a novelist, has laid down his pen to go behind the film camera once more with *Attenti al buffone*; Luigi Comencini is filming the cinema version of *La donna della domenica*, a successful novel written by a couple who normally work as a team, Fruttero and Lucentini; Lina Wertmüller is using, for the fourth time running, Giancarlo Giannini as the main protagonist of her *Pasqualino sette bellezze*. In short, at least from the point-of-view of quantity, the industry is recovering. It only remains to see what the public and critics will have to say when the films come out.

As regards the past season, from September 1974 to June 1975, it was undoubtedly better than the previous one.

Perhaps the most emblematic film was *C'eravamo tanto amati* by Ettore Scola, which covers, in a vein of thoughtful melancholy, the years immediately following the War to the present time, showing the sentimental, social and political life of three friends once all "comrades" together but now totally different from one another. One has allowed himself to be "integrated" into the "system" and lives a life of luxury through property speculation; another has transformed his own discontent into extremist rage; only the third (a magnificent performance by Nino Manfredi) continues to live a balanced life with dignity and to fight with conviction.

The most fascinatingly "ambiguous" film was undoubtedly *Allonsanfàn* by Paolo and Vittorio Taviani, a melodramatically structured description (while at the same time "cold" and full of *Verfremdung*) of the "middle-class" availability to revolution and treachery, the oscillation between ideology shaping the future and biology living out the present. The most discussed film was *Il sospetto* by Francesco Maselli, a Communist director who chose to go back to the period of the clandestine Thirties to find the sources (and both the positive and negative tradition) of the meaning of being Communist today. Paradoxically the most "chaste" film was *Il fiore delle mille e una notte* by Pier Paolo Pasolini, where the spectator was confronted exclusively with love-making between naked men and women but in such a fairly-tale atmosphere that sex appeared haloed like a lost sacral symbol. The most disappointing film was *Gruppo di famiglia in un interno* by Luchino Visconti, in which the great author of *La terra trema* and *Senso* seemed reduced to transforming into sumptuous museums of preciously moulded objects and artificial characters his own incapacity to understand

the present. The most opportunist film was *Anno uno* by Roberto Rossellini who, pretending that it was possible to have the same "objective" detachment for recent Italian history as for the history of France under Louis XIV, made a film (at the expense of the state which financed it, on a decision by the Christian Democrat majority, through the state company Italnoleggio) which, in order to provide propaganda for Christian Democracy, omitted and distorted truths about the postwar years more than any Christian Democrat meeting. Many considered the best film to be *Professione: reporter* by Michelangelo Antonioni who, far from "always repeating the same things"—as some French critics wrote at Cannes, and some Italian critics at Rome—developed his outlook coherently, enriching it with fresh nuances and wider implications, making it (as in the splendid final sequence) a film about the cinema, i.e. on the contrast between actual events and their impossible (because always omissive) depiction.

Other films appearing in the course of the season also contained things of interest, though these were primarily works of entertainment. While *Mio dio come sono caduta in basso*, by Luigi Comencini, had hilariously satyric moments, *Finchè c'è guerra c'è speranza*, by Alberto Sordi (leading player and director of the film), succeeded in introducing, even if in a climate of comedy *alla* Sordi, serious elements of pungent social criticism. While Alberto Lattuada surrounded the main actress of his *Le farò da padre* with smug Lolitism, Dino Risi managed to give the protagonist of his *Profumo di donna* persuasive accents of existential despair.

The year also marked the *débuts* of some newcomers, not all (indeed few) destined to pass into the history of the cinema but in certain cases showing a personal approach and poetic view of the world. This is undoubtedly the case with *Il tempo dell'inizio* by Luigi Di Gianni, with its Kafkaesque atmosphere of nightmarish political fiction; and of *Vermisat* by Mario Brenta, a severe X-ray of social demarcation.

Otherwise *L'età della pace* fully confirmed Fabio Carpi as one of the most interesting personalities to emerge in the Eighties; and *La prima volta sull' erba*, once more underlined the cinematographic talent and uncertainties of inspiration of Gianluigi Calderone.

One of the main events of the season was the rebirth of the Venice Biennale, better late than never. The first edition of the new Biennale took place during October–November 1974 and constituted essentially an experiment within the framework of which the film sector was by far the dreariest and most senseless. Perhaps the many criticisms received by Giacomo Gambetti (Director of the Cinema Section of the Biennale), apart from all those coming from the same sectors which called for the new formula, will have convinced the Cinema Section that it will need to show greater imagination as regards its programmes and a more intelligent selection policy. We will see if this happens or not between the end of August and the beginning of September, when the Biennale proposes to have its first "real" cinema meeting.

Meanwhile, the crisis afflicting the State cinema enterprises (Cinecittà, Istituto Luce, Italnoleggio, grouped together in the holding company of Ente Gestione Cinema) has gradually worsened. In March, when the Socialist members of the management board of the Ente Gestione Cinema resigned, it became obvious that the final crisis was looming dark on the horizon. The storm broke when, in July, the three representatives

of the dependent staff also resigned. In the summer of 1975 there began to be public talk of a re-foundation—that is, of a radical revision of the structures, methods and objectives—of direct state intervention in the cinema. If 1974—thanks to the Ente Gestione which paid for it—was the year of *Anno uno*, and 1975—thanks to the waste of public money such as *Anno uno*—is Year O of the Ente Gestione, 1976 could be the *anno uno* of a new way of conceiving and running the public cinema.

PROFESSIONE: REPORTER (The Passenger)

Script: Mark Peploe, Peter Wollen, and Michelangelo Antonioni, from an original story by Peploe. Direction: Antonioni. Photography (Metrocolor): Luciano Tavoli. Editing: Franco Arcalli, Michelangelo Antonioni. Music: (none). Art Direction: Piero Poletto. Players: Jack Nicholson, Maria Schneider, Jenny Runacre, Ian Hendry, Stephen Berkoff. For M-G-M (Carlo Ponti). 117 mins.

Like *La notte*, Antonioni's new film is about frustration. Like *The Eclipse*, it is about uncertainty. In short, *The Passenger* marks a return to the Italian master's great form of the early Sixties. David Locke (Jack Nicholson) is a distracted TV reporter who, like Pontano in *La notte*, has grown flaccid and liable to compromise. Suddenly, on an assignment in central Africa, he is presented with the chance of a new life. A guest named Robertson, who resembles him uncannily, dies in the tiny desert hotel. Locke stares at the corpse as if willing himself to assimilate its vanishing personality. But he is soon confronted with the realities of the dead man's occupation: gunrunning for the local guerrillas. There can be only one outcome: a fate that is a precise duplication of Robertson's. Locke, like the guerrilla whose execution by firing squad he has recorded on film, finally achieves extinction. He perishes on a hotel bed near Almeria, while the world around him continues to pulse with supreme indifference, and Antonioni's camera refuses to round on itself and witness the grisly act, preferring to advance like a robot through the bars of the bedroom window and out into the hot, lazy plaza.

In Jack Nicholson, Antonioni has found the ideal actor to personify the indolence, the listless charm, and the faded resolution of the contemporary West. And with *The Passenger*, Antonioni demonstrates once again that he is the only director in the world whose analysis of this malaise is as rigorous and concerned as it is free from contempt and self-indulgence.

PETER COWIE

Locke prepares to change identities in THE PASSENGER

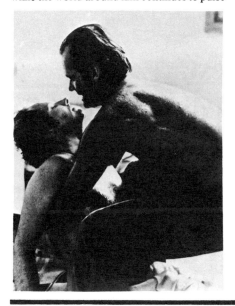

Art House Focus

In Trieste, **La Cappella Underground** (via Franca 17) has had some striking seasons in the past year: Italian Fascist cinema, Alfred Hitchcock, fantasy movies, and a remarkably full retrospective tribute to Griffith.

(continued from page 309)

Dinu Tănase. Art dir: Vasile Rotaru. Cost: Ileana Oroveanu. Music: Radu Serban. Players: Draga Oltteanu, Eliza Petrăchescu, ɔarmen galin, 'lna albu, Dan Nuţu, Gheorghe Dinică. For "Casa se Filme Trei."
NEMURITORII (The Immortals). Script and dir: Sergiu Nicolaescu. Phot (colour): Alexandru David. Art dir: Filip Dimitriu, Richard Schmidt. Cost: Hortensia Georgescu, Petre Veniamin. Music: Tiberiu Olah, Nicolae Covaci. Ed: Iolanda Mîntulescu. Players: Amza Pellea, Ion Besoiu, Ilarion Ciobanu, Sergiu Nicolaescu, Gina Patrichi, Jean Constantin, Colea Răutu. For "Casa de Filme Cinci."
FILIP CEL BUN (Philip the Kind). Script: Constantin Stoiciu. Dir: Dan Piţa. Phot (colour): Florin Mihăilescu. Art dir: Virgil Moise. Cost: Lidia Luludis. Music: Dorin Liviu Zaharia. Ed: Cristina Ionescu. Players: Mircea Diaconu, Ileana Popovici, Vasile Niţulescu, Gheorghe Dinică, Lazăr Vrabie, Ica Matache, Florina Luican. For "Casa de Filme Trei."

COMEDIE FANTASTICĂ (A Fantastic Comedy). Script and dir: Ion Popescu Gopo. Phot (colour): Grigore Ionescu, Stefan Horvath. Art dir: Marcel Bogos. Cost: Nelli Merola. Mus: Dumitru Capoianu. Ed: Eugenia Naghi. Players: Dem Rădulescu, Cornel Coman, Vasilica Tastaman, George Mihăiţă, Horea Popescu. For "Casa de Filme Cinci."
TATĂ DE DUMINICĂ (Sunday Father). Script: Octav Panculaşi. Dir: Mihai Constantinescu. Phot (colour): Dumitru Costache-Foni. Art dir: Vasile Rotaru. Cost: Ileana Oroveanu. Mus: Temistocle Popa. Ed: Lucia Anton. Players: Amza Pellea, Radu Beligan, Gina Patrichi, Olga Delia Mateescu, Monica Ghiuţă. For "Casa de Filme Trei."
DINCOLO DE POD (Beyond the Bridge). Script and dir: Mircea Veroiu. Phot (colour): Călin Ghibu. Art dir: Nicolae Drăgan. Mus: L. Zaharia. Ed: Dan Naum. Players: Leopoldina Bălănuţă, Mircea Albulescu, Ovidiu Iuliu Moldovan, Ion Caramitru, Irina Petrescu. A meditation on failure, love and death, seen through the destiny of a woman of 1848.

Japan

by Naoki Togawa

The recent *A Life of the Film Director*, produced and directed by Kaneto Shindo, is a remarkable documentary on the late director Kenji Mizoguchi, who is known world-wide for such masterpieces as *The Life of O-haru* and *Ugetsu monogatari*. Shindo, one of Mizoguchi's followers, made the film because of his great sympathy for many of his associates who had passed away during the nineteen years since the great director died. *A Life of the Film Director* is in a *cinéma vérité* style composed of Shindo's interviews with thirty-nine friends and collaborators on Mizoguchi's films, including actors and actresses, screenwriters and cameramen who used to work with him. The film describes in detail Mizoguchi's sternness, enthusiasm and devotion to films as a passionate artist through his life.

Akira Kurosawa completed his film *Dersu Uzala* in the U.S.S.R. in June 1975. It is regrettable, however, that such well-known directors as Nagisa Oshima and Hiroshi Teshigahara have had no work for the past few years. Some film-makers have been involved in TV: Yoshishige Yoshida is making a series of documentaries on fine arts in Europe; Susumu Hani has also been working on a series of wildlife films in Africa.

Daiei, the company that once produced *Rashomon* and *The Gate of Hell*, and one of the majors, has recently resurfaced after three-and-a-half years of silence since its declaration of bankruptcy at the end of 1971. The new Daiei's first production has been *The Days of My Youth*, and it is expected that Mr.

Masaichi Nagata, who used to be president of the old company, will return to the film world as a producer.

Since the success of *The Submersion of Japan* in 1973, disaster films have enjoyed great popularity. *Prediction by Nostradamus* and *Explosion in Tokyo Bay* are the new works of the season, a natural response to such foreign films as *Earthquake* and *The Towering Inferno*.

Yet Japanese film producers are still facing difficulties. Despite the fact that the number of thrill-seeking films have increased, audiences have not increased at all. Ticket prices of first-run theatres have risen to 1,000 yen or more. Sex and violence is still as widespread as in previous years, but most audiences are now tiring of the formula. Spectaculars are still being produced on a domestic scale. In the meantime, films of classic and contemporary literary works have been welcomed by the public as "eye-washers."

In the non-theatrical field, about 1,500 shorts were produced last year as in the previous year. The notable documentarist Noriaki Tsuchimoto has still been endeavouring to make a series of films dealing with the pollution problem since *Minamata*. The latest films in this series are *Minamata for Medical Science* (long enough at 271 minutes) and *Shiranui-kai*, 153 minutes long. The shortest film of the year was made by Yoji Kuri, a five-minute cartoon entitled *Parody of the Painter Brueghel*.

Though there have been some big

The back stage of the circus in Shuji Terayama's PASTORAL HIDE AND SEEK, now being released through Hiroko Govaers of Paris

successes, distribution of foreign films is undergoing a difficult time. M-G-M Japan was obliged to close down in February 1975; "Equipe du Cinéma", run by Mrs. Kashiko Kawakita and Miss Etsuko Takano, started another art house last year, enabling such foreign films as *Apur sansar* (Satyajit Ray) and *El mumiaa* (Shadi Abdelsalam), to be released. Three unreleased films by Ingmar Bergman are expected to be shown soon.

The Board of Culture of Japan has granted a prize of ten million yen to each of the ten best feature films selected by the committee from domestic product of the last year. The prize has yet to be extended to short films.

Finally, the National Film Centre has just begun work on the construction of a film vault to preserve old and famous works.

recent films

ARU EIGAKANTOKU NO SHOGAI (A Life of the Film Director). Dir: Kaneto Shindo. Phot: Yoshiyuki Miyake, Kiyomi Kuroda, Hisashi Shimoda. Prod: Kaneto Shindo for Kindai Eiga Kyokai. 150 mins. Documentary on Kenji Mizoguchi.
ASAKI YUMEMISHI (It Was a Faint Dream). Script: Shin Ooka. Dir: Akio Jissoji. Phot: Masao Nakabori. Players: Janet Hatta, Shin Kishida, Hisashi Hananomoto. Prod: Chusei Pro. for ATG. 120 mins.

DEN-EN NI SHISU (Pastoral Hide-and-Seek). Script and dir: Shuji Terayama. Phot: Tatsuo Suzuki. Art dir: Kiyoshi Awazu. Players: Kaoru Yachigusa, Masumi Harukawa, Yoshio Harada, Kantaro Suga. Prod: Jinriki Hikoki Sha for ATG. 102 mins.

IMOHTO (My Sister). Script: Ei-ichi Uchida. Dir: Toshiya Fujita. Phot: Kenji Hagiwara. Players: Kumiko Akiyoshi, Ryuzo Hayashi, Hideko Yoshida, Juzo Itami. For Nikkatsu. 92 mins.

NINGYO HIME (Princess Mermaid). Based on the novel by Hans Christian Andersen. Dir: Tomoharu Katsumada. For Toei. 67 mins. Feature cartoon.

SAKURA NO MORI NO MANKAI NO SHITA DE (Under the Fall of the Cherry Blossoms). Script: Taeko Tomioka, from the novel by Ango Sakaguchi. Dir: Masahiro Shinoda. Phot: Tatsuo Suzuki. Music: Toru Takemitsu. Players: Tomisaburo Wakayama, Shima Iwashita. Prod: Geien-sha for Toho. 95 mins.

SAIKAI (Meeting Again). Script: Koichi Saito, Shigeo Nakakura. Dir: Koichi Saito. Phot: Noritaka Sakamoto. Players: Goro Noguchi, Kyoko Enami, Ryo Ikebe. Prod: NP Pro. for Shochiku. 93 mins.

SANDAKAN HACHIBAN SHOKAN, BOHKYO (Sandakan). Story: Tomoko Yamazaki. Dir: Kei Kumai. Phot: Manji Kanau. Players: Kinuyo Tanaka, Komaki Kurihara, Yoko Takahashi. Prod: Haiyu-Za, Eiga-Hoso. For Toho. 121 mins.

SEISHUN NO MON (The Gate of the Youth). Script: Gyo Hayasaka, from the novel by Hiroyuki Itsuki. Dir: Kirio Urayama. Phot: Hiroshi Murai. Players: Ken Tanaka, Tatsuya Nakadai, Sayuri Yoshinaga. For Toho. 187 mins.

SHOWA KARESUSUKI (Elegy for Our Time). Script: Kaneto Shindo. Dir: Yoshitaro Nomura. Phot: Takashi Kawamata, Players: Hideki Takahashi, Kumiko Akiyoshi. For Shochiku. 87 mins.

SUNA NO UTSUWA (The Castle of Sand). Script: Shinobu Hashimoto, Yoji Yamada, from the novel by Seicho Matsumoto. Dir: Yoshitaro Nomura. Phot: Takashi Kawamata. Players: Tetsuro Tamba, Kensaku Morita, Go Kato. Prod: Hashimoto Pro. For Shochiku. 143 mins.

TOKKAN (Go for Break). Script and dir: Kihachi Okamoto. Phot: Daisaku Kimura. Players: Yusuke Okada, Etsuji Takahashi, Kyu Sakamoto, Hiroko Isayama. Prod: Kihachi Pro. For ATG. 93 mins.

WAGA SEISHUN NO TOKI (The Days of My Youth). Script: Ryu Tatsuhara, Hisashi Yamanouchi. Dir: Tokihisa Morikawa. Phot: Kiyomi Kuroda. Players: Komaki Kurihara, Kei Yamamoto, Rentaro Mikuni, Keiju Kobayashi. Prod: Daiei Eiga, Haiyu-za.

WAGAHAI WA NEKO DEARU (I am a Cat). Script: Toshio Yasumi, from the novel by Soseki Natsume. Dir: Kon Ichikawa. Phot: Kozo Okazaki. Music: Mitso

Fukudanji Katsura in ONI NO UTA, directed by Tetsutao Murano

Kinuyo Tanaka (right) won a Silver Bear in Berlin 1975 for her performance in SANDAKAN, directed by Kei Kumai

Tatsumi Kumashiro's STREET OF JOY, produced by Nikkatsu and available overseas through Shibata Organization

Toshitaka Ito and Hiroko Isayama in TOKKAN, directed by Kihachi Okamoto for Art Theatre Guild

Miyamoto. Players: Tatsuya Nakadai, Kuriko Namino, Juzo Itami, Mariko Okada, Nobuhito Okamoto, Mako Midori. Prod: Geien-sha. For Toho. 116 mins.

forthcoming films

BYAKU-YA NO SHIRABE (Leningrad-Kyoto). Co-production, Toho (Japan)/Mosfilm (U.S.S.R.).

HARAKARA (Brethren). Dir: Yoji Yamada. Players: Chieko Baisho, Yutaka Terada. For Shochiku.

KIMI YO FUNNU NO KAWA O WATARE (You, across the River of Wrath). Prod: Masaichi Nagata. Players: Tatsuya Nakadai, Machiko Kyo, Ayako Wakao. For Daiei.

KINKAN-SHOKU (Annual Eclipse). Novel: Tatsuzo Ishikawa. Dir: Satsuo Yamamoto. Phot: Setsuo Kobayashi. Players: Tatsuya Nakadai, Machiko Kyo, Jukichi Uno. For Daiei.

KITA NO MISAKI (Cape of the North). Novel: Kunio Tsuji. Dir: Kei Kumai.

ONI NO UTA (Demon Ballad). Novel: Giichi Fujimoto. Dir: Tetsutaro Murano. Players: Fukudanji Katsura, Yuko Katagiri. For ATG.

Statistics

Figures for the period April 1974 to March 1975, compared with the previous year in parenthesis.

Number of Cinemas:

total	2,468 (2,530)
for domestic films only	1,297 (1,332)
for foreign films exclusively	618 (632)
for both categories	553 (566)

Number of Films Released:

total	574 (657)
domestic films by major companies	163 (208)
domestic films by independents	170 (197)
foreign films	241 (252)

Box-office:

yearly attendance
185,500,000 (185,324,000)
gross theatre receipts without tax
116,300 million yen (92,682)
average admission fee without tax
627 yen (500)

Gross Film Rental:

total   43,500 million yen (35,200)
domestic films
22,500 million yen (19,700)
foreign films
21,000 million yen (15,500)
income from the export of films
$3,165,000 ($3,500,000)

Number of Television Sets Registered:
25,564,000 (24,900,000)

Kaneto Shindo prepares to film the tombstone of Kenji Mizoguchi for his A LIFE OF THE FILM DIRECTOR

The errant father and son in SUNA NO UTSUWA, directed by Yoshitaro Nomura

Lebanon

by Leon Torossian and Mohammed Rida

If there are in the world just a few countries where cinema-going has not suffered appreciably from the TV offensive, one of these is undoubtedly Lebanon. This tiny country, with just over 3,000,000 inhabitants, consumes more than 450 features a year (virtually all imported, mainly from the U.S., France, Egypt, Britain and Italy). Annual attendance has lately risen to about 18 visits per head of population, by far the highest of Arab countries. The main reason for this state of affairs is thought to be the extremely low seat-prices in first-run cinemas (roughly 20p for stalls and 30p for upstairs), competing in luxury with nothing less than the very best. In spite of inflation, ticket prices have not risen since the early Sixties. The privately-owned Lebanese TV broadcasts two to three Western features a week, usually more than ten years old and thus not satisfying filmgoers' hunger. Moreover, the average Lebanese distributor often manages to open major Western productions almost simultaneously with their European release (Polanski's *Chinatown*, Wilder's *The Front Page*).

The irony, however, lies elsewhere. This first-class consumer country, endowed with practically all the possibilities for a healthy and reasonably abundant national production, only turns out six to eight films a year, barely 2% of its needs. Yet Beirut is renowned as the cultural centre of the Middle East, and the first Lebanese attempt at a full-length features dates from 1931, providing a cinema tradition of over four decades. Beirut can count an impressive team of film-makers educated at different Western film-schools (George Nasser, Antoine Remy, Antoine Meshahwar, Silvio Tabet, Burhan Alawiya George Shamshum, Andre Gedeon, Suheil Jabbur), several first-class actors (Munir Maasri, Abdallah Shammas, Shawky Matta) and actreses (Habiba, alias Gladys Abu Jawdeh, Liz Sarkissian), some accomplished technicians, and the best colour processing laboratory in the Middle East. Moreover, the Wall Street of the Arab World lies in the Lebanese capital, with a profusion of money ready to be invested. Last, but not least, the picturesque countryside offers superb opportunities for location shooting. All these favourable conditions, however, fail to promote a satisfactory national output, and force many of the above film-makers to subsume their ambitions in TV.

L.T.

In an effort to improve the situation Lebanese producers and film-makers have begun to explore the possibilities of increasing cooperation with the government-supported Syrian Cinema Centre. Lebanese-Syrian cooperation over the past few years has resulted in several joint ventures and has led to new agreements concerning distribution rights, vital to the struggling industry. In the late Sixties production dropped from an average of seventeen films per year to five; and with this drop came a lowering in the quality of films being made. However, in the early Seventies a new group of directors began to emerge, young film-makers, some of them trained in Europe, eager to express themselves in terms of their own society. These included

Still from THE CHOSEN ONE, with Jan Harvey, written and directed with a keen sense of experiment and location by Souheil Jabbour, for The Hungry Days Film Production

George Shamshum (with two films to his credit to date: a short entitled *Inside Out*, and a feature *Salam after Death*), Samir Khoury (two features: *The Lady of the Seven Moons* and *Wolves Don't Eat Meat*, both of which have been bought by an English distribution company and are currently being translated), and Samir Ghoseini (*The Cats of Hamra Street*). All three are planning new productions.

By 1974 this new movement had gained momentum as more young directors returned to their native country after training in Europe. Two received prizes at the 1974 Carthage Film Festival: Burhan Alawiya for his feature *Kafr Kassem* (a re-staged documentary dealing with the massacre of the villagers of Kafr Kassem by Israeli soldiers in occupied Palestine in 1956) and Rafik Hajjar for his short *May ... the Palestinians*. Heini Srour is the first female director to emerge in this new movement; her film, *The Ticking Clock of Liberation ... Imperialism Must Go* comprises documentary footage of the continuing struggle of the Popular Liberation Front in independent Dhofar, and has enjoyed popular critical response on an international and local level. Last year also saw the return of director George Nasser after a silence of twelve years. Nasser's previous films, *Little Stranger* and *Where To?*, had been well received critically in the past, but until the recent Lebanese-Syrian production *One Man Wanted*, Nasser had consistently resisted all commercial propositions offered to him. *One Man Wanted* deals with the struggle of a Syrian village against the feudal system. This film, along with *Kafr Kassem*, ranks amongst the most important films ever made in Lebanon.

Next year offers more promise for the future. Marwan Baghdady, another new director recently returned from Europe, has just finished shooting his first feature *Beirut ya Beirut* which deals with the lives of four young Lebanese in flux following the 1967 war and prior to the death of Nasser. The four meet and influence each other as each struggles to resolve his problems, shown as a microcosm for the problems of the country as a whole. The New Wave has been helped extensively by critics who helped prepare the way for such productions and who continue to offer support and encouragement. Due to the critical acclaim afforded to such films as *Kafr Kassem* and *One Man Wanted*, and due to the success these films are enjoying on a national level, producers are again beginning to take an interest in the Lebanese film industry and are now ready to listen to the directors. A meeting was held recently in Beirut between producers and film-makers to discuss new projects, and the future looks promising for those with the ideas and the initiative to take advantage of this favourable change in the climate.

M.R.

Malaysia

by Baharudin A. Latiff

The future for Malay Films seems to be fruitful if the present rash of activity is any indication. A number of films are either currently shooting or slated for production during the year. Actors and directors have propitiously joined with financiers to set up companies, at present totalling (somewhat dangerously) more than thirty.

Though any move to create more independents is always welcome, over-enthusiasm can present its own problems. With companies unwittingly pitted against each other, their diversified resources, which do not amount to much in terms of either financial backing or material possessions, and their all-too-evident self-interest, are likely to frustrate them from achieving their original aim—to challenge the supremacy of the two distributing giants. Wisely, prompted by sheer economic need to survive, if not for the more noble purpose of producing quality films alone, the fledgling companies joined forces to form a confederation. This will hopefully finance future productions, projected to cost 200,000 Malay dollars (£40,000) each, with individual companies purchasing M$1,000 shares, quantity unlimited. A commendable idea on paper, but considering that such an ambitious idea entails innumerable problems, the confederation might well find itself defeated by its own ideals. Already plans have been bogged down by "personality clashes".

In sympathy the government set up a

Salmiah Dahlan as the insurance investigator in BONEKA PERMATA (THE DIAMOND DOLL), directed by Tony Azman. Photo by Baharudin A. Latiff

task force comprising senior officials from the Treasury and ministries to compile a comprehensive report on what should be done to protect the local industry. Its future may well depend on it. The task force has refused to divulge its findings, claiming that premature disclosure might be unwise. It fears that Shaw Brothers and Cathay, which at one time had planned to merge to form a single conglomerate with an estimated worth of US$ 70,000,000 might resort to protective measures and subsequently block whatever moves the ministry investigation proposes.

The findings, however, cannot be scandalously original or reverberatory in any sense. Only the usual measures can be recommended—a subsidy scheme, restrictions and a tax levy on imports, a theatre quota, compulsory use of local talent and equipment, etc. The two giants, who have been in business for many years, are not so naive that they have not already anticipated such moves.

A spokesman disclosed, however, that there are plans to set up a theatre in each of the thirteen states by 1980. These will be handled by the State Development Corporation (SDC), the National Corporation Berhad (PERNAS), the Majlis Amanah Raayat (MARA) or the Urban Development Authority (UDA). By then, the local industry will have attained a solid economic standing.

Censorship is still very prominent. The fourteen-member Film Censorship Committee has first call on all new films, while the eighteen-member Appeals Committee takes over when there are appeals against bans, cuts and classifications made by the first. The Advisory Panel is the last resort when further disputes arise. The Ministry for Home Affairs, in announcing its guidelines for passing films, emphasised that those glorifying sex, violence, politics, crime, bigotry, yellow culture, lesbianism, homosexuality, masochism, voyeurism, incest, sodomy, fetishism and exhibitionism are subject to strict scrutiny. Films already banned include *Last Tango in Paris, A Clockwork Orange* and *Straw Dogs*.

Meanwhile, Indonesian films, which were all the rage until recently, have now lost their box-office magnetism. Even a Wim Umboh film sank without trace, while a Hindustani film, *Bobby*, broke all records.

recent and forthcoming films

BONEKA PERMATA (The Diamond Doll). Script: Naz Achnas. Dir: Tony Azman. Players: Salmiah Dahlan, Dalila, Dali Siliwangi, Anita Jaafar, S. Zamilah, Norizan. For Pura Emas.

MALAYSIA 5. Script: Greg Macabanta. Dir: Jun Aristorenas. Players: Jun Aristorenas, Virginia, Sarimah, Aziz Jaafar, Anita Jaafar, Hamzah Hussein, Robin Aristorenas, Mona Sulaiman, Osman Botak. For Juver and Sari Artis.

PERMINTAAN TERAKHIR (The Last Wish). Script: H. M. Sutan. Dir: Jamil Sulong. Players: Uji Rashid, Nozie Nani, Saadiah, Ahmad Daud, Sonny Abdullah, Yusuf Haslam, Norizan. For Merdeka Studio.

SANDOKAN (Tiger of Malaya). Dir: Sarjo Solimo. Players: Carol Andre, Sarimah, Kabir Bedi, Aziz Jaafar, Dali Siliwangi, Normadiah, Malek Selamat, Osman Botak. For Sari Artist and Titanus Company.

RAHSIA HATIKU (My Heart's Secret). Script and dir: Naz Achnas. Players: Sharifah Hanim, Mariati, Maznah Ahmad, M. Amin, Gary Gideon, Ali Rahman. For Merdeka Studio.

MASTURA. Script and dir: Naz Achnas. Players: Hussein Abu Hassan, Maznah Ahmad, Noran Nordin, Norizan, Tony Azman, Merdawati. For Merdeka Studio.

SI BUTA (The Blind Warrior). Script and dir: Omar Rojik. Players: Hussein Abu Hassan, Mariati, Tony Azman, Dali Siliwangi, Idris Hashim, Shariff Baba. For Merdeka Studio.

BUNGA PADI BERDAUN LALANG. Script: Hashim Hamzah. Dir: Hussein Abu Hassan. Players: Hussein Abu Hassan, Mahyun Ismail, S. Zamilah, Razali Buyung, Kalam Hamidi. For Baiduri Film.

KELUARGA SI COMAT (Comat and Family). Dir: Aziz Sattar. Players: Aziz Sattar, S. Shamsuddin, Junainah, M. Amin, Ibrahim Pendek, Asmah Atan. For Sabah Films.

Mexico

by Tomás Pérez Turrent and Gillian Turner

The year 1974 was a poor one for Mexican cinema, both from the point-of-view of quantity and of quality: 54 films were made, of which 49 were wholly Mexican, one a co-production with France, and the remaining 4 American films made on Mexican territory. Of the 50 Mexican films, including the French co-production *No oyes ladrar a los perros?* (*Can't You Hear the Dogs Barking?*) by François Reichenbach, 26 were made in the Churubusco Studios, the most important in the country, and within the main Union (STPC). The remaining 24 were made in the América Studios and with workers from the "little" Union (STIC).

The State company CONACINE has taken over almost exclusively the production of the greater part of Mexican cinema, being

films made in the Churubusco Studios with workers from the STPC. CONACINE made or participated in 19 of the 26 films issuing from these studios; in four the company was the sole producer, in five it was co-producer with two of the few private producers still in action; and on three occasions with DASA (Directores Asociados), made up of a group of directors. The remaining co-production is the already mentioned *No oyes ladrar a los perros?* The other nine films were co-produced by CONACINE and the workers, artists and technicians, who intervened in the production by investing part of their salary, following the formula begun last year. An improvement can at last be seen in the productions made under this system, at least with regard to their ambitions, although these are

Scene from Alberto Isaac's TIVOLI

the films with the lowest budget. With this in mind, it can be said that the nucleus of Mexican production is becoming more and more state-controlled. Nationalisation is already a fact—confirmed in a speech made by the President of the Republic: "Cinema production should be in the hands of the workers." All that is needed is the decisive step or the formal procedure for this to be instituted effectively.

Private production, the majority of the producers being survivors from earlier days, clinging to an old-style way of film-making, has taken refuge in the América Studios and

with the "little" Union. This allows them to make lower-cost films, of extremely bad quality, repeating formulas of ten and twenty years ago: melodramas, vulgar comedies derived from TV, mediocre adventures, pseudo-westerns, cinema limited to the local market and the illiterate audiences of other Latin American countries. It is significant that of the twenty-four films made in the América Studios and with the STIC, the only one with certain ambitions, *Auandar Anapu*, by Rafael Corkidi, was made with the participation of CONACINE.

This does not mean that the state company guarantees an improvement in the quality and interests of the cinema, since on many occasions it just follows the old, traditional formulas. The production of 1974 was clear enough evidence of this, the general tone being one of mediocrity, with no really exceptional film having been made.

It may be that this is just a trial period. After the euphoria of previous years, when films were made with larger budgets and more equipment, the tendency now seems to be towards a lowering of costs, although a way has not as yet been found to conciliate a lesser degree of economic need with an increase in the quality, interest and authenticity of the films. For the moment, in view of the desertion of the private producers, it is imperative to make films to keep the industry on its feet and give work to cinema workers. What is lacking is a real plan, a real production policy, and thus a cultural policy. On the other hand, film-makers are confronted with habits created by the iron censure of the last thirty years, and by their own habits of self-censure.

To the initial total of 50 films two more must be added, both produced and made by CUEC (University Centre for Cinematographic Studies). Made together with a constant stream of shorts and documentaries, both are full-length features: *Meridiano 100* (*Meridian 100*) by Alfredo Joscowicz, and *Descenso al país de la noche* (*Descent to the Land of Night*) by Alfredo Gurrola (16mm). Production by CUEC does not have the same commercial and industrial imperatives, and distribution is very minor, if not nil. As has happened before, in order to gain a wider audience, films have to be "adopted" by the official system headed by the National Cinematographic Bank.

PRESAGIO
(Presage)

Script: Luis Alcoriza and Gabriel García Márquez.
Direction: Luis Alcoriza. Photography (colour): Gabriel
Figueroa. Editing: Carlos Savage. Art Direction: Rober-
to Silva. Players: David Reinoso, Fabiola Falcón, Lucha
Villa, Pancho Córdova, Enrique Lucero, Eric del
Castillo, Raquel Olmedo, José Galvez, Silvia Mariscal.
For Escorpion and Conacine.

This film, based on a story by the famous
Colombian writer Gabriel García Márquez, is
one of the more ambitious films of 1974. The
action takes place in a town where life is
difficult and its inhabitants are as dry and
bitter as the land they live off. One day an accident befalls the local midwife, an old
woman who is thought to have magic powers.
For her this accident is a presage that
something dreadful is to happen in the town.

This announcement lets loose fears, hates,
complexes, provokes irrational terror to such
a degree as to cause a lynching. There is a
chain reaction. The men stop working and
hunger becomes rampant; violence and cruelty become law; the situation becomes in-
tolerable, and in addition a series of strange
and inexplicable happenings occur. It
becomes necessary to leave the town, and
when the exodus begins the old woman
declares, satisfied: "I told you something
dreadful was going to happen in this town."
Alcoriza has tried to repeat what he has done
in previous films: examine more-or-less
typical behaviour, myths and attitudes in a

Still from Luis Alcoriza's PRESAGIO

specific place, and with representative characters, in the heat of an exceptional situation. But unhappily the context weakens, there is no action, it's a little bit Mexico and then it's not. The film is too much a slave of the anecdote: the initial announcement and its final confirmation seem to be the *raison d'être* for the rest of the film.

TOMÁS PÉREZ TURRENT

TIVOLI

Script: Alberto Isaac and Alfonso Arau. Direction: Alberto Isaac. Photography (colour): Jorge Stahl Jr. Editing: Rafael Ceballos. Music: Ruben Fuentes. Players: Alfonso Arau, Pancho Córdova, Lyn May, Carmen Salinas, Mario García H., Hector Ortega. For Dasa and Conacine.

This is the first Mexican film to follow the current fashion for nostalgia. It evokes the times of the Tivoli Theatre in the Forties and Fifties, the first revue theatre to base its fame on striptease numbers, at the time awakening the wrath of puritan organisations. The film exploits the memories of those who were then young, whose first erotic impulses were awakening. It narrates the last days of the theatre—condemned by pressure from certain sectors because of the city's growth and the land speculation provoked by this expansion—and also the struggles of a group of comedians and dancers to preserve their jobs. Isaac tries to reproduce exactly the style, choreography, and sets of the era, filming everything in the manner of contemporary Mexican cinema. The spaces between the musical numbers are filled with the story of the artists fighting for their jobs, combined with a timid attempt to criticise the corruption of certain authorities involved in large real estate concerns. In spite of its good moments the combination is both monotonous and repetitive, lacking the necessary strength for a nostalgic evocation of an era, and also the necessary distancing to analyse the customs of a social and political life still too near.

TOMÁS PÉREZ TURRENT

AUANDAR ANAPU

Script, direction and photography (colour): Rafael Corkidi. Music: Hector Sánchez. Editing: Rafael Landeres. Players: Ernesto Gómez Cruz, Aurora Clavel, Jorge Humberto Robles, Patricia Luke. For Cinemadiez and Conacine.

This is an original film which tries to shake off the narrative canons and habitual themes of Mexican cinema. It is spoken in Spanish and Purépecha, the dialect of the Indians living in the region where it was filmed, and mixes professional actors with the local people. *Auandar anapu* (which in Spanish means "He who came from the sky") evolves around a character who is part Christ, part Ché Guevara, part Camilio Torres, a Third World hero and mystic who fights for justice and against exploitation, works miracles, proclaims himself in favour of physical love—demonstrating this at every opportunity—and the Revolution. In the narration of his hero's adventures Corkidi mixes evangelical paraphrase with political allegory, folklore and photographic preciousness. There are evident influences from Glauber Rocha's cinema in its baroque violence, but the important influence of Miklós Jancsó can also be detected in the film's presentation as a pastoral allegory. Thus, at the end, all the characters, dead and alive, are reunited as a symbol of the undying revolutionary spirit. The synthesis, however, between Rocha's chaotic cinema and the perfect rationalism of Jancsó is never achieved. The result is confusion, with contradictory elements superimposed one on top of another, instead of integrating dialectically.

TOMÁS PÉREZ TURRENT

LA OTRA VIRGINIDAD
(The Other Virginity)

Script: Juan Manuel Torres, Luis Carrión. Direction: Juan Manuel Torres. Photography (colour): José Ortiz Ramos. Editing: Eufemio Rivera. Music: Gustavo Cesar Carrión. Players: Valentín Trujillo, Meche Carreño, Leticia Perdigón, Arturo Beristain, Victor Manuel Mendoza, Rita Macedo, Alejandro Cianguerotti. For Conacine and Cooperative Workers STPC.

This is the second feature film by Juan Manuel Torres, ex-pupil of the Polish Łódź Film School. It narrates the experiences of two young men and two girls as they pass through "the other virginity," that is, as they take their steps into the adult world: the girls work in a

Above: LA OTRA VIRGINIDAD

café frequented by old men; one of the boys is a student condemned to die, the other works for a company of film distributors. Their experiences acquaint them with the first emotions of love, disillusion, and solitude —their own and that of others. Torres builds his film on the volatile, the fragile, and the elusive; his intention seems to be to film feelings, and he is more at ease among the trivia of everyday existence than in weightier matters. At several points the film brings to mind the best of Truffaut, to whom there are constant references. Like Truffaut's Doinel, the young people in *La otra virginidad* are a little shy, a little indecisive, a little melancholy. It is a promising work, despite its deficiencies in rhythm and over-length.

TOMÁS PÉREZ TURRENT

new and forthcoming films

LA CASA DEL SUR (The House in the South). Script: Sergio Olhovich and Eduardo Lujan. Dir: Sergio Olhovich. Phot (colour): Rosalio Solano. Edit: Alberto Valenzuela. Mus: Gustavo Cesar Carrión. Art dir: José Rodríguez Granada, Carlos Grandjean. Players: David Reinoso, Helena Rojo, Salvador Sánchez, Rodrigo Puebla, Patricia Reyes Spindola. For Dasa and Conacine.

¿NO OYES LADRAR A LOS PERROS? (Can't You Hear the Dogs Barking?) Script: Carlos Fuentes, Jacqueline Lefevre, Noel Howard, from the novel by Juan Rulfo. Dir: François Reichenbach. Phot (colour): Rosalio Solano. Edit: Alberto Valenzuela. Art dir: Salvador Lozano, Carlos Grandjean. Mus: Vangelis O Papathanassiou. Players: Salvador Sánchez, Ahui Camacho, Ana de Sade, Salvador Gómez, Aurora Clavel, Gastón Melo, Patrick Penn. For Cinematografica Marco Polo—Conacine (Mexico) Les Films du Prisme—ORTF (France).

LA VENIDA DEL REY OLMOS (The Coming of King Olmos). Script: Julián Pastor and Eduardo Luján. Dir: Julián Pastor. Phot (colour): José Ortiz Ramos. Mus: Gustavo Cesar Carrion. Players: Jorge Martínez de Hoyos, Ana Luisa Peluffo, Maritza Olivares, Ernesto Gómez Cruz, Mario García González. For Conacine and Co-operative Workers STPC.

ACTAS DE MARUSIA (Proceedings in Marusia). Script and dir: Miguel Littin. Phot (colour): Jorge Stahl Jr. Players: Gian Maria Volontè, Claudio Obregón, Diana Bracho, Salvador Sánchez, Silvia Mariscal, Julián Pastor, Ernesto Gómez Crus, Arturo Beristain, Patricia Reyes Spindola, Mariana Lobo, Guillermo Gil. For Conacine.

CANOA. Script: Tomás Pérez Turrent. Dir: Felipe Cazals. Phot (colour): Alex Philips Jr. Edit: Rafael Ceballos. Players: Salvador Sánchez, Enrique Lucero, Ernesto Gómez Crus, Arturo Alegro, Roberto Sosa, Gerardo Vigil, Carlos Chavez, Jaime Garza, Alicia del Lago, Flor Trujillo, Salvador Garcini. For Conacine and Co-operative Workers STPC.

FOX-TROT. Script: Arturo Ripstein, José Emilio Pacheco, H. A. L. Craig. Dir: Arturo Ripstein. Phot (colour): Alex Philips Jr. Art dir: Lucero Isaac. Players: Peter O'Toole, Charlotte Rampling, Max von Sydow, Jorge Luke, Claudio Brook, Helena Rojo. For Conacine (Mexico) and Carbold (England).

THAT'S PIM & WIM

(Pim de la Parra and Wim Verstappen)

SCORPIO FILMS Postbox 581 **AMSTERDAM HOLLAND** Ph. **228674**

Netherlands

by Peter Cowie

Feature film production is now firmly established in the Netherlands. Visitors to the Dutch stand at the Cannes Festival have sensed a new cohesion, a new optimism, in the atmosphere. The pioneering days of the Sixties, when movies like *The Enemies* and *Paranoia* collapsed like pricked balloons at the box-office, seem far away. The Dutch public have at last accepted the idea of seeing Dutch films, and this means that the most interesting talents now go into features rather than shorts as hitherto.

In 1974, six Dutch features accounted for nearly 10% of the total receipts throughout the Netherlands, and nearly 9% of attendances. Nikolai van der Heyde's *Help, the Doctor's Drowning!* (reviewed here last year) was second only to *Jesus Christ Superstar* among the top grossing pictures. The number of filmgoers increased by 5.9% to well over 28 million. Gross takings rose by 14.5% to Dfl. 120 million. In 1974, 334 feature films were imported (382 in 1973). The average budget of a Dutch feature is now around $375,000, and the Production Fund for Dutch Feature Films contributes a portion of this to individual production teams and companies. The year 1975 promises to be the most spectacular period in recent Dutch film history, with no fewer than eleven full-length national features due for release. A Netherlands entry in the competitive section of each major festival is now a regular occurrence, and not the fluke of yesteryear. *The Family* went to Tehran in 1974, *Mariken van Nieumeghen* to Cannes in 1975, and more recently *Melancholy Fireside Tales* was invited to Berlin.

Among the most imaginative of the season's entries in Holland were René van Nie's *Child of the Daffodils* (see review below), Wim Verstappen's *Alicia* (also reviewed), and Samuel Meyering's *Rufus*, a vivid study of illegal gambling in the Netherlands, with a dramatic script by Arthur Benton and the twenty-eight year old Meyering, based on the novel by Anton Quintana. The screenwriter has in fact been the "missing link" in Dutch film production for a long time, but now the country can boast several teams that include gifted writers alongside experienced producers and ambitious directors. The government has observed all this activity with apparent approval, and the film budget has been increased in 1975 to Dfl. 7,678,000 (approximately $3 million).

In the realm of short films, the traditional Dutch speciality, there are signs of a revival after the disappointments of recent years. Animation is attaining international standards, and there are more experimental films as opposed to the more familiar brand of documentary. Graduates of the Netherlands Film Academy more often than not have an opportunity to make independent shorts, thanks to subsidies from the Ministry of Cultural Affairs, which acts on advice given by the Film Department of the Arts Council. The work of these young film-makers is distributed abroad by the Netherlands Information Service, although domestic release is still difficult to achieve; usually it is Dutch TV that comes to the rescue, programming Dutch shorts that have little chance of reaching audiences in cinemas.

Last year we saluted the independent, non-commercial distributors; a word, then, for Concorde Films of The Hague, which has remained independent of the big groups and has imported a wide spectrum of films, from *Don't Look Now* and *Sweet Movie* to *Nada* and *Le chaud lapin*.

KIND VAN DE ZON
(Anna, Child of the Daffodils)

Script: René van Nie, Jonne Severijn. Direction: René van Nie. Photography (colour): Mat van Hensbergen. Players: Josée Ruiter, Johan te Sla, Dora van der Groen, Huib Broos, Cox Habbema, Ramses Shaffy, Michel van Rooy. For Burgwal Films b.v. (René van Nie). 90 mins.

René van Nie has devoted most of his talented youth to working in Dutch TV (although foreign audiences may recall his searing, Franjuesque short about an old soldiers' home, *Brombeek, for Example*). This feature, however, indicates how boldly and smoothly he has seized on the complex potentialities of the modern film. He and his co-writer Jonne Severijn have organised the narrative in two parallel currents of thought, flowing alongside each other, yet in opposing directions. This format affords the ideal counterpoint for the story of a young girl recovering from schizophrenia. Various incidents and pressures that led to her illness are seen in different perspectives. Anna is typical of a generation that has been offered more emotional freedom than it can assimilate, and it is to the film's credit that all the characters—Anna, her bourgeois parents, her sister, her brother—appear sensitive and sympathetic, whereas the personalities in Ken Loach's *Family Life* are painted in all too black-and-white terms. The acting, particularly by Josée Ruiter, is excellent, and gone are the days when one had to apologise for the technical asperities of a Dutch feature film. This is an ambitious work, written and

Above: ANNA, CHILD OF THE DAFFODILS

directed with absolute control and persuasion, even if its elaborate mechanism may puzzle the impatient viewer.

PETER COWIE

ALICIA

Script: Charles Gormley and Wim Verstappen. Direction: Verstappen. Photography (colour): Marc Felperlaan. Editing: Jutta Brandstaedter. Music: Mozart. Players: Willeke van Ammelrooy, Hugo Metsers, Bob Verstraete, Carry Tefsen, Pim de la Parra. For Scorpio Films (Pim de la Parra). 105 mins.

The theme of the housewife suddenly awaking to her destiny and taking off from home is one that has strongly influenced a host of recent films. *Alicia* charts the rupture in an urban marriage with remarkable restraint and lack of pretention, and it ends not in a sentimental reconciliation but on a note of continuing dissatisfaction. Alicia has learned that life beyond the four walls of her domesticity does not have the champagne sparkle she had imagined; perhaps in conclusion she has to acknowledge that her husband is far from perfect too, as conscious of his own inadequacy as she is of hers.

Verstappen's gathering maturity as a director is apparent in the long opening sequence, as he observes Alicia at home, taking a bath, gauging her weight and her bodily charms, and almost subconsciously preparing for flight. Apart from one hilarious interlude in which Pim de la Parra tries vainly to play the lecherous neighbour, the film is wrapped in quietness and discretion. And finally it says more than many expensive American movies about the high price of admission demanded by modern morality.

PETER COWIE

From the closing shots of Nouchka van Brakel's episode in MELANCHOLY FIRESIDE TALES

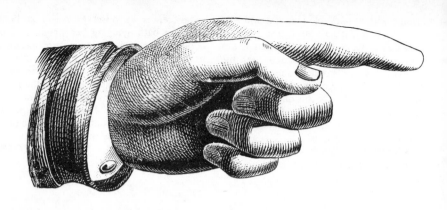

The four of us.

When we decided to join hands, we did so because we have so many activities in common. But mainly because we're so different.
Cinecentrum is famous for live action. Toonder Studios are great in cartoon animation. Geesink Film Productions are renowned for stop motion.
And Video Hilversum covers the whole field of colour video productions.
The four of us can put our hands to any job. In close cooperation and perfect harmony.

Partnership that works.

What the press said about "Anna, child of the daffodils"

Anna, child of the daffodils—a brilliant surprise in Dutch cinema.

JOSEE RUITER experiences the insane fears, the attacks of distress, the uncontrollable tears, hallucinations, bitter frustrations, and despair, in an astonishing way.

Anna, child of the daffodils, is better than 'Family Life'.

For 90 minutes I was watching the truth about myself. I have never seen a Dutch film that affected me so much,

RENE VAN NIE is clearly revealed as a talented director who knows how to show the dramatic conflict between people, and the way they live. This film concerns us all.

Rene's

recent films

MELANCHOLY FIRESIDE TALES. Script: Guus Luyters, from the stories by Heere Heeresma. Dir: Bas van der Lecq, Guido Pieters, Ernie Damen, Nouchka van Brakel. Phot (Eastmancolor): Theo van de Sande. Prod: Sigma Films/City Film Verhuur Mij. B.V. 85 mins.

RUFUS. Script: Arthur Benton, Samuel Meyering, Rogier Proper, from a novel by Anton Quintana. Dir: Meyering. Phot: Ton Buné. Players: Rijk de Gooyer, Cox Habbema, Pleuni Touw, Yoka Beretty. Prod: Cinecentrum N.V./City Produktie Mij. B.V. 90 mins.

MARIKEN VAN NIEUMEGHEN. Script and dir: Jos Stelling. Phot (colour): Ernest Bresser. Players: Ronnie Montagne, Sander Bais. Prod: Rob du Mée/Jos Stelling. 84 mins.

MIJN NACHTEN MET SUSAN, OLGA, ALBERT, JULIE, PIET & SANDRA (My Nights with Susan, Olga, Albert, Julie, Bill & Sandra). Script: Charles Gormley, David Kaufman, Harry Kümel, Carel Donck, Pim de la Parra. Dir: Pim de la Parra. Phot (colour, scope): Marc Felperlaan. Players: Willeke van Ammelrooy, Hans van der Gragt, Nelly Frijda, Franulka Heijermans, Marja de Heer. Prod: Scorpio Films (Wim Verstappen). 84 mins.

DE VIJF VAN DE VIERDAAGSE. Dir: René van Nie. Phot (colour): Mat van Hensbergen. Prod: Burgwalfilms. 100 mins.

ROOIE SIEN. Dir: Frans Weisz. Phot (colour): Ferenc Kálmán-Gaál. Prod: Rob du Mée/Parkfilm. 105 mins.

KEETJE TIPPEL. Dir: Paul Verhoeven. Phot: Jan de Bont. Prod: Rob Houwer Film Holland B.V. 105 mins.

Dutch Feature Film Producers

M.M. Chanowski B.V.
Prinsengracht 852–856
Amsterdam
City Produktie Maatschappij B.V.
Herengracht 102
Amsterdam
Fuga Film Produkties B.V.
Dirk van Hasseltssteeg 19–21
Amsterdam
Geesink Filmproduktie C.V.
Slotlaan 3
Nederhorst den Berg
Bert Haanstra Films B.V.
Verlengde Engweg 5
Laren (N.H.)
Rob Houwer Film Holland B.V.
Van Alkemadelaan 650
The Hague

Maggan Films B.V.
Dirk van Hasseltssteeg 19–21
Amsterdam
Rob du Meé Parkfilm B.V.
Sarphatipark 92
Amsterdam
Fons Rademakers' Produktie B.V.
Prinsengracht 685
Amsterdam
Rex Film
Thull 11a
Schinnen
Scorpio Films B.V.
Keizersgracht 230
Amsterdam
Sluizer Films B.V.
Singel 64
Amsterdam
René van Nie (Burgwalfilms)
O.Z. Voorburgwal 219
Amsterdam

Cinecentrum Group

In one of the most attractive and civilised settings one can imagine, the Cinecentrum Group in Hilversum is now the powerhouse of Dutch film technique. There are the Cineco Laboratories, a video department (the equipment here is really impressive, right up to the minute with film-to-tape facilities in both colour and monochrome, the now-famous "Video Train," and limitless possibilities for titling and sound amendments), five projection rooms, an editing department, and a massive sound department.

Many of Holland's most competent filmmakers have been seconded to Cinecentrum (Hattum Hoving, Frans Dupont, etc.), and it is also the home of the Polygoon Newsreel, edited each week by Philip Bloemendal. Toonder, Geesink, and Polyscoop are other companies—specialising in animation—within the Group.

the eyecatching art-houses in holland

AMSTERDAM

ROTTERDAM

THE HAGUE

HILVERSUM

NIJMEGEN

Laboratories and Studios

Cineco C.V.
's-Gravelandseweg 80
Hilversum.
Cinetone Studio's
Duivendrechtsekade 83
Amsterdam.
Color Film Center B.V.
Leeghwaterstraat 5
The Hague.
Bert Haanstra Filmproduktie
Verlengde Engweg 5
Laren (NH).
Bob Kommer Studio's CV
Riouwstraat 71
The Hague.
BV Nederlands Laboratorium voor Filmtechniek
Kerklaan 5
Loenen a/d Vecht.
Firma Proca Kleurenfilmtechniek B.V.
Prinsengracht 311
Amsterdam.
Renovo Film CV
Maziestraat 17a
The Hague.

Spectrum Film
Kloveniersburgwal 49
Amsterdam.
TITRA Film Laboratorium NV
Egelantiersgracht 82–86
Amsterdam.
Triofilm
Vondelstraat 72
Amsterdam.

Art House Focus

Visitors to the Netherlands can depend on seeing all foreign films with subtitles (as opposed to the dubbing in Italy and Germany that can make most movies incomprehensible to the nomadic buff). The Meerburg group of cinemas has an excellent range of programmes moving from one city to another. In June, there was a season entitled "Canada Today" which was seen in seven locations throughout the country. The

Kriterion, the **Uitkijk,** the **Leidseplein Theatre,** and other Meerburg art houses have screened such films as *Sweet Movie, The Gambler, The Night Porter, Nada, The Passenger, Alice Doesn't Live Here Anymore, Vincent, François, Paul . . . et les autres,* and Pascal Thomas's *Le chaud lapin.* The group has also given many opportunities to the new Dutch cinema, and recently opened the Rivoli, a new cinema aimed at giving a second chance to many European pictures.

Bioscooponderneming A. F. Wolff, located in Utrecht, also run some enterprising and valuable art houses. The **Studio** in Utrecht is the most famous, and the **Select,** in the same town, specialises in complete retrospectives. The organisation also runs the **Studio** in Groningen, where the accent is on first-run movies.

There are various non-profit-making film groups in Holland, among them **Fugitive Cinema** and **Film International,** both of which concentrate on bringing into the country films that might otherwise not see the light of day. Film International's distribution system covers fourteen of the most important Dutch towns and cities, and most films are projected on 16mm.

New Zealand

by Lindsay Shelton

One feature film was completed in New Zealand in 1975. It was begun two years ago as *Huia* (see IFG 1974) but when premiered at the Fourth Wellington Film Festival it had been retitled *Test Pictures,* representing two years work by three Aucklanders headed by Geoff Steven, founder of a co-operative film-makers' group known as Alternative Cinema.

While the makers of *Test Pictures* faced considerable financial sacrifices to complete their feature, there was still more talk about the need to aid local film-makers. At the start of 1975, the Arts Council handed out a meagre $15,000 in grants for short films. But by mid-year the Arts Council had been reorganised and its new chairman Hamish Keith was speaking of the need for more substantial aid. The first decision of this new council was to give $35,000 to Ardvark Films of Auckland to make a series of six films from short stories by New Zealand authors. Keith also supported the recommendation of a film report commissioned by the old council which said that aid to film-makers should be at least $300,000 a year, this representing the money earned by the New Zealand government in a film-hire tax paid by commercial film distributors. So hopes were high that a realistic film fund might at last be established.

Hopes were less high in the field of television films. Till 1975 the New Zealand Broadcasting Corporation's single television network had been the country's biggest single supporter of private film-makers. In the last twelve months of its existence it commissioned thirty major documentaries from independent companies—the total financial commitment would have been near $400,000.

But the new Labour Government carried out its policy of abolishing the NZBC and replacing it with two separate, competing networks. This brought the comment from veteran film-maker John O'Shea of Pacific Films that the change was a death-warrant for independent film-makers. Perhaps such statements were premature: the first of the new networks ended its first month by committing money to the Ardvark series, and it seemed there could be a change of emphasis which would move TV support more into the area of drama—a department headed by Michael Scott-Smith, the man who had been responsible for documentaries under the old NZBC.

Censorship continued as a major issue, with cuts being all too obvious in films such as *Chinatown*, *The Conversation*, and *Don't Look Now*. Three new members were appointed to the Appeal Board (which reconsiders disputed decisions of the censors) and their first rulings were eagerly awaited. A private members' bill to reform censorship was reintroduced after having been ignored the previous year. Australia's chief film censor spoke to a conference of New Zealand exhibitors (New Zealand's chief censor McIntosh was in the audience) and described how his system had changed from censorship to classification. The exhibitors were unmoved. What was of concern to them was a government plan to abolish the licensing system which for too long has protected a monopoly system of film exhibition—but everyone else welcomed this proposal.

The film society movement (Federation of Film Societies, Box 1048, Wellington) continues to grow in strength as a third circuit for 16mm distribution of a wide range of films (including *Savages*, *The Spirit of the Beehive*, *The Promised Land*) which would not otherwise have been seen.

New Zealand's two annual film festivals (Auckland Film Festival, Box 1411, Auckland. Wellington Film Festival, Box 1584, Wellington. Both in June/July) have also consolidated their position as a showcase for new films of merit, often earning reviews which edged some features into a general release which would otherwise have been lacking.

National Film Unit Report

Plans to move the National Film Unit from its present outmoded facilities to a new studio complex at Avalon, ten miles from Wellington, continued this year. Construction is proceeding and is currently ahead of schedule. Meanwhile, demands from public and private clients for speedier laboratory service have resulted in the installation of one new processing unit for 16 or 35mm, along with modifications to existing equipment to cater for new film stocks. The Sound Department, which added "Rock and Roll" recording last year, is this year concentrating on plans for a Neve console, along with new JBL monitor loudspeakers for amplifiers.

Shooting currently are two twenty-minute films on the *Visual Arts* and the *Visual Crafts* in New Zealand. This project was originally intended as a single film, but research opened up more possibilities than anticipated. Director David Sims has placed both films (dealing with artists and craftsmen now working in New Zealand) against a firm background of landscape and history.

Releases for 1975 also include an unusual view of New Zealand's past, tragically developing on a commune with four adults, a child, and several visitors. This film, Paul Maunder's feature-length *Landfall*, uses a sort of blank verse narrative style. In the film four young New Zealanders go back to the land, where they hope to live in an uncomplicated way. But their lives are directionless; living close to each other and cut off from their past, they find that tensions flare up and are not easily controlled. The tensions build and eventually explode into violence—and a killing takes place. To make sense of this for themselves, the four adopt a revolutionary ideology; and for a brief time they live happily and with purpose. But inevitably, it seems, violence begets violence. The question remains: did these things really happen or was this some sort of fantasy expressing the primitive feelings we all share?

Sam Neill, Gael Anderson, John Anderson, Rowena Zinsli and Denise Maunder in Paul Maunder's LANDFALL

The series of films on New Zealand birds has been expanded yet again, from nine to a total of thirteen films in all. Some birds included in this series are among the world's rarest, and these films are being used widely in New Zealand and overseas. *Tahere Tikitiki–The Making of a Maori Canoe* was released this year after nearly three years production. A documentary on the building of a ceremonial Maori war canoe, the 35mm colour film explains something of Maori culture through its attitude toward its own past and its living tradition of craftsmanship. From selection and felling of the original tree, each aspect of construction and carving is dictated by tradition, and is viewed through the most commonplace events—things like spring planting, the potato harvest, the long winter nights—all are part of the painstaking and affectionate shaping of the canoe. Its eventual launching is the occasion for a major celebration. Filmed at the Turangawaewae Marae, Ngaruawahia.

Other films completed during the year include *There Is a Place*, a 35mm colour production, with a not-too-serious approach to some typical New Zealand fobs and foibles . . . *The Kingston Flyer*, a trip to the Twenties aboard the country's last scheduled steam train . . . *The South Pacific Forum*, on New Zealand's relationship with its closest neighbours in Polynesia . . . and *Freshwater Dive*, a theatrical short subject about one of the world's unique natural springs.

(16mm prints of major productions are available from New Zealand diplomatic posts through the world, and from State and private film hire services in a number of countries.)

Norway

by Jan Erik Holst

The main bases for film activity in Norway are state production, municipal cinemas, and private distribution. Alternative film activities revolve round the film societies, the Film Centre (a distribution and information group for alternative cinema), and some film groups at colleges.

As a first step in a wide-ranging plan for reorganising national film production into state-financed groups, Norsk Film A/S, the main production company (owned by the state and the municipalities) has been given a production guarantee limited to 3,500,000 Norwegian kroner. This means that the firm can undertake long-term planning, and produce at least two features per annum apart from the productions guaranteed by the state production committee. This money has been used both to finance spectacular comedies based on Norwegian literature, in co-production with the private company EMI-Film A/S, and for producing more ambitious films such as *Hustruer* (*Wives*), by Anja Breien, from an original screenplay, and *Oss* (*Us*), by Laila Tuhus, from a script by Knut Faldbakken. Apart from these two female directors, the leading film personalities in

Norway are members of the Vampyrfilm group: Oddvar Bull Tuhus and Per Blom (directors), Erling Turmann Andersen and Halvor Naess (cinematographers). Norsk Film A/S has its own short film department and an experimental unit *cum* training section restricted, however, to a budget of less than a million Norwegian kroner.

Two other production companies of importance are Team Film A/S and Elan Film A/S. Team Film have made several successful feature comedies about the Olsen gang (three crazy bank-robbers and their many problems), and also two out of three very popular documentary recordings of stage shows—a *genre* that seems to be in vogue in Norwegian production at the moment—directed by Knut Bohwim. Knut Andersen is handling the more ambitious projects at the company, his latest film being *October 44*, in co-production with Lenfilm in Leningrad.

Norwegian feature film production has attained international standards during the past four years and participates more regularly at festivals like Moscow, Berlin, and London. In June 1975 the National Film Theatre

NORWEGIAN FILMS 1971-1974

The Norwegian film council issues catalogues of feature films and shorts, containing a cross-section of Norwegian films of interest to an international public.

During recent years several films have had a favourable reception at international film festivals, notably Berlin and Moscow. The catalogue gives information about these and other Norwegian films. For most films, producers offer a pre-viewing copy subtitled in foreign languages.

NORSK FILMRAD (Norwegian Film Council)

Kirke - og undervisningsdeparte-mentet

Oslo dep, Oslo 1 NORWAY

screened a special Norwegian Film Week, including features such as *Wives, Maria Marusjka, The Seed,* and *Strike!* The municipal Norwegian Cinema and Film Foundation, which gives technical and marketing assistance to the cinemas, was arranging a third film festival in 1975, with entries selected from the Cannes and Berlin Festivals that are being imported into the country.

The trend in contemporary Norwegian cinema is partly towards quality films based on classical writers like Hamsun, Vesaas, and Ibsen, and the well-known modern writer Knut Fladbakken, partly towards re-makes of older movies based on folk literature, turning them into musicals and comedies, and also partly towards semi-documentary features dealing with social and political problems, such as Anja Breien's *Wives* and Oddvar Bull Tuhus's *Strike!* These two films, together with a considerable portion of the annual short film production, most of the film societies, and the Film Centre, are the springboard of a new film policy in Norway, a radical and cultural policy in both the production and distribution areas.

STREIK!
(Strike!)

Script: Lasse Glom and Oddvar Bull Tuhus, from the novel "Sauda, Streik," by Tor Obrestad. Direction: Oddvar Bull Tuhus. Photography: Halvor Naess. Players: Kjell Pettersen, Kjell Stormoen, Kolbjørn Brenda, Bjarne Andersen. For NRK-TV and Markus Film.

Very few Norwegian features are discussing workers' problems. This feature, which has been banned by the Norwegian Broadcasting Corporation and condemned by the industrial organisations, tells of a serious conflict between the workers and an industrial company owned by the giant Union Carbide,

which ended in a strike in June 1970. *Strike!* is a simple, realistic, and outstanding example of radical film work in feature form. Several of the workers play themselves in the film, which also deals with tactics and relationships between social-democrats and Marxist-Leninists. Screened at the Cannes Festival this spring in the Director's Fortnight.

JAN HOLST

recent films

EINAR SCHANKES GLEDESHUS. Dir: Einar Schankes, from his own stage show at "Chat Noir," Oslo. Players: Jens Book Jensen, Inger Jacobsen, Dag Frøland, Tore Ryen, Gro Anita Schønn. For Castle Film.

FANEFLUKT (Desertion). Script and dir: Eldar Einarson. Phot: Erling Thurmann Andersen. Players: Aina Walle, Siemen Rühaak. For Norsk Film/Taurus Film. This well-directed film by a new director concerns a German soldier during the Second World War who escapes, together with his Norwegian girl-friend. They are forced live as refugees at the border until they are captured by the Swedish police in co-operation with the Germans. This collaboration between a neutral country and the Nazis remained concealed until long after the war. The story of the film is based on documentary material and a novel by Aksel Sandemose.

FLÅKLYPA GRAND PRIX. Dir: Ivo Caprino. For Caprino Film Centre. Ivo Caprino has been working on puppet films for many years, and is well-known in this field. This is his third feature, using much puppet work, and is inspired by the humorous short stories of Kjell Aukrust, known for his realistic fantasy figures.

FRU INGER TOL ØSTRÅT. Script: Sverre Udnaes and Åse Vikene. Dir: Udnaes. Phot: Odd Geir Saether. Players: Ingrid Vardund, Ulf Palme, Keve Hjelm, Fritz Helmut. For Norsk Film/EMI Produksjon. A film version of Henrik Ibsen's great play, "Lady Inger of Østråt," set in the Fifteenth century.

GLADE VRINSK. Dir: Knut Bohwim. Phot: Mattis Mathisen. For Teamfilm. Based on a stage show at the Oslo New Theatre. Players: Arve Opsahl, Aud Schønemann, Rolf Just Nilsen.

HISTORIEN OM LASSE OG GEIR (The Story of Lasse and Geir). Script and dir: Svend Wam. Phot: Paul Rene Roestad. Players: Torgeir Scherven, Lasse Tømte, Kjersti Døvigen, Liv Thorsen. For Elan Film. A film about young people in the suburbs, opposing the contemporary social-democratic "welfare" society. Svend Wam

deals mostly with social dilemmas in his films, and is becoming one of the more interesting young Norwegian directors.

HURRA-TA-TA. Script: Yngvar Numme. Dir: Knut Bohwim. Phot: Mattis Mathiesen. Players: Arve Opsahl, Grete Kausland, the Dizzy Tunes. For Teamfilm. A comedy featuring Norwegian show artistes.

HUSTRUER (Wives). Script and dir: Anja Breien. Phot: Halvor Naess (Super 16mm). Players: Frøydis Armand, Katja Medbøe, Anne Marie Ottersen. For Norsk Film. Anja Breien took her idea for this interesting film from a stage play about the situation of contemporary women, which she directed, and from Cassavetes's movie, *Husbands*. It is a realistic story about three women leaving their men and their families—possibly for a long period—to discuss and learn about their situation in relation to the new society. All the dialogue has been written in collaboration with the actresses.

KNUTSEN OG LUDVIGSEN. Script: Øystein Dolmen and Gustac Lorentzen. Dir: Ola Winger. Phot: Knut Gløersen. Players: Harld Heide Steen Jr., Rolf Just Nilsen. Arve Opsahl, Carsten Winger. For Filmconsult. Taken from some popular stories and a stage play based on them, this movie describes the antics of two very interesting fellows who dwell in a tunnel.

MIN MARION. Script and dir: Nils R. Müller, from the novel by Terje Stigen. Players: Ulrikke Greve, Sverre Anker Ousdal, Phot: Ragnar Sørensen. For Nils R. Müller Filmproduksjon. A film dealing with love between two handicapped people.

OLSENBANDENS SISTE BEDRIFTER. Script: Erik Balling, Henning Bahs. Dir: Knut Andersen. Phot: Knut Gløersen. Players: Carsten Byhring, Arve Opsahl, Sverre Holm, Rolf Søder. Number six in the series about the maverick Olsen gang.

Below: the three women in Anja Breien's WIVES

forthcoming films

HEKSESABBAT. Script and dir: Bredo Greve. For Fotfilm. A low-budget feature about witches.

INSEKTSOMMER. Dir: Knut Andersen, from the novel by Knut Faldbakken. For Teamfilm. This will be the third feature directed from works by the leading Norwegian writer of today, Knut Faldbakken. The first was *Mother's House*.

KJAERE MAREN. Script and dir: Jan Erik Düring, from the novel by Oskar Braaten. Phot: Odd Geir Saether. Players: Inger Lise Rypdal and Gisle Straume. For Norsk Film. Originally filmed in 1940, this movie deals with an unmarried mother in the early years of the century.

OSS. Script: Knut Faldbakken. Dir: Laila Tuhus. Phot: Erling Thurmann Andersen. Player: Knut Husebø. For Norsk Film. About pollution in the near future.

SKRAPHANDLERE. Script and dir: Bo Hermansson, from "Steptoe and Son" by Ray Galton and Alan Simpson. Phot: Erling Thurmann Andersen. Players: Leif Juster, Tom Tellefsen. Satirical comedy.

VÅRNATT. Script and dir: Erik Solbakken, from the novel by Tarjei Vesaas. Phot:Hans Nord. Players: Espen Schønberg, Svein Scharfenberg. Solbakken's second feature, this is also based on a novel by the famous writer Vesaas.

forthcoming co-productions

VICTORIA, from the novel by Knut Hamsun. Teamfilm in co-operation with Sweden. **DAGNY,** directed by Håkon Sandøy, set in the late Nineteenth century and involving Munch and Strindberg. Norsk Film/Film Polski.

Focus on Shorts

The short film situation is not too bright at present, as the cultural authorities are granting less money to serious productions, and prefer to support educational and informational shorts. Some films dealing with industrial and social problems have emerged recently, however. Svend Wam made *Tango Industri*, about the Norwegian industrial giant Norsk Hydro and its air pollution. Sølve Skagen is working on films about the aluminium industry in Western Norway, and others are dealing with oil questions. The film department of the student association in Oslo has released an interesting short protesting against the state plan to centralise hospitals. Norsk Filmsenter is involved in distribution, production, and policy planning for Norwegian shorts together with the film workers' association.

Production activity outside Oslo is sparse, although two industrial/cultural film companies are at work in Bergen. In Northern Norway, Knute Erik Jensen has made some outstanding films about cultural activities—reindeer keeping, fishermen in the poor outskirts, etc. Shorts are seldom screened at the municipal cinemas, as they are quite non-commercial, with no money flowing back to the producer. Most shorts are shown at film societies or by other groups.

Art House Focus

Oslo's two main art cinemas in recent years have been **Gimle** and the **Klingenberg** centre, the latter including the modern study cinema **Veslefrikk.** The centre presents outstanding films in original versions with Norwegian subtitles and special screenings of quality features and shorts from abroad. There are restaurants, modern equipment and rooms available for seminars. The municipal cinemas in Bergen, Trondheim and Tromsø have also selected cinemas for quality films. The **Sonja Henie** and **Niels Onstad** Foundations at Høvikodden near Oslo (the Henie—Onstad Art Centre) regularly show experimental shorts or present director's series. **Norsk Filminstitutt** offers special programmes with old Norwegian and foreign films in their own study cinema at Røa in Oslo and presents retrospectives in Veslefrikk in the Klingenberg centre. Furthermore, there are over sixty film societies scattered around Norway with interesting programmes once a week.

Useful Addresses

Film & Kino
(Norwegian film magazine)
Kommunale Kinematografers landsforbund
(National Association of Municipal Cinemas in Norway)
Norsk kino- og filmfond
(Norwegian Cinema and Film Foundation)
Nedre Voll gt. 9
Oslo 1.
Norske Filmklubbers Forbund
(Norwegian Association of Film Societies)
Kirke- og Undervisningsdepartementet—Film-opplæringen
(The Ministry's training course for professionals)
Fant—Tidsskrift for Film
(Fant—Norwegian Film Quarterly)
Norsk Filminstitutt
(The Norwegian Film Institute)
Aslakveien 14b
PO Box 5
Røa
Oslo 7.

Norsk Filmråd
(Norwegian Film Advisory Council)
Kirke- og Undervisningsdepartementet—kontoret for kunst og kultur
(The Ministry of Church and Education—Arts and Cultural Div.)
Oslo dep.
Oslo 1.
Norsk Filmsenter
(Norwegian Film Centre)
PO Box 7198
Homansbyen
Oslo 3.
Nordisk Film- og TV Union—Norsk seksjon
(Norwegian Film and TV Union—Norwegian section)
c/o Oslo Kinematografer
Stortingsgaten 16
Oslo 1.
Norsk Filmforbund
(Norwegian Film Association)
c/o Advokat Bjørn Pettersen

Biskop Gunnerus gate 2
Oslo 1.
Norsk Filmkritikerlag
(Norwegian Film Critics' Society—ass. with FIPRESCI)
Fr. Nansens plass 6 v. 403
Oslo 1.
Norsk Forening for film undervisning
(Norwegian Association for Film Teaching)
c/o Eidsvollkino
2080 Eidsvoll.
Norsk kinoforbund
(The Ass. of Private Cinemas in Norway)
PO Box 345
4801 Arendal.
Norske Filmbryåers forening
(Norwegian Film Distributors' Association)
c/o Advokat Arne M. Falch
Lille Grensen 7
Oslo 1.
Norske Filmprodusenters forening
(Norwegian Film Producers' Association)
c/o Advokat Einar Blanck
Drammensveien 30 VI
Oslo 2.
Statens Filmkontroll
(Board of Film Censors)
Klingenberggatten 5
Oslo 1.
Statens Filmsentral
(The Government Film Service)
Schwensens gate 6
Oslo 1.

Norwegian Producers

ABC Film—Studio ABC
St. Olavs gate 26
Oslo 1.
Caprino Film Centre
Snarøyveien 128
1335 Snarøya.
Centralfilm
Åkebergveien 56
Oslo 6.
Contactfilm
Fr. Stangsgate 41
Oslo 2.
Elan Film
Nordahl Bruunsgate 11
Oslo 1.

EMI Produksjon
Brynsveien 93
1300 Sandvika.
Informasjonsfilm
Akersgaten 64
Oslo 1.
KET Film
Røahagen 63
Oslo 7.
Landbrukets Film og Billedkontor
Frydenlundsgate 8
Oslo 1.
Løtvedt Film
Torvet 13
5000 Bergen.
Markusfilm
Ths. Heftyesgt. 35
Oslo 2.
NRC Film
Torsgate 10
Oslo 2.
Nils R. Müller Filmproduksjon
Knut Øyens vei 18
Ljan.
Norsk Dokumentarfilm
Bogstadveien 6
Oslo 1.
Norsk Film
Kirkeveien 59
Oslo 3.
and
Wedel Jarlsbergsvei 36
1342 Jar.
Statens Filmsentral
Schwensengate 6
Oslo 1.
Svekon Film
Seiersbjerget 7
5000 Bergen.
Teamfilm
Klingenberggata 5
Oslo 1.
Vampyrfilm
Damstredet
Oslo 1.
Zenith Film Scandinavia
Fearnleysgt. 8
Oslo 3.
Oslo Kinematografer
Stortingsgaten 16
Oslo 1.
and
Baerum Kinematografer
1300 Sandvika.

Norwegian Distributors

Centralfilm
Åkerbergveien 56
Oslo 6.
Cinema International Corporation
PO Box 1743
Vika
Oslo 1.
I.S. Columbia–Warner
Stortingsgaten 30
Oslo 1.
Elan Film
Nordahl Bruns gate 11
Oslo 1.
Europafilm
Stortingsgaten 30
Oslo 1.
Filmco
Waldemar Thranes gate 73
Oslo 1.
Fram Film
Fr. Nansens plass 6
Oslo 1.

Kommunenes Filmsentral
Nedre Voll gate 9
Oslo 1.
Kontinentalfilm
Stortingsgaten 28
Oslo 1.
Merkur Film
Fredrik Stangs gate 41
Oslo 2.
Fox
Stortingsgaten 12
Oslo 1.
Norenafilm
Klingenberggaten 5
Oslo 1.
Radio Films
Stortingsgaten 16
Oslo 1.
Syncron-Film
Klingenberggaten 5
Oslo 1.
T & O Film
Teatergaten 3
Oslo 1.
Thalia-Film
Bygdøy Allé 13
Oslo 2.

Triangelfilm
Pilestredet 15
Oslo 1.

Short Film Distributors

Norsk Filminstitutt
Aslakveien 14b
Røa.
Oslo 7.
Norsk Filmsenter
PO Box 7198
Homansbyen
Oslo 3.
Landbrukets Film og Billedkontor
Frydenlundsgate 8
Oslo 1.
Statens Filmsentral
Schwensensgate 6
Oslo 1.

Peru

by John Beauclerk

Peruvians witnessed their first cinema show in the summer of 1897, just two years after the Lumière brothers started their own shows in Paris; but it was eleven years before the first national production *Peruvian Centaurs*—a documentary on that year's cavalry manoeuvres—reached the new screens. If lost time tends to be a recurring theme of a film industry in which Peru lags well behind her neighbours in South America, valiant attempts have been made by both government agencies and individuals to redress the situation.

The first significant school of cinema sprang up in the Sixties in the pre-Colombian capital of Cuzco, where an unexpected collection of talents produced in 1961 *Kukuli*—the tragedy of a young Indian couple who become victims of a masked devil in a sierra fiesta. The subject was given an unselfconscious treatment that makes it the classic of Peruvian indigenous cinema. However, the promise of the Cuzco school did not survive attempts to exploit the success of its first work; *Jarawi*, made in 1966, failed to capture the popular imagination and the advent of the Argentinian co-producers in 1973 assured the failure of *Alpa Kalpa*, a film which unconvincingly attempts to combine a tragic theme of peon oppression with the antics of the hero, Limeno comic Tulio Losa.

A shadow of the Cuzco spirit lives on in the documentaries of Eulogio Nisiyama and Jorge Vignati, two Cuzquenos renowned for their resourcefulness in reaching the most isolated locations. The year 1975 produced two documentary features, *Yawar Fiesta* and *Batalla Ritual*, while a short that has already been accepted as a national classic in the social comment field is Luis Figueroa's *El cargador*, a sympathetic study of the subliminal life and expectations of a native bearer in Cuzco.

In the mid-Sixties the predominantly European film-makers from Lima retook the initiative, almost entirely owing to the work of veteran director Armando Robles Godoy who was producing convincingly authentic national features as early as 1966, the date of his first film *En la selva no hay estrellas* (*No Stars in the Jungle*). The film set a pattern of dramatic cinema later followed by *La muralla verde* (*The Green Wall*, 1969) and *Espejismo* (*Mirage*, 1973). Owing to the efforts of Robles Godoy and others, what may well prove to be the important factor in a re-birth of Peruvian cinema came in the 1973 promulgation of a cinematographic law which provided for the compulsory exhibition of national films duly approved by a commission, and in addition awarded attractive tariff reductions for film-makers wishing to import new equipment. Though the immediate effect of the new law has been what producer Bernardo Batievsky describes as a "poor man's gold rush" (bogus directors profiting from the ignorance of the commission—itself largely composed of soldiers—to promote quickly- and cheaply-made films) and although the majority of these shorts (some seventy-five in one year alone) continue to be of little merit, the law has at least given a shot in the arm to a flagging industry and encouraged the small corps of serious directors who would be

Helena Rojo and Miguel Angel Flores in ESPEJISMO

making features if the national investment situation permitted it.

Most skilled in the "argument short" is the young director Arturo Sinclair, who received (as, indeed, did Robles Godoy) his education in the United States. Sinclair's 1974 shorts include *Sisifus*, *The Veil*, *The Visitation*, and *Salt Water*—all black-and-white subjects of which the latter was awarded the Chicago Festival Golden Hugo Award. Silver Award in the same festival went to Robles Godoy for his own short *Elefant Cemetery*, a film that was originally refused for compulsory exhibition in Peru on the grounds of "lack of interest."

Cinesetenta stand head-and-shoulders clear of the many publicity companies trying their hand at the new industry. Bolivian cameraman Nicolas Smolij gave a virtuoso performance in *The Battle of Ayacucho*, a lavish historical short commissioned by the War Ministry to celebrate the 150th anniversary of independence. Peru's other first-rate lighting cameraman is Mario Robles Godoy (brother of the director), who received his training in Venezuela.

The majority of features shot in Peru are still co-produced with Argentine equipment, expertise and finance. The result invariably bears the indelible stamp of the glossy commercial Argentine feature that has little relation to life in Peru. The latest, *El inquisidor*, produced by Cine Andina and Marlo SCA, is also the best so far. Directed by Argentinian Bernardo Arias this horror thriller combines the legendary grim sites of the Peruvian

Armando Robles Godoy

balance of payments engendered by the export of exposed film for developing, and delaying with the necessary permissions sometimes up to six months after end of shooting). And on the personnel side film-makers still have much to learn in the area of co-operation, which tends to exist only long enough for an individual to acquire the very basics of the trade before setting up shop as fully-fledged director.

The first two years of operation of the cinema law will only be seen as a disappointment by those who expected the instant establishment of an industry along the lines of the Mexican, Venezuelan or Argentinian. Those in turn who regret the existing regime has not been able to inspire a new wave of Peruvian cinema art misunderstand the nature of military governments, not in themselves conducive to the production of masterpieces in any artistic field. The beginnings of an industry are here . . .

Inquisition with locations carefully selected from Lima's posh residential suburbs.

Robles Godoy has kept himself at arm's length from Argentine co-productions, which possibly explains why the only tried Peruvian director has not been able to make a film in two years. He has not benefited so very much from the law he sponsored himself, and its failings in this area can only be blamed on the very considerable obstacles to film-making existing in the country. On the production side the speedy and sophisticated requirements of a modern film are not entirely compatible with tardy business traditions hamstrung by legendary bureaucratic procedures. On the technical side Peru sorely lacks a worthy colour laboratory (the government intensely resenting the drain on the

important peruvian films

KUKULI. By Luis Figueroa, Eulogio Nisiyama and Villanueva. Players: Judith Figueroa and Victor Chambi. Ansachrome. Running time not available. 1961. A young Indian girl leaves her ageing parents high in the Andes to visit relatives and stay over for a fiesta in a distant town. On the way she is seduced by a traveller who leads her to town. The priest refuses to marry the couple and, as the fiesta develops, Kukuli is pursued by an all-too-real devil-dancer who murders her lover and makes off with her to his lair. She dies of shock before the priest can arrive with relief.

EN LA SELVA NO HAY ESTRELLAS (No Stars in the Jungle). Script and dir: Armando Robles Godoy, Phot (Eastmancolor): Mario Robles Godoy. Players: Ignacio Quiroz, Susana Pardal, Jorge Montoro and David Miro. 106 mins. 1966. A jungle adventurer kills his Indian guide after secretly stealing his family's *cache* of panned gold. He soon loses himself in the jungle but in spite of the threat of pursuing Indians and the dangers around him succeeds in reaching a river. After successfully ambushing his pursuers the rogue's efforts are all put to no avail when he slips into the water in an unguarded moment and is held down by the weight of the gold until drowned.

LA MURALLA VERDE (The Green Wall). Script and dir: Armando Robles Godoy. Phot (Eastmancolor): Mario Robles Godoy. Players: Julio Aleman, Sandra Riva and Raul Martin. 124 mins. 1969. The idyllic life of a jungle colonist is brusquely shattered by a deadly snake-bite inflicted on his son. By a vicious twist of fate the accident coincides with the visit of the President. Frantic search for the officials with keys to the hospital medical stores (where the serum is kept) is unsuccessful. The doctor is busy with the visiting dignitaries and the boy dies.

ESPEJISMO (Mirage). Script and dir: Armando Robles Godoy. Phot (Technicolor): Mario Robles Godoy. Prod: Bernardo Batievsky. Players: Helena Rojo (Mexico), Miguel Angel Flores, Orlando Sacha, Hernan Romero and Gabriel Figueroa. 90 mins. 1973. An adolescent dreamer lives alone in a delapidated *hacienda* surrounded by hallucinations of a tragic past. In the discovery of a letter and photograph the boy finds tangible evidence of the former existence of his "ghosts." The photograph is of a beautiful girl—the daughter of the house—who falls in love with a young foreman. In his dreams the boy takes on the role of the foreman, and the tragedy is re-enacted.

EL INQUISIDOR. Script: Gustavo Chirardi. Dir: Bernardo Arias (Argentina). Phot (colour): Pedro Marcialetti (Argentina). Players: Pablo Fernandez, Soledad Mujica, Hernando Cortez and Eduardo Cesti. For Industria Andina del Cine and Marlo SCA. Running time unavailable. 1974. An international (Argentine-Peru) ring of witches with insurance swindles on the side confront a psychotic who relives the inquisition's murderous past in the dungeons of an isolated castle. Bodies burn in suburban gardens and on crosses erected on the beach, limbs crack on the wrack as the PIP (Policia de Investigacion Peruano) wrestle with the thorniest case in memory.

forthcoming feature documentaries

YAWAR FIESTA. Full-length documentary of a fiesta where, in best Spanish tradition, the bulls are allowed free reign of the town for the day, wreaking havoc on the drunken Indian population which we then see "repaired" according to the prevailing medical code of hard liquor antiseptic and torn sheet bandages. (Vignati, Nisiyama).

BATALLA RITUAL. Annual battle for the virgins in which opposite teams of able-bodied and single Indian menfolk fight (often to the death) for first pick of the year's available virgins. (Vignati, Nisiyama)

Pablo Fernandez in EL INQUISIDOR

Production Companies

Audio Visual Productions
740 Av. la Republica
Lima.

Caycho Films SA
230 Malecon Pazos
Lima.

Caltari Films
457b Alcanfores
Lima.

Cinesetenta Productora Peruana de Peliculas SRL
362 Av. Mariategui
Lima.

Industria Andina del Cine
376 Av. Petit Thouars
Lima.

Nova Estudios Cinematograficas SA
Av. Cmdte Espinar 473
Miraflores.

Promoinvest Productores Cinematograficas
Av. Garcilaso de la Vega 955
Lima.

Telecine
Av. Mariategui
Lima.

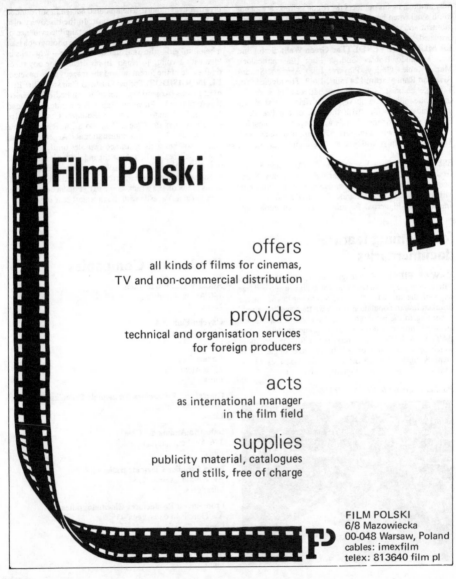

Poland

by Bolesław Lutosławski

Although only a sixth of all films premiered in 1974 were Polish in origin, the box-office success of the previous year was repeated, with 50,000,000 admissions from an overall total of 143,000,000. The most popular film of 1974/75, drawing an audience of 13,000,000 during its first four months, was *Potop* (*The Flood*), directed by Jerzy Hoffman and based on the historical novel by Henryk Sienkiewicz about the Swedish invasion of Poland during the Seventeenth century. Sienkiewicz's novels have often been filmed—*In the Desert and Virgin Forest*, *Colonel Wołodyjowski*, *Knights of the Teutonic Order*—finding a popularity to match his eighty-year-long success with the reading public ("Quo Vadis") both at home and abroad. Andrzej Wajda, who frequently bases his films on Polish literary material (*The Wedding*, by Stanisław Wyspiański), also directed a work based on Władysław Reymont's novel, *Ziemia obiecana* (*The Promised Land*), concerning the development of the great industrial and textile centre of Łódź in the Nineteenth century. Reymont's novels are almost as popular as Sienkiewicz's: *The Peasants* was filmed recently, and like Sienkiewicz in 1905, Reymont won the Nobel Prize in 1924.

The works by Hoffman and Wajda in-

Still from Wajda's recent film, LAND OF PROMISE

Tadeusz Łomnicki and Daniel Olbrychski in POTOP (THE FLOOD)

dicate an important trend in Polish cinema—historical films showing problems tied up with the evolution of the country. Other productions like *Gniazdo* (*The Nest*), *Kazimierz Wielki*, *Bolesław Smiały* and *Kopernik* all reflect this trend as well, though not based on literary material.

Films with contemporary settings embrace a wide range of subjects: from everyday town life in Krzysztof Zanussi's *Bilans kwartalny* (*Quarterly Balance*), through pathological problems in *Zapis zbrodni* (*Record of a Crime*), to a documentary treatment of a village party in *Kochajmy sie* (*Let Us Love*). The most popular of such works,

attracting 5,500,000 people, was Stanisław Chęciński's *Nie ma mocnych* (*No One Is Strong*). In all the films one notices that the central character, though individually characterised, is not only representative of his social group but also remains strongly tied to his particular environment. Stylistically works like *Record of a Crime* and *Let Us Love* are made in a naturalistic way that is quite different from the Polish school of Wajda and Has; aspiring to record occurrences in a documentary fashion, such new films on contemporary life are often made by young directors who received their training in TV.

DZIEJE GRZECHU
(The Story of Sin)

Script and direction: Walerian Borowczyk, from the novel by Stefan Żeromski. Photography (Eastmancolor): Zygmunt Samosiuk. Music: Mendelssohn (Violin Concerto in E minor, played by Konstanty Andrzej Kulka), Johann Pachelbel (Prelude in D minor, played by Feliks Rączkowski). Art Direction: Teresa Barska. Players: Grażyna Długołęcka, Jerzy Zelnik, Olgierd Łukaszewicz, Marek Walczewski, Roman Wilhelmi, Karolina Lubieńska, Zdzisław Mrożewski, Mieczysław Voit, Marek Bargiełowski. For "Tor" Unit (Helena Nowicka). 128 mins.

After making three films in France, Walerian Borowczyk returned to Poland for his latest, and in many ways, very Polish film. *The Story of Sin* is based on a melodramatic novel by Stefan Żeromski, an influential writer at the turn of the century who, in highlighting concepts of sin, virtue and retribution succeeded, in the views of some Polish critics, in making a criticism of the bourgeois order. Borowczyk has retained the melodramatic framework but, as it were, expanded the chinks and hidden allusions in the original work to make it into another of his studies of erotic tensions, emphasising the sexual energy implicit in the novel.

He does this through a narrative style which is more direct and uncomplicated than in his earlier work. The exposition is particularly brilliant—young working girl, living with her parents, becomes enamoured with the married man they take as a lodger. Later, when he goes off ostensibly to seek a divorce, she secretly has his child and then descends the ladder into prostitution until a final meeting with her old lover leads to a bloody climax. Throughout, Borowczyk emphasises the elemental passions surging within his protagonists—the love scenes, although somewhat less outspoken than in his French work, still have a coarse, carnal urge; the succession of betrayals, murders, robberies are presented quite unsentimentally and without any direct moral judgements. Somewhere in the middle the narrative tends to become tedious, even obvious, yet Borowczyk's unique visual style pulls him through at the end; once again, all the *objets d'art*, magazines, furniture, props which clutter these fetid interiors are given a life of their own, flashing past in swift close-ups and viewed with an eye which transforms them into a cold, dream-like image of a past era.

JOHN GILLETT

new and forthcoming films

JAROSŁAW DĄBROWSKI. Script: J. Nagibin. Dir: Bohdan Poręba. Phot: J. Czen-Ju-Łan, A. W. Szelenkow. Players: Zygmunt Malanowicz, Małgorzata Potocka, Joanna Jędryka, S. Szmidt, W. Awdiuszko. For Mosfilm (U.S.S.R.) and Panorama (Poland).

PIORUM KULISTY (Spherical Lightning). Three parts. Script and dir: R. Piwowarski (phot: W. Stok), P. Kędzierski (phot: W. Stok), Z. Kamiński (phot: Z. Kaczmarek). Players: Jadwiga Jankowska-Cieślak, Hanna Skarżanka, T. Budzisz-Krzyżanowska, W. Preyss, M. Glinka. For "X" Unit.

ZAKLĘTE REWIRY. Script: P. Hajný. Dir: Janusz Majewski. Phot: Miroslav Ondříček. Players: M. Kondrat, R. Wilhelmi, Stanisława Celińska. For Barrandov (Czech.) and "Tor" Unit (Poland).

OPADŁY LIŚCIE Z DRZEW (Fallen Leaves from the Trees). Script and dir: Stanisław Różewicz. Phot: Jerzy Wójcik. Players: M. Hryniewicz, M. Klejdysz, M. Kowalik. For "Tor" Unit.

KAZIMIERZ WIELKI (Kazimierz the Great). Script and dir: Ewa and Czesław Petelscy. Phot: Wiesław Rutowicz. Players: Krzysztof Chamiec, Z. Saretok, I. Machowski, Wiesław Gołas, Barbara Wrzesińska, W. Hańcza. For "Iluzjon" Unit.

DROGA NA FRONT (The Way to the Front). Script: Z. Safian. Dir: Andrzej Konic. Phot: R. Ranlau. Players: L. Pietraszek, J. Matałowski. For "Iluzjon" Unit.

DOKTOR JUDYM (Doctor Judym). Script: A. Szczypiorski. Dir: Włodzimierz Haupe. Phot: Maciej Kijowski. Players: Jan Englert, A. Nehrebecka. For "Pryzmat" Unit.

MAZEPA (Mazeppa). Script and dir: Gustaw Holoubek. Phot: Mieczysław Jahoda. Players: Magdalena Zawadzka, J. Bończa, K. Kolberger, Zygmunt Zapasiewicz. For "Pryzmat" Unit.

NASZ CZLOWIEK (Our Man). Script and dir: Krzysztof Kieślowski. Phot: Slawomir Idziak. For "Tor" Unit.

Portugal

by Fernando Duarte

Prior to April 25, 1974, the Portuguese cinema was severely hampered by several problems: censorship, a restricted market, and a total absence of any guiding policy. Studios, laboratories, film clubs and study courses each pursued their own course, and the result was inevitably bad. Nobody in the governments of Salazar or Marcelo Caetano recognised the value of a national cinema, and international films flooded the market. Portugal has about 300 cinemas and produces 4 or 5 films a year; it could have 1,000 cinemas and produce 20 or 30 films a year.

With the recent creation of the Instituto Português de Actividades Cinematográficas (Portuguese Institute of Film Affairs) and box-office control, things have suddenly brightened up. Though there were never any official statistics, box-office turnover (according to press reports) was in the region of seventy to eighty million escudos per year. Now film-makers should think in terms of

Luísa Neves in SOFIA AND SEXUAL EDUCATION

productions which cover the whole country, decentralising culture and democratising Portuguese cinema.

In Lisbon there is the National Cinematheque and many clubs operating. Three festivals will take place during 1975: the Fourth Figueira da Foz Festival (September 2–10), the Sixth Tourist Film Festival of Lisbon (September), and the Fifth International Film Festival of Santarem (October 20–26), the latter devoted to agricultural and rural works.

recent and forthcoming films
Released since April 25, 1974:

O MAL AMADO (Bad Love). Script: Fernando Matos Silva, João Matos Silva, Alvaro Guerra. Dir: Fernando Matos Silva. Players: João Mota, Maria do Céu Guerra, Zita Duarte. (May 3, 1974).

SOFIA E A EDUCAÇÂO SEXUAL (Sofia and Sexual Education). Script and dir: Eduardo Geada. Players: Luísa Neves, Io Apolloni, Artur Semedo, Carlos Ferreiro. (October 1, 1974).

CARTAS NA MESA (Cards on the Table). Script and dir: Rogério Ceitil. Players: José Jorge Letria, José Ceitil, Guida Maria, José Amador, Ricardo Nuno (January 6, 1975).

INDIA. Script and dir: António Faria. Players: Luis Ferreira, Maria Elisa Domingues, António Pacar. (February 14, 1975).

Recent films:

BENILDE OU A VIRGEM MÃE (Benilde or the Virgin Mother). Script: based on a play by José Régio. Dir: Manuel de Oliveira. Players: Maria Barroso, Glória de

Matos, Varela Silva, Augusto Figueiredo, Jacinto Ramos.

CÂNTICO FINAL (The Last Song). Script: based on a novel by Virgilio Ferreira. Dir: Manuel Guimarães (1915-75). Players: Rui de Carvalho, Manuela Carlo, Ana Zannati, Fernando Curado Ribeiro, Varela Silva.

BRANDOS COSTUMES (Sweet Costumes). Dir: Alberto Seixas Santos. Players: Luis Santos, Dalila Rocha, Isabel de Castro, Constança Navarro, Sofia de Carvalho, Cremilda Gil.

O PRINCIPIO DA SABEDORIA (The Beginning of Wisdom). Script: based on a story by Pero Claders. Dir: António de Macedo. Players: Sinde Filipe, Carmen Dolores, Guida Maria, Luis Cerqueira, Nicolau Breyner, Grece de Castro.

recent shorts

VILARINHO DE FURNAS. Dir: António Campos.
SEVER DO VOUGA. Dir: Paulo Rocha.
A CHAFARICA. Dir: António Faria.
QUEM ESPERA POR SAPATOS DE DEFUNTO MORRE DESCALÇO (Whoever Waits for the Shoes of a Dead Man Dies without Shoes). Dir: João César Monteiro.
GRANDE GRANDE ERA A CIDADE (Big, Big Was the City). Dir: Rogério Ceitil.
O BESTIÁRIO (The Bestiarius). Dir: Galvão Teles.
FESTA TRABALHO E PÃO (Feast, Work and Bread). Dir: Costa e Silva.
FALAMOS DE RIO DE ONOR (We Spoke about Onor River). Dir: António Campos.
JAIME. Dir: António Reis.
JULIO DE MATOS UM HOSPITAL (Julio de Matos in Hospital). Film by a group of university students about a mental hospital. Premiered at the Santarem Festival.
SAGRADA FAMÍLIA (Sacred Family). Dir: João César Monteiro.

Romania
by Manuela Gheorghiu

Rising attendances over the past couple of years testify to the popularity of Romanian films in their own country; ticket-sales, moreover, are over 30 % of the total figure. Last year production was so richly diversified that everyone was satisfied. Along with the highly sophisticated *Duhul aurului* (*Lust for Gold*), there was the romantic *Nemuritorii* (*The Immortals*) and the sharp *Filip cel bun* (*Philip the Kind*).

ZIDUL (THE WALL), directed by Constantin Vaeni

As Romania celebrated in 1974 the thirtieth anniversary of the national insurrection against the Nazi occupation, it was natural that some films commemorated that day of blood and glory. Mircea Mureşan's *Porţile albastre ale oraşului (The Blue Gates of the City)* tells the true story of a small battery whose soldiers sacrificed their lives on August 24, 1944, in order to protect the capital against the German reprisal. *Stejar, extremă urgenţă (Oak Tree, Top Emergency)*, directed by Dinu Cocea, is a counter-espionage film set during that stormy summer when certain elements at Romanian headquarters were plotting the uprising against the Germans. The decisive part played by the Communist party in that event is dealt with by young Constantin Vaeni in his excellent *début* work *Zidul (The Wall)* a film full of poetry in spite of its stern script. In *Actorul şi sălbaticii (The Player and the Savages)*, directed by Manole Marcus, who has lately specialised in big

socio-political canvases, the gloomy Fascist years when intellectual freedom was abolished are described through the story of a famous star and his struggle against the atmosphere of terror. In the leading role Toma Caragiu is superb and has good support from the up-and-coming young Mircea Diaconu, who also plays the leading role in *Filip cel bun*, the latest work of Dan Piţa. This film, undoubtedly one of the most interesting of the year—the portrait of a restless adolescent in search of a moral identity—confirms Pita's great talent revealed in *The Stone Wedding*, on which he worked with his gifted contemporary Mircea Veroiu. The same team recently offered *Duhul aurului (Lust for Gold)*, another subtle poem about life and death, another song of love to the beauty of film art. While the film was showing in Bucharest, news came that *The Stone Wedding* had won three prizes at the Panama Film Festival. *Lust for Gold*, which can be considered as a sequel to the previous work, not only has the same structure—two episodes—but also deals with the same world, one dominated by hatred and greed. The differences between the personalities of the two directors emerges more clearly: Veroiu shows a marked propensity for refinement of image and language, where each detail, each shadow has a meaning. This was noticeable in his latest work, *Hyperion*, a story of impossible love which, though having a science fiction setting, deals with loneliness in the modern world.

Director Andrei Blaier wrote his own script for *Ilustrate cu flori de cîmp (Postcards with Flowers)*, a sincere and moving plea for less male irresponsibility towards women. Inspired by a real event, the film describes the drama of a young girl who, after an affair with a married man, is forced by him to have an illegal abortion and dies as a result.

For enthusiasts of historical pictures,

Still from ILUSTRATE CU FLORI DE CÎMP, directed by Andrei Blaier

there has been the huge reconstruction of the Fifteenth century (when the Moldavian king Stefan the Great fought against the Turks, defeating them every time they tried to occupy his kingdom) called *The Martens Brothers*, directed by Mircea Drăgan. The most successful of the year, however, was the pseudo-historical *Nemuritorii* (*The Immortals*), in which Sergiu Nicolaescu proved once again to possess a magical touch with filmgoers. Moving easily from the thriller to the big historical fresco, from the psycological drama to the political film, he remains one of our most prolific and best directors, even though his previous job was ... engineering. *Nemuritorii* is a continuation *sui generis* of his previous *Mihai Viteazul* (*The Last Crusade/Michael the Brave*), in that it describes the adventures of a group of King Michael's ex-soldiers who, after years of exile, decide to return home. The brilliant cast, including Sergiu Nicolaescu in the main role, certainly accounted for the film's box-office success.

new and forthcoming films

DUHUL AURULUI (Lust for Gold). Script and dir: Mircea Veroiu, Dan Piţa. Phot: Iosif Demian. Art dir: Radu Boruzescu. Cost: Miruna Boruzescu. Mus: Dorin Liviu Zaharia. Ed: Cristina Ionescu. Players: Eliza Petrăchescu, Dora Ivanciuc, Liviu Rozorea, Ernest Maftei, Lucia Boga.

ZIDUL (The Wall). Script: Dumitru Carabăţ, Costache Ciobotaru. Dir: Constantin Vaeni. Phot: Iosif Demian. Art dir: Vittorio Holtier. Cost: Lidia Luludis. Mus: Cornelia Tăutu. Players: Gheorghe Dinică, Gabriel Oseciuc, Victor Rebengiuc. For "Case de Filme Trei."

ACTORUL SI SĂLBATICII (The Player and the Savages). Script: Titus Popovici. Dir: Manole Marcus. Phot (colour): Nicu Stan. Art dir: Virgil Moise. Cost: Florina Tomescu. Mus: George Grigoriu. Ed: Lucia Anton. Players: Toma Caragiu, Mircea Albulescu, Margareta Pogonat, Ion Besoiu, Mircea Diaconu. For "Casa de Filme Patru."

ILUSTRATE CU FLORI DE CÎMP (Postcards with Flowers). Script and dir: Andrei Blaier. Phot (colour):

(continued on page 255)

The SCOTTISH FILM COUNCIL
is a uniquely comprehensive agency
for promoting film culture and
educational technology in Scotland.
Its service and activities include:

the GLASGOW FILM THEATRE
a public cinema which combines the
best of the new films with retrospectives covering the major
directors, genres and movements in
world cinema past and present

the SCOTTISH CENTRAL FILM
LIBRARY
offering the most comprehensive
film hire service in the United
Kingdom with a catalogue listing
more than 7000 titles chiefly in the
educational and industrial fields

For further information, contact:

R. B. Macluskie,
Director,
Scottish Film Council,
16 Woodside Terrace,
Glasgow, G3 7XN.
Tel; 041-332-9988

Scotland

by Susan Andrews

Scottish film-makers have begun to break away from the traditional approach to documentaries over the last year, with greater emphasis on the directors' imagination and correspondingly less reliance on the technical tricks of the cameraman. However, despite the new enthusiasm for experimentation, it would be misleading to suggest that revolutionary changes have overtaken sponsored films, which provide the bulk of the output north of the border. We survey below the work of some of the liveliest independent companies.

INTERNATIONAL FILM ASSOCIATES (SCOTLAND)
19 North Claremont Street, Glasgow G3 7NR.

Under the inspiring guidance of Laurence Henson, IFA's position as one of Scotland's most active film companies seems assured by their continuing ability to put their finger on the pulse of Scottish life. *The Big Clubs*, a major co-production with Joachim Kreck, vividly illustrates the fanatical rivalry between the major Glasgow football clubs, Celtic and Rangers. With the stadiums able to hold more than 40% of the city's population, the total commitment of many Glaswegians to one club or the other is represented as a ritual ancient feud between rival Protestant and Catholic clans.

Sea City, a twenty-minute glimpse of Greenock Town, features a wee laddie who, like a Walter Mitty character, day-dreams himself into various adventurous roles. In production, *The Boat*, a comedy based on an idea by Henson, shows how Chic Murray tries to come to terms with an old inherited motor cruiser.

On a more serious note, Henson has just completed *At a Stone in the Heather*, a portrait of the late novelist Eric Linklater, and is working on an independent production about the family of King Robert the Bruce.

PELICULA FILMS
158 Queens Drive, Glasgow, G42 8QN.

Having completed their bread and butter sponsored work, Pelicula's Mike Alexander (director) and Mark Littlewood (cinematographer) eagerly seized the opportunity to concentrate their efforts again this year on a short fictional film. Alexander feels strongly that in their own category shorts are just as valid and important as full-length features. *The Tent*, currently being shot on the Isle of Arran, as a sequel to the highly successful *Home and Away*, explores an adolescent boy's obsession with a couple who are camping on his father's land and the effect this has on his father.

In addition to this venture, Pelicula have made a documentary featuring cellist Joan Dickson demonstrating different string techniques, and also an entertaining, free-wheeling production about a young man who comes to live in Livingston New Town.

TREE FILMS

Private Box, Glasgow G4 9DE.

Bill Forsythe and Charles Gormley, perhaps the most outspoken of the Scottish film-makers, feel that features are really long shorts and that feature writing is arguably less demanding than sponsored work.

Scriptwriter Charles Gormley, who commutes regularly to Holland to collaborate with Pim de la Parra and Wim Verstappen, is also working on a film for Films of Scotland and the DOI on environmental improvement in Possil, the massive prewar housing scheme that forgot to include basic amenities.

Bill Forsythe has just finished eighteen months' work on a film for the Highlands and Islands Development Board on Afforestation. Tree planting has become a subject of great controversy because of the objection to "tree factories" springing up overnight on formerly bare hillsides. The film simply shows that forests have always been part of the Scottish landscape and are an essential part of the environment.

VIZ

58 Queen Street, Edinburgh EH2 3NS.

As usual Murray Grigor and his colleagues are in filmic spate, with two new films following hard on the heels of *The Hand of Adam* (illustrated). *Blast!*, an essay on the Vorticists for the Arts Council, was completed this summer, with Ron Geesin generating the machine sounds and dance

The Venus in Newby Sculpture Gallery, Yorkshire, a shot from Murray Grigor's recent film for VIZ/Films of Scotland and the Scottish Arts Council, entitled THE HAND OF ADAM

rhythms so important to the Vorticists. It also includes some First World War footage, and some "dazzle camouflage, circa 1918."

Viz is finishing another architectural short for the Scottish Civic Trust, with the working title of *Scotland's Heritage*. The film pivots, says Grigor, on the only vernacular architecture which is uniquely Scottish: that is, the tower houses in post-Reformation style. Music is being concocted by a Swedish-Scottish medieval jazz band, "The Cowans."

SIDHARTHA

65a Montgomery Street, Edinburgh.

While two newcomers to the Scottish scene, Sidhartha's Bill Landale and Steve Clark-Hall, have increasingly specialised in cost saving audio-visual productions, they have also found time to make documentaries, as well as industrial and training films.

One of Sidhartha's most successful projects was *A Point in Time*, a forty-minute account of William Johnstone, the self-proclaimed painter, teacher, poacher (ex), author and rebel who after a long absence returned to his beloved border country.

Films of Scotland News

It was on January 14, 1954, that the formation of the Films of Scotland Committee of the Scottish Council Development and Industry was announced in Edinburgh by the Earl of Home, then Minister of State at the Scottish Office. The public announcement

TREE FILMS

Private Box Glasgow G4 9DE
041-331-1209

Low Budget Productions

had, of course, been preceded by much planning and preparation. The late Sir Alexander B. King had accepted the invitation of the Secretary of State to become the Committee's first Chairman—a position he was to hold until his death on February 12, 1973. Sir Alex in turn had persuaded the late Lord Fraser to become Hon. Treasurer of the new body and Lord Fraser had given its activities a firm foundation by making a contribution of £10,000 to its funds. The founder members of the Committee included the Late Dr. John Grierson, George Singleton, Robert Clark, John Gibson Kerr, Sir David Lowe, Charles Oakley, Neil Paterson and Norman Wilson.

Films of Scotland was set up to promote, stimulate and encourage the production and circulation of Scottish films in the national interest. In 1955 Forsyth Hardy was appointed director. He retired this year, 20 years and 140 films later, and was succeeded by

Lawrence Knight. Previous to joining Films of Scotland Lawrence Knight had been producing and directing entertainment and documentary films. The company of which he was a director was very much an international concern with offices in London, Amsterdam and Lagos. A Scot himself, he is happy to be back in his homeland and is eager to help put Scotland on the screens of the world.

The year 1975 opened for Films of Scotland with the completion of *The Hand of Adam* (Viz), which shows the work of Scotland's most celebrated architect, Robert Adam and was made as a contribution to European Architectural Heritage Year. The film was premiered at the Royal Festival Hall and has since received the Silver Medal at the Fifth International Festival on Architecture, Madrid. Another film to be completed was *Sea City—Greenock* (IFA) and in production is Films of Scotland's second story film, *The*

Boat (IFA), and a lyrical exercise in the beauty and importance of water, called *Raindrop*.

Towns are again much in evidence this year. Ogam Films are completing *Erskine New Town*, three years in the making, and Sidhartha Films, using cartoons and the voices of the townspeople, a film on Kirkcaldy. Tree Films, having completed *Keep Your Eye on Paisley* are in the final stages of a film on environmental improvement in Glasgow.

Penguins is the concise working title for a film Christopher Mylne is shooting, which looks at the idiosyncrasies of Edinburgh Zoo's unique breeding colony of penguins.

The Great Mill Race brings Films of Scotland's story films up to three. Now being made by Edinburgh Film Productions, it tells of a race between the Scottish woollen mills to shear a sheep and make a suit from its wool.

George Miller in SEA CITY . . . GREENOCK, produced by IFA Scotland

new and forthcoming films

THE HAND OF ADAM (Viz, for Films of Scotland and the Scottish Arts Council). Script and dir: Murray Grigor. Architectural and Historical Adviser: A. A. Tait. Phot: David Peat with Mike Coulter. Additional Phot: Jon Schorstein. Edit: Patrick Higson. Music: Frank Spedding. Technicolor. 33 minutes. An exploration of the life and work of Robert Adam, Scotland's most celebrated architect and interior designer.

KEEP YOUR EYE ON PAISLEY (Tree Films, for Films of Scotland and the Corporation of Paisley). Dir: Charles Gormley. Script: Gordon M. Williams and Charles Gormley. Narrated: Roddy MacMillan. Soloist: Kenneth McKellar. Music: Tom Ward and Charlie Soane. Phot: David Lewis, Jon Schorstein and Mark Littlewood. Edit: Brian Crumlish. Sound: Alex Brown. A look at a town with a robust and lively history that gave the world the Paisley pattern.

SEA CITY—GREENOCK (IFA Scotland, for Films of Scotland and the Corporation of Greenock). Dir: Laurence Henson. Script: Clifford Hanley. Phot: Edward McConnell and Mark Littlewood. Sound: Cyril McConnell. Instrumentals: Bobby Wishart. Asst: Mike Coulter, Gordon Hickey, Brian Lawrence, Iain Smith.

Players: George Miller, Jack Davidson, Ann Beveridge, Tom Steele, Tommy Sutherland, assisted by the Greenock and District Silver Band, the Toad Choir, the George Square Players, the Greenock Players and the Children of the Town. Technicolor. "The Green Oak Tree," the song of Greenock, runs through Clifford Hanley's web of fantasy and reality in a boy's eye view of his town.

THE BOAT (IFA Scotland, for Films of Scotland). Dir: Laurence Henson. Phot: Edward McConnell. Chic Murray inherits an old motor cruiser moored hard by Loch Lomond and enters into his inheritance.

AT A STONE IN THE HEATHER (IFA Scotland, for Films of Scotland and the Scottish Arts Council). Dir: Laurence Henson. Phot: Edward McConnell. A film study of Eric Linklater.

ERSKINE NEW TOWN (Ogam Films, for Films of Scotland and the County Council of the County of Renfrew). Dir: Oscar Marzaroli. The growth of a New Town over a period of years.

GLASGOW ENVIRONMENTAL IMPROVEMENT (Tree Films, for Films of Scotland and Glasgow Corporation). Script and dir: Charles Gormley. A film about the problems and early successes of a pioneering project to improve the face and quality of life of areas of Glasgow.

THE GREAT MILL RACE (Edinburgh Film Productions, for Films of Scotland and the National Association of Scottish Woollen Manufacturers). Dir: Robin Crichton. Script: Clifford Hanley. Players: John Cairney, Russell Hunter, Leonard Maguire, Elizabeth Brown and Ros Drinkwater. An attempt to break the record for shearing a sheep and making a suit of the wool becomes a race between all the mills of Scotland.

TALKING ABOUT KIRKCALDY ... (Sidhartha Films, for Films of Scotland and the Royal Burgh of Kirkcaldy). Dir: Stephen Clark-Hall. Phot: Gordon Coull. Animation: Donald Holwill. A study in depth of the town of Kirkcaldy with Donald Holwill's animation and the voices of the townspeople.

Scottish Film Council

The Scottish Film Council, with headquarters at 16 Woodside Terrace, Glasgow, is a grant-aided organisation whose purpose is to promote the use of audio-visual media in education and industry and to encourage serious study of the cinema.

The Council's new additional premises in Rose Street, which house the Glasgow Film Theatre and Scottish Centre for Educational Technology, are now in their second year of operation. The Educational Technology Centre consists of a large display area for semi-permanent exhibitions of hardware (from CCTV and video-tape to slide projectors and tape-recorders) and a comprehensive information library on all aspects of audio-visual media in education; the Centre is staffed by specialists, including a team of advisers covering primary, secondary and higher education and industrial training.

Although the Centre and Film Theatre serve different areas of the Council's interests, they are intended to complement one another as a central focus for everyone in Scotland concerned with film and related media. Along with the Council's existing services (such as

the Scottish Central Film Library, production of educational films, technical services, etc.) these new premises will enable the Council to meet the ever-increasing and ever-widening concern for film and audio-visual media.

Art House Focus

The Cameo's (34 Home Street, Edinburgh EH3 91Z) long-standing policy of screening special first-run and repertory programmes has paid off again this year with *Day for Night*, *The Last Detail*, *The Conversation*, *California Split* and Pasolini's *Arabian Nights*. Rather surprisingly, the biggest success was *Serpico* which appealed more to Scottish than English audiences.

At Film House, 3 Randolph Crescent, Lynda Myles organises the Edinburgh Film Theatre along necessarily spartan but enthusiastic lines, offering a host of neglected and off-beat movies at reasonable prices.

The Glasgow Film Theatre, now in its second year, has a 400-seat auditorium equipped for 16mm, 35mm and 70mm. Recent successes have included seasons devoted to Akira Kurosawa, Orson Welles, Robert Altman, Luchino Visconti and Frederick Wiseman. New films such as Fassbinder's *Fear Eats the Soul*, Erice's *Spirit of the Beehive* and Saul Bass's *Phase Four* have also been well received.

Senegal

by Viggo Holm Jensen

The Senegalese cinema has only existed for slightly more than a decade. The earliest works of importance were two shorts by Sembene Ousmane in 1964—*Borom Sarrett* and *Naiye*—followed the next year by *Et la neige n'était plus* by Ababacar Samb. In 1966 Ousmane directed the sixty-minute feature *La Noire de . . .*, two years later making the first African full-length feature, *Le mandat/Mandabi* ("African" defined as countries south of the Sahara, i.e. non-Arab).

In 1969 there appeared the important shorts *Badou-boy*, by Djibril Diop, and *Diankha-bi*, by Mahama J. Traoré. Traoré followed the latter work in 1970 with the hour-long feature *Diegue-bi*; three full-length works were made in 1971—*Emitaï* by Ousmane, *Codou* by Samb, and *Karim* by Momar Thiam.

The most important works since then have been: in 1972 the feature *Sérigné Hassane* by Tidiane Aw, and the one-hour works *Laambaye* and *Reou-Takh* by Traoré; in 1973 the one-hour film *Touki-Bouki* by Diop; and in 1974 the shorts *La brosse* and *Arrêt-car* by N'gaido Ba, and the features *Xala* by Ousmane, *Le bracelet de bronze* by Aw, *Garga M'bossé* and *N'Diangane* by Traoré. Projects for 1975/76 are a feature by Paulin S. Vieyra, *Et les fruits tinrent les promesses des fleurs*, and the works *Diamilou* (Cherif Adramou Seck), *Sona* (Arona Sarr), and *L'hivernage* (Mamadou Sarr).

Many more films have been produced recently in Senegal thanks to the state companies SIDEC and SNC (see IFG 1973/74/75 for details), though there have also been several works which have been both technically and ideologically sub-standard. The directors whose films contain the greatest potential are Sembene Ousmane, Mahama Johnson Traoré and Ababacar Samb.

South Africa

by Lionel Friedberg

It would seem that the age of enlightenment has at last reached the South African film industry. In a period where so much uncertainty prevails about its future, film-makers have displayed a hitherto unknown degree of daring and boldness in the subject-matter of local films. The most significant factors contributing to this situation are works which deal with controversial racial themes (albeit very delicately) and the large-scale production of feature films made expressly for Black audiences. In the latter case, great originality has been shown by the fact that a Black director has helmed two of the all-Black films.

While the artistic standards of local feature films remain as stagnant and unexciting as in previous years, the industry has made tremendous advances in box-office returns. The year's most financially successful film has been Jamie Uys's *Beautiful People*, which has grossed well over R2,000,000—more than double the receipts

for the next most highly successful film, *The Sting. Beautiful People* was perhaps the single most important factor which led to the decision by the Minister of Economic Affairs, Mr. C. Heunis, to increase the government's subsidy aid to local film-makers from R2,750,000 (last year) to R4,250,000. The subsidy system is as follows: once a film has received R50,000 in box-office returns, all additional recepits are subsidised by 55% for Afrikaans-language films, and 44% for English-language productions; films intended for Black audiences, and which are made in any of the tribal dialects, are immediately subsidised by 18c on every ticket sold.

State aid to the film industry is, in fact, the cornerstone of South African production. In a country more than twice the size of France, total cinema attendance is only about half that for an average week in London! Unfortunately the lifeline of the industry has also had a very detrimental effect on local films. The subsidy makes it too easy to achieve handsome profits on the domestic circuit, and as a result, there are far too many producers who make films merely for the sake of exploiting the subsidy facility. Local features have acquired a very poor reputation overseas because of these cheaply made, technically inadequate and artistically appalling features. It is time that the government instituted some sort of grading system in order to determine which films should qualify for subsidy, prior to their release. There should, at the very least, be a basic list of requirements concerning a film's technical and artistic standards.

A recent survey indicated a total of over 130 registered production companies, situated in the various metropolitan areas around the country. The majority of these are concerned with advertising commercials, training films and documentaries, although during the first quarter of 1975 no less than twenty-eight feature films were in various phases of preparation, production or in release. This healthy situation is in sharp contrast to many countries overseas, and the influx of foreign technicians and creative talents increases steadily.

Watershed Productions' *The Steam Pig* was a courageous venture into the arena of racial affairs. Directed by Francis Ferard and produced by Ross Devenish, the film is concerned with murder and its strong racial undertones, but is yet to be completed due to financial upsets. The film stars the outstanding young actor, Marius Wyers, and Black writer-actor, John Kani. *e Lollipop* is a Film Trust production, directed by Ashley Lazarus, and is destined to become another major success in the world market. It is the story of a White boy (played by Norman Knox) and his Black counterpart (played by Muntu Ben Louis Ndebele) who develop a friendship that eventually saves the life of the White child. The film unfolds against the magnificent backdrop of the Lesotho mountain kingdom, but includes important locations in New York City. *e Lollipop* is the most expensive local film ever made, and the first feature produced by brothers Philo and Andre Pieterse. They are already formulating exciting plans for the future, including a remake of *Bicycle Thieves* (which will be retailored to an African situation), *The Golden Rendezvous* (a co-production with Carlo Ponti) and a major production *When the Lion Feeds*. *e Lollipop* also features José Ferrer and Karen Valentine.

Shakespeare's "Macbeth" has already undergone a transformation to an African setting, and the result is Lynton Stephenson's

Simon Sabela directing Sudney Chama and Dick Sisilana during the shooting of the Heyns Film production U-DELIWE

powerful film *Maxhosa*. Made by Vansetex Productions, the entire film was shot on location in the traditional Xhosa tribal homeland, the Transkei. Stephenson is currently working on his forthcoming production *The Story of an African Farm*, which has become locked in a controversial race with two other local production houses who intend filming the classic story by Olive Schreiner.

The first two major films intended for all-Black audiences have been *U-deliwe* (*The Little One*) and *Inkedama* (*The Orphan*), produced by Heyns Films of Pretoria. Both films were directed by the distinguished Black actor, Simon Sabela, who was recently seen in Michael Klinger's *Gold*. The company has two more Black films scheduled for production before the end of 1975, including an ambitious musical.

Controversy also raged during the production of Cavalier Films' *The Diamond Hunters*, which stars imported actors David McCallum, John Cypher and Hayley Mills. Filming started under the direction of Lou Pastore, who was invited to make the film whilst living in America, but continued disagreements between him and the producers concerning the screenplay resulted in Mr. Pastore being replaced by local director Dirk de Villiers. Cavalier Films are, nevertheless, hoping to make their long-awaited inroad on the international market with this film.

As in the past, many companies have been here on location. The biggest was Michael Klinger's *Shout at the Devil*, with Lee Marvin, Roger Moore and Barbara Parkins. As with *Gold*, the film is based on a story by local author Wilbur Smith. In production during the first few months of 1975 was the Nat Wachsberger film, *The Diamond Mercenaries*. Significantly, the film utilises an all-South African crew, under the direction of Val Guest, and the features Telly Savalas, Peter Fonda and Jack Palance *African Express* is an Italian production, featuring Ursula Andress and directed by Michael Lupo. Much of the location shooting took place on the Zambesi River. Plans abound for further international productions in South Africa, and there can be no doubt that much of this activity is due to the widely-expanded technical facilities that experienced technical crews available here. Many producers are taking their films through post-production in this country, still very much less expensive than in Europe and America.

The question facing the local industry concerns the unknown effects which television will have on cinema attendances. To date, the South African Broadcasting Corporation has made little use of private producers for the supply of television programmes, and this future source of revenue for film-makers remains uncertain and unnerving.

With the British actors' Equity ban on the export of dramas and entertainment programmes to the South African Broadcasting Corporation, the country has been denied a great deal of potentially good television. The SABC is meanwhile aiming at about 50% local programming, and it is doubtful that they will be able to meet this objective for at least the next three or four years. Here is an ideal opportunity to inject new life into the film industry, but so far only a few documentary series have been awarded to private producers and, ironically, to the National Film Board (a state-owned organisation).

It is, understandably, far too early to critcise the SABC. Their efforts in bringing a nationwide colour television network to South Africa is a mammoth task, which has already consumed no less than R106,000,000. Many headaches will still have to be endured by the SABC Board of Directors before an official policy on programme supply can be established. The Television Centre in Auckland Park, Johannesburg, represents one of the biggest projects of its kind ever undertaken anywhere in the world, and the statistics are indeed impressive. The centre already includes seven major sound studios, and the entire complex sprawls over 45,000 square metres. By the time regular transmissions begin towards the end of 1975, the corporation will have a workforce of around 4,000 people.

The general development of the country's film and television industry has led to the formation of the South African Film and Television Technicians' Association. This is the first professional association which aims to serve local technicians and producers by establishing basic principles concerning working conditions, employment practices and contractual agreements. More important, however, is the aim to improve the technical and artistic standards of local films. SAFTTA provides an efficient contact between members of the film and television industries, and is working towards the consolidation of its members' hopes and aspirations.

Spain

by Roger Mortimore

The Spanish cinema is partly summed up by the absence of a Spanish entry at Cannes this year, after the successful *La prima Angélica* last year. Two notable films, *Furtivos* (José Luis Borau) and *Furia española* (Francisco Betriu), were requested by M. Bessy, but they were denied official permission. What is more serious is that there is still no Spanish national cinema of European calibre. Blame rests with the censor and state control of the film industry's finances. It remains impossible to make a film that deals with any important problem of contemporary Spanish life (strikes, ETA, Marxist priests). The films produced and written by José Luis Dibildos, regarded as pursuing a middle course between the vulgarities of Alfredo Landa and the hermeticism of Saura, have received acclaim, yet *Los nuevos españoles*, which describes the take-over of an insurance firm by an American corporation, was less incisive than films of Bardem and Berlanga twenty years ago. The most interesting new film was *El amor de Capitán Brando*.

The staples of the Spanish film industry remain the imitation and the sub-pornographic *genres*. *Exorcismo*, of obvious parentage, is set in England because the censor regards it impossible for a daughter of the Spanish *bourgeoisie* to be "possessed." Such inanity continues to hinder the formation of a mature cinema-going public. Similarly, the contents of banned films circulate by word-of-mouth from people who have seen them abroad, a false impression being created because of the taking of the sexual episodes out of context. Yet official approval is given to the sub-pornographic *genre* (doyen, Alfredo Landa), where marriage is seen, in the words of the old guard Archbishop of Cuenca, as "the remedy for concupiscence," a morality that allows the censor to permit the prior titillation. Spaniards remain *voyeurs*. Little wonder that the magazine "Cambio 16" now lists "Films that it's impossible to see *outside* Spain."

The most popular Spanish film last year was *Aborto criminal* (*Criminal Abortion*). Inquino, a kind of Catholic Andy Warhol, followed it with *Chicas de alquiler* (*Girls for Hire*), a farrago of prostitutes, pimps, drugs, lesbianism and corruption of minors that posed as a denunciation of a sector of contemporary Madrid but which was merely a pretext for a flagrant display of bad taste. Again, it only passed the censor because of its moralising conclusion. It starred Nadiushka, a Russian-Polish girl modelled on La Loren, "a symbol," as critic Fernando Lara observed, "of a cinema which wants to satisfy the longing for escape of a Triumphalist but repressed bourgeoisie." At one time she was starring in four new films in Madrid.

Due to the political *apertura*, there has been a slackening of censorship of foreign films, manifest in the uncut presence of *Blow-Up, Belle de Jour* and *Amarcord*. Hopefully this tolerance will extend to notable *Spanish* films like Berlanga's *The Executioner* (1963), yet to circulate inside Spain in a complete version. The *apertura* has also permitted the filming of two hitherto considered "dangerous" classics of Nineteenth-century Spanish literature, *Tormento* by Galdos and *La Regenta* by "Clarin," the Spanish Flaubert. Both were mediocre illustrations of

cinespaña, s.a

Av. Jose Antonio 42

MADRID

Tel: 231 66 05-06-07

* Exporter of Spanish films
* A broad organisation that enlarges
  commercial possibilities

the books, lacking the guts of the originals. The topic of a priest's affair with a maid in *Tormento* was easily assimilable by a *bourgeoisie* that is now allowed to see Brecht. Liberalisation in Spain has become a style.

The new censorship norms, promulgated in March 1975, merely substituted nudity for the freedom to treat important matters fully. As Bardem commented: "Censorship continues to prop up a cinema that is spineless and insubstantial, remote from the possibilities of expression of our European and American colleagues. Perhaps, as a gesture, more flesh, but the same insufficient dose of freedom of mind." The fact that scripts no longer have to be presented to the censor before permission is given to start shooting changes little. And the problem remains for a Spanish director that if he is successful he is expected to go on making the same kind of film, rather than being allowed more freedom of action as he would be by producers in other countries. A director either has to assent or shut up because, as the director Basilio Martin Patino observed, everyone who makes a film in Spain is "of the Right" because anything else would provoke police intervention. Worthwhile films are made in Spain despite, not because of, Francoism.

It has been reckoned that in the Forties the Spanish excluded 20 % of world cinema; now it is 50%. Spanish censorship in the Fifties was undoubtedly closer to European censorship than it is now; thus, a Spanish audience is not familiar with the language of modern cinema. *La dolce vita* remains banned. There was a two-year delay with *Summer of '42*. Scant Japanese and even less Indian cinema is shown. *Jesus Christ Superstar* made it, and provoked violence. *The Goat Horn* by the Bulgarian Andonov ran in Madrid for over a year, and enjoyed considerable success in provincial towns like

Saragossa. A clue to the reason why is given by the advertising, which plays on the rape sequence near the beginning of the film: "Don't miss the first quarter of an hour. You'll think that you're in Paris or London." *O Lucky Man!* opened in Madrid lacking forty-five minutes, the work of the distributor who felt the original length to be uncommercial. Not for nothing has it been suggested that there should be a law to protect audiences, who are also exposed to greatly misleading posters. The increase in seat prices, now close to European level, raised the point that this should mean European cinema, uncut and without absurd delays. The fan is also ill-served by the craze for blowing films up to 70mm and Cinerama, an expedient which destroyed the texture of the photography of *Cries and Whispers* and truncated legs in, of all things, *Singin' in the Rain*.

Festivals are numerous, often ludicrous, occasions for the parading of medals and gold braid, such as those of "Naval Cinema" at Cartagena and "Military Values" at Albacete, where everybody seems to win a prize. The retrospective of Nicholas Ray at San Sebastian last year was marred by black-and-white prints of colour films, others being shown in 16mm versions. Even the Filmoteca Nacional is not free from such problems, though its programmes remain magnificent. But what is one to think of a National Film Theatre that does not have its own premises, lacks adequate soundproofing, suffers incompetent reel-changing and has the projection box so ill-placed that the heads of late arrivals are reflected on the screen?

The presentation of films on Spanish TV remains no better—cuts, interruptions for the news, titles changed at the last minute, are frequent, coupled with errors in the presentation, like attributing *How Green Was My Valley* and *Viva Zapata!* to John Huston. As

Avenue d'Alfonso XIII, no. 75
telephone: 458-25-07, 458-24-17
MADRID—16 (Spain)
Cables: VOFILMS—MADRID

An organisation that stands for efficiency, dependability and experience in the fields of import, distribution, release and promotion of "Cinema d' Art et Essai" in Spain. At the service of the world's finest films.

VICENTE-ANTONIO PINEDA
CONSEILLER-DÉLÉGUÉ

compensation TV-owners near the border picked up *A Clockwork Orange* and other films screened on Portuguese TV, and for many it is more convenient to go to Portugal to see banned films than to France. Ironically, cinemas in the South of France now show Spanish films, like *Tarots*, that can be seen inside Spain, interspliced with material from genuine pornographic films.

Last year 460 films were distributed, of which 113 were American, 96 Spanish (including 23 co-productions) and 70 Italian. The most popular film was *The Sting*. In January 1975 a three-day programme of films about the Spanish Civil War was held in Perpignan. Sadly, it remains impossible for such an event to be held inside Spain, where there is not even freedom to treat historical subjects. A lavish project for a film about the Catholic Kings, Ferdinand and Isabella, called *La es-*

pada negra and to be directed by José Maria Forqué, had to be called off because of official disapproval. It is shameful that a notable film about a *conquistador* (*Aguirre, Wrath of God*) has to be made by a foreigner. As there have been no new films by Berlanga or Erice, the only hopeful signs are Arrabal's *Guernica*, with Gian Maria Volontè and Nuria Espert, being made in Italy, and Rosi's rumoured film of the Matesa affair. Finally, it is ironic to reflect that the same audiences who now watch the Yugoslav epic *The Fifth Offensive*, with the Nazis being defeated by Communist guerrillas, watched films in the Forties of the glorious *Wehrmacht* slugging the decadent democracies. All will be well in Spain when it is possible to make a *Carry On*-type film about July 18, 1936. Perhaps with Alfredo Landa as Franco. In Spain there is always a lot to look forward to.

EL AMOR DE CAPITÁN BRANDO
(The Love of Captain Brando)

Script: Juan Tebar and Jaime de Armiñán. Direction: Jaime de Armiñán. Photography (Eastmancolor): Luis Cuadrado. Music: José Nieto. Players: Fernando Fernán Gómez, Ana Belén, Jaime Gamboa, Amparo Soler Leal, Antonio Ferrandis, Julieta Serrano. For Incine/Impala (Alfredo Matas).

Armiñán's latest film reveals the sadness and frustration of a Castilian *pueblo*, where a triangular relationship develops between a young schoolteacher Aurora (Ana Belén), Fernando (Fernando Fernán Gómez), recently returned from exile, and Juan (Jaime Gamboa), aged thirteen. Juan's passion for Aurora, at first confined to his solitary game where he imagines himself to be a Seventh Cavalry officer, attracts her, but she herself falls in love with Fernando. Aurora is sacked because of her enlightened ideas on education, including sex education, and because of

complaints by Juan's mother. And she is incapable of sustaining a relationship with Fernando, who might well agree with Stephen Dedalus in "Ulysses" that "history is a nightmare from which I am trying to awake," and who has lost all his illusions in an exile that included entering Berlin with the Russians. Like Fernando in *The Spirit of the Beehive*, he is a man broken by the Civil War, whose only wish now is to record birdsong. The gulf between him and Aurora is well illustrated when both, separately, watch *The Gay Divorcee*, with Astaire and Rogers, on TV. For Fernando it is an important nostalgic occasion, while for Aurora it is just another Thirties film. Fernando is unable to comprehend the reality of contemporary Spain

Ana Belén, and Jaime Gamboa in EL AMOR DE CAPITÁN BRANDO

where, as he observes, everything has changed except the people.

El Amor de Capitán Brando is notable for its authentic reflection of reality, despite the implausibility of the schoolchildren's strike and demonstration in protest when Aurora is dismissed. The characters are three-dimensional, credible, including the minor ones: the mayor, with his empty Triumphalist rhetoric; the other schoolteacher, who tells the children a fable with a moral point to account for the building of the aqueduct during a day trip to Segovia; Juan's mother, deserted by her French husband, who, she tells Juan, is dead. The background is the austere beauty of Castile in winter, as bleak and bracing as the Fourth symphony of Sibelius, scrupulously recorded, it is otiose to add, by Cuadrado. The acting, too, is faultless, with another fine performance by Fernando Fernán Gómez, and Ana Belén reveals that, at the age of twenty-four, she is Spain's leading actress. All suggests that Armiñan is the man to film "The Forge," the first part of Arturo Barea's great autobiographical novel "The Forging of a Rebel," the Castilian equivalent of the *My Childhood*s of Gorki and Bill Douglas.

ROGER MORTIMORE

recent films

LA CRUZ DEL DIABLO (The Devil's Cross). Dir: John Gilling. Players: Adolfo Marsillach, Carmen Sevilla, Emma Cohen. For Bulnes (Madrid).

DUERME, DUERME, MI AMOR (Sleep, Sleep, My Love). Dir: Francisco Regueiro. Players: José Luis López Vázquez, Lina Canalejas, Laly Soldevila. For Goya (Madrid).

FURIA ESPAÑOLA (Spanish Fury). Dir: Francisco Betriu. Players: Cassen, Mónica Randall, Ovidi Montllor.

FURTIVOS (Furtives). Dir: José Luis Borau. Players: Lola Gaos, Ovidi Montllor, Alicia Sanchez.

LA REVOLUCIÓN MATRIMONIAL (The Matrimonial Revolution). Dir: José Antonio Nieves Conde. Players: José Luis López Vázquez, Analia Gade. For José Frade (Madrid).

LA LOBA Y LA PALOMA (The She-Wolf and the Dove). Dir: Gonzalo Suárez. Players: Donald Pleasence, Carmen Sevilla, Muriel Catala, Michael Dunn. For Eguilux-PAC (Madrid)/Sargon (Lichtenstein).

LOS NUEVOS ESPAÑOLES (The New Spaniards). Dir: Roberto Bodegas. Players: José Sacristan, María Luisa San José, Antonio Ferrandis, Amparo Soler Leal. For Agata (Madrid).

LOS PAJAROS DE BADEN-BADEN (The Birds of Baden-Baden). Dir: Mario Camus. Players: Catherine Spaak, Frederic de Pasquale, José Luis Alonso. For Impala (Madrid)/ARPA (Zürich).

LA REGENTA (The Regent). Dir: Gonzalo Suárez. Players: Emma Penella, Keith Baxter, Nigel Davenport, Adolfo Marsillach. For Emiliano Piedra (Madrid).

TOCATA Y FUGA DE LOLITA (Lolita's Toccata and Fugue). Dir: Antonio Drove. Players: Arturo Fernandez, Pauline Challenor, Amparo Muñoz, Francisco Algora. For Agata (Madrid).

TORMENTO (Torment). Dir: Pedro Olea. Players: Ana Belén, Conchita Velasco, Francisco Rabal, Javier Escriva. For José Frade (Madrid).

YA SOY UNA MUJER (Now I'm a Woman). Dir: Manuel Summers. Players: Cristina Ramón Guardiola, Jaqueline Rhodes, Beatriz Galbó. For Kalender (Madrid).

YO LA VI PRIMERO (I Saw Her First). Dir: Fernando Fernán Gómez. Players: Manuel Summers, Maria del Puy. For Kalender (Madrid).

Spanish Specialised Distributors

CB Films
Generalisimo Franco 407
Barcelona.
Cineteca, S.A.
Hurtado de Mendoza 11
Madrid.
Incine
Fernandez de la Hoz 5
Madrid.
V.O. Films, S.A.
Av. Alfonso XIII, 75
Madrid 16.

Art House Focus

Madrid and Barcelona contain the preponderance of art houses, which are called *salas especiales*. In Barcelona seek out the **Ars, Alexis, Balmes, Maryland, Moratin, Arcadia, Aquitania** and **Publi**; in Madrid the **Alexandra, Duplex** (Filmoteca Nacional), **Rosales, Palace, Galileo, Pompeya, California, Peñalver, Bellas Artes** and **Drygstore** can be recommended, although the visitor to Madrid is advised to consult the amusement pages in the press since some local cinemas, notably the **Carretas**, often run short seasons of films by such important contemporary Spanish directors as Saura and Fernán Gómez.

The rest of Spain also contains several *salas especiales*: in Alava, the **Aula de Cultura;** Alicante, the **Casablanca**; Bilbao, the **Abando**; Burgos, the **Tivoli** (summer only); Gandía, the **Colón** (ditto); Gerona, the **Oriente**; Gijón, the **Brisamar**; La Coruna, the **Goya**; Lerida, the **Bahiha**; Las Palmas, the **Vegueta** and **Canarias**; Manresa, the **Apolo**; Oviedo, the **Paladium**; San Sebastian, the **Pequeno Casino**; Santander, the **Monaco** and **Gran Casino**; Sevilla, the **Trajano**; Tarragona, the **Cesar**; Valencia, the **Xerea** and **Aula 7**; Vigo, the **Rosalia Castro**; Zaragoza, the **Eliseos.**

Sri Lanka (Ceylon)

by D. B. Warnasiri

The low ebb of production during the changeable years of the early Seventies seems to be at an end. With 90 films on the floor during the first quarter of 1975 (compared with 18–20 during the earlier period), a boom seems to be indicated. The reasons for such rejuvenation of the industry are mainly attributable to the State Film Corporation, established on January 21, 1972. Before the SFC's inauguration yearly production ran at about 18–20 features per year, but only 12–15 of these ever obtained release. Private distributors and exhibitors not only monopolised the local industry but also controlled the import of foreign and Indian films. The latter—glamorous, fairy-tale adventures—dominated the screens and hindered the emergence of any indigenous, socially-aware cinema. Such domination had been going on since the beginnings of the Sri Lanka industry in January 1947, but it was only in the Sixties that younger film-makers started to protest against such a state of affairs (chiefly due to the monopoly by two privately-owned companies of studios, laboratories and theatres on the island).

The State Film Corporation's avowed objectives were as follows: to make available credit and technical facilities; to provide screen time for Sinhalese films; to supply raw stock at subsidised rates; to reduce the competition of Indian cinema and thus re-educate public taste; and to train new talent for the industry. After four years the SFC has gone a long way towards realising its plans: importation of raw stock and foreign films is now totally in the SFC's control, and distribution is done in a strict order of preference. In place of the earlier two-circuit system, the SFC has opened up four circuits, thus allowing 25–30 new films to be screened every year (as compared with 12–15 previously). What is most needed now is some direct encouragement of younger film-makers, as well as a more understanding and liberal censorship board.

new and forthcoming films

DHUL MALAK. Script: H. L. Wijetunge. Dir: Wijaya Dharma Sri. Phot: Sumitra Amarasinghe. Players: Tony Ranasinghe, Nita Fernando, Ravindra Randeniya.
AEYA DEN LOKU LAMAYEK. Script and dir: Dharmasena Pathiraja. Phot: Donald Karunaratne. Players: Malini Fonseka, Wijaya Kumaratunge.
MADOL DUWA. Script: Philip Coorey. Dir: Lester James Peries. Phot: M. S. Anandan. Players: Joe Abeywickrema, Dhamma Jagoda, Jinne Hettiarachchi.

THE GOD KING

Script: Anthony Greville-Bell. Direction: Lester James Peries. Photography (Eastmancolor, Todd-AO 35): Willie Blake. Editing: Sumitra Peries. Music: Nimal Mendis (arranged and conducted by Larry Ashmore). Production Design: Herbert Smith. Players: Oliver Tobias, Leigh Lawson, Geoffrey Russell, Ravindra Randeniya, Irangani Serasinghe, Joe Abeywickrema, Anne Loos, Wijaya Kumarratunga, Douglas Wickremasinghe, Mano Breckenridge. For Dimitri de Grunwald. 99 mins.

Peries's *The God King* is Sri Lanka's biggest production ever undertaken (discounting *The Bridge on the River Kwai*) and bears every trace of having been conceived as a celebration of the country's achievement. Though set in the Fifth century, and nominally detailing the rise to power of the foundling King Kassapa, the film is more concerned with pointing up ever-present problems of power and government than simply telling a historical story. As such it possesses a universal quality which, combined with Peries's measured, visually opulent direction, raises it to epic status. *The God King* features three British actors in the leading roles, but it is to their, and the film's credit that their make-up never appears obtrusive amid the supporting cast of well-known Sinhalese players (Joe Abeywickrema, Ravindra Randeniya, etc.). Peries remains at all times in control of his epic canvas, only occasionally branching away from his inner circle of players to engage in large-scale set-pieces; in the latter one might have wished for a less stately approach, but it is the internal conflict which clearly concerns Peries more—and this he builds in an impressive and involving manner.

DEREK ELLEY

AMARNATH JAYATILAKA has played an important role in establishing serious cinema and its appreciation in Sri Lanka. His book "Chitrapata Parichaya" (Understanding Cinema) was the first comprehensive study to be published in Sinhala, and his two next works, "Cinema Chintana" (Thoughts on the Cinema) and "Chitrapata Adhyayanaya" (The Study of Films), were angled towards being used for teaching in schools. As well as serving on many panels and critical juries, and founding the Sri Lanka Cinematheque, Jayatilaka has himself taken up directing. His first venture into film production was with *Adarawanthayo* (*The Lovers*), released in 1968, followed by *Priyanga* and a *cinéma-vérité* short, *Thawath davasak*, in 1970. His third and most recent feature is *Thilaka and Thilakaa*, based on a trilogy of novels by T. B. Ilangaratne (Minister of Internal and Foreign Trade). Starring Karunaratne Hangawatta and Vajira Nirmalie in the title roles, the film

Amarnath Jayatilaka

(b&w, 114 mins.) has a quiet lyrical flow reminiscent of Satyajit Ray's early works and shows a new leadership emerging from the rural and middle classes to challenge those forces established through money, property and influence. In many ways it can be compared to the Indian film *Aandhi*, directed by Gulzar. Jayatilaka is currently directing *Nivenna ginna* (from another story by Ilangaratne), as well as finalising the first Indo–Sinhalese joint production and working for the establishment of an Afro-Asian Cinematheque in Sri Lanka.

FIROZE RANGOONWALA

Tony Ranasinghe and Nita Fernando in DHUL MALAK

The Swedish Film Institute

Presents 1975 - 76

Metamorphosis

Directed by Ivo Dvorak
Based on the short story by Franz Kafka

Hello Baby!

Directed by Johan Bergenstråhle
By and with the director's exceptional wife, Marie-Louise

Siesta Samba

Directed by Vilgot Sjöman
An exotic, erotic "I am curious" Brazilian adventure

Bang

Directed by Jan Troell
Before you know it, you're in your declining years

A Lover And His Lass

Just a comedy by Lasse Hallström

. . . and many others

The Swedish Film Institute

Filmhuset · Box 27 126 · S-102 52 Stockholm
Telephone 08 - 63 05 10 · Cable: Filminstitutet · Telex: 13326
Executive producer: Bengt Forslund

Sweden

by Peter Cowie

The long ideological feud between film and TV in Sweden may be coming to an end. During the past year, an agreement has been signed whereby the Swedish Film Institute and Sveriges Radio will jointly establish a fund worth 10 million Skr. (approximately $2,500,000) for the purpose of producing feature films.

It has always been difficult to understand the friction that endures between the two branches, for Swedish TV has one of the most imaginative and adventurous programming policies in Europe. Foreign films that have been spurned by local distributors pop up regularly on the small screen in Sweden, often introduced by critics and discussed in accompanying programmes. A reconciliation was inevitable, in spite of all the mud-slinging, because more and more directors were involving themselves with TV, notably Ingmar Bergman, with *Scenes from a Marriage*, and, more recently, *The Magic Flute* and his new four-part series, *Face to Face*.

The new revolving fund, to be administered primarily by Pelle Berglund (for Sveriges Radio) and Jörn Donner (for the Film Institute) will not be a mere hunting ground for esoteric directors. Strenuous efforts will be made to sell the films abroad, although as we go to press the actors' strike threatens to throw the year's plans into chaos.

And in 1974 the cinema industry in Sweden was in a strong negotiating position. Attendances were up by 10%, mirroring the trend in the United States and Britain, and box-office receipts increased by almost a quarter over 1973. *The Sting* and *The Exorcist* took over $4,500,000 between them

during the year, while even three new Swedish pictures (*Dunderklumpen*, *The Last Adventure*, and *The White Carnation*) combined to attract more than $2,000,000 worth of tickets.

It has also been a prolific year for Swedish films. Fifteen of them were released in the period ending April 1975, with a great many promising projects in the offing. They ranged from difficult, pretentious works like Kjell Grede's *A Simple Melody* and Michael Meschke's *Purgatory* to children's movies such as *Dunderklumpen* and *Agaton Sax and the Byköping Feast*. Familiar names like Vilgot Sjöman (*The Garage*), Jan Halldoff (*The Last Adventure*), and Hasse Alfredson (*Egg! Egg?*) all entered the lists with entertaining, commercial movies, while Bergman continued to lengthen the distance between him and all other Swedish directors with his sublime interpretation of *The Magic Flute*. His enormous success, particularly in the United States, only throws into relief the essential mediocrity of most other Swedish productions.

So the search is on for a new Bo Widerberg, a new Jan Troell. Two of the likeliest candidates for success are Lasse Hallström and Mats Arehn. Hallström surprised and delighted everyone with *It Was a Lover and His Lass*, a warm, understanding comedy about young people, while Arehn's first feature, *Maria*, revealed a director with a marvellous flair for catching the best moments in an actor's performance. Kenne Fant, head of Svensk Filmindustri, devoted his annual holiday to shooting a screen version of his play about the meaning

Karlsson on the roof

was written by ASTRID LINDGREN
directed by OLLE HELLBOM
photographed by LASSE BJÖRNE
and produced by OLLE NORDEMAR

AB SVENSK FILMINDUSTRI

Stockholm, Sweden. Phone 22 14 00
Telex ESSEFFS 17533 Cables "Filmindustri".

of liberty, *Monismania 1995*, with a first-class cast including Erland Josephson, Harriet Andersson, Ingrid Thulin, Holger Löwenadler, and Gösta Cederlund. The film, which was released theatrically but was really best seen on television, was little commented upon in the Swedish press because of its controversial message. Fant had dared to suggest that an open "democracy" of the Scandinavian type could easily drift into totalitarianism, and such unorthodox thinking is anathema to Stockholm's intellectual circles. *Monismania 1995* is a courageous statement by a thoughtful writer and director.

Awards

The main recipients of quality awards from the Swedish Film Institute in 1974 were: *A Handful of Love* (331,000 Kr.), *Seven Girls* (321,000 Kr.), *Stubby* (199,000 Kr.), *There's a Key to Every Door* (191,000 Kr.), *Ebon Lundin* (170,000 Kr.), *The Pistol* (164,000 Kr.), and *Emil and the Piglet* (106,000 Kr.).

The Gold Bugs (equivalent to U.S. Academy Awards in the Swedish film world) were given to Inga Tidblad, Vilgot Sjöman, Allan Edwall, and P. A. Lundgren.

TROLLFLÖJTEN
(The Magic Flute)

Direction: Ingmar Bergman, from the opera by Mozart and Schikaneder. Photography (Eastmancolor): Sven Nykvist. Editing: Siv Lundgren. Conducted by Eric Ericson, with the Swedish Radio Symphony Orchestra and Chorus. Players: Ulrik Cold, Irma Urrila, Josef Köstlinger, Håkan Hagegård, Ragnar Ulfung, Birgit Nordin. For Swedish Radio/TV2. 132 mins.

Whereas in most productions of Mozart's *Magic Flute*, there is an attempt to realise the opera on three distinct levels, all of equal force, namely the people's theatre, the magical aspect, and the mystical play, which the instinctive genius of Schikaneder in his

Bergman directing THE MAGIC FLUTE

limits, given a fresh interpretation. The sheer external and internal beauty, and boundless richness of Bergman's concept and production find an artistic equivalent in the expressive acting as well as in the overall style of performance. The singing is exquisite throughout, and Eric Ericson's conducting is particularly lucid. On the whole, then, there is undoubtedly an element of genius in Bergman's grasp and presentation of the opera.

FELIX BUCHER

MARIA

Script: Mats Arehn, Ingemar Ejve, Bertil Köhler. Direction: Mats Arehn. Photography (Eastmancolor): Lasse Björne. Editing: Ingemar Ejve. Music: Kjell Andersson. Art direction: Stig Boquist. Players: Lis Nilheim, Thomas Hellberg, Ulf Hasseltorp, Janne Carlsson, Peter Malmsjö, Sif Ruud. For AB Nordisk Tonefilm (Ingemar Ejve). 97 mins.

Maria is a hopeful beacon in the Swedish film landscape. It is not marred by aesthetic pretentions. It is not a prey to the complexes of "social commitment." Maria and Leffe are engaging characters who exult and suffer because they are ordinary human beings—and all the more ambiguous for that. Leffe will probably never be able to escape from his criminal tendencies; Maria will continue to fall in love with less than perfect partners. The point is that two souls have joined briefly in flight, and Mats Arehn's sensitive direction recalls the early Troell. The editing, by producer Ingemar Ejve, is brisk and intelligent, firmly banishing any hint of sententiousness from the film.

Two lesser personalities also shine. Magnus, Maria's fatherless son, is another Léaud, his ten-year-old face a mirror of the strain and anguish surrounding him. Rikard, the cartoonist who waits discreetly, warmly in the background as Maria's problems ac-

libretto has made possible, Bergman in his film version unifies these elements by imbuing the entire opera with humanity.

Everything in *The Magic Flute* can be explained in these humanistic terms, although in the final stages the vital magic of the "secret," the human secret, remains. Neither Sarastro nor the Queen of the Night are beings from another planet, and neither of them has an inexplicable appearance; they belong to the same world as Pamina and Tamino, Monostatos and Papageno. Bergman plays with great skill on the idea of a performance in the beautiful Drottningholm Theatre, although on several occasions, in spite of the restrictive framework of the stage, he communicates the drama in cinematic terms, and—probably for the first time—opera becomes a direct experience via the medium of film. Even the music is, within

Torbjörn Axelman
Lee Hazlewood

A HOUSE SAFE FOR TIGERS

Now ready for international release

In production:

SUMMER TRUMPET

Screenplay by Torbjörn Axelman,
Per Wästberg and Margareta Ekström

TAX PRODUCTIONS — TAX FILMS

cumulate, is another example of the non-conformist alive in an otherwise aloof society. And even Maria's parents are sympathetically drawn, far more flexible creations than the crass symbols endemic in this kind of production.

This is a real *début* film, the first feature assignment for the director, the producer, the composer, the actors, and several crew members. They can be proud of *Maria*.

PETER COWIE

DEN VITA VÄGGEN
(The White Wall)

Script and direction: Stig Björkman. Photography (Eastmancolor): Petter Davidsson. Editing: Stig Björkman, Margit Nordqvist. Music: S. O. Walldoff. Players: Harriet Andersson, Lena Nyman, Sven Wollter, Tomas Pontén. For Svenska Filminstitutet (Bengt Forslund). 75 mins.

This featurette, the screen equivalent of a short story, contains one of the year's best performances. Harriet Andersson plays the lonely, deserted wife, Monika Larsson, with a striking range of emotions, from coolness and despair to warmth and humour. The film describes a typical day in the life of the "emancipated" Scandinavian woman. Waking beside a strange man, applying

Lis Nilheim and Janne Carlsson in MARIA

fruitlessly for a job, trying to contact her vagrant husband, going to a gloomy dance hall with a friend ... It is a plaintive movie, almost a documentary on the individual at odds with the smooth, gleaming contours of social democracy. Unfortunately Stig Björkman fails to instil any kinetic energy into his style. Individual scenes are cold, like an abandoned dinner; some lines are delivered so flatly that they verge on the ludicrous (e.g. the comments of the personnel director, or the remarks of the immigrant worker whom Monika meets in a café). But *The White Wall* is saved by the acting of Harriet Andersson, a brief, pert appearance by Lena Nyman, and an accompanying lyric by Dory Previn. "Won't you stay a while and save my life?" asks the singer on the soundtrack as Monika drives home with yet another young pick-up, and music and imagery combine in a charge of appealing irony.

PETER COWIE

DUNDERKLUMPEN

Script: Beppe Wolgers. Direction, animation, and art direction: Per Åhlin. Photography (colour): Lennart Carlsson (live), Per Svensson (animated). Editing: Per Åhlin. Music: Toots Thielemans. Players: Beppe Wolgers, Jens Wolgers. For GK-Film (Gunnar Karlsson). 97 mins.

After many years in planning and production, *Dunderklumpen* amply fulfils the expectations of its producer, Gunnar Karlsson, and its director, Per Åhlin. Here is a Scandinavian full-length animated feature that can stand comparison with American movies like *Mary Poppins*. It blends live-action scenes (shot in the delightful expanses of Jämtland) with animated characters. A small boy is lured out of his home on Midsummer's Night, and his father (Beppe Wolgers) goes in search of him. Their adventures are rather nondescript, but the cartoon figures are enchanting. They include the villainous "One-Eye," who steals a treasure chest to take revenge on a money-seeking society and rides a spidery bike, the gigantic "John," literally composed of a mountain, whose favourite pastime is plunging his slopes into the lake, and a raddled hag known for obvious reasons as Elvira Fattigan. Dunderklumpen himself is a potato-faced creature who can breathe life into toys and lead his camp-followers in a genial procession. The infectious music, the songs, and the beautiful landscape all play their part in holding the attention of a young audience.

PETER COWIE

DET SISTA ÄVENTYRET (The Last Aventure)

Script and direction: Jan Halldoff, from the novel by Per Gunnar Evander. Photography (colour): Hasse Seiden. Editing: Peter Falck. Music: Sergey Rakhmaninov. Players: Göran Stangertz, Ann Zacharias, Marianne Aminoff, Thomas Bolme, For Hasse Seiden Film AB. 115 mins.

In the provincial world of Swedish cinema, Jan Halldoff has been a butt for the scorn of the intelligentsia throughout his career. Too prolific, too shallow, too winsome, say the critics. Of course Halldoff has made some really bad films; and it is true that, for all his energy, he lacks the immediately recognisable authority of a Godard or a Fassbinder. *The Last Adventure*, however, is a thoughtful, mature production by any standards, and its success at the Swedish box-office demonstrates once again that Halldoff is in tune with his public, which is more than can be said for many directors in Stockholm.

Based on a novel by Per Gunnar Evander, the movie tells of a young man's retreat from responsibility. Jimmy is suddenly appalled by the life that has been so carefully—and insensitively—mapped out for him by his parents. To his horror he finds

that the outside world is just as inhibiting and frustrating as the army camp where he has been completing his national service. So he turns tail and becomes a teacher, promptly falling in love with one of his pupils. Hedfrid. In a less percipient film, this couple's infatuation might justify Jimmy's rejection of society. Halldoff and Evander, though, pursue their hero inexorably to a different conclusion. It is not so much the social framework that buckles under the strain of our observation as Jimmy himself. He realises by degrees that he is as selfish, as possessive, and as dependent on *bourgeois* ideals as are his parents. Hedfrid drifts beyond his comprehension, her guilt-free attitude to love a baffling obstacle in his path to happiness. Jimmy has opted for neither attack nor defence in life. Like Jan in Halldoff's earlier film, *The Corridor*, he is last seen in a private limbo, from which a new, less temperamental, and more tolerant personality may emerge.

PETER COWIE

new and forthcoming films

METAMORPHOSIS. Dir: Ivo Dvorak, from the story by Franz Kafka. Phot: Jiri Tirl. Players: Ernst Günther, Gunn Wållgren. Prod: Svenska Filminstitutet.
GARAGET (The Garage). Script and dir: Vilgot Sjöman. Players: Agneta Ekmanner, Frej Lindqvist, Per Myrberg, Christina Schollin. Prod: Europa Film/Public Film/Vilgot Sjöman.
HALLO BABY. Script: Johan Bergenstråhle, Marie Louise de Geer. Dir: Bergenstråhle. Players: Marie Louise de Geer. Prod: Svenska Filminstitutet.
MONISMANIEN 1995 (Monismania 1995). Script and dir: Kenne Fant. Phot: Sven Nykvist. Players: Erland Josephson, Ingrid Thulin, Harriet Andersson. Prod: Kenne Fant/Sveriges Radio TV 2.
SKÄRSELD (Purgatory). Script: Michael Meschke, Silvano Agosti. Dir: Meschke. Phot: Agosti. Players: Jan Blomberg, Åke Nygren, Inger Jalmert-Moritz, Carin Rosén. Prod: Svenska Filminstitutet.

BORROW SWEDISH SHORT FILMS

from our distributors abroad:

AUSTRALIA

National Library of Australia
Film Collection
Parkes Place
CANBERRA A.C.T. 2600

AUSTRIA

Wirtschaftsförderungsinstitut
Hoher Markt 3
A-1011 VIENNA

Oesterreichischer Gewerk-
schaftsbund
Postfach 155
A-1011 VIENNA

BELGIUM

Sofedi-Films
147, avenue de l'Hippodrome
1050 BRUXELLES

FRANCE

Céfilm
15 bis, rue de Marignan
75008 PARIS

GREAT BRITAIN

Peter Darvill Associates Ltd
280 Chartridge Lane
CHESHAM, Buckinghamshire
HP5 2SG

Guild Sound & Vision Ltd
Woodston House
Oundle Road
PETERBOROUGH PE2 9PZ

NETHERLANDS

Technical Film Centre
Arnhemsestraatweg 17
VELP (Gld)

NEW ZEALAND

National Film Library
Amp Chambers
Featherson Street
WELLINGTON 1

SWITZERLAND

Schmalfilm-Zentrale
Erlachstrasse 21
3000 BERN 9

We have a variety of 16mm short films on different aspects of Swedish life and culture in English (or American), French, German and Spanish, most of them in colour.

ALSO AVAILABLE THROUGH SWEDISH EMBASSIES ABROAD.

In the *United States,* please contact Swedish Information Service
825 Third Avenue
NEW YORK, N.Y. 10022.

Most of the films are also available on short-term loan from the Swedish Institute's Film Service in Stockholm. *Requests should be made through Swedish diplomatic missions.*

Regarding *film sales* please contact

THE SWEDISH INSTITUTE
Film Section
P.O. Box 7072
S-103 82 STOCKHOLM 7, Sweden

Thommy Berggren and Mona Seilitz in the Sandrews production of GILIAP

ÄGGET ÄR LÖST! (Egg! Egg? A Hardboiled Story). Script and dir: Hans Alfredson. Phot: Lars Svanberg. Players: Gösta Ekman, Max von Sydow, Birgitta Andersson, Anna Godenius. Prod: Svenska Ord/SF-Produktion.

MINA DRÖMMAR STAD (My Dream City). Dir: Ingvar Skogsberg, from the novels by P. A. Fogelström. Prod: ST-Produktion.

BANG. Script and dir: Jan Troell. Prod: Svenska Filminstitutet.

ANSIKTE MOT ANSIKTE (Face to Face). Script and dir: Ingmar Bergman. Phot: Sven Nykvist. Players: Erland Josephson, Liv Ullmann, Gunnar Björnstrand. Prod: Cinematograph/Sveriges Radio.

SOMMARENS TROMPET (A Summer Trumpet). Script: Torbjörn Axelman, Per Wästberg and Margareta Ekström. Dir: Axelman. Prod: TAX Film.

Documentaries for Hire

The Swedish Institute has a wide variety of short films available on 16mm for hire from distributors and film depots throughout the world (Darvill Associates in Britain, for example):

FROM SWEDEN WITH LOVE. A film about stamps and at the same time a kind of film chat about Sweden, about the environment and the motives behind all stamps. 28 mins. Colour.

SWEDISH SCENES. A collage of pictures of the Swedish countryside, cities, people, and places of work. Evocative, wide-ranging, and lyrical in its way. 14 mins. Colour.

THE KARLSSON BROTHERS (Bröderna Karlsson). A warm, appealing film by Vilgot Sjöman that describes some of his cousins in Småland. Screened at Oberhausen in 1974, and one of this director's most relaxed works. 20 mins. Colour.

MODERN SWEDISH CINEMA. An updated version of a documentary film that has already proved to be of great value. Sequences from *Raven's End, Love 65, The Assault, A Swedish Love Story, The White Game,* and *Harry Munter* are included with an introduction by Nils Petter Sundgren. 35 mins. Colour and black-and-white.

VASA. The proud warship "Vasa" sank in Stockholm harbour in 1628 and was raised from the muddy depths 333 years later. 18 mins. Colour.

JOHAN EKBERG. A moving study of old age by Jan Troell, now famous for *Here Is Your Life* and *The Emigrants.*

Mathias Henrikson in MONISMANIA 1995

Useful Addresses

Sveriges Förenade Filmstudios
(Swedish Federation of Film Societies)
Box 27 126
S 102 52 Stockholm.

Svenska Filminstitutet
(Swedish Film Institute)
Box 27 126
S 102 52 Stockholm.

Statens Biografbyrå
Kungsgatan 38, VII
S 111 35 Stockholm.

Föreningen Sveriges Filmproducenter
(Swedish Federation of Film Producers)
Biblioteksgatan 9
S 111 46 Stockholm.

Swedish Specialised Distributors

Apollo Film AB
Kungsgatan 15
111 43 Stockholm.

AB Europa Film
Box 1316
111 83 Stockholm.

Filmarkivet
Box 43
S-200 72 Malmö.

Film Centrum
PO Box 171 01
104 62 Stockholm.

Minerva Film AB
Apelbergsgatan 58
111 37 Stockholm.

Pallas Film AB
PO Box 1522
111 85 Stockholm.

Sandrew Film & Teater AB
Box 5612
114 86 Stockholm.

Stockholm Film AB
Kungsgaten 24
111 35 Stockholm.

AB Svensk Filmindustri
Kungsgatan 36
101 10 Stockholm.

Svenska Filminstitutet
Borgvägen, Box 27126
102 52 Stockholm 27.

Swedish Film AB
Döbelnsgatan 12
113 58 Stockholm.
(16mm only)

Switzerland

by Felix Bucher

The general economic recession of the past year has been felt in the Swiss film industry. On the one hand the Film Section of the Confederate Department of the Interior will probably not be accorded an increasing fund from which to support Swiss cinema, and on the other individual directors will find the market less encouraging for the more difficult types of film, and consequently harder to finance and shoot them.

The Solothurn Filmdays in 1974, with eighteen features on show, will probably remain a peak for years to come, as feature film production has already slipped back in 1975, at least as far as the totally independent film-makers are concerned. The original group of Suisse romande directors—Tanner, Goretta, and Soutter—continue to produce films, however, almost unaware of the recession, chiefly because they can find support in the form of co-productions with France and are no longer totally dependent on government aid.

The inadequacy of the subsidy system is demonstrated by the fact that the Film Section only has two million francs at its disposal in 1975 (and out of this grants which could not be met in 1974 now have to be paid), and that this amount is subject to the ravages of inflation. It is still not quite clear if this sum should be divided among a few directors (thus providing substantial help) or among many (offering comparatively small amounts of aid). Since the Swiss Newsreels (founded in 1942) have had to be discontinued due to lack of interest by the cinema owners and in the face of competition from TV, the sum otherwise given to the Newsreels should be available and thus increase the amount of the subsidy.

It will be interesting to see how successful the various projects of the German-speaking TV in Zürich turn out to be, now that Zürich has followed the example of Geneva and is entering into collaboration with film-makers, arranging a scriptwriting competition among other things. As in Geneva, films co-produced with TV are expected to run for a certain period in the cinemas before they can be viewed on the small screen. New films by Alain Tanner, Claude Goretta, Michel Soutter, and Daniel Schmid have been announced.

The Swiss Film Centre, which groups together all supporters and friends of the "new Swiss cinema," functions as a private organisation (subsidised, however, by the federal government), and is now acknowledged as *the* promoter of Swiss films in general, both nationally and internationally (there have been some very successful "Swiss Film Weeks" abroad). It administers Film-pool, the distribution outlet for Swiss cinema. The Swiss Film Centre, the Swiss Association of Film-makers, and the Swiss Association of Animators, have united to produce a communal information sheet, in order to intensify and achieve their objectives (internationally, too).

Focus on New Films

Among more recent productions, Claude Goretta's *Pas si méchant que ça* deserves particular attention. Not only does the film show

CATALOGUE OF SWISS FILMS

published by the

SWISS FILM CENTRE
ZURICH

Vol. 1 1972—Vol. 2 (1 supplementary edition 1973) —
Vol. 3 (2 supplementary edition 1974)

This catalogue is the representative film list of Swiss
feature and short-films.

Mail orders to:
BUCH 2000, POSTFACH, 891o-AFFOLTERN a.A., SWITZERLAND.

● ● ● ● ● ● ●

The SWISS FILM CENTRE

POSTBOX 171, SPIEGELGASSE 7, 8o25-ZÜRICH Tel. o1/ 47 28 6o

is an independent organisation founded to promote Swiss
Filmmaking, supported by Filmmakers, the Film Industry of
Switzerland, private benefactors and the Swiss Department
of Home and Cultural Affairs.

The SWISS FILM CENTRE is presenting Swiss Films at
International Festivals—organising Swiss Film Weeks—
representing independent Swiss filmmakers in Switzerland
and abroad—distributing Swiss Films in Switzerland.

film-pool

how impressively Goretta knows how to communicate and experience unspoken, borderline emotional situations, but it proves how he seeks to perfect the art of human relationships, a theme already present in his earlier work. The idea of the outsider, who has to fend for himself, undergoes in *Pas si méchant que ça* a curious twist. Goretta describes a young business contractor who keeps going by stealing money in a series of hold-ups, during which he gets to know a girl who is willing to support him. But he does not tell his wife about this double, double-life: he is indeed a loner, but his various relationships fail to divert him from the cul-de-sac that confronts him. It is a film with French actors in the leading roles (Marlène Jobert, Gérard Depardieu, Dominique Labourier), who feel quite at home in the milieu of the Suisse romande.

Alain Tanner's *Le milieu du monde*, widely hailed as a small masterpiece in America and elsewhere, diagnoses the Swiss inability to change, to find oneself, and to communicate with others. The film achieves its end by analysing the way in which the leading man is too involved in—and committed to—his ambition in the world of politics and big business to fulfil his relationship with an girl immigrant worker. The film ends, inevitably, with the girl returning to Italy.

Two Swiss–German directors made a hopeful impact on the scene. Rolf Lyssy followed his *Eugen heisst wohlgeboren* (1970) with *Konfrontation*, and Markus Imhoof came up with *Fluchtgefahr*. The basis of Lyssy's film is the assassination of Wilhelm Gustloff, leader of the country's NSDAP branch group, by a Jew named David Frankfurter in Davos in 1936. Lyssy knows how to combine historical fact with dramatic elements. The personality of the assassin is

carefully built up, and the reasons for his action are extensively analysed. For long stretches the film succeeds admirably in mastering the comparatively recent past of Switzerland through the detached eyes of the present.

In *Fluchtgefahr*, however, the emphasis is on contemporary criticism of the Swiss penal system as well as on the portrayal of a small-time thief who becomes a hardened criminal during his prison term. The clean, precise direction blends with the unobtrusive playing of the leading actors to create a powerful documentary on the prison environment.

If these two features revealed some surprising aspects of the German-Swiss cinema, then Fredi Murer confirmed once again that the film-makers from Zürich are best in the field of documentary. In *Wie Bergler in den Bergen sind eigentlich nicht schuld, dass wir da sind* (*It's Not Really Our Fault That We Mountain Dwellers Are Where We Are*), he describes the people around Göschenen (near the northern entrance to the Gotthard tunnel), and from the Schächen and Madraner valleys, and formulates at the same time three typical styles of life of these mountain inhabitants.

other recent films

LE TROISIÈME CRI. Script and dir: Igaal Niddam. Players: Jacques Denis, Leyla Aubert, Christine Fersen, Camille Fournier, Roland Mahauden. Prod: Niddam and collaborators. Dist: Victor Film, Basle.
TAG DER AFFEN. Script: Elisabeth Gujer and Uli Meier. Dir: Uli Meier. Phot: Rob Gnant and Werner Zuber. Players: Michael Schacht, Hilde Ziegler, Norbert Schientek, Rolf Kadgin, Ingold Wildenauer. Prod: Cinémonde, ZDF and SRG (both TV, German and Swiss). Dist: Cinémonde, Kreuzstrasse 11, 8008 Zürich.
WER EINMAL LÜGT ODER VIKTOR UND DIE ERZIEHUNG. Script: June Kovach and Alexander J. Seiler. Dir and ed: June Kovach. Documentary about a

socially neglected young man and his experiences in various homes. Prod: Nemo Film Zürich. Dist: Filmpool, Zürich.

DIE KINDER VON FURNA. Script, dir., ed., prod: Christian Schocher (7504 Pontresina). Documentary about a mountain village in the Engadin.

Swiss Specialised Distributors

Cinema International Corp.
Kreuzstr. 26
Postbox
8032 Zürich.

Columbus Film KG
Steinstrasse 21
Zürich.

Domino Film AG
Militärstrasse 76
Zürich.

Idéal Film SA
14 rue Tronchin
1211 Geneva 7.

Majestic Films SA

6 rue de Grand Saint-Jean
Lausanne.

Monopole Pathé Films SA
3 rue de Chantepoulet
Geneva.

Monopol Films AG
Talacker 42
Zürich.

Park Film
7 avenue Léon-Gaud
1206 Geneva.

Rialto Film AG
Münchhaldenstrasse 10
Zürich.

Sadfi SA
8 rue de Hesse
Geneva.

Schweizer Schul- und Volkskino
Donnerbühlweg 32
Berne.

Septima Film
20 rue de Lausanne
Geneva.

Victor Film AG
Adlerstrasse 23
Basle.

Art House Focus

Most good films in Switzerland are screened in their original version with subtitles (usually French and German), which makes cinema-going a pleasure for the visitor from abroad. Some foreign films have enjoyed immense success in Switzerland, and are sometimes released there ahead of other mainland European countries.

In Zürich, buffs should call on the **Cinema Piccadilly,** the **Studio Nord-Süd,** the **Studio 4, Le Paris,** and the **Cinema Uto,** as well as the **Studio Commercio,** which runs revivals and off-beat films including Swiss documentaries and little-known features.

In Basel, there is the **Mascotte** and the **Studio Central,** while in Bern there is the reliable **Cinema Club.**

In Lausanne, Walter Beck has long regaled local residents and enthusiasts from throughout the Vaud with excellent revival and first-run programmes at his **Cinéma du Bourg.**

Geneva is probably the best of the Swiss cities as far as good films are concerned, for the general cinemas as well as the art houses maintain a high standard of programme. **L'Ecran,** which shows first-run films (such as *Lancelot du Lac*) in the winter and repertory items during the summer months, all chosen with taste and intelligence by Raphaël Jaquier, who is also responsible for various excellent cinemas in the city, is the haunt of students.

Some of the best art houses in Switzerland are off the beaten track. Michel Schwob's **Cinéma Bio** in Neuchâtel always has an attractive range of product on view, and recent programmes have included *Section spéciale, The Romantic Englishwoman,* and *Young Frankenstein.* Seats are 7 Sfrs. each. In La Chaux-de-Fonds the **Palace** is a good port of call, while in Saint-Gall, on the other side of the country, there is the **Studio Hecht.**

In Lucerne, Emil Steinberger runs the **Moderne,** which within the last few years has become the local centre for good films (most of which enjoy long runs). The **Ciné Studio** presents off-beat programmes of interest.

The **Centre d'Animation Cinématographique,** at the Cinema Roxy in Geneva, performs a fine task in developing the non-commercial circuit, as does Bernhard Uhlmann's **Filmpodium Zürich,** and the **Kellerkino** in Bern.

Syria

by Mohammed Rida

Syrian cinema began as a purely commercial enterprise specialising in poorly-made films: the first, *The Accused Innocent,* appeared in 1928, followed by *The Damascan Sky* in 1932. These two works set the standard until 1963, when the Syrian Government es-tablished a National Cinema Centre. Prior to that, attempts by the industry to establish itself had always been threatened by competition from the more experienced Egyptian cinema, which enjoyed an established star system guaranteed to pull the crowds. In addition, Egyptian Arabic was accepted throughout the Arab world, whereas Syrian was not always familiar to audiences (the same problem was encountered in Lebanon). The success of Egyptian films discouraged the domestic market, with the result that Syrians adopted a system of "borrowing" Egyptian stars and directors.

In 1963 the Government decided to intervene in the situation, and a National Cinema Centre was established with the aim of producing better-quality films on more serious subjects. The first, *The Truck Driver*, was directed by the Yugoslavian Boško Fočinić; another three years were to elapse before a second film emerged from the Centre. The efforts of the government did nothing to deter commercial producers who continued to churn out the same low-level comedies. Egyptian directors such as Saif El Din, Shawkat Abdul Minheim Shukri, Helmi Rafla, and Hassan Saifi, continued to work in Syria, and a few Syrian stars began to emerge from their films. Not the least of these were Douraid and Nouhad (a Syrian Laurel and Hardy) who appeared in some dozen films between 1968 and 1970. These included *The Eligible Man*, *The Two Friends*, *A Woman Lives Alone*, and *The Dwarfs*, all superficial comedies or farces.

In 1970, the National Cinema Centre decided to draw up a new plan of action. Its declared aim was to produce more serious, socially-oriented films, which at the same time would elicit popular response and prove commercially viable. It was not an easy task in view of how low-budget farces were able to draw the crowds. Nevertheless, the Centre went ahead with its new policy, and among the more successful films to emerge were *The Betrayed*, directed by Tawfik Saleh (a film which examines the plight of three generations of Palestinian refugees: those driven out in 1948, those born in exile after 1948, and the third generation who suffered defeat in the 1967 war), *The Panther*, by Nabil Maleh, *The Knife*, by Khalid Hamada, and *The Adventurer*, by Mohammad Shahine. In 1972 the Centre organised a festival for new directors. During the course of the question of an "alternative cinema" was much discussed, without reaching any real conclusions. The discussions continue. Among the new films to emerge from the activities of the Cinema Centre are *Kafr Kassem* (see Lebanese section), *The Progressive Gentleman*, directed by Mabil Meleh, *Al Yazerly*, by Kais Al Zoubaidy, and *One Day in the Life of a Syrian Village*, by Marwan Al Moazin (this film, which attempts to show how socialism has not yet reached all of Syria, is currently having difficulties with the censor since the authorities regard the premise of the film, its feudalistic bent, as unrepresentative of the actual situation). The aforementioned films, along with *The Betrayed*, are the best works produced since the founding of the Centre in 1963.

Documentaries of high quality are starting to appear more frequently, especially since the 1973 October War. Many of these deal with the damage inflicted on previously occupied land and include *Al Quenetra, My Love*, directed by Amin Al Bunni, *The Return*, by Marwan Haddad, *The Rose of the Golan*, by Salah Duhni, and an American-produced film, *Quenetra, the City of Death*, directed by Jim Crammer. (This film was involved in a law suit in England and was seized by police during a screening; it has not been seen in public since.)

The 1975/76 season promises to be the most fruitful period of Syrian cinema. Many of the above-mentioned films have just been completed and are waiting to be released; others are still in pre-production stages.

Turkey

by Giovanni Scognamillo

As predicted in last year's report the Turkish film industry is indeed trying a "new" gambit against television. Unfortunately it is far from new and it is obvious that it will not last long. It all started early in 1974 with some comedies—Ertem Eğilmez's *Köyden indim şehire* (*From the Village to the Town*), Atıf Yılmaz's *Salako*–introducing some theatrical actors, then turned abruptly, following the boom of foreign sex-pictures, to cheap, quickly-made sex-comedies. The year 1974 closed with 189 films having been released (182 in colour); in the first three months of 1975 100 films have been produced and according to reliable sources it is expected that, before the end of the year, about a further 150 will be shot, with sex being the main attraction.

Is that all that one can say about current Turkish cinema? Not exactly. Some interesting films have been produced and others will be, but they have been unable to influence the general spirit of production. The year's box-office hit, and without any doubt the best film of the period, remains *Arkadaş* (*Friend*) in which producer-director-screenwriter and actor Yılmaz Güney gives proof of a mature talent, enriching a politically-slanted social analysis with great sensibility. Other interesting films have also come from Guney's producing company, including *Endişe* (*Trouble*), directed by Şerif Gören, and *İzin* (*Leave*), directed by Temel Gürsü, the first a semi-documentary on the cotton plantation workers, the second a socially-involved story of a brief love-affair between a convict and a prostitute.

Social problems are also tackled in Lütfü Akad's *Diyet*, about factory workers, while Atıf Yılmaz's *Kuma* uses folk traditions to explore lyrically the theme of a "second wife" in a sterile marriage. A prostitute is again the heroine of young director Ömer Kavur's *Yatık Emine*.

Some of the above-mentioned films have been chosen to participate at a Week of Turkish Films in Paris—to be repeated in Geneva, Brussels and Lausanne—while three of Güney's most personal achievements, *Umut* (*Hope*), *Ağit* (*Complaint*) and *Arkadaş* (*Friend*), have represented Turkey at Royan's Festival.

It is interesting to note that some of Turkey's leading directors have been engaged by TV to shoot series of films based on classical novels and/or short stories. Thus, Halit Refiğ has directed his own adaptation of Halit Ziya Uşaklığıl's *Aşk-ı memnu* (*Forbidden Love*), Lütfü Akad a selection of Ömer Seyfettin's short stories, and Metin Erksan an anthology of Turkish writers.

As far as legislation is concerned nothing has been done so far to promote solutions for the benefit of the industry. Early in 1975 a 50% increase in the price of admission tickets was approved but with attendance down by 45% —and theatres closing—this measure was obviously ineffectual. "Wait and see" is the attitude now adopted by all leading producers and film-makers not willing to involve themselves in the "sex" rush. And "wait and see" is the only comment to be made at the present time on Turkish cinema.

recent films

ARKADAŞ (Friend). Script: Yılmaz Güney. Dir: Yılmaz Güney. Phot (colour): Çetin Tunca. Players:

Yılmaz Güney, Melike Demirağ, Kerim Afşar, Azra Balkan, Ahu Tuğbay. For Güney Film Production.

DİYET. Script: Lütfü Akad. Dir: Lütfü Akad. Phot (colour): Gani Turanlı. Players: Hülya Koçyiğit, Hakan Balamir, Erol Taş. For Erman Film.

ENDİŞE (Trouble). Script: Yılmaz Güney. Dir: Şerif Gören. Phot (colour): Kenan Ormanlar. Players: Erkan Yücel, Kâmuran Usluer, Emel Meşçi. For Güney Film Production.

İZİN (Leave). Script: Yılmaz Güney. Dir: Temel Gürsü. Phot (colour): Kenan Kurt. Players: Azra Balkan, Halil Ergün, Süleyman Turan. For Güney Film Production.

KUMA. Script: Atıf Yılmaz, from the play by Cahit Atay. Dir: Atıf Yılmaz. Phot (colour): Çetin Tunca. Players: Fatma Girik, Hakan Balamir, Nuran Aksoy. For Erman Film.

SALAKO. Script: Ertem Eğilmez and Sadik Şendil. Dir: Atıf Yılmaz. Phot (colour): Hüseyin Özşahin. Players: Kemal Sunal, Meral Zeren, İhsan Yüce. For Arzu Film.

YATIK EMİNE. Script: Turgut Özakman and Ömer Kavur, from the novel by Refik Halid Karay. Dir: Omer Kavur. Phot (colour): Renato Fait. Players: Serdar Gökhan, Neclâ Nazir, Bilâl İnci, Mahmut Hekimoğlu. For Günaydin Film.

ZAVALLILAR (The Poor Ones). Script: Yılmaz Güney and Atıf Yılmaz. Dir: Yılmaz Güney and Atıf Yılmaz. Phot (colour): Kenan Ormanlar and Gani Turanlı. Players: Yılmaz Güney, Yıldırım Önal, Güven Şengil. For Güney Film Production.

Melike Demirağ and Yılmaz Güney in ARKADAS (FRIEND)

U.S.A.
by Stuart Rosenthal

While most of the country struggled with inflation and recession, the American film industry thrived. MPAA figures reported in "Variety" put the total ticket sales for 1974 at 1,011,700,000, compared to 864,600,000 in 1973. The box-office gross was estimated at $1,650,000,000, which represents, roughly, a $150,000,000 increase over the preceding year. These statistics are the highest since 1946. There was even a rise in the number of movie theatres in operation, with about 150 new screens added to the nation's exhibition facilities. In fact, the only effect inflation seemed to have on the film business in 1974 was on admission prices, which rose nearly 7%. As the economic picture showed signs of brightening in the spring of 1975, however, box-office volume started to taper off.

Much of the filmgoing activity was fired by a mere handful of popular attractions. Mindless or pretentious epics like *The Towering Inferno*, *Earthquake* and *The Godfather Part II* dominated film commerce. Nonetheless, several intelligent works managed to find general release. Of these, the best by far was Robert Altman's *California Split*, an examination of our national obsession with "the big win." A lucky streak at roulette or the track, the film insists, can never really compensate for a losing record in everyday life. More than ever before, in *California Split*, Altman refuses to let narrative considerations confine his field of vision. His marvellously dense images and soundtrack make it clear that whenever Elliott Gould and George Segal win, their

good fortune is nothing more than a chance moment of order in an existence where entropy is inexorably expanding. Altman remains the best cinematic interpreter of America's romantic self-delusions.

Roman Polanski, whose work of late has been erratic, returned to Hollywood for *Chinatown*. The "Chinatown" of the title is a metaphor for the sinister, sordid side of human nature that we would like to pretend does not exist. The material is well suited to Polanski's taste for aberration, but much of *Chinatown*'s success is due to the contributions of Jack Nicholson and Robert Towne. Nicholson has proved himself to be the most reliable and versatile of actors, while Towne—on the weight of his scripts for *Chinatown*, *The Last Detail*, and *Shampoo*—is now a major figure among American screenwriters.

John Cassavetes's *A Woman under the Influence* attracted both critical and popular approval. However, Cassavetes's major achievement was getting his film shown at all. When the major releasing companies rejected his production, he despaired of ever finding distribution for it. Then a screening at the New York Film Festival helped stimulate public interest in the work and the director-producer decided to distribute it himself under the company name, Faces International. His unorthodox strategy included bookings in urban, black-oriented cinemas and previews at universities prior to local theatrical openings. As of May 1975, *A Woman under the Influence* has grossed in excess of $2,500,000. Cassavetes even penetrated the Academy Awards sanctuary with nominations for himself as "best director" and for Gena Rowlands as "best actress." While his experience may be exceptional, Cassavetes has demonstrated that it is not impossible for an independent with a good film to support his

enterprise outside of the all-powerful commercial production and distribution structure.

A limited, but reasonably profitable, market for foreign language films by major directors still exists in the United States. Three years ago, Roger Corman surprised almost everyone with his successful handling of *Cries and Whispers*. Last year his New World Releasing Company improved even on the Bergman film's record when it launched Fellini's *Amarcord*. Other foreign films that did moderately well across the country included *Scenes from a Marriage* (Cinema 5), *Stavisky* (Cinemation), *The Seduction of Mimi* (New Line Cinema) and *Lacombe Lucien* (20th Century-Fox).

new and forthcoming films

DOUBLE RANSOM. Script: Paul Schrader. Dir: Brian De Palma. Players: Cliff Robertson, Geneviève Bujold. Prod: George Litto for George Litto Productions.

AMELIA. Script: Pete Hamill. Dir: Lamont Johnson. Players: Shirley MacLaine. Prod: Frank Yablans for 20th Century-Fox.

I WILL, I WILL, FOR NOW. Script: Norman Panama and Albert E. Lewin. Dir: Norman Panama. Players: Elliott Gould. Prod: George Barrie for Brut Productions.

ALL THE PRESIDENT'S MEN. Script: William Goldman, from the work of Robert Woodward and Carl Bernstein. Dir: Alan J. Pakula. Players: Robert Redford, Dustin Hoffman. Prod: Walter Coblenz for Wildwood Productions and Warner Brothers.

W. C. FIELDS. Script: Bob Merrill, based upon Carlotta Monti's book, "W. C. Fields and Me." Dir: Arthur Hiller. Players: Rod Steiger, Valerie Perrine. Prod: Jay Weston for Universal.

THE SENTINEL. Script: Richard Alan Simmons, from a novel by Jeffrey Kontitz. Dir: Don Siegel. Prod: Siegel for Universal.

ULTIMATE VICTIM. Script: Michael Stanley. Dir: Jack Arnold. Prod: Maurice Silverstein.

THE DOG SOLDIERS. Script: from a novel by Robert Stone. Dir: Karel Reisz. Prod: Herb Jaffe and Gabriel Katzka for United Artists.

MAHOGANY. Script: Bob Merrill. Dir: Berry Gordy. Players: Diana Ross, Billy De Williams. Prod: Berry Gordy for Motown Productions.

THE SUNSHINE BOYS. Script: Neil Simon based on his own play. Dir: Herbert Ross. Players: Walter

Matthau, George Burns, Richard Benjamin. Prod: Ray Stark for M-G-M.

THE BLUE BIRD. Script: Alfred Hayes, Hugh Whitemore based on a play by Maurice Maeterlinck. Dir: George Cukor. Players: Elizabeth Taylor, Cicely Tyson, Will Geer, James Coco, Ava Gardner, Mona Washbourne, Richard Pearson, Todd Lookinland, Patsy Kensit. Prod: Edward Lewis for 20th Century-Fox.

ONE FLEW OVER THE CUCKOO'S NEST. Script: Lawrence Hauben, Bo Goldman. Dir: Miloš Forman. Players: Jack Nicholson, Louise Fletcher, William Redfield, Michael Berryman, Alonzo Brown, Peter Brocco. Prod: Michael Douglas, Saul Zaentz for Fantasy Films.

AN ACE UP MY SLEEVE. Script: Jesse Lasky Jr., Pat Silver, based on a novel by James Hadley Chase. Dir: Ivan Passer. Players: Omar Sharif, Karen Black, Joseph Bottoms. Prod: Barney Bernhard for Gloria Films.

WALKING TALL—PART II. Script: Howard Kreitsek. Dir: Earl Bellamy. Players: Bo Svenson, Robert Doqui, Bruce Glover, Richard Jaeckel, Luke Askew, Brooke Mills, William Bryant, Noah Beery, Lurene Tuttle, Angel Tompkins. Prod: Charles A. Pratt for BCP Productions.

FAREWELL MY LOVELY. Script: David Goodman, from the book by Raymond Chandler. Dir: Dick Richards. Players: Robert Mitchum, Charlotte Rampling, John Ireland, Sylvia Miles, Anthony Zerbe. Prod: George Pappas, Jerry Bruckheimer, Jerry Bick for Avco Embassy.

LUCKY LADY. Script: Willard Huyck, Gloria Katz. Dir: Stanley Donen. Players: Liza Minnelli, Burt Reynolds, Gene Hackman. Prod: Michael Gruskoff for Stanley Donen Enterprises.

BUFFALO BILL. Script: based on Arthur Kopit's play "Indians." Dir: Robert Altman. Player: Paul Newman. Prod: Robert Altman for Lionsgate.

THIS KING BUSINESS. Script: James L. Brooks, from a Dashiell Hammett short story. Prod: Hannah Weinstein for Paramount.

THE CHASE. Dir: Douglas Hickey. Players: Steve McQueen, Gene Hackman, Oskar Werner. For 20th Century-Fox.

THE GREAT SCOUT AND CATHOUSE THURSDAY. Dir: Daryl Duke. Prod: Jules Buck and Gerald Green for Bryanston.

HARD TIMES. Script and dir: Walter Hill. Players: Charles Bronson, James Coburn, Jill Ireland, Strother Martin, Maggie Blye, Bruce Glover. Prod: Lawrence Gordon for Columbia.

HEARTS OF THE WEST. Script: Rob Thompson. Dir: Howard Zieff. Players: Jeff Bridges, Andy Griffith, Alan Arkin, Donald Pleasence. Prod: Tony Bill for M-G-M.

HUSTLE. Script: Steve Shagan. Dir: Robert Aldrich.

Players: Burt Reynolds, Catherine Deneuve, Ben Johnson, Eddie Albert, Ernest Borgnine. Prod: Robert Aldrich for Paramount.

THE JUDGE AND HIS HANGMAN. Script: Bo Goldman, from a novel by Friedrich Dürrenmatt. Dir: Maximilian Schell. Players: Jon Voight, Jacqueline Bisset, Martin Ritt, Robert Shaw, Gabriele Ferzetti. Prod: Ben Arbeid for 20th Century-Fox.

THE HINDENBURG. Script: Martin B. Wehmeyer from a book by Michael MacDonald Mooney. Dir: Robert Wise. Players: George C. Scott, Anne Bancroft, Gig Young, Roy Thinnes, Burgess Meredith, René Auberjonois. Prod: Robert Wise for Universal.

DOG DAY AFTERNOON. Dir: Sidney Lumet. Players: Al Pacino, John Cazale. Prod: Martin Bregman, Martin Elfand for Warner Brothers.

THE DROWNING POOL. Script: Walter Hill, Lorenzo Semple Jr., Tracy Keenan Wynn, from the novel by Ross Macdonald. Dir: Stuart Rosenberg. Players: Paul Newman, Joanne Woodward, Tony Franciosa, Murray Hamilton, Gail Strickland, Richard Jaeckel. Prod: Lawrence Turman, David Foster for Warner Brothers.

WINTERHAWK. Script: R. R. Young. Dir: Charles B. Pierce. Players: Slim Pickens, Woody Strode, Elisha Cook Jr., Denver Pyle. Prod: Charles B. Pierce for Charles B. Pierce Productions.

THE KILLER INSIDE ME. Dir: Burt Kennedy. Players: Stacy Keach, Tisha Sterling, Keenan Wynn, Don Stroud, John Carradine. Prod: Michael Leighton for Devi Productions.

NINETY-TWO IN THE SHADE. Script and dir: Thomas McGuane, from his own novel. Players: Peter Fonda, Warren Oates, Elizabeth Ashley, Sylvia Miles. Prod: Elliott Kastner for ITC-EK Productions.

THREE DAYS OF THE CONDOR. Script: Lorenzo Semple Jr. Dir: Sydney Pollack. Players: Robert Redford, Faye Dunaway, Max von Sydow, John Houseman. Prod: Stanley Schneider for Dino De Laurentiis.

ALICE DOESN'T LIVE HERE ANYMORE

Script: Robert Getchell. Direction: Martin Scorsese. Photography (Technicolor): Kent L. Wakeford. Editing: Marcia Lucas. Music: various period songs. Art Direction: Toby Carr Rafelson. Players: Ellen Burstyn, Kris Kristofferson, Alfred Lutter, Billy Green Bush, Diane Ladd, Lelia Goldoni. For Warner Bros. (David Susskind-Audrey Maas). 111 mins.

Although Martin Scorsese now has four features behind him, and in spite of the full-

Ellen Burstyn with Kris Kristofferson

in love, is caught between these attitudes. He can exhilarate young Tommy by teaching him to ride; he can also lose his temper when the boy's impertinence goes too far.

Ironically, the film's real punch is not in the final scene (as Dave and Alice walk tamely off towards a silver lining) as in the idiosyncratic opening sequence, which flashes back to Alice the child in a cherry-red Monterey sunset, revealing herself to be every bit as foul-mouthed as her own eventual son.

PETER COWIE

A WOMAN UNDER THE INFLUENCE

Script and direction: John Cassavetes. Photography (colour): Mitch Breit, Chris Taylor, Bo Taylor, Merv Dayan, Caleb Deschanel. Editing: Elizabeth Bergeron, David Armstrong, Sheila Viseltear. Music: Bo Harwood. Art Direction: Phedon Papamichael. Players: Peter Falk, Gena Rowlands, Matthew Cassel, Matthew Laborteaux, Christina Grisanti, Katherine Cassavetes, Lady Rowlands. For Sam Shaw/John Cassavetes. 155 mins.

Mabel Longhetti is not so much under the influence as crinkling beneath the pressure of Laingian existence. Irritable, overwrought, wracked by a profound inferiority complex, she clings to her marriage with an almost catatonic impulse. Her hard-hat husband, Nick (Peter Falk), is sympathetic, but he is all too easily subservient to his mother, a vicious bitch who seeks to have Mabel confined at the first intimations of insanity.

Once again Cassavetes has chosen the marital arena as his region of concern; as usual, he brings the relationship into excruciatingly tight close-up, letting the drama accumulate within each scene rather than shaping and distorting it with spectacular editing. These "scenes from a marriage" are among the most sensitive that Cassavetes has ever caught: the huge spaghetti brunch, for example, that Mabel

blooded force of this new movie, he has not yet established the kind of personal signature in the wood that Cassavetes, for example, has done for so long. In fact, there's a strong argument for suggesting that *Alice* is an Ellen Burstyn film. This spunky, intelligent actress not only nursed the property to fruition at Warners (choosing Scorsese as director *en route*), but she also dominates every scene in the picture. It's a witty entertainment, and many will be inclined to accept it as a mere nod in the direction of Women's Lib.

Beneath the raw banter, however, the film is focusing on a clash of life-styles. Scorsese/Burstyn/Getchell pit the traditional American, Mildred Pierce hunger for success against the cynical inertia of a younger generation. Alice grows up yearning to outdo Alice Faye was a singer. When her husband is killed in a car crash and she takes to the road, she finds that such ambition is as out of fashion as her crooning. Tommy, her obnoxious young son, is typical of the modern world in his calculated disdain for rooted values, while Kris Kristofferson's Dave, the reticent rancher with whom Alice finally falls prepares for Nick and his mates and that ends, despite the bickering, with husband and wife reaching tenderly out for each other on the bed in a mood of lazy, post-prandial relief. Occasionally, the contrivance protrudes, and the wake-like party sequence on Mabel's return from asylum is as self-conscious in execution as its participants are in behaviour.

The abiding strength of John Cassavetes, from the unforgettable opening of *Shadows* to the dying-fall finale of this movie, has been his humanism in the face of disillusionment, his respect for the small gestures of domestic emotion, and for the inarticulacy that so often aggravates family strife. Peter Falk and Gena Rowlands are splendid interpreters of this confusion, while the soundtrack

Gena Rowlands in A WOMAN UNDER THE INFLUENCE

swells with appropriate background noise and chatter.   PETER COWIE

HESTER STREET

Script and direction: Joan Micklin Silver, from the novel "Yekl," by Abraham Cahan. Photography: Kenneth van Sickle. Editing: Katherine Wenning. Music: William Bolcom. Art Direction: Stewart Wurtzel. Players: Steven Keats, Carol Kane, Mel Howard, Dorrie Kavanaugh, Doris Roberts. For Midwest Film Productions Inc. 90 mins.

At first sight, *Hester Street* is dull and worthy, its monochrome images reinforcing its old-fashioned technique and acting style. But the film exerts a curious appeal long after other movies have faded in the mind. There is something disarmingly straightforward about Joan Silver's narrative method, and the care and sincerity with which she establishes time (1896), place (Manhattan's Lower East Side), and characters (Jewish immigrants). Jake has arrived in advance of his wife and little boy, and quickly falls to worshipping the Yankee ways of the world. He acquires a job in the garment district and a handsome, sophisticated mistress. When Gitl and her child join him, his problems begin. They talk

Yiddish among themselves, but Jake is aware of the need to speak English; Gitl refuses. "I won't be a Gentile, even for Jake," she tells a friend. Anger and frustration mount in Jake, and the marriage, in spite of an hilarious last-ditch effort by Gitl to acquire an American hairstyle, comes to ruin. The film records the elaborate ritual of the divorce proceedings, which have the same strength and solemnity as a wedding. And *Hester Street* concludes on a note of irony rather than sentimentality as Jake is forced to return to the sweatshops to earn his keep after being swindled by both wife and mistress. William Bolcom's woodwind score adds grace and favour to the production, and the acting is, for all its theatrical rhythm, persuasive to the last. *Hester Street* is simple and unadorned, well-meaning and well-made.

PETER COWIE

GU
ND

Art House Focus

Michael Webb terms his work at the **American Film Institute Theater** in Washington as "a year-round festival," and visitors to the John F. Kennedy Center for the Performing Arts, where the Theater is located, have been treated to weeks of Polish, Swiss, and Egyptian movies, as well as to seasons devoted to the *film noir* and the German classics. There are 200 seats, and screenings take place twice nightly.

Each year the Circle group of theatres in Washington seems to add satellites to its original **Circle** on Pennsylvania Avenue, NW (and the Circle, founded in 1911, is the city's oldest operating movie-house). In 1975, in addition to the Circle, **Inner Circle,** and **Outer Circle One** and **Two,** there is the **West End Circle,** on the corner of L and 23rd Streets. Kathleen Karr is the General Manager, while Ted and Jim Pedas continue to control the Circle group. Recent first-runs have included *Kamouraska* and *Swastika*, while the winter saw a massive French season, as well as Bergman and Fellini seasons.

The **Biograph,** at 2819 M Street NW, in Georgetown, is highly respected for its repertory programmes, and Alan Rubin and Leonard Poryles, who share the management, have recently twinned their **Biograph** in nearby Richmond, Virginia (814 W. Grace

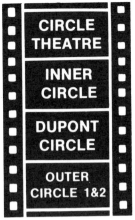

WASHINGTON'S FINEST REPERTORY AND ART THEATRES

2105 Pennsylvania Ave., N.W.   Phone 331-7480

Street), where *Lacombe Lucien, Amarcord,* and *Emmanuelle* have attracted large audiences. The atmosphere at both Biograph cinemas is lively and appealing.

In Philadelphia, Amos Vogel continues to select some really imaginative programmes for the **Annenberg Cinematheque** (Studio Theatre, Annenberg Center, 3680 Walnut Street). Seasons run in groups, as at the National Film Theatre, and the full houses that this comparatively new venture has been drawing suggests that until now Philadelphia has been poorly served with serious and experimental movies.

Stuart Samuels is attempting something similar on a smaller scale at the **Walnut Street Theatre** in Philadelphia. There are film showings, lectures, visits by film-makers, in an 80-seat screening room equipped with 35mm, 16mm, 8mm, and video capability.

In Detroit, the **Film Theatre** at the Detroit Institute of Arts (5200 Woodward Avenue) has an enthusiastic programme co-ordinator in Elliot Wilhelm. In a short time, the popularity of the Theatre has grown to such a degree that the 1,200 seat auditorium is often filled to capacity each Friday and Saturday at 7 and 9 p.m. The films come from all over the world, and there are also visits from film personalities like Robert Altman and Molly Haskell. On Sundays, short films and science fiction movies are frequently shown.

In the Mid-West, Bill Pence's pair of houses, **The Flick** (on Larimer Square, Denver, Colorado), continue their excellent work. There are first-run foreign movies, late-night shows, and a vast range of repertory items.

In New York there are fewer and fewer real art houses, now that the First Avenue Screening Room and the New Yorker have changed their once scrupulous commitment to foreign films. The **Museum of Modern Art** has film shows open to members on a first-come, first-served basis (though membership is in fact easily purchased), and a glance in "The Village Voice" will enable visitors to ascertain where the best films are being screened in any given week.

U.S.S.R.

by Derek Elley

The tragic death last year of Vasili Shukshin robbed Soviet cinema of one of its most fruitful (and controversial) talents. His *Kalina krasnaya* (*The Red Snowball-Tree*), despite having been heavily cut by both the censors and Shukshin himself, enjoyed tremendous public acclaim, not only because of the nature of its subject-matter (prison-camps) but also because of Shukshin's own performance in the central role. Born in Siberia in 1929, he started in the Fifties as an actor, only switching to direction in the Sixties. His death on October 2, 1974, of a heart attack while acting in Sergey Bondarchuk's *They Fought for Their Country* at the Moscow studios came as a great shock. At the time Shukshin had been trying to gain permission to direct a film on Stenka Razin—with difficulty; a screenplay he left behind, *Fellow Villagers*, has been filmed by Valentin Vinogradov.

Increased emphasis continues to be thrown on the national cinemas, with talents like Tolomush Okeyev and Bolot Shamshiyev working consistently within regional *genres*. The larger studios Lenfilm and Mosfilm, have recently been engaged on a heavy programme

Still from IVAN VASILYEVICH

Sergey Bondarchuk in THEY FOUGHT FOR THEIR COUNTRY

of Second World War dramas designed to celebrate the Thirtieth anniversary of the defeat of Nazi Germany (see Report from Sovexportfilm). This emphasis climaxed in the First International Festival of Anti-Fascist Films, held at Volgograd in May, at which 68 pictures and 34 documentaries were screened in one week, with twenty countries participating. Contemporary themes, however, remain equally important, with directors like Konchalovski, Panfilov and Mitta approaching their subjects in a wide variety of ways. And Soviet cinema has not lost the ability to react to current fads: *The Girl from Beryozovsk*, directed by Viktor Titov, gleefully cashes in on the gymnastic "rivalry" between Lyudmila Turishcheva and Olga Korbut, even to the point of picking actresses with remarkable physical resemblances.

On the co-production front, Japan continues to play a dominant role, Aleksandr Mitta's popular *Moscow, My Love* (with Toho) followed by Kurosawa's *Dersu Uzala*. Shooting on the latter (in the deepest *tayga*) has finally finished after a long germination. Similar delays have also afflicted the much-publicised, first-ever American-Soviet co-production, *The Blue Bird*. Filming was still progressing slowly in Spring 1975, under George Cukor's direction.

Report from Sovexportfilm

The year 1975 saw the thirtieth anniversary of the defeat of Nazi Germany. This was mainly brought about by the fighting strength of the Soviet soldier and the courage of its people to stay the course in spite of the loss of twenty million men, women and children.

Thus Soviet film producers and directors acknowledged this anniversary through the production of a number of outstanding wartime films set in different parts of the U.S.S.R., written by some of its most outstanding writers and acted by the cream of its cinematic film talent.

Easily the biggest and most audacious feature in its concept and scope was Sergey Bondarchuk's *They Fought for Their Country*, based on the famous novel by Mikhail Sholokhov. This outstanding 70mm production in two parts was shot in and around the village of Kletskaya, not far from the home of Sholokhov. It deals with the fate of a remnant of a regiment (117 men and officers) who are ordered to dig in on a hill and hold out whatever the cost. Bondarchuk treats the business of war in a realistic fashion but also shows that loyalty to one's people and country taught the Soviet soldier fearlessness in the fight against Fascism. Full of spectacular battle action, the film also makes good use of Sholokhov's rough and ready wit and humour to put over its dramatic concepts.

The partisan movement is excitingly depicted by Vitali Chetverikov in *Flames*, set in Byelorussia during the most savage periods of the German invasion of the Soviet Union. The script of *Flames* tackles the true story of the sixteen partisan units established in Byelorussia (where one out of four citizens were killed) and the havoc they wrought on the Third German Tank Army under General Reinhardt. Starring Yuri Kaurov, Mikhail Gluzki and Pyotr Glebov, *Flames* shows how the Soviet resistance movement came into being and developed into a nation-wide battle against Hitler's occupying armies.

Front without Flanks, directed by Igor Gostev and based on the documentary novel "We Shall Return" by Semyon Tsvigun, takes place in the early days of the war. The German Army has smashed its way through the units defending the border of the U.S.S.R. Panic sets in among the peasants and a group of soliders have been encircled by the enemy. Soviet actor Vyacheslav Tikhonov plays the central figure of Major Mlynski who inspires the villagers and teaches his men how to fight back against the invading German troops. Composer Venyamin Basner and poet Mikhail Matsusovski, who wrote the stirring music and verse for the film, fought in the forests of the North Western Front where the film was set.

Blockade, a two part film, is based on Alexandr Chakovski's Lenin Prize Winning novel of the same name. Directed by Mikhail Ershov, it tells the unbelievable story of the 900-day blockade of Leningrad in which one million folk (a third of the city's population) died of hunger or enemy action. *Blockade* mixes fiction with authentic documentary material, and real historical personalities appear side by side with characters created by scriptwriters Alexandr Chakovski and Arnold Vitol.

Motherland's Soldier describes a true and strange incident during the early days of the German invasion of the Soviet Union. A Soviet General, Dmitri Karbishev, a former Tsarist officer, was taken prisoner by the Nazis who tried to get him to work for the German Army. From this true story director Yuri Chulukin and scriptwriters Alexandr Gorokhov, Georgi Kushnirenko and Chulenko, have fashioned an exciting and moving story of a courageous man who remains true to his principles. No bribe was so attractive nor threat fearful enough to influence the tough, soldierly Karbishev. Played by Vladimir Sedov with a splendid integrity, the story of Karbishev is a magnificent study in characterisation and compulsive story telling.

Three other features worthy of mention are *Under a Sky of Stone*, a new Soviet–Norwegian film directed by Knut Anderssen (Norway) and Igor Maslennikov (U.S.S.R.), which tells of the liberation of Northern Norway and the city of Kirkenes by the Soviety Army and the co-operation between Soviet soldiers and Norwegian resistance fighters.

The Only Road is a Soviet-Yugoslav film

Still from SEMURG

directed by Vladimir Pavlović (Yugoslavia). This is an exciting tale of how Soviet prisoners of war and local partisans blow up a Nazi fuel convoy. A fast-moving and visually dramatic production. Finally there is *Sokolovo*, a massive Soviet–Czech co-production which describes the liberating battles that the Soviet Armies waged against the Nazis retreating into Czechoslovakia, and how the Czech freedom fighters collaborated with the Soviet units to save the destruction of Prague and other major Czech cities.

These are only a few of the excellent Soviet Films made during 1975 and distributed by Sovexportfilm. Many others, ranging from thrillers, musicals, children's productions, documentaries and cartoons are also available for exhibition in the United Kingdom.   S. V. LEKAREV
                                    (U.K. Representative)

Contemporary Soviet Filmgoing

The traditional yearly poll by the popular fortnightly "Sovyetski Ekran" (Soviet Screen) of its near-2,000,000 readership produced the following information about filmgoers' likes and habits.

The ten most popular Soviet films were, in descending order: *The Red Snowball-Tree, Shadows Disappear at Midday, Only Veterans Go to War, Those Whom I Love and Remember, High Rank, Kysh and Bag-on-Bag, Cabin-Boy of the Northern Fleet, Moscow, My Love, No Return, Lovers' Romance.* Among the most popular films from other Socialist Bloc countries were *Apachen* (GDR), *Živjeti od ljubavi* (Yugoslavia), and *Posledno lyato* (Bulgaria). From the rest of the world: *McKenna's Gold* and *The New Centurions* (U.S.A.).

new and forthcoming films

ONI SRAZHALIS ZA RODINU (They Fought for Their Country). Dir: Sergey Bondarchuk, from the work by Mikhail Sholokhov. Phot: V. Yusov. Players: Vyacheslav Tikhonov, Vasili Shukshin, Sergey Bondarchuk, Ivan Lapikov, Yuri Nikulin.

TSEMYENT (Cement). Script: Yevgyeni Mitko. Dir: Aleksandr Blank, Sergey Linkov. Phot: K. Ryzhov. Players: A. Dzigarkhanyan, V. Gaft, I. Gubanova, L. Zaytseva. For Lenfilm.

ANNA KARYENINA (Anna Karenina). Dir: Margarita Pilikhina. Music: Rodion Shchedrin. Players: Maya Plisetskaya, Yuri Vladimirov, V. Tikhonov, A. Godunov. For Mosfilm.

KRASNOYE YABLOKO (The Red Apple). Script: Chingiz Aytmatov, Tolomush Okeyev, Ye. Lyndinaya, from a story by Aytmatov. Dir: Tolomush Okeyev. Phot: Konstantin Orozaliyev. Music: Sándor Kallas. Player: Suymenkul Chokmorov.

DYEVOCHKA IZ BERYOZOVSKA (The Girl from Beryozovsk). Script: A. Lapshin, S. Puchinyan. Dir: V. Titov. Players: Ira Mazurkevich, Anya Zharova.

VOZVRATA NYET (No Return). Script and dir: A. Saltykov. Players: Nonna Mordyukova, V. Dvorzhetski. For Mosfilm.

LEGYENDA O TILYE ULENSHPIGELYE (The Legend of Till Eulenspiegel). Script and dir: A. Alov, V. Naumov. Phot: Valentin Zheleznikov. Players: Lembit Ulfsaak, Natalya Belokhvostikova, I. Budraytis, I. Ledogorov, Ye. Leonov. For Mosfilm.

MATERIK GIGANTOV (The Land of Giants). Dir: Andrey Mikhalkov-Konchalovski. For Mosfilm.

KOMMUNISTI (Communists). Dir: Yuri Ozerov. For Mosfilm.

SINYAYA PTITSA (The Blue Bird). Dir: George Cukor. Players: see listing in U.S.A. section.

PROSHU SLOVA (I Forgive the Words). Script and dir: Gleb Panfilov. Phot: Alexandr Antipenko. Music: V. Bibergan. Players: Inna Churikova, I. Gubenko. For Lenfilm.

MOSKVA, LYUBOV MOYA (Moscow, My Love). Script: E. Radzinski, T. Kasikur. Dir: Alexandr Mitta. Players: Oleg Vidov, Komaki Kurihara. For Mosfilm (U.S.S.R.)/Toho (Japan).

AFONYA (Afonya). Dir: Georgi Daneliya. Phot: Sergey Vronski. Players: Leonid Kuravlyov, Raisa Kurkina, Zhenya Simonova, N. Maslova.

DERSU UZALA (Dersu Uzala). Dir: Akira Kurosawa. Phot: Asakazu Nakai. Players: Yuri Solomin, Maxim Munzuk.

MELODII VERIYSKOVO KVARTALA
(Melodies of the Veriyski Neighbourhood)

Script: Georgi Shengelaya, Anzor Salukvadze. Direction: Georgi Shengelaya. Phot (colour): Alexandr Mgebrishvili. Music: Georgi Tsabadze. Art Direction: Vakhtang Rurua, Eduard Lapkovski. Choreography: Yuri Zaryetski. Players: Vakhtang Kikabidze, Sofiko Chiaureli, Iya Ninidze, Maya Kankava. For Gruzia-Film. 97 mins.

From no less a director than Georgi Shengelaya—of *Pirosmani* fame— comes this high-spirited celebration on Georgian life in Tsarist Russia. Shot, unlike its predecessor, entirely in Georgian (which bears not the slightest relation to the Russian language), it has many similarities, both visually and choreographically, with Western counterparts, notably *Fiddler on the Roof*, *Oliver!* and *Seven Brides for Seven Brothers*. The film's resonances, however, are completely Georgian, and though lacking *Pirosmani's* conscious stylisation, the work can be seen to spring from the same source with its pictorial compositions and mellow use of russets and browns. Yuri Zaryetski's choreography is muscular and invigorating, worthy of comparison with that of Michael Kidd or Onna White. Most of the acting laurels go to Sofiko Chiaureli as Vardo, a laundress in pre-Revolutionary Tiflis (Tbilisi) who uses all her guile to raise the money for two young girls to

The local police force on parade in Georgi Shengelaya's MELODIES OF THE VERIYSKI NEIGHBOURHOOD

attend the local ballet school. The opening number with Vardo and her fellow-launderesses ("That's Our Life") sets the tone, later pursued by the girls Tamro and Maro in "What Joy." Between the more overtly satirical numbers, featuring the foppish dancing teachers and crooked local gendarmerie (all realised with a surprising lightness of touch), there is quieter reflection in solos by both Vardo (singing voice dubbed by Nana Bregvadze) and Pavle, the girls' father. Shengelaya's ingenuous approach is most rewarding in the final number, a moving carol performed with touching simplicity by the four principals. As the father, Vakhtang Kikabidze is perhaps the more faceless of the quartet, but in the face of such utterly charming playing by Iya Ninidze and Maya Kankava (as Maro and Tamro) even Sofiko Chiaureli has difficulty maintaining a presence.   DEREK ELLEY

ROMANS O VLYUBLYONNYKH
(Lovers' Romance)

Script: Yevgyeni Grigoryev. Direction: Andrey Mikhalkov-Konchalovski. Photography (Sovcolor, 70mm): Levan Paatashvili. Music: Alexandr Gradski. Art direction: Leonid Pertsev. Players: Yelyena Koreneva, Yevgyeni Kindinov, Innokenti Smoktunovski, Iya Savvina, Irina Kupchenko, Yelizaveta Solodova. For Mosfilm. 129 mins.

With the demise of Cinerama, only the Soviet film industry remains to develop the full potential of the 70mm process. Mikhalkov-Konchalovski's new film, *Lovers' Romance*, starts on an almost overwhelmingly intimate note, as the young Sergey and Tanya gaze rapturously at each other in the depths of a lush sylvan environment. As the stereophonic music climbs ecstatically, and the lovers chase each other through the woods, the hectic camera movements convey an exhilaration rare even in the classic American musicals.

When the scene switches to contemporary Moscow, however, the magic is dispelled, although the technical courage of the film remains impressive. There is even a fashionable *Verfremdungseffekt* when the director and the film crew come into shot during certain sequences, and Innokenti Smoktunovski stage-manages the romantic entanglements with the cheerful guile of a *meneur de jeu*. While Sergey is doing his national service, rock music imaginatively accompanies the traditional images of military exercises in full swing, and the huge screen is alive with close-ups of TV monitors, naval manoeuvres, tanks on the offensive, etc.

Mikhalkov-Konchalovski lacks the delicate touch that enabled Demy to balance *Les parapluies de Cherbourg* on the head of a pin, and only in the final moments, as Sergey's new wife sings a lullaby to their baby, does the fragile romance of the first sequence impinge once more on the film. Sergey has lost his first love, but he has learned the secret of emotional happiness.

With its adroit choreography and its sense of pace, this is certainly one of the liveliest and most adventurous Soviet productions of the past two years, and Yelyena Koreneva as Tanya is a real discovery, her insouciance and intensity recalling the young Shirley MacLaine. It's also good to see Iya Savvina, the heroine of *The Lady with a Little Dog*, playing a maternal role with dignity rather than sentimentality.

PETER COWIE

Venezuela

by Jacobo Brender

As prophesied in last year's IFG, 1974 was a decisive year for film production in this country. The change of government was largely responsible, its greater understanding of the medium's growing potential being shown in the grant of the Ministry of Development (with Conahotu) of 5,000,000 bolivars of credit for the production of ten exclusively Venezuelan features. The following directors received 500,000 bolivars each: Clemente de la Cerda, Roman Chalbaud, Manuel Diaz Punceles, Maria Carbonell, Giancarlo Carrer, Alfredo Lugo, Julio Cesar Mármol, Juan Santana, Enver Cordido, Alberto Vázquez Figueroa. Though such grants are not enough to finance any production com-

pletely, they nevertheless have brought considerable encouragement to film-makers who have struggled for years to develop the home industry.

Legislation to protect the industry and ensure adequate distribution throughout the country has still not been drafted, though its appearance is soon likely. The fact is that Venezuelan films are now big business, and this has resulted in a spate of activity previously unknown here. Last year six features (including the documentary *Juan Vicente Gomez*, by Manuel de Pedro) were released, and the number is confidently expected to increase this year. New talents are returning from film schools abroad to swell

the ranks of directors, and Venezuelan pictures have been screened at festivals in Moscow, Berlin and San Sebastian, as well as nearer home in Mexico and Colombia. In addition, the Tourist Corporation is finally supporting the production of *Erendira* which Margot Benacerraf has been trying for years to set up. The script is by Gabriel García Márquez from his own well-known book.

At the time of writing, a meeting of Latin-American directors is being organised in Caracas, and another in June (of Venezuelan film-makers) will discuss the recent developments and plan for the future.

important shorts

MARIELA HA DESAPARECIDO (Mariela Has Disappeared). Script and dir: Carlos Camacho. Phot (colour): Jesús Roseelón. For Soc. Comun. School of Univ. Cent. Ven. Fiction; experimental. 30 mins.
AL FINAL DEL CAMINO (At the End of the Road). Script and dir: Antonio Castellet and Jorge Canudas, based on a real episode from the Second World War. Phot: A. Castellet, Vincente Castellet, Halejandro Avendaño. Players: Canudas, A. Castellet, Angel Matéos, Antonio C. Vila. For Casnic. Fiction. 40 mins.
EL FARO DE CAYO SANGRE (The Lighthouse of Blood Rock). Script: Angel Matéo. Dir: Antonio Castellet. Phot: Canudas, Nicolau, Castellet. For Casnic. Horror-fiction. 40 mins.

(Continued on page 512)

CRONICA DE UN SUBVERSIVO LATINO-AMERICANO
(Chronicle of a Latin-American Subversive)

Script: José Ignacio Cabrujas, Luis Correa, Mauricio Walerstein. Dir: Mauricio Walterstein. Phot (colour): Abigail Rojas. Editing: Alberto Torrija. Music: Miguel Angel Fuster. Players: Miguel Angel Landa, Claudio Brook, Orlando Urdaneta, Maria Eugenia Dominguez, Pedro Laya, Perla Wonasheck, Eva Mondolfi, Oscar Mendoza, Lucio Bueno, Asdrubal Meléndez, Julio Mota. For Walerstein-Landa.

Walerstein's film is based on a real occurrence which took place in Venezuela a few years ago. A group of young guerrillas, members of the Communist party, kidnap an American colonel named Whitney (Claudio Brook), their object being to prevent the execution of an important Vietnamese Communist leader held prisoner in Saigon. While the officer is kept captive in the room of an unsuspected couple and the police search frantically for the abductors, the news of the kidnapping provokes a stay of execution in Vietnam. Through the panic of one of the guerrillas the police manage to arrest the youngster and secure his confession. The end of the film leaves room for individual conclusions; the audience may sympathise with either side. Cabrujas, Correa and Walerstein have written an ambiguous, tightly-constructed script, and as in *Cuando quiero llorar no lloro* the director employs a modern style which makes spare but revealing use of dialogue.

Playing is convincing, especially Landa as the leader of the guerrilla group and Brook as the tall American officer.

JACOBO BRENDER

new and forthcoming films

LA QUEMA DE JUDAS (The Burning of Judas). Script: Roman Chalbaud, José Ignacio Cabrujas, from the play by Chalbaud. Dir: Roman Chalbaud. Phot (colour): Abigail Rojas, Cesar Bolivar. Edit: A. Torrijas. Music: Miguel Angel Fuster. Prod: Chalbaud, Landa, C. Bolivar, Rojas, Walerstein. Players: Miguel Angel Landa, Hilda Vera, Maria Teresa Acosta, Arturo Calderón, Claudio Brook, William Moreno, Rafael Briceño, Pablo Gil, Raúl Medina, J. I. Cabrujas, Eladio Lárez. For Gente de Cine. During a bank robbery a policeman is killed, and it is only later that it is discovered that the dead man was in fact the leader of the gang, Jesus Carmona. Through reminiscences of people who knew him a picture is built up of his double life, and the "burning of Judas" (a Catholic custom in South America) takes on a symbolic significance for Carmona at the end. Through flashbacks Chalbaud and Cabrujas de-mystify the dead man as a false hero, and the film's atmosphere is aided greatly by the camerawork of Rojas and Bolivar, working in sombre colours and *chiaroscuro* effects. Chalbaud, also a very experienced theatre and TV director, draws fine playing from his cast to produce one of the best films ever made in Venezuela.

NO ES NADA MAMA, SOLO UN JUEGO (It's Nothing, Mama ... Just a Game). Script: Hermógenes Sainz, José Maria Forqué. Dir: José Maria Forque. Phot (Eastmancolor, CinemaScope): Alejandro Ulloa. Edit:

Mercedes Alonso. Music: Adolfo Waitzman. Art dir: Leo Anchoriz. Prod: Renny Otolina, José Maria Forqué. Players: David Hemmings, Alida Valli, Francisco Rabal, Andrea Rau, Galeazzo Bentivoglio, Rudy Hernandez, Aquiles Guerrero, Gonzalo Fernandez de Cordoba Jr., Lucila Herrera. For Alfa Films-Orfeo. Venezuelan– Spanish. Though made entirely in Venezuela the film has an international cast (British, Spanish, German, Italian) and under the expert direction of Forqué is a palpable hit, its mixture of violence and eroticism given a commercial gloss by Alejandro Ulloa's beautiful colour photography. The story, set on a South American ranch, concerns the cruel attempts of an embittered son (Hemmings) to restore his father's once rich and powerful ranch to its former status. His mother (Valli) is his accomplice, and the attractive Lola (Andrea Rau) his victim who finally gains her revenge.

MARACAIBO PETROLEUM COMPANY. Script: David Alizo, Daniel Oropeza. Dir: Daniel Orpoeza. Phot (scope): Carlos Beltrán, José Jimenez, Emilio Ramos.

Edit: Juan Martínez. Music: José Verdú. Players: Pierina España, Rafael Sebastian, Alfonso Montilla, Rafael Rodrigues Rars, Daniel Oropeza, Salvador Prasel, Raquel Ruiz, Roger Silver. For Cinesistemas. Oropeza has followed his particular line in stark realism ever since he returned from Europe where he studied direction. Here he deals (a little belatedly but certainly with concern) with foreign oil exploitation in Maracaibo, and although he does not provide a coherent survey of the problems at issue he at least manages to bring to life the personal drama of his young protagonists, Melina and Samuel (España and Sebastian). The decline of their originally beautiful love through violence, fraud and opposing circumstances is very touching to watch. Economic difficulties have forced Oropeza to shoot in black-and-white, and many scenes are not as clearly constructed as they might have been, but in Pierina España he has found a photogenic actress who shows much promise as the tragic heroine.

Yugoslavia

by Ronald Holloway

Although most of the veterans and important young directors of Yugoslav cinema have either left the country (Petrović and Makavejev live in Paris) or were without work in 1974 (the Serban directors Puriša Djordjevic, Želimir Žilnik, Miša Radivojevic and Miroslav Antić, the Croatians Vatroslav Mimica, Ãnte Babaja and Krsto Papić, the Bosnian Bato Čengić, and the Slovenian Matjaž Klopčić), a small core of old and new directors are effectively keeping a pressured national cinema alive and promising for the present. In the Sixties the Yugoslav cinema reached its height of world recognition through a string of lyrical, poetic, semi-documentary "black films" (particularly Žika Pavlović's *The Rats Wake Up* and *When I Was Dead and White*); today only a faint echo of those striking achievements seen up to three years ago can be found in that magnificent Pula arena (dating from Vespasian in the

Second century), and it is doubtful whether the political situation will make a change for the better in the near future.

Instead of "black cinema", black humour underscores the irony of the times. A book of "Forbidden Sayings" under the pen name "Zarko Petan" makes the rounds indiscreetly, many of the sayings lamenting the crippled condition of the renowned socially-engaged film, as: "Shooting documentaries with near-sighted cameras is not very fruitful." And: "The state has hired a translator who can translate foreign thoughts." The latter has a sting in view of the recent dismissal of eight Marxist theorist-philosophers associated with the Zagreb journal, "Praxis," from chairs at the Belgrade University, along with the stretch of imagination that condemned Naive Painting (Croatia has a corner on the world market) as detrimental to the tenets of Social Realism.

With the film industry sinking rapidly into a whirlpool of intrigue, it was natural for the Pula festival on the Adriatic to reflect the conditions realistically and metaphorically as matters drew to a head. The economy (inflation has risen 25 %), the divided interests of a dividend nation—a land of six republics, five nations, four religions, three languages, two alphabets and only one Yugoslav: Tito – and an escape into the past through romanticised partisan themes (the "Eastern") and literary adaptations: all these bubbled to the surface in the overcrowded Pula arena (seating 12,000) and during a week-long succession of press conferences on the state, and future, of Yugoslav cinema. The 1975 Pula event focused on young directors.

The young film-makers had the most to say, and perhaps newcomer Karolj Viček's *début* film, *The Neglected Land*, can be taken as symbolic of the troubled *status quo* in the industry itself. Produced by the progressive Neoplanta Films in Novi Sad, Viček and cameraman Dušan Ninkov used a father-son conflict in a Vojvodina village as the starting point for an examination of mismanaged land-reform and national conflicts in the agriculturally rich, autonomous province just north of Belgrade. Considering that the film is severely critical of the acres of fallow land used only for hunting, both with and without co-op farming, and that it parodies officials only interested in prestige and self-gain, it is remarkable that so much was allowed to be said—but this is a literary adaptation of Veljko Petrović's well-known novel, and artistic freedom was given to make it on a shoestring. *The Neglected Land*, as its title indicates, is a pessimistic film etched in striking, melancholy images (fog spreading over the land) and drawing its force from the erosion of past traditions: a land of milk and honey overgrown with weeds.

By contrast, Rajko Grlić's *Whichever Way the Ball Bounces*, produced by Jadran Film and Croatia Film, scores its points by involving the audience indirectly in a whacky, irreverent, fatalistic quest for something different than the doldrums of everyday life. Another *début* film, its main criticism is society itself, challenged through the rebelliousness of a youth and his well-to-do, pregnant girlfriend by enlisting a film crew to make them and their search for an identity a catalyst for the mass media. The game works for a while, as advice and help mounts through the press, radio and television—until rebellion alone gets on everyone's nerves, and the film crew needs a sacrifice to end the story. The same theme has been handled often enough in the West, but the accusations levelled at the amorality of a decayed consumer society is something different for the East.

The partisan film fits the Pula arena to a tee. More than one wag has uttered the quip: "In the old days lions tore Christians apart in this arena, today Christians tear films apart here"—and the remark usually is dropped after the experience of deafening hoots and whistles greeting a partisan epic. Žika Mitrović's *67 Days* and Stole Janković's *The Partisan*, an international production, both deal with real events (more or less) in 1941 in pure blood-and-guts fashion. More than half of the present Yugoslav film production is slated for the action epic, while most of the others take their cues from literary adaptations.

Two veterans, France Štiglić and Žika Pavlović, made representative but disappointing films in Slovenia: the former a children's tale, *Shepherds*, the latter a chronicle on seasonal workers, *Dead Bird's Flight*; both are commendable as portraits of contemporary life in the predominantly agricultural, pastoral republic to the north, but they are not up to the standard of their directors' earlier, path-breaking works. The future of Yugoslav cinema, however, may be stamped by their vision and integrity.

new and forthcoming films

PARLOG (The Neglected Land). Script: Ferenc Deak. Dir: Karolj Viček. Phot (colour): Dušan Ninkov. Music: Kiralj Erne. Players: Stevo Žigon, Šolti Bertalan, Irena Prosen, Rada Djuričin, Ibi Romhanji, Mića Tomić, Mira Nikolić, Miodrag Lončar. For Neoplanta Film, Novi Sad, and Centar FRZ, Belgrade.

KUD PUKLO DA PUKLO (Whichever Way the Ball Bounces). Script: Rajko Grlić, Srdjan Karanović, Aleksandar Koenigsmark. Dir: Rajko Grlić. Phot (colour): Živko Zalar. Music: Brane Živković. Players: Mladen Budišćak, Jagoda Kaloper, Feliks Smitka, Srečko Ptiček, Slobodan Šembera. For Jadran Film and Croatia Film, Zagreb.

UŽIČKA REPUBLIKA (67 Days). Script: Ana Marija Car, Arsen Diklić, Zika Mitrović. Dir: Mitrović. Phot (colour): Predrag Popović. Music: Zoran Hristić. Players: Boris Buzančić, Božidarka Frajt, Branko Milićević, Rade Šerbedžija, Neda Arnerič, Ivan Jagodić, Aljoša Vučović, Marko Nikolić, Miodrag Lazarević, Vasa Pantelić, Bogoljub Petrović, Petre Prličko, Mija Aleksić, Ružica Sokić, Marko Todorović, Dragan Ocokoljić. For Inex Film, Belgrade.

DEPS. Script and dir: Antun Vrdoljak. Phot (colour): Vjenceslav Orešković. Music: Alfi Kabiljo. Players: Bekim Fehmiu, Milena Dravić, Fabijan Šovagović, Relja Bašić, Zvonko Lepetić, Krešimir Zidarić, Vlado Puhalo, Mato Ergović. For Jadran Film and Croatia Film, Zagreb.

SB ZATVARA KRUG (The Security Service Closes In). Script: Dragan Marković, Dušan Perković, Miomir Stamenković. Dir: Miomir-Miki Stamenković. Phot (colour): Milivoje Milivojević. Music: Darko Kraljić. Players: Slobodan Dimitrijević, Dušica Žegarac, Dragomir Felba, Rade Marković, Voja Mirić, Faruk Begoli. For Centar FRZ, Belgrade.

PROTIV KINGA (Against King). Script: Gordan Mihić. Dir: Dragovan Jovanović. Phot (colour): Bogoljub Petrović. Players: Slobodan Perović, Božin Djulaković, Eugen Verber, Dragoljub Milosavljević-Gula, Stojan Dečermić, Mira Vacić, Branko Milenković, Nadežda Vukićević. For Centar FRZ, Belgrade.

PASTIRCI (Shepherds). Script: Ivan Potrč. Dir: France Štiglic. Phot (colour): Rudi Vavpotić. Music: Alojz Srebotnjak. Players: Miha Levstek, Ksenija Sinur, Andrej Čevka, Bogo Ropotar, Jože Zupan. For Viba Film, Ljubljana, and Kinematografi, Zagreb.

Still from KOŠAVA, directed by Dragoslav Lazić

OTPISANI (Written Off). Script: Dragan Marković. Dir: Aleksandar Djordjević. Phot (colour): Milorad Marković. Music: Milivoje Marković. Players: Dragan Nikolić, Voja Brajević, Miki Manojlović, Vladan Holec, Čeda Petrović, Rade Marković, Dragomir Felba, Slobodan Aligrudić. For Centralni Filmski Studio "Košutnjak" and Radiotelevizija Belgrade.

KOŠAVA (They Call the Wind Košava). Script: M. M. Lango. Dir: Dragoslav Lazić. Phot (colour): Milorad Jakšic-Fandjo. Music: Arsen Dedić. Players: Bekim Fehmiu, Bata Živojinović, Jovan Janićijević, Tatjana Bošković, Milena Dapčević, Ilija Milhajiović. For Centar FRZ, Belgrade.

STRAH (Fear). Script and dir: Matjaž Klopčič. Phot: Tomislav Pinter. Players: Ljuba Tadić, Milena Zupančić, Milena Dravić, Marjeta Gregorač. For Viba Film, Ljubljana.

HITLER IZ NAŠEG SOKAKA (Hitler from around the Corner). Script: Zoran Petrović, Vladimir Tadej. Dir:

Tadej. Players: Nikola Simić, Boris Dvornik, Ružica Sokić, Dušan Bulajić, Zvonko Lepetić, Mira Banjac. For Jadran Film and Croatia Film, Zagreb.

SARAJEVSKI ATENTAT (The Sarajevo Assassination). Script: Stevan Bulajić, Vladimir Bor, Veljko Bulajić. Dir: Bulajić. For Jadran Film, Zagreb, Kinema, Sarajevo, Centar FRZ, Belgrade and Studio Barrandov, Prague.

SELJAČKA BUNA 1573 (The Peasants' Revolt 1573). Script and dir: Vatroslav Mimica. For Jadran Film, Zagreb.

CRVENI UDAR (The Miners' Detachment). Script: Branislav Božović, Ratko Djurović, Predrag Golubović. Dir: Golubović. Phot (colour): Milivoje Milivojević. Music: Boris Bizetić. Players: Bata Živojinović, Boris Dvornik, Abdurahman Šalja, Dževad Čena, Bert Sotlar, Faruk Begoli, Olivera Katarina, Istref Begoli. For Kosova Film, Priština, Avala Film, Belgrade, and Centar FRZ, Belgrade.

26th BERLIN INTERNATIONAL FILM FESTIVAL
JUNE 25—JULY 6, 1976

Competition of latest outstanding films from all over the world
Retrospective of film classics
International Film Fair for interested professionals

5th International Forum of Young Cinema

Information:
Berliner Festspiele GmbH
Berlin 15, Bundesallee 1–12
Phone: (030) 882 20 81

Film Festivals

Note: the number of film festivals seems to increase annually, and we try here to list only those events that occur regularly and are conducted on a serious basis. Not all of these forty-odd festivals are recognised by FIAPF— *Editor*.

Adelaide—Auckland

June 1976

The Adelaide Film Festival is now the only FIAPF endorsed Festival of New Cinema in the world. It is thus the focal point for new works by new directors in the English speaking world. The Festival is held in the Adelaide Festival Theatre, a $16 million performing Arts complex. The Festival is supported financially by the South Australian State Government and prizes are awarded to the best films (First Feature, Asian and Grand Prix—which includes other than new Cinema) to assist their commercial distribution in Australia and New Zealand. Auckland, the sister Festival City of Adelaide, provides the only major Film Festival outlet for film in New Zealand. *Inquiries to*: Adelaide Film Festival, Box 2019, GPO, Adelaide, S. Australia 5001.

American Film Festival

May 1976

Over 300 films are screened during this very much loved and respected gathering, which is devoted primarily to educational and short films. There are Blue Ribbon Awards in five sections. Registration in advance is imperative. *Inquiries to*: Educational Film Library Association, 17 West 60th Street, New York, NY 10023, U.S.A.

Brisbane

Every July

Since 1966 this annual event has gone from strength to strength. It is presented and organised by Brisbane Cinema Group, the city's leading film society. The festival tries to show a diverse array of features and shorts, particularly those of merit that might not otherwise be seen by Queensland audiences. *Inquiries to*: Brisbane Cinema Group, Box 166, GPO Brisbane, Queensland, Australia 4001.

Berlin

June–July 1976

One of the oldest and most respected festivals in the calendar, Berlin has four principal advantages: the main programme itself (which often features films ignored for the wrong reasons by Cannes), the "Forum des jungen Films," organised by Ulrich Gregor and his colleagues as a counterpart to the Directors' Fortnight in Cannes, the retrospectives (devoted in 1975, the festival's Silver Jubilee year, to Greta Garbo and Conrad Veidt), and the Film Fair, which comprises stands and screenings from the trade of many countries. *Inquiries to*: Bundesallee 1–12, 1 Berlin 15.

AWARDS 1974

Golden Bear (features): **The Apprenticeship of Duddy Kravitz** (Canada), Kotcheff. *Silver Bears*: **Little Malcolm** (Britain), Cooper; **Tabiate bijan** (Iran), Shahid-Saless; **L'horloger de Saint-Paul** (France), Tavernier; **La Patagonia rebelde** (Argentina), Olivera; **Pane e cioccolata** (Italy), Brusati; **In Namen des Volkes** (West Germany), Runze. *Otte-Dibelius Prize*: **Effi Briest** (West Germany), Fassbinder.

Stratford Shakespearean Festival Foundation of Canada

STRATFORD, ONTARIO, CANADA

Stratford Festival 1975

June 9 - October 11

International Film Festival

Opening September 13 – Avon Theatre

Eleventh International
Film Festival
September 13 to September 20

Stratford's Eleventh International Film Festival again presents outstanding works of cinema from around the world together with notable films from the Canadian film industry, retrospective showings, and unusual short subjects. Distinguished guests from the world of film are in attendance throughout the week. Specially priced memberships again available.

 ONTARIO FILM INSTITUTE

Cannes

May 13–28, 1976

Cannes has become the enormous hub of the international film world, a festival at which all the major distributors, producers, critics, and often directors congregate each sunny May to trade and talk. Between 400 and 500 films are unspooled during the fifteen days of Cannes, and the Market is larger than at any comparable event. Parallel with the main competition there is the Critics' Week and the Directors' Fortnight, as well as innumerable special screenings and events. *Inquiries to*: Mme. Louisette Fargette, Festival International du Film, 71 rue du Faubourg Saint-Honoré, 75008 Paris.

AWARDS 1975
International Grand Prix: **Chronique des années de braise** (Algeria), Lakhdar-Hamima.
Best Actor: Vittorio Gassman for **Profumo di donna** (Italy).
Best Actress: Valerie Perrine for **Lenny** (U.S.A.).
Special Jury Prize: **The Enigma of Kaspar Hauser** (West Germany), Herzog.
Best Director (*shared*): Michael Brault for **Les ordres** (Canada), and Costa-Gavras for **Section spéciale** (France).
Grand Prix (*shorts*): **Lautrec** (Britain), Dunbar.
FIPRESCI Prize (*shared*): **The Enigma of Kaspar Hauser** and **The Troupe** (Greece), Angelopoulos.

Chicago

November 1975

Now firmly established as one of the world's leading festivals, Chicago owes its success to the single-mindedness, the ceaseless travel, and the flair of Michael Kutza, who has brought more unusual films to the U.S.A. than anyone apart from Dan Talbot! Chicago is the only competitive festival in the States, and there are now twelve prize categories, as well as retrospectives. *Inquiries to*: Michael J. Kutza, 415 North Dearborn Street, Chicago, Illinois 60610, U.S.A.

Gina Lollobrigida, whose exhibition of photographs was a highpoint of the 25th Berlin International Film Festival

AWARDS 1974
Golden Hugo (*features*): **Pirosmani** (U.S.S.R.), Shengelaya.
Silver Hugo: **Angst essen Seele auf** (West Germany), Fassbinder.
Bronze Hugo: **La prima Angélica** (Spain), Saura.
Bronze Hugo for a First Feature: **Why Rock the Boat** (Canada), Howe.
Golden Plaque: **A Bigger Splash** (Britain), Hazan.

Cork

June 1976

Each year more countries send films to Cork, a mark of tribute for Dermot Breen and his colleagues. Cork concentrates on showing films of high *technical* qualities, with special emphasis on the work of the writer and cameraman. Richard Lester was honoured with a retrospective in 1975. There is a "Film Techniques" course given during the Festival.

Cracow

June 1976

Since 1972 money prizes of 30,000, 20,000 and 15,000 złotys have been awarded at Cracow, which began its career over a dozen years ago. All directors, producers, critics, and short film fans are welcome at the mid-summer event, which is Poland's only international festival and a much respected short film showcase. *Inquiries to*: Festival Bureau, 6/8 Mazowiecka Street, 00-950 Warsaw, Poland.

AWARDS 1974

Grand Prix—Golden Dragon: **First Love** (Poland), Kieslowski.

Special Prize: **Hawks** (Poland), Niedbalski and Manturzewski.

Edinburgh

August-September 1976

Lynda Myles has been busily touring European centres to maintain the admirable momentum built up by the Edinburgh Film Festival during the past few years. Special events in 1975 included "Brecht and the Cinema." The strong suit in the Edinburgh selection is its firm commitment to the experimental and off-beat. The Festival is non-competitive. *Inquiries to*: Edinburgh Film Festival, 3 Randolph Crescent, Edinburgh EH3 7TH.

Film International

March 1976

This festival takes place each year in Rotterdam in the Netherlands, under the energetic guidance of Hubert Bals and Frank Visbeen. During the event, new films which Film International has agreed to import (exclusively on a percentage basis, to avoid competition with distributors), are promoted. Film International also organises a film week in June during the Holland Festival. *Inquiries to*: Film International, Kruisplein 30, Rotterdam, The Netherlands.

Grenoble

June 1976

Some sixty films are in competition here with two solid days of French shorts apart from this. There is also a market for film buyers. *Inquiries to*: 85 rue du Cherche-Midi, Paris 6, France.

AWARDS 1974

Prize for Committed Films: **Last Grave at Dimbaza** (Britain), anon.

Prize for Reportage Films: **Le journal de Naryn** (U.S.S.R.), Viduguiris.

Prize for Fiction Films: **Marc** (U.S.A.), Obenhaus.

FIPRESCI Prize: **Last Grave at Dimbaza.**

International Animation Film Festival in New York

Every September

The only animation festival in North America

**21st
CORK FILM
INTERNATIONAL**

June 5th—June 12th, 1976

FEATURES AND SHORTS
IN COMPETITION

FILM INTERNATIONAL
KRUISPLEIN 30. ROTTERDAM
THE NETHERLANDS
PHONE 10-362758 & 10-115811
HUBERT BALS AND FRANK VISBEEN

film international

organises its fifth festival from 20 february till 1 march 1976 in Rotterdam and Antwerp

---

FILM INTERNATIONAL non profit distribution organisation in 16 mm. In Holland and Belgium over 100 features with the most recent films by MIKLOS JANCSO. ROBERT KRAMER. SHUJI TERAYAMA. WERNER HERZOG. PAOLO AND VITTORIO TAVIANI. DENYS ARCAND. PHILIPPE GARREL. WIM WENDERS among others.

of its kind, this East Coast gathering has been founded and organised by Fred Mintz, as a non-profit-making event sponsored by the N.Y. State Council for the Arts, and other contributors. There is a strong emphasis on the American cartoon form, and this year the Festival held the first full Walt Disney retrospective, together with tributes to George Dunning, Walter Lantz, Chuck Jones, Tex Avery, and UPA. *Inquiries to*: Fred Mintz, Suite 1905, 342 Madison Avenue, New York, NY 10017.

Internationale Hofer Filmtage

October 30–November 2, 1975

Regarded by many as the most intimate and important festival in West Germany, the Hofer Film Days scooped Cannes in 1974 with the world *première* of Herzog's *The Enigma of Kaspar Hauser*. *Inquiries to*: Heinz Badewitz, Wolgemutstr, 10, D–8 Munich 90, West Germany.

Leipzig

November 1975

This winter festival in the German Democratic Republic maintains a competition for documentaries and shorts, whether made for the cinema or television, and directors compete for awards of Gold or Silver Doves. The theme of the festival is "Films of the World for the Peace of the World." *Inquiries to*: Burgstrasse 27, 102 Berlin, G.D.R.

Locarno

August 1976

This Swiss festival offers several parallel sections: an international competition for

3RD INTERNATIONAL ANIMATION FILM FESTIVAL IN NEW YORK
SEPTEMBER 30 · OCTOBER 4 1975
COLUMBIA UNIV. NEW YORK CITY – S.I.A. BUILDING

features, a FIPRESCI Week, a retrospective, and an information section devoted to Swiss cinema. There is also an "Open Forum." The aim of the festival is to promote films that are new in style or content. *Inquiries to*: Moritz de Hadeln, Festivals Internationaux de Cinema, 11 rue d'Italie, CH 1204 Geneva, Switzerland.

AWARDS 1974
Grand Prix: **Tüzoltó utca 25** (Hungary), Szabó.
Grand Jury Prize: **Céline et Julie vont en bateau** (France), Rivette.
Second Prize: **Palec bozy** (Poland), Krauze; **A Bigger Splash** (Britain), Hazan.
Special Prize: **Maa on syntinen laulu** (Finland), Mollberg.
FIPRESCI Prize: **La circostanza** (Italy), Olmi.

London

November 1975
Each year the London Film Festival grows larger in its range and number of pro-grammes. Ken Wlaschin and his contacts hurtle from festival to festival to round up the celebrated and the obscure, not forgetting the finest shorts of the year from other festivals, and the best children's films. Even more praiseworthy is the emphasis on British films that might otherwise flower unseen. Directors often appear to introduce their works at this non-competitive festival, and the National Film Theatre is the perfect headquarters for this fortnight in November. *Inquiries to*: British Film Institute, 81 Dean Street, London W1V 6AA.

Los Angeles International Film Exposition (FILMEX)

March 1976
The unique location of this event has great impact on the HQ of the American film industry

(with residual sales potential for entrants), and over 80,000 people attended the various programmes in 1975. Choices cover a broad spectrum not so much of the star directors' work, as of interesting first films, and films that might otherwise be neglected in the States. The 1975 event sparkled with eight world *premières*, and nineteen American *premières*. There was also a special presentation of the five Academy Award nominees for Best Foreign Language Film, and a "Film Tribute to Nobel Prize-winning Authors" whose work has been interpreted on film. The festival is presented in co-operation with the Academy of Motion Picture Arts and Sciences, the American Film Institute, the Los Angeles County Museum of Art, and the film schools in the area. *Inquiries to*: Gary Essert, Director, Filmex, PO Box 1739, Hollywood, U.S.A. 90028.

Lübeck
Every October
Created in 1956, the Lübeck Festival is concerned exclusively with Scandinavian films, features and shorts as well as animation. In addition to screenings there are discussions, lectures, and special retrospectives. New and old films are presented. *Inquiries to*: Nordische Filmtage, PO Box 1888, D-24 Lübeck, West Germany.

Mannheim
Every October
This is an annual competition for first features, long and short documentaries, featurettes and animation films, which are judged by a jury of young film-makers. There is always a retrospective screening too. A Grand Prize of DM 10,000 is awarded for the best feature; the Josef von Sternberg prize of

DM 2,000 to the most original film; and there are also awards of five Mannheim Film Ducats, each accompanied by DM 1,500. *Inquiries to*: Filmwochenbüro, 6800 Mannheim, Rathaus, E5, West Germany.

AWARDS 1974
Grand Prize of the City of Mannheim: **Vegül** (Hungary), Maár.
Special Prize of the Mayor of Mannheim: **Last Grave at Dimbaza** (Britain), anon.
Josef von Sternberg Prize: **The Innerview** (U.S.A.), Beymer.
Ducats: **Wer einmal lügt oder Viktor und die Erziehung** (Switzerland), Kovach; **Frame-Up: The Imprisonment of Martin Sostre** (U.S.A.), Blatt, Sucher, Fischler; **Zapis zbrodni** (Poland), Trzos-Rastawiecki; **O mal amado** (Portugal), Silva; **27 Down Bombay-Varanasi Express** (India), Kaul. *FIPRESCI Prize*: **Zapis zbrodni.**

Melbourne
June 1976
One of the dozen oldest festivals in the world, Melbourne is unique in its equal interest in features and shorts. In 1975, a record number of 50 features and 150 shorts were screened, including *The Passenger, Céline et Julie vont*

The venue of the MIFED—the International Film, TV Film, and Documentary Market—in Milan

FESTIVAL INTERNATIONAL CINÉMA EN 16mm MONTRÉAL

"THE MOST IMPORTANT IN TOMORROW'S CINEMA"
EVERY LAST WEEK IN OCTOBER

FOR INFORMATION CONTACT:
Dimitri Eipides,
Director,
Montreal International Festival of Cinema in 16mm.
2026 Ontario East, Montreal 133, P.Q. Canada.

---

en bateau, *La circostanza*, and *Shampoo*, as well as a retrospective of the experimental films of Piotr Kamler. For its Twenty-fifth Anniversary, the cash awards at the festival have been increased to $6,000 for the best three shorts, with a top prize of $3,000. *Inquiries to:* Erwin Rado, PO Box 357, Carlton South, Melbourne, Victoria 3053, Australia.

AWARDS 1974
Grand Prix: **Edward Burra** (Britain), Peter K. Smith.
Second Prize: **Druge** (Yugoslavia).
Third Prize: **Chester, Portrait of a City** (Britain).

MIFED (Milan)
April and October 1976
MIFED— the International Film, TV Film and Documentary Market—was founded in 1960 at the time of the thirty-eighth Milan Fair. It is held twice a year: in April to coincide with the Milan Fair, and in October. This Film Market is reserved solely for producers, renters and distributors of feature and documentary films for cinema and TV presentation. MIFED offers several international film awards at its two annual sessions. Among these are the "Five Continents Trophy" and the "TV Pearl." The former is awarded to the best entertainment feature; the latter to the best full-length or serialised film, and to the best short film produced for TV transmission. For clients who are unable to attend the whole time, there is a special assistance bureau which undertakes to represent their interests. In October MIFED also offers the "Indian Summer," a market for the latest film production. *Inquiries to*: MIFED, Largo Domodossola 1, 20145 Milan, Italy (Telex: 37360 Fieramil).

Montreal 16mm

Every October

With its motto "The Most Important in Tomorrow's Cinema" this is a non-competitive festival, with the stress on independently produced 16mm films from around the world. In addition to screenings there are discussions, lectures and special retrospectives. About twenty features and forty shorts are shown annually to audiences that include North American directors, distributors, and press. *Inquiries to*: Dimitri Eipides, Director, 2026 Ontario East, Montreal 133, Canada.

Moscow

July 1977

The ninth Moscow International Film

V International Sport Film Festival
Oberhausen

President
Willi Weyer
General Management
Wolfgang Ruf

END OF OCTOBER 1977

Already with the first
International Sport Film
Festival Oberhausen became
the best one in this
category   *Variety*

D-4200 Oberhausen, Grillostr. 34

Festival took place in July 1975 (it alternates with Karlovy Vary in Czechoslovakia). Over seventy countries take part and while the festival affords a splendid opportunity to the Soviet audiences to see the latest Western films, it also enables visitors from the capitalist countries to catch a glimpse of Soviet production from the various republics, and also to note the latest films from other Eastern European countries. There are restrospectives of classic Soviet films too, and children's films are always given emphasis at Moscow. *Inquiries to*: 33 Vorovski Street, Moscow, U.S.S.R.

New York
Every September

Although it is non-competitive, and although it takes place in a city where more films are screened than anywhere else in the West, the New York Festival has established a name and an image that result in SRO signs almost as soon as the schedule is announced. Richard Roud, the Programme Director, is respected by many of the world's leading directors, and for that reason New York has had some notable world *premières—Le charme discret de la bourgeoisie*, for instance, and *Last Tango in Paris. Inquiries to*: New York Film Festival, Film Society of Lincoln Center, 1865 Broadway, New York, NY 10023.

Nyon
Every October

Created in 1969, with its rules admitting a wide range of films (animation, short features, social documentaries etc.), the Nyon Festival has established a reputation for being concerned with contemporary issues. The event is organised by the Department of Public Education of the Vaud, although financial straits have severely restricted the efforts of the organisers this past year. Like Locarno, this Swiss event is run with unremitting devotion by the widely-travelled Moritz de Hadeln. *Inquiries to*: 27 rue de la Gare, CH-1260 Nyon, Switzerland.

AWARDS 1974
Golden Sesterce: **Broken Treaty at Battle Mountain** (U.S.A.), Freedman.
Silver Sesterces: **Gardarem lo Larzac** (France), Bloch, Levy, Haudiquet; **Ich war, ich bin, ich werde sein** (West Germany), Heynowski, Scheumann, Hellmich.
Jury Prize: **To Live in Freedom** (Britain).

Oberhausen
May 1976

The tragic and early death of Will Wehling flung the Oberhausen Festival into chaos only a few weeks before it was due to take place in 1975. Great credit is due to Wolfgang Ruf, who took over at short notice and produced a programme that was well accepted by visitors and local audiences alike. Oberhausen can

A World class performance.
The Melbourne Film Festival.
One of the few to celebrate a Silver Anniversary,
Melbourne has an unequalled exhibition
record in Australia.
Special Silver Anniversary.
International prizes for short films.

Box 357 Carlton South Victoria 3053 Australia

25th
Melbourne Film Festival

SAN FRANCISCO INTERNATIONAL FILM FESTIVAL

15-26 OCTOBER

Inquiries to: George Gund, Claude Jarman, Lorena Cantrell
and Mark Chase

1409 Bush Street, San Francisco, CA 94109 Tel: (415) 928-8333

still arguably be regarded as the world's best short film festival, but it needs to open its doors more cheerfully to experimental films. *Inquiries to*: Westdeutsche Kurzfilmtage, Grillostrasse 34, 42 Oberhausen 1, West Germany.

AWARDS 1975
Prize of the City of Oberhausen: **Ein Streik ist keine Sonntagsschule** (Switzerland), Stürm, Kanuer.
Main Prizes: **Psalm 18** (G.D.R.), Heynowski and Scheumann; **Izrada i otkrivanje spomenika velikom srpskom satiriečaru Radoju Domanoviću kao i druge manifestacije povodom proslave 100-godišnjice njegovog rodjenja** (Yugoslavia), Babić, ... **As We Are** (Canada), Gross; **Rozmova** (Poland), Adriejew; **Fuji** (U.S.A.), Breer.

Oberhausen Sportfilmtage
October 1977
The Oberhausen Sports Film Festival held its fourth meeting in 1975. The festival aims to show the relationship between film, television and sports, and especially the extraordinary potential that the communication media have in sport instruction. The festival is organised jointly by the city of Oberhausen and the Provincial Sports Association of Nordrhein-Westfalen, and is under the patronage of Minister Willi Weyer. *Inquiries to*: Grillostrasse 34, 42 Oberhausen 1, West Germany.

Perth
August 1976

This Australian event has moved ahead by leaps and bounds, and this summer welcomed Louis Malle and the world *première* of his *Black Moon*. Other unusual films presented in August 1975 were Jørgen Leth's *Good and Evil*, Lutz Eisholz's *Bruno the Black*, and Marguerite Duras's *India Song*. Perth is a member of the International Federation of Independent Film Festivals, along with the Directors' Fortnight in Cannes, the Forum in Berlin, the Edinburgh Film Festival, Film International in Rotterdam, and Pesaro, and as such places its emphasis on finding distribution for the films it presents in Australia as well as attracting critical appraisal of them. Guest directors from overseas are invited to the event. *Inquiries to*: Sylvie Le Clezio, Director, Perth Film Festival, PO Box 149, South Perth, Western Australia 6151.

Pesaro
September 1976
The "Mostra Internazionale del Nuovo Cinema" is particularly concerned with the work of new directors and young cinemas—in other words, with innovations at every level of the film world. There are many round table discussions. The "Mostra," under the lively leadership of Lino Miccichè, also does all it can to secure distribution of the films that it screens, certainly as far as Italy is concerned. There is a special section for *début* films as well as an Information section. *Inquiries to*: Mostra Internazionale del Nuovo Cinema, Via della Stelletta 23, 00186 Rome, Italy.

Philadelphia International Film Festival
April–May 1976
This major attraction of the month-long Philadelphia Festival, presents around two dozen features plus shorts. There was the world *première* of Sembene Ousmane's *Xala* on the opening night in 1975. *Inquiries to*: Philadelphia Festival, PO Box 1928, Philadelphia, Pennsylvania 19105, U.S.A.

Pula

July 1976

One of the most important of Yugoslav film gatherings, and one that over the past twenty years has become a traditional review of artistic quality in the Yugoslav cinema, particularly as regards feature films. There are usually fifteen films shown in the arena, while the remainder are screened in morning programmes. Projections take place in Pula's historic amphitheatre. *Inquiries to*: Jugoslavija Film, Knez Mihailova 19, Belgrade.

AWARDS 1974
Grand Golden Arena: **Užička republika,** Mitrović.
Grand Silver Arena: **Derviš i smrt,** Velimirović.
Grand Bronze Arena: **Crveni udar,** Golubović.

Sanremo

March 1976

Formerly sited at Bergamo, the "Mostra Internazionale del Film d'Autore" has now entered a new phase at the seaside resort of Sanremo. There is a prize of 5,000,000 Lire for the best film, and the principal regulation is that entries should be *auteur* films and should not have been screened in other festivals. Nino Zucchelli is the energetic force behind the event. *Inquiries to*: Rotonda dei Mille 1, 24100 Bergamo, Italy.

AWARDS 1975
Gran Premio: **Takiji Kobayashi** (Japan), Imai.
Best Actor: no award.
Best Actress: no award.

San Sebastian

September 1976

The San Sebastian festival has become a useful film market, and can always boast a good retrospective. The festival is competitive, and films are always screened in their original language, with Spanish or French subtitles. *Inquiries to*: Festival Internacional de Cine, Teatro Victoria Eugenia, San Sebastian, Spain.

AWARDS 1974
Golden Shell: **Badlands** (U.S.A.), Malick.
Golden Shell (shorts): **Simparela** (Cuba).
Special Jury Prize: **Boquitas pintadas** (Argentina), Torre Nilsson.
Silver Shell: **La femme de Jean** (France), Bellon; **The Wicket Gate** (Poland), Różewicz.

Solothurn Film Days

January 1976

This six-day gathering provides the Swiss and foreign observers a chance to see all independent Swiss films made during the preceding year, together with all shorts produced in Switzerland. A selection *is* made, but *all* features are screened. Directors are on hand, and there are daily press conferences. *Inquiries to*: Stefan Portmann, PO Box 4500, Solothurn, Switzerland.

Sorrento

September 1976

Sorrento is the *only* festival that has the courage to devote its entire attention to one particular country's films (Yugoslavia in 1975). The result is that in this attractive setting just south of Naples and opposite Capri, one can meet all the directors, stars, and film personalities from one country as well as see the latest productions. *Inquiries to*: Dr. Gian Luigi Rondi, Ente Provinciale di Turismo, Naples, Italy.

Stratford, Ontario

September 1976

A delightfully unpretentious international festival, this event owes much of its appeal to the intelligent programming of Gerald Pratley. The main programme includes

TEHRAN

INTERNATIONAL FESTIVAL OF FILMS FOR

CHILDREN AND YOUNG ADULTS

2 - 9 NOVEMBER 1975

TAKHTE TAVOUS AVE., NO. 31 JAM ST., TEHRAN, IRAN TEL: 836891 . 8
CABLE KANOON TEHRAN

features from many countries, and there is a retrospective, as well as a day with Canadian film-makers. Many distinguished guests come to Stratford. The Festival is supported by the Ontario Film Institute, the Government of Ontario, and of course the famous Shakespearian Festival. *Inquiries to*: The Director, Stratford International Film Festival, Avon Theatre, Stratford, Ontario.

Sydney
June 1976

The Twenty-second Sydney Film Festival opened with the most important new Australian film of the year, *Sunday Too Far Away*, and closed with John Schlesinger's *The Day of the Locust*. In between these two, forty features and dozens of shorts were presented to packed audiences in the magnificent old State Theatre. Features shown include *Céline et Julie vont en bateau*, *Cousin Angelica*, *The Passenger*, Jancsó's *Elektreia*, *The Orders*, *The Sandglass*, *The Circumstance*, *The Phantom of Liberty*, *A Private Enterprise*, *A Bigger Splash*, *The Mouth Agape*, *Alice in the Cities* and many others. Warren Beatty (*Shampoo*), Dušan Makavejev (*Sweet Movie*), King Hu (*The Valiant Ones*) and Philippe Mora (*Brother Can You Spare a Dime?*) introduced their films and participated in spirited question and answer sessions. A major feature of the Festival was a comprehensive retrospective of Australian feature films from 1911–1971. *Inquiries to*: David Stratton, Director, Box 4934, GPO, Sydney, NSW 2001.

Tampere
February 19–22, 1976

The fifth international short film festival in this well-known Finnish cultural centre was held in 1975 and 190 films from 40 countries were entered for competitions, besides which an admirable series of animated films produced by the Zagreb studio was shown, along with a retrospective compilation entitled "Four Decades of British Documentary Films." On two preceding days, February 18–19, 1976, the Seventh International Conference of Short, Animation and Documentary Film Festivals is being held here. *Inquiries to*: Tampere Film Festival, PO Box 305, SF-33101 Tampere 10, Finland.

AWARDS 1975
Grand Prix: **Wise Masters and Clever Mechanisms** (Hungary/Bulgaria), Lakatos.
First Prizes: **The Three Fools and the Cow** (Bulgaria), Donov (Animation); **A Day with the Builders** (India), Shukla (Documentary); and **Experimental** (Britain), Lehman (Sports).

Tehran
November 26–December 7, 1975

After three years, Tehran has settled into place as *the* winter film festival (although the Iranian weather in November–December is usually superb), and is competitive for both features and shorts. Recognised by FIAPF, Tehran places special emphasis on films from Africa and the Far East, and while Western participation is strong, the Market and Retrospectives offer items unfamiliar at other festivals. Hospitality is impeccable. *Inquiries to*: Hagir Daryoush, Secretary-General, Tehran International Film Festival, Ministry of Culture and Arts, Tehran, Iran.

AWARDS 1974
Grand Prix (Golden Winged Ibex): **Shazdeh Ehtejab** (Iran), Farmanara.
Special Jury Prize: **Football of the Good Old Days** (Hungary), Sándor.
Best Actor: Behruz Vosuqi for **The Deer** (Iran).
Best Actress: Olimpia Carlisi for **Le milieu du monde** (Switzerland).
Best Direction: Richard Lester for **Juggernaut** (Britain).
Grand Prix (shorts): **The Night It Rained** (Iran), Shirdel.

thessaloniki
international
film festival

COMPETITIVE   FOR   SHORT   LENGTH   FILMS

NON COMPETITIVE FOR FEATURE LENGTH FILMS

● RETROSPECTIVES   ● FILM MARKET

INFORMATION THESSALONIKI INTERNATIONAL FILM FESTIVAL TEL.031-220.440 CABLE FOIRINT TELEX 291 THESSALONIKI-GREECE

Tehran (Children and Young Adults)

November 1976

Founded by Her Imperial Majesty Farah Pahlavi, this Festival is now in its eleventh year, and is recognised by FIAPF. The event is competitive, and an international jury dispenses awards to both shorts and features. Tehran is now established as the world's leading children's film festival. An offshoot of the festival's activities is the institute for the Intellectual Development of Children and Young Adults, which has produced several interesting films. *Inquiries to*: Fereydoun Moezi-Moghaddam, Secretary-General, Takhte Tavous Ave., No. 31 Jam St., Tehran, Iran.

AWARDS 1974

Grand Prix: **Vinegar** (Czechoslovakia), Pinkova.
Golden Plaque (*6 to 10 Age Group*): **Roly** (Poland), Sokolowska.
Golden Plaque (*10 to 14 Age Group*): **Automatic** (Czechoslovakia), Bedřich.
Golden Plaque (*14 to 18 Age Group*): **Life of the Birds** (Czechoslovakia), Mačurek and Doubravá.
Golden Plaque (*General*): **Wind** (*Canada*), Tunis.

Telluride

Every August

This short but remarkably imaginative festival in one of Colorado's most beautiful towns is the brainchild of Tom Luddy, James Card, and Bill Pence. There are tributes to stars, and screenings in the Sheridan Opera House of new and controversial movies. *Inquiries to*: Bill Pence, Janus Films Inc., Larimer Square, Denver, Colorado, U.S.A.

Thessaloniki International Film Festival

June 1976

Now in its fifth year, Thessaloniki's International Film Festival, approved by FIAPF, is competitive for shorts from all over the world. The 1974 event, which took place in October after the collapse of the junta *régime*, was a great success, in spite of the fact that the international jury did not dispense the honorary awards (gold effigies of the Nike of Samothrace). There were programmes of feature films too, from the Balkan countries, the U.S.S.R., the U.S.A., England, France, West Germany and China and tributes to the Latin-American cinema and the contemporary Italian cinema, as well as a children's film programme and a retrospective of Greek postwar satirical features. *Inquiries to*: International Film Festival Secretariat, Thessaloniki, Greece.

Thessaloniki (Domestic Festival)

September 1976

Over the past seventeen years, this annual gathering, which follows the closure of the Thessaloniki Fair, and lasts seven days, has become an extremely important support for the local industry and an outlet for new talents, both for features and shorts. *Inquiries to*: Greek Film Festival Secretariat, Thessaloniki, Greece.

AWARDS 1974

Best Film: **Kierion**, Theos; and **Model**, Sfikas.
Best Productions: **Megara**, Maniatis–Tseberopoulos; **Gazoros**, Hatzopoulos.
Best Direction: **The Murderess**, Ferris.
Best Photography: **The Colours of the Rainbow**, Panayotopoulos.
Best Short: **Antigone's Life Story**, Netas.

Trieste

July 1976

Now in its fourteenth year, Trieste is the only festival devoted exclusively to science-fiction films. Screenings take place in the magnificent Fourteenth century castle of San Giusto above the ancient port of Trieste. In recent years the festival has also concerned itself with films of scientific achievement. *Inquiries to*: Festival Internazionale Film di Fantascienza, Castello San Giusto, Trieste, Italy.

AWARDS 1974

Golden Asteroid: **Sanatorium pod klepsydrą** (Poland), Has.

Special Jury Awards: **The Silence of Dr. Ivens** (U.S.S.R.); **Miss Golem** (U.S.S.R.).

Best Actor: John Ryan for **It's Alive** (U.S.A.).

Best Actress: Zhanna Bolotova for **The Silence of Dr. Ivens.**

Golden Seal for Best Short: **The Making of "Silent Running"** (U.S.A.), Barbee.

U.S.A. Film Festival

March 1975

This annual event spotlights the best American movies from the season ahead, as selected by leading national critics. All films screened are *premières*, except for the retrospective (devoted in 1974 to Joseph L. Mankiewicz). Directors and stars are in attendance, and there is a useful section for short films. *Inquiries to*: Mary MacFarland, U.S.A. Film Festival, PO Box 3105, Dallas, Texas 75275.

Academy Awards: 1975

Best Picture: *The Godfather Part II*.

Best Direction: Francis Ford Coppola for *The Godfather Part II*.

Best Actor: Art Carney for *Harry and Tonto*.

Best Acresss: Ellen Burstyn for *Alice Doesn't Live Here Anymore*.

Best Supporting Actor: Robert De Niro for *The Godfather Part II*.

Best Supporting Actress: Ingrid Bergman for *Murder on the Orient Express*.

Best Screenplay (based on material from another medium): Francis Ford Coppola and Mario Puzo for *The Godfather Part II*.

Best Screenplay (based on material not previously published): Robert Towne for *Chinatown*.

Best Cinematography: Fred Koenekamp for *The Towering Inferno*.

Best Art Direction: Dean Tavoularis and Angelo Graham for *The Godfather Part II* (set dec: George R. Nelson).

Best Costume Design: Theoni Aldredge for *The Great Gatsby*.

Best Editing: Harold F. Kress and Carl Kress for *The Towering Inferno*.

Best Original Song: Al Kasha and Joel Hirschhorn for "We May Never Love Like This Again" from *The Towering Inferno*.

Best Scoring Adaptation: Nelson Riddle for *The Great Gatsby*.

Best Original Dramatic Score: Nino Rota and Carmine Coppola for *The Godfather Part II*.

Best Sound: Ronald Pierce and Melvin Metcalfe Sr. for *Earthquake*.

Best Documentary Feature: *Hearts and Minds*.

Best Documentary Short: *Don't*.

Best Foreign Language Feature: *Amarcord*.

Best Live-Action Short: *One-Eyed Men Are Kings*.

Best Cartoon Short: *Closed Mondays*.

Film Music

Soundtrack Albums of the Year
by Tom Vallance

It was another lean year for the film musical, with only three new full-scale productions. **Funny Lady** (Arista ARTY 101), **At Long Last Love** (RCA ABL2 0967), and **Tommy** Polydor Deluxe Double 2657 014). The M-G-M compilation **That's Entertainment!** proved slightly disappointing in its two-record album (MGM Super Double 2659 033), for much of it was previously issued material from the record company's vaults, tracks edited long ago to "78" length, rather than as presented in the film. There is enough material taken from the compilation's soundtrack, however, such as the early vocal efforts of Gable, Stewart and Grant, the Garland-Rooney montage, Lena Horne's "Honeysuckle Rose," Garland and O'Brien's "Under the Bamboo Tree" and the marvellous opening sequence from *Show Boat*, with its irresistible Conrad Salinger orchestration, to make the album essential.

The Garland–O'Brien song was one of many memorable moments in the M-G-M classic **Meet Me in St. Louis,** and a valuable reissue coupled Garland's studio recordings of the songs from that film with the score of another in which she starred, **The Harvey Girls** (MCA MCFM 2588). Other welcome reissues included **Deep in My Heart** (MGM Select 2353 090), in which an all-star cast headed by former Metropolitan star Helen Traubel does fine justice to the songs of Sigmund Romberg, **Carmen Jones** (RCA AHL1 0046), the surprisingly successful Hammerstein–Bizet collaboration with Marilyn Horne singing the title role, and a second tribute to

Busby Berkeley taking its title **Hooray for Hollywood** (United Artists UAG 29644) from the Richard Whiting–Johnny Mercer song composed for *Hollywood Hotel.* Seven of the ten songs on this album are the work of Harry Warren and Al Dubin, including three numbers from *42nd Street* that enable the collector who has the companion album on the same label to possess the complete score from that early classic. Though musically weaker than the first record, which skimmed off the cream of the Berkeley scores, it is never less than enjoyable and is beautifully produced with dialogue extracts skilfully integrated.

The outstanding vintage issues of the year came with the appearance of four Astaire–Rogers soundtracks on two LPs, one coupling **Top Hat** with **Shall We Dance?** (EMI EMTC 102), the other **Swing Time** with **The Gay Divorcee** (EMI EMTC 101). Classic scores all, none of them previously available on disc, and all of them excellently edited with relevant dialogue snippets and all the numbers (though the marathon "Continental" has been necessarily shortened).

It was a particularly grand year for the voice of Astaire, as befitted the great dancer-vocalist in his seventy-fifth year, for besides the classic soundtracks with Rogers, there were three super compilation albums which spanned the three greatest decades of his film career. **Starring Fred Astaire** (CBS 88062) included all thirty titles recorded by Astaire for the American Brunswick label between June 1935 and March 1938, remastered in crystal clear mono sound of the highest quality and sumptuously packaged with six pages of copious notes, photos and sheet music reproductions. At a special low price, this set was the year's Best Buy! Equally valuable was **Easy to Dance With** (MCA MCFM 2698), a seventeen-song selection taken from that post-RKO period of the early Forties which until now has been poorly represented on disc. With *Easter Parade* (1948) Astaire emerged from retirement to start another brilliant decade in which many of his finest hours were spent at M-G-M; these were represented by **A Shine on His Shoes** (M-G-M Select 2353 112), giving one the chance to savour again the magnificent M-G-M orchestra backing the Astaire voice in many unjustly neglected delights. Other Hollywood personalities represented by compilation albums were Judy Garland **(The Best of Judy Garland,** MCA CDSP 803, two records), soprano Deanna Durbin **(Sweetheart of Song,** MCFM 2579) and "Brazilian Bombshell" Carmen Miranda with her superb backing group the Bando da Lua **(South American Way,** MCA Coral CDLM 8029).

Several of the year's new background scores made prominent use of songs both old and new: Curtis Mayfield's heavily-accented score **Claudine** (Buddah Super 2318 097), Elmer Bernstein's bracing **Gold** (Philips 9299 225), plus **Blazing Saddles** (Warner Bros. K 16414) and **Young Frankenstein** (ABC ABCL 5108). **Phantom of the Paradise** (A&M AMLS 63653) mixed parody and genuinely funny lyrics (notably one about posthumous success in the pop field) with some beguiling soft-rock melodies. The year's Oscar-winning song was "We May Never Love Like This Again" by Al Kasha and Joel Hirschhorn, sung by Maureen McGovern in **The Towering Inferno** (Warner Bros. K 56102). The film's main score by John

Williams had a surging main theme, its pulsating rhythms and counter-melodies effectively suggesting both the architect's aspirations and the flawed reality. The composer's orchestrations are colourful, and for the tense final sequence he employs muted xylophone notes to punctuate the suspense. The same composer scored the year's other big disaster film **Earthquake** (MCA MCF 2580), producing a majestic long-lined melody reminiscent of the big-city themes of Newman and Rózsa, injecting rhythms beneath to represent day-to-day life. Some engaging jazz-tinged sections showcasing top-class soloists were another distinctive feature of this enjoyable score (though the grooves failed to reproduce "Sensurround").

Two of the year's best scores were imbued with nostalgia. A pastiche Thirties dance-tune is one of the two main themes for **Murder on the Orient Express** (EMI EMC 3054), wittily orchestrated by composer Richard Rodney Bennett. This and the stately waltz which symbolises the train are performed with panache by the Covent Garden Opera House Orchestra under Marcus Dods. For **The Great Waldo Pepper** (MCA MCF 2707) Henry Mancini composed his best score in some time, a lively, nostalgic and tuneful mixture of musical styles with an emphasis on the band music that proliferated at the fairs and carnivals where the barnstorming pilots of the Twenties performed their dare-devil feats.

Jerry Goldsmith used a lazily beautiful trumpet theme, sinuously played by Uan Ramsey, to suggest an aura of *film noir* for **Chinatown** (ABC ABCL 5068) and also worked in some authentic standards including Bunny Berigan's timeless performance of "I Can't Get Started." This was a more impressive score than Goldsmith's jangly and repetitive music for **Ransom** (Dart ARTS

65376). Andrew Lloyd Webber's second original film score **The Odessa File** (MCA MCF 2591) was richly varied, ranging from a Teutonic anthem to polkas, a pop song for Perry Como and a fugue for cello, rock group and orchestra. Other new scores included Nino Rota and Carmine Coppola's Oscar-winning music for **The Godfather Part II** (ABC ABCL 5128), an atmospheric and tuneful collection through which Rota's original themes from the first film insistently weave; Vladimir Cosma's primarily jaunty and jolly music to accompany **The Mad Aventures of "Rabbi" Jacob** (Decca SKL 5199); John Cacavas's partially electronic but primarily unimaginative **Airport 1975** (MCA MCF 2583); and the piquant themes of Pierre Bachelet and Hervé Roy for **Emmanuelle** (Warner Bros. K 56084).

Three new recordings and one reissue provided potent reminders of three of the finest composers of film music. RCA's series of Classic Film Scores happily resumed with tributes to Franz Waxman and Bernard Herrmann. **Sunset Boulevard: Classic Film Scores of Franz Waxman** (RCA ARL1-0708) took the German-born composer from his first Hollywood assignment *The Bride of Frankenstein*, with its rivettingly errie "Creation of the Female Monster," through the composer's own favourite score *Rebecca* with its breathless climactic waltz, to *A Place in the Sun*, with its luscious romantic theme, its high alto saxophone solos depicting the film's tormented protagonists, and its exciting chase fugue later to be echoed by Shostakovich, to the later pieces for *Prince Valiant* and *Taras Bulba*. **Citizen Kane: Classic Film Scores of Bernard Herrmann** (RCA ARL1- 0707) took its title from the composer's first film assignment, presented in a suite which leads from the sombre opening to the powerful climax as the identity of Rosebud is revealed. The suite

here is different to the one Herrmann himself arranged and recorded under the title "Welles Raises Kane" and includes the first recording of the recitative and aria for the fictional opera "Salammbô," brilliantly sung by Kiri Te Kanawa. Four other films were also represented with scores of power and beauty: *Beneath the 12-Mile Reef*, *White Witch Doctor*, *Hangover Square* (a complete performance of the intense, bravura "Concerto Macabre," played with requisite *brio* by Joaquím Achucarro), and a brief chase sequence from *On Dangerous Ground*, utilising eight horns and an augmented brass section for a savagely driving, breathlessly effective piece. Both these RCA records were superbly performed by the National Philharmonic Orchestra under Charles Gerhardt.

Bernard Herrmann himself conducted the National Philharmonic in **The Fantasy Film World of Bernard Herrmann** (Decca PFS 4309), containing four extended selections by this most individual and non-compromising of Hollywood composers. Few scores are less overtly commercial than the composer's first excursion into science-fiction. *The Day the Earth Stood Still*, but his trend-setting work, balancing the otherwise conventional orchestra with a large electronic group, was to prove a major influence in film scoring. *Journey to the Center of the Earth*, for which Herrmann suggested the atmosphere inside the bowels of the earth by eliminating strings and using only instruments of low registers, includes a moment of considerable emotional power as a burst of full orchestra and organs signifies the revelation of the way to the earth's centre. The celebrated score for *The Seventh Voyage of Sinbad* includes a lilting waltz for the duel with the skeleton, a xylophone punctuating the rapid rhythms of the woodwind. A haunting love theme demonstrates Herrmann's ability to write beautiful romantic music, as does his lovely suite from the neglected *Fahrenheit 451*.

Jungle Book and **The Thief of Bagdad** (United Artists UAS 29725) not only feature two classic scores by Miklós Rózsa, but the former is noteworthy for being the first major film score to be put on disc, when RCA issued a set of 78s in 1942 with star Sabu providing a narration. The current disc was recorded in 1959 by the Frankenland Symphony Orchestra conducted by the composer. The narratives for both suites are read rather drily by Leo Genn, while the playing and recording are adequate; the music, however, is splendid, rich in descriptive and witty orchestrations, and it is good to have these fine scores back in the catalogue.

Films for Young People

by Peter Cowie

Several European countries are now at last following the example of the United States in persuading educational authorities and municipal libraries to use film alongside literature as a pedagogic tool. The Netherlands Information Service, for instance, is making a concerted effort to sell prints of Dutch shorts to their own local authorities; amazingly enough, the films of Bert Haanstra are better known to foreign audiences than they are to the Dutch. The Danes too have restructured their audio-visual policy, incorporating the work of the Statens Filmcentral into a wider programme that will ensure the release of visual materials throughout the schools and educational establishments of Denmark.

The signals of an improvement in the American economy may not affect the educational film market in the States for some time. Library budgets are still much lower than they should be, and there are more companies than ever before fighting for a share of the market. The small, specialised firms are best equipped for survival, alongside the giants like Macmillan and McGraw-Hill. If there are any trends to be discerned in the past twelve months, then the decline of animation may be one of them. Only the finest animated subjects are acceptable in schools today; and it is harder than ever to persuade educational authorities to purchase foreign movies with subtitles (how sad it would be if everyone's efforts on behalf of educational films resulted in a generation that could not read!).

The death of Julien Bryan in October 1974 deprived everyone in the field of a stimulating and immensely gifted individual. As head of the International Film Foundation he had become a legend long before celebrating his seventy-fifth birthday, and was able to charm even the most truculent of classroom audiences. Julien was a perfectionist in the best sense of that word, and his immense personal achievements never turned his head; no one, indeed, was more welcoming

INTERNATIONAL FILM BUREAU INC.

the oldest distributor of documentary films in the U.S.

FOUR FILMS ABOUT FILMMAKING FOR BEGINNERS

A FILM ABOUT FILMMAKING
MAKING A SOUND FILM
A FILM ABOUT FILM EDITING
A FILM ABOUT CINEMATOGRAPHY

ANIMATED FILMS

from Belgium.................. CHROMOPHOBIA
GOLDFRAME
THE FALSE NOTE
SIRENE
TO SPEAK OR NOT TO SPEAK
OPERATION X-70
PEGASUS

from Switzerland .... NAILS
A LINE IS A LINE IS A LINE

from Czechoslovakia .... THE FISH
JANOS AT THE RIVER

And many other 16mm films in all categories. Enquiries invited.

INTERNATIONAL FILM BUREAU INC.
332 South Michigan Avenue
Chicago, Illinois 60604

to a newcomer than Julien Bryan. He was, of course, profoundly curious about other countries and other peoples. Traveller extraordinary (he was trapped inside Warsaw in 1939 and brought back that brilliant film *Siege* as a consequence), he pioneered the non-narration film with an enthusiasm and conviction that made his own International Film Foundation productions celebrated throughout the States. We have lost not merely a most civilised friend and colleague, but also the symbol of the personal touch in film distribution. Julien had foreseen the Day of the Giant Conglomerate, but to the end he knew that one rough-hewn short by a man of talent was worth a hundred assembly-line productions.

We append below details of the principal American companies offering films for young people, in the hope that such notes may be useful to teachers and also to independent producers seeking a distributor for their work.

ACI FILMS

35 West 45th Street, New York, NY 10036. (212) 582-1918.

ACI manages to add around sixty new releases to its catalogue annually, and a wondrous selection they always are. "The History Makers," a series of documentary biographies, offers a panorama of modern American history, while *Sioux Legends* (20 mins.) won a Cine Golden Eagle for its portrayal of Indian lives and beliefs. Maynard Orme's *Sam Maloof: Woodworker* took a Red Ribbon at the 1974 American Film Festival, and shows how hard, sustained creative work can lead to a balanced family life. Agnes de Mille's *Cherry Tree Carol* tells a holy legend in ballet and folksong form.

In animation ACI has released the unusual, and very carefully thought out *Boasting*, an Iranian film that shows how war games lead to trouble and how difficult it is to learn to survive. *Eternal Change: Story of a Mountain* (14 mins.) is a spectacular, awesome study of Mount Ranier, a volcanic peak in Washington state. Time-lapse photography detects the ominous and inexorable movement of the glaciers, and, quite apart from the geological revelations it provides, this film should stimulate classroom discussion on the role of nature and its processes.

Finally, from Australia, there is *What Have You Done with My Country?* (20 mins.), a challenging documentary about the Aborigines, the dilemmas and pressures that face them, and their sense of loss in the face of urban progress. This is a film that questions

I Seem To Be A Verb

A cinematic interpretation of the philosophy of Buckminster Fuller based on the book of the same name.

USA Film Festival

23 minutes

AGUA SALADA
(Bitter Waters)

A modern-day Passion, dramatically constructed to Bach's "Passion According To Saint John."

Gold Hugo Award, International Chicago Film Festival

12 minutes

EL VISITANTE
(The Visitation)

A contemporary woman reacts powerfully to her own child, and her own life.

9 minutes

Mime and cinema elegantly interweave to tell a witty, ironic tale.

EXCHANGE PLACE

10 minutes

the values of our modern society with disquieting intelligence.

BENCHMARK FILMS

145 Scarborough Road, Briarcliff Manor, NY 10510. (914) 762-3838.

The small but choice selection of films offered by Mike Solin's Benchmark organisation can stand comparison with the giants in terms of craftsmanship and imagination. Films are available for both purchase and rental and cover the Social Sciences as well as the Humanities, Drug Abuse, Human Reproduction, and Natural Science. Several of the Benchmark titles are international award-winners. Recent acquisitions include *You*

Irresistible You, a satire on male cosmetics, *One Man's Garden*, an allegory about recycling of garbage, and *Gals Guys and Dolls*, a puppet film about sex roles.

CAROUSEL FILMS

1501 Broadway, New York, NY 10036. (212) BR 9-6734.

Carousel, under the management of Dave Dash, has been broadening its distribution network this past year, and now has an office in Los Angeles. The company specialises in reaching public libraries, and is interested in acquiring new films from Europe. Carousel aims at productions for

A striking shot from ETERNAL CHANGE: STORY OF A MOUNTAIN, released in the U.S. by ACI Films

primary grade use, and CBS and ABC Television are good sources for its library. Carousel owns overseas rights on several films in its catalogue.

Recent releases include *A Watersnake in Coney Valley*, a bristling satire on the Nixon affair directed by Steve Ujlaki. President "Vixen" uses strongarm tactics to rig a small-town decision as to his guilt, and the hand-coloured still pictures make him and his henchmen look like fugitives from a horror movie. A witty and unusual film. *The Dam at Nagarjunasagar* is a documentary on the building of a dam on the Krishna River over a fourteen-year period—during which time the population increases by millions. The film conveys a sense of people working in unison and thus striving to overcome their poverty.

A French short, *Eclosion*, uses speeded-up photography to register the growth of an egg to a caterpillar to a butterfly. The music track is mysterious and evocative, and the film is infinitely superior to the average Disney study of a similar subject.

THE ECCENTRIC CIRCLE

PO Box 4085, Greenwich, Connecticut 06830. (203) 661-2278.

In a comparatively short time, Ted Fairchild's Eccentric Circle Cinema Workshop has built up a reputation for carefully prepared and promoted film materials. Eccentric Circle believe in a close collaboration with each film-maker, and involve him as much as possible in the distribution process. They regularly include directors in their screenings and workshops around the country and are frequently asked for consultation by producers while their film is in production.

Recent releases include *Tout en l'air*, directed by Grant Munro for NFBC, a percipient study of two ballet dancers; *The Saga of Macrame Park*, by Ben van Meter, a lyrical documentary about the ancient sailor's art of knot-tying; and *With Intent to Harm*, by Scott Siegler and Stephen Ujlaki, which takes the viewer inside the prisons of Massachusetts and shows the need for penal reform.

FILMS INC.

1144 Wilmette Avenue, Wilmette, Illinois 60091.

This gigantic enterprise has grown enormously since Charles Benton acquired the company from Encyclopaedia Britannica in 1968. It distributes high quality films from sources as far apart as the British Film Institute, Japan Broadcasting System (NHK), National Film Board of Canada, and

Trevor Howard and Martin Sheen in CATHOLICS, distributed in the U.S. by Carousel Films

Zagreb Film. Each year nearly one hundred new titles are added to the catalogue, but outdated films are ruthlessly pruned to ensure a high level of material at all times. The Films Inc. catalogue is attractively designed.

GROVE PRESS

53 East 11th Street, New York, NY 10003. (212) 677-2400.

Although best known for its library of foreign and *avant-garde* feature films, Grove Press has a strong division devoted to educational movies. The "Life Encounters" series includes all three of Robert Snyder's acclaimed portraits of Henry Miller, Anaïs Nin and Buckminster Fuller. There is also a group of films from the People's Republic of China, and a startling documentary, *Twilight of the Mayas*, about the surviving Indians of southern Mexico.

INTERNATIONAL FILM BUREAU

332 South Michigan Avenue, Chicago, Illinois 60604. (312) 427-4545.

This reliable company more than lives up to its name, and many of the hundreds of films on its books are also available for sale throughout the world. The 1974 supplement to the main catalogue includes films on Art, Music, Film as Art and Film Study, Language Arts, Literature, Modern Languages, Maths, Education and Welfare, Science, Soc ̄ial Studies, and Safety. IFB has supported the w   orks of individual European directors such as   ecently *Pegasus* and animated shorts (most re   ses in the U.S.A. *Operation X-70*) it now releas   es in the U.S.A.   McLaren, The hour-long tribute to Norma.   so dis- *The Eye Hears, The Ear Sees*, is a   will tributed by IFB, and music students w. welcome the series of six composer profiles covering Bach, Mozart, Beethoven, Schubert, Chopin, and Debussy. Filmstrips are also within the bailiwick of IFB, and for purchase and preview details readers should write to them in Chicago.

INTERNATIONAL FILM FOUNDATION

475 Fifth Avenue, New York, NY 10017. (212) 685-4998.

In our Introduction above we have paid tribute to the late Julien Bryan. But IFF is a continuing entity, under the vigorous and thoughtful supervision of his son, Sam Bryan, himself a skilled cinematographer and observer of far-flung cultures. *The Changing*

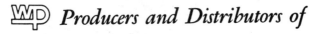

An enchanting moment caught, from THE VIOLIN, one of the many award-winning shorts released by Learning Corporation of America

Middle East (25 mins.) is a mosaic of intelligent impressions of "the world's first crossroads." The film contrasts the old and the new, describes the birth of the three great monotheistic religions, the role of education, of oil, water, and land reform. Twelve countries are represented in the survey, which promises to be as popular as the Foundation's *South America Today.*

Mention should also be made of *The American Super 8 Revolution*, a virtuoso film by Stan Woodward about film-making in the classroom. It's a movie about history and about film technique, all in one stimulating mix.

LEARNING CORPORATION OF AMERICA

1350 Avenue of the Americas, New York, NY 10019. (212) 397-9330.

LCA is one of the few organisations to be both large *and* personal in the educational field. Bill Deneen and his team are sensitive to the latest trends in classroom cinema, and the LCA catalogue includes everything from feature films like *The Autobiography of Miss Jane Pittman* to animated delights of the standard of Eli Noyes's *The Fable of He and She*, which sketches, with the aid of brightly spangled plasticines, the fundamentals of community living and non-sexism.

The company is also sponsoring the work of creative film-makers like Bert Salzman, whose *Me and You Kangaroo* is set in Australia and tells a story, without narration, that is bound to move and entrance any young audience. Salzman's latest movie, *The Shopping Bag Lady* (21 mins.) was shot mainly in Central Park and features Mildred Dunnock as a lonely woman rejected by society and the young generation. Again there is a palpable sense of loss, echoed in the exquisite music score, accompanied by a recognition of the inevitable disillusions of life.

LCA specialises in series, and one of the best of these is entitled "Comparative Cultures and Geographies." In one film, London and New York are compared and their urban values discussed. In another, a factory in Osaka, Japan, is compared with a similar plant in the United States. Such films not only open a window on the wider world; they force an audience to think for itself.

Other recent LCA releases include the *Handy Dandy Do It Yourself Animation Film*, which, presented by three children, shows how the basic principles of animation can be applied to everything from clay to sand; *The Poem as Imagery*, which supplies thoughtful and provocative imagery for a poem by Margaret Atwood; and *The Family That Dwelt Apart*, based on a 1937 story from "The New Yorker," and deliberately animated in the style of that era.

MASS MEDIA ASSOCIATES

1720 Chouteau Avenue, St. Louis, Missouri 63103. (314) 436-0418.

Mass Media houses one of the country's most unusual and stimulating collections of 16mm films and multi-media. The aim of each film is to make the pupil or student respond; not to spoon-feed him, but to provoke him into meaningful dialogue with his teacher and the world about him. The catalogue subdivides all films into such intriguing groups as "Fear," "Evil," "Feminism," "Forgiveness," and "Dissent." Many of Mass Media's acquisitions are from Europe, with Yugoslav films figuring prominently. *Death of a Peasant, I Think They Call Him John, The Hat, Scabies,* and *Two Men and a Wardrobe* are just some of the many award-winners in the 1974/75 catalogue. Rental and purchase rates are reasonable; materials are in good shape always.

McGRAW-HILL FILMS

1221 Avenue of the Americas, New York, NY 10020.

This most complex and enormous of all film libraries covers literally every category of education imaginable. Many of the films are produced specifically for McGraw-Hill; others are imported from Europe. It is in the area of the documentary that McGraw-Hill is justly renowned, with such classics as *Future Shock* and *The Lion Hunters* offering food for thought and for discussion. Contemporary Films, a division within the company, is now releasing *One Eyed Men Are Kings,* the Academy Award winning live-action short directed by Edmond Séchan.

PHOENIX FILMS

470 Park Avenue South, New York, NY 10016. (212) 684-5910.

Within a couple of years, Phoenix has risen in the ranks of educational film distributors, and boasts a selection of first-class shorts. Robin Lehman, whose work we survey on another page, owes his American success in large part to the efforts of the Phoenix team, while an older master, Jiři Trnka, is almost exclusively distributed by this firm. The team of Heinz Gelles, Leo Dratfield, and Barbara Bryant is well-known throughout the world, particularly as Mr. Dratfield searches out potential new acquisitions at the major European festivals. Other fine Phoenix offerings include a documentary on the actress Helen Hayes, and Charles Huguenot van der Linden's *This Tiny World*, a charming evocation of the fantasy toyland that every child delights in. See our U.S. Non-Theatrical section for coverage of the Phoenix feature list.

PICTURA FILMS DISTRIBUTION CORP.

43 West 16th Street, New York, NY 10011. (212) 691-1730.

Roslyn Appelbaum and Alfred Wallace have a discriminating taste that is reflected in their excellent Pictura catalogue. In addition to imported shorts such as *The Hidden Truth* (a middle eastern puppet tale) and Mr. Wallace's own series, *A Nation Is Born* (commissioned for the Bi-centennial celebrations), Pictura has some outstanding individual films. *The Two Faces of China* evokes the rituals, customs, and geography of mainland China, and stresses the family loyalty and individual outlook that transcend the slogans of

the day. *The Magic Pear Tree* is a Chinese folk tale by Wan-go Weng, told in audacious animation, using a stylised, cut-out technique. *The Toymaker* has sold over 4,000 prints during the past quarter-century, and Alfred Wallace, a skilled puppeteer in his earlier life, conveys beautifully the concept of two identical puppets being created and manipulated by the same maker, while yet having different personalities. *Lucy*, scripted and directed by Paul Glickman, describes the emotional turmoil of a sixteen-year old girl who finds herself pregnant. The film makes no value judgements, and ends on a warm, positive note. Note finally that Pictura has world nontheatrical rights to *The Book of Kells*, which is a record of that superb illuminated manuscript of the Ninth century.

PYRAMID FILMS

Box 1048, Santa Monica, California 90406. (213) 828-7577.

There is no doubt that David Adams and his Pyramid Films produce the most handsome catalogue in the field. Superbly designed by Saul Bass & Associates, the catalogue includes stills and text on hundreds of high-quality films, many of them, like *Frank Film*, *Iran, The Bolero*, and *Why Man Creates*, prize winners around the world. Each film is chosen for its contribution to learning by sharing the experiences of others, says Mr. Adams. Pyramid also has on offer many European classic short films such as *Un chien andalou* and *The Apple*.

Recent additions to the Pyramid collection include *An Adventure in Film Lighting*, by Paul Burnford and Jerry Samuelson, *Be Fit and Love*, by Ralph Luce, Flaherty's classic, *Industrial Britain*, *A Time Out of War*, by the Sanders brothers, and the long-lost documentary on the 1936 Winter Olympics by Carl Junghans.

ROA FILMS

1696 North Astor Street, Milwaukee, Wisconsin 53202. (414) 271-0861.

In addition to many feature films, the Roa library contains a large Disney selection, and several discussion films for young people. Some of these are available from other sources, but Roa Films designs its catalogue intelligently so that items are grouped under sub-headings that enable teachers to choose shorts to fit their discussion topics.

TEXTURE FILMS

1600 Broadway, New York, NY 10019. (212) 586-6960.

Herman Engel and Sonya Friedman have added several fine, idiosyncratic works to their very extensive Texture Film library this year. Although the films are as a rule geared toward an educational market, they are exceptionally well-crafted and, on the whole, of interest to a wide age bracket.

Two films by a new Peruvian director—Arturo Sinclair F.—will be of particular interest to film students and enthusiasts. Both *El visitante* (*The Visit*) and *Agua salada* (*Salty Water*) are elliptical works—technically complex and viscerally beguiling, *El visitante* is a disturbing melange of segments of a mother's day—told to a skilfully varied musical soundtrack–culminating in the horror-ecstasy of the visitation (at lunch). *Agua salada* superimposes the piercing tones of Bach's "Passion according to Saint John" over the silent contemporary tragedy of two fishermen—father and son—shot along the Peruvian coast. The subtle intensity and scrupulous stylisation of the director's images—particularly in this film—are extraordinary, and he is most certainly an original.

Also highly recommended is the less obscure *Sex and the Professional*—a frank, good-natured investigation of a new breed of doctor, nurse, teacher learning to deal specifically with sexual guidance and/or disorders. Although the film has earned some notoriety for its male frontal nude (flashing on the screen for less than a second), its most memorable segments deal with various group encounters. *Exchange Place*, another new Texture offering, is an extremely well-constructed mime with masks and a vagrant quarter.

(Diane Jacobs)

TRICONTINENTAL FILM CENTER

333 Sixth Avenue, New York, NY 10014.

Primarily active in Third World feature material, Tricontinental has recently caused quite a stir in American educational film circles with *The History Book*, a series of nine animated films on the history of Western civilisation from the Middle Ages to the present day. History is interpreted not so much in terms of statesmen and royalty as through the eyes of the ordinary working men and women. These nine movies were produced by the Statens Filmcentral in Denmark.

UNITED NATIONS

Radio & Visual Services Division, Office of Public Information of the United Nations, NY 10017. (212) 754-1234.

The 1975/76 English-language 16mm film catalogue from the United Nations describes almost 200 films, ranging in subject matter from basic information about UN Charter and organisations, to issues of such urgent global concern as world population and development, the food and energy crises, UN peace keeping in the Middle East, and the changing status of women. All titles are available for purchase on a worldwide basis, and for rental in the U.S.A. and Canada. Selected films may be borrowed from over fifty UN Information Centres round the world. Daphne Brooke, Chief of the Distribution section of the Radio & Visual Services, is a familiar figure at conventions and screenings, and has a distinguished background with the National Film Board of Canada and ACI Films.

Still from THE MOUNTAIN PEOPLE, available through Wombat Productions

WOMBAT PRODUCTIONS

77 Tarrytown Road, White Plains, NY 10607. (914) 428-6220.

The international scope of the Wombat library increases year by year, and there are films here from the United States, Britain, France, Yugoslavia, Italy, Australia, Canada, Bulgaria, and West Germany. Although there are only forty films in the catalogue, these same films have won thrity-five awards and citations from festivals and organisations around the world. Recent releases include *The Fire*, which won the Gold Medal at the 1974 Belgrade Festival, *The Mill*, another Yugoslav film by Živko Nikolić, and Film Australia's *The Road to Charlie*, an effective drug-abuse and guidance movie.

The Mountain People, glimpsed so dramatically in John Boorman's film *Deliverance*, live in Southern Appalachia, and this documentary delineates their plight—and also their strong spirit of kinship. *I'm the Prettiest Piece in Greece* is a portrait of the vaudeville singer and actress of the Thirties and Forties, Billie Haywood. *My Son, Kevin* is a profile of a child born without arms and legs, due to thalidomide. All these Wombat films are accompanied by the most searching and valuable sets of notes.

EDUCATIONAL MEDIA AUSTRALIA

237 Clarendon Street, South Melbourne, Victoria, 3205.

Founded eight years ago by Ken Widdowson, Educational Media Australia provides an outlet in Australia for overseas produced 16mm films and has fostered the much-needed local production of educational films and multi-media material.

Now one of the largest 16mm distributors in the country, EMA represents many prominent producers, including the National Film Board of Canada, Films Inc., Pyramid, the British Film Institute, and the National Film Unit of New Zealand.

A boy in Jordan, from Sam Bryan's film, THE CHANGING MIDDLE EAST

EDWARD PATTERSON ASSOCIATES

68 Copers Cope Road, Beckenham, Kent. (01) 658-1515.

William Orr is now well-known and respected for his distribution in Britain of such excellent libraries as International Film Bureau of Chicago and Time-Life Films. Since 1974, his firm has also released the superb collection of Julien Bryan's International Film Foundation. One of Mr. Bryan's last trips before his death at the age of seventy-five was to England, to introduce his films to audiences around the UK. Mr. Orr also has a number of British productions for TV and non-theatrical distribution—Peter Bayliss's *A Set of Slides* and *The Worlds of Rudyard Kipling*, for instance.

CENTER FOR SOUTHERN FOLKLORE

3756 Mimosa Avenue, Memphis, Tennessee 38111. (901) 323-0127.

This non-profit organisation has been established by William Ferris and Judy Peiser, in order to document folktales, crafts, and music that are rapidly disappearing in the southern United States. The Center researches and documents folk culture which is threatened by modern industrial society. To document these traditions, the Center produces and distributes films, records, photographs, and books for use by educators, museums, and libraries.

Some films currently available include *Delta Blues Singer, James "Sonny Ford" Thomas, Gravel Springs Fife and Drum, Ray Lum: Mule Trader, Greene Valley Grandparents, Black Delta Region*, and *Mississippi Delta Blues*.

EMA has produced over twenty 16mm educational films in conjunction with local education authorities. Releases this year to date are *Hospital at Work, Malaysian Village, Bicycle Stall in Malaysia*, and a five-film series on *Weaving*.

From its inception, Educational Media Australia has also produced and distributed multi-media material, such as sets of slides and study prints, with sound cassettes and teachers' guides which are priced to allow schools to purchase a range of titles for library and individual use. EMA has now opened a London office at 3 Elsham Road, London W14.

Robin Lehman

Winning the Golden Bear award in Berlin in 1972 with *Flyaway*, his first film and one of the official British entries, Robin Lehman began his career as a short film-maker with a flourish. Since then, making three or four films a year, he has managed at various festivals to gain thirty-three gold, silver and bronze awards and four certificates of merit. In April 1975 he crowned his achievement by winning an Oscar. In a very short period of time Robin Lehman has become a leading name.

Born in 1936, Lehman was for many years a full time student of painting and then of music, studying composition in Paris in the early Sixties. He turned to film-making by chance, partly as a result of his lifelong hobby of underwater diving and exploration which led him to take up underwater photography. Modest in his approach, Robin Lehman's confidence grew as he saw that the rushes of the film he took compared well with those of professional film-makers with whom he was working.

Flyaway (U.K., 1972, 12 mins, colour; with Roy Evans) which has won seven awards, is about a man who launches a model aeroplane on a hillside and follows it across country on its seemingly independent flight. A cameo without words, the film in its cutting and coverage reveals a natural talent. *Wings and Things* (U.K., 1973, 18½ mins, colour), which Lehman made next and which has won six awards, is about different kinds of model aeroplanes and their devotees. Dissatisfied with the first version he recut it to reduce its length and to eliminate the speech tracks, becoming convinced that he wanted his films without commentary or speech.

This technique is brilliantly realised in his outstanding third film, *Undercurrents*

Robin Lehman shooting COLTER'S HELL

(U.S.A., 1973, 10 mins, colour), a study of underwater life, shot in the Caribbean and full of colour and activity as the fish weave close to the camera. This won the Silver Medal for Lehman at the 1973 Moscow Festival and subsequently six other awards. The extraordinary beauty of this unusual view of nature, a world unseen by us, was matched by the film released in 1973 called *Colter's Hell* (U.S.A., 10½ mins, colour). This won Lehman a Gold at Berlin for the second year running. Made in the Yellowstone Park it reveals his artist's eye for colour. Full of strange close-ups of bubbling geysers which in their sinister turbulence evoke the Creation, the film takes on the form of a symphonic concerto. Material from this film is to be seen in Ken Russell's *Tommy* (with a screen credit to Lehman).

At this stage his imagination, as formidable as his world-wide filming programme, dwelt on human problems and conceived a space flight film that would imply a comment on the future of mankind. Set construction, using *2001: A Space Odyssey* expertise, took place at Elstree and animal filming was set up in Africa but for a number of reasons the film, to be called *Once upon a Time*, was never made. Instead Lehman brought human comment in visual terms to a work about the butterfly called *Don't* (U.K., 1974, 18½ mins, colour). With photography which delighted experts at the Natural History Museum (where the Lehman films have all been shown) the film traces the butterfly's progress from chrysalis stage to the reactions it produces in the streets of New York. Completed in 1974 and shown on BBC television that summer along with all the other Lehman films (at peak hours), it was this short which won him the Academy of Motion Pictures Oscar in 1975.

Sea Creatures, *Hotspot*, and *Experimental* were three more films released in 1974 along with *Don't* and which have also won prizes. *Sea Creatures* (U.K., 1974, 12 mins, colour) was shot in the heat of a Red Sea summer and again captures the beauty of the underwater world. Lehman had put in a considerable amount of research to find the right equipment for underwater filming, and all his films are made in 35mm. For *Hotspot* (U.K., 1974, 8½ mins, colour) Lehman took himself down into the crater of the active Niragongo volcano in Zaire to capture the spellbinding explosion of molten lava at its source. The film is edited to the musical accompaniment of Bach's Toccata and Fugue in D minor. *Experimental* (U.K., 1974, 11 mins, colour), which was short-listed in 1975 for the Grierson Film Award by the British Federation of Film Societies, has already collected gold and silver awards; it is a fascinating look at the world of human flight, from the antics of men leaping into a river with home-made wings to the supremacy of the Concorde.

In 1975 Lehman has been in Paris editing *See*, another underwater film made in the Red Sea and which he considers is superior to *Sea Creatures*. He has made another underwater film in the Irish Sea and is also making a picture called *The End of the Game*, a conservation film about African animals. Already completed is *The Mugger*, a love story set in New York City.

With his films shown first at the London Academy Cinema, then on BBC television, and distributed widely by Contemporary Films; with wide distribution in the United States and in France; with magnificent international festival awards, Robin Lehman has become a truly international figure, recognised as an artist who looks at nature and the human world with a unique visual sense and feeling for colour; possessing a mastery of rythmm and structure, and a concern for humanity. With this unique talent the interesting question is, will Lehman tread the thorny path from shorts to features?

KEN GAY

Robin Lehman's Films are available in the U.K., on 16/35mm from Contemporary Films Ltd., 55 Greek Street, London, W1V 6DB (Tel: 01-734 4901), and in the U.S.A. from Phoenix Films Inc., 470 Park Avenue So., New York, NY 10016 (Tel: 684 5910).

The Children's Film Foundation

The Children's Film Foundation is a non-profit-making organisation set up in 1951 by the British Film Industry to ensure the production and distribution of entertainment films especially designed for children. Although the films are primarily intended for screening at the 725 commercial cinemas which run special matinees for children throughout the United Kingdom, they are also available in 16mm and are in great demand in numerous overseas territories. The Directors of the Foundation are nominated by the five trade associations and the Federation of Film Unions, who also appoint the Chairman (Sir John Davis), and all serve voluntarily. The day to day running of the Foundation is in the hands of a small permanent staff and Henry Geddes has been the Executive Producer since 1964. Its films are mainly stories of achievement, adventure, comedy and drama and almost invariably have young people in the leading roles. The stories are selected by a voluntary Production Committee, and made into films by commercial producers at a fixed budget. Production finance is provided mainly by a grant from the British Film Production Fund, but this is augmented by special discounts and donations from all branches of the Industry. The co-operative attitude adopted by the Unions and by artists and senior technicians, who invariably accept far below the normal commercial rates on Children's Film Foundation films, ensures that high quality films are produced at a very modest cost.

The films are distributed to every children's matinee in the United Kingdom on a rotation basis. As the audience is constantly growing up and therefore changing, films are re-issued every eight years.

During 1975, the Children's Film Foundation will make seven one-hour features, and twelve short comedies, bringing the Foundation library up to 120 tailor-made features, thirty-two serials and numerous shorts. In addition to its own production, the Foundation also adapts suitable overseas films and distributes them through the United Kingdom.

Overseas 35mm Distribution is handled for the Children's Film Foundation by Rank Film Distributors. 16mm Home Distribution is handled for the Children's Film Foundation by the Rank Film Library and Columbia-Warner. The Children's Film Foundation is now the major distributor of children's matinees, despatching well over 1,150 prints each week.

HENRY GEDDES

John Halas, Chairman of the International Jury of BBC TV Icograda Asifa annual contest for children, presents the Olivetti Trophy for the best designed film to John Karatson for his winning entry in a TV programme in Budapest—June 1975

Children and Film in Scotland

With its twin concerns for education and film culture, the Scottish Film Council is particularly well placed to stimulate children's and young people's interest in film. The Council encourages the development of film study in the classroom, and has recently initiated a slide/tape competition for children, which has drawn entries, all of a remarkably high standard, from all over Scotland.

The Council is, of course, not the only agent in this field. Two ambitious non-professional film-making groups have recently produced films specially aimed at the younger audience. Tycho Productions of Motherwell are responsible for *Jack Snell*, an elaborate and imaginative medieval fantasy (with a cast of over a hundred) about a cobbler who wins the hand of a princess by overcoming a fearsome giant. Group Five,

from Aberdeen, chose a different subject and a different approach in *Donald of the Colours*, an adventure story of a boy after the Battle of Culloden, bringing to it all the skill of their earlier productions *Vortex* and *Race to Nowhere* which reached a wide audience through television.

Still from BOASTING, an animated fairy tale released in the States by ACI Films

ON THE AIR

The owl is our symbol. It has been on the air in Finland for 17 years. It's also spreading across the frontiers and has already been seen flying in more than 30 countries.
This year it's been crossing the big oceans.

Make sure that the owl will land in your company, too. Contact us now for. nature programmes, other documentaries, as "Alvar Aalto the Humanization of Architecture", drama, entertainment, animation, and even co-productions.

dynamic programming and quality

 OY MAINOS-TV-REKLAM AB
Foreign Relations Department
Pasilankatu 44, 00240 Helsinki 24, Finland
tel. 413 300 cables COMTELE telex 12-1544

1975: Crisis and Change

by David Wilson

Last year, introducing IFG's new section, I predicted a further year of crisis for European television. It was not a difficult prediction to make, at least for Western Europe, since inflation (the immediate but by no means the only cause of the crisis) seemed likely to be with us for some time. And so it is. Production costs have soared, and the result has been a general paring down of budgets—and, some would say, a general decline in standards. Reports from the major television festivals of the year have been depressing; and there may be some significance in the fact that the Eastern European countries have picked up some of the major prizes.

If anything, inflation has hit TV even more than the cinema. Television, after all, has no box-office returns with which to recoup costs. Companies have responded by making production economies (a case in point being the BBC's much-heralded *Churchill's People* series, whose shoestring budget has been almost laughably obvious). Another European strategy has been to spread costs by co-production agreements, either with one of the major American companies or with another European country. Warners and Universal are increasingly familiar names on the credits of home-produced Western European television programmes. And it is not simply because of the EEC that Britain, West Germany, France, Italy and so on are finding an expanding market for each other's television output. In Europe, at least, McLuhan's global village has as much to do with the economics of making television as with the technological advances in disseminating it.

A year of crisis also promised to be a year of change. If the promise has not been fulfilled, that is probably because the largely monolithic structure of television in most European countries does not easily lend itself to radical change. As our report from France shows, the dismantling of ORTF in favour of a television structure with at least the potential of greater independence has in fact been a case of "Tout ça change, tout c'est la même chose." The same is broadly true of the changes in Italian television. And in other countries, like Portugal and Greece, it is too soon to predict the likely effect on TV of recent political change. Less negatively, perhaps, the wall which used to separate television from the cinema has crumbled further. Made-for-TV films are now a universal phenomenon. And it is now not uncommon to see films made for the cinema having their first showing on television.

This year's section includes reports from a number of countries not covered last year. The focus is still Europe, though we also have reports from North and South America. Next year, space permitting, we hope to go further afield.

Britain

British television, like the nation itself, is in the doldrums. While inflation runs riot and economic Cassandras warn of worse to come, television adopts the familiar British posture of showing two faces at once, the one bemoaning (and usually exaggerating) the crisis, the other pretending that it doesn't exist. An evening's television in Britain is quite likely to produce the bizarre conjunction of political pundits warning of Armageddon, a nostalgic drama series trying to show how much better things used to be, and *Monty Python's Flying Circus* demonstrating with zany logic that the world is mad and always has been, all rounded off with late night hints on chess and transcendental meditation. A *potpourri* of facts and fantasy is in the nature of television: the flux of images is making

visual schizophrenics of us all. But television, like the press, also reflects the mood it tends to help create. Was it just fortuitous programme planning which brought British viewers a new BBC drama series called *The Survivors*, in which the population has been decimated by a nationwide epidemic and the few that remain have to scrabble in the woods for sustenance?

The Survivors has attracted neither critical approval nor audience ratings, but survival is a serious business for the BBC. Faced with pay increases (which incurred official criticism) and the government's reluctance to raise television licence fees beyond a level which might cost votes, the BBC responded by cutting jobs as well as budgets. The budgetary cuts have been evident in a number of ways, most obviously in yet more repeats of programmes already aired two and three times (the late Dr. Jacob Bronowski's monumental series on scientific/philosophical evolution, *The Ascent of Man*, has recently been screened for the fourth time). New programmes have been manifestly short on the reliable production finesse which makes BBC drama series so attractive to the international market. The most notorious example has been the prestigious *Churchill's People* series, based on Churchill's epic history of "the English-speaking peoples" (and co-produced by Universal Pictures Television), whose embarrassingly obvious studio economies earned a good deal of critical scorn which rapidly knocked the series off its peak-time viewing pedestal. Cardboard rocks and hastily erected miniature forests did not seem quite the right style for a series commemorating Churchill.

The cash crisis has also hit the fifteen commercial television companies. Advertising revenue may gradually have increased during the year (and some companies were able to declare record profits), but in real terms revenue is not keeping pace with inflation. The dilemma facing the ITV companies is cruelly simple: since their lifeblood is advertising revenue, and advertising revenue depends on high viewing figures, the temptation is to go for larger audiences by increasing the ratio of "entertainment" to "serious" programmes. But this is a move which would earn the disapproval of ITV's monitoring um-

Still from AKENFIELD, the Peter Hall film shown on British TV as well as in cinemas

brella, the Independent Broadcasting Authority, which requires the companies to maintain a reasonable balance between *This Is Your Life* and Verdi.

The dilemma has been exacerbated this year by industrial disputes within ITV which resulted in an almost nationwide blackout of programmes—and gave the BBC the rare satisfaction of recording undisputed higher audience ratings. Unless this problem is resolved by the end of 1975 (which seems unlikely), it will come as no surprise to find some of the smaller ITV regional companies merging with their bigger brothers, a development which many would regard with alarm at a time when regional development is being locally demanded and officially encouraged.

All this has happened against a background of continuing uncertainty about the future of British television. The Annan committee of inquiry into broadcasting, set up by the government last year, has received a flood of evidence from pressure groups large and small. It is too early to predict what the committee, which still hopes to report some time in 1976, will recommend; and, in any case, the government is under no obligation to implement all or even any of their recommendations. It seems likely, however, that it will be economics as much as anything which determines the general drift of the committee's proposals. Significantly, the major television debating point of the last few years—the allocation of the fourth channel—is now little heard. No one is talking about a new fourth channel when the existing three channels are faced with so many apparently intractable problems, and when rumour has it that the minority channel, BBC-2, may not even survive in its present form.

Meanwhile, for the "least worst tele-

vision in the world" (one former TV critic's view of British television), this has not been a year to remember. ITV still dominates the audience ratings (taking a week at random, in February 1975, one finds not a single BBC programme in the national top twenty ratings), mostly with tried and tested light entertainment pap. On the other hand ITV continues to produce better television in areas traditionally dominated by the BBC, particularly current affairs and documentary. Granada's *World in Action* and London Weekend's *Weekend World* are consistently livelier than the BBC's now rather tired *Panorama* and *Midweek*. The Granada programme, for instance, pulled off a notable coup—and provoked a government inquiry—in its *exposé* of conditions in the mostly British-owned tea plantations of Sri Lanka. In the documentary field ITV companies like Yorkshire and Thames have made programmes which put to shame the generally staid and stilted productions now filling the BBC's regular documentary slot, which has recently found nothing better to offer than Lord Chalfont interviewing the Shah of Iran and a celebration of railways which provided a painful reminder of the *Look at Life* programme fillers long familiar to British cinema audiences.

That the BBC can still produce good documentary film-making is occasionally demonstrated in long-running series like *Man Alive*; but the general trend is increasingly towards orthodoxy and against anything likely to upset the BBC's notion of "balance," which usually pivots on a point between the consensus view and the received idea. This was graphically illustrated by the coverage of Britain's EEC referendum campaign, when, despite the BBC's declared intention (and statutory obligation) to keep a general balance between the "Yes" and "No" cam-

paigners, there was never any doubt about which side would get the better coverage. Though, as with last year's two General Elections, television's contribution to "the great debate" was depressingly superficial.

If ITV has taken the year's major honours (and this year it was ITV companies who scooped the national television awards), there are still areas in which the BBC excels. One of them is comedy, which provided some of the year's most inventive television. *The Goodies*, a cross between the Goon Show and the Keystone Cops, carried off one of the major prizes at the Montreux festival. The similarly lunatic *Monty Python's Flying Circus*, which has now spawned a second feature film, has been sold to several foreign television networks; while British audiences have been blessed with *Rutland Weekend Television*, eccentric though erratic brainchild of one of the Monty Python team. And a much admired series was *The Last of the Summer Wine*, which brought a refreshingly original approach (not least the fact that it was largely filmed on location) to situation comedy.

Originality was what was lacking in the year's television drama. With some exceptions, like Colin Welland's *Leeds United!* (a spirited reconstruction of a strike by women at a clothing factory), original drama has lacked enterprise and imagination. The most interesting productions have usually been short plays tucked away in series like the BBC's *Centre Play*, or in a late-night series called *Eleventh Hour*, which makes the best of increasingly limited budgets by improvising plays from start to finish within a week. ITV offered an adventurous series of Restoration comedies, but has also been short on good original drama.

The mood of the nation has been reflected in the viewing figures for escapist entertainment. One of the BBC's most pop-

From Thames TV's THE SWEENEY

ular programmes has been the New York police series *Kojak*, which for sheer production finesse puts all the British TV cops (with the possible exception of Thames's glossy series *The Sweeney*) in the shade. Another index of national habit has been television's continuing nostalgia boom, with drama series like Thames's *Affairs of the Heart* (versions of Henry James stories), the BBC's *Ten from the Twenties* and ATV's highly successful serial biography of *Edward the Seventh*.

Looking back is now a national pasttime, encouraged if not prompted by television. Looking forward, in the present climate, is a more difficult exercise. But some television prospects at least look hopeful, like Lew Grade's expansive plans for ATV, which include the showing of an epic *Moses* (made with Italy's RAI) and a twenty-four-part adaptation of Arnold Bennett's *Clayhanger*. One of the BBC's brightest promises is *Days of Hope*, a series of four films about the experiences of an English working-class family of fifty years ago, made by the Ken Loach-Tony Garnett partnership which has been responsible for some of the best in television

drama as well as for films like *Kes* and *Family Life*.

Which prompts a final note about one of the year's developments that is probably here to stay. The TV version of Bergman's *Scenes from a Marriage* (marred for most people by the dubbing) was shown after the film version had been seen in cinemas. But there were also several feature films—like Alain Resnais's *Stavisky* and Peter Hall's *Akenfield* (backed by London Weekend Television)—which were shown either simultaneously with or even before their release to cinemas. It is too soon to say what effect this innovation will have on both television and the film industry, but it could be substantial.

DAVID WILSON

Telly Savalas as KOJAK

Still from VIBRATION, by Jack Bond and Jane Arden, a film "which unites Sufic meditation practices with advanced film/video techniques." An Indigo Production

Finland

Television was introduced into Finland in the second half of the Fifties; after a brief experimental period, regular TV broadcasts were started in 1958. At the present time, 99 % of the Finnish population are within reach of at least one of the country's two television networks. By October 1974, 1.3 million TV licences had been issued. Colour has also been introduced on both channels, and the number of colour licences should soon start approaching the 200,000 mark.

The overall organisation of the Finnish television system is rather unusual. The sole licence for radio and television broadcasting in Finland is held by Oy Yleisradio Ab (YLE), a government-controlled company which operates two radio networks, two television units and a separate Swedish-speaking radio and TV unit, which is in charge of programmes for the Swedish-speaking minority in the country (about 7 % of the population). Helsinki-based TV-1 has traditionally been considered the nationwide network, but its position is now significantly challenged from Tampere, the second largest city, by TV-2, which covers about 80 % of the population and can boast a brand new production centre fully equipped for colour production. The Swedish-speaking section (RTV) has programmes on both channels; and there is also an extensive network of regional production centres, though their potential is yet to be fully realised.

What makes the Finnish TV-system so unique, however, is the presence of a private, commercial company, Oy Mainos-TV-Reklam Ab (MTV), on both YLE-networks. According to its charter, YLE is allowed to make use of MTV as an additional programme source, and MTV, on the other hand, is the only unit which is allowed to use advertising within and between its programmes. Together with money from radio and television licences, revenue from TV advertising forms the bulk of YLE's budgeted income. The ever-present economic crisis in the company has recently once again given rise to discussions on the size of MTV's share of the budget cake. Licence fees are also on the upswing, and new sources of income (state financing of educational programmes, for instance) have been explored.

For the record, one might also add that cable television is about to be added to the complicated Finnish TV scene. Privately owned and operated, it is reaching its experimental first stage, especially in the Helsinki area.

The total amount of television broadcasting time is now something like 80 hours per week, of which roughly 25 % is handled by commercial television. According to 1973 statistics, the annual total was 2,885 hours for YLE and 772 hours for MTV—surprisingly high figures for a relatively small country. The ratio of foreign and domestic production has been wavering on both sides of the fifty-fifty mark. Of programmes transmitted by Yleisradio in 1973, about 35 % was of foreign origin. The prominence of Anglo-Saxon attitudes is still evident in the choice of foreign material—more so in the programme policy of MTV—but there is also a genuine desire to cover as large an international programme span as possible. It is not now unusual, for example, to find at least 25 countries from all over the world represented in YLE's annual output of about 150 feature films.

In the area of international television co-operation, Yleisradio occupies an unrivalled mediating position by being the only full member of both the European Broadcasting

Still from THE MOCKER, produced by Oy Mainos TV of Helsinki

Still from DALES OF YORKSHIRE, the award-winning documentary from Oy Mainos TV of Helsinki

Still from the Finnish production, SOLVEIG's SONG

Union (EBU) and its East European equivalent, the International Radio and Television Organisation (OIRT), and engaging fully in the programme exchange and co-production activities of the Scandinavian Nordvision countries. Excluded from membership in these organisations, MTV has its own wide network of contacts, including co-productions with European and even American companies.

While theatrical film production has recently been hitting rock-bottom in Finland, there have appeared signs that the earthy, socially engaged trend of film-making for which Finnish cinema has gained international acclaim, has also reached the small screen. The most worthwhile television productions in this area have usually been adaptations of recent Finnish fiction. These include *Solveigin laulu* (*Solveig's Song*), a powerful and far-reaching working class ballad of three women and three generations in Helsinki, based on a novel by Lassi Sinkkonen and directed by Reima Kekäläinen. Another success has been *Simpauttaja* (*The Mocker*), a longish, realistic and unusually outspoken "western" from the Finnish backwoods, based on a novel by Heikki Turunen, and directed by MTV's Veikko Kerttula, a reliable adapter of many a piece of modern Finnish fiction, including a few masterpieces by Veijo Meri.

Mikko Niskanen, whose *Eight Deadly Shots* (originally made for TV) reached the Top Ten list in the 1974 edition of International Film Guide, has since been busy with projects of a widely different nature. After sharing directorial credits with Hannu Heikinheimo in the TV-opera *Pagliacci*, Niskanen was finally able to complete his long-cherished project *Omat koirat purivat* (*Bitten by His Own Dogs*), a lengthy, passionately acted (Niskanen himself in the main role) and patient analysis of the fate of a sensitive creative talent at the mercy of a hostile society. The film was based on the personal experiences of Finnish classic writer Ilmari Kianto during the Second World War. Niskanen's new project is a television documentary on Finland.

During the years, Finnish TV has received its fair share of international awards. Children's programmes have been regarded especially favourably by the various juries—probably because the prevailing characteristic of these films has been a straightforward look at life's problems through the eyes of a child. Recent international acclaim has been showered on *Äiti menee naimisiin* (*Mother Gets Married*), directed by Raili Rusto, which won the first prize at the Prix-Jeunesse contest in 1974, and *Jasons Sommar* (*Jason's Summer*), a surprise winner of the animation category in the Hollywood Television Festival of 1975. At the New York Television Festival of 1974, a bronze medal was awarded in the documentary category to *Dales of Yorkshire*, an MTV/Yorkshire Television co-production directed by Juhan af Grann, whose 1975 credits include a film portrait of Finnish President Urho Kekkonen.

OLLI TUOMOLA

France

The end of 1974 and the beginning of 1975 was a hectic time for French television, with the so-called "reform" of ORTF being announced, implemented and commented on amid much commotion. As it turned out, it appeared that the present government saw the situation as one of its now familiar publicity stunts. Spicing his natural sense of occasion with a paternalist crowd-pleasing flavour, M. Giscard d' Estaing has taken to inviting

Raymond Bussières (centre) in LE PAIN NOIR, an ORTF presentation

himself to dinner with his tax-payers. In this spirit he presided over a televisual carve-up whose only visible consequence has been the removal of a large number of practitioners (for example, 261 journalists dismissed from a total of 1,080), musical chairs at the top management level, and the invasion of the small screen by feature films (following a strike by actors, the projected number of films to be shown by the three channels tops five hundred a year).

What has not changed, and indeed has increased, is the number of advertising spots—always a come-on and usually both sexist and silly—and variety shows, in which the same artists, short on talent if not on con-

nections, mercilessly bludgeon the viewers. The controller of the second channel (himself the author of a series about a French family, the Fargeots, which was a thoroughly cliched view of French family life) was pleased to announce that "literary" programmes no longer talked about books but current events. These are invariably seen through the eyes of an interchangeable group of "personalities" whose role is to talk about everything under the sun. The "new television," in fact, is afflicted by a peculiarly French disease—official gobbledegook. On any conceivable pretext (a fire, a racist crime, a literary prize) the television screen is filled with official (the President, a Minister), or semi-official (journalists, intellectuals, actresses) personalities, government mouthpieces talking blandly and interminably to each other.

The swan song of the old-style ORTF was a vast series about a family (traditionally a highly-regarded *genre*), budgeted at 1,000 million old francs, two years in the making, and daringly entrusted to a director not yet thirty. The series, entitled *Le pain noir*, captured a large and wide-ranging audience as week by week it told its story—at a very slow pace and in a highly-wrought visual style—of several families involved in the struggles of the peasants and the workers at the end of the Nineteenth century.

The new broadcasting "companies" are making television on the cheap, reducing the number of plays and under-employing (or not employing at all) producers and directors of proven talent. The result has been the dawning of commercials television: the second channel is now authorised to sell morning airtime to private companies. Marcel Bluwal, an experienced director of good popular programmes, was reported in "Le Monde" as predicting that in future "it will be quantity, the commercial basis, that will count. We are moving away from the notion of a public service to one based on money. We are asked to work faster and less diligently. The whole thing is being turned into a push-button operation."

In these circumstances it is difficult to see how Jean-Paul Sartre will be able to safeguard the making, not to mention the transmission, of the series of programmes which he has taken on, and in which at the age of seventy he will appear for the first time on his own country's television. Brigitte Bardot (appearing on television seems to depend on having a famous name or being a spokesman for an organised group) has already made a stir by denouncing the activities of certain zoo directors. And it is not difficult to predict the consequences if anyone were to dare to attack political taboos through the auspices of the very medium which for almost twenty years has been obliged to broadcast the propaganda of the powers that be ...

There has been a two-year delay, for instance, in the transmission of a play about the Resistance (from a novel by Elsa Triolet) which made the mistake of referring to the Communists and of actually being directed by a Communist. Another programme, a documentary critical of nuclear force, is still on the shelf—certain scientists having disapproved and ensured that their own contributions were cut. The viewing public, meanwhile, is expected to content itself with promises about being left to judge for itself.

True to themselves, and to the President of the Republic, the new controllers of the ex-ORTF have announced that the making and broadcasting of all programmes will be geared to the tested reaction of the viewing public. The consequences of this fake democratic approach are easy to see. One need only recall what Roland Barthes said not so long ago: "If it were possible to make a scientific analysis of fatuity, the whole of television would collapse."

BRUNO VILLIEN

Greece

Now that democracy has returned to Greece, it looks as though the national television service will be able to develop beyond its former rather retarded state. Born on the eve of the junta *coup*, Greek television's development was slow and irregular, with advertising far exceeding the official six minutes per hour limitation, and programmes consisting for the most part (or so it seemed) of tedious melodrama series, soap operas and propaganda speeches and debates.

Sir Hugh Greene, former Director General of the BBC and a friend of democratic Greece, has now submitted to the government a report on the reforms necessary for a revitalised television service. It is to be hoped (though there are no clear signs of this as yet) that the independence of broadcasting will be guaranteed under the new constitution and the new broadcasting law. Meanwhile, the National Radio-Television Institute's (EIRT) Director General and Programme Director (Anghelos Vlahos and Alexis Solomos—the first a former Minister, diplomat and writer, the second a distinguished Athens stage director) are taking the first gradual steps towards a general improvement in the quality of programmes. The junta years left television in the doldrums; now we can hope that it will emerge into the light.

The signs so far are auspicious. Among the programmes broadcast recently or

QUEEN AMALIA, one of the most successful series on Greek TV (EIRT), and produced by DYAS-TV Production

currently being prepared are documentaries about the poet George Seferis, the actress Katina Paxinou, the singers Maria Callas and Nikos Zahariou, the composer and conductor Dimitris Mitropoulos, and the internationally known painters Moralis, Vasiliou and Hatzikiriakos-Ghikas. There have also been three series based on Greek novels (*Christ Recrucified* by Nikos Kazantzakis and *The Violet-Crowned City* by Anghelos Terzakis) and a historical play (George Roussos's *Queen Amalia*). And there is increasing emphasis on discussion and argument in programmes like *Free Debate*.

One legacy from the junta remains controversial. The opposition parties and the press have claimed that the continuing existence of the second network, Greek Armed Forces Radio and Television (YENED), is an unpalatable anomaly now that democracy has returned. But at the time of writing YENED is still operating, and there is no sign at the moment of its being absorbed by EIRT.

MIRELLA GEORGIADOU

Italy

The latter part of 1974 and almost all of 1975 were synonymous with a power vacuum at RAI, Italy's state-run TV-Radio network which has enjoyed a monopoly over broadcasting since the war. A decision by the Constitutional Court in 1974 that this monopoly was unconstitutional came at a moment when the political parties in parliament were debating a new statute for RAI (the old one had expired in 1973 and was being given six-months renewals until new legislation could be passed). In practice, RAI's monopoly has always meant that the political parties in power could divide up the jobs between them, from the key posts on the top floor of the smart RAI building in Viale Mazzini, Rome, to those of the journalists of the television news bulletins (the contents of which in terms of "importance" and slant, not to mention omissions, were decided in the antechambers of the government and the powerful Christian Democrat party secretariat).

The Constitutional Court decision opens the way to regional television stations (something the central government has always feared because several of Italy's regions are governed by a Communist-led majority) and to private networks. These have been slow to get going, but the first result during 1975 of the new opening outside of RAI was to permit—or rather no longer to be able to forbid—transmissions in colour from Switzerland and France which are beamed at least as far as Rome (Northern Italy had for some time been receiving transmissions from these countries and from Yugoslavia but without the seal of legality). With the government deciding to opt for the PAL colour system, Italian industry were hoping that colour would finally be introduced by early 1976. But no sooner had this announcement been made than one of the political parties in the government coalition expressed doubts as to whether the economic situation permitted Italian families to indulge in this luxury (for it is generally assumed that in terms of "keeping up with the Bianchi" most Italian families will want a colour set whether they can afford it or not—and at £400 each the "average" family will not be able to do so). Most Italian programmes have been filmed or taped in colour and the quality is exceptional (TV critics always see everything in colour, though their readers have to resign themselves to black-and-white viewing). In the case of RAI's two biggest productions of the 1974/75 season, Ronconi's *Orlando Furioso* and Gianfranco De Bosio's *Moses, the Lawgiver*, the absence of colour considerably diminished the impact, and provoked many a yawn and protest from common mortals who had not been privileged to see them in "the original."

After months of debate in parliament which at one time almost brought down the government (because of filibustering by the neo-fascist deputies, who were adamantly against the new reform since theirs was the only party which would never gain any jobs for their members or much space beyond that "democratically" allotted to them at election time as one of the parties in parliament) the law was finally passed, with the Communists abstaining and rather angry: in spite of the good intentions behind the new legislation (to which Communists had contributed as members of the parliamentary commission preparing it), when it came down to practical interpretation (i.e., appointments) it was very much a case of the same as before. Once again, the main parties were dividing up the jobs between them. The main novelty was that RAI is now divided into two networks, one Catholic-slanted and the other lay (meaning the parties, for example, who were in favour of divorce in the 1974 referendum). Naturally, however, the men chosen for the jobs were decided by the party secretariats. The Socialists, who currently play a double game in Italian politics (siding with Communists on a local level and with Christian Democrats for the central government), had their fair share of the sliced cake, including the post of RAI President for one of their most

able men, Beniamino Finocchiaro. But the key post of Director General naturally went to a Christian Democrat, Michele Principe.

It will need time to see how the two networks will function, but at least the two newsreels should give viewers a more impartial version of home and world news than has been the case in the past. In reply to Communist complaints about the cake-slicing (though as soon as they enter the area of government—which may be quite soon—they too will obviously be claiming jobs for their members), the Socialists say that they have put their best men into the jobs, and this is certainly true. It is thanks to Socialist infiltration into RAI since they joined the first Centre-Left government in the early sixties that many of RAI's more courageous projects, such as the film production programme, have opened up viewing to fresh talent and new ideas. If two Communist party card-holders like the Taviani brothers could make a film such as *Saint Michael Had a Rooster* (much acclaimed at the London and New York Film Festivals), it means that a certain degree of democratisation had been achieved even before the new reform.

In spite of internal crises, RAI still managed to produce some ·outstanding programmes in 1975. They won the Golden Rose at Montreux for the first time with a musical show. And history was made by the four plays filmed by Eduardo De Filippo, the great Neapolitan actor-dramatist-director. De Filippo had done some of his own plays in the early years of Italian television, but for personal (and political) reasons had kept away for at least a decade. At the age of seventy-five he was finally enticed back and the result was sensational: as one critic put it, "As if Molière had had the chance to put on record his productions at the Palais Royal." For his cycle, De Filippo did three plays by

Still from the Italian TV/ITC (London) production, MOSES

Massimo Foschi as Orlando in Ronconi's ORLANDO FURIOSO, screened on Italian TV

his father Eduardo Scarpetta and one by another of the family, Vincenzo Scarpetta. It was something quite new in Italian TV—a recreation of the theatrical style of another age. Such was the success of these plays that De Filippo has followed them up with a new cycle, this time of four of his own plays, three written in the last decade and one written in the Twenties.

Because of the power vacuum, film production in recent times has slowed down. *Orlando Furioso* turned out to be a highly expensive production, and though several international networks have bought it (Sweden showed it before Italy itself), the six-hour version of Ariosto's epic poem about the Paladins cannot be edited into a cinema version (as the producers of *Moses* have been able to do, and as was done with another RAI

series of a few years ago, *Ulysses*). Ronconi was obliged in the end to give the cinema distributors two episodes of the TV series (because he was committed to producing a film version) and this gave little idea of the whole scope of the work. *Orlando* is a mixture of the theatrical, the cinematic and the literary, with splendid design by Pier Luigi Pizzi and photography from Vittorio Storaro (Bertolucci's regular lighting director) and Arturo Zavattini. But Ronconi failed to find a television equivalent of the extraordinary invention which he displayed in his internationally acclaimed stage version of the same work. The visual enchantment was not enough and the mixed acting styles, ranging from the lyrical to the histrionic, so successfully on the stage as a parody of Italian acting, on the small screen just seemed in many cases like bad acting. The choice of Sunday night peak viewing-time for the series caused a national scandal. But Ronconi may have his vindication when the series is repeated in colour; meanwhile he has directed a version of a Goldoni play in the TV studios.

Though production of feature films has slowed down, the Experimental TV Films section has managed to keep going, and this has resulted in a number of interesting off-beat works (one of which is Gianni Amelio's film about the making of Bertolucci's *1900*). Otherwise, RAI has been involved in the co-production of colossals which have taken the place of the old Cinecittà blockbusters like *Ben-Hur* and *Cleopatra*. An Italian producer who formally worked for 20th Century-Fox, Vincenzo Labella, is the man behind most of these projects, which are co-produced with Sir Lew Grade's ITC and with certain guarantees from U.S. networks (*Moses*, for example, was bought by CBS). Anthony Burgess, who wrote *Moses* with Italian scriptwriters Bonicelli and Zapponi and director De Bosio, has written a *Life of Shakespeare* which is co-authored by Masolino D'Amico and directed by Peter Wood. Burgess is also writing the Life of Jesus, which is to be shot on location in Tunisia, probably with Franco Zeffirelli directing. The same group has also made a series on the Mafia. If the political barometer continues to move towards the Left in Italy, as seems likely, one can visualise that after Moses, Jesus, Shakespeare and the Mafia, Labella's next project will have to be a life of Marx.

JOHN FRANCIS LANE

Netherlands

Tell someone who is not familiar with Dutch society how Dutch broadcasting is organised and the reaction is likely to be confused. Not surprisingly, since Dutch broadcasting is as complicated as Dutch society itself. It has attracted much attention abroad, but that is as nothing compared with the amount of time, space and talk expended on the subject in the Netherlands itself.

To indicate how the broadcasting system works in the Netherlands, one must go back to the Twenties. This was the time of emancipation, when every religious and ideological faction in Dutch society— political parties, the organisations for education and welfare, the broadcasting companies—felt the need to express its own exclusive identity. So this was a time of fragmentation, with Roman Catholics, Calvinists, Protestants, Socialists and so on all involved in the communications business according to their own particular principles. After the Second World War there was a general reaction against the rigid sectarianism of the past. But the divisions persisted; and the result of years of in-fighting is, inevitably perhaps, a compromise. Holland today has more than twenty political parties—and seven broadcasting organisations.

The current Dutch television system derives from a government law of 1966, which determined that broadcasting in Holland should be both non-commercial and pluralistic. One of the results is that any non-profit-making organisation with enough members has access to the system, provided that its aims are approved by the Minister of Culture. Finance for broadcasting comes from special taxes, and from contributions from the various organisations given air-time. A secondary source of finance, instituted a few years ago, comes from a non-profit-making, state-controlled foundation which makes commercials for radio and television.

This apparently haphazard structure was bolstered by the foundation of a central organisation, the NOS (Nederlandse Omroep Stichting), which provides technical facilities for programme-making, is responsible for general administration, and is itself involved in making programmes. These NOS programmes, however, are by law strictly limited to subjects likely to meet the approval of the general consensus. So NOS broadcasts, for instance, the Eurovision Song Contest, football, American presidential elections, events in space, and so on. Recently, however, the NOS has shown an increasing tendency to bend the rules, and has been broadcasting films, children's programmes and quiz games. The consequence of this policy is increasing competition, not only between the broadcasting companies themselves, but also between the companies and their technical and administrative umbrella organisation, the NOS.

But there is an even more serious problem now confronting Dutch television. The broadcasting organisations can only survive as long as they are publicly supported. That support, however, depends on the programmes broadcast, and public interest in information and documentary programmes has been declining. What the viewing public prefers, apparently, is escapist entertainment: drama series, films, nature documentaries and the like. A network concerned to broadcast serious information programmes now has to face the fact that it is likely to lose public support. This situation has been exacerbated by the recent establishment of a new broadcasting organisation, known as TROS, which is wholly geared to producing entertainment programmes: quiz games, imported series like *The FBI*, big budget films like *QB7*, not to mention a fair number of the nature films sponsored by the Shell oil company.

And in Dutch television entertainment pays dividends: TROS is winning audiences from the other broadcasting companies. The result has been a Catch-22 situation. Worried by declining audiences, the other companies are now imitating TROS by going for entertainment programmes in a big way. The socialist company has imported American film series like *McCloud* and *MacMillan and Wife*; the Protestant company has *Kojak* from America and *Sam* from Britain; and the Catholics have come up with *Gunsmoke* and a series of Danny Kaye films. This phenomenon has even acquired a name, *vertrossing*, derived from TROS, mention of which immediately provokes a debate about the pros and cons of the new programming trend. The word even appeared in an official report issued by the left-wing Minister of Culture, Mr. H. W. van Doorn (who is also, incidentally, the former director of the Catholic broadcasting organisation). The report provided guidelines for future press and broadcasting policy. The Minister declared himself anxious to oppose *vertrossing* and to defend the open, pluralist, non-commercial Dutch broadcasting system. Sceptics are suggesting that the battle may already be lost.

SUSANNE PIËT

Why the Hilversum video train will fit in with your schedule.

Our latest idea has just hit the road. It's called Video Train and as you'd expect, it's three video services in one.
An OB van.
A VTR van.
And an equipment van.
The crew? Skilled video technicians backed up by the Cinecentrum staff. All-in-all it means that you can have a fast and full video service anywhere in the Netherlands and surrounding countries. Give us a call: 2150 - 16131. And find out that our video train is just the very ticket.

A train load of video experience

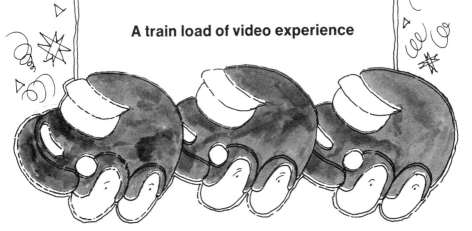

Public Television in America

In 1973 the Exxon (Standard Oil) Corporation announced the funding of a new series of domestically produced dramas to be broadcast over public television as *Theater in America*. These were not, like BBC productions, to be specially produced for television, but rather videotaped versions of existing shows that had been performed at various theatres around the country. Most were classics (Shakespeare, O'Neill, Chekhov, Rostand), but an occasional new play—such as *Who's Happy Now* by Oliver Hailey—was included.

At the same time, Exxon prepared an extensive series of commercials to promote the series. One of these is particularly noteworthy: a sixty-second spot, widely broadcast on the commercial networks, showing a fully-fledged theatre troupe arriving at the front door of a typical American family in order to put on a play in their living room. This commercial was prepared by Exxon's advertising agency, and it is extraordinarily well done. Although Exxon will not divulge its production cost, it is apparent that a great deal of time, talent and money went into those sixty seconds—not to mention the $80,000–$100,000 that it costs in advertising fees each time it is aired nationally. Although the general standard of the productions on *Theater in America* is high, they all have a somewhat threadbare look—the look of stage plays recorded in the simplest and most expeditious way possible. None have the made-for-television look or attention to detail of that sixty-second commercial—and it is a safe bet to say that none cost as much, either.

This discrepancy symbolises the dilemma of American Public Television today, a dilemma so deeply ingrained in the system that all attempts to resolve it result in an uneasy compromise. Public broadcasting in the United States has only existed in its present form since 1967—prior to that, the sole function of non-commercial television was educational programming. Indeed, the call letters of the country's largest public broadcasting station, WNET in New York, reflect its origins as National Educational Television.

An act of Congress in 1967 established the Corporation for Public Broadcasting, whose fifteen-member board of directors is appointed by the President, and which is responsible for the piloting and development of new programmes. Within five years, CPB was embroiled in the middle of a political thicket as the result of former President Nixon's war on the media. Public television was a particular object of scorn in the Nixon administration, and the President's control over CPB's board of directors made that organisation particularly susceptible to Presidential displeasure. Relations between the 200 non-commercial stations throughout the country and the CPB in Washington grew steadily worse, and by early 1973 it appeared as if the entire structure of non-commercial broadcasting was in danger of collapse.

The danger was averted by the disclosure of the Watergate scandals and the subsequent weakening of Nixon's power and his eventual resignation. A new organisation, the Public Broadcasting Service, was created by the stations in order to regain a measure of control over policy. Unlike CPB, which is funded by Congress, PBS is owned and funded by its member stations, and distributes programmes according to a fairly complicated system of balloting. The tensions of the past five years have thus been eased, but

An Egyptian couple whose son was killed in the Yom Kippur War. From ARABS AND ISRAELIS

the net result is a somewhat unwieldy system, involving two distinct bureaucracies in Washington, whose functions often overlap.

Decision-making is further hampered by the divergent needs of the many organisations which make up the mosaic that is public television in America today. These include the major foundations (Rockefeller, Ford, etc.), the National Endowment for the Arts, the National Endowment for the Humanities, the large corporations (Exxon, Mobil, IBM, Xerox, etc.) whose financial contributions are essential for the system, and the two hundred individual stations themselves, all of them entities of very different character whose needs are determined not only by the size, location and relative power within the system, but also by their own ownership. State and city-owned stations, for example, are concerned primarily with daytime programming as a means of supplementing their educational curricula. Community-owned stations, on the other hand, are primarily interested in obtaining a broad range of general interest programmes for the evening hours. The objectives of university-owned stations fall somewhere in between, depending primarily on the philosophy and objectives of the university trustees.

In addition to these organisational structures, one must also take into account the considerable influence of the commercial broadcasting lobbyists, who are determined to see that public television never becomes a

Comedy on American TV: THE BOB AND RAY SHOW

potent competitor to their own interests. (Thus far, they have little to worry about: non-commercial TV virtually never garners a rating higher than 4% of the potential audience.)

There are many measures that could be taken in order to strengthen public television in the United States—licence fees for set owners or a special tax on the commercial stations' advertisements are among the more obvious proposals. Those familiar with the system, however, universally regard such "European" measures as utopian, and there is virtually no chance of any such system coming into effect. The forces that would oppose such measures are powerful and well-organised; no executive of CPB or PBS would publicly endorse them (although, in private conversation, many see such a solution as ideal); and public apathy towards the whole concept of non-commercial broadcasting is very high. A certain degree of optimism exists at the moment, partly because there are no more Spiro Agnews railing against "socialised media," and partly because, for

the first time, a long-range funding proposal shows a good chance of being passed by Congress. But it is also clear that even if the new Public Broadcasting Act becomes law, non-commercial television will still have to search for operating funds from a wide range of sources, including direct appeals to the viewing public. And although such appeals are often ingeniously planned and successfully executed, it is difficult to imagine the Director General of the BBC riding through the streets, as did the President of one of America's largest PBS stations, perched on the back of a circus elephant.

Television in America, as it is presently constituted, can be seen as a single, interlocking system, with public TV functioning as a complement, but not a competitor, to the commercial networks. Indeed, the major commercial networks have always spoken very highly of public broadcasting, since it imparts a degree of respectability to the entire medium—without endangering profitability.

For the viewing public, not only in America but also overseas, the net result is singularly unfortunate. During the early days of television, the flood of cheap (as low as $2,000 an hour) American exports of westerns and situation comedies made the development of an indigenous television culture among the smaller countries extremely difficult. Now, however, when the public broadcasting stations are thirsting for quality productions, the economics of the system work heavily against domestic production. Evening hours are dominated by British imports, not only from the BBC but also from the ITV stations. It is indicative of public TV's inability to generate its own identity that its most popular and successful figure, Alistair Cooke, is not only an Englishman but also a commentator who established his American reputation more than twenty years ago on the commercially produced programme *Omnibus*.

The discrepancy between the potential of public television in America and its present reality was brought into poignant relief during a programme in one of PBS's best public affairs series, *Bill Moyer's Journal*, which featured an interview with Huw Wheldon, Managing Director of BBC Television. At one point, Mr. Wheldon was asked how the decision was made to produce Jacob Bronowski's brilliant series, *The Ascent of Man*. He looked surprised at the question, and replied that it just seemed like a marvellously exciting thing to do. That philosophy, which has given the BBC its reputation as "the least worst television in the world," is—for American television in its current form—beyond any hope of attainment.

PAUL MARETH

Emmy Awards 1975
(Primetime Entertainment)

Best Drama Special: *The Law* (NBC, "World Premiere Movie").

Best Variety or Music Series: *Carol Burnett Show* (CBS).

Best Drama Series: *Upstairs, Downstairs* (LWT, London).

Best Comedy Series: *The Mary Tyler Moore Show* (CBS).

Actor of the Year, Comedy Series: Tony Randall for *The Odd Couple* (ABC).

Actor of the Year, Drama Special: Laurence Olivier for *Love among the Ruins* (ABC).

Actress of the Year, Drama Special: Katharine Hepburn for *Love among the Ruins* (ABC).

Actor of the Year, Series: Robert Blake for *Baretta* (ABC).

Actress of the Year, Series: Jean Marsh for *Upstairs, Downstairs* (LWT, London).

Supporting Actor of the Year, Special: Anthony Quayle for *QB VII* (ABC).

Supporting Actress of the Year, Special: Juliet Mills for *QB VII* (ABC).

Best Children's Special: *Yes, Virginia, There Is a Santa Claus* (ABC).

Director of the Year, Drama Special: George Cukor for *Love among the Ruins* (ABC).

Director of the Year, Series: Bill Bain for *Upstairs, Downstairs* (episode: "A Sudden Storm"; LWT, London).

Writer of the Year, Drama Series: Howard Fast for *The Ambassador—Benjamin Franklin* (CBS).

Writer of the Year, Drama Special: James Costigan for *Love among the Ruins* (ABC).

Best Sports Programme: *Wide World of Sports* (ABC), and Jim Mackay, presenter.

(N.B. There are 71 Primetime Emmy Awards, of which the above is a selective list.)

Montreux Television Festival Awards: 1975

Golden Rose: *Fatti e fattacci—spettacolo in piazza* (RAI, Italy; director, Antonello Falqui).

Silver Rose: *The Goodies* (BBC, G.B.; director, Jim Franklin).

Bronze Rose: *Mad in Austria* (ORF, Austria; director, Herbert Grunsky).

Press prize: *Fatti e fattacci—spettacolo in piazza*.

Philips Video Cassette Recorder.

This system offers everything needed. Recording and replay in black and white *or colour*. Recording from a domestic TV aerial, or a TV camera. Easy-loading video cassettes that you can replay or re-record time and time again. Fast wind and rewind for quick selection or replay of any section of track. And simple operation.

Comedy prize: *Mad in Austria.*
Special prize: *Cirque Alfonso* (MTV, Hungary; director, Nándor Bednai).

Monte Carlo Television Awards

Golden Nymph: *Death of a Guide* (ORTF, France).

Silver Nymphs: Best script or direction: *Witness for the Prosecution* (Czechoslovakia); Best acting: Tatyana Lavrova in *The Flight Is Held Up* (USSR); Best children's programme; *Lucky* (JRT, Yugoslavia); Special jury mentions: Celia Johnson for her performance in *Love Affair* (LWT, GB), and *The Shroud* (Spain); Cino del Duca Prize: John Jacobs, director of *Love Affair* (LWT, GB); Critics' Prize: *The Bird That Was Not for the Cat* (Belgium).

Society of Film and Television Arts Awards: 1975

Best Single Play: Jon Scoffield for *Antony and Cleopatra* (ATV).

Best Drama Series/Serial: James Ormerod for *South Riding* (Yorkshire).

Best Factual Programme: Frank Cvitanovitch for *Beauty, Bonny, Daisy, Violet, Grace and Geoffrey Morton* (Thames).

Best Factual Series: Peter Goodchild and Bruce Norman for *Horizon* (BBC).

Best Light Entertainment Programme: David Bell for *The Stanley Baxter Moving Picture Show* (London Weekend).

Best Situation Comedy Series: Sydney Lotterby for *Porridge* (BBC).

Best Specialised Programme: Brian Gibson for *Joey* (from *Horizon*) (BBC).

Best Specialised Series: Humphrey Burton for *Aquarius* (London Weekend).

Best Design: Bill McPherson for *The Stanley Baxter Moving Picture Show* (London Weekend).

Technical Craft Award: Lynda Beighton; make-up, particularly for *The Stanley Baxter Moving Picture Show* (London Weekend).

Best Actor: Peter Barkworth for *Crown Matrimonial* (LWT).

Best Actress: Lee Remick for *Jennie* (Thames).

Best Light Entertainment Performance: Stanley Baxter for *The Stanley Baxter Moving Picture Show* (London Weekend).

Richard Dimbleby Award, for the year's most important personal contribution on the screen in factual television: Robin Day for his enormous contribution in the realms of political journalism in television.

Desmond Davis Award, for an outstanding creative contribution to television: Denis Mitchell.

Rediffusion Star Awards: "Harlequin" (Children's Entertainment): Pamela Lonsdale for *Rainbow* (Thames) and Carol Wilkes for *Soldier and Me* (Granada). "Flame of Knowledge" (Schools Programmes): Roger Tonge for *What Does Money Matter?* (BBC).

Shell International Award: Peter Jay for *Weekend World* (London Weekend).

GUIDE TO MAJOR TV COMPANIES

AUSTRIA

Oesterreichische Rundfunk, *Argentinierstr. 30a, 1041 Vienna. Tel. (0222) 653794. Telex: 01-2397.*

Director General: Otto Oberhammer. *Television Director:* Gerhard Weiss, Franz Kreuzer. *Sales Director:* Walter Skala. *Hours of broadcasting per week:* 95. *TV sets reached:* 1,740,000. *Commercials:* Yes.

BELGIUM

Radiodiffusion-Télévision Belge (RTB)/Belgische Radio en Televisie (BRT), *Place Eugène Flagey 18, 1050 Brussels. Tel: (02) 359060 (RTB), (02) 496050 (BRT).*

Director General: Robert Wangermee (RTB), Paul Vandenbussche (BRT). *Programme Director:* A. Massinger (RTB), Nic. Bal (BRT). *Sales/ Purchasing Director:* Paule Herreman (RTB), Jozef Coolsaet (BRT). *Hours of broadcasting per week :* 120. *TV sets reached:* 3,150,000.

BULGARIA

Bulgarian Television, *T. Shashimirov 2, Sofia. Tel: 44-63-21. Telex: 22581.*

Director: Ivan Slovkov. *Hours of broadcasting per week:* 58. *TV sets reached:* 1,367,360.

CZECHOSLOVAKIA

Československá Televize, *náměstí M. Gorkého 29-30, Prague 1. Tel: 225070. Telex: 121800.*

Director: Gennadij Codr. *Programme Director:* Dr. Vladimír Diviš. *Technical Director:* Ing. František Kajňák. *Sales Director:* Ing. Josef Vaněk. *Purchasing Director:* František Marvan. *Co-Productions Director:* Ing. Josef Vaněk. *Hours of broadcasting per week:* 65. *TV sets reached:* 3,444,587. *Commercials:* Yes.

DENMARK

Danmarks Radio-TV, *TV-Center, 2860 Soeborg. Tel: 01-671233. Telex: 2695.*

Director: Hans Sølvhøj. *Programme Director:* Laurits Bindsløv. *Technical Director:* Peter Hansen. *Purchasing Director:* Henning Skaarup. *Hours of broadcasting per week:* 55. *TV sets reached:* 1,497,000. *Commercials:* No.

EIRE
Radio Telefis Eireann, *Donnybrook, Dublin 4. Tel:*
69311. Telex: 5268.
Director General: Thomas P. Hardiman.
Programme Controller: Michael Garvey. *Sales*
Director: Gerald M. McLaughlin. *Hours of broad-*
casting per week: approx 51. *Commercials:* Yes.
TV sets reached: 560,000.

FINLAND
Oy Yleisradio Ab, *Pasila, SF-00240 Helsinki 24*
(Programme 1). Tel: 418811. Telex: 12–849.
Oy Yleisradio Ab, *Tohlopinranta 23, SF-33270*
Tampere 27 (Programme 2). Tel: 931–455 455.
Telex: 22–315, 22–176.
Director: Sakari Kiuru (Programme 1), Pertti
Paloheimo (Programme 2). *Purchasing Director:*
Kaarle Stewen. *Hours of broadcasting per week:*
43½ (Programme 1), 27½ (Programme 2).
Oy Mainos-TV-Reklam Ab (Commercial
network), *Pasilankatu 44, 002400 Helsinki 24.*
Tel: 413300. Telex: 12-1544.
Director: Pentti Hanski. *Programme Director:*
Leo Meller. *Purchasing Director:* Jaakko Ter-
vasmäki. *Sales Director:* Dennis Livson. *Co-*
production Manager: Dennis Livson. *Hours of*
broadcasting per week: 18. *TV sets reached:*
1,375,178 (1974).

FRANCE
Office de Radiodiffusion-Télévision Française
(ORTF), *116 avenue du President Kennedy,*
Paris 16. Tel: (01) 224-22-22. Telex: 20002.
Director General: Marceau Long. *Programme*
Directors: Jean Cazeneuve (Programme 1),
Marcel Jullian (Programme 2), Claude Contamine
(Programme 3). *Hours of broadcasting per week:*
66 (1), 45 (2), 21 (3). *TV sets reached:* 12,400,000
(1973). *Commercials:* Yes (1 and 2).

GERMANY (BRD)
ARD, *PO Box 3111, Bertramstr. 8,*
Frankfurt/Main. Tel: (0611) 59 06 07. Telex:
04-11127.
Programme Director: Hans Abich. *Hours of*
broadcasting per week: 53 (Programme 1).
Commercials: Yes (Programme 1 only).

ARD companies:
Bayerische Rundfunk (BR), *Rundfunkplatz 1, 8*
Munich 2. Tel: (0811) 59001.
Director: Reinhold Voeth. *TV Director:* Helmut
Oeller.
Hessischer Rundfunk (HR), *Bertramstr. 8, 6*
Frankfurt/Main. Tel: (0611) 1551.
Director: Werner Hess. *TV Director:* Hans-Otto
Gruenefeldt.
Norddeutsche Rundfunk (NDR), *Rothen-*
baumchaussee 132–134, 2 Hamburg 13. Tel:
(0411) 4131.
Director: Gerhard Schroeder. *TV Director:*
Dietrich Schwarzkopf. *Technical Director:* Horst
A. C. Krieger.
Radio Bremen (RV), *Heinrich-Hertz-Strasse 13,*
2800 Bremen. Tel: 0421-427 (1). Telex:
02451815.
Director: Klaus Bölling. *Programme Director:*
Dieter Ertel. *Technical Director:* Heinz Heyer.
Commercials: No.
Saarländischer Rundfunk (SR), *Funkhaus*
Halberg, 66 Saarbrücken. Tel: 6021.
Director: Franz Mai. *TV Director:* Karl
Schnelting.
Sender Freies Berlin (SFB), *Masurenallee 8–14, 1*
Berlin 19. Tel: (0311) 3081.
Director: Franz Barsig. *TV Director:* Erich
Pröbster.
Süddeutscher Rundfunk (SDR), *Postfach 837,*
7000 Stuttgart 1. Tel. 07151/2070 (1). Telex:
723074.
Director: Prof. Dr. Hans Bausch. *Programme*
Director: Horst Jaedicke. *Techʳical Director:* Dr.
Helmut Rupp. SDR is a non-profit corporation.
Südwestfunk (SWF), *Hans-Bredow-Strasse, 757*
Baden-Baden. Tel: 07221-2761. Telex:
07842368.
Director: Helmuth Hammerschmidt. *TV Director:*
Dieter Stolte. *Sales Director:* Ulrich Weber.
Westdeutscher Rundfunk (WDR), *Appellhofplatz*
1, 5 Köln. Tel: (0221) 2201.
Director: Klaus von Bismarck. *TV Director:*
Werner Hoefer.

ZDF, *PO Box 4040, 6500 Mainz. Tel: 131. Telex:*
04-187661.
Director General: Karl Holzamer. *Programme*

Director: Gerhard Prager. *Purchasing Director:* H. Blank. *Hours of broadcasting per week:* 51. *Commercials:* Yes.

TV sets reached (by both ARD and ADF combined): 18,040,000.

GERMANY (DDR)
Deutsche Fernsehfunk, *Rudowenchaussee 3, DDR-1199 Berlin. Tel: 632 64 361. Telex: 011-2885.*
Hours of broadcasting per week: 88. *Commercials:* Yes. *TV sets reached:* 4,600,000 (1973).

GREAT BRITAIN
BBC, *Television Centre, Wood Lane, London W12. Tel: 01-743 8000. Telex: 22182.*
Director General: Charles Curran. *Managing Director, TV:* Huw Wheldon. *Director of Programmes, TV:* Alastair Milne. *Controller of BBC-1:* Bryan Cowgill. *Controller of BBC-2:* Aubrey Singer. *Chief Engineer:* S. N. Watson. *Sales Director:* P. J. F Lord. *Purchasing Director:* Gunnar Rugheimer. *Co-productions Director:* J. J. Stringer. *Hours of broadcasting per week:* approx. 100. *Commercials:* No. *TV sets reached:* 17,200,000.

ITV
Independent Broadcasting Authority (IBA), *70 Brompton Road, London SW3 1EY. Tel: 01-584 7011. Telex: 24345.*
Chairman: Lady Plowden. *Director General:* Brian Young.

ITV companies:
Anglia Television, *Anglia House, Norwich NOR 07A. Tel: Norwich 28366.*
Area: East of England. *Administration Controller:* J. F. M. Roualle. *Production Controller:* P. Garner. *Station Engineer:* A. Barnett. *Sales Controller:* J. P. Margetson.
ATV, *ATV Centre, Birmingham B1 2JP. Tel: 021-643 9898.*
Area: Midlands. *Managing Director:* Sir Lew Grade. *Director of Programmes:* Bill Ward. *Chief Engineer:* Gerry Kaye. *Director of Sales:* John Wardrop.
Border Television, *Television Centre, Carlisle CA1 3NT. Tel: Carlisle 25101.*

The best available source of software for video installations.

5/7/9 BEADON ROAD   LONDON W6
TELEPHONE 01-741 0011 TELEX 934386

Area: The Borders and Isle of Man. *Managing Director:* James Bredin. *Controller of Programmes:* James Bredin. *Chief Engineer:* H. J. C. Gower. *Sales Director:* B. C. Blyth.
Channel Television, *The Television Centre, St Helier, Jersey, Channel Islands. Tel: Jersey Central 23451.*
Area: Channel Islands. *Managing Director:* K. A. Killip. *Operations Manager:* Brian Turner. *Head of Sales:* Phill Mottram Brown. *Head of News and Features:* John Rothwell.
Grampian Television, *Queen's Cross, Aberdeen AB9 2XJ. Tel: Aberdeen 53553.*
Area: North-East Scotland. *Chief Executive:* Alex Mair. *Programme Controller:* James F. Buchan. *Station Engineer:* Alex Ramsay.
Granada Television, *Granada TV Centre, Manchester M60 9EA. Tel: 061-832 7211.*
Area: Lancashire, Cheshire. *Joint Managing Directors:* Alex Bernstein, Denis Forman. *Programme Controller:* David Plowright. *Controller of Engineering:* Keith Fowler. *Sales Director:* Peter M. Rennie.
HTV, *HTV Wales, Television Centre, Cardiff CF1 9XL. Tel: Cardiff 26633.*
HTV West, Television Centre, Bath Road, Bristol BS4 3HG. Tel: Bristol 70271.
Area: Wales and West of England. *Managing Director:* A. J. Gorard. *Programme Controller, Wales:* A. Vaughan. *Programme Controller, West of England:* P. Dromgoole. *Chief Engineer:* T. Marshall. *Sales Director:* R. W. Wordley.
London Weekend Television, *South Bank Television Centre, Kent House, Upper Ground, London SE1 9LT. Tel: 01-261 3434.*
Area: London (weekends). *Chief Executive:* John

Freeman. *Controller of Programmes:* Cyril Bennett. *Chief Engineer:* Roger Appleton. *Sales Director:* Ron Miller.

Scottish Television, *Cowcaddens, Glasgow G2 3PR. Tel: 041-332 9999.*

Area: Central Scotland. *Managing Director:* William Brown. *Director of Programmes:* Anthony Firth. *Technical Controller:* J. R. Miller. *Sales Director:* Hugh W. Henry.

Southern Television, *Southern Television Centre, Northam, Southampton SO9 4YQ. Tel: Southampton 28582.*

Area: South of England. *Managing Director:* C. D. Wilson. *Controller of Programmes:* Berkeley Smith. *Chief Engineer:* Basil Bultitude. *Sales Director:* B. G. Henry.

Thames Television, *Thames Television House, 306–16 Euston Road, London NW1 3BB. Tel: 01-387 9494.*

Area: London (weekdays). *Managing Director:* George A. Cooper. *Director of Programmes:* Jeremy Isaacs. *Director of Studios and Engineering:* J. Stuart Sansom. *Director of Sales:* James F. Shaw.

Tyne Tees Television, *The Television Centre, City Road, Newcastle-upon-Tyne NE1 2AL. Tel: Newcastle-upon-Tyne 610181.*

Area: North-East England. *Managing Director:* Peter S. Paine. *Director of Programmes:* Arthur E. Clifford. *Technical Director:* Dennis Packham. *Sales:* Trident Management Ltd., 15–16 Brooks Mews, London W1Y 1LF.

Ulster Television, *Havelock House, Ormeau Road, Belfast BT7 1EB. Tel: Belfast 28122.*

Area: Northern Ireland. *Managing Director:* R. B. Henderson. *Programme Controller:* S. R. Perry. *Chief Engineer:* F. A. Brady. *Sales Director:* M. R. Hutcheson.

Westward Television, *Derry's Cross, Plymouth PL1 2SP. Tel: Plymouth 69311.*

Area: South-West England. *Managing Director:* Ronald Perry. *Production Controller:* Terry Fleet. *Technical Controller:* D. Dickinson. *Regional Sales Manager:* H. Stracey.

Yorkshire Television, *The Television Centre, Leeds LS3 1JS. Tel: Leeds 38283. Telex: 557232.*

Area: Yorkshire. *Joint Managing Directors:* G. E.

Ward Thomas, E. Stuart Wilson. *Director of Programmes:* Paul Fox. *Director of Engineering:* Philip Parker. *Sales Controller:* Clive Leach.

Independent Television News, *ITN House, 48 Wells Street, London W1P 3FE. Tel: 01-637 2424.*

Editor: Nigel Ryan. *Production Controller:* Michael Batchelor. *Chief Engineer:* Peter Ward.

GREECE

Ethnikon Idrima Radiofonias ke Tileorasis (EIRT), *Aghia Paraskevi, Athens. Tel: 6595970. Telex: 216066, 215181* (Studios and Head Offices). *16 Mourouzi Street, Athens. Tel: 724811* (Other Offices).

Director General: Anghelos Vlahos. *Deputy Director:* Alexis Solomos. *TV Director:* Spiros Pafatakis. *Hours of broadcasting per week:* 45.

Ipiresia Enimeroseos Enoplon Dinameon (YENED), *136 Messogion Avenue, Athens. Tel: 7701911, 7707060.*

Director General: Sotirios Vavaroutsos. *Programme Director:* Marios Vallindras. *Hours of broadcasting per week:* 52.

HUNGARY

Hungarian Radio and Television, *Szabadsag ter 17, Budapest V. Tel. 113–200. Telex: 225568.*

President: István Tompe. *Television Director:* Ferenc Pecsi. *Head of Co-productions:* Endre Gellert. *Hours of broadcasting per week:* 39. *TV sets reached:* 2,734,861.

ITALY

Radiotelevisione Italiana (RAI), *Direzione Centrale TV, Viale Mazzini 14, 00195 Rome. Tel: 38781. Telex: 61142.*

President: Umberto Delle Fave. *General Director:* Ettore Bernabei. *Television Directors:* Villy De Luca, A. Romano, F. Fabiani, P. E. Gennarini. *Hours of broadcasting per week:* 82 (National Programme), 20 (Programme 2). *Commercials:* Yes. *TV sets reached:* 10, 900,000.

NETHERLANDS

Nederlandse Omroep Stichting (NOS), *PO Box 10, Hilversum. Tel: 81110. Telex: 13186.*

Director: Emile A. Schüttenhelm. *Programme Director:* C. A. Steketee. *Technical Director:* Dr. A. W. W. van den Bos. *Sales Director and Purchasing Director:* J. C. Beumer. *Hours of broadcasting per week:* 73 hours $11\frac{1}{2}$ mins. *TV sets reached:* approx. 4,000,000. *Commercials:* Yes.

NORWAY
Norsk Rikskringkasting, *Oslo 3. Tel: (472) 469860. Telex: 11794.*
Director General: Torolf Elster. *Programme Director:* Otto Albert Nes. *Hours of broadcasting per week:* 40. *TV sets reached:* 950,000 (1974). *Commercials:* No.

POLAND
Polskie Radio i Telewisja, *Woronicza 17, Warsaw. Tel: 443251. Telex: 813421.*
President: Maciej Szczepański. *Director General:* Michał Gardowski, Włodzimierz Loziński. *Director, Film Programmes:* Jacek Fuksiewicz. *Hours of broadcasting per week:* 56. *TV sets reached:* 5,199,950.

PORTUGAL
Radiotelevisão Portuguesa (RTP), *PO Box 2934, Rua de S. Domingos (à Lapa) 26, Lisboa 1. Tel: 666134/9. Telex: 12576 (RtpP).*
Currently run by a military commission. Personnel changes due in late 1975. *Sales Director:* Condorcet da Silva Costa. *Hours of broadcasting per week:* 77 (divided into 2 channels—UHF and VHF). *TV sets reached:* 616,628. *Commercials:* Yes.

ROMANIA
Radiodifuziuneă şi Televiziuneă Română, *Televiziuneă Română, Calcea Dorobanti 191, PO Box 111, Bucharest. Tel: 162080. Telex: 251.*
Director General: Juliu Fejes. *Hours of broadcasting per week:* 77 (Programme 1), $25\frac{1}{2}$ (Programme 2). *TV sets reached:* 1,900,000.

SPAIN
Televisión Española, *Prado del Rey, Madrid. Tel: (01) 711-99-18. Telex: 22053.*

Director General: Juan José Roson. *Programme Director:* Narciso Ibáñez Serrador. *Sales Director:* Mariano Gonzalez-Arnao. *Hours of broadcasting per week:* 90 (Programme 1), $36\frac{1}{2}$ (Programme 2). *TV sets reached:* 6,500,000.

SWEDEN
Sveriges Radio, *Radiohuset, Oxenstiernsgatan 20, S-105 10 Stockholm. Tel: (08) 63-10-00. Telex: 100 00.*
Director-General: O. Nordenskiold. *Programme Directors, Television:* Bo Johan Hultman (Programme 1), Nils Petter Sundgren (Programme 2). *Purchasing Director:* Thomas Alexanderson. *Film Buyer:* Arne Weise. *Hours of broadcasting per week:* 46 (plus schools broadcasting). *TV sets reached:* approx. 3,400,000.

SWITZERLAND
Swiss Broadcasting Corporation (SBC), *Giacomettistr. 1, CH-3000 Berne 16. Tel: (031) 44.55.55. Telex: 33116.*
Director General: Stelio Molo. *Director, Television:* Edward Haas. *Programme Controller:* Frank R. Tappolet.
German-Language Programme, *Fernsehstr. 1, CH-8052 Zürich. Tel: (051) 50.05.00. Telex: 57-756.*
Director: Guido Frei.
French-Language Programme, *6 av. de la Gare, 1001 Lausanne. Tel: (021) 20.59.11.*
Director: René Schenker.
Italian-Language Programme, *CH-6903 Lugano-Besso, Lugano. Tel: (091) 3.20.21.*
Director: Franco Marazzi.

Hours of broadcasting per week: 66 (German), 58 (French), 57 (Italian). *TV sets reached:* 1,668,000. *Commercials:* Yes.

U.S.S.R.
Sovyetskoye Televideniye, *Television Centre, Akademik Korolev St. 12, Moscow. Tel: 181-78-98. Telex: 136, 137, 138, 139.*
Chairman: S. G. Lapin. *Deputy Chairman, Television:* E. N. Mamedov. *Head of Programme Exchange:* L. N. Korolev. *Hours of broadcasting*

per week: 80 (Programme 1). *TV sets reached:* 42,000,000.

VENEZUELA
Radio Caracas Television (Channel 2), *Barcenas a Rio, Carcas. Tel: 418971. Telex:* 21221.

Director General: Peter Bottome. *Production Director:* Dr. José Antonio Guevara. *Technical Director General:* Dr. Marcel Graniere. *Sales Director:* Odon Escoté. *Administration Director:* Dr. Jorge Dahdah. *Investigation Department:* Diana Dominguez. *Hours of broadcasting per week:* 126. *Commerials:* Yes. *TV sets reached:* about 1,700,000.

Venevision (Channel 4), *Avenida La Salle, Colina de Los Caobos, Caracas. Tel: 742444. Telex: 21379 Ventel.*

Director General: Valeriano Humpirrez. *General Manager:* Henrique Cuscó. *Programme Director:* Angel del Cerro. *Technical Director General:* Engineer Raúl Lopez Guiral. *Sales Director:* Rodolfo Rodriguez. *Administration Director:* Sergio Gómez. *Hours of broadcasting per week:* 112. *Commercials:* Yes. *TV sets reached:* about 1,700,000.

Venezolana de Television (Channel 8), *Apartado de Correo 2739, Caracas. Tel: 34957179. Telex: 25401.*

Director General: Don Pedro Beroeta. *General Manager:* Enrique Faillace. *Programme Directors:* Julio Ibarra (Drama), George Stone (Plays), Luis Duque (News), Victor Bollet (Sport), Luis Villarroel (Comedy). *Technical Director General:* Efraim Sauri. *Executive Director and Narrator:* Efraim de la Cerda. *Assistant Executive Director:* Angel Genaro Escobar. *Hours of broadcasting per*

week: 105. *Commercials:* No. *TV sets reached:* about 1,700,000.

YUGOSLAVIA
Jugoslovenska Radiotelevizija (JRT), *Borisa Kidrica 70/1, Belgrade. Tel: 443-693. Telex: 11469 Yu Yurate.*

Secretary General: Ivko I. Pustisek. Yugoslav television comprises 8 public networks: Television Belgrade, Television Ljubljana, Television Novi Sad, Television Pristina, Television Sarajevo, Television Skopje, Television Titograd, Television Zagreb. Each network operates a separate programme, broadcasting an average of 70 hours weekly. *Commercials:* Yes. *TV sets reached:* 2,492,937.

Polytel International

One of the best links between German TV and other countries is Polytel International Film- und Fernseh GmbH (Tonndorfer Hauptstr. 90, 2 Hamburg 70), which handles the distribution and production negotiations for TV productions and co-productions, together with all related business. Polyphon Film also deals in similar areas and is run from the same headquarters by Gyula Trebitsch and his colleagues.

Venezuela

Venezuela has three television networks. Venezolana de Television is run by the state

(*Continued on page 500*)

(*Continued from page 456*)

WEST GERMANY. Wolfgang Urchs's *The Hostage* gave a somewhat cryptic account of urban guerrillas, but not in a very decorative or effective style.

YUGOSLAVIA. The official entry was *Chameleon* by Branko Rainitović, fully up to the Zagreb standard for wit and originality. It

showed a compulsive orator who carries his lectern and microphone about with him and even harangues his lady-love from the foot of the bed. Zlatko Grgić's contribution from Canada has been already mentioned and there was also *Seven Little Flames* by Pavao Stalter, a tale of peasants turned into pigs by a sorceress.

Animation

ANNECY SURVEY
by Ralph Stephenson

The tenth Annecy Festival presented a wide selection of cartoon and puppet films from all over the world. It is evident that animation work is on the increase in most countries. Many animation features are reported to be in production and the Festival showed Per Åhlin's *Dunderklumpen* and Ralph Bakshi's *Coonskin*. Annecy was marked by extensive student participation and there were five sessions organised by BLIFA (Bureau de Liaison des Instituts du Film d'Animation) showing very competent work from some forty art and film colleges in different countries. Another feature was the exhibition of drawing, painting, engraving and sculpture by leading animators—Alexeïeff (there was also a retrospective of his films), Grimault, Bartosch, Laloux, Watrin, Indelli and Emile Cohl. Attendance was so large that three sessions were necessary but the organisation was excellent, programmes were punctual and well-documented, projection and sound impeccable. On the jury was the legendary Len Lye and also Mustapha Alassane, a Nigerian animator, the Russian writer Sergey Assenin, and from Tehran the animator Farshid Mesghali.

AUSTRALIA. *Mother's Little Helper*, by Gary Jackson, upheld Australia's newly-acquired reputation in the cartoon field with a sympathetic send-up of Flossie the dog-lover and her pet.

BELGIUM. *The Meat Machine Is Broken Down*, by Roland de Salency, gave a grim picture of modern life with its organisation jamming and breaking down. Also interesting were *The Red-Headed Revolver*, by Gerald Frydman, best known for his *Scarabus*, and *La sclérose calcaire*, a publicity film for water-softener by Raoul Servais, who made *To Speak or Not to Speak* and *Syrène*.

BRAZIL. Antonio Moreno's *Reflections* gave a pastiche of colour to the music of Villa-Lobos and Guarnieri.

BULGARIA. The Bulgarian entry included two amusing short cartoons, Georgi Shavdarov's *Fortress* and Stoyan Doukov's *Sisyphus*. The latter, a send-up of classical mythology, showed Jove in trouble with his thunder and poor Sisyphus the victim of endless gags.

CANADA. The Canadian entry was one of the largest, and as usual was strong both in art work and in cartoon humour. *Climates*, by Suzanne Gervais, was in oils, a mixture of moving faces and landscapes with fine painting and colours. Also finely drawn was *The Marriage of the Owl*, based on an Eskimo legend and done in soft charcoal. One of the best abstracts was Ishu Patel's *Perspectrum*, with delicate moving lines and masses set to Japanese music. *Satellites of the Sun* was a new view of the solar system with excellent models. On the comic side was *Who Are We?*, a light pageant of Canadian history by the visiting Yugoslav animator Zlatko Grgić. *Mr. Frog Went A-Courting*, by Evelyn Lambart, was a children's film based on a Scottish folk song, but in such glowing colours, so well controlled and sweetly presented as to appeal equally to adults.

Strongest of the Canadian entries was Ken Wallace's *Thanksgiving* in which a turkey's carcass ready for the oven tries to escape—a pathetic, maimed creature. It was enough to turn the greediest meat-eater into a vegetarian.

CZECHOSLOVAKIA. *The Miner's Rose* (*dir*: Jiří Brdečka) had some fine images by Z. Hajdová and told the sad story of a miner killed by a fall in the pit. There is a sudden shock when the miner's wife starts up in the night to see her husband's ghost at the window. *Please Excuse Me*, by Lubomir Beneš, used the usual splendid Czech puppets to tell the story of a timid little man who finally revolts, only to be run over when he refuses to obey the traffic lights.

FRANCE. The Grand Prix went to Piotr Kamler's *Le pas*, an extraordinary abstract film in which green sheets go floating through the air. The technique was a mystery and its perfection of control made it compulsive viewing. Peter Foldes showed *Rêve*, an extract from a longer work entitled *Daphnis and Chloë*. In his usual Picasso-like fluid line it explored a mobile world of fantasy. Jan Lenica broke new ground in *Paysage*, instead of his usual crowded scene describing a deserted, dark land where bodiless skulls chased and bit one another. Bernard Palacios's *Oiseau de nuit* showed the reaction of a conventional man who encounters a winged bird-woman hitch-hiker, a being from another world. His fear of the unknown leads him to "destroy what he does not understand." Also on serious themes were Henri Lacam's *L'empreint* and *Comme il pleut sur la ville*. In the first a child is brought up wearing a vice on his head and chest, designed to mark a footprint on his back—a footprint that will fit the overseer's boot when he reaches manhood. The second film by Didier Pourcel takes its title from Verlaine—

Il pleut dans mon coeur
Comme il pleut sur la ville

and it showed a city drenched in blood when an innocent bird is killed.

G.D.R. Klaus Georgi's *Stolen Happiness* showed that international art thieves are not only taking property, but depriving those who love art of an important part of their life and enjoyment.

GREAT BRITAIN. As usual Britain produced some of the best comic films. Bob Godfrey's *Great* is a very funny account of Isambard Brunel, the bridge- and ship-builder and engineer. It successfully mixed every conceivable style from live-action to the wildest animation and excelled in them all. Bill Mather showed several films including a puppet clip of Arthur Negus and a satire on the shipwrecked mariner theme—*The Castaway*. A pleasant fantasy on two young peoples' thoughts as they sit opposite in a café was Alison de Vere's *Café Bar*. Rowland Wilson's *Trans-Siberian Express*, drawn in the grand manner, worked up to an enormous climax as the train rushes to Vladivostok where aristocrats gather in glittering splendour to toast the achievement in—so-and-so vodka! Ted Rockley and Stan Hayward showed a never-ending film-within-a-film, *Way Out*, Terry Gilliam presented *The Miracle of Flight* packed with gags about airlines, and—cruellest satire of all—Thalma Goldman in *Amateur Night* depicted with deadly accuracy the agonies of amateur strippers in a workers' club.

HUNGARY. Outstanding in a bold painting style was *Ça ira*, an evocation of the French Revolution. This is the finest example of György Kovásznai's impressive technique of ever-changing oil painting. *Let's Keep a Dog*, by Béla Ternovszky, was a hilarious series of gags on the reasons why everyone should have a dog. Dogs are useful, practical, house-trained, good for children, faithful—well, sometimes.

INDIA. The only cartoon was *Fire*, by Bhim Sain from Bombay, shown out of competition, and it seems production in India is still very limited.

ITALY. Manfredo Manfredi's *Clouds* was a liquid abstract composition. Giuseppe Lagana's *Wild Man* told the gay story of an *enfant terrible* in a colourful style.

JAPAN. Taku Furukawa's *Phenakistascope* described light-coloured designs revolving in a circle. Kihachiro Kawamoto's *A Poet's Life*, in a sombre style rather like that of Alexeïeff, told of the "vanished dreams and hopes of the working class." There was an impressive Japanese restrospective, mostly of silhouette films à la Lotte Reiniger, from the Twenties and Thirties.

NETHERLANDS. The Dutch entry included a good publicity film for fruit, *It's a Good Pear Year This Year* by Ton van der Meijde, and Niet Ren's *Tekenfilm,* a children's cartoon.

POLAND. *The Legend of Łódź*, by Andrzej Piliczewski, in colourful images, offered the story of a smoke devil plaguing a factory neighbourhood and only being killed when the chimneys are removed. Ryszard Antoniszczak's *Goodbye Steam* gave lively glimpses of steam engines, while Jerzy Kalina's *In the Grass*, made in paper cut-outs, was an allegory of the struggle for existence.

ROMANIA. Popescu-Gopo again produced his little man in *Intermezzo for an Eternal Love* with two contrasting episodes—first in a natural, rural environment, man makes of earth a terrestial paradise, secondly through pollution, over-production, over-population, and over-industralisation he destroys his environment.

SWITZERLAND. Ernest and Gisèle Ansorge in *Smile 1 and 2* showed first a man lifted up by a balloon marked PAX but weighed down by chains on his legs and finally torn in two by the opposing forces. Second a pregnant woman whose baby grows up inside her body with dire consequences.

U.S.A. This was one of the biggest entries and animation, whether in the *avant-garde* or commercial field, is obviously flourishing. In a pleasant *plume-de-ma-tante* style, *The Beast of Monsieur Racine* by Gene Deitch told the genial story of a strange new creature who turns out to be a children's hoax. Pieter van Deusen's *Cloudmaker* showed a tiny man on stilts labouring amid vast machines. *Closed Mondays* by Will Vinton and Bob Gardiner won the Critics' Prize for its unusual story of a spectator who wanders into a deserted museum and finally stays as one of the exhibits, and also for its technique. The medium used was modelling clay and the life-like control of facial expression, eyes and mouth were quite outstanding. There was a satire on the Marx Brothers in Levin and Hadley's *Frootsie* and a surrealist vision in John Haugse's *This Is Not a Museum*. Faith Hubley in *WOW Women of the World* showed some nice graphics, but, lacking any commentary, the Women's Lib message of the film was somewhat muted.

U.S.S.R. *The Heron and the Stork* was a fine cartoon by I. Nordstein with a *décor* of faded elegance. It is the story of human futility since neither heron nor stork will accept the other in marriage. Doomed to eternal proposal and refusal, the two giant birds parade against an overgrown park and ruined classical architecture, dignified, ungainly and frustrated to the end.

(Continued on page 452)

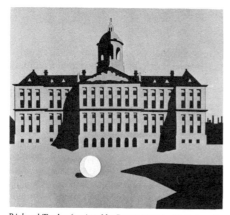

Richard Taylor (assisted by Roger McIntosh) designed a presentation composed of slides and animation for the Philips "Evoluon" pavilion in Holland

Richard Taylor has been continuing his work for the COI (Central Office of Information) with, among other things, two excellent shorts about safer cycling, which have been screened on TV during children's viewing hours. Both feature a crusty, distinguished rider named Augustus Windsock, the oldest living cyclist of them all, who has stayed alive thanks to his impeccable road manners, some of which are shown (in three-dimensional animation) in these two shorts.

Taylor's skills have also been employed in a multi-screen display presentation in "Evoluon," the Philips technology pavilion in the Netherlands. He and his assistant Roger McIntosh used eleven screens to trace the history and development of human communications, from a baby's mouthing to perpetual TV. Taylor's fondness for olive greens, chocolate browns, and Atlantic blues ("Stanley Spencer's colours," he calls them) is beautifully expressed in these visuals, which reduce concepts to easily identifiable symbols. Dick Taylor is undoubtedly one of the few British animators who is as skilful a draughtsman/painter as he is an animator.

For all their enthusiastic forays into the field of live-action, Larkins are known for their animation expertise, and *Operation Tea Strainer*, one of their most recent productions, is a racy cartoon history of Naval provisioning, from Pepys to the computerised present-day system. Lots of in-jokes. After all, Larkins are among the few studios that still believe in *amusing* animation, and not in metaphysical codswallop. The studio has also done two full-length teaching films on the character of electricity for the Electricity Council, as well as some commercials for Barclays Bank travellers' cheques, for showing on board ship. Then there have been slide presentations, recruiting strips for BP, a learning seminar package for Courier Express, and some elaborate animation for the Qatar Museum—"How Allah formed the world in ten seconds flat but took a little longer over Qatar," to quote the essential Beryl Stevens.

"Around the World in 80 Ways" with Barclays Travellers' Cheques; designed by the Larkins Studio

Training the Artists and the Craftsmen
by E. Smith-Morris

The production of animated films on any scale requires a large staff of artists and technicians. The volume of work and the factory conditions under which many television series are made can be daunting, and the economic considerations which define the style and content of this type of production make it difficult to retain any creative impetus.

Anyone seeking to escape from this faces the difficulty of finding a market for his work and, if a lone worker, many weeks, months or years of effort to realise a project which can well lose in time the freshness of the original concept.

It could be argued that the delegation which occurs in a commercial studio allows the director to inject enthusiasm, alter and modify, viewing the project as a whole and protecting the concept from decay. The lone worker can fail because of lack of support and criticism but it is perhaps significant that at international animation festivals the most applauded films are often the product of the lone worker or small studio, perhaps short on technical quality, but having that spontaneous appeal which is unique to animation and which comes from an idea-rich original mind. The films are also very often brief. It is difficult to understand why in a technique where every additional foot of film is directly related to time, work and money, so many animated films are excessively long.

Animation studios engaged in commercial work can rarely afford to maintain staff over the dead period between productions. Senior executive staff must be held, but erratic productions or a lost contract can create local gluts and shortages of trained supporting staff. In times of shortage there comes the chance for a new entrant to learn the game by being part of a working team, and this can provide valuable experience as well as conditioning to budgets, schedules and standards. Employment in this section of the film industry appears more stable than in other branches, where casualisation is almost universal, but it may be just that the films are longer in production.

When there are shortages of staff the question of training for the industry is inevitably given an airing. At the London Film School we were frequently asked to supply "students trained in trace and paint" at a moment's notice from our animation department. Only rarely were we able to help as the requests usually came in mid-term or mid-course, and it was necessary to explain that we did not train students for entry into the various grades of competence in the animation studios.

The policy of the School in animation training was clear-cut: Robert Dunbar, the Principal, wisely regarded the Animation Department as a supplement to the normal two-year Diploma Course in Film Production, and offered the course in animation as a third-year extension. It was felt that a basic understanding of film-making and the techniques of camera, sound and editing would be a pre-requisite for entry into the Animation Department. This meant that in the department we could specialise without needing to digress on every small technical question. The rules for entry were waived occasionally in cases where previous industry or amateur production experience could be assessed.

Because of the time scales which enabled students of live cinema to produce evidence of work and merit in a few weeks, which the

Heinz Schmid's ONE OF THOSE QUIET DAYS AT THE TUBE FACTORY

animation student working alone could produce only after months of effort, it was essential to evolve a system where animation students could be brought into productive film-making as quickly as possible and be given something to show as evidence of their work on the course. Many students, having already spent two years on the Diploma course, could spend only a limited time on animation, especially if they were self-financed, and therefore results were called for in the minimum time. It was obvious that any course with detailed instruction in all the techniques of animation would require a long period of study, certainly three years; this has been demonstrated by schools in other countries, where a very full curriculum has been attempted. The alternative was, in any case, more in line with our general philosophy of teaching; firstly, to encourage individual expression of ideas, and secondly, to feed in the techniques as required, to the extent necessary for realisation. Technique is necessary to art, but it can also stifle the delicate creative idea.

We believed that to appoint well-known commercial animators to head a course would perhaps have been an attraction to students, but the danger of thus imposing style and patterns of thought was very great. No one has a monopoly on ideas and our purpose was to develop whatever our students had which was *unique to them*. Adequate technical knowledge to provide for practical matters of animation technique and camera work already existed and was supplemented by bringing in from outside various experts and well-known animators to show and discuss their work and techniques.

The selection of students entering from the Diploma course was made easier by familiarity with person and performance. The most difficult to assess was the art school student with a portfolio depressingly similar to others from art schools, both here and abroad. Few had the fluency of drawing to make natural animators and some had little more than the urge, as yet unsatisfied, to create. But in a remarkable way, the lack of drawing ability was not always a handicap. More than one student joined the course with the intention of furthering his general knowledge of film-making techniques rather than as a potential animator and went on to produce exceptional work.

Initial training was aimed at developing a feel for timing and action. By drawing directly on to clear 35mm film, animating dots or lines as simple forms, timing related to the number of frames of film could be studied. A moviola in the studio gave instant playback and the system proved valuable for teaching the technique of lip-sync, simple mouth shapes being drawn to a recorded soundtrack. Analysis of the work of professional animators on large-screen editing machines helped to demonstrate timing and technique, and line tests of animation were screened and discussed.

Every student was a special case, with varying capabilities, and as time passed it became more and more obvious that no ordered curriculum could do justice to the variety of talent presented and to the range of ideas both creative and technical which

students wished to develop. In spite of restricted equipment and workshop facilities, many techniques were attempted. Several puppet films provided experience in making, jointing and moving stop-motion puppets, but one of the most successful, *Emmanuel* by Israel Hevrony, used match-boxes. Pierre Gaudry in *Zero Growth* used a rotoscope which he built himself, around a vintage 400ft Newman camera, and in another film he experimented with ultra-violet lamps and fluorescent paints. Richard Lowe, in *Princess and the Frog* used modelled Plasticine figures with elaborate *appliqué* decoration and multiple exposure to achieve a tapestry effect, and in *Bird Spirit* he dressed and painted living actors to resemble drawn and painted characters and then animated them! Max Bannah in *Carrier Pigeon* animated in coloured chalk on a vertical blackboard, and John Verbeck made *The Oldest Trick in the Book* by drawing directly on film. Thalma Goldman, in *Variations on a Yellow Woman* used cut-outs in paper; others used optical effects and the bi-pack camera.

The course attracted both introverts and extroverts, but to those with uncompromising ideas the opportunity to go it alone was appealing. If they succeeded their film would be praised at festivals, shown maybe on television, and earn compliments from the critics. *Puttin' on the Ritz* by Antoinette Starkiewicz was a great personal triumph for her at Zagreb and came close to winning the John Grierson Award, proving that if talent exists, the opportunity to sit and develop it is the first requirement. It may be that we should be more active in seeking out talent and, when found, giving it more time, money and facilities, than spending our substance on bringing all up to the uniform level of mediocrity demonstrated by the portfolios of many students.

The training of trace and paint artists, in-between artists, background artists and many other grades in the commercial animation industry would, if the demand was large enough, fall naturally to the art schools, but only in London and perhaps one or two provincial centres could such training be even contemplated. At the London Film School we were looking for originators, but it is also necessary to train the craftsmen, who are equally important in the structure of the industry and of the art.

Unfortunately the unstable nature of the cartoon film industry provides little encouragement for a formal training pattern. Nevertheless, the need for a centre where young people can find freedom to express themselves in the medium is very great.

AM Films

Peter Arthy's company works on a wide range of commercials and instructional films; they are at present engaged on producing a weekly animated segment for London Weekend Television's *Weekend World*, a current affairs programme presented by Peter Jay. They emphasise the speed with which they work, unusual in animation, receiving their scripts for *Weekend World* every Friday, shooting on the Saturday for transmission on Sunday.

Bob Godfrey's year achieved its climax at Berlin, where his long-awaited film on Isambard Kingdom Brunel, *The Great*, was screened in competition and made most other shorts on display look very scrappy. It is a 28 minute tribute to the Nineteenth-century inventor who designed the Clifton Suspension Bridge, umpteen ships and railway systems, and a fifteen-hundred bed hospital in the Crimea for good measure. Ironically, however, the personality of Brunel does not really come to life in this wild blend of cartoon, musical, and documentary, and the best sequence describes the items that Brunel *failed* to invent (everything from the violin to chocolate *mousse*). As so often with Bob's work, the commentary is funnier than the imagery, but there are so many rich moments in IKB, so much visual invention, and so much refreshing impudence, that one is content to sit back and enjoy the fun. With its hectic variety of styles, IKB is probably the best film to emerge from a British animation studio since *Yellow Submarine*.

Below: from Godfrey's Brunel film

Phil Kimmelman

Bill Peckmann

Sid Horn

We Animate

PHIL KIMMELMAN & **ASSOCIATES** 65 E. 55 Street, New York, N.Y. 10022, Tel; 371-1850

"Cheezy Rider," a commercial designed by Bill Peckmann at Phil Kimmelman & Associates

Harvey Kurtzman's SESAME STREET "BOAT"

I'M JUST A BILL, designed by Tom Yohe

The character Prospero as he appears in "The Tempest" in progress at TVC London. Drawings by George Dunning.

PROSPERO.

'T is time
The hour's now come;

And thy no greater father.

FROM "SAFETY SENSES"—JIM DUFFY
FOR THE NATIONAL COAL BOARD

TVC LONDON
70 CHARLOTTE STREET
LONDON WIP ILR

This page: Dick Williams (above) inspects his animated creation of Blake Edwards's Pink Panther. At right, a composite from the opening sequence of Murder on the Orient Express. *Some audiences were unaware of the skilled work that was devoted to this haunting episode showing the kidnapping of the Armstrong baby.*

In a year liberally sprinkled with prizes, **Richard Williams** has leapt ahead both commercially and creatively. He is now involved in projects on both sides of the Atlantic. In New York he is directing and supervising the Lester Osterman–Richard Horner production of *Raggedy Ann and Andy* (the first feature funded by ITT), and in London he is completing *The Thief and the Cobbler*. The latter will be a 100-minute animated feature in colour and scope. Two sequences already stand out: the Thief trying desperately to extricate some glowing green crystals from a decanter, and wobbling and undulating hilariously on a tight-rope far above the minarets as he strives to grasp the "Three Golden Balls." Williams looks upon the film, tongue in cheek, as "the *War and Peace* of animation, a Hollywood-style *Thief of Bagdad*." Ken Harris has been animating the Thief, and Vincent Price speaks the part of Zig-Zag, the Grand Vizier, while Anthony Quayle speaks King Nod.

Commercials from the Richard Williams Studio have gathered numerous awards in 1975, including two Clios, and Silver and Bronze Lions at Venice. Many of these TV segments are wonderfully original in conception and graphics: the "Tic-Tac" Flick a Mint series, for instance, based on old comic strips; a "Maroc" Clementine stripping before an excited off-screen crowd; and a Barclays Bank cheque changing magically into a host of practical objects and people.

Above: the achievement of 1975 at the Richard Williams Studio has undoubtedly been the animated credits and inserts for The Return of the Pink Panther. *Williams's graphic work here has won praise throughout the United States.*

Europe's Oldest and Newest Animation Studio

During April 1975 John Halas and Joy Batchelor, the original founders of the unit, bought back their old company Halas and Batchelor Ltd. The previous owners—ATV networks and Trident Television—have offered the unit to John Halas and Joy Batchelor upon completion of the half-hour television series THE COUNT OF MONTE CRISTO and THE ADDAMS FAMILY. They felt that with the recession in the U.S. television market, the company should specialise in the production of television commercials and industrial projects, which are not entirely within the activities of major television networks. Jack King, who previously acted as executive producer for television commercials, has been appointed Joint Managing Director of the company.

The new Halas and Batchelor Animation will undertake a wide range of top-quality animation—TV commercials, TV series, industrials or special productions. In addition, Halas and Batchelor will be able to call on the resources of Educational Film Centre Ltd., and Multinational Visual Products Group, which have been under John Halas's personal guidance for three years and have made a feature film and prestige industrial films in live action and animation. The unit now offers decades of experience plus a range of new stars which includes the latest technology in computer animation as well as in the developing video techniques.

It is the only studio in Europe able to offer both the competence of a long tradition and a new outlook of the seventies. The combination of the two makes the oldest and the newest unit in Europe a big contender in the world of animation.

H. & B. Cartoon "Butterfly Ball" wins Grierson Award 1975

This year's Grierson Award, given by the British Federation of Film Societies to the best short film of the year, went to THE BUTTERFLY BALL, produced by Halas and Batchelor Animation. The animated film, which won by popular vote of the audience at the National Film Theatre, was made to promote a song of the same name based on a best-selling book of the same name. Its success marks something of a departure from recognition of the documentary tradition which the Grierson Award, in name at least, might be expected to foster. This may, of course, be a reflection of the quality of documentary production at the moment. Also interesting is the fact that two of the most favoured entries were by film school students.

The late John Grierson's cable for Halas and Batchelor's Twenty-first anniversary:

"John Halas and Joy Batchelor have given international standing to the work of animation in Britain. That is a great thing to have done. They will always have a place in the history of the British Cinema."

The addresses of the Halas and Batchelor Group are as follows:–

Halas & Batchelor Animation Ltd.
Multinational Visual Products Group
Educational Film Centre
3–7 Kean Street
London WC2.

Telex: 269496
Telephone: 240 3888/836 1623
Cables: Habafilm WC2.

Three Halas & Batchelor productions. Above, THE ADDAMS FAMILY, animated for Hanna and Barbera, Hollywood. Below left, Lee Mishkin's BUTTERFLY BALL, winner of the Grierson Award 1975. Below right: KKB BANK, Baums, Mang and Zimmerman, Düsseldorf, West Germany, with INTERTEAM, Munich

B.M.ANIMATION LTD.

20 OLD COMPTON ST, LONDON W1V.5PE. TEL. 01-437 1257

1) **Left:** an example of the animated graphics used as a programme title in the recent BBC's PASSWORD.

2) Kennomeat Dog Food
   30 second TV commercial.

3) Homepride Flour
   30 second TV commercial.

4) Below: rough visuals from Barrie Merritt's marathon new project —
   THE RIME OF THE ANCIENT MARINER.

The artist at work: from Geoff Dunbar's LAUTREC, which deservedly won the Grand Prix for Short Films at Cannes 1975

Dutch Animation Facilities

Toonder Studios and Geesink Filmproduktie are unique in Europe with their staff of forty specialists in two- and three-dimensional animation. Since 1967 both companies have been based in a charming medieval castle in Nederhorst den Berg, which is an ideal place for working—no traffic, no noise, no vibrations. Toonder have been producing comics (e.g. "Tom Puss") and cartoon animation since 1939, and Geesink is known for its puppetoons. Both companies have won several awards at international festivals and specialise in live action, stop motion and tape production etc.

From Alison de Vere's CAFE BAR, a hit at Annecy 1975

From SWISS BATHROOM. a commercial made for TV in Zürich

The combination live action/animation folk dance from Tetley Tea Bags' commercial, by Wyatt Cattaneo

ZAGREB ROUND-UP
by Ronald Holloway

Saul Steinberg's comment that satire illuminates truth could be taken as the masthead of Zagreb Film, for from Vukotić's *Cowboy Jimmie* (1957) to Dragić's *Diary* (1974) the tiny Zagreb studio in the foothills of Croatia has consistently captured the world's respectful attention. Nedeljko Dragić's *Diary* was finished just in time (he does his best work at a fevered pitch over short stretches) for the 1974 Zagreb Animation Festival—won the Grand Prize—and could still qualify the next spring for the Belgrade Short Film Festival—winning First Prize again. The next stop is the Oberhausen Short Film Festival, where it could easily score a third time for the "Grand Sweep" in animation. It ranks as one of the best cartoon satires ever made.

Diary is a collection of Dragić's impressions of New York City on a recent visit: a nightmarish vision of tumbling images photographed as they spilled on to his drawing board. Highways tie into knots, building-blocks teeter under huge ads like a forbodeing scrabble-pile, a cocktail party

merges into a sardonic allegory on power and ostentation, and so on. As fantastic and wickedly scurrilous as it sounds, the cartoon-satire runs at such a delightful pace that the bitterness of technology choking itself is buried in awe and wonder. Dragić's wit puts him easily in the good company of Steinberg (also a born East European) and such caustic American newspaper caricaturists as Block, Mauldin and Oliphant. The remarkable element in *Diary* is that Dragić's memory could absorb so much, and that he could hit the bull's-eye of American capitalist *mores* on the first try—more than one critic has credited him with a natural genius.

Dušan Vukotić's *The Grasshopper* is another of his patented live action-animation story films, a fifteen-minute co-production with Viba Film. The theme is nostalgia, a salute to the past heroics of partisan-fighting, viewed through the eyes of a young boy about ten absorbed in the magic of his drawing board. In the first part of the film Vukotić satirises the petty-bourgeois manners of a well-to-do family on a picnic in the woods,

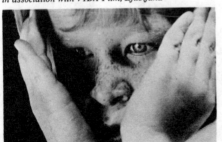

Still from GRASSHOPPER, produced by Zagreb Film in association with VIBA Film, Ljubljana

EPIDEMIOLOGY, a Zagreb cartoon directed by Duško Petričić

reducing the parents' idle prattle to musical buffoonery on the soundtrack. Stealing away to a tree stump, the youth communicates with a boy his own age recreated in the cut-outs, who was killed on this very spot during a skirmish with the enemy. The combination of real-life and animated sequences is extremely effective through compact editing and the boy's own disarming world of fantasy.

Pavao Štalter's *The Seven Little Flames* compares more than favourably with his earlier painted, frame-by-frame, adaptation of Edgar Allan Poe's *The Mask of the Red Death*. A master of painting in miniature, Štalter this time reveals a fine hand for movement and colour tones to enhance this mediaeval tale of mystery and bewitching magic. A family of honest peasants live in a clearing of a forest, threatened by a witch in a nearby swamp who prowls as a black knight after dark. The family is protected by the seven little flames in the hearth, and after nearly all is lost in a grim, menancing story of enticement and enchantment, the seven little flames rise from a razed cottage to restore order and harmony. A simple story, but the drama is inseparable from mood: the fishing scene is tranquil and idyllic in light, soft colours; the witch ravaging the forest charges the imagination with forboding images of doom (eyes peeping through tall grass); and the perspective of a young boy throughout renders the whole in a dream-world of elegaic poetry. Štalter's best film, in the style of a manuscript illumination.

Ante Zaninović's sardonic sense of humour is put to full use in *Disinfection*, reminiscent of Bob Godfrey and the English school of cartoon nonsense. A daydreaming eccentric gentleman sits in his study encased in an arm-chair, drifting off on imaginary voyages with a book in his lap—only to be shaken back to reality by his wife obsessed with the dusting and cleaning. The mood changes when a friendly fly is abruptly rubbed out by the intruding female, and the husband revolts by changing into an insect—only to be effectively eliminated by disinfectant from a spray can! Zaninović as of late is given to gentler caprices than usual, but underneath this one has all the whimsical bitterness of Thurber's Carnival.

The regulars of the Zagreb studio—Zlatko Grgić, Boris Kolar, Borivoj Dovniković, Aleksandar Marks, Vladimir Jutriša—are kept busy, perhaps too busy on international co-productions and developing "series" cartoons for the world market. Grgić spends a good deal of time at the National Film Board of Canada in between turning out mini-films on "Maxi Cat" and contributing to the successful children's series, *Professor Balthasar*, a co-production with Windrose-Dumont-Time in Cologne for West German Television. One of the studio's most ambitious projects was the one-hour television special in co-production with the NFBC: *Man the Pollutor*, featuring commentary with animated sequences by Zaninović, Bourek, Štalter, Dragić, Marks, Jutriša, Blažeković, Kolar and Vukotić.

Nevertheless, the Zagreb studio has not lost its "family" character. Following the second World Animation Festival in Zagreb in 1974, plans were made to move out of the cramped quarters on Vlaška 70 to larger ones up the hill in a former monastic convent. The old coffee shop at the other end of a shaded courtyard will be no more, but times are changing and new impulses demand that a move be made. Satire, however, remains eternal, and this fickle spirit will surely find its way to the house of Nova Ves with the proud, prancing horse over the door.

Films on 16mm (U.K.)

by Derek Elley

The brightest arrival on the 16mm scene during the past year has without doubt been **Cinegate**, a distribution library* under the same management as the well-known repertory cinema in Notting Hill Gate. Particular emphasis is placed on the films of Fassbinder and other (less well-known) young German directors, notably two features by Wim Wenders, *Die Angst des Tormanns beim Elfmeter/The Goalkeeper's Fear of the Penalty* and *Alice in den Städten/Alice in the Cities*. Both works are odyssey-like in structure, the first showing a murderer's own fascination with his pursuit by the police, the second a moving and affecting portrait of a friendship between a nine-year-old girl and an out-of-work reporter. Wenders uses a cool, but never clinical, approach to his subjects; *Alice in the Cities* is perhaps the greater work of the two, though *Goalkeeper* carries a strange feeling of disorientation in its refusal to surrender to the simple thriller format. Cinegate's library is consciously social-oriented, though this takes many forms: from Louis Malle's hypnotic seven-part study of *Phantom India*, through Peter K. Smith's flawed but impressive *A Private Enterprise*, to the Fonda/Hayden/Wexler *Vietnam Journey*. Almost as a bonus come Mizoguchi's 1952 *Saikaku ichidai onna/The Life of O-haru* and Ozu's 1959 *Ohayo/Good Morning*.

At the other end of the entertainment scale, **FDA**'s major release has been Dick Lester's buoyant and inventive *The Three Musketeers* (*The Queen's Diamonds*). Lester's feel for *life as it was lived* gives the film an authenticity which no amount of detailed set re-creation can ever equal, while the large—and, one might imagine, cumbersome—cast never suffocates the action. Two films which won mixed receptions on their theatrical release were Mankiewicz's *Sleuth* and Boorman's *Zardoz*, both in their separate ways (whodunnit vs. futuristic fantasy) bending the medium to their own ends. Louis Malle's *Lacombe Lucien*, on the other hand, is as discreet as one expects from this director, particularly in the detail of its period setting. FDA have also acquired a large number of Thirties and Forties classics—Curtiz's *The Adventures of Robin Hood, Angels with Dirty Faces, Captain Blood, The Charge of the Light Brigade* and *The Private Lives of Elizabeth & Essex*, Hawks's *The Big Sleep*, Dieterle's *Juarez*, and many other works by Walsh, Lloyd Bacon and others. From FDA's other contemporary releases, most of which speak for themselves, one should draw attention to John Hough's masterly exercise in horror, *The Legend of Hell House*, every way as good as Robert Wise's *The Haunting* in its pacing of shocks amid sustained atmosphere.

EMI's major release for the forthcoming year will naturally be Sidney Lumet's *Murder on the Orient Express*, remarkable as much for Richard Rodney Bennett's skilful pastiche score as for its well-integrated gallery of players. Michael Apted's *Stardust*, which featured a surprisingly good performance from Adam Faith as the embittered manager, is also of interest. Less well-known titles jostle for interest: Brian Clemens's *Captain Kronos—Vampire Hunter* is a tiny gem in its own field, a rural period piece which has an almost mythic feel to many of its scenes; *Dillinger*, by up-and-coming John Milius; and Chang Ch'eh's visually and thematically rich *The New One-Armed Swordsman*, with David Chiang. Especially welcome also is Claude Whatham's third feature, *All Creatures Great and Small*. Based on the autobiographical books of the North Country vet James Herriot, the film has a lyrical feel for country life which, while romanticised through photography and montage, never becomes indigestible—merely very engaging and boasting winning performances from Anthony Hopkins, Simon Ward and newcomer Lisa Harrow.

Columbia–Warner also have many popular works now on 16mm: Friedkin's *The Exorcist*, Winner's *Death Wish* and Coppola's *The Godfather*. Particularly recommended is the off-beat *The Prisoner of Second Avenue*, Neil Simon's black comedy on urban nervous disorders, with Anne Bancroft partnering Jack Lemmon in quieter style. Robert Altman's *California Split* features another unexpectedly successful partnership—the flamboyant Elliott Gould, part-and-parcel of Altman's "continual dialogue" style, and the quieter George Segal who (as in *A Touch of Class*) shows a fine sense of comic timing. In more fantastic regions, Robert Clouse's *Enter the Dragon* is an uneasy mixture of East and West but is handsomely mounted and includes Lalo Schifrin's best musical score for years; likewise, *The Golden Voyage of Sinbad*—miraculous animation from Ray Harryhausen and a welcome return to film music by Miklós Rózsa.

Ron Harris, as well as having several foreign features which have not been released theatrically to date—Etienne Perier's *And Hope to Die*, with Lea Massari and Michel Bouquet; Yves Robert's *The Bit Player*, with Mastroianni and Françoise Fabian; Edouard Molinaro's *Hostages*, with Bulle Ogier—also have Jean Chapot's *The Lumière Years 1895–1900*, a ninety-minute compilation from Lumière's vast legacy of almost two thousand sequences.

The **BFI**'s addition of many German classics to their library (announced last year) progresses slower than expected due to technical difficulties, but many other works have since been included. Kurosawa's neglected *Dodeska-den* and Fellini's almost forgotten *Luci del varietà/Variety Lights* are at last available, while such staple diet as Hawks's *Bringing Up Baby*, Ford's *The Informer*, Ray's *They Live by Night* and Tourneur's *Cat People* are available at reasonable prices. Slightly more expensive, but still well worth investigating, are Chabrol's *Les bonnes femmes*, one of the finest works of his early period, and Renoir's *La bête humaine*, recently resurrected in its complete form and featuring an ambiguous central performance by Jean Gabin.

Classics are also the keynote of **London Films**, chiefly concerned with showcasing the Thirties work of Sir Alexander Korda. All are extremely valuable additions to the viewing catalogue, many already seen during the past year on TV: Michael Powell's intriguing *The Spy in Black*, William K. Howard's *The Squeaker* (a good example of British Thirties film noir), Zoltán Korda's *Sanders of the River*, *The Drum* and *The Four Feathers*, plus others including Robert Flaherty's *Elephant Boy* (which catapulted Sabu to international fame).

For vintage American cinema enthusiasts, **Robert Kingston** has become indispensable. His new catalogue bulges more than ever with a mass of well-known classics and reputable B-features at rock-bottom

prices. Major recent additions have included the two Gabriel Pascal/G.B. Shaw features, *Androcles and the Lion* and *Major Barbara*. The first is a notable example of Shavian wit brought to bear on an historical subject, alternately touching and hilarious, and memorable for fine playing from Jean Simmons and Robert Newton. Other gaps filled by Robert Kingston include David Lean's colourful *Summer Madness*, with Katharine Hepburn and Rossano Brazzi in Venice, and Preminger's controlled *The Court-Martial of Billy Mitchell*. Generally, however, directors count less than actors in Kingston's library, which is a rich hunting-ground for well-known players in little-publicised (or now forgotten) works.

Intercontinental Films also have a similarly eclectic, though smaller, collection of American and foreign features, ranging from Italian *peplum* epics to such recent releases as Fritz Lang's 1948 *Secret beyond the Door* (the last of his trilogy of Joan Bennett pictures, a psychological Gothic thriller with fine camerawork by Stanley Cortez) or George Stevens's *A Double Life*. Of note is Steve Sekely's remarkable *The Day of the Triffids*, which, though flawed, has some excellent uses of special effects and sound to achieve maximum menace. Scenes such as that showing hundreds of rampant Triffids gathered together outside a perimeter fence, the air alive with their speech, remain in the memory.

Of those libraries specialising in foreign cinema, **Contemporary** have added a trio of little-known but meritorious Finnish films to their collection. Edvin Laine's *Täällä pohjantähden alla/Here beneath the North Star* and its sequel *Akseli ja Elina/Akseli and Elina* reveal themselves as richly-drawn portraits, traced through several generations of a tenant-farmer's family, from the troubled period of Finland's history during the first decades of the present century. Like his famous 1955 work, *The Unknown Soldier*, Laine's films are adaptations of the epic novels of Väino Linna, and show that the country's oldest active film director is still in full command of his powers. Rauni Mollberg's first feature, *Maa on syntinen laulu/The Earth Is a Sinful Song* is a less consciously "cinematic" work, at times coming close to the ethnic documentary *genre*: the rough, tough lives of the Laplanders are shown with unblinking honesty, the story of a buxom young girl's first sexual awakenings providing a framework for a diverse flow of incidents. From across the border in the Soviet Union, Contemporary have also acquired Eisenstein's *Battleship Potemkin* (with the *original* orchestral score by Edmund Meisel—a fascinating experience) and Pudovkin's *Storm over Asia* (re-edited with synchronised dialogue and music, under the director's supervision). Contemporary also share, with **Connoisseur**, both Erice's *El espíritu de la colmena/The Spirit of the Beehive* (see IFG 1975) and Bo Widerberg's *Fimpen/Stubby*, the story of a young football champion which represents a distinct change of direction for the Swedish director. Connoisseur have also taken Joan Silver's *Hester Street* (reviewed in our U.S. section) and Clive Donner's *The Caretaker*, as well as having two recent Chabrol works available on 16mm. *Nada* is certainly the more fascinating of the pair, if only for the unlikely choice of subject for Chabrol (modern-day terrorists), though *Les noces rouges/Blood Wedding* is the more engrossing work—a perfectly-honed study of the *bourgeoisie* trapped by their own actions, with Michel Piccoli and Stéphane Audran giving their finest performances for some time.

Peter Darvill Associates is now a force to be reckoned with in the foreign field, with

still more Swedish features, both old and new, supplementing the lists. Of the recent works Johan Bergenstråhle's *Jag heter Stelios/Foreigners* should not be overlooked. A study of Greek immigrant workers in Sweden, it uses authentic players to draw a convincing picture of the unhappy, but inevitable, isolation of a tightly-knit minority in a foreign land. Bergenstråhle focusses on the fortunes of a young man in his family, work and sexual life, contrasting his nascent hope with the dead-end existence of an older relation, whose only wish is to return to Greece before he dies. Older works include Bergman's two Fifties pictures, *Kvinnodröm/Journey into Autumn* and *Gycklarnas afton/Sawdust and Tinsel*, while Jonas Cornell's *Puss & kram/Hugs and Kisses* (schematic comedy) and Susan Sontag's *Duett för kannibaler/Duet for Cannibals*

(rigorous emotional drama) become re-available.

Smaller-scale but featuring a number of fine films is **Amanda Films,** with Satyajit Ray's *Charulata* and Arrabal's *Viva la muerte* alongside Marco Ferreri's *Dillinger Is Dead* (stylistically the exact opposite of *La grande bouffe*, and worth re-viewing for that very reason) and Volker Schlöndorff's *Der junge Törless/Young Törless*, a gritty examination of the suppressed tensions in a male boarding school in Germany. Amanda also have Toshio Matsumoto's riveting and bloody *Shura/Pandemonium* (reviewed in IFG 1973) and Godard's colourful "musical" *Une femme est une femme*—among others.

From **ETV** comes Martin Smith's film of Victor Jara, entitled simply *Compañero*. Jara, a Chilean folk singer sprung from peasant origins, was imprisoned, tortured and killed

Educational & Television Films

present

"COMPANERO" — Victor Jara of Chile
Music: Victor Jara. Eastmancolour. 55mins.
Cert. U. 16mm A film by Martin Smith &
Stanley Forman. "Golden Dove" award
Leipzig 1974

Victor Jara. Chilean folk singer
born: September 28, 1938
murdered: September 15, 1973

MANIFESTO

I don't sing for love of singing
or to show off my voice
but for the statements
made by my honest guitar
for its heart is of the earth
and like the dove it goes flying . . .
tenderly as holy water
blessing the brave and the dying
so my song has found a purpose
as Violetta Parra would say.
Yes, my guitar is a worker
shining and smelling of spring
my guitar is not for killers
greedy for money and power
but for the people who labour
so that the future may flower.
For a song takes on a meaning
when its own heartbeat is strong
sung by a man who will die singing
singing his song.

I don't sing for adulation
or so that strangers may weep.
I sing for a far strip of country
narrow but endlessly deep.

In the earth in which we begin
in the earth in which we end
brave songs will give birth to a song
which will always be new.

details of this remarkable film and many others from:
ETV Ltd. 247a Upper Street, Highbury Corner,
London N1 1RU   Tel: 01 226 2298/9

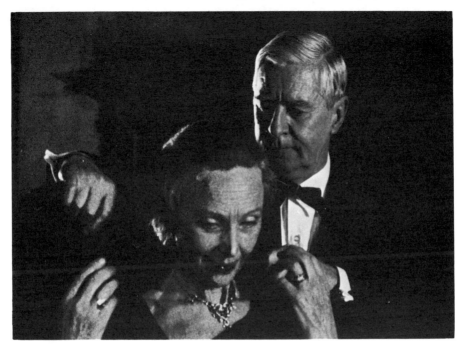

Inga Tiblad and Gunnar Björnstrand in THE PISTOL, now available from Darvill Associates

for supporting President Allende's Popular Unity Government by the military junta which took over the country in September 1973. Smith, who has directed several of Thames TV's *World at War* programmes, uses archive material and a detailed interview with Jara's wife to draw his portrait. ETV, from their large collection of recent Czechoslovak features (the majority hardly seen in this country), have František Vláčil's *Údolí vcel/Valley of the Bees*, made in 1968 immediately after his acknowledged masterpiece *Markéta Lazarová*. Almost Bressonian in its control, the film shows the psychological conflict of a Thirteenth-century crusader who deserts his religious order. Filmed in real locations, it has the feel of a social study of the age rather than a period epic.

Of the newer libraries, **Derann Film Services** sport an energetic collection of popular entertainment, as diverse as Chang Ch'eh's *Hellfighters of the East*, and Kien Lun's superb *Wang Yu—Ten Fingers of Steel*, to Pete Walker's eminently scarey *House of Whipcord* (better than its title suggests) and such John Wayne classics as *The Quiet Man* and *The Fighting Kentuckian*. Their major release of this year is the resurrected Herbert

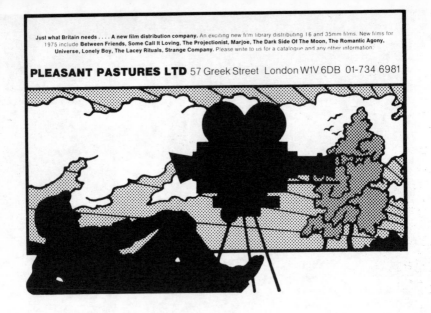

Wilcox production, *Sixty Glorious Years*, dating from 1938. From **Concord Films Council** is available a fasinating study of the artist *Lautrec*, while **Leshar Films,** the country's largest distributor of independent documentaries, has *Chabot Solo* (first part of a projected three-part study of Charles Chabot, the world's oldest active aviator) and *Okavango Delta*, a one-hour film concerning the drainage programme in Botswana to provide water for the country. Leshar, run by ex-BBC Les Harris, also has its own "dramatised" documentary about the discovery of the Tutankhamun treasures, called (appropriately) *In Search of Tutankhamun*. Finally, **Pleasant Pastures,** a new company which also now runs **Fair Enterprises** (now static as regards any fresh acquisitions), have several musical shorts—*The Dark Side of the Moon* (Pink Floyd), *Paint the City with Music* (country), *Within Southern Louisiana* (ethnic)—plus some out-of-the-way features. Chief among these are Henry Jaglom's ambitious exploration of a child-woman's fantasies, *A Safe Place*, with Tuesday Weld and Orson Welles, and *Marjoe*, a frightening documentary about a revivalist in singer's guise.

* British readers are advised to consult the special BFFS insert for details of catalogues and addresses, etc., of this and other 16mm libraries.

THE DAY OF THE TRIFFIDS, available on 16mm from Intercontinental

TRIDENT PREVIEW THEATRE

All facilities including DOLBY SYSTEM ®

for theatre bookings contact:

DICK SLADE

Trident House,
17, St. Anne's Court,   734-7595
London W.1.   734-9901/4

Preview Theatres

BOB'S PLACE, *118 Wardour St., W1. Tel. 437.1871.*

CONTEMPORARY PREVIEW THEATRE, *55 Greek St., W1V 6DB. Tel. 734.4901.*

HUMPHRIES PREVIEW THEATRE, *111 Wardour St., W1V 4JA. Tel. 636.3636.*

MERCURY THEATRES (Baronet, Coronet, Crown A, Little Gem, Bijou, and Sapphire), *84–88 Wardour St., W1V 3LF. Tel. 437.2233.*

A group of well-organised theatres of various sizes.

MAYFAIR STARLIGHT THEATRE, *Mayfair Hotel, Berkeley St., W1A 2AN. Tel. 629.7777.*

THE MINEMA, *45 Knightsbridge, SW1X 7NL. Tel. 235.4226.*

SUDBURY CONFERENCE HALL, *15 Newgate St., EC1. Tel. 248.1202.*

Seating 214 viewers, the Sudbury Conference Hall is one of London's largest preview theatres, and is excellent for general meetings requiring discussions (in up to four languages if required!) with film as an integral part of the proceedings. There is a separate reception/display/refreshment area of 3,000 square feet. There are projection facilities on 8mm, 16mm, and 35mm up to scope format.

TRIDENT PREVIEW THEATRE, *Trident House, St. Anne's Court, Wardour St., W1 Tel. 734.9901–4.*

This luxurious, acoustic-treated theatre has 35mm and 16mm double head projectors, rollback 35mm, all picture ratios, record replay facilities, and seats between thirty-five and forty people. Arrangements can be made for catering and for additional seating, and the theatre is air-conditioned.

WARDOUR PREVIEW THEATRE, *92 Wardour St., W1. Tel. 734.4949.*

Film Insurance

Established in 1921, the firm of Jauch & Hübener, Gr. Reichenstr. 2, Hamburg 11, West Germany, now look after all the production insurance for the second television channel in Germany, and for a majority of the feature films produced in that country. They have special branches in Berlin, Mülheim, Vienna, Munich, Frankfurt and Zürich so as to maintain direct links with producers, whether in the studio or on location. But Jauch & Hübener do not confine their activities solely to Germany. They work closely with foreign companies and particularly with Lloyd's in London. Another useful contact for producers working in Europe.

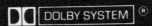
490 FILM SERVICES

Film Transporters

AUSTRIA

Frey & Co., *Lindengasse 43, Vienna.*
Karl Vrablitz, *Neubaugasse 36, Vienna.*

BELGIUM

Import Film Service, *13 Blvd Badouin, Brussels.*
Van de Moortel, F., *17 avenue Galilée, Brussels.*

BRAZIL

Transportes Fink, *Rio de Janeiro.*

BRITAIN

Air Express Ltd, *8 Lorenzo Street, London WC1.*
Bob Burge, Ltd, *7 Chalcot Road, London NW1. Tel. 01.586.4411/7.*

This firm can call on over thirty years' experience in film shipments, import and export. Mr. Burge specialises in TV work also. His London Airport office is in the Air Cargo Terminal, with extensive office accommodation and a large warehouse. The address there is Room 128/G/1, Building 521, Air Cargo Terminal.

D.A.C. Air Services Ltd, *Building 30, London Airport, Hounslow, Middlesex.*

Film Transport Specialists (G.B.) Ltd, *Fairfield House, N. Circular Rd., London NW10. Tel. 965.7181.*
Müller, Wm H. & Co. (Batavier) Ltd, *58 Old Compton Street, London W1. Tel. 437.8131.*

DENMARK

Copenhagen Forwarding Agency A/S, *Amager Strandvej 350, DK-2770 Kastrup. Tel. (01) 50 35 55.*

CFA's turnover increased in 1974 quite substantially, and about 75% of Danish film organisations route their films through the company now. Financial security has now been added to CFA's professional expertise thanks to the merger with the huge ASG concern, which has an annual turnover of more than $200,000,000. So now CFA is able to concentrate only on service.

FINLAND

Internationella Transport AB, *Glogatan 3, Helsinki. Tel. 11771.*

FRANCE

Donot, Paul et Cie, *175 rue de Courcelles, 75017 Paris.*

Express Transport, *27 rue de Flandres, Paris.*
Michaux, R. et Cie, *2 & 5 rue de Rocroy, 75010 Paris. Tel. 878 72-72.*

GERMANY

Hagens Anthony & Co, *Sonninstr. 24, 2 Hamburg 1. Tel. 24 82 71.*

The oldest firm of transporters on the continent is—technically—Hagens Anthony & Co. The actual firm was started at the end of the last century, and for many years Hagens Anthony have been IATA agents in air-freight traffic, with a non-stop service at Hamburg Fuhlsbüttel Airport, as well as at Bremen.

Kroll, Franz & Co, *Lindenstr. 39, Berlin. Tel. 251.50.51.*

Kroll, Franz & Co, *Airport Freight Centre, Düsseldorf. Tel. 422671 and 426565.*

Kroll, Franz & Co, *Mainzer Landstr. 168, Frankfurt-am-Main. Tel. 253029.*

Kroll, Franz & Co, *Airport Freight Centre, Hannover. Tel. 7305407 and 735313.*

Kroll, Franz & Co, *Schertlinstr. 10, Munich. Tel. 789986.*

GREECE

Greca Transport, *96 Academy St., Athens.*

ITALY

Cippolli & Zanetti, *Via Nomentana 257, Rome.*

NETHERLANDS

Ruys Aeronaut, *Vrachtgebouw Schiphol Airport, P.O. Box 7540. Tel. 020.170922.*

Ruys Aeronaut's Bonded Stores has its HQ in the magnificent new Amsterdam airport at Schiphol. It handles efficiently, and at low prices, all kinds of films, tapes, and equipment. The recent merger of Ruys and Aeronaut has enabled the company to offer much improved services at every level, with an experienced staff of 200. There are branches in Rotterdam, Hilversum, and The Hague.

SOUTH AFRICA

Jet Freight Services, *Jan Smuts Int'l Airport, Johannesburg. Tel. 975-6814, 975-6818.*
Van's Airfreight, *New Freight Agents Building, Jan Smuts Int'l Airport, Johannesburg. Tel. 975-2647.*

SWEDEN

AB Transportkompaniet, *Hornsbruksgatan 28, Stockholm 9. Tel. 680580.*

AB Transportkompaniet has more than forty years' experience in the handling of film and film units. Crews from abroad can be cleared at the border towns with a minimum of delay. Branch offices are available for clearance at Stockholm, Gothenburg, Malmö, Halsingborg, Trelleborg, Norrköping, Borås, Örebro, Karlstad, and Eskilstuna. Special airport offices are maintained at the international airports in Stockholm, Gothenburg and Malmö.

U.S.A.

Barnett/Novo International Corp., *425 East 53rd St., New York, NY 10022.*
Beckmann and Beckmann, Int'l, *152–32 Rockaway Blvd., Jamaica, NY 11434. Tel. 723.7627-28-29.*

TRANSPORTERS **493**

Subtitling

BELGIUM

LABORATORIES TITRA S.A., *98 rue des Plantes, 1030 Brussels.*

BRAZIL

TITRA FILM DO BRASIL S.A., *17 rue Sâo Luiz Gonzaga, Rio de Janiero.*

FRANCE

NEUE MARS-FILM PETERS KG, *4 rue Christophe Colomb, 75008 Paris. Tel. 723. 9178.*

LABORATOIRES TITRA S.A., *66 rue Pierre Rimbaud, 92230 Gennevilliers.*

GERMANY

NEUE MARS-FILM PETERS KG, *Friedrichstr. 235, Berlin 61. Tel. 251.0865.* This lively firm is responsible for subtitling all important features screened at the Berlin International Film Festival and the Forum of Young Cinema. Its titles, printed in modern IBM Univers, are always recognisable for their accuracy and clarity. Mr. Lundewall is the technical director and the company works in every major language. Neue Mars-Film produces and sells subtitling machines, and has served such majors as CIC and Warners.

NETHERLANDS

TITRA FILM LABORATORIUM N.V., *82–86 Egelantiersgracht, Amsterdam C.*

COLOR FILM CENTER, *Leeghwaterstraat 5, P.O. Box 1083, The Hague. Tel. 88.92.07.*

A subtitling machine produced by Neue-Mars Film of Berlin

This organisation specialises in the sub-titling of positive prints, both colour and black-and-white, in 35mm and 16mm, and also in the reduction of 35mm subtitled positive prints to 16mm positive or reversal colour prints. Modern equipment and punctilious attention to detail have established the reputation of this laboratory far beyond the borders of Holland.

SWITZERLAND

CINETYP, *Grünaustrasse 10, 3084 Wabern-Bern. Tel. 541754.*

TITRA FILM S.A., *29 rue de Lancy, 1227 Geneva.*

Studios and Laboratories

AUSTRALIA

SUPREME SOUND STUDIOS, *11–15 Young St., Paddington, Sydney.*

AUSTRIA

WIEN-FILM GmbH, *Sievering Studios, Sieveringerstr. 135, 1190 Vienna. Tel. 322153.*

BRAZIL

CINEDIA S. A., *Estrada da Soca 400, Jacarepagua, Rio de Janeiro.*

STUDIO HAMBURG
2 HAMBURG 70, TONNDORFER HAUPTSTRASSE 90
TEL: 66 88 5350/5351 TELEX: 0214 218

PRODUCOES CINEMATOGRAFICAS **HERBERT RICHERS S. A.,** *Rua Conde de Bimfim 1331, Rio de Janeiro.*

COMPANHIA CINEMATOGRAFICA VERA CRUZ, *São Bernardo do Campo, São Paulo.*

BRITAIN

EMI ELSTREE STUDIOS, *Borehamwood. Tel. 953.1600.*

BRAY INTERNATIONAL FILM CENTRE, *Down Place, Windsor Road, Windsor, Berks. Tel. (0628) 22111.*

PINEWOOD STUDIOS, *Iver Heath, Bucks. Tel. (75) 33441.*

SHEPPERTON STUDIOS, *Shepperton, Middx. Tel. (09328) 62611.*

TWICKENHAM FILM STUDIOS, *The Barons, St. Margarets, Twickenham, Middx. Tel. 892.4477.*

HUMPHRIES FILM LABORATORIES, *71 Whitfield Street, London W1A 2HL.*

Together with its sister companies (De Lane Lea and Mole-Richardson), Humphries offers a first-class laboratory service for all sponsors, film-makers, and educational publishers, with an emphasis on documentaries, shorts, TV programmes, cinema commercials, and of course feature films. All gauges—35mm, 16mm, 8mm and even Super 8—are accorded equal attention by the Humphries staff. A twenty-four hour service is the norm for rushes. There is also a laboratory in Manchester.

STUDIOSOUND, *84–88 Wardour St., London W1V 3LF. Tel. 437.2233 and 734.5000.*

WARWICK DUBBING THEATRE, *153 Wardour St., London W1.*

Full range of dubbing services available. Five fully-equipped cutting rooms.

CANADA

CRAWLEY FILMS, *19 Fairmont Avenue, Ottawa 3, Ontario.*

DENMARK

THE DANISH FILM STUDIO, *52 Blomstervaenget, DK 2800 Lyngby. Tel. (01) 87 2700.*

NORDISK FILMS KOMPAGNI, *Mosedalvej, DK-2500 Valby. Tel. (01) 301033.*

RIALTO/SAGA STUDIO K/S, *Ledøjevej 1, DK-2620 Albertslund. Tel. (01) 649646.*

STEEN HERDEL FILM & TV PRODUCTION, *Nygård Terrasserne 242D, 3520 Farum. Tel. (01) 95 49 19.*

Known as a successful producer, Steen Herdel also offers outstandingly good technical facilities for the independent film-maker. He has an Arriflex 35 BL, Nagra and MWA sound equipment, 1mm and 33mm cutting tables, and can arrange processing through local labs.

FINLAND

SUOMI-FILMI, *Bulevardi 12, Helsinki 12. Tel. 642112.*

This old-established firm has studios and laboratories among the best in Scandinavia. There is a sister company for international TV commercial spots. Mr. Risto Orko, the famous head of the firm, introduced the word and idea of "documentary" films in Finland. Shorts of this type on the wood industry, on ice-breaking, and sport have been successfully made by and at Suomi Film studios.

FRANCE

PARIS STUDIOS CINEMA, *50 Quai du Pont-du-Jour, Billancourt, Seine.*

STUDIOS DE BOULOGNE, *137 avenue Jean Baptiste Clément, Boulogne, Seine. Tel. MOL 6580.*

STUDIOS ECLAIR, *avenue de Lattre-de-Tessigny, Epinay-sur-Seine. Tel. PLA 39–60.*

SAINT-MAURICE, *Epinay-sur-Seine.*

FRANSTUDIO, *4 rue des Reservoirs, Epinay-sur-Seine.*

GERMANY

STUDIO HAMBURG, *Tonndorfer Hauptstr. 90, 2 Hamburg 70. Tel. 66882291.*

This impressive complex in northern Germany provides German and overseas producers with virtually all the facilities they could hope for. There are 11 studio stages (each 450 to 1,000 square metres), a variety of dubbing and recording studios, rehearsal stages for TV production, 5 editing areas and 43 cutting rooms for all gauges, underwater, post-synch, processing and re-wind facilities. Trained, specialised personnel in all audio-visual sectors are available, and Studio Hamburg can offer dubbing facilities for all foreign languages for TV, documentary, and other kinds of film. More and more big productions are being handled by the Studio.

BAVARIA ATELIER GmbH, *Bavaria-Filmplatz 7, Geiselgasteig, Munich. Tel. 47691.*

GREECE

FINOS FILMS, *53 Chiou St., Athens. Tel. 815–087, 823–566.*

HUNGARY

MAFILM STUDIOS, *Lumumba utca 174, Budapest XIV, Budapest.*

NORWAY

NORSK FILM A/S, *Wedel Jarlsbergs vei 36, 1342 Jar. Tel. (02) 121070.*

WARWICK DUBBING THEATRE

151-153 WARDOUR STREET, LONDON, W1V 3TB
Telephone 01-437 5532/3

POLAND

LÓDŹ FEATURE FILM STUDIO, *Łakowa 29, 90–554 Łódź.*

WROCŁAW FEATURE FILM STUDIO, *Wystawowa 1, 51–618 Wrocław.*

WARSAW FEATURE FILM STUDIO, *Chełmska 21, 00–724 Warsaw.*

All the above studios have electromagnetic sound recording facilities, printing laboratories, and all necessary means for feature productions. The Łódź studio has four stages (most modern: 400 sq. metres), the Wrocław two (biggest: 1,300), and the modern Warsaw one, completed in 1961, two (each of 600).

DOCUMENTARY FILM AND NEWSREEL STUDIO, *Chełmska 21, 00–724 Warsaw.*

Besides usual technical facilities, this also has a large library of historical material.

EDUCATIONAL FILM STUDIO, *Kilińskiego 210, 93–106 Łódź.*

CARTOON FILM STUDIO, *Cieszyńska 24, 43–300 Bielsko Biała.*

FEATURETTE STUDIO "SEMAFOR," *Kościuszki 48, 90–514 Łódź.*

MINIATURE FILM STUDIO, *Puławska 02–595 Warsaw.*

SPAIN

BALCAZAR STUDIOS, *Calle San Antonio María Claret s/n. Esplugas de Llobregat, Barcelona. Tel. 271 2854.*

ESTUDIOS ROMA, *Carretera de Burgos 11.7, Madrid. Tel. 209 1346.*

SEVILLA FILMS, *Pio XII 2, Madrid. Tel. 2-59-03-00.*

SOUTH AFRICA

KILLARNEY FILM STUDIOS, *P.O. Box 2787, Johannesburg.* (Studio, crew, and equipment hire.)

NATIONAL FILM BOARD, *P.O. Box 600, Silverton, Pretoria.* (Sound stage.)

CAVALIER FILMS, *P.O. Box 35071, Northcliff, Johannesburg.* (Sound stage.)

S.A. FILM STUDIOS, *Lone Hill, P.O. Box 67448, Bryanston, Transvaal.* (Studio and technical facilities.)

SWEDEN

SVENSK FILMINDUSTRI, *Stocksund.*

EUROPA FILM, *Box 200 65, S-161 20 Bromma 20.*

SVENSKA FILMINSTITUTET, *Filmhuset, Borgvägen, 102 52 Stockholm.*

SWITZERLAND

PETER BLASER PRODUCTIONS, *Oberdorfstrasse 19, 8001 Zürich. Tel. 01. 32 77 48.*

Mr. Blaser can arrange shooting and location work in Switzerland with speed and efficiency.

(*Continued from page 452*)
and directed by Pedro Beroeta, an experienced journalist and writer. The other two networks are under private management: Radio Caracas Television, directed by Peter Bottome, and Venevision, directed by Valeriano Humpirrez. All three are based on Caracas. A fourth network, which had a broad cultural programme policy, has been suspended (audience ratings reign supreme in Venezuela). This network, Channel 5, had broadcast documentaries, concerts and, most notably, a series of plays (including Shaw's "Candida," Lorca's "Yerma," and so on) featuring the great Venezuelan television actress America Alonso and directed by her husband Daniel Farria. Both have since left for Spain, and have said that they will only return when Channel 5 is re-opened with an adequate budget, as has been promised.

Meanwhile, the remaining three networks continue with their staple diet of news, documentaries, light entertainment, interviews and so on. Venezolana de Television is distinguished by the fact that its programmes are not interrupted by commercials, but on the whole there is really not much to choose between the three networks. On the drama side Venezuelan television is afflicted by long-running and generally sentimental teleplays, called *novelas* but also known (sardonically) as *culebras* (snakes). These soap operas, which feature such talented players as Eva Moreno, Doris Wells, Tomás Henriquez, Martin Lantigua, etc., are artificially prolonged, sometimes running as much as a year, by means of absurd scriptwriters' inventions.

But it would be wrong to give the impression that Venezuelan television is all pap. Programmes like the political interviews of Sofia Imber and Carlos Rangel, or the admirably wide-ranging series by Arturo Uslar Pietri under the title *Valores humanos*, are just some of the more interesting highlights. There are also the programmes imported from the United States: special shows (Liza Minnelli, Barbra Streisand, etc.) and filmed series like *Kojak, Hawaii Five-O, Mannix*, as well as cartoons for children, and on Sunday evenings there is usually a good film shown without commercials. Colour television has not yet been introduced, but it is only a matter of time. Whether it will change the present balance and standards of Venezuelan television remains to be seen.

JACOBO BRENDER

Sponsored Films

by Susan Andrews

While some of this year's sponsored films have been spoiled by banal scripting, many have pioneered a refreshingly original approach. Surveyed below are a selection of films from some of the major film libraries.

For my money the outstanding sponsored film of the year was *Drive Carefully Darling*, produced by Graphic Films for the Department of the Environment; surprisingly it was only given a bronze award at Brighton. It has deservedly been given TV time, and its message is a warning to experienced drivers who tend not to be as careful on the roads as they ought. The driver in the film is setting off for work, his movements controlled by three characters in the "Control Room" of his head—Brain, Memory and Ego. The dramatic ending brings to a close a fascinating and powerful film.

BP

Petroleum Films Bureau, 4 Brook Street, London W1.

Conveying all the excitement and technical precision of the early moonshots, *Location North Sea* describes how a giant 30,000-ton oil rig was carefully raised from its side to an upright position and lowered to an exact spot on the seabed some 400 feet down. This was the climax of the laborious journey of the giant steel structure which was floated on buoyancy tanks and towed 250 miles to develop an oilfield in the North Sea. *Location North Sea* (colour, 16 mins.) is a tribute to technical progress, although the rusty-looking set of scaffolding sticking out of the sea seems a rather pathetic shrine.

BRITISH GAS

British Gas Film Library, 16 Paxton Place, London SE27 9SS.

Super Natural Gas (colour, 10 mins) features Kenneth Williams as the legendary Will O' the Wisp crawling through a maze of underground pipes and trying to escape through a leaky pipe. The film explains how natural gas is brought ashore at high pressure and how this pressure is gradually reduced by governor valves to the right level for domestic use. All this technical information is made attractive by Nicholas Spargo's charming animation.

Kitchen Think (colour, 10 mins) is a light-hearted cartoon that traces the development of the kitchen from a fire in a prehistoric cave to the streamlined split-level style of today. Frank Muir's script and narration, spiced with the inevitable puns, compensates for the rather disappointing animation.

BRITISH TRANSPORT

Transport and Travel Film Library, Melbury House, Melbury Terrace, London NW1 6LP.

Midland Country is another film in the series focusing on the British countryside, showing historic cities and tempting green landscapes not always associated with this part of Britain.

Other new additions include *Sea Road to Britain*, a film to lure Europeans to Britain for their holidays, and *Age of Invention*, which reflects the current interest in our industrial heritage.

Films to interest everyone

1933 steel tape recorder demonstrated in
Cough, and you'll deafen thousands

A still from the Mullard film
The Electrons Tale

A microcircuit going through the eye of a
needle in *Something big in Microcircuits*

...from the Mullard Film Library

The Mullard Film Library offers an exceptional range of 16mm sound films on subjects related to electronics.

The special feature of the films is the way they bring to life many of the things which affect our everyday life – like transistors, tv tubes, and computers.

Because of this, the films are of wide general interest and at the same time appeal to the technically minded audience. Films like 'Cough, and you'll deafen thousands', which was made to mark the 50th anniversary of the BBC and features some of the men who have helped pioneer broadcasting since it began in the 1920s.

Films are classified under four main groups – Manufacturing, History, Science, and General. Running times vary from 10 to 50 minutes, so the films can be used as a complete evening's viewing or as a novel and entertaining 'filler'.

A full list of over 50 titles, with synopses, is available now.

Write to the Mullard Film Library, Woodston House, Oundle Road, Peterborough PE2 9PZ, or telephone Peterborough 63122.

THE COMMUNICATORS

Marketing, informing, instructing

We can help you audio-visually
in so many different ways

Producing, writing, distributing

Contact the experts

British Transport Films

Melbury House Melbury Terrace London NW1 6LP 01-262 3232

FILM AUSTRALIA

Canberra House, Maltravers Street, London WC2R 3EH.

A dramatic radio warning heralded Cyclone Tracey and put the people of Darwin, Australia in fear of their lives. Two days later Film Australia had a documented account of the devastation: pitiful scenes of people rummaging to salvage fragments of their possessions or just staring in disbelief at the scattered piles of corrugated iron and bricks that had once been their home. *Cyclone Tracey* (colour, 9 mins) has deserved its widespread screenings in British cinemas.

Film Australia have also extended their series of wildlife films to include *Crocodile*, which was co-produced with the BBC.

MIDLAND BANK

Public Relations and Advertising Department, Midland Bank Limited, Head Office, Poultry, London EC2P 2BX.

The Event Horse (colour, 53 mins) is a marathon production by the Midland Bank based on a book by Sheila Wilcox. Most of the filming took place in the Cotswolds and was skilfully directed by Robin Crane. The film tells the story of the training of a young horse up to its first official outing at a novice horse trail. Eventing is a tough sport which is divided into three sections: dressage, cross country and show jumping. After a rigorous training programme, horse and rider are ready to enter the Bucklebury horse trials where they come in second, narrowly beaten by Princess Anne on her horse "Black Jack."

Still from one of three films made for the Electricity Council by the Larkins Studio, about the nature of electricity

NATIONAL CHILDREN'S HOMES

85 Highbury Park, London N5 1UD.

They Can Be Helped (colour, 21 mins) follows the progress of four multi-handicapped children over a period of six months. As the film was made primarily to assist the training of child care staff, emphasis was on practical ways of providing an interesting environment, especially for immobile children. It is particularly encouraging to see children responding to a programme of regular, planned stimulation.

NCB

NCB Films, National Coal Board, Hobart House, Grosvenor Place, London SW1X 7AE.

Two films recently added to the Coal Board's extensive library are both concerned with safety but completely different in approach. *Out of Control* by Terry Edwards makes the point that many of the accidents

NCB FILMS

N.C.B. Films
National Coal Board
Hobart House
Grosvenor Place
London SW1X 7AE
Tel. 01-235 2020

underground are the result of shifting heavy loads. Either loads are insecurely fastened or the routes have not been properly checked for possible obstructions beforehand. By simulating realistic accident situations the importance of checking every detail is clearly emphasised. To anyone not involved in coalmining it is very alarming to see the terrible dangers and hazards that the miners must face in the semi-darkness.

As a complete contrast, *Safety Senses* is a short animated film using vivid colours and loud blaring music to stress the importance of being constantly alert for danger signals. In a short one-and-a-half-minute sequence each sense—sight, hearing, taste, feel and smell—is taken in turn.

RSPB

Royal Society for the Protection of Birds, The Lodge, Sandy, Bedfordshire.

Look Again at Gulls provides twenty-five minutes of lively entertainment, exploring the complexities of community life in gull colonies. The birds go to great lengths to protect their territories and their successful survival is attributed largely to their ingenious adaptability. They can thrive just as well on litter and rubbish that humans leave around as on the more traditional fish and worms. We follow the maturing of gulls, in close-up, from their emergence as speckled chicks from their eggs, through adolescence when their voracious appetites keep their parents constantly searching for food, to the first attempts at flying and independence.

SHELL

Shell Film Library, 25 The Burroughs, Hendon, London NW4 4AT.

How an Aeroplane Flies, a new four-part

series of films from Shell, forms the introduction to the subject of heavier-than-air, low-speed flight. The parts are subtitled "Lift and Weight" ($16\frac{1}{2}$ mins), "Thrust and Drag" ($11\frac{1}{2}$ mins), "Balance and Stability" ($11\frac{1}{2}$ mins), and finally, "The Controls and Their Effect" (17 mins). Much technical information is crammed into each film but, by combining shots of a small Cessna plane in flight with animation and intriguing smoke tunnel demonstrations, the information is conveyed in a readily digestible form.

Acting in Turn (colour, 20 mins) is another superbly-made film from the Shell Film Unit, which traces development of the gear wheel from its earliest crude form over two thousand years ago to its widespread use today. The film contains some striking sequences of a car engine which will delight any motoring enthusiast.

Finally, a re-release of *The Rival World* (colour, 24 mins), originally made in 1955, shows the insect menace and how to combat it. Bert Haanstra directs this award-winning production brilliantly, and there are innumerable close-up shots of ravenous insects and the frightful destruction they cause. Not for the squeamish, the film spares us nothing of the misery and disfigurement of insect-borne disease. A new generation of audiences will undoubtedly find this documentary as gripping as their parents did.

UKAEA

United Kingdom Atomic Energy Authority, Film Library, 11 Charles II Street, London SW1.

Although *The Liquid Drop Model of Nuclear Fission* (colour, 13 mins) appears rather dreary and uninspiring, it is in fact a highly lucid account of a very complex process. The fission of nuclei is demonstrated

How to borrow films on atomic energy

GREAT BRITAIN

A film catalogue listing all
UKAEA films is available.
Please write to
The Film Library,
U.K. Atomic Energy Authority,
11 Charles II Street, London, SW1.

OVERSEAS

Many of our films are obtainable
through the British Information
Services or the British Council
in your country. In the countries
shown below, copies are
obtainable from:

U.S.A. Senior Representative of the UK
Atomic Energy Authority, British Embassy,
3100 Massachusetts Avenue,
Washington 8, DC

CANADA National Science Film Library,
Canadian Film Institute, 1762 Carling,
Ottawa 13, Ontario.

AUSTRIA International Atomic Energy
Agency, Vienna 1, Kaerntnerring.

FRANCE European Nuclear Energy Agency,
38 Boulevard Suchet, Paris 16.

NETHERLANDS Reactor Centrum
Nederland, s'Gravenhage.

UK Atomic Energy Authority

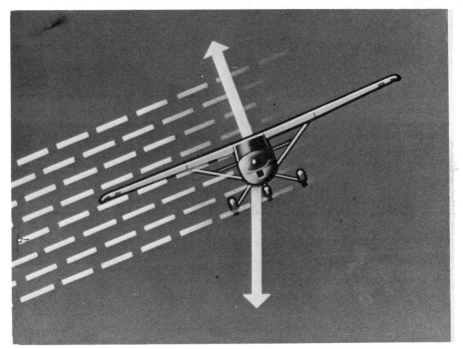

Still from the Shell film, HOW AN AEROPLANE FLIES. Shell celebrated its fortieth anniversary in films during 1975

in slow motion by applying an electric current to an oil droplet in a tank of water. The film attempts to answer two questions: Why do some heavy nuclei undergo fission and why do nuclei undergoing fission emit such enormous energy? In production is a film on the Boiling Water Tube Reactor System which is being built in Britain as part of the Third Nuclear Power Programme.

From ALICE IN LABEL LAND, produced by Richard Taylor Cartoon Films for the Ministry of Agriculture, Fisheries and Food

MINISTRY OF AGRICULTURE, FISHERIES AND FOOD

Central Film Library, Government Building, Bromyard Avenue, Acton, London W3 7JB.

Alice in Label Land (colour, 13 mins) is an animated production made by Richard Taylor Cartoon Films. Using the Lewis Carroll characters, the film succeeds in being amusing and informative at the same time. As much of the food we buy is pre-packed before sale, we are completely dependent on the label for information about the contents. Alice shrinks to a diminutive size after drinking from a bottle labelled only "drink me" and is bewildered by endless shelves of strangely marked tins in a supermarket. The Ministry, in the person of the White Knight, comes to her rescue with the "Labelling of Food Regulations 1970 Act" which went into force in January 1973.

British Sponsored Film Festival Awards: 1975

It was encouraging to see that the number of entries for the 1975, British Sponsored Film Festival at Brighton was well up on last year. With several film libraries closing and other companies cutting out so-called "extraneous" activities it is reassuring to know that so many organisations still value sponsored film as a means of providing information in an easily digestible and hopefully memorable way. A total of 211 entries were judged in 17 categories.

Category 1: Education to "A" level.
Gold Award:
SUPER NATURAL GAS
British Gas Corporation (Nicholas Cartoon Films)
Silver Award:
THE INDUSTRIAL REVOLUTION
Education Foundation for Visual Aids (Hugh Baddeley Productions)

Category 2: Education: University and Further Education
Gold Award:
INTRODUCTION TO ECOSYSTEMS
The Open University (BBC Open University Productions)

Category 3: Career Opportunities
Gold Award:
GIBSON'S GAME
Lloyds Bank Limited (Illustra Films Limited)
Silver Award:
DESIGN AND THE ENGINEER
Central Office of Information (Anvil Films and Recording Group Limited)

Category 4: Management Training and Related Subjects
Gold Award:
THE GOYA EFFECT
Rank Aldis Industrial Services (Rank Aldis Industrial Services)

Category 5: Sales Training and Related Subjects
Gold Award:
THE CHALLENGE OF OBJECTIONS
Rank Aldis Industrial Services (Rank Short Films Group)

Category 6: Staff and Operative Training and Related Subjects
Gold Award:
IN SAFE HANDS
Millbank Films Limited (Millbank Films Limited)
Silver Award:
MORE AWKWARD CUTSOMERS
Video Arts Limited (Video Arts Limited)

Category 7–Safety: Including Accident and Fire Prevention
Gold Award:
THE FIRE RAISERS
Ministry of Defence (Navy) (Films of Today)
Silver Award:
FLIGHT SAFETY—YOUR BUSINESS

Ministry of Defence (Navy) (World Wide Pictures Limited)
Bronze Award (1):
... AND THEN THERE WERE TWO
Imperial Chemicals Insurance Limited (Millbank Films Limited)
Bronze Award (2):
DRIVE CAREFULLY DARLING
Central Office of Information (Graphic Films Limited)

Category 8: Public Welfare and Social Questions, Including Health and Rehabilitation
Gold Award:
THEY CAN BE HELPED
The National Children's Home (Hugh Baddeley Productions)
Silver Award:
THE LOSERS
COI for the Home Office (Illustra Films Limited)

Category 9: Films Made by Non-Profit or Charitable Organisations to Raise Funds for or Promote Interest in their Field
Gold Award
LOOK AGAIN AT GULLS
The Royal Society for the Protection of Birds (RSPB Film Unit)
Silver Award:
RIDING TOWARDS FREEDOM
Riding for the Disabled Association (Wessex Film & Video Productions)

Category 10—Medical: For the Medical Profession
Gold Award:
PREVENTIVE DENTISTRY
Ministry of Defence (Navy) (Antony Barrier Productions Limited)
Silver Award:
THE HIDDEN HYPERTENSIVES
CIBA Laboratories Limited (Videological Productions Limited)

Category 11: Travel and Tourism, Recration and Sport
Gold Award:
EVENT HORSE
Midland Bank Limited (Robin Crane Films)
Silver Award:
THE QUIET LAND
Northern Ireland Tourist Board (Ronald H. Riley & Associates Limited)

Category 12: Public Relations and Prestige
Gold Award:

FACETS OF GLASS
Pilkington Brothers Limited (Charles Barker Films Limited)
Silver Award:
COLOUR
Imperial Chemical Industries Limited (Millbank Films Limited)
Bronze Award:
FLIGHT FOR SURVIVAL
The Royal Society for the Protection of Birds (RSPB Film Unit)

Category 13: Films about Products, Materials or Projects, Excluding Sales Films
Gold Award:
LOCATION NORTH SEA
The British Petroleum Company Limited (Pelican Films)
Silver Award:
BREAD—SOMETHING OF A MIRACLE
The Flour Advisory Bureau (Anthony Gilkison Associates Limited)
Bronze Award:
CONQUEST OF LIGHT
Waterford Glass Limited (Louis Marcus Films Limited)
Certificate:
VERSATILITY IN GLASS
Pilkington Brothers Limited (World Wide Pictures Limited)
Prix d'Honneur:
PROJECT WATERHAIL (South Africa)
Sentraoes (Co-operative) Limited (Insight Films (Pty) Limited)

Category 14: Films to Sell Products
Gold Award:
THE ANSWER IS ESCORT
The Ford Motor Company (Illustra Films Limited)
Silver Award:
VARIATIONS ON A THEME
Philips Electrical Limited (Millbank Films Limited)
Bronze Award:
CYANAMID AVENGE
Cyanamid Corporation of America (Cygnet Films Limited)
Certificate:
GIN IS GILBEYS
Gilbeys Limited (Films of Today)

Category 15: Films to Sell Services
Gold Award:
THE STRONGEST LINK
The Building Societies Association (Chatsworth Film Productions Limited)

Silver Award:
RAILFREIGHT, ECONOMY OF SCALE
British Railways Board (British Transport Films)

Category 16: Viedeo Tape: Training (as 4, 5 and 6)
Gold Award (1):
INFLATION ACCOUNTING
The Institute of Chartered Accountants in England and Wales)

Gold Award (2):
SELLING ON THE TELEPHONE
Rank Aldis Industrial Services (Rank Short Films Group)

Category 17: Video Tape: Sales Promotion (as 14 and 15)
Gold Award:
BURKE ON PAINT
ICI Paints Division (World Wide Pictures Limited)

Category 18: Video Tape: Medical (as 10)
Gold Award:

PSYCHOLOGICAL AND CLINICAL ASPECTS QF CARDIAC AUSCULTATION
Medi-Cine Limited & ICI Pharmaceuticals Division (Medi-Cine Limited)
Financial Times Export Award:
AGE OF INVENTION
British Tourist Authority/British Railways Board (British Transport Films)

The Times Newcomers Award:
KNOCKDOWN AND KILL
J. L. MacEwen (C2M Scientific Productions)

The Clifford Wheeler Memorial Award:
HISTORY OF THE MOTOR CAR PART II—THE VETERANS
The British Petroleum Company Limited.

Specially Commended:
FARMING WITH WILDLIFE
Royal Society for the Protection of Birds.

(*Continued from page 368*)
FESTIVAL OF THEATRE. Dir: Fernando Gómez. Phot (colour): George Balevich. Edit: Carlos Molina, Hector Aparicio. For Bolivar Films.
COMPETENCIA DE LANCHAS. Dir: Javier Blanco. Phot (colour): Ildefonso Rodriguez. Edit: Frank Rojas. For Bolivar Films.
PRESIDENTS OF VENEZUELA. Dir: Oziel Rodriguez. Phot (colour): Oswaldo Girardi. Edit: F. Rojas. For Bolivar Films.
HOMES FOR INFANTILES. Dir: Manuel de Pedro. Phot (colour): G. Balevich. Edit: Carlos Molina. For Bolivar Films.
PANTEON NACIONAL. Dir: Alfred Brandler. Phot (colour): Luis Jaco, Martin Alvarez. Edit: C. Molina. For Bolivar Films.
BATTLE OF AYACHUCHO. Dir; Eduardo Camacho. Phot (colour): Balevich. Edit: Rojas. For Bolivar Films.
SIDERURGICA DEL ORINOCO. Dir: Eduardo Camacho. Phot (colour): O. Girardi. Edit: Rojas. For Bolivar Films.
RECOUNT OF DR. RAFAEL CALDERA'S GOVERNMENT. Dir: Eduardo Camacho. Edit: Rojas. For Bolivar Films. In colour.
PIÑERUA ORDAZ. Script and dir: Carlos Molina. For Bolivar Films. In colour.
TOWN DIEGO DE LOSADA. Dir: Oziel Rodrigquez.

Phot (colour): O. Girardi. Edit: Hector Aparicio. For Bolivar Films.
LA RECLUTA (The Recruiting). Dir: De Pedro. Phot (colour): Martin Alvarez. Edit: C. Molina. For Bolivar Films.
SOTO MUSEUM-GUGGENHEIM-NEW YORK. Dir: Eduardo Camacho. Phot (colour): Girardi. Edit: F. Rojas. For Bolivar Films.
FERIA DEL SOL-MERIDA. Dir: Eduardo Camacho. Phot (colour): Girardi, Emilio Fernandez. Edit: H. Aparicio. For Bolivar Films.
VISIT OF THE PRESIDENT TO ALGIERS. Dir: Eduardo Camacho. Phot (colour): E. Fernandez. Edit: F. Rojas. For Bolivar Films.
VISIT OF THE PRESIDENT OF MEXICO TO VENEZUELA. Dir: Eduardo Camacho. Phot: O. Girardi, E. Fernandez. Edit: Rojas. For Bolivar Films.
ASESINATO EN EL BLOQUE UNO (Assassination in Blockhouse One). Story, script, dir and edit: Alfredo Lugo. Phot: Gustavo Chami. Music: Vivaldi. Players: Azdrubal Melendez, Luisa Motta, Jacobo Borges. For Pepeca & Lugo. Fiction. 40 mins.
ANDRES ELOY BLANCO. Script: Clemente de la Cerda, S. M. Sozio. Dir: Silvia Manrique Sozio. Phot (colour): José Jimenez. For Neo Cine. Documentary.

(*Continued on page 605*)

Film Collecting

by Anthony Slide

The year 1975, as everyone by now must be aware, saw the hundredth anniversary of the birth of David Wark Griffith. In this introduction I would like, therefore, to present a quick coverage of what Griffith productions are available for purchase in the U.S., and from where.

Blackhawk Films offer the widest selection of Griffith works on Standard and Super 8mm, including eight of the director's feature-length productions: *Judith of Bethulia* (also available on 16mm), *The Mother and the Law* (also 16mm), *Intolerance* (also 16mm), *Hearts of the World* (also 16mm), *Broken Blossoms, Way Down East, Orphans of the Storm* and *America*. For some time, Blackhawk has been selling—on all gauges—prints of a number of Griffith Biographs, including his first film as a director, *The Adventures of Dollie* (1908). Now the company is presenting some of the lesser-known Biographs, which are deserving of greater attention. Blackhawk has access to the original negatives of the Biograph productions at the Museum of Modern Art, and from these negatives has struck fine grain masters, which are the pre-print materials from which come their Standard 8mm, Super 8mm and 16mm prints. Among the new Biograph titles currently available, I would recommend four in particular, *In the Border States* (1910), *The Girl and Her Trust* (1912), *The Mothering Heart* (1913) and *The House of Darkness* (1913). The print quality of these is unbelievable. One wishes that all films available to collectors could be as close to the original negatives since it is such prints which help to dispel the myth that all silent films were badly photographed. Projected at the correct speed—sixteen to eighteen frames per second—these Blackhawk items are a joy to behold.

Glenn Photo Supply also offers a number of Griffith Biographs on 8mm and 16mm, some of which are not available elsewhere. This company also offers "colour" footage from two of Griffith's finest productions, *Intolerance* (1916) and *Hearts of the World* (1918). As most people are aware, silent films were never simply released in the form of black-and-white prints, but were tinted in various colours. Glenn Photo has taken original nitrate prints of these two features, and struck colour negatives on four reels of *Intolerance* and one reel of *Hearts of the World*. Also available exclusively from Glenn Photo—on 8mm and 16mm—are *True Heart Susie, The Idol Dancer, Way Down East* and *Isn't Life Wonderful*.

A little-known, but interesting Griffith feature, *The Greatest Question*, in many scenes very reminiscent of *True Heart Susie*, is available on Standard 8mm only from Milestone.

The Essex Film Club has available three Griffith features on 8mm and 16mm—*Intolerance, Broken Blossoms* and *Hearts of the World*—a number of Biograph shorts, the best of which is *The Painted Lady* (1912) with Blanche Sweet, and, most excitingly, a filmed interview between Griffith and Walter Huston, intended as a prologue to the sound reissue of *The Birth of a Nation*. Essex also has two Griffith-supervised productions for

sale: *A Child of the Paris Streets* and *Hoodoo Ann* (also available from Blackhawk).

There are two magazines devoted entirely to the interests of film collectors. The bible is Sam Rubin's "Classic Film Collector" (734 Philadelphia Street, Indiana, Pa. 15701), a quarterly newspaper containing articles, news items and general information on all the latest film releases, both in the U.S. and Great Britain. It even features a column devoted to 9.5mm. "The Film Collector's Registry" (PO Box 66393, Houston, Texas 77006), edited by Earl Blair, also contains general information on new film releases for collectors. It is particularly valuable to collectors of B-features, especially westerns.

BRITAIN

Breakspear Films, 66 Derby Street, Leek, Staffs, ST13 5AJ.

John Cunningham's company has been fairly inactive of late, which is a pity, because there was no other concern offering the same excellent print quality. However, promised for release during 1976 are: a compilation of early films produced by Edison, Hepworth and Williamson between 1898 and 1902; a delightful 1919 feature, *The Best Man*, with Lois Wilson and J. Warren Kerrigan; *Back to God's Country* (1919), with Nell Shipman. Standard 8mm only.

Robert Kingston (Films) Ltd., 645/7 Uxbridge Road, Hayes End, Middlesex.

Robert Kingston's non-theatrical rights in the RK library of 700-odd features and shorts enables him to offer titles for purchase to collectors on 16mm. Although Kingston seems unwilling to sell any complete features outright, he does have available—at reasonable prices—a number of the *Flicker Flashback* series; extracts from Fred Astaire and Ginger Rogers musicals; and a one-reel *King Kong* condensation.

Novascope Ltd., 14 Gowan Avenue, London SW6 6RF.

Novascope, run by two enthusiasts, Paul van Someren and Patrick Moules, continues to be the only company offering new releases on 9.5mm. The number of films available is small, but there are many interesting titles, including: *Belles of Liberty*, with Monty Banks; a 1926 *British Screen News*; Lloyd Hamilton in *Moonshine*; *Felix in Hollywood*.

Perry's Movies, 129 Kingston Road, London SW19.

Keith Perry continues to offer the cheapest 8mm releases. His catalogue and shop are crowded with films—Perry also acts as British agent for Thunderbird—film books, stills and posters. He recently entered the Super 8mm sound field with releases of *Dick Turpin* (1953), with Victor McLaglen, and Carol Reed's *The Stars Look Down* (1939), with Michael Redgrave and Margaret Lockwood.

Walton Films, 87 Richford Street, London W6 7HN.

Walton is without a doubt Britain's leading home movie distributor, with a vast array of features and shorts available on both Standard and Super 8mm, silent and sound. Shorts include Tom and Jerry cartoons, Laurel and Hardy comedies and several Chaplin two-reelers. Recent feature releases include: *Witchfinder General*. (U.S.: *The*

Conqueror Worm), with Vincent Price; *The Curse of the Crimson Altar*, with Boris Karloff; *Doctor in the House*, with Dirk Bogarde and Kenneth More; *Hannie Caulder*, with Raquel Welch.

U.S.A.

Blackhawk Films, 1235 West 5th Street, Davenport, Iowa 52808.

As always, the most exciting films for collectors come from Blackhawk. David Shepard is quite definitely making his presence felt here. In the shorts field, Blackhawk is releasing a number of Ub Iwerk cartoons, including the "Flip the Frog" and "Willie Whopper" series. Also, the company has acquired prime materials, in many cases the original negatives, on the twelve Chaplin Mutuals, which Blackhawk will issue with the original titles and musical scores taken from the Van Buren reissues. Feature releases include: three

Robert Flaherty productions, *Louisiana Story*, *Man of Aran* and *Nanook of the North*; *As You Like It*, with Laurence Olivier and Elizabeth Bergner: Lon Chaney's *Oliver Twist*; three Russian classics, *Bezhin Meadow*, *Earth* and *The End of St. Petersburg*, with prints struck from pre-print material imported from the Soviet Union; and a series of "B" action pictures, including nine starring Frankie Darro.

Cambridge Film Institute and Silent Film Museum, RFD1, Cambridge, Maine 04923.

William Donnachie was a familiar name to film collectors a few years ago. Now his daughter, Julie Lombard, has entered the film collecting field with a number of titles, previously available from her father, plus some new releases. Recommended: Tay Garnett's *The Spieler*, with Renée Adorée; *The Unknown Soldier*; with Charles Emmett

Mack and Henry B. Walthall; Douglas Fairbanks' *Flirting with Fate*; Betty Compson in *The Belle of Broadway*.

Cinema Eight, Middlesex Avenue, Chester, Conn. 06412.

Cinema Eight is an unusual company, offering films from most other distributors, generally at lower prices than the original companies themselves. The 1975 catalogue lists over 1,000 films available on 8mm and 16mm, everything from Dovzhenko's *Arsenal* to Douglas Fairbanks' *Wild and Woolly*. The catalogue is intelligently laid out, with films listed under features, documentaries, serials, subjects, personalities and cartoon characters. Cinema Eight also offers a wide selection of film books and equipment, plus one or two exclusive releases, the most important of which is Dušan Vukotić's animated classic, *Piccolo*.

Columbia Pictures, 8mm Division, 711 Fifth Avenue, New York, NY 10022.

Columbia has gone into the Super 8mm Sound business in a big way, with the release of dozens of their features in two-reel condensations. Print and sound quality is excellent, as it should be, and the features have been intelligently edited. Titles available include: Marlon Brando in *On the Waterfront*; Howard Hawks's *Only Angels Have Wings*; *The Awful Truth*, with Irene Dunne and Cary Grant; *Platinum Blonde*, with Jean Harlow; *Twentieth Century*, with John Barrymore and Carole Lombard.

Edward Finney, 1578 Queens Road, Hollywood, Calif. 90069.

Ed Finney's 8mm and 16mm distribution business has been around for some time now, and it has been quite some time since he had a new release, although there is talk of his issuing Yale University's *Chronicles of America* series in time for the American Bicentennial celebrations. Recommended is his reel of Claire Windsor home movies, featuring a host of glamorous Twenties stars.

Essex Film Club, 263 Harrison Street, Nutley, New Jersey 07110.

Bob Lee's Essex Film Club, combining with Griggs Moviedrome, has been around since 1939, and is one of the most reliable distributors in the U.S., offering films on Standard and Super 8mm and 16mm. Print quality is always good, and many films offered by other dealers have been duped from Lee's library. Recommended: William S. Hart's *Tumbleweeds*; Maurice Tourneur's *The Wishing Ring* and *A Girl's Folly*; Leni Riefenstahl's *Tag der Freiheit*; interview between D. W. Griffith and Walter Huston; Sidney Olcott's *Timothy's Quest* (1922).

Glenn Photo Supply, 4931 Gloria Avenue, Encino, Calif. 91436.

One can always expect something interesting from Murray Glass's Glenn Photo Supply. Over a period of years, Glass has built up an exciting library of films for sale on 8mm and 16mm, and also available for rental from his Em Gee Film Library. Recent releases: Douglas Fairbanks' *A Modern Musketeer*; John Grierson's *Granton Trawler*; *Isn't Life Wonderful* and *The Idol Dancer*, both directed by D. W. Griffith; G. W. Pabst's *The Joyless Street*, with Greta Garbo; Eisenstein's *Ten Days That Shook the World*.

Hart Industries, PO Box 452, Birmingham, Michigan 48012.

A wide selection of Standard and Super 8mm releases.

Independent Film Associates, 1425 South Main, Tulsa, Oklahoma 74119.

A new company, formed by United Films, to offer for sale to collectors on 16mm a number of films currently available for rental from the parent company. This is possibly the first time that copyrighted films have been legally made available to collectors on 16mm—and at most reasonable prices. Apart from twelve Universal *Sherlock Holmes* features, starring Basil Rathbone and Nigel Bruce, IFA offers: *Long Day's Journey into Night* with Katharine Hepburn and Ralph Richardson; George Pal's *Destination Moon*; Raoul Walsh's *The Naked and the Dead*; Robert Altman's *That Cold Day in the Park*; Mark Robson's *The Champion*.

Milestone Movies Corporation, 212 Shelton Road, Monroe, Conn. 06468.

Hartney Arthur's Milestone Movies continues to release more and more desirable items to collectors, but on Standard 8mm only. Print quality has improved considerably, and it is always a pleasure to leaf through Milestone's intelligently and attractively laid out catalogue. Recent releases: D. W. Griffith's *The Greatest Question* (1919); Rin-Tin-Tin in *Tracked by the Police* (1927); G. W. Pabst's *Secrets of a Soul* (1926); *Are Parents People?* (1925), with Betty Bronson and Florence Vidor. Milestone is eager to contact buyers in Britain.

Mizzell Films, 784 Locust Street, Pasadena, Calif. 91101.

A small concern, offering a number of titles in 16mm sound, including: *My Man Godfrey* (the best quality print around), with Carole Lombard; *Jungle Jitters*, a 1938 Merrie Melodies Cartoon; *Song of Texas* (1943), with Roy Rogers and the Sons of the Pioneers; *Daffy and the Dinosaur*, a 1939 Merrie Melodies cartoon.

National Cinema Service, 333 West 57th Street, New York, NY 10018.

National Cinema Service has been in business since 1936, selling new and used 16mm movies throughout the world. Its twice-monthly lists feature one-of-a-kind items, usually "B" westerns and "B" British films from the Forties and Fifties, and a host of special releases, including many early Hitchcock productions: *Secret Agent, The Thirty-Nine Steps, Young and Innocent* and *The Man Who Knew Too Much.*

Niles Film Products Inc., 1141 Mishawaka Avenue, South Bend, Indiana 46615.

Niles's regularly-issued newspaper-style catalogues offer a wide range of films on all gauges, released by Niles, Castle and Walt Disney, plus a selection of used prints. The highlight of Niles releases is the 1926 M-G-M studio tour, a three-reel short copied from an original 35mm nitrate print. Recent releases: *A Free People* (1971); *Off the Horses*, with Bert Lahr; Alfred Hitchcock's *The Lodger.*

Northwest Custom Movies, 4600 Union Bay Place NE, Seattle, Washington 98105.

A wide choice of Standard and Super 8mm silent and sound releases.

Nostalgia Films, PO Box 666, Gracie Station, New York, NY 10028.

A fairly new company, offering a multitude of features and shorts on 16mm only. Releases include: William Wellman's *A Star Is Born*, with Janet Gaynor; *The Beachcomber*, with Charles Laughton; Howard Hawks's *His Girl Friday*, with Cary Grant and Rosalind Russell; Fay Wray and Joel McCrea in *The Most Dangerous Game.*

Select Film Library Inc., 115 West 31st Street, New York, NY 10001.

Select Film Library is a seemingly, and hopefully, permanent fixture within Willoughby-Peerless's world-renowned photographic store, but as owner Milton Menell points out to me, it is an entirely independent operation. Apart from operating a vast rental library, Select has many films available for sale. Recent Super 8mm sound releases include: *Visit to a Small Planet* (1960), *Sad Sack* (1957) and *Don't Give Up the Ship* (1959), all with Jerry Lewis; seven Elvis Presley features; *All in a Night's Work* (1961) with Dean Martin and Shirley

MacLaine; *Topper Returns* (1941), with Roland Young and Joan Blondell; *Jungle Book* (1942), with Sabu.

Thunderbird Films, PO Box 65157, Los Angeles, Calif. 90065.

Tom Dunnahoo recently issued a twenty-page catalogue overflowing with desirable films on Standard and Super 8mm and 16mm. Features, shorts and trailers are all there, and print quality is generally excellent. Recommended: Frank Capra's *Meet John Doe*, with Gary Cooper; Leslie Howard in *The Scarlet Pimpernel*; *Bitter Sweet*, with Anna Neagle; Marcel Carné's *Daybreak*; Raoul Walsh's *Dark Command*, with John Wayne; Lewis Milestone's *Of Mice and Men*.

CANADA

Cine Books, 692a Yonge Street, Toronto, Ontario.

Cine Books offers only one film to collectors in both the U.S. and Canada, but it is a rare one: highlights from *King Kong*, available in Standard and Super 8mm silent and 16mm sound version. For Canadian readers, Cine Books always has in stock a large selection of Standard and Super 8mm films.

CABARET

Winner of 8 Academy Awards

BEST ACTRESS:
Liza Minnelli.
BEST SUPPORTING ACTOR:
Joel Grey.
BEST DIRECTOR:
Bob Fosse.
BEST ART DIRECTION
BEST CINEMATOGRAPHY
BEST FILM EDITING
BEST MUSIC SCORING
BEST SOUND

Allied Artists and ABC Pictures Corp. present An ABC Pictures Corp. Production Liza Minnelli Michael York
Helmut Griem in A Feuer & Martin Production Cabaret with Marisa Berenson Fritz Wepper and Joel Grey as "Emcee"
Based on the Musical Play "Cabaret" Book by Joe Masteroff Music by John Kander Lyrics by Fred Ebb Based on the Play by John Van Druten and Stories by Christopher Isherwood
Produced on the New York Stage by Harold Prince Dances and Musical Numbers Staged by Bob Fosse Screenplay by Jay Allen Music by John Kander
Lyrics by Fred Ebb Produced by Cy Feuer Directed by Bob Fosse Technicolor® Distributed by Allied Artists

Non-Theatrical (U.S.A.)

by Stuart Rosenthal

This year has seen a sizeable expansion of the 16mm, non-theatrical market in the United States. A number of new companies added their names to the list of those in the business of distributing feature films to universities, film societies and other institutions while companies already in business added new titles to their catalogues. Minimum rental rates for recent commercial titles reached new peaks and the prices on some classic films actually declined. Many films which were not previously available in any format found first release in 16mm.

The Non-Theatrical Film Distributors Association, the 16mm trade organisation, welcomed several new members to its roster and mounted a campaign against illegal showings and duplicating of copyrighted motion pictures. In a letter to college presidents, the NFDA cited copyright infringement, film piracy and lack of administrative control over film exhibitions on campuses as major problems. The letter was part of an informational campaign begun by the group last year to make 16mm movie users aware of the spectrum of the bootleg print and illegal videotaping problems currently plaguing the industry. Anyone with a question regarding the legality of an institutional videotaping programme or the legitimacy of any source of rental films is invited to contact the NFDA at 40 West 57th Street, New York 10019. Tel. (212) 977-9700.

AUDIO BRANDON FILMS

34 MacQuesten Parkway South, Mount Vernon, New York 10550. (914) 664-5051. Branches in Brookfield, Ill., Dallas, Los Angeles, and Oakland, California.

Audio Brandon's International collection is the largest and most diverse offering of foreign films in the United States. In addition, Audio Brandon's catalogues contain nearly every American title handled by the various independent libraries. Rental rates depend upon whether or not admission is charged and upon audience size. A discount of $2.50 per film applies to orders of six or more titles. Classroom rates are available, upon application, when enrollment is less than 75 students.

The Adventures of Robinson Crusoe (Dir: Luis Buñuel). After many years out of circulation, Buñuel's version of the Defoe novel is again available. *The Adventures of Robinson Crusoe* follows the classic format of the adventure film, but Buñuel's distinctive touch shines through every now and then. Even on his island, for example, Crusoe's work ethic is strong. After growing his own grain and building baking facilities the shipwrecked man reports, with obvious satisfaction, "I could at last say that I worked for my bread."

The Man with the Balloons (Dir: Marco Ferreri). Ferreri's allegory features Marcello Mastroianni as a candy manufacturer who becomes obsessed with determining the exact maximum capacity of balloons. One can pinpoint this measurement, of course, only after

the balloon has burst—a paradox which plays havoc with the industrialist's precisely planned life, eventually destroying it. The collaboration between Ferreri (best known in the U.S. for *La grande bouffe*) and Mastroianni produces the wry quality that makes the film so successful.

New Japanese Films. Audio Brandon has significantly expanded its selection of important Japanese features. Among the new titles are Kurosawa's first film (*Sanshiro sugata*), Kobayashi's epic "Human Condition Trilogy," Shinoda's *Double Suicide*, and the last two instalments of Inagaki's *Samurai*. There are six Ozu films in this group: *Passing Fancy* (1933), *The Only Son* (1936), *Brothers and Sisters of the Toda Family* (1941), *There Was a Father* (1942), *Early Summer* (1951), and *Twilight in Tokyo* (1957).

Other new releases from Audio Brandon include: *Ossessione* (Visconti), *Love* (Károly Makk), *E' primavera* (Renato Castellani), *Quick Billy* (Bruce Baillie), *Ostia* (Sergio Citti).

CINEMA 5: 16mm

595 Madison Avenue, New York 10022, (212) 421-5555.

Besides handling the releases of Cinema 5, Cinema 5: 16mm has acquired several new titles from other companies. Among these are Lina Wertmüller's *Love and Anarchy* and Resnais's *Stavisky*. Rental rates are based upon a minimum guarantee vs. a percentage of any admission charge collected. Classroom rates are available on some films.

Scenes from a Marriage (Dir: Ingmar Bergman). This is among the most intimate and intense of Bergman's films. Its tone progresses from barely suppressed antagonism as a seemingly ideal marriage begins to fray, to a paralysing sense of physical pain when the break suddenly occurs. The subsequent process of dissolving, changing and rebuilding the relationship is agonising and fraught with frustration. Running nearly three hours, the film was distilled into its present form by Bergman from a six-episode series he made for Swedish television. This compression, superimposed upon Bergman's frighteningly perceptive screenplay and *tour-de-force* performances by Liv Ullmann and Erland Josephson, makes *Scenes from a Marriage* all the more explosive and emotionally exhausting.

Distant Thunder (Dir: Satyajit Ray). "Distant Thunder" is the sound of planes flying overhead on their way into battle during the Second World War. Although the war itself takes place far from the Bengali villagers in the film, the effects of the conflict strike disastrously close to home. Ray's depiction of the war-induced famine of the early Forties movingly dwells upon the crisis' effect at the most basic level of human behaviour. Still, in the midst of violence and moral deterioration, Ray's essential optimism is embodied in the condescending Brahmin who, faced with adversity, discovers his own dependence upon and obligation to others.

Other Cinema 5: 16mm titles: *Monty Python and the Holy Grail*, *The Glass Menagerie*, *WR: Mysteries of the Organism* (Dušan Makavejev), *The Sorrow and the Pity* (Marcel Ophuls), *Putney Swope*, *Z* and *State of Siege* (both by Costa-Gavras), *The Garden of the Finzi Continis* (Vittorio De Sica), *Trash* (Morrissey-Warhol), *Gimme Shelter*, *The Firemen's Ball* (Miloš Forman), *The Hellstrom Chronicle*, *Visions of Eight*, *Marjoe*, *Ramparts of Clay*.

CLASSIC FILM MUSEUM

4 Union Square, Dover-Foxcroft, Maine 04426.

Although Classic Film Museum has a general catalogue of more recent titles, its booklet "50 Years of Forgotten Classics" is of special interest, including reproductions of some of the original advertising (both public and trade) for many of the films listed. Rental rates are for one showing and are flat rates. Certain institutions are eligible, upon application, for special rental terms.

The Front Page (1931: dir: Lewis Milestone). Unlike *His Girl Friday* (which Classic Film Museum also offers) or the recent Billy Wilder remake, Milestone's film centres on the movements of the reporters who populate the press-room in the criminal courts building. The sardonic newsmen are much more interestingly drawn than in any other version of the Hecht-MacArthur play. Consequently, the conflict between the abrasive, conniving editor, Walter Burns, and his star hireling, Hildy Johnson, loses its prominence. This shift of emphasis is unfortunate since Adolphe Menjou is the perfect incarnation of the diabolical Burns.

CLEM WILLIAMS FILMS

2240 Noblestown Road, Pittsburgh, Pa. 15205. (412) 921-5810. Branches in Chicago, Atlanta and Houston.

Clem Williams Films handle releases from Universal, Columbia, Warner Brothers and other theatrical distributors. Their prices are moderate and service is good. Rental rates for a day's use are flat rates (except on Universal titles which require a guarantee against 50% of any admission collected).

The Producers and **The Twelve Chairs** (Dir: Mel Brooks). *The Producers* was already a cult film of sorts when *Blazing Saddles* touched off a flurry of interest in Mel Brooks's earlier films. Lunacy is rampant from the very start of *The Producers*, but reaches a peak in "Springtime for Hitler," a comically tasteless play staged by the fly-by-night impresarios. By comparison, *The Twelve Chairs* is restrained, relying upon the character humour furnished by Mel Brooks and Ron Moody.

Other new Clem Williams releases include: *The Black Windmill* (Don Siegel), *Come Back Charleston Blue*, *Frenzy* (Alfred Hitchcock), *In Search of Ancient Astronauts*, *Oklahoma Crude* (Stanley Kramer), *Summer of '42, The Valachi Papers.*

CONTEMPORARY FILMS/McGRAW HILL

Princeton Road, Hightstown, NJ 08520. (609) 448-1700. Offices in Evanston, Ill. and San Francisco.

The Contemporary library is rich in its sampling of French films from the Thirties and Forties. Their collection of foreign features is absolutely superb. In addition, they have McGraw-Hill's extensive catalogue of short films available for rental or sale (see Films for Young People section). Discounts ranging from 10-20% apply on orders of 3 or more films: (3-5 films—10%, 6-9 films—15%, 10 or more films—20%). When admission is taken, the catalogue rate is a minimum guarantee against a percentage of the gross receipts.

The Last Millionaire (1934, Dir: René Clair). *The Last Millionaire* is Clair's satiric assault on totalitarianism, which he characterises as government by whim. To save itself from bankruptcy, the Monte Carlo-like kingdom of Casinario accepts the ab-

Audio Brandon Films

Outstanding new releases, available for non-theatrical rental in 16mm in the United States only. Write for a free copy of Volume 2 of our International Cinema Catalog.

Audio Brandon Films, Inc., Dept. IFG-75, 34 MacQuesten Pkwy. So., Mt. Vernon, N.Y. 10550

solute rule of its richest citizen. Unfortunately, he begins his reign while in the throes of insanity and issues such arbitrary edicts as the one calling for all men to wear bermuda shorts. But when his temporary madness abates, he becomes all the more dangerous. Clair makes his social statement forthrightly, but without sacrificing any of his renowned wit or grace.

Other Contempoary releases by René Clair include: *Italian Straw Hat, Two Timid People, A nous la liberté, Beauty and the Devil, Beauties of the Night, Sous les toits de Paris* and *Le million.*

Master of the House (Dir: Carl Dreyer). *Master of the House* operates on an everyday level far removed from the spirituality of some of Dreyer's later work. It deals sympathetically with a middle-class family ruled by a domineering husband/father. This domestic tyrant is tamed by two old women who recognise the needs and the love that lie beneath his arrogance. Their conspiracy to reform "the master of the house" unfolds with a warm humour that leads naturally to a tender moment of reconciliation.

Elena et les hommes (Dir: Jean Renoir, with Ingrid Bergman). The charm of *Elena et les hommes* is almost entirely visual. Renoir designed this period comedy to appeal primarily to the eye, filling it with vivid colours, boisterous crowds, unceasing movement and people who are caricatures of their vices and virtues. The farce is all the more enthralling for taking place in a beautiful world that could never really have existed.

Other Renoir films distributed by Contemporary: *Boudu Saved from Drowning, Madame Bovary, Toni, A Day in the Country, The Lower Depths, La Marseillaise, Picnic on the Grass, The Elusive Corporal.*

Contemporary has added two new foreign titles to its collection: Roberto Rossellini's *Europa '51* and an Israeli film, *Marriage, Jewish Style.*

FILM IMAGES/ RADIM FILMS

17 West 60th Street, New York, NY 10023. (212) 279-6653. Branches in Oak Park, Illinois and San Francisco.

The Film Images collection includes unusual features of all descriptions and education films. Their film history section is particularly rich in its selections from the very early international cinema. Many prints are available for lease or sale. Rental rates vary according to the nature of the sponsoring organisation.

Alternate Cinema. *Alternate Cinema* is a programme of short films, many of them student efforts, all made by independent filmmakers. The best of the group is a crazy comedy called *Manhattan Melody*, written and directed by Ken Wiederhorn. It deals with a teenage bicycle thief who falls for a runaway high school baton twirler, only to have her reclaimed by her drum major. Besides parodying the conventions of the musical success story, the film is loaded with absurd sight gags. Another film of particular interest is *It's Not Just You, Murray*, a student film by Martin Scorsese. *A Night at the Sunset* by Paul Newell is a nostalgic treatment of the drive-in movie, and *Hot Dogs for Gauguin* by Martin Brest is the saga of a mad photographer who plans to blow up the Statue of Liberty in order to get a sensational news photo. The package is rounded out by *Balloon* by Sebastian Schroeder and *6344* by Joseph Pipher. None of these movies are meant to be taken very seriously, so *Alternate*

PARAMOUNT & BOGDONOVICH & BERG-
MAN & BUNUEL & METRO-GOLDWYN-
MAYER & MELVILLE & NICHOLS &
WELLES & FORD & HAWKS & WIDER-
BERG & ABC PICTURES & SKOLIMOWSKI
& HITCHCOCK & ALDRICH & LEONE &
RKO RADIO & BROOKS & BROWN &
BROWNING & ＿＿＿ & DE MILLE &
HUSTON & LA＿＿＿EY & SIEGEL &
TWENTIETH C＿＿＿Y-FOX & MAN-
KIEWICZ & MINNELLI & WALT DISNEY &
LEWIS & TASHLIN & RENOIR & FELLINI
& VON STROHEIM & ANTONIONI &
VISCONTI & CAYATTE & PECKINPAH &
ALLEN & KADAR & MAMOULIAN &
INGRAM & PARKS & DEMY & LEAN

From Films Inc., Att. Doug Lemza, 1144 Wilmette Ave. • Wilmette, Ill. 60091

528

Cinema is well suited for general audiences looking for a good time.

Other Film Images releases include: *Native Land* (Hurwitz), *Demons* (Toshio Matsumoto), *Bleak Moments*, *Loving Moments* (Mike Leigh), *The Emerging Woman* (The Women's Film Project), *The Hidden Fortress* (Akira Kurosawa), *Shakespeare Wallah* (James Ivory), *Zagreb Festival* (a collection of films from the world's most famous animation studios), *Behind the Wall* (Krzysztof Zanussi), *Bride of the Andes* (Susumu Hani).

FILMS INC.

1144 Wilmette Ave., Wilmette, Ill. 60091. (312) 256-4730. Branches in Atlanta, Boston, Dallas, Hollywood, New York City, Salt Lake City, San Diego, Hayard, Calif. and Skokie, Ill.

Films Inc. is the 16mm, non-theatrical outlet for the releases of Paramount (post-1948 only), M-G-M and 20th Century-Fox, as well as for the productions of ABC pictures, and occasionally an important film from various, small, independent distributors. The library is particularly valuable for the Fox and Metro output of the Twenties and Thirties. Rentals vary from a base rate attached to each film, according to audience size and type of showing. Usually, percentage terms are 50%, except for a group of recent box-office hits for which the guarantee is set against a *per capita* charge of 65¢ per viewer, whether admission is charged or not. Films Inc. is the theatrical distributor for M-G-M product in 16mm.

The Raymond Chandler/Philip Marlowe films. The recent flurry of interest in *film noir* has prompted several studies of Raymond Chandler's writings and of the films that were made from them. Of the actors who played Philip Marlowe, Chandler's hard-boiled private eye, the author's personal preference was for Dick Powell in *Murder My Sweet* (*Farewell My Lovely*). Powell seems more emotionally open than, say Bogart—a quality that emphasises Marlowe's intrinsic romanticism. Although the screenplay for *Murder My Sweet* represents a condensation of the novel, the spirit of the film comes very close to that of its source. Physically, the characters match Chandler's descriptions perfectly. Mike Mazurki is at once pathetic and frightening as the love-sick, muscle-bound Moose Malloy, and Otto Kruger, as Amthor the Psychic, oozes civilised malice from every pore. Director Edward Dmytryk uses some adventurous visual effects to take Marlowe through the drugging sequence.

Films Inc. has several other Philip Marlowe stories, including *The Brasher Doubloon*, taken from the book "The High Window"; *The Lady in the Lake* in which Robert Montgomery, using a purely subjective camera, directed himself in the Marlowe role; *Marlowe*, based on the book "The Little Sister," with James Garner in the title role; and *The Falcon Takes Over* which is based, in part, on "Farewell My Lovely."

The Fearless Vampire Killers (Dir: Roman Polanski). In his only film with Sharon Tate, Polanski satirises the sexual fears that have been sublimated into vampire lore. Several sequences, like the vampire's slow motion descent into the heroine's bathtub are eerily beautiful. Under the title *Dance of the Vampires* the film met with critical success in Europe. In the United States, however, M-G-M shortened, redubbed and re-edited it. This tampering led to a disastrous American reception. Films Inc. is now offering this underrated work in Polanski's original version.

Other new releases from Films Inc: *Les violons du bal*, *Black Thursday*, *Lacombe Lucien* (Louis Malle), *The Mad Adventures of Rabbi Jacob*, *The Apprenticeship of Duddy Kravitz*, *The House on Chelouche Street*, *The Harder They Come*, *Fantastic Planet*, *Chariots of the Gods?*, *Chinatown*, *The Conversation*.

Hanging and *Boy* (both by Nagisa Oshima), *I Am Curious* (*Blue* and *Yellow*) (Vilgot Sjöman), *Mandabi* (Sembene Ousmane), *Antonio das Mortes* (Glauber Rocha), *The Devil in Miss Jones*, *Titicut Follies* (Frederick Wiseman), *Pinter People*, and the following films by Jean-Luc Godard: *Weekend*, *Vladimir and Rosa*, *Pravda*, *See You at Mao*.

GROVE PRESS FILM DIVISION

53 East 11th Street, New York, NY 10003. (212) 677-2400.

Although the high point of the Grove Press catalogue is its collection of shorts and independent films, there is a limited number of impressive features available for rental and sale. Rental rates are for single showings and apply against 50% of the gross receipts when admission is charged.

The Henry Miller Odyssey (Dir: Robert Snyder). In this remarkable document, Henry Miller reconstructs his past—from his childhood in Brooklyn through his days as an expatriate in France. In piecing those years together, Miller makes use of his friends, writings, notebooks, letters, drawings, and watercolours. He points out the places where he lived and worked in France, recalling the meaning they had for him then. It is during this tour that we start gaining insight into both the artist himself and the forces that animate his books.

The Henry Miller Odyssey is one of a trio of documentaries, all by Robert Snyder, that Grove Press has available for rental or sale. The others are: *Anaïs Observed: A Film Portrait of a Woman as Artist* and *The World of Buckminster Fuller*.

Other Grove Press releases: *Innocence Unprotected* (Dušan Makavejev), *Death by*

HURLOCK CINE-WORLD

13 Arcadia Road, Old Greenwich, Conn. 06870. (203) 637-4319.

The Hurlock Cine-World library includes all the releases of Allied Artists. Among them are a number of important foreign films, several commercial successes and some durable American classics. Base rental rates are for one showing only and serve as a minimum guarantee against 50% of the gross when admission is charged. Hurlock's service is meticulous, prints always arrive in plenty of time and in fine condition. This small but efficient firm offers its customers a personalised service that is hard to find elsewhere.

Portraits of Women (Dir: Jörn Donner). This comedy is, in fact, a sardonic portrait of Finnish attitudes. Donner pictures the Finns as outwardly puritanical; but this proudly flaunted show of propriety covers drives and appetites all the more voracious for lack of open expression. Even films about love-making must be pornography made respectable with a self-consciously arty surface. Pertti (a film director played by Donner himself) declares war upon such cinematic hypocrisy only to find his personal life complicated by the very affectations he is challenging in his films. Donner's dry, detached humour makes for ferocious satire.

Belle de Jour (Dir: Luis Buñuel). "Through surrealism", Buñuel once said, "I learned that man is not free." *Belle de Jour* goes further in explaining this remark than any of his other films. Séverine is the captive of her *bourgeois*, Catholic inhibitions. Her attempts to free herself lead her into other forms of enslavement—a frigid marriage, prostitution, a jealous lover and the fear of exposure. Catherine Deneuve's elegance and the sheer beauty of Sacha Vierny's images heighten the irony of this story of self-defeat.

Other Hurlock releases: *Papillon, Cabaret, Day of the Triffids, The Bridge, This Man Must Die* (Claude Chabrol), *Black God White Devil* (Glauber Rocha), *Little Shop of Horrors* (Roger Corman), *Gun Crazy* (J. Lewis).

IMAGES

2 Purdy Avenue Rye, New York 10580. (914) 967-1102.

Images is the ambitious project of Bob Harris who promises to stock his library with major foreign classics as well as the best available prints of other titles already in distribution. The care he is lavishing on his operation is apparent in his first handsome, informative catalogue. His tastes and priorities are indicated by the package of French films he is putting together. Besides the productions of Marcel Pagnol, he has acquired many previously uncirculated titles by Gance, Franju and Cocteau. Whenever possible, Images plans to go to original negatives and fine grain masters for printing materials. This preprint material will be deposited with the Museum of Modern Art to ensure its continued availability.

Bonaparte and the Revolution (1971 version, Abel Gance). When Abel Gance made his first version of *Napoléon* in 1927, he was already anticipating the coming of "talkies." In 1934 he added sound and dialogue to the silent footage and filmed additional material. In 1971, with the financial backing of Claude Lelouch, Gance re-worked the 1934 version and shot some new sequences for it. Even if the latest edition is not the legendary silent masterpiece, it provides the best presently available indication of Gance's wizardry. The camera movements and angles are as dazzling as the tour-de-force optical effects. Gance's pyrotechnics, however, are more than just show. After sitting through this epic, one feels as though he has spent its more than four hour running time in the presence of Napoléon himself.

The Films of Marcel Pagnol. Images will have available the major productions of Marcel Pagnol's studio. This group includes: *Marius, César, Fanny, Letters from My Windmill, The Baker's Wife, The Well Digger's Daughter, Harvest, Le Schpountz, Angel.*

Other Images releases: *La roue* (Gance), *Ivan the Terrible* (Eisenstein), *Le gai savoir* (J.-L. Godard).

IVY FILM

165 West 46th Street, New York, NY 10036. (212) 765-3940.

The sheer bulk of Ivy's many catalogues is an invitation to the film programmer to sift this massive inventory in search of lost or forgotten masterpieces. It is an enjoyable experience simply to browse through the "Directory of Feature Films" which lists titles, stars, directors and releases dates of several thousand movies. For the less adventurous, there is a "Director's Catalogue" containing an abundance of famous work by major artists. Included in this group are three

by Don Siegel (*Invasion of the Body Snatchers*, *Private Hell 36*, and *Riot in Cell Block 11*), two by Jean Renoir (*The Southerner* and *Diary of a Chambermaid*), the Marx Brothers' *Night in Casablanca* and *Love Happy*, and Sternberg's *Docks of New York*. Most of Ivy's films are available for sale on super 8mm sound, and several are on offer worldwide. This sale catalogue is available on request.

Ivy pioneered the release of vintage cartoon packages with *The Betty Boop Scandals*. Now they have put together a sequel, *The Betty Boop Goodies*. Their short film catalogue contains specimens from the output of Max Fleischer, Noveltoons, and George Pal, as well as newsreels and *The Little Rascals*. Another catalogue itemises 66 serials from *Adventures of Captain Marvel* to *Zorro Rides Again*.

Film rental is determined on a sliding scale and there are discounts for classroom and series (3 or more films) users.

A sampling of Ivy titles includes: *Pitfall* (with Dick Powell, featured in Ivy's "Film Noir" catalogue), *Becky Sharp* (Rouben Mamoulian), *The Bigamist* (Ida Lupino), *Johnny Guitar* (Nick Ray), *Letter from an Unknown Woman* (Max Ophüls), *Behind Locked Doors* (Budd Boetticher), *No Minor Vices* (Lewis Milestone). *Macbeth* (Orson Welles), *Strangers in the Night* (Anthony Mann), *The Wrong Road* (James Cruze), *Father Goose* (one of several Cary Grant pictures handled by Ivy).

JANUS FILMS

745 Fifth Avenue, New York, NY 10022. (212) 753-7100.

The Janus collection includes the most important works by Bergman, Truffaut, Renoir and others. The Janus library is particularly rich in German, British and French films. Janus has standard prices for all rentals, regardless of title, with special discounts available to high schools, classrooms, religious groups and series (six or more films) users. Colour works are priced slightly higher than those produced in black-and-white, and there is a *per capita* charge on audiences exceeding 300 persons.

Shoeshine (Dir: Vittorio De Sica). For years *Bicycle Thieves* was the only member of Vittorio De Sica's neo-realist trilogy available in the United States. Not long ago, Janus resurrected *Umberto D.*; now the company has returned *Shoeshine* to distribution. In *Shoeshine*, De Sica first charms his audience with the friendship and aspirations of two street urchins. Then the boys are arrested for their unwitting role in a robbery, and De Sica uses our affection for the pair to draw us into his searing attack upon the juvenile penal system. *Shoeshine's* skilful integration of its dramatic and social elements gives the viewer an extraordinary feeling for the Italian postwar tragedy.

The Fiancés (Dir: Ermanno Olmi). It is a great loss to everyone who appreciates the cinema that Ermanno Olmi's films are so seldom screened in this country. *The Fiancés* is certainly of the same stature as the best work of Fellini and Antonioni. Beneath its casual, amusing, perfectly fluid surface, the film probes the state of mind of industralised Italy. The northern worker's view of the south illustrates the national repercussions of the "economic miracle." At the same time, the correspondence betwen the separated *fiancés* reflects the boom's impact upon individuals and their relationships. In addition to *The Fiancés*, Janus carries Olmi's *Il posto*, another masterful insight into the depersonalising, corporate monster.

The New Collection. The New Collection is a special group of films (in both 16 and 35mm) that are available from Janus's theatrical division on special terms. Many of these properties are first-run attractions, including Claude Goretta's *The Invitation*, Jacques Demy's *Donkey Skin*, Kurosawa's *Dodes'ka-den*, Jaromil Jireš's *Valerie and Her Week of Wonders*, and Claude Jutra's *My Uncle Antoine*. More information can be obtained from: Janus Films, Larimer Square, Denver, Colorado 80202.

Other recent Janus releases: *La strada* (Fellini), *Street of Shame* (Mizoguchi), *The Love Goddesses* (Turell & Ferguson), *Miracle in Milan* (De Sica), *Two English Girls* (Truffaut), *Paris Belongs to Us* (Jacques Rivette).

KILLIAM SHOWS, INC.

6 East 39th Street, New York, New York 10016. (212) 679-8230.

With his Killiam Shows Collection, Paul Killiam hopes to correct the misconceptions that most people have about the silent cinema. Many still believe that silent movies were technically crude, jerky in their reproduction of motion, and projected in deathly silence. Killiam has been collecting and restoring silent films for years and is now making available a long list of these pictures in 16mm prints that do justice to the artistry and technical virtuosity of the pre-talkie cinema. Killiam's prints are produced from the best preprint material he can find (a far cry from the nth generation dupes of these titles that are in general circulation). They have been tinted following the pattern of the originals and boast specially composed musical scores appropriate to each individual picture.

In addition to the feature length films,

Killiam Shows has numerous short subjects, television programmes that treat various aspects of Motion Picture history, and half hour and hour long condensations of some of the feature offerings. The Killiam Shows films are fully described in the company's attractive catalogue.

Some of the feature films include: *Sally of the Sawdust* (W. C. Fields, directed by D. W. Griffith), *Seventh Heaven* (Frank Borzage), *Hearts of the World* (D. W. Griffith), *The Iron Horse* (John Ford), *The Mark of Zorro* (Douglas Fairbanks), *What Price Glory?* (Raoul Walsh), *Orphans of the Storm* (D. W. Griffith), *Peck's Bad Boy* (Sam Wood), *The Iron Mask* (Allan Dwan), *The Extra Girl* (Mack Sennett), *College* (Buster Keaton), *Blood and Sand* (Rudolph Valentino), *The Beloved Rogue* (John Barrymore).

LIBRA FILMS CORPORATION

171 Eighth Avenue, New York, NY 10011. (212) 243-8200.

Libra Films is a brand new organisation, established by Ben Barenholtz, which currently offers three films for the non-theatrical market and a few others for theatrical outlets. Two of Libra's features were saved from obscurity, at least in America, when Barenholtz arranged to take them over from a major distributor which had no intention of putting them into release. Philippe de Broca's *Touch and Go* (*La poudre d'escampette*) was made in 1972 and stars Michel Piccoli, Michael York and Marlène Jobert. Claude Chabrol's *Just before Nightfall* was produced at about the same time and, like *Touch and Go*, sat on Columbia's shelves with little hope of ever reaching American theatre screens. Perhaps the most interesting

of Libra's films, though, is Jean-Pierre Melville's version of Cocteau's *Les enfants terribles* which has not been seen in the United States for almost ten years.

NEW LINE CINEMA

853 Broadway, New York, NY 10003. (212) 674-7460.

New Line's repertory continues to be an incongruous mixture of classic and contemporary foreign, experimental, American independent, exploitation, and porno films. Prices in the New Line Catalogue are flexible and satisfactory terms can almost always be negotiated for any type of showing.

The Seduction of Mimi (Dir: Lina Wertmüller; original title translation: *Mimi the Metalworker, His Honour Betrayed*). New Line has performed a commercial miracle

with this Lina Wertmüller film. Because of a title change and a few cuts, *The Seduction of Mimi* underwent a remarkable general release, attracting viewers who once would never have dreamed of patronising a foreign language picture. Once inside the theatre, few ticket buyers were disappointed. This fast-moving farce with its betrayals and counter-betrayals, vendettas of honour, political absurdities and one outrageous seduction is a natural crowd pleaser.

Films of Claude Chabrol. New Line Cinema has done more than any other group to make Chabrol's films available to the American public. The company currently distributes *The Nada Gang* (original title: *Nada*), *La rupture*, *Ophélia*, and *Wedding in Blood*.

Other New Line Cinema releases: *Soldiers and Skirts* (Dir: Michael Apted; original title: *The Triple Echo*). *Shadow Man* (Georges Franju; original title: *Man without a Face*), *Lulu the Tool* (Dir: Elio Petri; original title: *The Working Class Goes to Paradise*), *A Very Natural Thing* (Dir: Christopher Larkin), *Porcile* (Dir: Pier Paolo Pasolini), *The Girls* (Mai Zetterling).

New Line also has an excellent lecture presentation service, with many prominent directors and critics available for appearances at film societies and on campus.

NEW YORKER FILMS

43 West 61st Street, New York, NY 10023. (212) 247-6110.

Dan Talbot has made his New Yorker Films Library indispensable to anybody with a serious interest in cinema. Talbot singlehandedly introduced American audiences to Ozu, and continues to bring in and support important films which might otherwise never been seen in this country.

Price structure varies according to title, type of showing and print availability. A package of pertinent xeroxed information and reviews is provided automatically with each booking.

The Merchant of Four Seasons (Dir: Rainer Werner Fassbinder). In this half-realist, half-absurdist film, Fassbinder views a man who has no alternative but to die since nobody will accept him as he is. His calling as a fruit vendor, his height, his stupidity, and his natural passions, among other things, subject him to continual humiliation. Finally, he ritualistically drinks himself to death, dedicating each deadly swallow to one of those who resented his existence. *The Merchant of Four Seasons* is one of several Fassbinder films, including *Ali*, that are being offered by New Yorker.

A Free Woman (Dir: Volker Schlöndorff; original title translation: *Summer Lightning*). The American title *A Free Woman*, like the film itself, is meant to be ironic. Elisabeth emerges from the divorce court to find that she is still constrained by the full weight of social, cultural and legal tradition. Ultimately, these pressures drive her back into marriage. *A Free Woman* is, perhaps, the most direct and effective statement of the problems that the feminist movement is confronting.

Black Holiday (Dir: Marco Leto). In *Black Holiday* the commandant of one of Mussolini's colonies for subversives walks along the beach with a history professor who refused to sign an oath of allegiance to Il Duce. "These days," he tells the teacher, "the best people do as the old socialists do—neither support nor sabotage." At that moment, the academician understands that he has been playing into the hands of the

Charles Farrell and Janet Gaynor in SEVENTH HEAVEN (1927), available in superb prints from Killiam Shows

Fascists by espousing non-militancy as long as the government does not cause him to violate his personal principles. The people who really keep a *régime* in power are those who are well-intentioned, but uncommitted. Marco Leto's first feature is a thoughtfully mounted, thoroughly convincing attack against such compromisers.

New Releases from New Yorker: *Don't Cry with Your Mouth Full* (Pascal Thomas), *Middle of the World* (Alain Tanner), *Arthur Rubinstein—Love of Life* (Dir: François Reichenbach and S. G. Patris), *Lancelot of the Lake* (Robert Bresson), *Record of a Tenement Gentleman* (Dir: Yasujiro Ozu), *Human, Too Human* (Dir: Louis Malle), *The Train Rolls On* (Chris Marker), *Floating Weeds* (Dir: Ozu; silent version).

PHOENIX FILMS

470 Park Avenue, South, New York, NY 10016. (212) 684-5910. Office in Chicago.

Although Phoenix handles mainly short films (see the Films for Young People section), they do list several features in their inventory.

The Little Theatre of Jean Renoir. Originally produced for French television, these three vignettes constitute what is almost certain to be Renoir's last film. The final episode, the best of the trio, is about a middle-aged man whose loving young wife falls for a family friend. It is through defiance of the standard expectations of society that the triangle resolves, assuring the happiness of all three parties. Although it is not nearly as powerful as Renoir's previous features, *The Little Theatre* is a moving reaffirmation of the things he has stood for throughout his awesome career.

Phoenix also releases *Farrebique* by Georges Rouquier and Leni Riefenstahl's *Olympia.*

RBC FILMS

933 North LaBrea Avenue, Los Angeles, California 90038. (213) 874-5050.

In addition to the Chaplin feature film collection and the more recent BBS productions, RBC Films has been acquiring titles from other sources. Customers are furnished with professionally designed promotional material to help boost attendance at their showings. RBC has a number of rental schemes available and these are often tailored to suit the specific exhibition situation. Classroom and series rates are available on many titles.

Hearts and Minds (Dir: Peter Davis). More than a year after the end of American combat involvement in Vietnam, Peter Davis's documentary stirred up enough controversy to prevent its distribution for nearly ten months. In *Hearts and Minds*, the horror, insanity and immorality of the war itself are established by battle footage and interviews with Vietnamese, Vietnam veterans and American policy-makers like Walt Rostow. (Although the attitude of U.S. government and military was evident all along, it is still chilling to see Westmoreland face the cameras, without embarrassment, and state that Orientals don't value life as highly as westerners.) But Davis is more interested in trying to define the values that made the people of the United States support the continued intervention. To this end, he has devoted considerable screen time to American patriotic activities, competitive events and even cultural and informational media like the movies and television news. This emphasis makes the Academy Award-winning *Hearts* *and Minds* of more than just historical interest at this late date.

The Gentleman Tramp. In this tribute to Charles Chaplin, excerpts from his films, newsreels, stills, dramatised voices, production footage and Oona Chaplin's home movies trace the story of his life from his London boyhood to the present. *The Gentleman Tramp* may be the definitive film biography of the star. It was written, directed and edited by Richard Patterson and features contributions by Walter Matthau, Laurence Olivier, Jack Lemmon, and, of course, Chaplin himself.

Other RBC releases: *That'll Be the Day* (Dir: Claude Whatham, with David Essex and Ringo Starr), *Walls of Fire* (documentary on the art of Siqueiros, Orozco and Rivera), *Five Easy Pieces* and *The King of Marvin Gardens* (both by Bob Rafelson), *Drive, He Said* (Dir: Jack Nicholson), *The Last Picture Show* (Dir: Peter Bogdanovich), *Easy Rider* (Dir: Dennis Hopper), *City Lights, Modern Times, The Great Dictator, A King in New York, The Chaplin Review.*

ROA FILMS

1696 North Astor Street, Milwaukee, Wisc. 53202. (414) 271-0861.

Roa Films has a large selection of films oriented primarily toward entertainment and educational purposes. The company's films come from Warner Brothers, Columbia, Universal, Walter Reade and a number of smaller distributors. Roa frequently offers bargain prices, but in no way compromises service or quality. There is a separate catalogue of educational films available (see Films for Young People section).

The Loneliness of the Long Distance Runner (Dir: Tony Richardson). This powerful study of class warfare in England neatly absorbs its audience with what seems to be the story of a young tough's rehabilitation. But Richardson is cynical in appraising his subject's chances for success. In the enigmatic ending, the title character, who has all but won his race, stops short of the finish line and deliberately loses. This tantalising film, brimming with social awareness, is typical of the angry British films of the early Sixties.

New releases by Roa Films include: *The Autobiography of Miss Jane Pittman, David and Lisa* (Frank Perry), *Dead End* (William Wyler, with Humphrey Bogart), *The Little Foxes* (William Wyler), *Hamlet* and *Henry V* (Olivier versions), *Lord of the Flies* (Peter Brook), *Night of the Living Dead, Metropolis* (Fritz Lang), *Rebecca* (Alfred Hitchcock), *A Tale of Two Cities, Wuthering Heights* (William Wyler), *Gilbert and Sullivan.*

RŌNIN FILM

43 West 61st Street, New York, NY 10023. (212) 757-5715.

Rōnin Film's inventory ranges from a quintet of Russ Meyer's features (*Faster Pussycat Kill Kill!, Finders Keepers, Lovers Weepers, Cherry Harry & Raquel, Vixen,* and *Super Vixens*) to the immensely successful cult film, *The Groove Tube.* Some other titles of interest include: *Summer Soldiers* (Hiroshi Teshigahara), *Heat* (Warhol-Morrissey), *Montreal Man* (Frank Vitale), *The Free Life* (Ronnie Hersh, Russel Schwartz, Ken Searls), *Ciao! Manhattan* (John Palmer and David Weisman), *Daddy* (Niki de Saint Phalle and Peter Whitehead), *Castle of Purity* (Arturo Ripstein), and *Vampir* (Pedro Portabella). Rental rates are negotiable and classroom terms are available.

TRANS-WORLD FILMS, INC.

is one of the leading U. S. distributors of foreign and
American 16mm features and short film subjects.

Almost all titles are

available with or without

English subtitles.

Write for our FREE catalog.

TRANS-WORLD FILMS, INC.

332 South Michigan Avenue, Chicago, Illinois 60604
Area Code 312/ 922-1530

WE SET THE FILM INDUSTRY BACK FIFTY YEARS!!

Though probably more silent films are available now for rental than since their golden age, often the prints are incomplete, poor quality, later generation dupes, lacking the vitality and beauty experienced by early audiences.

Working from original negatives and prints, Paul Killiam and his staff have painstakingly restored and re-issued many of the great classics of the silent era, complete with color tints and specially composed music scores. For picture quality and authenticity, the films in The Killiam Collection offer the ultimate achievement in silent film presentation.

FOR A NON-THEATRICAL RENTAL CATALOG, WRITE ON YOUR ORGANIZATION LETTERHEAD TO:

THE KILLIAM COLLECTION
6 EAST 39th STREET NEW YORK, N.Y. 10016

Still from Jacques Tati's PLAYTIME, available in the U.S.A. through Select Film Library

SELECT FILM LIBRARY

115 West 31st Street, New York, NY 10001. (212) 594-4450.

Select Film Library is a multifaceted enterprise encompassing 16mm feature film rental, educational films, sales of films in 8mm and Super 8mm (see Film Collecting section), film books and audio-visual equipment. The rental library features many fine titles—foreign, silent, specialised and general entertainment—at agreeably low prices. A number of their offerings, like the *Topper* series and several Sam Fuller pictures, are not to be found elsewhere. Select is also unique in that it stocks an extensive inventory of 16mm CinemaScope prints. Anamorphic lenses are available from them for either sale or rent. Rental rates are flat, regardless of whether admission is charged, and are for one day's use. Special discounts are offered for regular volume users and for institutions with summer film programmes.

Playtime (Dir: Jacques Tati). Considered by many to be Tati's masterpiece, *Playtime* is even more important now that *Mr. Hulot's Holiday* and *Mon oncle* have been withdrawn from circulation. *Playtime* casts a jaundiced eye upon the "new" Paris, satirically demolishing modern architecture, frenetic night-spots, traffic jams, package tours and insipid consumer goods. The film has no real dialogue (eliminating the need for subtitles), and relies entirely upon visual incongruities to make its points. Tati's knack for gags predicated upon absurdities of motion and geometry has never been more effectively or hilariously displayed.

What's Up Tiger Lily? (Dir: Woody Allen). For his first feature film, Woody Allen took a fourth-rate Japanese thriller and, without regard to its original plot or dialogue, dubbed it into English. The result is a steady barrage of idiocy in the free, uninhibited manner that has become his trademark. Allen has interpolated musical numbers by The Lovin' Spoonful as well as his personal, on-screen introduction and commentary.

Some new Select releases include: *Alexander Nevsky, Carnal Knowledge, Murder* (Alfred Hitchcock), *Rififi* (Jules Dassin), *Woman in the Moon* (Fritz Lang), *Sundays and Cybele, The Girl Most Likely, Night of the Living Dead, Sante Fé Trail, Faust* (F. W. Murnau).

SWANK MOTION PICTURES

201 South Jefferson, St. Louis, Missouri 63166. (314) 534-6300. Offices in New York City, Los Angeles, Houston, Boston and Chicago.

Swank is the exclusive non-theatrical distributor of films from Cinerama Releasing, Cinema Center, National General, Bryanston, and many Columbia releases. Swank also rents films from Universal's library and selected Warner Brothers, AIP and Disney titles. Rental base rates are for one day's showing and most recent films use a guarantee against 50% of any admission collected. A good number of movies are available at a flat, per day rate.

Payday (Dir: Daryl Duke). *Payday* focuses on Maury Dann, a country and western singer on his way to the top. In Dann's field, advancement is dependent upon the ability to represent certain homespun

Laurence de Monaghan in CLAIRE'S KNEE, available in the United States from Swank

standards. But in America, success and corruption are inseparable and the singer not only becomes debauched in his own right, but degrades everyone who comes into contact with him. Dann's boyhood home has fallen to waste; his marriage has disintegrated. He exploits and discards his friends, fans, girls, and loyal employees. By undermining the values that he embodies for millions, he destroys himself. In this handsome film, Daryl Duke captures the unique ambience of the country music circuit and uses it to study an insidious form of national decay.

Chloe in the Afternoon and **Claire's Knee** (both by Eric Rohmer). The characters in Eric Rohmer's films are continually analysing and reassessing their feelings and actions. They compulsively reassure themselves about their own behaviour. But Rohmer challenges his protagonists with dilemmas that put their justifications to the test. The major conflict in his films comes from the often intellectual contortions these characters go through as they attempt to maintain their belief in their own rationalisations. In *Claire's Knee*, Jean-Claude Brialy plays a man about to marry simply because he feels that it is the right thing to do. How then, does he cope with his attraction to a girl he meets on vacation, when he has declared himself ready to make a commitment to one woman? He abstracts his desire into a craving to touch the girl's knee. Under Rohmer's guidance, the resolution of Brialy's dilemma is simultaneously ridiculous, thoughtful, and erotic. *Chloe in the Afternoon* views another man who lies to himself—this time about the nature of his relationship with Chloe, a voluptuous friend from his bachelor days. Chloe plays on his vanity and self-confidence until he becomes more involved with her than he had intended. Only when he is on the verge of marital infidelity does he realise how flimsy his self-assurance really is.

Other new releases from Swank: *California Split* (Robert Altman), *Andy Warhol's Frankenstein*, *Holiday* (George Cukor), *The Odessa File*, *The Gravy Train*, *Le boucher* (Claude Chabrol), *Masculine-Feminine* (Jean-Luc Godard). Swank also has new prints of nearly all of Frank Capra's Columbia films.

TRANS-WORLD FILMS

332 South Michigan Avenue, Chicago, Ill. 60604.

A small but select list of fine features from Spain, Britain, France, Germany,

Belgium, India and Japan is included in the Trans-World catalogue. Many films are available either with or without subtitles for the benefit of language classes. Rentals are modest and well within the budget of most teaching programmes. Trans-World also offers a wide range of animated shorts, including the work of Raoul Servais.

The Man Who Had His Hair Cut Short (Dir: André Delvaux). Of André Delvaux's films (*Rendez-vous à Bray, Belle, Un soir, un train*), only *The Man Who Had His Hair Cut Short* is available in the United States. Delvaux's ongoing preoccupation with the irretrievability of the past begins with this macabre story of a teacher who cannot tell a graduating student of his love for her. Though the *dénouement* is calculatedly vague, the slick manipulation of time and memory is continually stimulating.

La mandragola (Dir: Alberto Lattuada). The best thing about *La mandragola* is the presence of Jean-Claude Brialy as a renaissance confidence man. He not only plays his victims against one another, making them happy in the process, but organises his intricate schemes in a way that provides him with self-satisfaction as well as material benefits. The smug, bemused Brialy is the embodiment of the film's cynicism and the catalyst which keeps this sex-farce moving at an ever accelerating pace.

Other films from Trans-World: *Les jeux sont faits* and *La symphonie pastorale* (both by Jean Delannoy), *Emil and the Detectives* (Dir: Gerhardt Lamprecht), *Tonio Kroger, Charulata* and *Nayak* (both by Satyajit Ray), *I'll Never Cry* (Kenji Yoshida), *The Lavender Hill Mob*, and the following films of Pierre Etaix: *Le grand amour, Insomnie, Happy Anniversary, Tant qu'on a la santé*. Trans-World's catalogue also features a section of American classic and popular films.

TRICONTINENTAL FILM CENTER

333 Sixth Avenue, New York, NY 10014. (212) 989-3330. Offices in Berkeley, Calif. and Oak Park, Ill.

In the United States, Tricontinental is the most comprehensive source of films from and about Third World countries. Most films are available for rental and sale and special rates are available for classroom use and for political groups.

The Hour of the Furnaces (Produced by Grupo Cine Liberación; Dir: Fernando Solanas and Octavio Getino). The authors of *Hour of the Furnaces* refer to it as a "film act." Its immediate purpose is to stir Argentinian audiences into political awareness and then into action. There are even breaks for discussion of the material that has been presented.

The film develops in three separate, self-contained parts. The first defines neo-colonialism and discusses its insidious workings. The second examines nationalism as an antidote to neo-colonialism by chronicling the Perónist movement both before and after Perón's exile. The final segment delves into the need to meet oppressive violence with revolutionary violence. Taken as a whole, *The Hour of the Furnaces*

UNITED FILMS

1425 SOUTH MAIN
TULSA, OKLA. 74119

(918) 583-2681

D.O.A.	**WUTHERING HEIGHTS**
CREAM	**YELLOW SUBMARINE**
SUPER SHOW	**THE GRADUATE**
SPIRITS OF THE DEAD	**SOLDIER BLUE**
THE MAGIC CHRISTIAN	**REBECCA**
AND THEN THERE WERE NONE	**RAIN**
THE PEOPLE NEXT DOOR	**NOTORIOUS**
COUNT DRACULA	**BRIAN'S SONG**
THE HURRICANE	**AFRICAN QUEEN**

I NEVER SANG FOR MY FATHER

demonstrates that the pattern of history in Argentina is essentially that of all Third World countries. The problems of South America are also the problems of South-East Asia and of the emerging African nations. So, despite the fact that its documentation is specifically Argentine, the film does not lose its power beyond the borders of Latin America, nor has that power been diminished by the passage of time.

Other Tricontinental releases: *Lucia* (Humberto Solas), *The Traitors, Mexico, The Frozen Revolution, The History Book* (animated), *Blood of the Condor* (Jorge Sanjines), *Memories of Underdevelopment* (Tomás Gutiérrez Alea), *Jackal of Nahueltoro, Tupamaros, Alliance for Progress.*

TWYMAN FILMS

329 Salem Avenue, Dayton, Ohio. (513) 222-4014.

The Twyman catalogue now includes titles from Walter Reade, Columbia, Warner Brothers, Universal, the Goldwyn library, and others. A number of foreign language pictures without subtitles are available for language class study. Rental rates are based upon one day's use and are flat (with the exception of Universal titles). A discount of $2.50 is allowed on each film when six or more are booked at once.

The Private Life of Henry VIII (Dir: Alexander Korda). Charles Laughton's robust performance in the title role is, of course, the major attraction in Korda's famous comedy. Laughton's Henry is so single-minded in his pursuit of self-indulgence that he is easily manipulated by everyone from chambermaids to opportunistic, upper echelon members of his court. The bustling,

often bawdy, period atmosphere receives careful attention, especially in the crowd scenes associated with the executions of his wives.

Other new Twyman releases: *Go Ask Alice* (John Korty), *A Doll's House* (Joseph Losey), *The Glass House* (Tom Gries), *La belle américaine* (Robert Dhery), *The Hurricane* (John Ford), *Judex* (Georges Franju), *Dead End* (William Wyler), *Monsieur Vincent, THX 1138* (George Lucas).

UA: 16

729 Seventh Avenue, New York, NY 10019. (212) 575-4715.

This year UA: 16 has added additional United Artists releases to its catalogue as well as a selection of films from the old Monogram library. This is the first time the Monogram titles have been offered in 16mm. UA: 16 handles all the releases of its parent company, United Artists, plus the entire pre-1950 Warner Brothers library. The company has also expanded its selection of shorts and newsreels. UA: 16 rents films for a flat, per show rate when no admission is charged and for a guarantee vs. a percentage of the gross (varying from 50–65%) when admission is collected. There are also a number of films available for a flat $35/day rental.

The Manchurian Candidate (Dir: John Frankenheimer, with Frank Sinatra, Laurence Harvey). Watergate and the war in Vietnam have given *The Manchurian Candidate* a somewhat different complexion than it had when it was first released in 1962. Nonetheless, its snide view of the cold war with its McCarthyite senators, "Red Peril," and brainwashings retains its sting. Beyond the political innuendo, George Axelrod's offbeat screenplay (which, at one point, transforms an evil gathering of Communist operatives into a ladies' garden party) and Frankenheimer's sense of staging sustain the intrigue. The shooting of the senator through the milk carton is the high point of Frankenheimer's career to date.

Last Tango in Paris (Dir: Bernardo Bertolucci, with Marlon Brando). Bertolucci's flawless film has been widely hailed as a cinema landmark and requires little introduction here. UA: 16 has taken great pains in preparing it for 16mm release. Theatrically, *Last Tango* tended to draw large, sensation seeking crowds. On the college circuit, the remarkable experience offered by the work should be enhanced by the presence of a properly appreciative audience.

The Taking of Pelham One Two Three. To be sure, *The Taking of Pelham* contains a great deal of hokum, most of it intentional, and much of it quite funny. A large portion of the first half is a burlesque of certain familiar characteristics of New York and New Yorkers. But when it comes time to get serious and follow the tense course of the subway hijacking, *Pelham* becomes quite gripping. Many people might classify the film as an "ark picture"—that is, one where a number of stereotyped personalities are confined to close quarters during a stressful situation. But its character interest lies not with the hostage passengers, but with Robert Shaw as the head hijacker, an ex-mercenary more concerned with running a flawless, quasi-military operation than with the million dollar ransom. With this role, Shaw is well on his way toward becoming one of today's best heavies.

Other recent UA: 16 releases include: *Sleeper* (Woody Allen), *Fellini's Roma* (Federico Fellini), *Thieves Like Us* (Robert Altman), *Where's Poppa?* (Carl Reiner), *An Infinite Tenderness* (Pierre Jallaud), *Thunderbolt and Lightfoot*, *Adventures of Robin Hood* (with Errol Flynn), The Charlie Chan and Mr. Wong series.

UNITED FILMS

1425 South Main, Tulsa, Oklahoma 74119. (918) 583–2681.

United Films has a wide selection of feature films of every variety, including American and foreign classics, recent major releases, silent films and serials. All rentals are at a flat rate and prices are very reasonable. Prints are good and the service is efficient. United has recently acquired the libraries of Crown International, American National, and Sun International, including controversial documentaries like *The Outer Space Connection* and numerous nature and wildlife films.

The Shuttered Room (with Oliver Reed, Carol Lynley, Gig Young). Despite its low budget, *The Shuttered Room* generates a good deal of suspense and even an occasional shock. The story of a young woman and her demon sister was taken from a book by H. P. Lovecraft and is far superior to *The Dunwich Horror*, another film adapted from that book. When the woman and her husband visit the island where she was born, they were trapped between two equally unnerving sources of danger. On one hand, there is the supernatural threat of the monstrous sibling. On the other, a gang of mentally deficient punks threaten the couple with physical and sexual violence. The film sustains an aura of tension between the two menaces.

The Gold of Naples (Dir: Vittorio De Sica, written by Cesare Zavattini). *The Gold of Naples* (made in 1955) harks back to De Sica's neo-realist years in that the camera seems to assume a passive role, thus allowing the material to speak for itself. But the resemblance to the director's immediate postwar films ends there. The cast is professional and includes Sophia Loren. Silvana Mangano and De Sica himself. Most importantly, the object of the film is far removed from that of *Bicycle Thieves* and *Shoeshine*. Instead of documenting the social conditions of an era, De Sica and Zavattini are celebrating the vitality and good nature of a people. The four funny, touching episodes that comprise the film all emphasise character. The people of Naples are the "gold" referred to in the title.

Cindy Williams in AMERICAN GRAFFITI, available in the U.S. through Universal 16

Other recent releases from United: *The Secret Life of Walter Mitty, Guys and Dolls, Taste the Blood of Dracula, Soldier Blue, Notorious* (Alfred Hitchcock), *DOA* (Rudolph Maté), *And Then There Were None* (René Clair), *To Be or Not To Be* (Ernst Lubitsch, with Jack Benny), *Under Capricorn* (Alfred Hitchcock), *Made in Sweden* (Johan Bergenstråhle), *Rancho Notorious* (Fritz Lang), *The Lusty Men* (Nick Ray).

UNIVERSAL 16

445 Park Avenue, New York, NY 10022. (212) 759-7500. Offices in Atlanta, Chicago, Dallas, Los Angeles.

Universal 16 handles not only the product of its parent company, Universal, but also the MCA library which includes all of Paramount's pre-1948 releases. Features are booked on the basis of a minimum guarantee vs. 50% of the gross (if admission is charged).

Duel (Dir: Steven Spielberg) is an enigmatic chase film involving a terrified, bewildered motorist and a sinister gasoline tanker which, for no obvious reason, is bent upon killing him. The film was originally made for television, but it drew a great deal of critical and popular attention during its European theatrical release. It is difficult to imagine *Duel* ever being appreciated on the small screen. However, when the film is properly projected and run without commercials, the high level of unremitting suspense becomes absolutely exhausting.

My Man Godfrey (Dir: Gregory La Cava, 1936). This famous screwball comedy bears the unmistakable imprint of the mid-Thirties. Its tone is preposterously optimistic, and lurking behind the insane dialogue, there is a moral about the need for productivity and social unity. The scenes between William Powell as the "tramp"-turned-butler and Carole Lombard as the silly society girl who falls for him are often spectacularly funny. Universal 16 offers many other comedies from that era including *Midnight* (Scr: Wilder-Brackett, with Claudette Colbert), *Easy Living* (Dir: Preston Sturges), *Girls about Town* (Dir: George Cukor), as well as films by the Marx Brothers, W. C. Fields and Mae West.

New releases from Universal 16 include: *The Sting, American Graffiti, The Sugarland*

Express (Dir: Steven Spielberg), *Animal Crackers*, *Outside the Law* (Dir: Tod Browning; sound version), *Breezy* (Dir: Clint Eastwood), *The Don Is Dead* (Dir: Richard Fleischer), *The Ra Expeditions*, *Ladies and Gentlemen the Rolling Stones*. Universal 16 has recently restored the deleted first reel (containing Dietrich's swimming sequence) to its prints of *Blonde Venus*.

VISION QUEST

7715 North Sheridan Road, Chicago, Illinois 60626. (312) 338-1116. Branches in New York City and Mill Valley, Calif.

Vision Quest is active not only in 16mm distribution, but also in video tape, educational films, sales, television and theatrical distribution. The films cover a broad spectrum from American *avant-garde* and political works to ethnographic films and films on psychology. Rental arrangements are flexible. A large selection of short films is also available at Vision Quest.

Snapshots (a film by Mel Howard, Ken Schwartz, Paul Goldsmith, Judy Sobol and Turid Aarsted). When someone makes a film about his own family, it usually turns into a thinly disguised study of himself. *Snapshots* begins this way, but soon abandons the pretence of modesty and becomes a movie about the film-makers and their attempts to capture themselves on celluloid. However, even these people have inhibitions. They find that when it comes to baring one's life and feelings before the camera, honest self-expression is neither comfortable nor easy. To complicate matters further, the act of working together on the picture precipitates personal crises that are difficult to record frankly. If the film-makers finally achieve a measure of truthfulness, it is in their sense of humour at

not being able to be completely honest about themselves.

Other Vision Quest releases include: *The Mirages* (Armando Robles Godoy), *Tidikawa and Friends* (Jef and Su Doring), *Kodou* (Ababacar Samb), *Heroes* (Rick Becker), *American Revolution 2* (The Film Group), *Asylum* (Peter Robinson), *Alexeieff at the Pinboard* (Alexandre Alexeieff and Claire Parker), *In Order to Change* (William Mahin), *In the Streets of Harlem* (Robert Macbeth), *Here Comes Everybody* (John Whitmore).

WALTER READE 16

241 East 34th Street, New York, New York 10016. (212) MU-36300.

Walter Reade 16 handles the product released theatrically by The Walter Reade Organization. Many of the titles are exclusive to the company. When admission is charged, the rental rate is a guarantee against 50% of the gross receipts. Some films are available for annual lease and classrooms rates are offered.

General della Rovere (Dir: Roberto Rossellini, with Vittorio De Sica). *General della Rovere*, a minor Rossellini film, is a highlight of Vittorio De Sica's acting career. The story calls for a charming incorrigible swindler to metamorphose into a self-sacrificing hero of the partisan movement. The film could never realise its implausible vision were it not for the emotional vulnerability that De Sica gives the character. Because of his sensitivity to misery—be it his own or someone else's—he convincingly brings off the transition from smooth-talking con man to martyr.

Other releases from Walter Reade 16 include: *The Shooting* and *Ride in the Whirlwind* (both by Monte Hellman), *Playtime* (Jacques Tati), *The Wrong Arm of* the *Law* (with Peter Sellers), *High and Low* (Akira Kurosawa), *Seduced and Abandoned* (Pietro Germi), *Faces* (John Cassavetes), *Gervaise* (René Clément).

WARNER BROTHERS FILM GALLERY

Warner Brothers, Inc., Non-Theatrical Div., 4000 Warner Blvd. Burbank, Calif. 91522. (213) 843-7280.

The Warner Brothers Film Gallery carries the cream of recent Warner releases, as well as some of their classics and some films acquired from independent distributors. Rental is based on a minimum guarantee vs. 50 % of any admission charged. Base rates apply per day, rather than per showing. With 4 films, a discount of 10 % is allowed. When 7 films are ordered at one time, a discount of 20 % is applied.

Ten from Your Show of Shows. This is an *hommage* to the days when television comedy was both inventive and spontaneous. The film is simply a collection of kinescopes from "Your Show of Shows," the zany Fifties programme that featured the work of Sid Caesar, Imogene Coco, Mel Brooks, Carl Reiner and Louis Nye, among others. Of the ten sketches presented, two are masterpieces of television choreography. One cannot help but marvel at the precision of movement at-

Pierre Lindstedt in THE NEW LAND, available in the U.S. through Warners

tained in "The Little Sewing Machine Girl," a parody of silent movie technique, or in the mechanical clock routine. *Ten from Your Show of Shows* will be in demand because of the nostalgia craze, but it can stand on its own against any era's standard of humour.

Warner Brothers' new releases this year are: *Badlands* (Terrence Malick), *Black Belt Jones, Damn Yankees, Day for Night* (François Truffaut), *Enter the Dragon, Jimi Hendrix, The Mackintosh Man* (John Huston), *Mean Streets* (Martin Scorsese), *McQ, The New Land* (Jan Troell), *Our Time, The Pajama Game, The Terminal Man, Zandy's Bride* (Jan Troell), *Uptown Saturday Night*.

Film Archives

ALBANIA
Filmarshiva Republikes Popullore te Shqiperise, Rruga Alexandre Moissi, Tiranë, Director: V. Aristidhi.

ARGENTINA
Cinemateca Argentina, Lavalle 2168–1°–37, Buenos Aires. Curator: Guillermo Fernández Jurado. Stock: 2,000 film titles, 5,000 books, 250,000 film stills, 3,000 posters. The Cinemateca operates a Film Theatre, screening films from 3 p.m. to 1 a.m.

AUSTRALIA
*National Library of Australia, Film Division, Parkes Place, Canberra, A.C.T. Curator: A. P. Fleming. Stock: 3,400 film titles, 500 books, 53,000 film stills, 2,000 posters.

AUSTRIA
*Österreichisches Filmarchiv, Rauhensteingasse 5/3, 1010 Vienna. Chairman: Dr. Alfred Lehr. Director: Dr. Ludwig Gesek. Dep. director: Dr. Walter Fritz. Stock: 8,295 film titles, 160,000 stills, 25,000 posters, 3,000 books, 800 periodicals, reference index of 100,000 fiches.

*Oesterreichisches Filmmuseum, Augustinerstrasse 1, 1010 Vienna. Directors: Peter Konlechner and Peter Kubelka. Stock: 3,600 film titles, 100,000 stills, 4,000 books. Now with 11,000 members, the Museum holds daily screenings at the Albertina Gallery, collects and projects original undubbed prints, and shows silent films at the original speed without musical accompaniment. Has also published nine books.

BELGIUM
*Cinémathèque Royale de Belgique, 23 Ravenstein, Brussels 1. Curator: Jacques Ledoux. Stock: more than 5,000 film titles, 200,000 film stills, 8,000 books and large collection of posters. Publishes useful brochures and screens three films daily. Enthusiastically run.

BRAZIL
Fundacão Cinemateca Brasiliera, Caixa Postal 12900, 04113 São Paulo. Director: Rudá Andrade.
Cinemateca do Museu de Arte Moderna, Caixa Postal 44 (ZC-00), 2000 Guanabara. Director: Cosme Alves Neto.

BULGARIA
*Bulgarska Nationalna Filmoteka, Gourko St. 50, Sofia. Curator: Georgi Stoyanov-Bigor. Stock: 16,800 film-titles, 6,000 stills, 4,800 posters, 2,500 books, 580 bound volumes of periodicals. The Filmoteka holds four regular screenings a day and also organises film weeks abroad. It also publishes the quarterly "Kino i Vreme."

CANADA
Canadian Film Archives, 1762 Carling, Ottawa K2A 2H7. On May 1, 1975 the entire holdings of the Canadian Film Archives (films, stills, posters, books and periodicals) were deposited in the National Film Archives, leaving the Canadian Film Institute, parent of the CFA, free to concentrate on exhibition, publications, and distribution. The CFI remains a private non-profit organization. Executive director: Frederik Manter.

Cinémathèque Québecoise, 360 rue McGill, Montréal, Québec. Director: Robert Daudelin. The Cinémathèque specialises in animation (many early films) and Canadian (particularly Québec) production. In 1974 a new vault was built to house the film collection.

Conservatoire d'Art Cinématographique, 1455 de Maisonneuve W., Concordia University, Room H-109, Montréal, Québec. Director: Serge Losique. Stock: 3,000 films, several thousand stills and posters. The Conservatoire holds regular weekly programmes and specialises in festival participation.

National Film Archives, 395 Wellington, Ottawa K1A ON3. Director: Sam Kula. Stock: 20,000,000 ft. of film (3,000,000 ft. on nitrate), plus stills, books, etc.

Ontario Film Institute, 770 Don Mills Road, Don Mills, Ontario. Director: Gerald Pratley. Stock: several hundred film titles, stills and posters, 3,500 books, 50 magazine titles, card-index of 100,000 entries, 2,000 film music records.

CHILE
Cineteca Universitaria, Amuñategui 73 of. 12, Santiago. Director: Pedro Chaskel. Stock: 220 film titles, 200 books, 10,000 film stills.

COLOMBIA
Cinemateca Colombiana, Apartado Nacional 1898, Bogata. Director: Hernando Salcedo Silva.

CUBA
*****Cinemateca de Cuba,** Calle 23 n° 1155, Vedado, Havana. Director: Hector Garcia Mesa. Stock: 1,000 film titles, 110,000 film stills.

CZECHOSLOVAKIA
*****Czechoslovak Film Archive of the Czech and Slovak Film Institute,** V jámě 1, 110 00 Prague 1. Director: Slavoj Ondroušek. Stock: c. 8,000 features, plus the same number of shorts and documentaries, including newsreels, 13,148 stills, 3,800 posters, 64,200 books, 10,800 periodicals.

DENMARK
*****Det Danske Filmmuseum,** Store Søndervoldstræde, 1419 Copenhagen K. Director: Ib Monty. Stock: 5,900 film titles, 962,200 stills, 8,900 posters, 21,000 books, 4,000 volumes of periodicals, plus index of 23,000 film cards, 11,500 personality cards and 250 boxes of subject clippings. The Museum has a permanent exhibition of film apparati, and also publishes "Kosmorama." From September to June, fourteen screenings a week are presented by the Museum in its own 158-seater theatre.

FINLAND
*****Suomen Elokuva-arkisto,** Eteläranta 4 B, SF-00130 Helsinki 13. Director: Mr. Seppo Huhtala. Stock: 2,000 film titles, 7,000 books, 150,000 film stills, 10,000 posters. The archive arranges "Finnish Film Weeks" abroad, as well as regular screenings in Helsinki and the provinces.

FRANCE
Cinémathèque Française. Curator: Henri Langlois. Since 1968, the Cinémathèque has been an independent body, relying on private support to continue its excellent screenings of old films at the cinemas in the Palais de Chaillot and the Rue d'Ulm.

*****Cinémathèque de Toulouse,** 3 Rue Roquelaine, Toulouse. Conservator: Raymond Borde.

Service des Archives du Film, 78-Yvelines, Bois D'Arcy. Curator/Director: F. Schmitt. Stock:

Det Danske Filmmuseum
Store Søndervoldstraede
Copenhagen K

18,000 film titles, 3,000 stills, 2,000 posters, 700 books/periodicals. A new archive, founded in 1969 by the Centre National de la Cinématographie, with magnificent film vaults capable of holding 300,000 reels of film. Already 37,540 reels are deposited there, together with a vast amount of newsreel material.

Comité de Fondation du Musée du Cinéma et de la Cinémathèque de Lyon. Rue Jean-Jaurès, 69 Villeurbanne. Curator: Dr. Paul Genard. A unique collection of films and apparati which once belonged to the Lumière brothers.

GERMANY (EAST)
*****Staatliches Filmarchiv der Deutschen Demokratischen Republik,** Hausvogteiplatz 3-4, 108 Berlin. Curator: Wolfgang Klaue. Stock: 40,000 film titles, plus documentation material on c. 25,000 titles. With its own theatre, the Filmarchiv holds exhibitions and a yearly retrospective on documentaries at the Leipzig Festival. Enquiries on production should go to: Staatliches Archiv für den wissenschaftlichen Film der DDR, Breites Gestell 1, 1502 Potsdam-Babelsberg.

GERMANY (WEST)
*****Deutsche Kinemathek,** Pommernallee 1, Berlin 19. Director: Dr. Heinz Rathsack. Stock: 5,000 film titles, 1,700 books, 170,000 film stills, 6,000 posters. The Kinemathek also has a collection of 650 film scripts and 7,000 sketches, and designs by art directors. Its book collection has been transferred to the library of the Deutsche Film-und Fernsehakademie Berlin (same address).

Seminars, retrospectives and exhibitions are also held.

*Deutsches Institut für Filmkunde, Schloss, 6202 Wiesbaden-Biebrich. Directors: Dr. Theo Fürstenau and Ulrich Pöschke. Deputy Director: Eberhard Spiess. Curator: Dorothea Gebauer. Stock: 2,000 film titles, 399,715 stills, 22,513 posters, 20,969 books, 277 periodical titles. Also 2,165 scripts, 11,256 German dialogue sheets.

Arsenal Kino der Freunde der Deutschen Kinemathek e.V, Welserstrasse 25, Berlin 30. Programme Director: Ulrich Gregor. The nearest German equivalent to Britain's National Film Theatre. Mr. and Mrs. Gregor are also responsible for an excellent series of brochures which contain archive material difficult to find elsewhere (see Germany section for further details).

GREAT BRITAIN

*National Film Archive, 81 Dean Street, London W1V 6AA. Curator: David Francis. Deputy Curator: Clyde Jeavons. Head of Information (incl. "British National Film Catalogue"): Brenda Davies. Librarian: Gillian Hartnoll. Stock: 23,000 film titles, 24,000 books, 225 current magazine titles, 4,000 scripts, reference index of 250,000 cards, about 1,000,000 stills, about 3,000 posters. Viewing services for film students and researchers; frequent exhibition of holdings at NFT and FIAF cinemas.

Imperial War Museum, Lambeth Road, London S.E.1. Head of Film Dept: Clive Coultass. Founded in 1920, the Museum's archive of over 31,000,000 feet of film is believed to be the oldest in the world.

Barnes Museum of Cinematography, Fore Street, St. Ives, Conrwall. Curator: John Barnes. Established in 1963, the Museum is the only one of its kind in the British Commonwealth. John and William Barnes spent over thirty years gathering together this unique collection, which is divided into three main groupings: Precursors of the Cinema, Pre-Cinema and Cinematography.

GREECE

Tainiothiki tis Ellados, 1 Kanari Street, Athens 138. Curator: Aglaya Mitropoulou. Stock: 1,000 film titles, 300 books, 800 film stills, 1,000 posters. The archive has a special collection on Greek cinema, and in collaboration with the Cinema Club runs the best-attended seasons (every afternoon and Sunday morning) in Athens. In 1974/75 as well as revivals and retrospectives (Renoir, Godard, Antonioni tributes, a René Clair week attended by the director himself, and a Greek panorama with the complete works of Cacoyannis, Koundouros, Gregg Talas, etc.) there were many first showings of new Italian, Brazilian and Cuban cinema.

HUNGARY

*Magyar Filmtudományi Intézet és Filmarchivum, Népstadion ut 97, 1143 Budapest XIV. Director: Dr. Sándor Papp. Curator: Dr. István Molnár. Stock, 4,930 feature titles, 6,848 shorts, 5,208 newsreels, 46,260 stills, 6,400 posters, 6,100 books, 2,100 periodicals.

INDIA

National Film Archive of India, Ministry of Information and Broadcasting, Government of India, Law College Road, Poona 411004. Curator: P. K. Nair. Stock: 1,062 film titles, 7,578 stills, 2,120 posters, 4,779 books, 150 periodicals. Arranges daily screenings of Indian and foreign classics for students at Film Institute (Poona); also weekly screenings at Poona and Bombay for public. Conducts periodical lecture programmes and short courses in film appreciation. Publishes monographs on Indian film pioneers.

ITALY

*Cineteca Nazionale, Via Tuscolana N. 1524, 00173 Rome. Curator: Dr. Lodoletta Lupo. Director: Dr. Leonardo Fioravanti. Stock: 15,000 film titles, 190,000 stills, 2,000 posters, 15,000 books/periodicals. The Cineteca is an adjunct of the Centro Sperimentale di Cinematografia.

JAPAN

Japan Film Library Council, Taisei-kensatu Yomiuri Bldg., 2-3-12 Ginza, Chuo-ku, Tokyo. Director General: Mrs. K. Kawakita.

National Filmcenter, 3–11 Kyobashi, Chuo-ku, Tokyo. Curator: Yukinobu Toba. Stock: 2,000 film titles, 1,800 books, 5,000 film stills, 150 posters.

KOREA

Fédération Coréene des Archives du Film, Pyong-Yang. Director: Kim Han Kyoo.

MEXICO

Cinemateca Mexicana, Cordoba 45, Mexico 7, D.F. Director: Galdino Gómez-Gómez. Stock: 1,000 film titles. 500 books, 500 film stills, 300 posters. The Cinemateca also has a collection of early apparati dating from 1900, and a special collection devoted to the Mexican film industry from 1930–40.

Departamento de Actividades Cinematograficas, Direccion General de Difusion Cultural, Universidad Nacional Autonoma, Torre de la Rectoria, 10° Pisco, Mexico City.

NEDERLANDS

*Stichting Nederlands Filmmuseum, Paviljoen Vondelpark, Vondelpark 3, Amsterdam. Director: Jan de Vaal. Stock: 6,000 film titles, 6,500 books, 250,000 film stills, 15,000 posters. The Museum has a publications programme, and also arranges screenings in its own theatre. Also avilable for research are a large collection of music scores for silent films and the Joris Ivens archive.

Ervede, 43 Noordeinde, The Hague. A collection of 20,000,000 feet of Dutch newsreel film dating back to 1898.

NEW ZEALAND

National Film Library, Clifton Terrace, Wellington, C.I. Director: R. L. Hayes. The collection is limited to films made in New Zealand, and does not include books, posters, etc.

NORWAY

*Norsk Filminstitutt, Aslakveien 14b, Oslo 7. Curator: Jon Stenkiev. Stock: 5,360 film titles, 28,000 stills, 4,300 posters, 5,645 books/ periodicals. Also over five hundred pieces of early cinema apparatus, and a fine cinema for screenings of old films. The Institute also distributes quality films to film clubs throughout Norway.

Henie-Onstad Art Centre, 1311 Høvikodden, Oslo. Director: Ole Henrik Moe. Stock: 100 film titles, 3,000 stills, 200 posters, 3,000 books/ periodicals. A large collection of documentary material on experimental film, plus regular showings of them, distinguishes this Centre. The film society has a membership of 700.

PARAGUAY

Cinemateca Paraguaya, Estrella 496, Oficina 10, Assuncion. Director: Oscar Trinidad.

PERU

Cinemateca Peruana, Apartado 456, Lima. Director: Miguel Reynel Santillana.

POLAND

*Filmoteka Polska, u. Puławska 61, 00–975 Warsaw, skr. poczt. 65. Director: Jan Zbigniew Pastuszko. Stock: 7,510 film titles, 7,720 books, 511,000 film stills, 6,280 posters. Plus 137 early film projectors and a reference index. Holds reviews of old films twice a week.

PORTUGAL

*Cinemateca Nacional, Palacio Foz Restauradores, Lisbon. Director: F. Ribeiro. Stock:. 850 film titles, 5,500 books, 20,000 stills.

ROMANIA

*Arhiva Natională de Filme, Bd. Gh. Gheorghiu formacion y Turismo Planta 9 , arcnida del Stock: 4,500 feature titles, 10,000 shorts, 240,000 stills, 19,000 posters, 3,500 books, plus a reference index. The Arhiva also has a collection of clippings, scripts and periodicals.

SOUTH AFRICA

Killarney Film Studios, PO Box 2787, Johannesburg. Much valuable material is kept at this studio, which also has material dating from 1912.

South African Film Institute, National Film Board, PO Box 600, Silverton, Pretoria. Director: J. H. de Lange. Stock: more than 1,700 film titles, 7,500 stills, 190 posters, 3,700 books and periodicals, 700 scripts, 23,400 clippings. Founded in 1964, the Institute has two theatres for daily screenings and a permanent exhibition of apparatus and archive material.

SPAIN

*Filmoteca Nacional de España, Ministerio de Información y Turismo, Planta 9ª, avenida del Generalísimo 39, Madrid 16. Director: Florentino Soria Heredia. Stock: 5,000 film titles, 2,000 stills, a few posers, 1,000 books, 700 Spanish film scripts, and periodicals. Shows four programmes a day, and publishes monographs, etc.

Archivo Cinematográfico Internacional, Calle Mascaró 26, Barcelona, 16. Directors: Manuel Ferrer Salvador, Francisco Rialp Cases, José María Ibañez Llurba. Stock: over 25,000 stills, over 43,000 press-books, 8,745 books, 21 magazine titles, over 850,000 fiches. A purely "amateur" archive, founded in 1968, which freely collaborates with other publications.

SWEDEN
*Cinemateket, Filmhuset, Box 27 126, 102 52 Stockholm 27. Stock: 5,300 film titles, 19,000 stills-titles, 30,000 posters (inc. dupes), 19,000 books, 200 magazine titles, 950 Swedish feature film scripts. The film club annually screens about 550 films for its 15,000 members. The publication dept. is currently preparing an extensive Swedish filmography, to be published in 1975 and thereafter.

SWITZERLAND
*Cinémathèque Suisse, 12 Place Cathédrale, Case Ville 850, 1000 Lausanne. Curator: Freddy Buache. Stock: 2,500 features, 1,500 shorts, 50,000 film references, 5,000 books, 100,000 film stills.

TURKEY
Türk Film Arşivi, Sinema Televizyon Enstitüsü, Devlet Güzel Sanatlar Akademisi, Fındıklı, İstanbul.

URUGUAY
Cinemateca Uruguaya, Paysandú 830, Casilla de

Michel Simon, who was to die some weeks later, with Freddy Bauche, curator of the Cinémathèque Suisse in Lausanne, at the opening of an exhibition to mark the Silver Jubilee of the Swiss Film Archive in 1975

Correo 1170, Montevideo. Executive Directors: Luis Elbert, M. Martínez Carril, Nelson Pita. Stock: 1,200 films, 3,000 stills, 500 posters, 1,100 books, 90 periodicals.

U.S.A.

*American Film Institute, John F. Kennedy Center for the Performing Arts, Washington, DC 20566. Archivist: Lawrence F. Karr. Assistant archivist: Anthony Slide. Stock: 10,500 film titles. The AFI works in close collaboration with the Library of Congress, and all films in the AFI's collection are housed at the Library.

American Film Institute Library, 501 Doheny Road, Beverly Hills, Calif. 90210. Librarian: Anne G. Schlosser. Stock: 2,250 books, 153 periodicals, plus a large script collection which includes over 1,000 M-G-M titles, with scrapbooks and interview transcripts. Started in October 1969, the (Charles K. Feldman) Library has recently begun an extensive cross-indexing project.

*The Museum of Modern Art, Department of Film, 11 West 53rd Street, New York, N.Y. 10019. Acting Director: Margareta Akermark. Other executive staff include Eileen Bowser, Adrienne Mancia, Laurence Kardish, Mary Corliss, and Charles Silver. Stock: 4,500 film titles, one million film stills, 500 posters. Publishes much valuable material on the cinema and arranges extensive seasons of rare films in its own theatre.

George Eastman House, 900 East Avenue, Rochester 7, N.Y. Curator: James Card. Associate Curator: George Pratt. A magnificent private collection of over a million film stills, plus a film collection particularly rich in German and American silents. The Museum holds nightly screenings in its own theatre.

*University of California, Theater Arts Library, University Research Library, Los Angeles, Calif. 90024. Librarian: Audree Malkin. Stock: 2,000 film titles (housed in UCLA Film Archive, Theater Arts Dept.), 45,000 stills, 414 posters, 9,000 books, 150 magazine titles, 4,000 screenplays, 1,144 festival programmes and press-books, 15,000 entries in clipping file.

U.S.S.R.

*Gosfilmofond, Stantsia Byelye Stolby, Moscow oblast. Director: Viktor Privato. Stock: 39,000 film titles, 136,000 stills, 29,000 posters, 11,500 books, 15,000 periodicals. Shows films publicly, and has viewing facilities for the serious student. Also owns restoring and copying equipment.

Central Documentary Film Archive, Krasogorsk, near Moscow. Director: N. Myshko.

VENEZUELA

Cinemateca Nacional, Museo de Ciencias Naturales, Edf. Anexo, Plaza Morelos, Los Caobos, Caracas. Director: Rodolfo Izaguirre. Stock: 285 film titles, 7,900 stills, 600 books. Founded in 1966 by Margot Benacerraf. Daily screenings in the Sala del Museo de Bellas Artes.

YUGOSLAVIA

*Jugoslavenska Kinoteka, Knez Mihailova 19/1, Belgrade. Director: Vladimir Pogačić. Stock: 11,000 film titles, 6,500 books, 85,000 film stills.

* Denotes member of F.I.A.F. (International Federation of Film Archives, 23 Ravenstein, Brussels, Belgium).

THE NATIONAL FILM SCHOOL

A professional school for training directors, producers, writers and cameramen, with studios and offices at Beaconsfield, Buckinghamshire, near London.

Training commenced October 1971. The next intake of students (approximately twenty five) will be in 1976. Applications can be submitted between January 1st and February 29th, 1976.

Address all enquiries to:

**The Director,
NATIONAL FILM SCHOOL,
Beaconsfield Film Studios,
Station Road,
Beaconsfield, Bucks.**

Film Schools

by Miles Smith-Morris

AUSTRALIA

The Film and Television School, PO Box 245, Chatswood, NSW 2067. Director: Jerzy Toeplitz. Offers a three-year course of intensive practical training in production, direction, writing, editing, cinematography, sound recording and production management. About 25 students are enrolled each year; all students take a common first-year introductory course, followed by increased specialisation in the second and third years. The courses are designed to qualify students to work in the film industry or alternatively in education as teachers of film or in the production of educational films. Admission requirements are flexible.

AUSTRIA

Akademie für music und darstellende Kunst, Abteilug für Film und Fernsehen, Türkenstrasse 4, 1090 Vienna. President: Dr. Hans Sittner.

BELGIUM

Académie Royale des Beaux-Arts/Koninklijke Akademie voor Schone Kunsten—Gent, Academiestraat 2, B-9000 Gent. Animation department, director: Raoul Servais; assistant: Rembrand Hoste. Four-year course in the experimental and commercial use of animation on film and video. Tuition is in Flemish.

Institut des Arts de Diffusion, Avenue de Tervueren 15, B-1040 Brussels. Director: Jean-Louis Luxen. 140 students and 80 staff. Four-year course in direction or production in film, television, radio and the theatre. Three-year courses in photography, sound, editing and writing. Films made by students include features, documentaries and animated shorts.

Institut National Supérieur des Arts due Spectacle et des Techniques de Diffusion (INSAS), Rue Thérésiane 8, B-1000 Brussels. Director: Raymond Ravar. 171 students and 97 staff. Four-year course, leading to a degree, concerned with all aspects of film/radio/television production, or three-year courses giving more specialised instruction in photography, sound, editing, writing or acting. The Institute is equipped with 4 8mm cameras, 8 16mm and 1 35mm; 2 sound studios, 1 fully-equipped television studio, 3 video machines, 5 editing rooms and 3 processing laboratories.

BRAZIL

Escola Superior de Cinema, Faculdade São Luis, Av. Paulista 2324, São Paulo.

Escola Superior de Cinema, Pontificia Universidade Catolica, Av. Brasil 2033, Belo Horizonte, Minas Gerais.

Instituto de Arte e Comunicação Social, Universidade Federal Fluminense, Rua Miguel de Frias 9, 24.000 Niterói, Rio de Janeiro.

CZECHOSLOVAKIA

Ministry of Culture, Academy of Arts, Faculty of Film (FAMU), Valdesjnska ulice, Prague III.

DENMARK

Danish Film School, Danish Film Institute, Store Søndervoldstraede, DK·1419 Copenhagen K. Completely re-organised in 1973 under a new director, Jens Ravn, the school now offers a series of courses in different aspects of professional filmmaking. The school has an average of 30 students, 8 full-time and 15 part-time staff. Danish-speaking students only.

FINLAND

Taideteollinen korkeakoulu, Kuvallisen viestinnäu laitos, Elokuva- ja tv-linja, Institute of Industrial Arts, Faculty of Visual Communications, Films and TV Studies, Vesitorni 1D, SF-00240 Helsinki 24. Director: Ywe Jalander. Qualifications for admission: matriculation exam and the admission course of two weeks. Foreign students admitted with knowledge of Finnish. Average duration of studies: four years. Main subjects: directing, camerawork, screenwriting, sound. Production on 8, 16 and 35mm films plus videotape. Production facilities: professional film equipment and mini TV studio and photographic equipment.

FRANCE

Ecole Technique de Photographie et de Cinématographie, 85 rue de Vaugirard, Paris VI.

L'Institut des Hautes Etudes Cinématographiques (I.D.H.E.C.), Voie des Pilotes, 94360 Bry-sur-Marne. President: Jean Delannoy.

Conservatoire Libre du Cinéma Français (C.L.C.F.), 16 rue de Delta, 75009 Paris.

Institut Supérieur de Cinéma, Radio et Télévision (I.S.C.R.T.), 65 Bd. Brune, 75014 Paris.

GERMANY (EAST)

Hochschule für Film und Fernsehen der deutschen demokratischen Republik, Karl-Marx-Strasse 27, 1502 Potsdam-Babelsberg. Rector: Dr. Lutz Koehlert.

GERMANY (WEST)

Deutsche Film- und Fernseh-Akademie Berlin GmbH, Pommernallee 1, 1 Berlin 19. Director: Heinz Rathsack. Three-year course dealing with all aspects of practical film and television production; direction, photography, sound, editing and special effects. Students make films in each of their three years and are encouraged to gain experience in as wide a variety of techniques as possible.

Hochschule für Fernsehen und Film, Ohmstrasse 11, 8000 München 40. Director: Dr. Helmut Jedele. 99 students, 40 staff. Course of three to three-and-a-half years providing instruction in the theory and practice of film and television techniques. Students make two short films and one longer diploma film. Facilities for work on 8, 16, and 35mm as well as video equipment.

GREAT BRITAIN

London International Film School, 24 Shelton Street, London WC2. Two-year diploma course, one year animation. Half of each term devoted to production work, practical training plus film analysis and study of film history. The School is equipped with studios, two viewing theatres for both 35 and 16mm, fifteen editing rooms, sound recording and transfer equipment, 35, 16 and 8mm cameras. Tuition is given by professionals from the industry. Three courses start each year, in January, April and September.

National Film School, Beaconsfield Film Studios, Station Road, Beaconsfield, Bucks. Director: Colin Young. 75 students at present. 12 full-time teaching staff supplemented by tutors from the profession. Three years. The emphasis is on the creative aspects of film-making rather than strictly technical instruction, designed to equip the school's graduates for immediate employment in the industry. The admission process is described as an open competition among the candidates. The school is fully-equipped and films are made on Super-8, 16 and 35mm.

Polytechnic of Central London, School of Communication, 309 Regent Street, London W1R 8AL. Post-graduate Diploma in Film Studies: Two-year part-time evening course exploring the intellectual basis of film study, by close study of individual examples of important film styles. Course leader: Vincent Porter. BA(Hons) degree in Media Studies: three-year full-time course examining the dissemination of information by the mass media with the aim of developing "media Awareness" through academic study and "media literacy" through practical study. Course leader: Nicholas Garnham. BA Degree in Photographic Arts: Three-year full-time course in the practice and theory of motion-picture and still photography. One-year introductory course is followed by specialisation in either film or still photography. Course leader: David Faddy.

Royal College of Art, Department of Film and Television, Queen's Gate, London SW7. 55 students. Three-year post-graduate course.

Outside London:

Birmingham Polytechnic, Department of Visual Communication, Corporation Street, Birmingham B4 7DX. Head of Department: W. H. Price. 10 students. One-year post-graduate course; syllabus determined by individual needs but accent on animation.

Bournemouth and Poole College of Art, Department of Visual Communications, Royal London House, Lansdowne, Bournemouth BH1 3JL. Head of Department: Frank Turland. 36 students. Qualifications for admission: five GCE 'O' level passes (or equivalent) including English and Maths or Science subject; attend for interview. Three years. Students are trained for situations in industrial film units in which the skills both of photography and of film production are required.

Bristol University, Department of Drama, Radio, Film and Television Studies, 29 Park Row, Bristol BS1 5LT. Undergraduate courses in practical criticism, historical and theoretical film studies. Post-graduate: Certificate in Radio, Film and Television, predominantly practical, provides an introduction to a variety of technical skills. One year, second year in exceptional cases. Film production entirely on 16mm; animation rostrum available.

Croydon College of Design and Technology, School of Art and Design, Television, Film and Animation Unit, Barclay Road, Croydon. Fine Art TV, option, and one-year intensive course for graduates or applicants with experience in related fields. Film work on 16mm, fully-equipped video studio.

Harrow College of Technology and Art, School of Photography, Northwick Park, Harrow HA1 3TP. Head of School: Dennis Boxall. 70–80 students (Film and television, 2nd and 3rd year: 10–20). Three years, five GCEs, two of which must be 'A' level. Film history, film appreciation; the art, science and technical operations of film-making. Emphasis on the technical training of cameramen, editors and sound recordists.

Middlesex Polytechnic, Faculty of Art and Design, Advanced Studies/Film and Television, Badmington Suite, Alexandra Palace, London N22 4BA. Course leader: Roy Armes. A one-year postgraduate course in Film and Television in Education, offering a general background education in film and television rather than a detailed professional training; specialisation is actively discouraged, the course demands an imaginative response to the possibilities given by the whole range of basic film and video equipment.

Newport College of Art and Design, Clarence Place, Newport, Monmouthshire. In charge of Film: Harley Jones. Facilities for production on 8, 16, 35mm and video. BA(Hons) in Film and Television; from September 1975 the college is offering in addition a one-year advanced Documentary Film-Making course.

West Surrey College of Art and Design, Guildford Centre, Stoke Park, Guildford, Surrey. Head of Department: Arthur J. Evans. 30 students. Entry requirements: five "O" levels; also preliminary year for students wishing to gain entry to main Film and Television Production course. Two years (plus preliminary year if applicable). History of film and television, practical film production with emphasis on professional technical training.

HUNGARY

Szinhaz és Filmmuveszeti Foiskola, Vas u.2/c, Budapest VIII. Director: Lászlo Vadász.

INDIA

Ministry of Information and Boradcasting, Film

Institute of India, Chiplunker Road, Poona 4. Director: Shri Girish Karnad. 176 students, 25 teaching staff. Three years. Courses in direction and screenplay, writing, editing, photography, sound recording and engineering, acting. Basic orientation course in first year for all students included lectures on film appreciation. All students make several films including a documentary, an advertising short and a two-reel diploma feature.

Institute of Film Technology, Department of Information and Public Relations, Government of Tamil Nadu, Madras, Adyar, Madras-600020. Principal: B. Sivathanu Pillay. 94 students, 21 teaching staff. Three-year courses in direction, cinematography, sound engineering and recording, film processing. Two years for editing and acting. Fully-equipped studios and processing facilities. The Institute also has a production department, where film and production facilities are rented to commercial film producers; this scheme helps the students to gain experience in aspects of actual film production.

IRAN

Madressey alie Cinema va Television, Djame Djam Avenue, Tehran. Director: Fereydoon Mekanik.

Dramatic Arts Faculty, Film Section, 291 Jalé Avenue, Abé Sardar, Tehran. Director: Dr. Mehdi Forough. 75 students, 10 teaching staff. Four-year course; third and fourth year students make short films; to graduate each student must submit a 15-minute sound film and a written thesis. Equipped for work on 8 and 16mm.

ITALY

Centro Sperimentale di Cinematografica (C.S.C.), Via Tuscolana 1524, Rome, Director: Dr. Leonardo Fioravanti.

JAPAN

Nihon University College of Arts, Asahigoaka 2–42, Nerima-ku, Tokyo 176. Head of Film Department: Professor Toru Otake.

NETHERLANDS

Netherlands Film Academy, Overtoom 301, Amsterdam. Head of School: Anton Koolhaas, 103 students, 23 staff. Four years.

PHILIPPINES

The Film Instiute of the Philippines, 36 P. Tuason Boulevard, Cubao, Quezon City. Director Ben G.

Pinga. About 250 graduates each year, staff of 12. Separate specialised courses of varying length, usually between four and ten months, part-time or full-time. Recently the Institute has organised workshops in film direction, writing, motion picture photography, sound effects and animation. Particular stress is laid on work in the field of documentary film-making, in which the Institute has a distinguished record.

POLAND

Państowa Wyższa Szkoła Teatralna Filmowe, Ul. Targova 61, Łódź, and Al Armü, Ludowej 6 m. 165, Warszawa 10.

ROMANIA

Institutul de Arta Teatrala si Cinematografica "I. L. Caragiale," Bd. Schitu Măgureanu 1, Bucharest. Director: Eugenia Popovici.

SOUTH AFRICA

Pretoria College for Adult Education. Offers a basic technical course lasting one year.

SPAIN

Ciudad Universitaria, Escuela Oficial de Cinematografia, Carretera de la Dehesa de la Villa s/n, Madrid 25. Director: Professor J. J. Baena Alvarez. 200 students, teaching staff of 60 and 40 technicians. Three-year course with specialisation in directing, production management, photography, art direction, acting and writing. Students make four films during their three years. Fully-equipped studio, two dubbing theatres, five editing rooms, two projection rooms, 8, 16 and 35mm.

SWEDEN

Lund Institute for Cinematic Arts, Studieförbundet Vuxenskolan, St. Gråbrörsgatan 13B, S-222 22 Lund. Principal: S. N. Rehrman. 20 students, 3 full-time staff. Diploma courses of two years in directing, production, screenwriting, cinematography and editing. Certificate (one-and-a-half years)—Film Promotion, Continuity and Production Assistant. 16 and 35mm cameras, small studio for film and television work. Editing and processing facilities.

Dramatiska Institutet (The Swedish Dramatic Institute), Filmhuset, Borgvägen, Box 27090, S-102 51 Stockholm 27. Principal: Pierre Fränckel. Administrative Director: Bertil Lauritzen. Formed in 1970, the Institute is intended to provide instruction in production techniques for theatre, radio, television and film. A two-year course aims to equip students to a professional standard in one of these fields; there is also a one-year course designed for those such as teachers, youth leaders, etc., who require a working knowledge of small-scale media techniques as an aid to their work. 30 students are accepted each year for the two-year course, 16 for the one-year course. The Institute also runs seminars and shorter courses on various subjects throughout the country; it is equipped with film and television studios, 14 editing rooms for 8, 16 and 35mm, sound mixing studios and portable video equipment.

U.S.A.
Information on film courses is contained in **The American Film Institute's Guide to College Film Courses,** available at $3.50 from the American Library Association, 50 East Huron Street, Chicago, Illinois 60611.

U.S.S.R.
Vsesoyuzny Gosudarstvenny Institut Kinematografii (All-Union State Institute of Cinematography), ulitsa Testiltsilov, Moscow. Rector: Vitali Nikolayevich Zhdan. No. of students: 1500. No. of instructors: 250. Length of courses: writers, actors, economists—4 years; cameramen—$4\frac{1}{2}$ years; directors—5 years; designers—6 years. Specialisation is always taken into account during training. The various disciplines taught can be divided into three groups: economic (e.g. philosophy—140 hours), general knowledge (e.g. history of Fine Arts—160 hours—history of theatre, Soviet and foreign literature), and specialist instruction (e.g. for cameramen: 320 hours on operating, 110 on lighting). Practical work undertaken on all courses. The Institute has a training studio (with four stages of 1,000 sq. metres and more than 100 cameras of various types), an information department, its own textbooks and teaching manuals, and also auxiliary instruction quarters for Soviet cinema, foreign cinema, camera operating, direction, etc.

YUGOSLAVIA
Fakultet Dramskih Umetnosti (pozorišta, filma, radija i televizije), Ho Ši Mina 20, 11070 Beograd. Director: Desan Kosanović. Four-year course equivalent to undergraduate level; specialisation in direction, production, photography or editing. Students make films on 8 and 16mm, and a final diploma film on 35mm; film and television companies often provide facilities for students to gain experience of work under professional conditions.

Ann Rosander, Kevin Benn and Birgitta Hjalmarsson in GREEN LEAVES OF WINTER, produced at the Lund Institute for Cinematic Arts, Sweden, by Tony Broadwick.

THE CINEMA BOOKSHOP
13-14 GREAT RUSSELL ST., W.C.1. Tel. 01-637 0206

Europe's Largest Collection
of New, Rare, and Out of Print
Film Books, Magazines,
Stills, Posters, Pressbooks,
Programmes, Lobby Cards
and Ephemera.

Proprietor: Fred Zentner

Film Bookshops

AUSTRALIA

Anchor Bookshop, *Crystal Palace Arcade, George St., Sydney.*

John Brink's is one of the best collections of film books in Australia (and, incidentally, he is the agent in Australia for this book and all other Tantivy titles). Rare stills are also available for sale.

BRITAIN

Book City, *8–12 Broadwick St., London W1V 1FH. Tel. 437.2603.*

Book City began as a specialist firm for *technical* film literature. Now, however, the range is comprehensive, and Irene Holloway has brought her flair and knowledge to Book City. TV and photographic items are also stocked.

The Cinema Bookshop, *13–14 Great Russell St., London WC1. Tel. 637.0206.*

Fred Zentner's hard work, enthusiasm, and, one should add, considerable knowledge, have made his shop one of the world's most famous and respected source of film books, whether they be new or rare, and also of posters, press books, memorabilia, magazines, even early toys, and especially *stills.* In short, no visit to London is complete without a call at this cheerful establishment.

Cox, A. E., *21 Cecil Rd., Itchen, Southampton.*

This is a postal business (or by appointment), and a current copy of Mr. Cox's comprehensive list can be obtained cheaply. Many rare annuals, and runs of old movie magazines are to be found in these lists, as well as foyer posters, stills, and even souvenir theatre programmes.

Motley Books, *Mottisfont Abbey, Romsey, Hampshire SO5 0LP. Tel. Lockerley 278.*

Motley Books offer a selection of scholarly material in different languages; no "fan" material. Business is by post or appointment only.

Peter Wood, *20 Stonehill Road, Great Shelford, Cambridge CB2 5JL.*

Mr. Wood specialises in books and ephemera on all the Performing Arts. Catalogues are issued regularly (sample for 15p.). Scarce items can be found here.

Zwemmer, A., *78 Charing Cross Rd., London WC2. Tel. 836.4710.*

With their side window in Charing Cross Road a familiar landmark to all film enthusiasts in London, Zwemmer's have established a peerless reputation among film booksellers, and apart from the stock available to callers, there is a most efficient mail order service.

CANADA

Cine Books, *692a Yonge St., Toronto, Ontario. Tel. 964.6474.*

David Beard and his friends have established Cine Books as *the* Canadian centre for film books. Their burgeoning stock (both new and second-hand) is attractively arranged in the shop, but they also provide a most efficient mail order service (send for a catalogue at $2.50). Stills, posters, memorabilia, screen soundtracks, and now 8mm and 16mm films can be obtained.

DENMARK

Busck, Arnold, *Fiolstraede 24, Copenhagen.*
Here is a rewarding stock of *second-hand* books on the cinema at very moderate prices. Write to the manager if you are looking for standard works of the prewar era, or if you want to *sell* such items.

FRANCE

Librairie Contacts, *24 rue du Colisée, 75008 Paris. Tel. 256.1771.*
Visitors to this handsome little establishment, just behind the Champs-Elysées, will find a large selection of film *magazines* and books, predominantly in French and now English and Italian. Write detailing specific wants. Librairie Contacts sells other books apart from film items.

Librairie La Dame Blanche, *54 rue du Faubourg du Temple, 75011 Paris.*

Le Minotaure, *2 rue des Beaux-Arts, 75006 Paris.*

For sheer character and extent of stock, Le Minotaure is hard to beat among film bookshops. There are models, optical toys, and other memorabilia as well as long runs of out-of-print magazines, comics, and a vast array of new items of film literature.

Volume 31, *31 avenue MacMahon, 75017 Paris.*

A bright young bookshop near the Arc de Triomphe, offering all types of books in English, French and Italian Language.

Le Zinzin d'Hollywood, *7 rue des Ursulines, 75005 Paris.*

Michel Volatron has created a pleasing atmosphere in his film bookshop, just near the Blvd St. Germain and much patronised by students and film buffs.

GERMANY

Autoren Buchhandlung, *Wilhelmstr. 41, 8 Munich 40.*

Founded in 1973 by nearly 150 German writers, this establishment has already issued an excellent catalogue.

Schoeller, Marga, *Knesebeckstr. 33, 1000 Berlin 12.*

The film department of this legendary bookshop (now situated near the University) is always worth a visit.

Buchhandlung Walther König, *Breite Strasse 93, 5 Köln 1.*

This firm's latest catalogue contains some 1,400 items on film, which makes it an invaluable source for anyone in Europe looking for that out-of-print book or magazine. Write stating wants.

Wolfgang Gielow, *Theatinerstr. 35, 8 Munich 2.*

For over a decade Wolfgang Gielow has prepared catalogues, bibliographies, and built up a worldwide clientele. Write to him with specific wants, and note his stock of *soundtrack records*.

Sautter & Lackmann, *Klosterstern, 2 Hamburg 13.*

A North German source for books and magazines on the cinema as well as on related arts. Lists issued.

SOUTH AFRICA

Butch Burman's Bookshop, *Plein Street, Johannesburg.*

Exclusive Books, *Pretoria Street, Hillbrow, Johannesburg.*

The Magazine Center, *Commissioner Street, Johannesburg.*

SPAIN

Liberia R. Seriña, *Calle Aribau 114,
Barcelona 11.*

SWITZERLAND

Hans Rohr Buchhandlung und Antiquariat,
Oberdorfster. 5, 8024 Zürich.

Rohr's have not only issued regular and
exhaustive catalogues; they have reprinted
several famous film texts (such as Hans
Richter's "Expressionismus und Film") that
were hitherto beyond the reach of a new
generation of film enthusiasts. The stock of
current literature on the cinema is also
excellent, and owes much to the celebrated
skill and knowledge of Hanspeter Manz.

U.S.A.

Cinemabilia, *10 West 13th St., New York,
NY 10011. Tel. 989.8519.*

In conveniently large premises just off
Fifth Avenue, Ernest Burns's Cinemabilia is
justly renowned for its enormous stills collection, as well as for its wide range of film
books, magazines, and posters from all over
the world. The jumbo catalogue (No.
5–"Original Film Graphics") costs $2.50.

Drama Bookshop, *150 West 52nd St., New
York, NY 10019. Tel. JU 2.1037.*

Arthur Seelen and Allen Collins run a
hive of activity at Drama Bookshop, located
upstairs at 150 West 52nd Street. Known
primarily for its theatrical stock, the shop also
covers cinema and boasts one of the country's
finest mail order services.

Gotham Book Mart, *41 West 47th St., New York, NY 10036.*

As its regular "GBM Film Bulletins" will testify, Gotham has achieved a remarkable pre-eminence in the film bookshops field, and has been flourishing since 1920. Philip Lyman, the General Manager, has worked hard to expand the film section.

Hampton Books, *Route 1, Box 76, Newberry, S.C. 29108. Tel. 803.276.6870.*

For $1, one can obtain "Cinema 8," the latest in a long line of fascinating catalogues from Hampton Books. This firm specialises in movie, TV, and photography items, but also, note, in aeronautics literature and in material devoted to the Carolinas. Lobby cards, stills, and portraits are available, too—in profusion.

Larry Edmunds Bookshop, *6658 Hollywood Blvd., Hollywood, California 90028. Tel. 213.463.3273.*

In terms of turnover and display of current titles, Larry Edmunds is the world's nearest equivalent to a film-book supermart. But there is also the personal enthusiasm that Milton Luboviski, his brothers, and his wife Git (who prepared the splendid catalogue—$2.95) bring to the business. Their stills collection alone is a goldmine for any film buff.

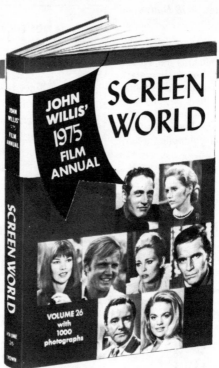

Book Reviews

We review virtually all books on cinema that are sent to us each year, but the following notes make no mention of our own range of more than one hundred titles on film (for a descriptive list, write to The Tantivy Press, 108 New Bond Street, London W1Y OQX).

REFERENCE AND HISTORY

Le Cinéma Colonial, by Pierre Boulanger (Editions Seghers, Paris, 1975). With the proliferation of film books in recent years, it has become harder and harder to treat fresh topics. Here is a study that covers a field hitherto untouched—films concerning, and films emanating from the French "Third World," Morocco, Tunisia, Algeria. As history it is first-class; as anti-racist propaganda it is a little outmoded.

The Critical Index, edited by John C. Gerlach and Lana Gerlach (Teachers College Press, Columbia University, New York and London, 1974). A singularly useful bibliography of articles on film in English, arranged by names and topics, from 1946 to 1973. Over 700 pages of invaluable source material for any library or archive. Excellent indexing.

Films and the Second World War, by Roger Manvell (A. S. Barnes & Co., South Brunswick: J. M. Dent & Sons, London, 1974). A major contribution to film literature, both scholarly in detail and profuse in illustrations. Films by all the warring nations are discussed, throughout the various phases of the conflict.

Filmlexicon degli autori e delle opere (Edizioni di Bianco e Nero, Rome, 1973-4). Two volumes that have emerged most valuably from the aftermath of the publication of the seven-tome Italian "Filmlexicon."

Here are entries devoted to personalities not covered in the main set, as well as additional information about directors and stars who have died in the meantime, or radically developed their career. Indispensable to libraries or individuals already in possession of the main dictionary.

Indian Films 1973, by B. V. Dharap (Motion Picture Enterprises, Poona, 1974). Complete credits for all feature films made in India during 1973, together with listings of all short films. Illustrations on each page, too.

Nazi Cinema, by Erwin Leiser (Secker & Warburg, London, 1975). Cleanly translated monograph of the films of the Hitler period in Germany, written by the man whose *Mein Kampf* was one of the first major documentaries on the Third Reich. The book is notable for its use of source materials, contemporary letters, etc.

Stumfilmen i Sverige—Kritik och debatt, edited by Elisabeth Liljedahl (Proprius Förlag/Svenska Filminstitutet, Stockholm, 1975). A quite entrancing selection of Swedish film reviews from the silent era, edited by Sweden's first feminine Doctor of Film. There is a summary in English.

Yoseloff/Tantivy

All the Bright Young Men and Women
Skvorecky/on Czech cinema
£2.70/$5.95

The American Musical
Vallance £1.25/$3.50

The Animated Film
Stephenson £1.10/$2.95

Basil Rathbone
Druxman £4.25/$10.00

Boris Karloff and His Films
Jensen £3.75/$8.95

Bound and Gagged
Lahue/on silent serials
£2.50/$7.50

Cads and Cavaliers
Thomas/on swashbucklers
£6.25/$15.00

Cinema in Britain
Butler/illustrated history
£5.75/$15.00

Cinema of Andrzej Wajda
Michalek £1.10/$2.95

Cinema of Carl Dreyer
Milne £1.10/$2.95

Cinema of David Lean
Pratley £5.00/$12.50

Cinema of François Truffaut
Petrie £1.10/$2.95

Cinema of Fritz Lang
Jensen £1.10/$2.95

Cinema of John Ford
Baxter £1.10/$2.95

Cinema of John Frankenheimer
Pratley £1.10/$2.95

Cinema of Josef von Sternberg
Baxter £1.10/$2.95

Cinema of Luis Buñuel
Buache £1.10/$2.95

Cinema of Otto Preminger
Pratley £1.10/$2.95

Cinema of Roman Polanski
Butler £1.10/$2.95

Coming Next Week
Sweeney/movie adverts
£4.75/$12.95

Concise History of the Cinema
Cowie/2 vols
£1.25/$3.50 each

DeMille: The Man & His Pictures
Essoe and Lee £3.50/$8.50

Directing Motion Pictures
Marner/Screen Textbook
£1.25/$3.95

Dreams for Sale
Lahue/history of Triangle
£3.25/$8.50

Early American Cinema
Slide £1.10/$2.95

Eastern Europe
Hibbin £1.25/$3.50

Faces of Hollywood
Bull and Lee/great star portraits £3.75/$9.50

The Film Actor
Pate/acting technique
£3.75/$9.50

Film Design
Marner/Screen Textbook
£1.50/$3.95

Film Fantasy Scrapbook
Harryhausen £6.00/$15.00

Films of Mary Pickford
Lee £3.50/$8.95

Films on the Campus
Fensch/student film-making
£6.00/$15.00

Fit for the Chase
Lee/cars in movies
£3.15/$8.50

Forty Years in Hollywood
Freulich and Abramson
£5.00/$12.50

France
Martin/illustrated dictionary
£1.25/$3.50

French Cinema since 1946
Armes/2 vols
£1.10/$2.95 each

The Gangster Film
Baxter £1.25/$3.50

Gentlemen to the Rescue
Lahue £3.50/$8.50

Germany
Bucher/illustrated dictionary
£1.25/$3.50

Gloria Swanson
Lee £3.50/$8.50

Golden Age of Sound Comedy
McCaffrey £5.75/$15.00

Good Dames
Parish £6.00/$15.00

The Great Movie Series
Parish £6.00/$15.00

The Griffith Actresses
Slide £3.75/$8.95

Hollywood's Other Men
Barris £6.25/$15.00

Griffith and the Rise of Hollywood
O'Dell £1.10/$2.95

A Handbook of Canadian Film
Beattie £1.25/$2.95

Hitchcock's Films
Wood £1.10/$2.95

Hollywood in the Twenties
Robinson £1.10/$2.95

Hollywood in the Thirties
Baxter £1.10/$2.95

Ten Years in Paradise, compiled and edited by Paul A. Scaramazza (Pleasant Press, New York, 1975; distributed by Cinemabilia, New York). Another compilation, this time from the pages of "Photoplay" between 1921 and 1930. There are excerpts from comments on some 4,200 features, and an introduction by Anthony Slide.

To Kinoumeno Skhedio, by Yanni Vasiliadi (Ekdosis Kastanioti, Athens, 1975). A comprehensive international review of Animation, from the editorial team responsible for the Greek magazine "Film." Though the text will remain a closed shop for most people, the 1890–1974 filmography at the end is useful and readily understandable.

MONOGRAPHS AND BIOGRAPHIES

Bogart, by Allen Eyles (Macmillan, London, 1975). An outstanding selection of stills (including one *colour* picture from *Treasure of the Sierra Madre*!) make this one of the best of Macmillan's new series, "The Movie Makers." Eyles concentrates on the films rather than the legend, the character Bogart created rather than the off-screen personality. Full filmography.

Brando, by David Shipman (Macmillan, London, 1974). Another entry in the well-designed "Movie Makers" collection. Shipman's style is flippant and often patronising (he implies, for instance, that *The Godfather* is a less valuable film than *The Sound of Music* because it is less likeable), but perhaps this is due to his subject, whose work has never had the consistent cult appeal of Bogie's.

Chaplin, by Denis Gifford (Macmillan, London, 1974). The illustrations, some in brash colour, again save this "Movie Makers"

volume. Gifford's historical survey is accurate, but his critical intelligence is blunt—for example, he dismisses *The Circus* as being pathetic and primitive.

Chaplin, by Roger Manvell (Hutchinson, London; Little, Brown, Boston, 1974). This is among Manvell's best books, for it thoughtfully places Chaplin in the entire context of his time, relating his attitudes to contemporary history and his style to the mime and theatrical traditions in which he was reared. Reading this biography, one feels that it must be the first ever devoted to Chaplin; and that is the best tribute one can offer.

James Dean, by John Howlett (Plexus, London, 1975). A large-format monograph on Dean that skirts most of the pitfalls and most of the *clichés*, and contains some of the most unfamiliar photographs of Dean, both on and

off screen. There is a fluency to the writing that by degrees makes a rather distant, unsympathetic figure appear timely and alluring.

Rainer Werner Fassbinder, by Peter W. Jansen and Wolfram Schütte (Carl Hanser Verlag, Munich, 1974). The first book—and a fine one—on the continent's most exciting new director. Fassbinder's work in theatre is well covered alongside his many films, and there are interviews and a full filmography.

John Ford, by Joseph McBride and Michael Wilmington (Secker and Warburg, London, 1975). Like much of Robin Wood's work, this auteurist profile is good on some films, slighting of others (*She Wore a Yellow Ribbon* is virtually ignored), and excessively generous to a third group (notably *The Searchers*). There are some informal glimpses of Ford, however, that make the book humane as well as cerebral in approach.

Hitchcock, by George Perry (Macmillan, London, 1975). The fourth in the new "Movie Makers" series. Pictorially, the book is a delight. But the text has the quality of a reheated dish; after all, Perry has already said much the same things in his Hitchcock monograph for Studio Vista (1965).

The Films of Sophia Loren, by Tony Crawley (LSP Books, London, 1974). Based on the Citadel series of pictorial surveys, this British book follows Sophia Loren's career from *Aida* (1953) to *Verdict* (1974). Good for reference and browsing. The illustrations are superbly assembled,

Marilyn Monroe, edited by Pierre Lherminier (Cinéma d'Aujourd'hui, Paris, 1975). The most challenging and rewarding event of the film book year in France has been the resuscitation of the "Cinéma d'Aujourd'hui" series, in a new format and as a quarterly magazine-cum-book. The Monroe volume contains much fresh and intriguing material,

> THE LITTLE FILM GAZETTE
> OF NDW
> APARTMENT 32
> 227 WEST 11 STREET
> NEW YORK, NEW YORK 10014
>
> Monographs on Selected Film Topics

such us an interview with Yves Montand and reproductions of MM's actual letters.

Ozu, His Life and Films, by Donald Richie (University of California Press, Berkeley, 1974). For all his formidable scholarship and familiarity with the craft of writing, Richie is not as at home with Ozu as he was with Kurosawa—even the filmography is sketchy—and the illustrations are not so beautifully keyed to the text as they were in the earlier book. There are certain passages, however, of exquisite understanding with which the modest Ozu himself would surely have been delighted.

Jean Renoir, edited by Claude Beylie (Cinéma d'Aujourd'hui, Paris, 1975). The second in Pierre Lherminier's fascinating series, stuffed with good things, such as a filmography of scrupulous accuracy, a profile of Renoir at work that captures the man and his personality, and a host of rare pictures.

My Life and My Films, by Jean Renoir (Collins, London, 1974). *The* film book of the year, an autobiography in which Renoir expresses with the utmost limpidity the wisdom he has gained from his career and his environment. There are neat comments on all his films, in which he seizes on the essential, revelatory detail. But it is the warmth of his disposition that illuminates this book— Renoir's belief in the oneness of man and the world.

My Life in Pictures, by Charles Chaplin (The Bodley Head, London, 1974). One of the most sumptuous picture books ever issued on the cinema, laid out with imagination and affection by David King, who uses a variety of duotone effects to conjure up the far-off faces and moments revealed in Chaplin's scrapbook. There is also a folio of full-colour material, and an introduction by Francis Wyndham. It is an ironic paradox that pictures like *The Circus*, so neglected by Chaplin in his autobiography, are here accorded proper attention. The Bodley Head can be proud of producing this volume.

T. J. Särkkä, legenda jo cläessään, by Kari Uusitalo (WSOY, Helsinki, 1975). A biography of one of the portal figures in Finnish cinema, with a career stretching from 1935 to 1965, during which time Särkkä produced 233 features, directing no fewer than 49 himself. Researched with Kari Uusitalo's customary zeal and accuracy.

Raoul Walsh, edited by Phil Hardy (Edinburgh Film Festival, 1974). A well-meaning but pretentious and ultimately opaque study of a Hollywood director whose action movies are light-years away from the schematic, semiological criticism of this monograph. There is a useful interview with Walsh, though.

classes, for example—but publishers will still not learn that frame enlargements make poor illustrations. Most film buffs would surely prefer the crisp, well-lit artifice of production stills. Why, too, are some shots "larger" than others? Libraries, however, will clearly wish to acquire these volumes as they appear.

Scenes from a Marriage, by Ingmar Bergman (Pantheon Books, New York, 1974). Launched with commendable speed by Random House to coincide with the opening of the movie, this screenplay contains the full version of Bergman's TV series from which he himself condensed the threatrical release. Like all Bergman's scripts, this one reads beautifully. The dialogue is both complex and spare; Bergman's introduction brief but compassionate.

The Complete Wedding March of Erich von Stroheim, edited by Herman G. Weinberg (Little, Brown, Boston, 1974, for the American Film Institute). Another luxurious tribute to the memory of von Stroheim. Weinberg's introduction is long and fulsome, Olympian in its grasp of detail and in its recreation of the Viennese atmosphere Stroheim himself sought to convey in the movie. In place of a screenplay, there is a splendid collection of stills, which tell the story more eloquently than words ever could.

SCRIPTS

James Whale's Frankenstein, edited by Richard J. Anobile (Macmillan, London; Darien House, New York, 1974). An attempt to capture the spirit of a film by reproducing every shot, with dialogue laid out beneath the pictures. This is the *raison d'être* for a new series that has also covered *Psycho, Casablanca,* and *The Maltese Falcon.* Up to a point the technique is successful—individual sequences can be analysed in film

GENERAL

About Documentary: Anthropology on Film, by Robert Edmonds (Pflaum Publishing, Dayton, 1974). This theoretical work concentrates not so much on individual documentaries but on the social philosophy behind all documentary as such. It is likely to spark off plenty of classroom discussion.

American Film Genres, by Stuart M. Kaminsky (Pflaum Publishing, Dayton, 1974). Subtitled "Approaches to a Critical

THE MOVIEMAKERS

BRANDO
David Shipman   £1.95

CHAPLIN
Denis Gifford   £1.95

BOGART
Allen Eyles   £2.50

HITCHCOCK
George Perry   £2.50

A lively, illustrated series which gives a critical survey of the development and entire film output of major screen figures. Fully illustrated in colour and black and white, each book has a comprehensive filmography and index.

THE FILM CLASSICS LIBRARY

Edited by Richard J. Anobile

THE MALTESE FALCON

CASABLANCA

PSYCHO

FRANKENSTEIN

£4.50 each

The most accurate and complete reconstructions of classic films in book form, containing over 1,400 frame blow-ups coupled with the complete dialogue from the original soundtrack

For more information, write to: Publicity Department, Macmillan London, Little Essex Street, London WC2

MACMILLAN LONDON

Theory of Popular Film," this educational manual covers the familiar *genres*, but also dwells on the work of directors like Ford and Siegel. Like all Pflaum books, it is well annotated and intelligently designed.

The Celluloid Literature, by William Jinks (Pflaum Publishing, Dayton, 1974). This is a second edition of Jinks's study of film language (in spite of its title, the book is not a bibliography), and uses diagrams as well as stills to illustrate a director's point of view.

Celluloid Rock, by Philip Jenkinson and Alan Warner (Lorrimer Publishing, London, 1974). An alluring picture book for those with nostalgic memories of the Fifties and Sixties, though the text is flawed by the inescapable fact that most of the movies concerned were really very, very bad.

Crossroads to the Cinema, by Douglas Brode (Holbrook Press, Boston, 1975). A cheaply produced anthology of good writing on the cinema in general—its *genres*, its themes, its transitions.

Elokuva television aikakaudella, by Modest Savchenko (Otava, Helsinki, 1975). A distinguished Finnish critic relates film to the TV era, and traces back deep into film history to find the antecedents of today's video revolution. This is a book that covers movies of all types and sizes and yet still speaks freshly about them (even the stills are unexpectedly good).

Film Is, by Stephen Dwoskin (Peter Owen, London, 1975). At last one of the portal figures in the British underground cinema has written his own study of the international "free cinema." He proves himself a fine analytical critic. The indexes and stills are outstandingly good.

From Reverence to Rape, The Treatment of Women in the Movies, by Molly Haskell (Holt, Rinehart and Winston, New York/ Penguin Books, New York, 1974; New

English Library, London, 1975). The best of the recent spate of feminist polemics on film. Ms. Haskell writes clearly and with a dry wit. Her book is impressive because it shirks few eras and few movies; in a sense, it is a brand-new history of the cinema, especially good on the Twenties and the European directors of recent times. If you want to be converted to Women's Lib in three quick hours, read this book.

Hal in the Classroom: Science Fiction Films, by Ralph J. Amelio (Pflaum Publishing, Dayton, 1974). Nine articles that discuss the theory, *genre*, analysis and practical use of science fiction movies. There is also an annotated filmography of over 150 short and feature films. Another worthy educational manual from Pflaum.

Kung Fu, Cinema of Vengeance, by Verina Glaessner (Lorrimer Publishing, London, 1974). If anyone can make Hongkong kick-flicks seem serious, then Verina Glaessner is that person. She writes with just the right degree of scholarship and verve, disclosing the underlying themes behind these Chinese films. Plenty of stills and statistics sprinkled throughout the book.

Marshall Delaney at the Movies, by Robert Fulford (Peter Martin Associates/Take One, Toronto, 1974). A collection of reviews by a leading Canadian critic. Chatty remi-niscences rather than analysis and cant.

The Media Reader, edited by Joan Valdes and Jeanne Crow (Pflaum Publishing, Dayton, 1975). One of the year's most unusual and exciting books, not entirely devoted to films, but covering a wide spectrum of bright prose involving the performing arts and the media. Everything from still photography to pop music is covered, how it's created, how it's interpreted, how it's sold.

Screen Test, A Quiz Book about the Movies, by Peter Bowen, Martin Hayden, and Frank Riess (Penguin Books, London, 1975). One of the year's most useless film books, a paper handkerchief to be deployed for half an hour and then relegated to the shelves of the Great Unread. Its single virtue is its comprehensiveness—questions on literally thousands of films and topics.

Stroheim, A Pictorial Record of His Nine Films, by Herman G. Weinberg (Dover Publications, New York, 1975). Weinberg is a latterday Boswell to Stroheim's Johnson. This contribution is short on text but ravishing in its panoply of stills. Original posters and lobby material add to the book's value.

Talking Pictures, by Richard Corliss (Overlook Press, Woodstock, NY, 1974). A lengthy and ambitious study of the screenwriter in American cinema, an attempt, indeed, to oust the director from his pedestal

in the auteurist's Pantheon. Corliss's own language is resolutely American, rippling with references to U.S. life and *moeurs* that may puzzle the overseas reader. He is excellent on the scribes of Hollywood's heyday (Howard Koch, Ben Hecht, Garson Kanin, etc.), but less sympathetic to moderns like Buck Henry (why no appraisal of the tautly-written *Taking Off*?).

Theories of Film, by Andrew Tudor (Secker and Warburg, London, 1974). The critics criticised: an analysis of the influence and meaning of John Grierson, Kracauer, Bazin *et al.*

Women in Focus, by Jeanne Betancourt (Pflaum Publishing, Dayton, 1974). An annotated dictionary of female films and filmmakers, seen from a feminist standpoint. A practical source guide.

Film Magazines

Except with British and American magazines, prices quoted are for subscriptions taken outside the country of origin. Abbreviation n.p.a. = numbers per annum.

L'AVANT-SCENE CINEMA

Ed: Jacques-G. Perret, 27 rue Saint-André-des-Arts, Paris 6. 11 n.p.a.: 79.60 francs (£8.00 from British agents, The Tantivy Press, 108 New Bond Street, London W1Y 0QX). 60pp approx. The monthly screenplays released by "L'Avant-Scène" are particularly valuable because they contain the text of the actual *film*, unlike most published scripts, which deviate from the movie on several points. The magazine offers ancillary delights such as posters and the supplement "Anthologie du Cinéma," which builds into a magnificent encyclopaedia through the years. Finally there are the boxes of slides from the work of directors like Bergman, Buñuel, Renoir, and Fellini.

Number 148: *Sunrise* (Murnau).
Number 149/50: Animation issue, devoted to *La planète sauvage* (Laloux-Topor).

Number 151: *Le fantôme de la liberté* (Buñuel).
Number 152: *Ana y los lobos* (Saura).
Number 153: *Vincent, François, Paul ... et les autres* (Sautet).
Number 154: *Dance of the Vampires* (Polanski).
Number 155: *The General* (Keaton-Bruckman).
Number 156: *Stavisky* (Resnais).
Number 157: *Les doigts dans la tête* (Doillon).
Number 158: *L'important c'est d'aimer* (Żuławski).
Number 159: *Violence et passion* (Visconti).

CHAPLIN

Ed: Lars-Olof Löthwall, Svenska Filminstitutet, Box 27 126, S 102 52 Stockholm 27, Sweden. 6 n.p.a.: 30 Kr. (£3.40 or $7.50 approx.). 40pp. Scandinavia's leading film magazine, with detailed filmographies and attractive presentation making it accessible to non-Swedish-speaking readers. Emphasis on interviews, reviews, and debate.

Number 131: Interviews with Martin Scorsese and Francis Ford Coppola; long coverage of Vilgot Sjöman's career.
Number 132: Article on the growth of the camera apparatus, by Torsten Jungstedt, and other studies of the

SOME OF YOU ARE STILL NOT READING FOCUS ON FILM

Of course, not everyone wants to read the kind of magazine that starts where most others leave off—documenting the more obscure areas of film history in a lively and entertaining fashion. But perhaps because of the magazine's restricted distribution you've not yet heard of FOCUS ON FILM or seen a copy. Yet with more than twenty issues behind us, we've gained a keen and devoted readership and we've been recognised by the "International Index to Film Periodicals" as a magazine of lasting value and significance.

Each issue has 68 pages in a distinctive wide format, starts with a section of reviews of new films with profiles of some of their leading artists; continues with long interviews or career studies concerned with actors, directors, writers, etc. (plus the occasional general article), always well illustrated and usually accompanied by richly detailed filmographies; ends with a department of concise book reviews (including many publications not reviewed in other British magazines); often includes reappraisals of old films; and provides space for readers' comments, corrections and additions consolidating the research of past issues.

Recent numbers have included interviews with John Wayne, Allen Garfield, Eleanor Powell, Fritz Lang, Barré Lyndon, Jule Styne and Fernand Gravey; career studies of Conrad Veidt and Nick Lucas; a history of the Private Eye in the Hollywood movie; reappraisals of "The Last Flight" and "Smart Money"; and concise profiles of such figures as Claude Lelouch, John Vernon, Gerry Fisher, Ellen Burstyn, Martin Scorsese.

Each issue costs 60p or $1.75 by post from The Tantivy Press (publishers of International Film Guide), 108 New Bond Street, London W1Y 0QX (England), or 50p—$1.75 from bookshops specialising in film magazines.

cinematographer's art, including an interview with Robert Surtees.

Number 133: Focus on Swedish animation.

Number 134: "Amerikanska bilder," by Olle Sjögren, a study of four aspects of American life as reflected in cimema.

Number 135: Interview with Jack Nicholson.

Number 136: Splendid double issue devoted to horror and fantasy films.

Number 137: Reports on film in Iran, Hungary, and Poland.

CINEMA 75 . . . 76

Ed: Gaston Haustrate, 6 rue Ordener, 75018 Paris. 10 n.p.a.: 90 francs (£9.50 or $20 abroad). 160pp. The special value of this long-running French magazine is its in-depth inquiries into *genres* or national cinemas. Film reviews are frequently quirky, but coverage is large. Useful interviews.

Number 198: Interviews with Kate Millett, Léonce-Henry Burel, Yoshishige Yoshida, Joël Santoni; "La folie dans le cinéma américain."

Number 190/91: A 200-page examination of Italian cinema, with filmographies, reports, etc.—something at which "Cinéma" excels.

Number 192: Cuban and New German cinema; interviews with Michel Simon and Daniel Schmid.

Number 193: Interviews with Rainer Werner Fassbinder, Sam Fuller, Jack Hazan.

Number 194: Third World cinema; "Le cinéma et le cirque" (with filmography).

Number 195: Eisenstein and "Das Kapital"; New German cinema (part two); interview with Andrzej Żuławski.

Number 197: Hongkong martial arts cinema; Syrian cinema; interview with Claude D'Anna.

Number 198: Interviews with Werner Herzog, Bertrand Tavernier, and Otto Preminger.

Number 199: Portuguese and Belgian cinema.

CONTINENTAL FILM REVIEW

Ed: Gordon Reid, Eurap Publishing Co., 71 Stoke Newington Road, London N16. 12 n.p.a.: £3.96 ($10 abroad). 36pp. Beneath the acres of titillation which light up this monthly lies a serious appreciation of all aspects of world cinema.

Jun 1974: Hungarian report; cinema and the history of art.

Aug 1974: Italian, French, Berlin Festival reports.

Oct 1974: Extensive report on Edinburgh Festival.

Dec 1974: Australian report; article on *The Abdication*; marathon French films.

Feb 1975: Article on Swiss cinema.

Apr 1975: Truffaut's *L'histoire d'Adèle H.*; interview with Romy Schneider.

May 1975: Robbe-Grillet's *Le jeu avec le feu*, plus interview.

ECRAN '75

Ed: Marcel Martin, Guy Braucourt, Editions de l'Atalante, 60 avenue Simon-Bolivar, 75019 Paris. 12 n.p.a.: 115 francs (£11.50 or $27). 96pp. Although economic exigencies are restricting most magazines of this kind to a focus on only the best films and directors, "Ecran" is still a goldmine for anyone wanting to find a film-maker's comments on his work, some advance news on a project, reviews of books in French, and in-depth discussions of new releases.

Number 26: "Le secret de Maître Pagnol," by Claude Beylie; "Liliana Cavani: le mythe, le sexe, la révolte," by Claire Clouzot.

Number 27: Interviews with Resnais, Altman, and Coppola, together with studies of *Stavisky, Thieves Like Us,* and *The Conversation.*

Number 28: Special summer issue on women in the cinema.

Number 29: "Luis G. Berlanga, Createur, Grandeur, Nature," by Guy Braucourt.

Number 30: Study of Dino Risi's work; dossier on new trends in African cinema.

Number 31: Focus on Fassbinder and Renoir.

Number 32: Special issue on *film noir.*

Number 33: Excellent, informative study of Orson Welles and his most recent films; also a round-table discussion of current French cinema.

Number 34: Interview with Paul Strand, together with a rare filmography.

Number 35: Focus on Billy Wilder.
Number 36: Studies of Chabrol, Antonioni, and Frank Lloyd.

FILM

Ed: Peter Cargin, British Federation of Film Societies, 72 Dean Street, London W1. 12 n.p.a.: £4.10 ($12). 24pp. Though available at a discount to BFFS members, "Film" is still rather pricy for its size. A consistently attractive lay-out and excellent festival coverage do much to compensate, however, and for 16mm enthusiasts the magazine is indispensable.

Jul 1974: Cannes; Canadian cinema, by Gerald Pratley; interview with Otto Preminger.
Aug 1974: Zagreb; interview with Bertrand Tavernier; Louis Malle.
Sep 1974: Berlin and Cork.
Oct 1974: Locarno; New German cinema.
Nov 1974: Edinburgh; František Vláčil.
Dec 1974: New York; interview with Ann Sheridan.
Jan 1975: Interviews with Daniel Mann and Ann Sheridan (cont.).
Feb 1975: Welles's *Hearts of Age*; interview with Dick Lester.
Mar 1975: Hungarian cinema; interviews with Pablo Ferro, and Juliet Berto and Dominique Labourier.
Apr 1975: Delhi and Cork; Memorial Enterprises.
May 1975: Interviews with John Cassavetes. Louise Brooks, Robert Redford; Antwerp and Rotterdam.
Jun 1975: Zagreb Studio.

FILM COMMENT

Ed: Richard Corliss, Film Society of Lincoln Center, 1865 Broadway, New York, NY 10023. 6 n.p.a.: $9 ($10.50 abroad). 72pp approx. This glossy, well-presented bi-monthly covers a broad range of material and opinion, and can be relied upon for some attractive special numbers during each year.

May–Jun 1974: Interviews with Howard Hawks and Keith Carradine and Shelley Duvall; *Tout va bien*, Dick Lester, and Stroheim.
Jul–Aug 1974: Focus on Rossellini; interview with Francis Ford Coppola, and with Jack Clayton; re-assessment of *The Incredible Shrinking Man*, by Martin Rubin.
Sep–Oct 1974: Interviews with Jacques Rivette, Gene Hackman, and Hal Mohr; festivals round-up, and a major study of Robert Altman.
Nov–Dec 1974: Superbly-produced issue on *film noir*, as well as an interview with Alexander Kluge.
Jan–Feb 1975: 96-page special issue on Animation, with colour pictures and several important historical articles on the growth of American cartoons.
Mar–Apr 1975: "Old Hollywood"; interview with Martin Scorsese.

FILMGUIA

Ed: Manuel Ferrer Salvador, Marquesa Caldas de Montbuy 27, Barcelona 16. 12 n.p.a.: 600 pesetas. 40pp. A well-produced, well-documented and lively Spanish monthly which is international in outlook while not forgetting the native cinema (an exhaustive cumulative list of *every* film released in Spain between 1939 and 1974 is a particularly valuable section in each issue). Full of filmographies.

Number 1 (Nov. 1974): Mythology in the cinema.
Numbers 3 and 4: Filmography of women directors.
Number 5: Rome in the cinema.
Number 6: Robert Aldrich; John Cassavetes; Oscar Wilde in the cinema.

FILM-MAKERS NEWSLETTER

Ed: Suni Mallow, H. Whitney Bailey, PO Box 115, Ward Hill, Massachusetts 01830. 11 n.p.a.: $8 ($10 abroad). 80pp. Now produced on clean, coated paper, this technical magazine can claim to be the finest and most successful of its kind in the world. Specialises in interviews *in extenso*.

Vol 7, Number 9–10: "The Art of Comedy: Woody Allen and *Sleeper*," by Judith Trotsky; interview with Steven Spielberg on *The Sugarland Express*.
Vol. 8, Number 1: Dossier on *The Taking of Pelham One Two Three*.

Vol. 8, Number 2: "Alain Resnais: The Freeing of Film Form," by Wim Sharples Jr.; interview with Walter Murch on sound editing.

Vol. 8, Number 3: Interview with John Cassavetes on *A Woman under the Influence*.

Vol. 8, Number 4: "*Lenny*: A Filmic Critique," by Andrew C. Bobrow; interview with Bob Fosse, and conversation with Brian De Palma on *Phantom of the Paradise*.

Vol. 8, Number 5: Martin Scorsese discusses *Alice Doesn't Live Here Anymore*; interview with Marcel Marceau.

Vol. 8, Number 6: "The Making of *Hearts and Minds*," an interview with Peter Davis.

Vol. 8, Number 7: Neil Simon discusses *The Prisoner of Second Avenue*; "The Film Art of Jordan Belson."

FILM QUARTERLY

Ed: Ernest Callenbach, University of California Press, Berkeley, California 94720. 4 n.p.a.: $6 ($7 abroad). 64pp. Valuable for its long, often theoretically-inclined articles and reviews, but lacking the verve and wide spectrum of information that are needed to rejuvenate such a scholarly quarterly.

Summer 1974: "Rossellini's Case Histories for Moral Education," by Louis Norman; "Structures of Narrativity in Fritz Lang's *Metropolis*," by Alan Williams.

Fall 1974: "Rebel without a Cause: Nicholas Ray in the Fifties," by Peter Biskind; "Footnote to the History of Riefenstahl's *Olympia*," by Hans Barkhausen.

Spring 1975: "In Defense of Sam Peckinpah," by Mark Crispin Miller; "Style, Grammar, and the Movies," by Bill Nichols.

FILMS AND FILMING

Ed: Robin Bean, Hansom Books, Artillery Mansions, 75 Victoria Street, London SW1. 12 n.p.a.: £6.50 ($16.10 abroad). 60pp. "f&f" continues to vacillate between the alarming and outrageous, its number of pages shrinking as fast as its editorial matter. Compulsively readable, all the same.

Jul 1974: Cannes '74, by Ken Wlaschin; American Sons, by Gerald Jones; recent Czech cinema, by Derek Elley.

Aug 1974: Interview with Arthur Hiller; *Casablanca*, by Barry Day; Zagreb and Cork reports; interview with Robert Gordon Edwards.

Sep 1974: Start of a long series of picture-spreads and articles devoted to Fifties cinema; interview with Gregory Peck.

Oct 1974: Interviews with Dick Lester and Monte Hellman; *North by Northwest*, by Gordon Gow.

Nov 1974: Brando, by Gordon Gow; Bulgarian cinema, by Derek Elley; Felix the Cat, by Julian Fox.

Dec 1974: Interviews with "Monty Python" and Pete Walker; Orson Welles, by Gordon Gow.

Jan 1975: Interview with Robert Evans; *King Kong*, by Gordon Gow.

Feb 1975: Interview with Liliana Cavani; *The Night of the Hunter*, by Gordon Gow.

May 1975: British cinema, by Michael Winner; Swanson, Loy and Karen Black, by Eric Braun.

Apr 1975: Fifties American acting, by Gordon Gow; Winner on British cinema (continued).

Mar 1975: Interviews with Sidney Lumet and scriptwriter Kenneth Ross; *Sweet Charity*, by Derek Elley.

Jun 1975: Interviews with George Chakiris and Pete Townshend.

Jul 1975: Interview with Mel Brooks; *Zabriskie Point*, by Gordon Gow.

FILMS ILLUSTRATED

Ed: David Castell, Independent Magazines Ltd., Bridge House, 181 Queen Victoria Street, London EC4V 4 DD. 12 n.p.a.: £4.50 ($11). 40pp. No slackening in quality this year: still an admirably comprehensive review section, and a wide range of interviews and on-set reports. "Portfolio," a new section showcasing the work of still photographers, is an enterprising addition.

Jul 1974: Oscar Homolka, Lee Marvin, *The Conversation*.

Aug 1974: Jean Seberg, Jon Voight, Oliver Reed.

Sep 1974: Anthony Newley, Richard Attenborough, Edith Head, Bob Simmons.

Oct 1974: Alan Price, David Essex, Mickey Rooney, Helen Hayes.

Nov 1974: Gene Kelly, Liza Minnelli, Jack Haley Jr.,
Omar Sharif.
Dec 1974: Rod Steiger, Gloria Swanson, David Puttnam.
Feb 1975: Billy Wilder, Ted Kotcheff, *Man Friday*.
Mar 1975: Michael Winner, Robert Stevenson.
May 1975: Warren Beatty, Otto Preminger, Cybill
Shepherd, Peter Bogdanovich.
Jun 1975: George Kennedy, George Roy Hill.

FILMS IN REVIEW

Ed: Charles Phillips Reilly, 210 East 68th
Street, New York, NY 10021. 10 n.p.a.:
$10.50 ($12 abroad). 64pp. By working along
set lines for a number of years, FIR has established a respected place for itself among
American film magazines. It is best collected
for its career articles of stars and directors,
and for its correspondence columns, bursting
at the seams with all manner of recondite information, accurate and inaccurate.

May 1974: "David Lean," by Roy Pickard; "Homage to
James Cagney," by Kenneth G. Lawrence.
Aug–Sep 1974: "Mabel Normand," by Stephen Nor-
mand; "Paulette Goddard," by Jeffrey Gorney.
Oct 1974: "Jetta Goudal," by DeWitt Bodeen; "William
Keighley," by George Geltzer.
Nov 1974: "Garson Kanin," by Janice R. Welsch and
Patricia Erens, plus a history of Radio City Music
Hall.
Dec 1974: "Betty Bronson," by DeWitt Bodeen.
Jan 1975: "Gene Hackman," by Herbert G. Luft; "Lili
Damita," by Alfonso Pinto.
Feb 1975: "Rex Ingram and Alice Terry," by DeWitt
Bodeen; "The Ealing Story," by Roy Pickard.
Mar 1975: "Universal's Golden Age of Horror," by
Stephen Pendo.
Apr 1975: "Jane Wyman," by J. E. A. Bawden; "Brian
Donlevy," by Gregory Mank.
May 1975: "Rock Hudson," by Jimmie Hicks, plus
reports on the Academy Awards ceremony and the
text of Orson Welles's acceptance speech at the AFI
presentation.

FOCUS ON FILM

Ed: Allen Eyles, The Tantivy Press, 108 New
Bond Street, London W1Y 0QX. 4 n.p.a.:

£2.00 ($7.00 abroad). 68pp. Our own magazine, so naturally we think highly of its design, its accuracy, its carefully-selected pictures, and its eclectic enthusiasm for all corners of the cinema.

Number 19: Interview with Eleanor Powell: article on the Sennett Bathing Beauties, by DeWitt Bodeen; final part of Robert Wise interview.
Number 20: Interviews with John Wayne, Allen Garfield, and Fritz Lang; conclusion of Eleanor Powell interview; Sjöström's *Terje Vigen*, by John Fullerton; Nick Lucas, by Michael R. Pitts.
Number 21: Article on Conrad Veidt, by Herbert Holba, with David Robinson; interviews with Jule Styne and Barré Lyndon; Dieterle's *The Last Flight*, by Jeffrey Richards.
Number 22: "Private Eyes—From Sam Spade to J. J. Gittes," by Don Miller; interview with Fernand Gravey.

ISKUSSTVO KINO

Ed: Yevgyeni Surkov, 9 ul. Usiyevicha, 125 319 Moscow. 12 n.p.a.: 1 rouble per copy. 192pp. The long-running and prestigious Soviet monthly, unchanged in format, critical weight or indispensability.

Number 5, 1974: Interview with Yuri Ozerov; posthumous working papers of Kozintsev.
Number 6, 1974: Continuation of Kozintsev's papers; profile of Larisa Malevannaya.
Number 7, 1974: Discussion on directing; final part of Kozintsev's papers; script of Vasili Shukshin's *My Brother* ...
Number 8, 1974: Production reports; profile of Anatoly Solonitsyn.
Number 9, 1974: Articles celebrating Dovzhenko anniversary.
Number 11, 1974: Profiles of Kozintsev; interview with Kurosawa at work on *Dersu Uzala*.
Number 12, 1974: Interview with Tamara Makarova.
Number 2, 1975: Essay by Trauberg on Design; interview with Satyajit Ray; script of Kazimierz Kutz's *Pearl in the Crown*.
Number 4, 1975: Hungarian cinema, including article by Félix Máriássy.
Number 5, 1975: Sholokhov in the cinema.

KINO

Ed: Ryszard Koniczek, ul. Puławska 61, 02-595 Warsaw. 12 n.p.a.: 15 złoty per copy. 66pp. Not a trace of fatigue in this energetic Polish monthly, now with space-age covers. Few magazines can equal "Kino" in its visual appeal or international outlook, while remaining definitive on home matters.

Number 4, 1974: Profile of Jerzy Stefan Stawiński; Iranian cinema.
Number 5, 1974: Sylwester Szyszko's *Ciemna rzeka*; interview with Wajda on the set of *Ziemia obiecana*.
Number 6, 1974: Interviews with Roman Bratny and Sergey Gerasimov.
Number 7, 1974: Polish film posters at home and abroad.
Number 8, 1974: Jerzy Hoffman's *Potop*; profile of Wacław Kowalski; Cannes 1974.
Number 9, 1974: Profiles of Henryk Kluba, and Andrzej Trzos-Rastawiecki's *Zapis zbrodni*; Swedish cinema.
Number 11, 1974: Discussion on acting; profile of Vasili Shukshin; African filmography.
Number 12, 1974: Wajda's *Ziemia obiecana*; article on Bo Widerberg.
Number 1, 1975: Zanussi's *Bilans kwartalny*; "Agnès Varda and others."
Number 2, 1975: Profile of Maja Komorowska; Polish filmography for 1974.
Number 3, 1975: Interview with Wajda; profile of Bertolucci.
Number 4, 1975: Interview with Walerian Borowczyk; Polish TV; profile of Andrey Mikhalkov-Konchalovski.
Number 5, 1975: Interviews with documentary filmmakers; Polish TV series.

KOSMORAMA

Ed: Per Calum, Det Danske Filmmuseum, Store Søndervoldstraede, 1419 Copenhagen K, Denmark. 4 n.p.a.: 45 Kr. (£3.50 or $8.50). 48pp approx. A bold, imaginative Danish quarterly that has undergone several metamorphoses, and is disposed to rewarding double issues.

Number 121: "Sovjetisk ortodoski," by Peter Schepelern; "Rowland Brown—ugleset, overset og glemt," by Ron Mottram.

Number 122: "Hal Ashby—en auteur?" by Ul Jørgensen; "Martin Ritts sociale holdning," by Kaare Schmidt.

Number 123/24: Jumbo number with interviews with John Boorman and Francis Ford Coppola.

Number 125: "Om Hasseåtage," by Peter Hirsch; "Alan J. Pakula fortaeller om *Sidste vidne*," by Andrew C. Bobrow; "Frankenstein-myten," by John Ernst.

POSITIF

Ed: various, Editions Opta, 39 rue d'Amsterdam, 75008 Paris. 12 n.p.a.: 100 francs (£11 or $25.50). 80pp approx. Although it has passed through the hands of several publishers, the editorial board of "Positif" remains intact, together with its forthright championship of the underrated director. Whatever the magazine does, it does well and in depth.

Number 160: Interviews with Alain Corneau and Dušan Makavejev, plus coverage of the contemporary animation scene.

Number 161: First part of a study of King Vidor (most dossiers of this kind in "Positif" are supported by interviews), and of Francis Ford Coppola.

Number 162: Focus on Rivette, Buñuel, and Saura.

Number 163: Focus on Sautet, Risi—and the second part of the King Vidor companion.

Number 164: Special issue devoted to movies in Latin America.

Number 165: A wide selection of articles on fantasy films, science fiction films, Marilyn Monroe, and Japanese cinema.

Number 166: Interview with Robert Altman during the shooting of *Nashville*.

Number 167: Memorable and indispensable Orson Welles issue.

Number 168: Interviews with Barbara Loden and Jean Aurenche.

Number 169: An exemplary number, with three major focal points: Hongkong cinema, the Yugoslav director Klopčić, and the latest work of Werner Herzog.

SIGHT AND SOUND

Ed: Penelope Houston, British Film Institute, 81 Dean Street, London W1V 6AA. 4 n.p.a.: £2 or $6. 66pp. Almost unnoticed, "Sight and Sound," the world's oldest established quarterly, has begun to cover TV during the past year, with some fine, detailed studies of various aspects of British TV. Otherwise the magazine is notable for its interviews and long reviews.

Summer 1974: "Threads through the Labyrinth: Hongkong Movies," by Tony Rayns; "Profession: Actor: an interview with Jack Nicholson," by John Russell Taylor; "Swedish Retrospect," by John Gillett.

Autumn 1974: "Spain: Out of the Past," by Roger Mortimore; interview with Jacques Rivette.

Winter 1974/75: "The Case of Sergo Paradjanov," by Herbert Marshall; interviews with Fassbinder, Wenders, and Syberberg.

Spring 1975: "Vittorio De Sica," by Gideon Bachmann; "The Communal Touch: the Television Plays of Colin Welland," by Paul Madden and David Wilson.

TAKE ONE

Ed: Peter Lebensold, Unicorn Publishing, PO Box 1778, Station B, Montréal, Québec H3B 3L3. 6 n.p.a. but subs only for 12 issues: $5 ($7.50 abroad). 40pp. By far the liveliest film magazine in the North American continent, still extraordinarily reasonable in price, and bursting with enthusiasm for movies of all kinds, times, and countries. The zestful design makes even the most sober article seem exciting.

Vol 4, Number 3: "Interview with Salvador Allende," by Roberto Rossellini.

Vol 4, Number 4: "Porn Films: an In-Depth Report," by John Morthland; interview with Rossellini.

Vol 4, Number 5: "Just a Dancer Gone Wrong," profile of James Cagney by Patrick McGilligan; "Pasolini Today," by Gideon Bachmann.

Vol 4, Number 6: "Fassbinder's Holy Whores," by Christian Br. Thomsen.

Vol 4, Number 5: First part of superb centenary tribute to D. W. Griffith, by Alanna Nash.

Vol 4, Number 8: Second Part of Alanna Nash's Griffith dossier, plus an interview with William Clothier.

Other Magazines

ACTION, 7950 Sunset Blvd, Hollywood, California 90046. The elegant house magazine of the Directors' Guild of America. Fine inside stories, interviews, and book review column.

CAHIERS DU CINEMA, 9 passage de la Boule-Blanche, 75012 Paris. Now not even a pale shadow of its former self, this monthly is bare, polemical and of limited appeal.

CATHOLIC FILM NEWSLETTER, Suite 4200, 405 Lexington Avenue, New York, NY 10017. Issued fortnightly by the National Catholic Office for Motion Pictures, this provides extended reviews of new films, features, and also shorts and specialist subjects.

CELULÓIDE, Rua David Manuel da Fonseca 88, Rio Maior, Portugal. Seventeenth year of publication. Monthly magazine in Portuguese.

CINE AL DIA, Apartado 50, 446, Sabana Grande, Caracas, Venezuela. Venezuelan monthly magazine.

CINEASTE, 333 Sixth Avenue, New York, NY 10014. If the Alternative Cinema ever elects an official magazine, then "Cineaste" should top the poll. Edited with persistence and good sense by Gary Crowdus, this periodical covers film theory and political cinema, and its interviews are always extensive.

CINE CUBANO, Calle 23 no. 1155, Havana, Cuba. Vital information on all Latin American cinema, unfortunately only in Spanish. Often includes interesting theoretical articles.

CINE DOSSIERS, L'Action Cinématographique, 30 rue de l'Etuve, 1000 Brussels. Belgian review, edited by well-known critic and historian Francis Bolen.

CINEFANTASTIQUE, 7470 Diversey, Elmwood Park, Ill. 60635. An enthusiastic attractive quarterly with a special emphasis on science fiction films. A modern "successor" to the French "Midi-Minuit Fantastique."

CINEMA, Postfach 1049, CH 8022 Zürich, Switzerland. The splendid first issue of 1975 looked back in depth at Swiss cinema in the previous decade, and its book-like format and distinguished editorial board make the magazine (printed in French and German) essential for film archives abroad.

CINEMA, PO Box 1574, Johannesburg. Glossy picture magazine entirely devoted to features.

CINEMA CANADA, 6 Washington Avenue, No. 3, Toronto. Canadian bi-monthly which enthusiastically champions its native cinema with professional aplomb.

CINEMA 53, c/o Tehran International Film Festival, Avenue Kamal-ol-molk, Tehran. Edited by Jamal Omid, this is the only serious film monthly in the Persian language. International in its choice of contents, it usually tries to achieve a balance between film history and new cinema (especially Third World). Fully illustrated.

CINEMA JOURNAL, 17 West College Street, Iowa City, Iowa 52242. A scholarly and respected American quarterly, edited by Richard Dyer MacCann.

CINEMA PAPERS, 143 Therry Street, Melbourne, Australia 3000. One of the world's most imaginatively designed movie quarterlies, its large format embracing a host of pictures, capsule comments, and serious reviews and interviews. Colour tinting adds impact to the layout.

CINEMA QUEBEC, CP 309, Station Outremont, Montréal 154, Quebec. French-Canadian periodical (10 issues a year) which is slimmer, more polemic, and generally less readable than the English-language **Cinema Canada.**

CLASSIC FILM COLLECTOR, Contact Inc., PO Box 391, Indiana, Penn. 15701. A good source for film buffs eager to enlarge their library of movies, and a highly readable paper besides.

CTVD, Hampton Books, Rt. 1, Box 76, Newberry, S.C. 29108. A concise digest of foreign-language writing on film, with additional reports by an ever-increasing group of overseas correspondents.

DIRIGIDO POR ..., Pujol 9-1.1, Barcelona 6. This handsomely-produced Spanish monthly throws the spotlight each issue on a particular director of international renown. Very good documentation on all personalities.

EIGASHI KENKYU, c/o Tadao Sato, 5-10-4

Matsubara, Setagaya-ku, Tokyo, Japan. An interesting new Japanese quarterly, edited by Tadao Sato, with a full English translation in each issue.

EKRAN, Dalmatinova 4/II, Soba 9, 61000 Ljubljana. Slovenian film periodical that contains an enormous wealth of articles, reports, statistics, and reviews. Intriguing design.

FANT, Ths. Heftyesgt. 37, Oslo 2. Outspoken and polemical Norwegian quarterly.

FILM, Panepistimiou 39, Athens. A brave new Greek venture, edited by Thanasis Rentzis, directed at a particularly high-brow readership. Both reprinted foreign articles and original Greek criticism.

FILM, ul. Puławska 61, 02-595 Warsaw. Popular Polish weekly with international slant, now in a much improved format.

FILM, P.K. 307, Beyoğlu, Istanbul. Turkish monthly, the official organ of the "Sinematek Derneği."

FILM A DOBA, Václavské nám. 43, Praha 1. The principal Czech film monthly.

FILME CULTURA, Rua Mayrink Veiga 28, ZC 05, Rio de Janeiro, Guanabara. The leading Brazilian film magazine (in Portuguese).

FILM DOPE, 5 Norman Court, Little Heath, Potters Bar, Hertfordshire EN6 1HY. Not so much a magazine, more a part-work film dictionary, this British quarterly is to be welcomed for its exhaustive research.

FILM EN TELEVISIE, Olmstraat 10, 1040 Brussels. Reliable and informed Belgian magazine (printed in Flemish).

FILMFACTS, P.O. Box 213, Village Station, New York, NY 10014. The fortnightly checklist (with extracts from major press reviews) of all feature films released in the U.S.A.

FILM FAN MONTHLY. 77 Grayson Place, Teaneck, New Jersey 07666. Naive in conception and rather amateurishly produced, this magazine has some interest for fans of the old Hollywood.

FILM HERITAGE, College of Liberal Arts, Wright State University, Dayton, Ohio 45431. Quarterly journal of criticism, tending towards the high brow.

FILMIHULLU, c/o Suomen Elokuva arkisto, Eteläranta 4B, Helsinki 13. Finnish film and TV magazine with critical approach, appearing eight times a year and published by film consumers' and cultural organisations.

THE FILM JOURNAL, Box 9602, Hollins College, Virginia 24020. Lavishly-designed quarterly which devotes each issue to an in-depth study.

FILM-KORRESPONDENZ, Romanstrasse 20, 8 München 19. Edited by Günther Pflaum, this long-standing German publication contains articles and interviews immaculately typed in stapled form. The modest presentation should not be allowed to detract from the rich content.

FILMKRITIK, Filmkritiker-Kooperative, Kreittmayrst 3, 8 Munich 2. Polemical West German magazine.

FILM KULTÚRA, Nepstadion út. 97, Budapest XIV. The major Hungarian film periodical, with articles of a high intellectual calibre, and a useful summary of contents in English.

FILMKUNST, Rauhensteingasse 5, 1010 Vienna. Old and distinguished Austrian magazine. Contents often of research value.

FILM LIBRARY QUARTERLY, Box 348, Radio City Station, New York, NY 10019. Bill Sloan's editorial flair has kept this educational film quarterly on the shelves of everyone interested in good movies and their classroom use. Each issue contains some challenging topics and well-researched comment.

FILM NEWS, 250 West 57th Street, New York, NY 10019. The U.S. review magazine of 16mm films, filmstrips, education TV and equipment. An excellent materials source periodical, run with devotion for thirty years and more by Rohama Lee.

FILMOGRAPH, 7926 Ashboro Drive, Alexandria, Virginia 22309. Quarterly journal with good career articles and factual pieces.

FILMOWY SERWIS PRASOWY, ul. Mazowiecka 6/8, 00-950 Warsaw. A mine of information: a Polish MFB with production and trade details.

FILM REVIEW, The Old Court House, Old Court Place, 42–70 Kensington High Street, London W.8. Known to scores of thousands of cinema patrons, this monthly is brightly coloured and illustrated and up to the minute with its coverage of new films.

FILMRUTAN, Granängsringen 50 B (3), 135 00 Tyresö. The magazine of the Swedish Federation of Film Societies, well-printed and often containing long and serious articles on world cinema.

FILM WORLD, 8 Horniman Circle, Botawala Building, 2nd Floor, Bombay 400 023. Lively and outspoken Indian monthly, similar to the British "Photoplay." Large survey of world cinema in January 1975 issue.

GUIA DE FILMES, Rua Mayrink 28–5° andar, Rio de Janeiro, Guanabara. Bi-monthly Brazilian magazine, an equivalent to "Monthly Film Bulletin."

HABLEMOS DE CINE, Libertadores 199, San Isidro, Lima 27. Principal Peruvian film magazine.

JOURNAL OF THE SOCIETY OF FILM AND TELEVISION ARTS, 80 Great Portland Street, London W1N 6JJ. A long-established and respected quarterly, containing many articles about the film *industry.*

LITERATURE/FILM QUARTERLY, Salisbury State College, Salisbury, Maryland 21801. This quarterly contains many valuable articles on the relationship of the printed word to film, and provides interesting background.

MASS MEDIA, 2116 N. Charles Street, Baltimore, Maryland 21218. Fine bi-weekly newsletter that reviews new films (notably shorts), filmstrips, recordings, books on the media, and miscellaneous resources.

MILLIMETER, 139 East 43rd Street, New York, NY 10017. An American technical monthly that covers the spectrum from animation to video, boasts off-beat interviews, and gains from some zestful page design.

MONTAGE, London Regional Group of the British Federation of Film Societies, 2 Colnbrook Street, London SE1. Although composed of duplicated, typed sheets stapled together, this quarterly bursts the bonds of financial constraint and contains some of the liveliest writing and reviewing on the British scene, by some of the best-known critics.

MONTHLY FILM BULLETIN, British Film Institute, 81 Dean Street, London W1V 6AA. Provides commendably full and usually accurate credits, synopses and reviews (less objective) of all new films released in Britain.

PHOTOPLAY, 12–18 Paul Street, London EC2A 4JS. Much improved fan monthly that contains good interviews and useful titbits.

LA REVUE DU CINEMA, 3 rue Récamier, Paris 7. French monthly that is better known still under the title of "Image et Son."

LA REVUE INTERNATIONALE D'HISTOIRE DU CINEMA, L'Avant-Scène, 27 rue St.-André-des-Arts, Paris 6. A series of immaculately-produced micro-fiches, issued regularly on a subscription basis, which place information on various subjects at the researcher's fingertips. (Available through British agents, The Tantivy Press.)

SEQUENCE, Vintage Publications, 152 Azimpur Road, Dacca 283463, Bangladesh. A new quarterly (in English), edited by Alamgir Kabir and covering Satyajit Ray, the Bangladesh domestic scene, and theatrical topics.

SEQUENCES, 1474 rue Alexandre-Desève, Montréal 133. French-Canadian quarterly that has an enthusiastic mixture of reviews, comment and production news.

SHOWBIZ, PO Box 700, Durban, Natal. South African monthly containing local news and views, with interviews and production details.

SINEMA TV, Yıldız Yolu, Gayrettepe, Istanbul. Monthly Turkish magazine, the official organ of the "Turk Film Arşivi."

SINGHRONOS KINIMATOGRAFOS '75, Ipatias 5, TT 118, Athens. Attractive and well-produced mixture of serious articles and valuable data, plus criticism designed to improve the state of Greek cinema. Thoughtfully illustrated.

SKOOP, Boekencentrum NV, Scheveningseweg 72, The Hague. The well-known Dutch movie magazine, with a spectrum of news, reviews, interviews, and a lavish selection of pictures. Colour covers are always striking.

SKRIEN, Postbus 318, Amsterdam 1000. Excellent Dutch magazine that appears with regularity and enthusiasm. Fine historical articles.

SOVYETSKI EKRAN, ul. Chasovaya 5B, Moscow A-319, U.S.S.R. 125319. Popular fortnightly founded in 1925 with up-to-date news of current cinema. Similar to Polish "Film."

SPOTLIGHT, Hans Egedesgade 7/3, DK-2200 Copenhagen N. Enthusiastic little Danish quarterly, edited by Bo Torp Pedersen with an independent outlook.

STARS ET CINEMA, 7 place Georges Brugmann, 1060 Brussels. Glossy Belgian monthly with international slant. Similar to the British "Films Illustrated."

TIME OUT, 374 Gray's Inn Road, London WC1X 8BB. Weekly guide to London, whose nearest transatlantic equivalent would be "The Village Voice." Informative cinema section.

WHAT'S ON IN LONDON, 79 Temple Chambers, London EC4. The oldest and largest of the London film and entertainment round-ups, still run with devotion by critic F. Maurice Speed.

UNIVERSITY VISION, 72 Dean Street, London W1V 5HB. Journal of the British Universities Film Council, dealing with film as a medium rather than as entertainment.

YEDİNCİ SANAT, P.K. 654, Beyoğlu, İstanbul. Monthly Turkish magazine.

ZOOM-FILMBERATER, Postfach 1717, 3001 Bern. Edited by Urs Jaeggi, this trim Swiss Catholic magazine features detailed reviews as well as full-length analyses.

Trade and Technical

AMERICAN CINEMATOGRAPHER, ASC Agency Inc., 1782 North Orange Drive, Hollywood, California 90028. High quality monthly for professionals and cameramen in particular.

BKSTS JOURNAL, 110–112 Victoria House, Vernon Place, London WC1B 4DJ. Important monthly specialising in technical trends and developments in Cinema.

BRITISH NATIONAL FILM CATALOGUE, 81 Dean Street, London W1V 6AA. Quarterly that provides essential particulars of all non-fiction films (British and foreign) becoming available in Britain.

LE FILM FRANCAIS, 9 Avenue Hoche, 75 Paris 8. The leading French trade weekly.

FILM & TV, FilmCentrum, Kungsholmstorg 2, 112 21 Stockholm. Polemical magazine issued by FilmCentrum, intended to improve the state of the Swedish film world, Superb design.

FILM-ECHO/FILMWOCHE, Wilhelmstrasse 42, 62 Wiesbaden. Regular West German trade paper.

FILM OG KINO, Stortingsgt. 16, Oslo 1. Norway's monthly trade review.

GREATER AMUSEMENTS, 1600 Broadway, Suite 5140, New York, NY 10019. American trade paper, now in its sixtieth year.

HOLLYWOOD REPORTER, 6715 Sunset Blvd, Hollywood, California 90028. All the news from the Coast. There is also a European edition.

KINOLEHTI, Kaisaniemenkatu 3 B 24, 00100 Helsinki 10. Film business organ for Finland, published five times each year, with various articles, reviews, news items, statistics, attractively presented.

MOVIE TV MARKETING, Box 30, Central Post Office, Tokyo, 100–91 Japan. A remarkable monthly enterprise pioneered from Japan by Glenn F. Ireton—in English.

S.A. FILM AND TELEVISION WEEKLY, PO Box 10137, Johannesburg. Bright weekly trade paper published in South Africa by Harry Jones. Often controversial and always informative.

SCREEN INTERNATIONAL, 142–150 Wardour Street, London W1V 4BR. Revamped version of "CinemaTV Today," the British weekly trade paper now under Peter Noble's energetic editorship.

THEAMATA, Athinon 64, Aharnai Attikis, Greece. Informative fortnightly containing statistics, reviews, news, etc.

TM (TEKNISKT MEDDELANDE), Svenska Filminstitutet, Box 27126, 102 52 Stockholm 27, Sweden. Scandinavian technical magazine that is designed and assembled with consummate care and knowledge by Lars Swanberg, one of Sweden's most gifted cinematographers.

VARIETY, 154 West 46th Street, New York, NY 10036. Long-established, and invaluable for anyone interested in films—gossip, statistics, advance production news, good reviews, etc.

National Organs

BULGARIAN FILMS, FilmBulgaria, 135a Rakovski Street, Sofia. Appears eight times a year, and now is partly in colour. Large format, fully illustrated.

CINEMA, CINEMA, Ministère de la Culture Française, avenue de Cortenburg 158, 1040 Brussels. Neat, stapled newsletter, appearing three times a year and containing "nouvelles du film belge d'expression française." Illustrated.

CZECHOSLOVAK FILM, 28 Václavské náměstí, Prague 1. Handsomely-illustrated, large format. Short on credits, etc.

FINLAND-FILMLAND, Suomen Elokuvasäätiö, Kaisaniemenkatu 3 B 25, 00100 Helsinki 10. One of the best of the national organs, large format and filled with information. With bulletin "Facts about Film Finland." Colour cover.

GERMAN FILM NEWS, 47 Dean Street, London W1V 5HL. A modest, neatly-produced booklet with interleaved picture-spreads, similar to Unifrance Film News.

HUNGAROFILM BULLETIN, Báthori utca 10, Budapest V. Reliable and comprehensive, including films produced for TV. Appears four or five times a year.

ISRAEL FILM CENTRE INFORMATION BULLETIN, Ministry of Commerce and Industry, 30 Agron Street, Jerusalem. Very high quality stapled bulletin with comprehensive editorial matter.

JUGOSLAVIJA FILM NEWS, Jugoslavija Film, Knez Mihailova 19, Belgrade. Large in size but few in pages. Good on credits and gives equal space to shorts and cartoons.

NEW CANADIAN FILM, La Cinémathèque québécoise, 360 McGill Street, Montréal 125, Québec. Stapled broadsheet, lightly illustrated, but very readable and excellent for facts and credits.

POLISH FILM, Film Polski, Mazowiecka 6/8, Warsaw. This valuable large-format publication has recently resurfaced in a modernised lay-out. Extensive coverage of TV films, also.

SOVIET FILM, Sovexportfilm, 14 Kalashny pereulok, Moscow 103009. Now in its eighteenth year, this handsome monthly continues to be indispensable for students of Russian film. Colour spreads.

SWEDISH FILMS NEWS BULLETIN, Svenska Filminstitutet, Box 27 126, S-102 52 Stockholm. Regularly-mailed information sheets which build up into a comprehensive dossier. A handsomely-produced annual appears every year in addition.

UNIFRANCE FILM NEWS, 77 avenue des Champs-Elysées, Paris 8e. Accurate, up-to-date information makes this stylish booklet transcend its economical layout. Occasional interleaved picture-spreads.

UNIJAPAN FILM QUARTERLY, UniJapan Film, 9–13 Ginza 5-chome, Chuo-ku, Tokyo 104. This well-published little booklet is now published only irregularly.

UNITALIA FILM NEWS, Via L. Luciani 1, Rome. Considering the quality of Unitalia's handsome yearbook, this duplicated newsletter is disappointing, although information and material is always readily supplied by this organisation.

Distribution of IFG

Outside the United Kingdom and the United States of America, *International Film Guide* is distributed through the following outlets:

AUSTRALIA
Anchor Books Pty. Ltd., Shop 5, Crystal Palace Arcade, 590–592 George Street, Sydney, NSW, Australia 2000.

FRANCE
Idea Books, 46–48 rue de Montreuil, 750111 Paris, France.

INDIA
Lakhani Book Depot, Ramchandra Building, Girgaum, Bombay 4, India.

ITALY
Idea Books, 21 via Cappuccio, 20123 Milano, Italy.

SOUTH AFRICA
Informafilm, P.O. Box 96, Sea Point, 8060 Cape, South Africa.

(Continued from page 512)

TECHNICONSULT. Script and dir: L. A. Roche. Phot (colour): Chami. Edit: Ferrioli. For Arsiete-Techniconsult SRL. Documentary.

HACER NUESTRO, NUESTRO PETROLIO (To Make Our Own Oil). Script: Alonso Gamero, Roche. Dir: Roche. Phot (colour): Chami. Edit. Ferrioli. For Arsiete-Conicit. Documentary.

MERIDA NO ES UN PUEBLO (Mérida Is Not the Village). Script and dir: Luis Armando Roche. Phot (colour): Chami. Edit: Ferrioli. Music: Fulgencio Aquino, Anselmo Lopez, Julian Plaza. Song ("Nostalgia") sung by: Anibal Troilo. Players: Omaira Churrion, Victor Millán, Gran Lotario. For Arsiete. Surreal experimental short about the painter Manuel Mérida.

TESTIMONIOS DEL PASADO (Testimonies of the Past). Text: Pedro Berroeta, based on authentic historical material. Dir: Manuel Diaz Punceles. Edit: José Bañados, Carlos Molina, Diaz Punceles. For Cinesa-Cant. V. 50 mins. Printed in one colour. Documentary.

ACADEMIA MILITAR (Military Academy). Script and dir: Manuel de Pedro. Phot (colour): Martin Alverez. Edit: José Garrido. For Cinesa. Documentary.

VENEZUELA SALUDES. Script: Isa Dobles. Dir: De Pedro. Phot: Jorge Balevich. Edit: Oscar Montanti. For Cinesa. Documentary.

HIERRO (Iron). Script and dir: De Pedro. Phot (colour): Rafael Giraldi. Edit: Garrido. For Cinesa. Documentary.

OPERACION CANAIMA. Script and dir: Javier Blanco. Phot (colour): Hildefonso Rodriguez. Edit: Humberto Carballo Luque. For Nucineca. Documentary.

NUESTROS RIOS SON NAVEGABLES (Our Rivers Are Navigable). Script: Nestor Lovera de Lima. Dir: J. Blanco. Phot (colour): H. Rodriguez. Edit: Carballo Luque. For Nucineca. Documentary.

METRO DE CARACAS. Script and dir: Nestor Lovera de Lima. Phot (colour): Javier Lovera de Lima. For Nucineca. Documentary.

EL LARGO VIAJE DE AZUCAR (The Long Voyage of Sugar). Script: Caupolican Ovalles. Dir and edit: Bruno Scheuren. Phot (colour): Jimmy Nasser. Narr: Luis Salazar. For Creativos Audovisuales. Documentary.

TOMA DE POSESION DE CARLOS ANDRES PEREZ (The Takeover of Carlos Andrés Perez). Script: B. Scheuren. Dir: Luis Felipe Correa. Phot (colour): José Vicente Scheuren, Bruno Scheuren, Jimmy Nasser, José Camero. Edit: B. Scheuren, J. Nasser. Narr: Luis Alberto Maldonado. For Creat. Aud. Documentary.

100 YEARS BOLIVAR SQUARE IN CARACAS. Dir and edit: Bruno Scheuren. Phot (colour): J. Vicente Scheuren. Narr: Iván Diaz Millán. For Creat. Aud. Documentary.

LA FLOR DE CAFETAL (Flower of Cafetal). Script: Caupolican Ovalles. Dir: Bruno Scheuren. Phot (colour): J. Nasser. Edit: Oscar Montauti and J. Nasser. Narr: Luis Gerardo Tovar. For Creat. Aud. Documentary.

OPERATION SEMANA SANTA (Operation Holy Week). Dir and edit: B. Scheuren. Narr: L. G. Tovar. For Creat. Aud. Documentary.

TIERRA LIBRE HOMBRES LIBRES (Free Land, Free People). Dir: Ana Maria Cazullo. Phot: Héctor Gonzalez, J. Nasser. Edit: O. Montauti. Narr: Luis Gerardo Tovar. For Creat. Aud. Documentary.

MODULOS RETICULARES DE APURE. Script and dir: Oziel Rodriguez. Phot (colour): Oswaldo Girardi. Edit: Hector Aparicio. Anim. sequences: Ricardo Boquete, Mauricio Antori. For Texaco (MOP). Documentary.

CAMINO DEL FUTURO (Road of the Future). Script and dir: O. Rodriguez. Phot (colour): Jorge Balevici. Edit: Luis Bañados. For Cinesa (Creole). Documentary.

THE PRESIDENT'S TAKE-OVER. Script and dir: O. Rodriguez. Edit: Hector Aparicio. From the archives of Bolivar Films. Music and sound: Eduardo Andersen. For Cinesa (OCI). Documentary.

PRUINCA. Script and dir: Luis Armando Roche. Phot (colour): Gustavo Chami. Music. Freddy Reyna. Edit: Giuliano Ferrioli. Narr: Porfirio Torres. For Arsiete. Documentary.

MINES AND METALLURGY. Script: Alonso Gamero, Roche. Dir: L. A. Roche. Phot (colour): Chami. Edit: Ferrioli. Music: Reyna. For Arsiete-Prod. Educ. and Conicit. Documentary.

COMO ISLAS EN EL TIEMPO (Like Islands in Time). Script: Charles Brewer Carias, Roche. Dir: Luis Armando Roche. Phot (colour): Gustavo Chiami. Edit: Giuliano Ferrioli. For Arsiete & Venez. Society of Natural Sciences. 55 mins. Scientific Documentary.

Index to Advertisers